# HAND BOOK OF AGRO CHEMICAL INDUSTRIES (INSECTICIDE & PESTICIDES)

# HAND BOOK OF AGRO CHEMICAL INDUSTRIES (INSECTICIDE & PESTICIDES)

*Written By*

EIRI BOARD OF CONSULTANTS & ENGINEERS

ENGINEERS INDIA RESEARCH INSTITUTE

4449, Nai Sarak, Main Road, Delhi - 110 006 (India)

Ph:. 91-11-3918117, 3916431, 3920361, 3960797

Fax: 91-11-391 6431

* E-Mail : eirisidi@bol.net.in

* Website: www.startindustry.com

Sole Distributor :

INDIAN INSTITUTE OF CONSULTANTS, 4/27, ROOP NAGAR, DELHI - 110 007

PRINTED & PUBLISHED BY

**ENGINEERS INDIA RESEARCH INSTITUTE**

**4449, Nai Sarak, Main Road, Delhi - 110 006 (India)**
**Ph:. 91-11-3918117, 3916431, 3920361, 3960797**
*** Fax: 91-11-3916431, 3918117**
*** E-Mail : eirisidi@bol.net.in**
*** Website: www.startindustry.com**

DISTRIBUTED BY

**SMALL INDUSTRY RESEARCH INSTITUTE**
**INDIAN INSTITUTE OF CONSULTANTS**



**ISBN : 81- 86732-46-2**
**Printed in New Delhi (INDIA)**



**Rs. 900**

Printed & Published by Sudhir Gupta for **"Engineers India Research Institute"** 4449 Nai Sarak, Main Road, New Delhi - 110 006 and Printed at Swastik Offset, Shahadra, Delhi - 32

# Preface

The book ***'Hand Book of Agro Chemical Industries (Insecticide and Pesticide)'*** covers almost all the basic and advanced details to setup own Agro Chemical Unit. The major chapters and details of the book are : Agro Chemical Industries, Pesticides, Insecticides Technology, Fungicides, Nematicides, Rodenticides, Molluscicides, Fumigants, Acaricides, Herbicides, Plant Growth Regulators, Repellents, Attractants, Pheromones, Synergists, Synthetic Inhibitors and Proinsecticides, Toxicology and Safe Use of Pesticides, Insecticide Act, Pesticide Formulations, Pesticide Mixtures, Modern Equipments for a Pesticide Formulation Laboratory and Pilot Plant, Aerosol Formulations, Advances in Pesticides Formulations Packaging, Packaging in Pesticide Industry, Emulsifier for Pesticides, Pesticide Preparation Using Neem Fruit and Seeds (Margosa), Insecticides for Rats, Termites, Rodents, Mouses, Cockroaches, Monthicide, Mosquito Coil and Mats, Mosquito Larva Destroyer, Pesticide Formulations, Insecticides for Neem Seeds, Neem Oils and Neem Leaves, Air Freshners (Odonil Type), Phenyl (Black and White), B.H.C., Aerosol and Mosquito Repellent Spray (Baygon, Hit, Mortein Type), Mosquito Repellent Agarbatti (Insense Sticks), Allethrin Mosquito Repellent Oil etc. Plant and Equipments Suppliers, Packaging Suppliers, Apart from these details, the book also discloses the major other untold chapters which are quite important for those who wish to enter into Agro Chemical manufacturing trade. Frankly speaking- the book is also quite indispensable for those who have also setup their industry.

The book has been written for the benefit and to prove an asset and a handy reference guide in the hands of new entrepreneurs & well established industrialists.

Director

**ENGINEERS INDIA RESEARCH INSTITUTE**

Nai Sarak, New Delhi (INDIA)

E-Mail : eirisidi@bol.net.in

# Contents and Subject Index

# 1

# Agrochemical Industries

## Introduction

**India has one of** the most dynamic generic pesticide industries in the world. Exports of generic agrochemicals will hold the key to profitable operations for players in the Indian agrochemical industry. Industry is in the process of developing and manufacturing environment-friendly formulations such as flowable; water dispersable granules and suspension concentrates with better bio-efficiency and shelf life. These products are having a huge world market of approximately US $ 1 billion and in the next three years India will be exporting these products worth Rs. 300 crore if sincere efforts are made.

The Indian industry is fortunate to have the expertise of organisations such as the institute of Pesticide. Formulation Technology which is aided by UNIDO. Also the credit goes to various CSIR laboratories particularly national Chemical laboratory (NCL), Pune and the Indian Institute of Chemical Technology (IICT), Hyderabad. These laboratories worked on processes for a number of technicals, and transferred this is the industry as a complete engineering package, which led to the development of the industry. Thus the agrochemical industry, in particular, is seeing dramatic developments, involving the constant phase-out of old molecules, and their replacement by environ-friendly, low dosage, more potent moieties, Fluorinated pyrethroids, including, Tefluthrin, Bifenthrin and Acrinathrin which have good activity when applied to soil, are now on the anvil to replace organophosphates, and aryl heterocyclics have been developed as a new class of compounds.

A new class of respiration inhibitors which kill pests by preventing oxidative phosphorylation are also now available, and these include pyridaben and tebufenpyrad. Aryl heterocylics are a new class of neutrotoxic insecticides, of which Fipronil, the first compound, along with some others, have shown greater activity than synthetic pyrethroids. New avenues should be explore, so that industry is in a position to offer broad-based product for use for the national and international markets.

Backward integration is a must to make production cost effective and, diversification into fine chemicals segments is necessary. Both the pharmaceuticals and the agrochemicals industries need various chemicals and many of these products are still imported.

Structurally, pesticide molecules will undergo significant changes in the future to become more specific and eco-compatible. From the process point of view, shortened and high performance synthesis enriched through novel chemistry and biotechnology will provide immense opportunities and challenges to the researchers in the Asia-Pacific region. A number of enabling science have to be employed to provide the cutting edge to these technologies. These include process science and engineering, computational and combinational chemistry, molecular modelling to relate structure with the mode of pesticidal action, analytical measurements and environmental sciences. Biotechnology will play an increasing role in process technologies, as will assymmetric synthesis and chiral separations. However, the integrated pest management is the likely trump card for the future growth process. The product processes waste paradigm will undergo significant transformation to ensure sustainability of agrochemical sector in this region.

Changing customer priorities in USA, Europe and domestic markets will create excellent opportunities for agrochemical sector in Asia-Pacific region to create new business designs. The health risks posed by chemical pesticides which arise during manufacture, transportation and application are still much lower than for may harmless looking operations. This is mainly due to abundant precautions taken during pesticides manufacture. Notwithstanding these facts it has become increasingly difficult for the industry to convince the public at large, that not every pesticide plant is a 'Bhopal' in the making.

## INORGANIC INSECTICIDES

Some or the inorganic insecticides are discussed below.

### Lead Arsenate

Lead arsenate is a very poisonous, colourless and crystalline compound and is usually employed for the potato beetle and for the codling moth in apple orchards.

It is soluble in nitric acid and insoluble in water, sp. gr. 5.8 m.p. 1024°C. It is usually employed for the potato beetle and for the coding moth. in apple orchards. It is used as an insecticide and herbicide. Due to its high toxicity 1 gm. is lethal to man, may cause skin irritation.

### Calcium Arsenate

It can be prepared by interaction of calcium chloride, calcium hydroxide, and sodium arsenate. It is a white powder, slightly soluble in water, soluble in dilute acids. Decomposes on heating. It is used as an insecticide and germicide. It is toxic by ingestion and inhalation. Tolerance, 1 mg per cubic metre of air (as As). It is applied to leaves in the form of dust.

## ORGANIC INSECTICIDES

### Dinitrophenol

It can be prepared : (i) by heating phenol with dilute sulphuric acid, cooling the product, and then nitrating, keeping the temperature below 50°C; (ii) by nitration with mixed acid with careful temperature control. It can be purified by crystallisation. It is in the form of yellow crystals, sp. gr. 1.681; m.p. 144°C (2, 4 dinitrophenol), sp. gr. 1.683; m.p. 114–115°C. m.p. 63°C (2,6 dinitrophenol). Soluble in alcohol, ether, benzene and chloroform; slightly soluble in water. It is used in dyes, especially sulphur colours; picric acid; picramic acid; preservation of lumber; manufacture the photographic developer diaminophenol hydrochloride; explosives manufacture; indicator and can be used as a reagent for K and $NH_4$ ions. It is highly toxic; absorbed by skin. Dust inhalation may be fatal. Severe explosion hazard when dry.

### Dichloro Diphenyl Trichloroethane (DDT)

It can be prepared by condensing chloral or chloral hydrate with chlorobenzene in presence of sulphuric acid. It is in the form of colourless crystals or white to slightly off-white powder. Odourless or with slight aromatic odor. Insoluble in water; soluble in acetone, ether, benzene, carbon tetrachloride, kerosene, dioxane, and pyridine. Not comparable with alkaline materials.

It is toxic by ingestion, inhalation, and skin absorption, especially in solution, Acute oral toxicity for man said to be 0.25 g/kg of body weight. Since DDT is not biodegradable and is ecologically damaging. Claims of human carcinogenicity have not been proved. DDT can be used for a few specialised purposes, e.g., to combat the tussock moth. Tolerance, 1 mg. per cubic metre of air; 5 ppm in foods. May accumulate in the soil incompatible with alkaline materials. It should not be stored in iron containers. Toxic to bees Accumulates in the body fat of animals. It is used as an insecticides, especially for tobacco and cotton; pesticides (tussock moth).

**Methoxychlor (Methoxy DDT; DMDT)**

It can be prepared by reaction of methyl phenyl ether and chloral hydrate. It is in the form of white, crystalline solid; m.p. 89°C; insoluble in water; soluble in alcohol. Not compatible with alkaline materials. It is used as an insecticide, effective against mosquito larvae and house flies. Especially recommended for use in dairy farns. It is moderately toxic. Tolerance, 10 mg per cubic metre in air.

**BHC or Benzene Hexachloride**

BHC or benzene hexachloride or more correctly 1, 2, 3, 4, 5, 6 hexachlorocyclohexane is another important insecticide, which exists in a number of stereoisomers, the gama being the most toxic.

The commercial BHC possesses 5 main geometrical isomers. The percentage of each of the isomer in the commercial BHC is alpha (55–70%), beta (5–14%), gamma (10–13%), delta (6–8%), epsilon (3–4%). Later on various isomers were separately prepared or separated from the mixture and it was found that BHC has insecticidal property of gamma $\alpha$-isomer.

The gamma BHC is usually known as gammexane or lindane. It is refined material containing 99% of gamma isomer of BHC. The BHC is prepared by the chlorination of benzene in presence of sunlight.

The product is a mixture of five out of eight possible isomers of which the physiologically active isomer does not exceed 18%. The amount and formation or isomer has been found to increase in presence of some substances such as sulphur, selenium, tellurium, notrotoluenes. dialkyl peroxy dicarbonates etc.

Excess of benzene is used in order to keep the products in solution and to continue the reaction under homogeneous-conditions. The reaction can also be carried out in presence of $\gamma$-radiation or fluorine (elemental) instead of uv radiation.

The manufacture can be carried out by batch process or by continuous process. In batch process technical grade benzene and chlorine are reacted in a lead lined vessel provided with cooling arrangements and mercury vapour lamp is used as a uv source. The temperature is kept between 15–20°C and pressure is maintained slightly above atmospheric pressure, in order to minimise the loss of benzene. The reaction is continued till the BHC concentration attains 12–15%. The excess of chlorine is air blown and the mother liquor is concentrated and finally fractionally crystallised to isolate the biologically active isomer.

In continuous process chlorination is carried out in a glass lined pipe chlorinator in the central tube of which benzene is taken and uv source is two 40 watt fluorescent lamps. The temperature is 40–60°C and pressure is atmospheric. The chlorination is continued till the concentration of BHC reaches 13–14.5%. The chlorinated liquor is concentrated at 85–88°C till it becomes saturated in isomer and almost all the $\gamma$ -and $\beta$ -isomers are crystallised out. The crystals are separated by filtration and the filtrate or mother liquor is subjected to steam distillation. The molten residue in the vessel is cooled to get lumps of crude BHC containing 25% of the isomer. The isomer is then extracted by solvent extraction using hexanenitromethane solvent mixture. The ground solid is then deodourised treatment with oleum or agitation in air with kaolin and manganese linoleate. Isomer of BHC is more soluble than other in most organic solvents. It kills or controls insects, grass hoppers and common pests and used in the form of dust containing 5–10% of the ingredients in emulsion containing 25% of the $\gamma$- isomer and also as granules having 6–10% of the active principal.

**Gammexane**

Crude BHC is generally not suitable for food crops, because of its strong musty odour. Gammexane or lindane, a refined containing 99% of the BHC, has largely overcome the odor, Benzene hexachloride is a colourless, practically odourless crystalline solid, insoluble in water, but soluble in organic solvents.

Gammexane has exceptional insecticidal activity, comparable to that of DDT and may be used in food crops. Insects that are not killed by DDT are killed by gammexane. Gammexane has also been applied successfully against the common disease carrying insects, household stock, horticulture, stored food and agriculture pests. Gammexane has widely been used also as an agricultural pesticide. 99% pure BHC, called lindane or gammexane is prepared by its selective crystallisation followed by repeated solvent extraction. Lindane or gammexane is sparingly soluble in water but soluble in acetone. It is stable to air, heat and light. It is also stable to strong acids but decomposes in contact with hot alkalies. It has no contact action on human system and so it is safe insecticide for domestic use. It is applied as dust, emulsion, granules and as water dispersion.

**Chlordane**

Chlordane is a chlorinated hydrocarbon, insecticide showing contact, stomach poison, and fumigant action with long residual effects. It is colourless, odourless, viscous liquid; sp.gr. 1.57–1.67 (60/60°F); viscosity SSU 100 seconds (38°C); organic chlorine 64–67% by wt, purity 98%; b.p. 175°C (2 mm); refractive index (n 25/D) 1.56–1.57; soluble in many organic solvents; insoluble in water; miscible in deodorised kerosene; decomposes in weak alkalies. It is used as an insecticide and fumigant. It is toxic by ingestion, inhalation, and skin absorption. Tolerance, 0.5 mg per cubic metre of air.

**Heptachlor**

Hepatachlor is a chlorinated hydrocarbon, insecticide with contact and stomach poison action, especially effective on soil insects. It is a white, waxy solid; m.p. 95–96°C; sp. gr. 1.57–1.59. insoluble in water; soluble in xyiene, and alcohol. It is used as an insecticide, in soil treatment, seed treatment and on the plant foilage. It is toxic by ingestion, inhalation and skin absorption. Tolelance, 0.5 mg per cubic metre of air.

**Aldrin**

Aldrin is a chlorinated hydrocarbon insecticide with contact and stomach poison action. It is in the form of brown to white crystalline solid, m.p. 104–105°C; insoluble in water ; soluble in most organic solvents. Not affected by alkalies or dilute acids; compatible with most fertilisers, herbicides, fungicides, and insecticides. It is valuable as a soil insecticide for termites. It is highly toxic by ingestion and inhalation; absorbed by skin. Tolerance, 0.25 mg per cubic metre of air. It is a suspected carcinogen, It's use restricted to non-agricultural applications.

**Endrin**

Endrin is isomeric to dieldrin and can be prepared by first preparing hexachloro bicylochlorinated by an inorganic base. Hexachloro bicycloheptane can also be prepared by adding Hex to acetylene in a tubular nickel alloy reactor at 150°C and 300 psi pressure. The hexachloro bicycloheptadine is then heated with cyclopentadience at 70–100°C to obtain isodrin, the endoendo isomer of aldrin. The isodrin on epoxidation with paracetic acid produces endrin, the endoendo isomer of aldrin. Endrin is also used as contact cum stomach poison and employed as dust or emulsion.

**Toxaphene**

Toxaphene is a chlorinated hydrocarbon insecticide showing contact with stomach poison activity. It is amber, waxy solid with a mild odour of chlorine and camphor; melting range 65–90°C; sp.gr. 1.66 (27°C). Soluble in common organic solvents. It is used as an insecticide (primarily for cotton and early growth stage of vegetables). It is toxic by ingestion, tolerance 0.5 mg per cubic metre of air inhalation, skin absorption. Causes cancer in mice. It is corrosive to iron. Lactating dairy animals should not be treated. Birds feeding on treated areas may be killed. Use may be restricted.

**Malathion**

Malathion is an organic phosphate insecticide-acaricide. It can be prepared from diethyl maleate and dimethyl di-thiophosphoric acid. It is in the form of yellow, high-boiling liquid; (b.p. 156–157°C, under 0.7 mm with slight decomposition); m.p. 3.0°C; refractive index (n 25/D) 1.4985; sp. gr. 1.2315 (25°C); vapour pressure (20°C) approximately 0.00004 mm. Miscible with most polar organic solvents. Slightly soluble in water. It is toxic by ingestion and inhalation. Absorbed by skin. Tolerance 10 mg per cubic metre of air. Chloinesterase inhibitor.

### Parathion

Parathion is an organic phosphate insecticide, a caricide with both contact and stomach poison activity. It can be prepared from sodium ethylate, thiophosphoryl chloride and sodium para-notrophenate. It is deep brown to yellow liquid; usually has faint odour. Refractive index (n 25/D) 1.5367; sp. gr. 1.26 (25/4°C) b.p. 375°C; f.p. 6°C; vapour pressure 0.003 mm (24°C); very slightly soluble in water (20 ppm); completely soluble in esters, alcohols, ketones, ethers, aromatic hydrocarbons, animal and vegetable oils; insoluble in petroleum ether, kerosene, spray oils. Stable in distilled water and in acid solution. Hydrolysed in the presence of alkaline materials slowly decomposes in air. It is highly toxic by skin contact, inhalation or ingestion. Cholinesterase inhibitor. Repeated exposure may, without symptoms, be increasingly hazardous. Fatalities have resulted from its accidental use. Tolerance 0.1 mg per cubic metre of air. Use has been restricted.

## FUMIGANTS

A toxic agent in vapour form that destroys rodents, insects, and infectious organisms; a type of pesticide. The most effective temperature for their use is about 70°F. They are used chiefly in enclosed or limited areas (barns, greenhouses, ships holds, and the like); also are applied locally to soils, grains fruits and garments. Some commonly used fumigants are formaldehyde, sulphur dioxide and other sulphur compounds, hydrogen cyanide, methyl bromide, carbon tetrachloride, p-dichlorobenzene, and ethylene oxide. Care must be used when handling and applying fumigants in view of their toxicity. Some of the fumigants are discussed below.

### Ethylene Dibromide

It can be prepared by the action of bromine on ethylene. It is colourless, nonflammable liquid having sweetish odour and emulsifiable. Miscible with most solvents and thinners; slightly soluble in water. sp. gr. 2.17–2.18 (20°C); wt/gal 18.1 lb; b.p. 131°C; vapour pressure 17.4 mm (30°C);f.p. 9°C; refractive index 1.5337 (25°C); flash point, none. It can be used as scavenger for lead in gasoline; grain fumigant; general solvent; water proofing preparations; organic synthesis; fumigant for tree crops. It is toxic by inhalation, ingestion, and skin absorption. Carcinogen in test animals. Strong irritant to eyes and skin.

**Ethylene Dichloride**

It can be prepared by the action of chlorine on ethylene with subsequent distillation, with metallic catalyst; also by reaction of acetylene and HCl. It is colourless, oily liquid; chloroform-like odour; sweet taste. Stable to water, alkalies, acids, or active chemicals, Resistant to oxidation and will not corrode metals. Miscible with most common solvents; slightly soluble in water. B.p 83.5°C; f.p.-35.5°C sp. gr. 1.2554 (20/4°C); wt/gal 10.4 lb; refractive index 1.444; flash point 56°F (13.3°C).

It is used in vinyl chloride solvent; lead scavenger in anti-knock gasoline; paint, varnish and finish removers; metal degreasing; soaps and scouring compounds; wetting and penetrating agents; organic synthesis; ore floatation It is toxic by ingestion, inhalation, skin absorption. Strong irritant to eyes and skin. Tolerance, 10 ppm in air. Flammable, dangerous fire risk; explosive limits in air 6 to 16% and it may be carcinogenic.

**Para-dichlorobenzene**

Para-dichlorobenzene is prepared by the chlorination of monochlorobenzene. It is in the form of white crystals; volatile (sublimes readily); penetrating odour and it is combustible. Sp.gr. 1.458; b.p. 173.7°C; m.p. 53°C; flash point 150°F (6.5.5°C) (closed cup). Soluble in alcohol, benzene, and ether; insoluble in water. It is used as moth repellent; general insecticide; germicide; space odorant; manufacture of 2,5–dichloroanililne; dyes; intermediates; pharmacy; agriculture (fumigating soil). It is toxic by ingestion; irritant to eyes. Tolerance, 75 ppm in air.

**MITICIDES**

Miticide generally is a pesticide which kills mites, small animals of the spider class, among them the European red mite and the common red spider which infest fruit trees.

**RODENTICIDES**

Both inorganic (zinc phosphide) and organic compounds are used as rodenticides. They all kill rodent when they penetrate through the gastrointestinal tract, although the mechanism of action of each pesticide is different. Rodenticides are mainly used for preparing poisoned baits. Grains of wheat, rye, corn, etc. are used as the bait material for controlling gophers, voles midday gerbils and mice in field conditions. Grain bait can be used to control voles only in cold weather. In summer, they do not eat such bait. To eradicate them in warm weather, and also the great gerbil in spring and autumn, green bait is used such as alfalfa, clover, and other succulent food.

To exterminate rats and mice in premises (granaries, livestock, buildings, greenhouses, etc.), bread crumbs, porridge, grain, minced meat and fish,etc.are used as the bait. At stock-raising farms, bait is prepared on the fodder forming the ration of the livestock and is placed in the feed bunks in stalls freed of animals. Baits must include adhesive (stickers). Vegetable oils are the best for this purpose. In controlling gophers, motor oil is mainly used as the adhesive.

Water-soluble poisons are used in the form of aqueous solutions and the bait is soaked in them. A very small assortment of substances is used in practice for poisoned baits. This is associated with the difficulty of preparing substances with a narrow selective toxicity.

### Zinc Phosphide (Phosvin)

The active ingredient in $Zn_3P_2$. The pure substance is a dark grey odourless powder with a high melting point. It is insoluble in water and ethanol, and soluble in benzene and carbon disulphide. It is thermally stable. When reacted with acids, even weak organic ones, zinc phosphide decomposes with the evolution of the very poisonous phosphine, capable of spontaneous flammation :

$$Zn_3P_2 + 6\,HCl \longrightarrow 2PH_3 + 3ZnCl_2$$

Such a process also occurs in an animals's stomach upon the souring of baits consisting of bread, dough, porridge, or greens. Such baits lose their toxic properties in a few days. Zinc phosphide decomposes comparatively slowly in other poisoned baits, and their toxicity persists during a month and more. Consequently, when zinc phosphide is used, domestic and wild animals and birds may be poisoned.

The toxic action of zinc phosphide on rodents is due to the fact that when it is ingested into the stomach, it decomposes into phosphine, which is the toxic substance. Phosphine penetrates with the blood stream into the animals's nervous system and results in violation of its functions. The death of animals is preceded by vomitting, weakening of the heart's activity, emphysema, and convulsions.

The toxicity of zinc phosphide to rodents depends on the quality of the poison and on the natural resistance of the animals to its action. The quality of the rodenticide is determined by the fineness of grinding, which underlies the dimensions of the poison's reactive surface coming into contact with the acid in an animals's stomach. Finer particles accelerate and amplify the action of the poison. The fineness of grinding is determined by the relevant USSR State Standard. The resistance of rodents to zinc phosphide depends on their mass, physiological state, age, and specific features. Animals with a high vitality (in the period of intensive reproduction) are more resistant to poisons.

The specific resistance of rodents to zinc phosphide is associated with the features of their feed in. The high resistance of gophers is apparently explained by the lower acidity of their gastric juice. The amount of acid evolved in the stomach depends on the composition and quality of the food and on the time when it enters the stomach. It has been established that the more the food corresponds to the needs of rodents in the given conditions of their existence, the higher is the acidity of their gastric juice and the more rapidly does poisoning with zinc phosphide occur. Baits with zinc phosphide have no repelling taste or odour and are readily eaten by rodents.

As regards its toxicity to humans and warm-blooded animals, zinc phosphide belongs to strong poisons with selective toxicity; it has no chronic toxicity. It completely decomposes in the stomachs of killed animals, therefore the secondary poisoning of predators is excluded.

**Fungicides**

Any substance which kills or inhibits the growth of fungi is known as fungicide. Older types include mixtures of lime and sulphur, copper oxychloride, and Bordeaux mixture. Copper naphthenate has been used to impregnate textile fabrics such as tenting and military clothing. Mercury compounds are also effective, but have been discontinued because of their toxicity to humans. Hypochlorite solutions are used in swimming pools and water-cooled heat exchangers. Some types of fungi that infect the human body are extremely hard to eradicate and require highly specific medical treatment.

**Eptam**

It is trade-mark for a selective herbicide containing ethyl-N, N-di-n-propylthiolcarbamate.

2, 3-dichloroallyl diisopropylthiolcarbamate (Diallate)

It is in the form of brown liquid; b.p. 159°C (9 mm). Almost insoluble in water; soluble in acetone, benzene, chloroform, kerosene, and xylene. It is generally used as herbicide. It is toxic and absorbed by skin.

**Ferbam**

It can be prepared by addition of carbon disulphide to an alcoholic solution of dimethylamine and precipitation with a ferric salt. It is in black or dark coloured fluffy powder; decomposes above 180°C; usually readily dispersible but very slightly soluble in water; pH of saturated solution 5.0. It is used as a fungicide. It is irritant to eyes and mucous membranes. Tolerance, 10 mg per cubic metre of air.

**2, 4, 6-trichlorophenol**

It is in the form of yellow flakes with strong phenolic odour; sp. gr; (25/4°C) 1.675; f.p. 61°C; b.p. 248–249°C; no flash point. Soluble in acetone, alcohol, and ether. It is non-flammable. It is used as fungicide, herbicide, defoliant. It may cause skin irritation.

**Para-chlorophenol**

It can be prepared by chlorination of phenol; from chloroailine through the diazonium salt. It is the form of white crystals (yellow or pink when impure) with unpleasant penetrating odour. Slightly soluble in water; soluble in benzene, alcohol, and ether. Volatile with stream; b.p. 217°C; m.p. 42–43°C; sp. gr. 1.306; refractive index (n40/D) 1.5579. A 1% solution is acid to litmus. Flash point 250°F (121°C). It is combustible. It is used as an intermediate in synthesis of dyes and drugs; denaturant for alcohol; selective solvent in refining minerals oils; antiseptic. It is toxic by skin absorption, inhalation or ingestion. Strong irritant to tissue.

**Glyodin**

It can be prepared by the action of ethylenediamine on stearic acid. It is in the form of light orange crystals; m.p. 62°C; sp. gr. 1.03; insoluble in water. Toxicity probably low. It is used as fungicide (fruits and vegetables).

**HERBICIDES**

A pesticide, either organic or inorganic, used to destroy unwanted vegetarian, especially various types of weeds, grasses, and woody plants. Until 1924 inorganics such as sodium chlorate, sodium chloride, ammonium sulphamate, arsenic, and boron compounds were used. At that time the more specific organics were introduced, typified by 2, 4-dichlorophenoxyacetic acid (2, 4-D) Herbicides may be of two major types : (i) selective, such as 2, 4-D; 2, 4, 5-T; phenols; carbamates, and urea derivatives, permitting elimination or weeds without injury to the crop; and (ii) non-selective, comprising soil sterilants (sodium compounds) and silvicides (ammonium sulphamate). The latter kill wood plants and trees. Some types act as overstimulating growth hormones. Many herbicides are highly toxic and should be handled and applied with care; use of chlorinated types may be restricted.

**2, 4-dichlorophenol**

It can be prepared by chlorination of phenol. It is in the form of white, low melting solid; b.p. 210°C; m.p. 45°C; flash point 237°F (113°C);' combustible. Soluble in alcohol and carbon tetrachloride; slightly soluble in water. It is used in organic synthesis. It is strong irritant to tissue; moderately toxic by ingestion.

**Sodium Trichloroacetate**

It is toxic by ingestion. Irritant to skin and eyes. It is used as herbicide and pesticide.

**Chloro-IPC**

It is a light tan powder; m.p. 41.4°C; vapour pressure (149°C) 2 mm; sp. gr. 1.18 (30°C)j; very slightly soluble in water. It is a pre-emergence herbicide; prevents sprouting of potatoes. It is toxic by ingestion.

**Sesone**

It is a cystalline solid m.p. 245°C; soluble in water. It is toxic and is used as pre-emergence herbicide.

**MCPA**

It is a white crystalline solid; m.p. 118–119°C. Free acid insoluble in water but sodium and amine salts are soluble. It is used as selective herbicide.

**Synthetic Insecticides**

These insecticides, unlike other types, are absorbed by the plant roots and foliage and translocated through the plants. In this manner, they render plants toxic to aphides, red spider mites and other sucking insects that are otherwise difficult to be killed. These insecticides remain within the plants and so remain effective for much longer time than the other insecticides sprayed on their surface. If synthetic insecticides are applied to seeds, they are capable of protecting the young plants for a considerable period of time. *Schradan, dimefox, systax,* and *dimetholate* etc. are well known and important synthetic insecticides. These are described briefly as under :

(1) Schradan is octamethyl pyrophosphoramide and can be prepared by the reaction of tetramethyl diamido chlorophosphate with water in the presence of tertiary amine. Treatment of ethyl tetramethyl diamidophosphate with tetramethyl amidochlorophosphate at 40°C give schradan in a good yield. It is soluble in water as well as in most organic solvents. It provides long term protection from aphides and mites after absorption into plants.

(2) Dimefox is bis (dimethylamino) phosphoryl fluoride and can be prepared by the following important methods :

(a) By the reaction of dimethylamine with dimethylamido difluorophosphate.

(b) By the action of sodium fluoride on bis (dimethyl amino phsophoryl chloride).

It is a colourless mobile liquid, which is soluble in water as well as in common organic solvents. It is most suitable for foilage application. It is an insecticide for sucking pests of hops and vactors of a virus disease of Cocao trees.

(3) Systax or Demeton can be prepared by the action of diethyl chlorothiophosphate with 2-hydroxy diethyl sulphide in presence of NaOH. It is in the form of yellow colour liquid which soluble in organic solvents. It is long-lasting, rapidly absorbed by roots, stems or foliage.

(4) Dimethoate can be prepared by the reaction of potassium salt of dimethyl dithio phosphoric acid with N-methyl chloroacetamide. It is in the form of white crystalline solid, which is soluble in water as well as in common organic solvents. It is used for fruit larvae and for side dressing of soil.

# 2

# Introduction of Pesticide

## Introduction

Pesticide means any substance intended for preventing, destroying attracting, repelling or controlling any pest inciuding unwanted species of plants or animals during production, storage transport, distribution and processing of food, agricultural commodities, or animals feeds or which may be administered to the animals for the control of ectoparasites. The term includes substances intended for use a plant growth regulator, defoliant, desiccant, fruit thinning agent or sprouting inhibitor and substances applied to the crops either before or after harvest to protect the commodity from deterioration during storage and transport. The term normally excludes fertilizers, plant and animal nutrients, food additives and animal drugs. Pesticide is a general terms used in connection with any pest. More specific terms are available for individual pest categories. Pests are any organisms, insects, rodents, nematodes, fungal diseases, weeds, herbs, bacteria etc. which are injurious to the health of man or to rnans economic efforts.

| | |
|---|---|
| Insecticides: | are substances that prevent, destroy kill mitigate insects (belonging to class insects, Phylum athropoda). |
| Fungicides: | are substances that prevent, destroy or inhibit the growth of fungi/diseases in crops. |
| Herbicides: | are substances which are used for preventing or inhibiting growth of plants or for killing weeds. |
| Rodenticides: | are substances that inhibit growth, destroy or kill rodents (Class Mammalia, order Rodentia) |
| Nematicides: | are substances that prevent, destroy, repel or inhibit the nematodes. |
| Chemosterilants: | are substances that sterlize the pests. |
| Molluscicides: | are substances that prevent, repel, destroy or inhibit the growth of the Phylum Mollusca. |

| | |
|---|---|
| Plant growth Regulators: | are substances that cause the acceleration or retardation of the rate of growth or rate maturation. |
| Defoliants: | are substances that cause the plant leaves to die and fall away. |
| Desiccants: | are substances that cause to drain moisture out of the plants causing them to dry. |
| Attractants: | are substances that attract the pests. |
| Repellents: | are substances that repels the pest from a treated plant. |

### *Ideal pesticide*

It should have the following properties:

1. It should have a broad spectrum to kill the pests.
2. It should be non-toxic to mammals.
3. It should be non-toxic to plants.
4. It should have low production cost.
5. It should be easily formulated.
6. It should have optimal residue persistence.
7. It should have low toxicity to beneficial insects.
8. It should be compatible with other pesticides.
9. It should not produce off taste on vegetables on which it is sprayed.
10. It should be non inflammable and should have non corrosive action on metals.

### Steps involved in commercial development of pesticide starting from laboratory synthesis.

1. Synthesis
2. The preliminary screening.
3. Formulation
4. Toxicity studies, (acute, oral, dermal etc.)
5. Metabolism studies.
6. Residue studies.
7. Registration
8. Promotion
9. Pilot plant studies.
10. Commercial Development.

## Reasons for use of pesticides

1. Pesticides are used to ensure better protection at harvest against unpredictable losses caused by plant diseases and pests.
2. Pesticides are used to improve both quality and quantity of food.
3. Pesticides are used to decrease the extent of vector born and other diseases in humans and animals.

## Production of pesticides in organised sector in India.

Of the total pesticides used in India, 80 per cent are insecticides, 11 per cent are fungicides, and 7 per cent are herbicides. In India, total production of pesticides has increased from 250 metric tonnes in 1947-48 to 80,000 metric tonnes during the year 1996-97. India has installed capacity of infrastructure of manufacture of 62 technical grade pesticides (Table 1).

**Table 1 : Indian production of major technical grade pesticides**

| *Product* | *Production (1000 tonnes)* | | | *% of installed* |
|---|---|---|---|---|
| | *1995-96* | *% change* | *1996-97* | *capacity* |
| **Insecticides** | | | | |
| Acephate | 0.5 | 0.0 | 0.5 | 100.0 |
| BHC | 30.2 | +1.0 | 30.5 | 82.4 |
| Chlorpyrifos | 0.2 | 0.0 | 0.2 | 25.0 |
| Cypermethrin | 1.0 | +10.0 | 1.1 | 100.0 |
| DDT | 6.0 | –16.7 | 5.0 | 54.9 |
| dichlorvos | 1.6 | 0.0 | 1.6 | 61.5 |
| dimethoate | 1.7 | 0.0 | 1.7 | 73.9 |
| endosulfan | 7.4 | –5.4 | 7.0 | 95.9 |
| ethion | 0.8 | 0.0 | 0.8 | 88.9 |
| fenitrothion | 0.03 | –33.3 | 0.02 | 4.0 |
| fenthion | 0.2 | 0.0 | 0.2 | N.A |
| fenvalerate | 1.2 | +16.7 | 1.4 | 100.0 |
| malathion | 2.9 | +3.4 | 3.0 | 39.5 |
| metasystox | 0.4 | +50.0 | 0.6 | 100.0 |
| monocrotophos | 7.8 | +7.7 | 8.4 | 81.6 |
| parathion-methyl | 2.4 | 0.0 | 2.4 | 53.3 |
| phorate | 3.3 | +15.2 | 3.8 | 97.4 |

Contd......

| | | | | |
|---|---|---|---|---|
| phosalone | 0.4 | 0.0 | 0.4 | 40.0 |
| phosphamidon | 2.0 | +5.0 | 2.1 | 65.6 |
| quinalphos | 2.5 | +20.0 | 3.0 | 100.0 |
| temephos | 0.3 | 0.0 | 0.3 | N.A |
| **Fungicides** | | | | |
| captan/captafol | 0.5 | 0.0 | 0.5 | 83.3 |
| carbendazim | 0.7 | −14.3 | 0.6 | 50.0 |
| mancozeb | 4.0 | −5.0 | 3.8 | 95.0 |
| thiram | 0.02 | 0.0 | 0.02 | 10.0 |
| tridemorph | 0.2 | 0.0 | 0.2 | 40.0 |
| ziram | 0.1 | 0.0 | 0.1 | 25.0 |
| **Herbicides** | | | | |
| 2,4–D | 0.9 | +11.1 | 1.0 | 55.6 |
| butachlor | 1.2 | -33.3 | 0.8 | 17.8 |
| fluchloralin | 0.14 | -35.7 | 0.09 | 30.0 |
| isoproturon | 2.70 | +11.1 | 3.0 | 96.8 |
| **Fumigants** | | | | |
| aluminium phosphide | 1.50 | -6.7 | 1.4 | 100.0 |
| methyl bronmide | 0.08 | 0 | 0.08 | 26.7 |
| Total | 85.50 | +0.4 | 85.8 | 73.6 |

## Level of pesticides consumption in various countries

The consumption of pesticides kg/ha in developing countries is low as compared to the developed countries. India use only 0.3 kg/ha of pesticides while in Korea and Japan it is 6.60 and 10.80 kg/ha respectively (Table 2)

**Table 2 : Pesticide used on major crops in some countries**

| *Country* | *Pesticide used (Kg/ha)* | *Country* | *Pesticide used (Kg/ha)* |
|---|---|---|---|
| 1. Japan | 10.80 | 6. Indonesia | 0.60 |
| 2. Korea | 6.60 | 7. India | 0.30 |
| 3. Europe | 1.90 | 8. Latin America | 6.22 |
| 4. USA | 1.50 | 9. Oceanic | 0.13 |
| 5. Thailand | 1.40 | 10. Africa | 0.13 |

## Present consumption and future demand

The planning commission's working group on Pesticide Industry has placed the demand for technical grade pesticides at 107, 864 metric tonnes for the year 1994-95 (Table 3). The production and consumption of pesticides have not witnessed an increase at the desired pace in spite of the fact that the area under plant protection has been increasing considerably year after year.

**Table 3 : Demand pattern during VIIIth five year plan**

| Group of pesticides | (Tonnes) Demand as proposed by working group | | |
|---|---|---|---|
| | 1989-90 | 1991-92 | 1994-95 |
| Fungicides | 11,387 | 13,858 | 15,564 |
| Weedicides | 5,710 | 6,541 | 8,125 |
| Rodenticides& Fumigants | 1,790 | 2,062 | 2,615 |
| Acaridies | 145 | 154 | 170 |
| Total | **79,482** | **91,040** | **1,07,864** |

*Source :* Report of the working group on Pesticide Industry (VIIIth Five Year Plan), November 1989, Government of India, cited from David B.V. (ed) (1992) Pest Management and Pesticides: Indian Scenario, Namrutha Publications, Chennai, p.250.

## Cropwise consumption of pesticides

The figures of cropwise consumption indicate that cotton claims most of the pesticides 44.5% while for paddy it is 22% of the total pesticide used followed by jowar (8.9%) and wheat (6.4%). The consumption of pesticide on fruits and vegetables is only 7% (Table 4)

**Table 4: Cropwise consumption of pesticides**

| *Crop* | *Estimated pesticide consumption (in million Rs.)* | *% to total pesticides consumption* |
|---|---|---|
| Paddy | 1272.05 | 22.0 |
| Wheat | 354.18 | 6.4 |
| Jowar | 495.40 | 8.9 |
| Bajra | 95.05 | 1.8 |
| Barley | 0.00 | 0.0 |
| Ragi | 24.04 | 0.4 |
| Maize | 63.62 | 1.1 |
| Arhar | 155.20 | 2.8 |

Contd.....

| | | |
|---|---|---|
| Gram | 12.20 | 0.2 |
| Jute | 15.38 | 0.3 |
| Cotton | 2462.13 | 44.5 |
| Sugar cane | 38.41 | 0.7 |
| Groundnut | 136.84 | 2.5 |
| Rape and mustard | 9.10 | 0.2 |
| Soybean | 0.95 | 0.0 |
| Sunflower | 3.04 | 0.1 |
| Onion | 10.92 | 0.2 |
| Potato | 2.45 | 0.0 |
| Tobacco | 3.93 | 0.1 |
| Tapioca | 0.10 | 0 0 |
| Fruits and vegetables (excluding Onion and Potato) | 389.38 | 7.0 |
| Total | 5555.37 | 100.0 |

## Statewise consumption of pesticides in agriculture

Amongst the states in terms of highest consumption of pesticides, Tamil Nadu is highest with 16.5%. The share of Andhra Pradesh, Uttar Pradesh, Maharashtra in total consumption of pesticides is abcut 13.0, 14.0 and 11.24 per cent respectively. Other states account for less than nearly 7 per cent, but most of the states account for less than 3 per cent (Table 5).

**Table 5 : Consumption of pesticides in various states/union territories**

| *Sl. No.* | *State/Union Territories* | *Consumption (Metric tonnes)* |
|---|---|---|
| 1. | Andhra Pradesh | 9,910 |
| 2. | Arunachal Pradesh | 30 |
| 3. | Assam | 595 |
| 4. | Bihar | 1,700 |
| 5. | Gujrat | 5,500 |
| 6. | Goa | 22 |
| 7. | Haryana | 4,500 |
| 8. | Himachal Pradesh | 7·8 |

Contd....

| | | |
|---|---|---|
| 9. | Jammu & Kashmir | 110 |
| 10. | Karnataka | 3,900 |
| 11. | Kerala | 1,100 |
| 12. | Madhya Pradesh | 4,500 |
| 13. | Maharashtra | 6,020 |
| 14. | Manipur | 50 |
| 15. | Meghalaya | 45 |
| 16. | Mizoram | 15 |
| 17. | Nagaland | 12 |
| 18. | Orissa | 1,800 |
| 19. | Punjab | 5,770 |
| 20. | Rajasthan | 2,758 |
| 21. | Sikkim | 20 |
| 22. | Tamil Nadu | 12,500 |
| 23. | Tripura | 164 |
| 24. | Uttar Pradesh | 8,480 |
| 25. | West Bengal | 5,000 |
| 26. | Andaman & Nikobar | - |
| 27. | Chandigarh | - |
| 28. | Delhi | 60 |
| 29. | Dadra & Nagar Haveli | 4 |
| 30. | Daman & Diu | - |
| 31. | Pondicherry | 135 |
| 32. | Lakshadweep | 0.70 |
| | Total | 75,417.70 |

## Pesticides Registered, not approved for use, banned, restricted for use and under review

The list of pesticides Registered, not approved for use, banned, restricted for use and under review are given in Tables 6,7,8,9 and 10.

**Table 6 : List of insecticides registered on regular basis under section 9(3) of the insecticides act, 1968"**

| Name of the Insecticide | | | |
|---|---|---|---|
| 1. | Acephate | 2. | Alachlor |
| 3. | Aldicarb | 4. | Allethrin |
| 5. | Alphanapthyl Acetic Acid | 6. | Aluminium phosphide |
| 7. | Anilophos | 8. | Atrazine |
| 9. | Alphacypermethrin | 10. | Aureofungin |
| 11. | Barium Carbonate | 12. | Benzene Hexachlcride (BHC) |
| 13. | Benthiocarb (Thiobencarb) | 14. | Benomyl |
| 15. | Bitertanol | 16. | Bromadiolone |
| 17. | Butachlor | 18. | Calcium Cyanide |
| 19. | Captafol | 20. | Captan |
| 21. | Cartap Hydrochloride | 22. | Carbaryl |
| 24. | Carbendazim | 24. | Carbofuran |
| 25. | Carboxin | 26. | Chlorbenzilate |
| 27. | Chlorfenvinphos | 28. | Chlormequat Chloride (CCC) |
| 29. | Chlorothalonil | 30. | Chlorpyriphos |
| 31. | Copper Oxychloride | 32. | Copper Sulphate |
| 33. | Coumachlor | 34. | Coumatetralyl |
| 35. | Cuprous Chloride | 36. | Cypermethrin |
| 37. | Cyfluthrin | 38. | Dalapon |
| 39. | Decamethrin (Deltamethrin) | 40. | Dichloro Diphenyl Trichloroethane (DDT) |
| 41. | Dichloropropane and Dichloropropanes mixture (DD mixture) | 42. | Dichlorvos(DDVP) |
| 43. | Dicofol | 44. | Diflubenzuron |
| 45. | Dimethoate | 46. | Dinacap |
| 47. | Dithianon | 48. | Diuron |
| 49. | Dodine | 50. | Diazinon |
| 51. | Dieldrin (Restricted for Locust Control by PPA) | 52. | 2,4-Dichlorophenoxy Acetic Acid (2,4-D, Sodium Amine and Ester Salts) |
| 53. | Ethylene Dibromide and Carbon Tetrachloride mixture (EDCT mixture 3:1) | 54. | Edifenphos |

Contd.....

| | | | |
|---|---|---|---|
| 55. | Endosulfan | 56. | Ethofenprox (Etofenprox) |
| 57. | Ethephon | 58. | Ethylene Dibromide (EDB) |
| 59. | Ethyl Mercury chloride | 60. | Ethion |
| 61. | Fenitrothion | 62. | Fenarimol |
| 63. | Fenobucarb (EPMC) | 64. | Fenthion |
| 65. | Fenvalerate | 66. | Ferbam |
| 67. | Fluchloralin | 68. | Fluvalinate |
| 69. | Formothion | 70. | Fosetyl-Al |
| 71. | Gibberellic Acid | 72. | Glyphosate |
| 73. | Iprodione | 74. | Isoproturon |
| 75. | Kitazin | 76. | Lime Sulphur |
| 77. | Lindane (Gamma BHC) | 78. | Malathion |
| 79. | Maleic Hydrazide (MH) | 80. | Mancozeb |
| 81. | Menazon | 82. | Metaldehyde |
| 83. | Methabenzthiazuron | 84. | Methoxy Ethyl Mercury Chloride (MEMC) |
| 85. | Methyl Bromide | 86. | Methyl Bromide + Ethylene Dibromide (1:1 & 3:1) |
| 87. | Methyl Chlorophenoxy Acetic Acid (MCPA) | 88. | Metalaxyl |
| 89. | Metoxuron | 90. | Methomyl |
| 91. | Metribuzon | 92. | Metolachlor |
| 93. | Monocrotophos | 94. | Mono Sodium Methane Arsonate (MSMA) |
| 95. | Myclobutanil | 96. | Methyl Parathion |
| 97. | Nickle chloride | 98. | Nicotine Sulphate** |
| 99. | Oxadiazon | 100. | Oxycarboxin |
| 101. | Oxydemeton-methyl | 102. | Oxyfluorfen |
| 103. | Para dichlorobenzene | 104. | Paris Green (Copper Acetoarsenite) |
| 105. | Paraquat dichloride | 106. | Pendimethalin |
| 107. | Permethrin | 108. | Phenthoate |
| 109. | Phenyl Mercury Acetate (PMA)** | 110. | Phorate |
| 111. | Phosalone | 112. | Phosphamidon |
| 113. | Pirimiphos-methyl | 114. | Profenofos |

Contd....

| | | | |
|---|---|---|---|
| 115. | Propanil | 116. | Propetamphos |
| 117. | Propoxur | 118. | Pyrethrum |
| 119. | Quinalphos | 120. | Sevidol (Carbaryl and Gamma BHC) |
| 121. | Simazine | 122. | Sirmate |
| 123. | Sodium Cyanide | 124. | Streptocycline (Streptorrycin) |
| 125. | Sulphur | 126. | Temephos |
| 127. | Trichloro Acetic Acid (TCA) | 128. | Triallate |
| 129. | Trichlorphom | 130. | Tricyclazole |
| 131. | Tridemorph | 132. | Tirfluralin |
| 133. | Thiometon | 134. | Thiram |
| 135. | Thiophanate Methyl | 136. | Triazophos |
| 137. | Triadimefon | 138. | Warfarin |
| 139. | Zinc Phosphide | 140. | Zineb |
| 141. | Ziram | 142. | Hexaconazole |
| 143. | Pretilachlor | 144. | Propiconazole |

** for export only

**Table 7: List of pesticides not approved for use**

| *Name of Pesticides* | | | |
|---|---|---|---|
| 1. | Calcium aresenate | 2. | EPN |
| 3. | Azinphos-methyl | 4. | Lead Arsonate |
| 5. | Mevinphos (Phosdrin) | 6. | Carbophenothion |
| 7. | Vamidothion | 8. | Mephosfolen |
| 9. | Azonphos Ethyl | 10. | Binapacryl |
| 11. | Dicrotophos | 12. | Thiodmeton/Disulfoton |
| 13. | Fention Acetate | 14. | Fention/Hydroxide |
| 15. | Chinomethionate (Morestan) | 16. | Ammonium Sulphamate |
| 17. | Leptaphos (Phosvel) | | |

**Table 8 : List of banned pesticides**

| Name of Pesticides | | | |
|---|---|---|---|
| 1. | Dibromochloropropane | 2. | Endrin |
| 3. | Pentachlornitobenzene (PCNB) | 4. | Pentachlorophenol (PCP) |
| 5. | Toxaphene | 6. | Ethyl Parathion |
| 7. | Chlordane | 8. | Heptachlor |
| 9. | Aldrin (w.e.f. 1.1.1994) | 10. | Paraquat-di-methyl Sulphate |
| 11. | Nitrofen | 12. | BHC |
| 13. | Tetradifen | | |

**Table 9 : List of pesticides restricted for use in India**

| Sl. No. | Name of Pesticides | Type of restriction (s) imposed |
|---|---|---|
| 1. | Aluminium Phosphide | It is to be sold only to Government Undertaking/Organisations and to be used under the strict supervision of Government Expert of Pest Control Operations whose expertise is approved by the plant protection Adviser to the Government of India. |
| 2. | B.H.C. | The use of BHC on vegetables, fruits, oilseed crops and preservation of foodgrains is banned. |
| 3. | Chlorbenzilate | Use in agriculture is banned. If required it can be imported by Govt./ Semi. Govt. Organisations for pre folbex strips for making it available to bee keepers for controlling mites of honeybees. |
| 4. | Captafol. | Shall be used only as seed dresser. Its use as foliar spray is banned. |
| 5. | D.D.T. | Use of DDT in agriculture is banned. Use of DDT for the public health programme upto 10,000 MTs per annum is restricted. |
| 6. | Dieldrin | Use of Dieldrin shall be restricted for locust control in desert areas by plant protection adviser to the Government of India. |
| 7. | Ethylene dibromide (EDB) | Use of EDB shall be restircted as a fumigant for foodgrains through Central Government, State Government, State Government Undertakings, Government Organisations such as Food Corporation of India, Central Warehousing Corporations, State Warehousing Corporation and Pest Control |

| | | |
|---|---|---|
| | | Operators whose expertise is approved by Plant Protection Adviser to the Govt. of India. |
| 8. | Methyl Bromide | Methyl Bromide is to be used as a fumigant in the manner in which Aluminium Phosphide is used. |
| 9. | Sodium Cyanide | Use of Sodium Cyanide shall be restricted for fumigation of cotton bales by Plant Protection Adviser to Govt. of India under Expert supervision. |
| 10. | Phenyl mercury acetate (PMA) | Use of PMA is prohibited in India w.e.f. 1.1.73 but it may continue to be produced in the country only for export. Nonconsumed stock as on 1.1.73 shall be used for Export purpose only and shall be subject to the modification in the Certificate of registration to this effect. |
| 11. | Lindane | Use of Lindane formulation generating smoke for indoor use is prohibited in India provided that lindane may be continued to be produced in the country for use for control of insect pests of field crops and subject to the modification in the Certificate of registration to this effect. |
| 12. | Nicotine Sulphate | Use of Nicotine Sulphate is prohibited in India provided that may be continued to be produced in the country only for Export purpose and subject to the modification in the Certificate of Registration to this effect. |

**Table 10 : List of pesticides which are under review by government of India**

| *Name of Pesticides* | |
|---|---|
| 1. Alachlor | 2. Benomyl |
| 3. Copper acetoarsenite | 4. Diuron |
| 5. Ethyl Mercury Chloride | 6. Fenarimol |
| 7. Menazon | 8. Methomyl |
| 9. Oxyflourfen | 10. Sodium Methane Arsonate |
| 11. Calcium Cyanide | 12. Phosphamidon |
| 13. Thiometon | 14. Triazophos |
| 15. Tridemorph | 16. Monocrotophos |
| 17. Ziram | 18. Zineb |

## List of quality control laboratories in India

In India the number of pesticide testing laboratories in state/union territories are 40 and capacity per annum for testing of samples for quality control is 45,556 (Table 11).

**Table 11 : Pesticides testing laboratories in state/union territory**

| *State/Union Territory* | *No. of labs* | *Location* | *Capacity annum* |
|---|---|---|---|
| Andhra Pradesh | 4 | Rajendranagar, Guntur Anantapur & Tadepalligudem | 8,520 |
| Assam | 1 | Guwahati | 166 |
| Bihar | 1 | Patna | 500 |
| Gujarat | 2 | Junagarh & Gandhinagar | 2,000 |
| Jammu & Kashmir | 1 | Srinagar | 600 |
| Karnataka | 2 | Bangalore & Bellary | 2,400 |
| Kerala | 1 | Trivandrum | 2,000 |
| Madhya Pradesh | 1 | Jabalpur | 1,000 |
| Maharashtra | 4 | Pune, Amravati, Thane & Aurangabad | 3,840 |
| Manipur | 1 | Mantripukhri | 30 |
| Mizoram | 2 | Aizwal | |
| Orissa | 1 | Bhubaneswar | 1,000 |
| Punjab | 3 | Ludhiana, Bhatinda & Amritsar | 900 |
| Rajasthan | 2 | Durgapura (Jaipur) & Bikaner | |
| Tamil Nadu | 9 | Coimbatore, Kovilpatti, Madurai, Trichurapalli, Aduthurai, Salem Erode, Kanchepuram & Cuddalore | 16,200 |
| Uttar Pradesh | 3 | Meerut, Lucknow & Varanasi | 3,000 |
| West Bengal | 1 | Midnapore | 450 |
| Pondicherry | 1 | Pondicherry | 450 |
| Total | 40 | | 45,556 |

# 3

# Insecticides

Insecticides can be defined as any substances or mixture of substances intended for preventing, killing, repelling or controlling insects.

## Classification of Insecticides

Insecticides are classified on the basis of :

1. Chemical nature
2. Mode of entry
3. Mode of action

## Based on Chemical Nature

Insecticides are classified based on the chemical nature as follows :

1. Inorganic compounds : arsenicals, fluorine compounds etc.
2. Organic compounds : DDT, HCH, Carbaryl, phorate etc.
3. Botanicals : Nicotine sulphate, pyrethrum etc.

## Based on Mode of Entry

1. **Stomach Insecticides :** The insecticides are applied to that part of the crop which serves as food for the pest and is required in the normal process of eating, for example DDT, HCH. Their application is through food and entry through the midgut of the insect. Stomach poisons are necessarily, therefore to be ingested during feeding.
2. **Contact Poisons :** Contact poisons are those which kill the pest only due to contact or absorbed action. Their application is through the body surface and entry through the cuticle and tracheae. For example pyrethrum, rotenone, toxaphene, and chlorodane.
3. **Fumigants :** Gaseous poisons used for killing insects are called fumigants. These are applied in vapour state and their entry is through tracheae e.g. HCN, chloropicrin, methyl bromide, DDVP, aluminum phosphide.
4. **Systemic Insecticides :** Systemic Insecticides are toxicants which when applied to the root, stem, or leaves of plants are rapidly

absorbed and translocated to various parts of the plants in amounts lethal to insects feeding on these e.g. phorate, aldicarb, carbofuran. Translocation of these pesticides takes place mostly through xylem vessels only.

The main properties of the systemic insecticides are :

(a) The compound should have sufficient solubility to enable the compounds to move in the plant sap.

(b) It should have ability to penetrate into the plant through roots, stems and leaves.

Repper has given the following classification of systemics :

(a) **Stable systemics :** Insecticides which don't metabolise in the system e.g. sodium fluorosilicate, sellinum.

(b) **Endolytic systemics :** Systemic insecticides in which the toxic compound is present in 98% in its original form, which is taken up by the insects e.g. Schradan.

(c) **Endometatoxic :** Systemic insecticides in which the toxic compounds gets converted into more toxic form e.g. systox, metasystox.

**Based on Mode of Action**

1. **Physical Poisons :** These compounds exert a physical rather than a biochemical effect and these actually kill the insects by suffocation.

2. **Inert Dusts :** They effect a loss of body moisture from insects by two types of action. Abrasive dusts e.g. aluminum oxide cause water loss by lacerating the epicuticle and water adsorbents e.g. charcoal remove water as a consequence of their hygroscopic properties.

3. **Heavy Mineral Oils:** These may exert a purely asphyrient effect killing scale insects slowly by exclusion of air.

4. **Protoplasmic Poisons:** The action of these poisons apears to be associated primarily with the precipitation of proteins e.g. heavy metals, nitrophenols, nitro cresols.

5. **Respiratory Poisons:** They combine with cytochrome oxidase and other oxidases containing Fe and thus inhibit their catalytic action e.g. HCN, $H_2S$, CO.

6. **Nerve Poisons:** The action of these poisons is associated primarily with their solubility in the tissue lipids. e.g. chlorinated hydrocarbons, organophosphates, botanical insecticides

## ORGANOCHLORINE INSECTICIDES

### DDT

(1,1,1, -trichloro,2,2-di(p-chlorophenyl) ethane)

This insecticide was first discovered by Zeidler (1874) but its powerful insecticidal properties were discovered by Paul Muller of the Swiss Geigy Company in 1939.

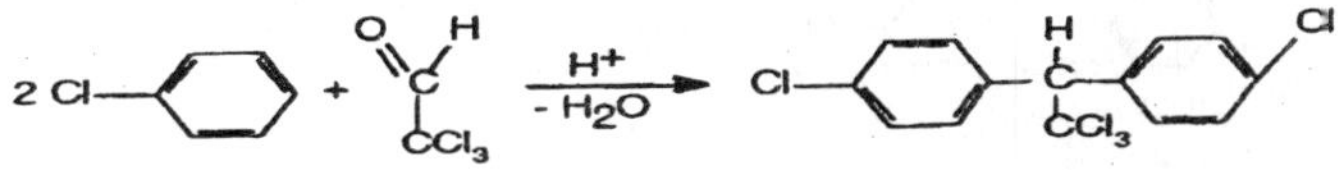

(1) 80%

+

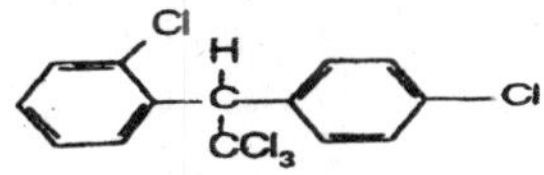

(2) 20%

DDT is prepared by the condensation of chloral and chlorobenzene in the presence of excess concentrated sulphuric acid.

The crude product consists of about 80% of the desired p,p' DDT (1) compound together with approximately 20% of the o,p' isomer (2) and trace of o,o' isomer. Only p,p' isomer has significant insecticidal activity. Pure p,p' DDT can be obtainted by recrystalization from ethanol.

### Reaction with Caustic Soda

DDT on treatment with alcoholic KOH is converted into 1,1-dichloro-2,2-bis (p-chlorophenyl) ethylene (DDE) (3)

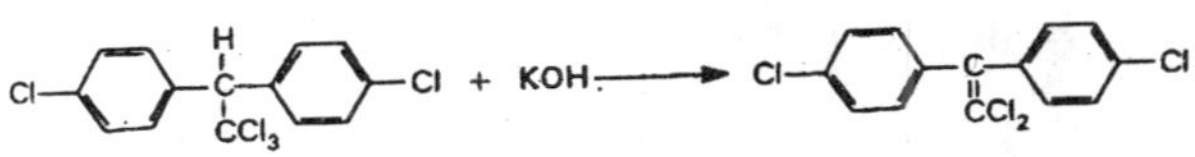

(3)

### Structure activity relationships

1. DDT type molecule must be substituted in the p,p' position with halogen or short chain alkyl or alkoxy groups. Replacement of Cl by H, Br, I, OH, higher hydrocarbons, $NH_2$, $NO_2$, COOH, CN, CNS. groups decreases the activity than DDT. Replacement by F, $-OCH_3$-$CH_3$, $-C_2H_5$ does not decrease the insecticidal activity but mammalian toxicity is reduced.
2. Replacement of Cl of $CCl_3$ by F, Br, alkyl decreases the activity.
3. If H in CH-$CCl_3$ is replaced by OH, insecticidal activity is nil but the compounds shows the acaricidal activity.

4. If $CCl_3$ is replaced by $CHCl_2$, $CH(NO_2)$, $CH_3$, $C(CH_3)_3$ the activity is decreased as follows.

$$CCl_3 > CHCl_2 > CH(NO_2) > CH_3 > C(CH_3)_3$$

5. If benzene rings of DDT are replaced by napthyl rings, then the compound is nontoxic to insects.

The metabolism of DDT is as follows

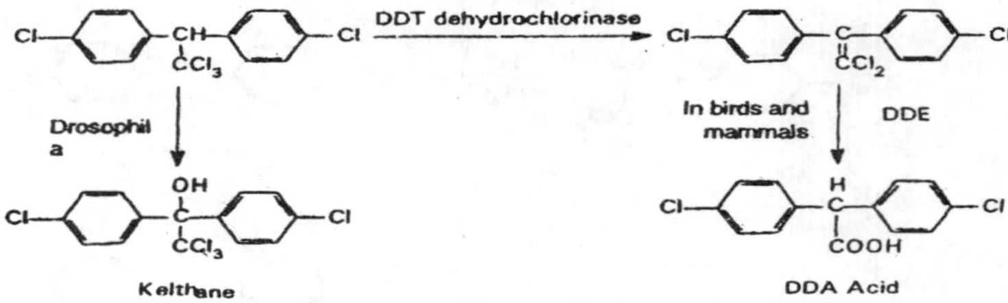


**Methoxychlor**

(1,1,1 trichloro-2,2-bis (p-methoxy phenyl) ethane)

It is prepared in good yield by the condensation of anisole and chloral in the presence of sulphuric acid.

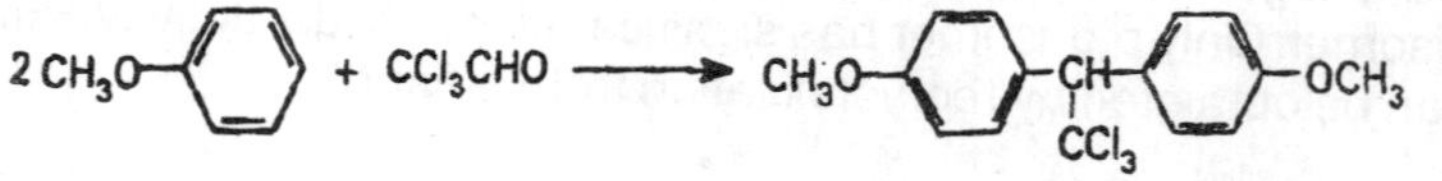

**DDD**

1,1-dichloro-2,2, bis (p-chlorophenyl) ethane)

Also known as TDE is prepared by the condensation of chlorobenzene with dichloroacetaldehyde

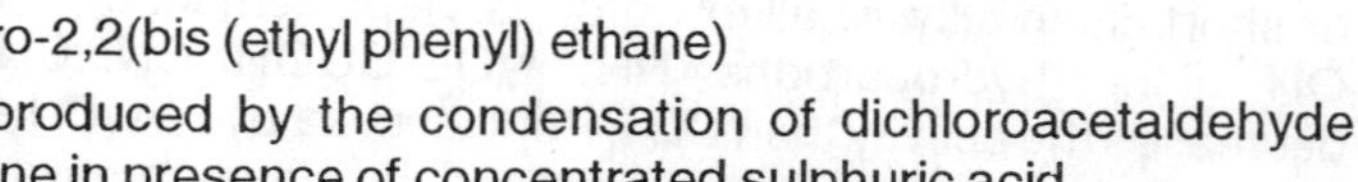

**Perthane**

(1,1-dichloro-2,2(bis (ethyl phenyl) ethane)

It is produced by the condensation of dichloroacetaldehyde with ethylbenzene in presence of concentrated sulphuric acid

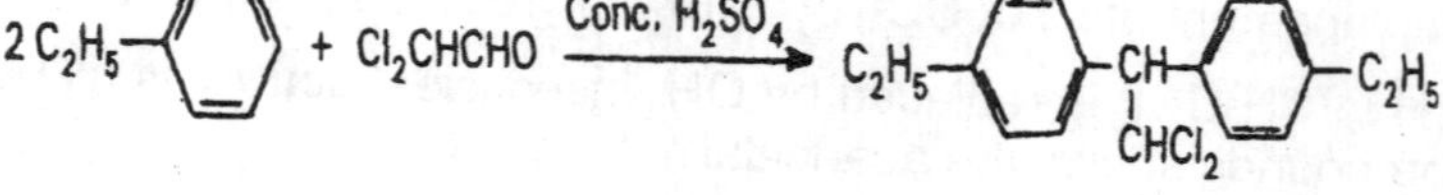

**DFDT**

(1,1,1-trichloro,2,2-bis (fluorophenyl) Ethane)

DFDT is prepared by treating fluorobenzene with chloral

**Chlorobenzilate**

(2-hydroxy 2,2-bis (p-chloro phenyl) acetate)

This is prepared from p-chlorobenzaldehyde via benzoin condensation.

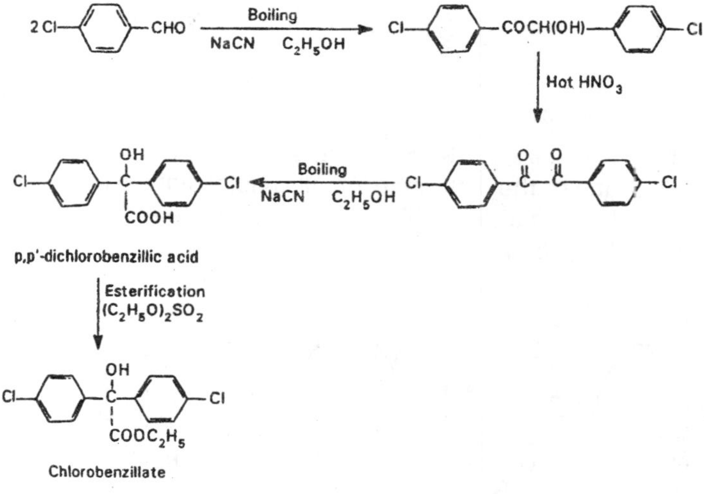

**Dilan**

Dilan is a mixture of Bulan 1,1' (2-nitrobutylidene) bis -(4-chlorobenzene) and prolan (1,1'-(2-nitropropylidene) bis (4-chlorobenzene). Bulan is prepared by addition of nitropropane to 4-chlorobenzaldehyde to give the carbinol which is then condensed with chlorobenzene to give Bulan

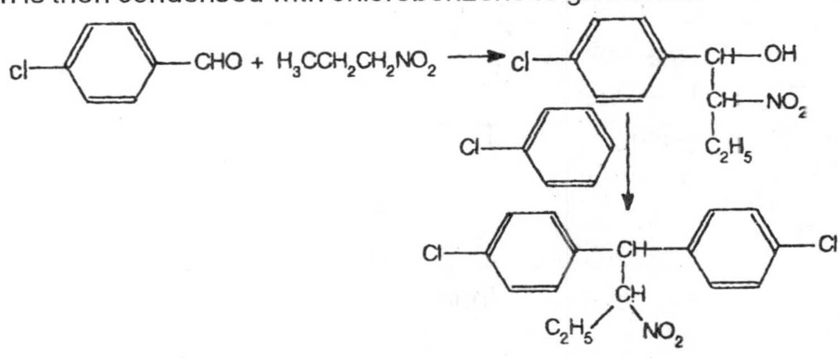

Prolan is prepared by treating nitroethane and 4-chlorobenzaldehyde to give carbinol and this is condensed with chlorobenzene to give Prolan

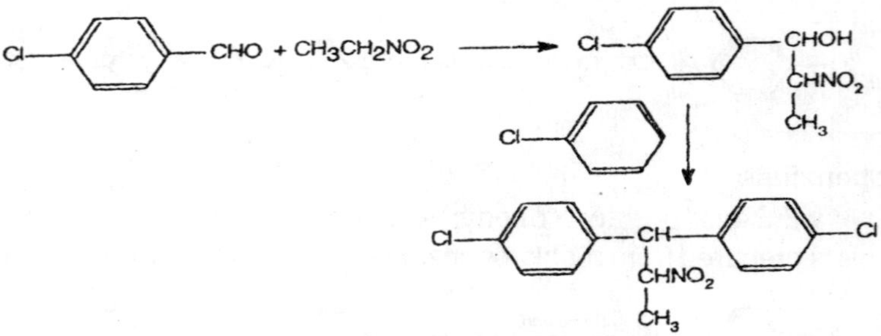

### HCH

(Hexacchlorocyclohexane)

HCH (Hexachlorocyclohexane) is prepared by treatment of benzene with chlorine under the influence of ultraviolet light without catalyst. Hexachlorocyclohexane can exist in eight different stereo-isomers of which five are present in product.

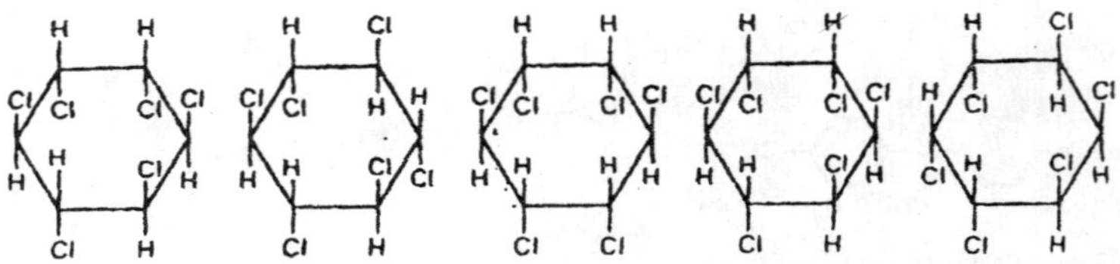

α β γ δ ε

The chlorination is carried out in excess of methylene chloride. In chlorination of benzene, mixture of isomers of HCH is obtainted with the following contents.

— α-isomer 53.70%
— β-isomer 3—14%
— γ-isomer 11—18%
— δ-isomer 6—10%
— ε-isomer 3—5%
— Heptachlorocyclohexane 3—4%
— Octachlorocyclohexane 0.5—1%
— Oily compounds 0.3—3%

The τ-isomer or lindane has insecticidal properties. The γ-isomer from the curde product is obtained by extraction with hot methanol followed by fractional crystallization to give pure γ-isomer. α and β isomers are insoluble in methanol.

τ-HCH (Lindane) exerts fumigant action but not as DDT because it has an appreciably higher vapour pressure $9 \times 10^{-6}$ mm Hg at 200°c than DDT ( $2 \times 10^{-7}$ mm Hg), so that it can exert a significant fumigant action.

**Action with caustic soda**

With caustic alkalies in alcoholic solution, HCH splits into three molecules of HCl giving trichlorobenzene.

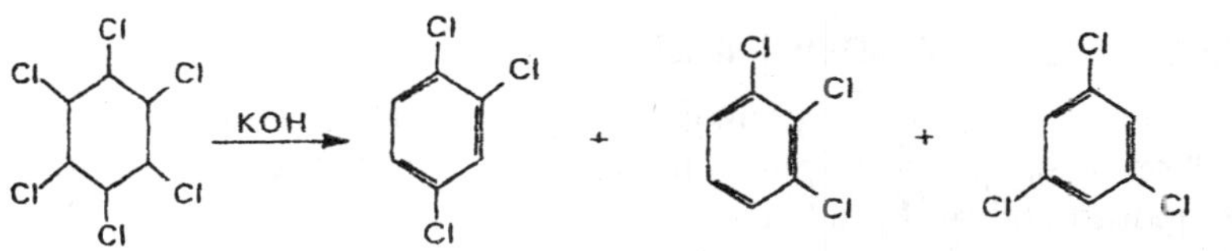


The main product of the reaction is 1,2,4-trichlorobenzene.

**Metabolism of HCH**

HCH is metabolised in the plants as follows:

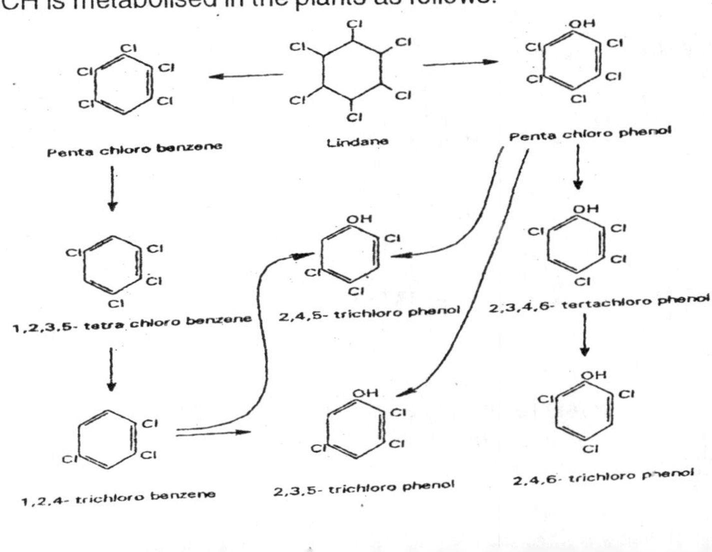

Structure Activity Relationship of HCH

1. γ-isomer of HCH has insecticidal property and is about 50 to 10,000 times toxic than a and b isomers.
2. If Cl in HCH is replaced by F, Br, I, CH3, activity is reduced than γ-HCH
3. Six chlorine atoms are essential for activity.

**Use of DDT and HCH in India**

Use of DDT is withdrawn in agriculture by the Ministry of Agriculture vide notification dated 26.5.1989. However the use of DDT for public health will be continued limited to 10,000 metric tonnes per annum.

The use of HCH is withdrawn on preservation of food grains, pulses, oilseeds etc. and in storage by ministry of Agriculture, Government of India.

**THE CYCLODIENE GROUP INSECTICIDES**

Most of the compounds of this group are prepared by Diel's-Alder reaction. A simple example of the Diel's-Alder reaction is the addition to conjugated diene of an ethylenic compound in which the double bond is adjacent to a carbonyl group e.g. butadiene combines with acraldehyde to form tetrahydrobenzaldehyde.

In general the diene synthesis is of the following type.

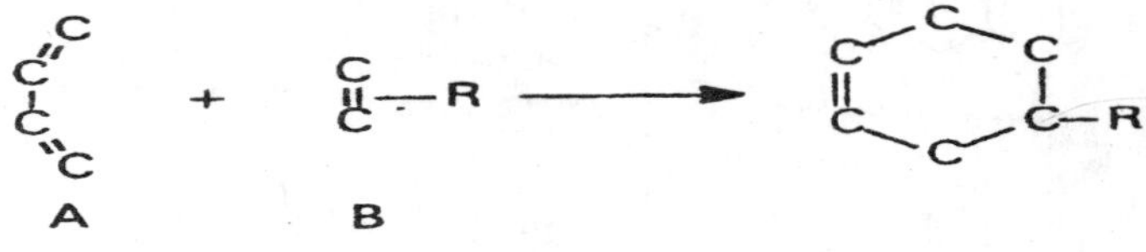

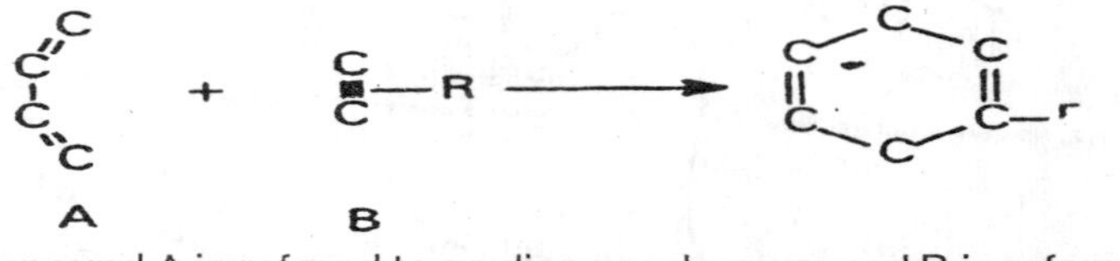

Compound A is refered to as diene and compound B is referred to as dienophile. R is usually a group which contains a carbonyl.

Characteristics of cyclodine Insecticides:

1. They are polycyclic structures
2. They are polychloro compounds
3. They contain methylene bridge
4. Their preparation is based on the Diels-Alder reaction
5. Action of alkalies- Resistant to alkalies but chlorodane and toxaphene are hydrolysed.

**Heptachlor**

(1,4,5,6,7,8,8, heptachloro-3a, 4,7, 7a tetrahydro-1, 7-methanoindene)

Heptachlor is prepared by chlorination of chlordene with sulfuryl chloride. Chlordene is prepared by the reaction of hexachloro cyclopentadiene with cyclopentadine

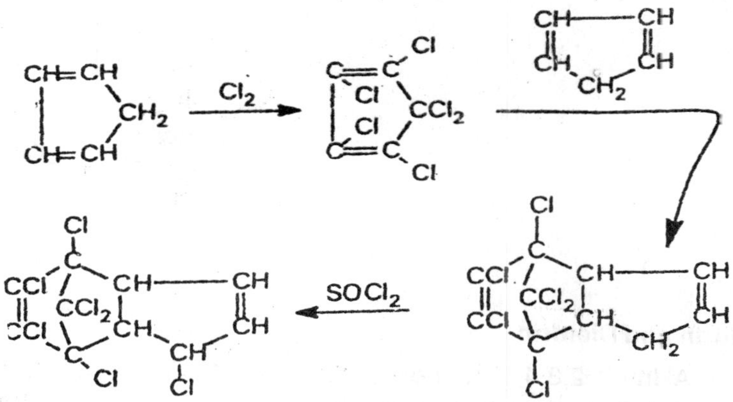

Heptachlor is also obtainted in good yield by the action of thionyl chloride with hydroxy chlordene.

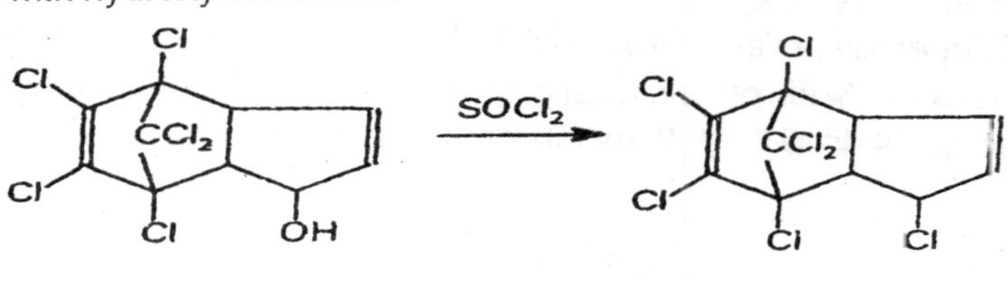

Heptachlor is used to control soil inhibiting pests. It has an advantage over BHC since it is stable in alkaline soils.

**Chlordane**

1,2,4,5,6,7,8,8-Octachloro-2,3,3a,4,7,7a-hexahydro-4,7-methano-IH-indene

Chlordane is prepared by treating hexachlorocyclopentodiene with cyclopentadiene to give chlordene which is converted to chlordane by treating carbon tetrachloride or with sulfuryl chloride in the presence of iron chlorine

Technical chlordane is brown liquid. It is almost insoluble in water. Chlordane is stable towards acid but losses hydrogen chloride under the influence of alkali. Its $LD_{50}$ is 283—590 mg/kg is broadly active contact, stomach and respiratory poison and is suitable for control of soil pests, white grubs and termites.

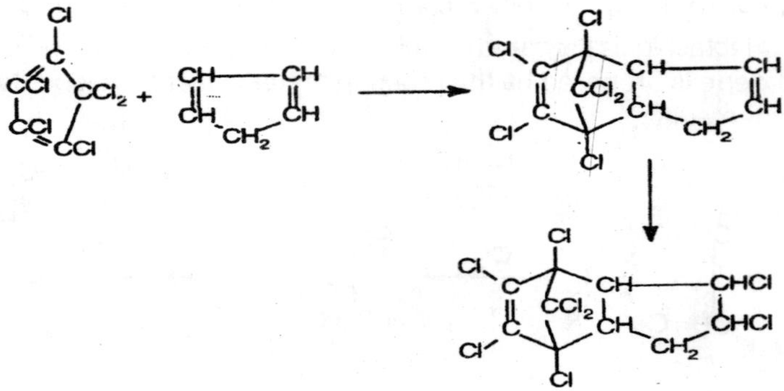

**Aldrin and Dieldrin**

Aldrin (1,2,3,4,10,10 hexachloro) - (1,4,4a, 5,8,8a hexahydro) - (1,4-endo, exo-5,8) - dimethano napthalene). Aldrin is obtainted by the reaction of hexachlorocyclopentadiene with an excess of bicyclo (2,2,1) -hepta-diene-2,5 at 100°C. Bicyclo (2,2,1) -heptadiene-2,5 is obtained by the action of cyclopentadine and vinyl chloride followed by treatment with potassium hydroxide. Aldrin on epoxydation gives Dieldrin, 1,2,3,4,10,10-hexachloro,6,7 epoxy, 1,4,4a, 5,6,7,8.8a-octahydro-1,4-endo, exo-5,8-dimethanonapthalene

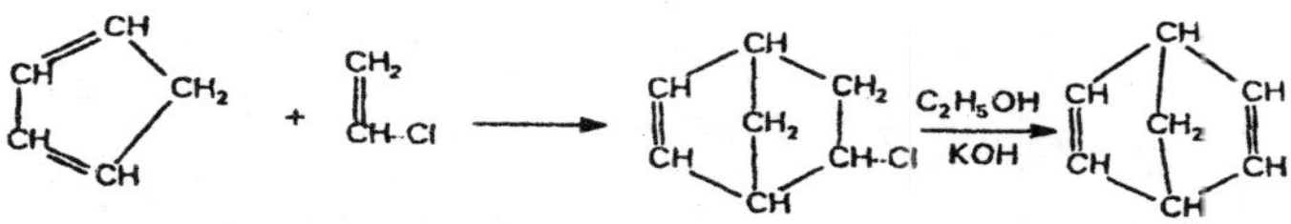


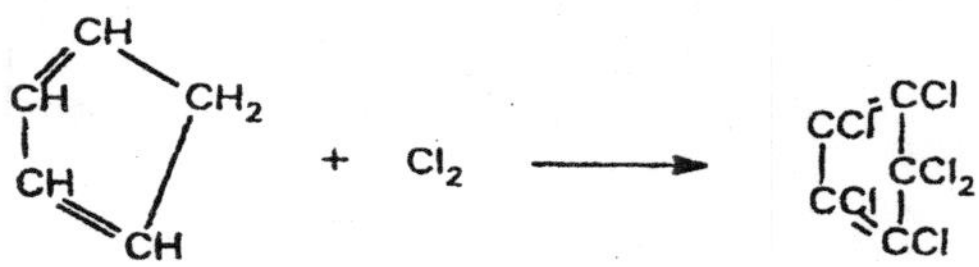

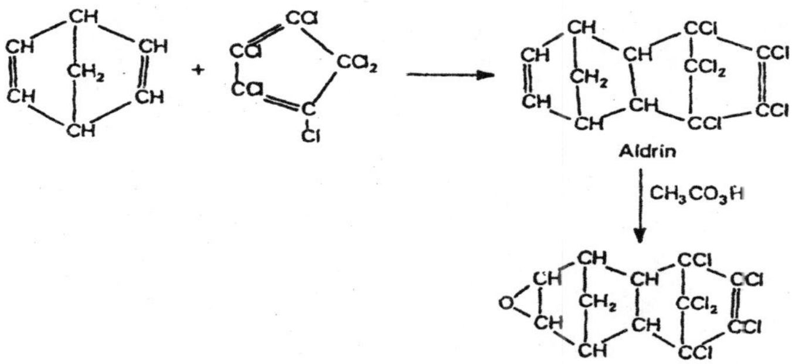


**Dieldrin**

## Endrin

(1,2,3,4,10,10 hexochlor-6, 7-epoxy-1,4,4a, 5,6,7,8,8a, octohydro, 14, 5,8, endo-dimethano napthalene.)

Endrin is produced by the oxidation of isodrin with hydrogen peroxide in acetic acid.

Heptachlor, chlordane, aldrin, and endrin are used to control soil inhibiting pests. These cyclodiene pesticides have an advantage over HCH since these are stable in alkaline soils.

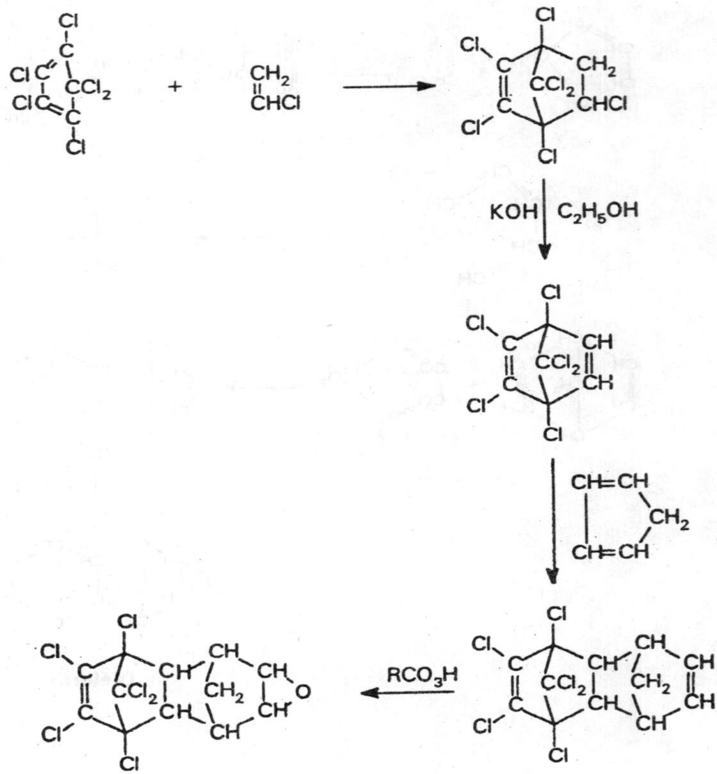

**Endosulfan**

(6,7,8,9,10,10-hexachloro-1,5,5a,6,9,9a-hexahydro 6, 9 metheno-2,4,3-benzodioxathiepin-3-oxide)

Endosulfan is prepared by treating endosulfan alcohol with thionyl chloride. Endosulfan alcohol is prepared by treating butene-2-diol-1,4-diacetate with hexachlorocyclopentadiene in xylene solution and subsequent hydrolysis in acid medium. The technical, material consists of 4 parts of α-endosulfan and one part of β-endosulfan.

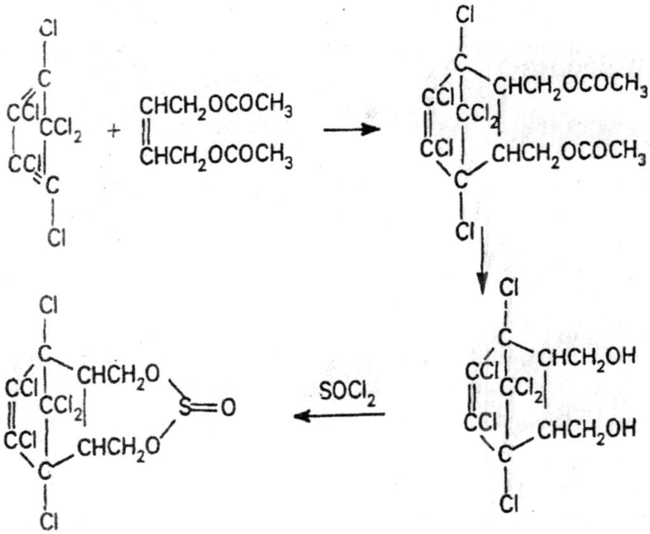

Endosulfan

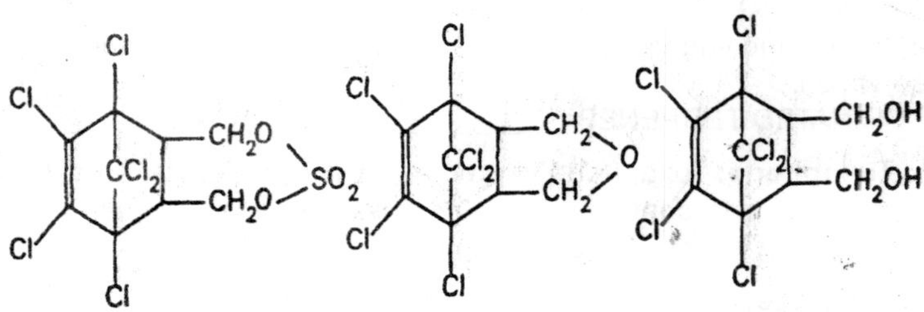

Endosulfan sulphate Endosulfan ether Endosulfan diol

Endosulfan is slowly converted at high temperature to endosulfan sulphate. In plants, endosulfan is converted into different metabolites endosulfan sulfate, endosulfan ether and endosulfan alcohol.

Uses of endosulfan -Endosulfan is a broad spectrum non-systemic, contact and stomach insecticide and is used for control of pests on various crops.

**Structure-activity relationship**

1. Increase in number of chlorine atoms in molecule increases the activity.

2. If all the chlorines are replaced by bromine, activity is reduced.
3. If two chlorine of cyclopentadine rings are replaced by F, then activity is increased.
4. Replacement of Cl of methano bridge by $-OCH_3$ group reduces the activity.
5. Highest activity is shown by these compounds that contain a polychlorinated centre together with another electronegative site such as double bound or Cl, O, S, or N atoms.
6. Configuration of rings, e.g. endo, oxo or endo, endo- has a substantial effect on insecticidal activity.
7. Removal of double bonds in aldrin by the addition of different groups like hydrogen, halogen, leads to decrease in activity.

**Use of cyclodiene Pesticides in India**

Registeration of endrin was withdrawn vide Ministry of Agriculture notification dated 15.5.90. Use of dieldrin is restricted for locust control by Plant Protection Adviser to Government of India only w.e.f. 15.5.90. Use of heptachlor and chlorodane has also been banned. Aldrin due to its proven termiticide properties and safety in low dosages is retained for termite control in soil and for seed treatment. But, its use is banned for use directly on food, fodder and vegetable crops or for directly mixing with food grains for preservation.

**CHLORINATED TERPENES**

— **Toxaphene:** Toxaphene is prepared by the chlorination of bicyclic comphene to contain 67 to 70% chlorine. It has emperial formula $C_{10}H_{10}Cl_8$. The oral $LD_{50}$ value to rates is 69 mg/kg.

— **Storbane:** Storbane is prepared by the chlorination of mixture of comphene and pinene to contain 66% chlorine. The oral $LD_{50}$ to rats is 200 mg/kg.

— **Polychloropinene:** Polsychloropinene is obtainted by the chlorinatin of bornyl chloride to contain 64 to 67% chlorine. The general formula is $C_{10}H_{10}Cl_8$. The oral $LD_{50}$ to rats is 200—500 mg/kg.

**Mode of action of chlorinated hydrocarbons**

Living organisms, which are elaborately ordered assays of organic and inorganic components, may be lethaly disordered by disrupting the essential life processes by mechanical, physical or chemical means. Chorinated hydrocarbons show a marked dependence of activity and structure and also cause specific modifications of the electrical properties of a nerve component.

**Mode of action of DDT and its derivatives**

It is agreed now that the primary effect of DDT is on the nervous system in both, vertebrates and invertebrates as indicated by the following evidence.

1. Nervous impairment is indicated by DDT jitters along with hyperexcitability followed by ataxia (loss of motion and apparent paralysis.
2. When applied to isolated tissues and enzymes, only nervous tissues are sensitive to low concentrations.

A positive correlation between the level of DDT in central nervous system of a rate and the intensity of symptoms exist. (Dale et al,).

All these evidences indicate that DDT is a neurotoxicant

Multiplication effect of DDT in nerve impulses was shown by Yeager and Munson. Single nerve impulse arriving at a DDT trated region gives rise to prolonged volleys of impulses. DDT acts on axonic rather than on synaptic transmission.

Roeder and Weiant showed that sensory nerves were more sensitive than the motor nerves in case of American cockroach, which was later confirmed by Welsh and Gordon.

Yamasoki and Narahashi, who started their study in 1957 have shown that in case of crural nerves of American cockroach, DDT increased the Negative after Potential' (NAP), which is associated with potassium efflux They suggested that DDT inhibited this efflux. Matsumura and O'Brein (1966) have finally shown that DDT greatly increased the $K^+$ permeability of cockroach nervous tissues.

Brown reviewed the structure activity relationships in DDT analogues and concluded that any attempt to obtain any complete quantitative correlation with any single property ends in failure and that symmetry is the only hallmark of all the good DDT analogus.

Toxin Theory', introduced by Sternburg and Kearns suggests the presence of a blood borne paralysis factor in cockroach treated with DDT. This factor was also introduced by other chemicals like TEPP and dieldrin. This theory does not explain the primary lession, presumably the membrane destabilization.

A theory that DDT acts upon the cholinesterase also exists. Tobias et.al. reported a two fold elevation in acetylcholine level in the housefly or cockroach nervous system, at later stages of poisoning, while cholineterase was unaffected. Similar effects of lindane and aldrin have been reported but, Kearns found that much of the so called acetyl choline was, in fact, trichloroacetic acid from the extraction procedure. Colhoun concluded that the acetylcholine effect was only secondary effect of DDT poisoning. The effect of DDT on the acetylcholine synthesis was reported by Lewis in case of *Calliphora erythrocephata*. He showed that the synthesis was reduced first and then increased, indicating that some enzyme is first inhibited and then activated.

DDT has a negative temperature coefficient of activity, being more active at low temperatures in contrast to organophosphates, pyrethrins and several chlorinated hydrocarbons.

DDT causes a sharp and substantial increase in the oxygen consumption of insects (Harvey and Brown). This may be due to the increased muscular activity due to excessive nervous activity.

Disturbance of amino acid metabolism caused by DDT is also know. Carrigan and Kearns (1965) showed that treatment of American cockroach at 150° C caused decreas of 71% and 61% of tyrosine and proline, respectively and increase of 131% of phenylalanine with small changes in 11 other amino acids. Similar effect were found with DDT in housefly and with DDT in cockroaches.

In 1954, Millins proposed a theory that the activity of DDT is due to physically sleepe of its molecule, which is such that it fits into the intermolecular lattice. The insecticidal molecule entering the interspace of lipoprotein in the axonic memberane is firmly attached to the surrounding lipoprotein molecule. This brings some distortion which cause nerve 'disorder' of DDT molecule enters interspaces from its trichlorocarbon group. The dichlorophenyl carbon group spreads enough to make a triangle so that it constitutes two stable feet. In order to make this arrangement, the benzene ring should be able to rotate, DDE which posses the double bond between two carbon atoms is unable to fit in the interspace. Its double bound prevents the rotation of the benzene ring making it non-toxic. The structure-activity relationship of various isomers of DDT can be explained on the basis of this hypothesis. In p,p' DDT, the chlorine atoms are attached at para position which allows the rotation of phenyl group, but if chlorine atom is attached to ortho position as in o,p' DDT, the rotation of phenyl group becomes difficult and in o,o' DDT is becomes impossible. It is for this reason the insecticidal activity of various insomers is p,p'>m,p>m,'>o,o' DDT.

## Mode of action of lindane and HCH

Like DDT, lindane and BHC too are neuroactive agents as indicated by symptoms like tremors, ataxia convulsion and prostration, stimulated respiration, increase in acetylcholine levels, excessive electrical activity in poisoned axons (Lalonde & Brown 1954) and a negative temperature coefficient though smaller than that of DDT (Guthrie, 1950).

Comparative studies of individual isomers on various insects revealed that γ-isomer of BHC is 60—10000 times as active as, α, β and d iscmers depending on insect species. Separation of γ-isomer is important from view point of human toxicology, because on one hand it considerably decreases the total quantity of BHC used and on the other hand, α, β and δ iscmers which are without insecticidal effects, accumulates most easily in various organisms. The activity of γ-isomer may be due to its molecular configuration. In gamma isomer, out of the six isomers of chlorine in benzene ring, three (1,2,3) are distributed alternately above and below at right angles to the equitorial plane of the benzene ring and rest of three atoms at 4,5 6 are located approximately in the equitorial plane of the benzene ring, no other isomers of BHC has this type of molecular configuration.

According to Mullins the molecular diameter in the plane of ring of gamma isomer due to its special molecular configuration has a value of 8.5 A° for all the three maximum diameters where as other isomers have these values more than 8.5 A°. Because of this reason only γ-isomer can enter the interspace of liporoteins causing distortion of pores and consequent excitation of nerve impulse transmission.

On the other hand lindane has been reported to be an antimetabolite of myornositol in a number of fungi, but it has been disporved in case of insects and mammals. Thus, BHC and lindane (γ-BHC) may be regarded as neurotoxicants.

## Mode of action of cyclodiene

Experiments conducted by Gianotti et al. with aldrin and dielcrin on the American cockroach have revealed that tremors in the legs were caused due to the effect of the poison on central nervous system. Effect of cyclodienes like chlordane, aldrin, dieldrin was shown by Lalonde and Brown (1954) using a crural nerve of the American cockroach. Short trains of impulses, typically lasting 0.2 seconds were produced just as in the case of DDT.

Increased levels of acetylcholine in the nervous system as a result of aldrin and dieldrin poisoning have also been reported though the implications of this rise are obscure and one might guess it to be a consequence of nervous hyper-activity.

Studies by Hart et.al. Schultice et.al. and Fouts have shown that Chlordane have a stimulatory effect on hepatic cell microsomal activity for the metabolism of certain drugs, probably by stimulating the enzyme activity.

Orser and Brown (1951) reported that the injection of chlordane or toxaphene into Periplanata americana resulted in an irregularity of heart pulsation in both normal and decapitated insects. With chlordane the heart stopped in diastole and with toxaphene in systole.

**Mode of action of halo-derivatives of aliphatic hydrocarbons**

Halogen derivatives of aliphatic hydrocarbons are biologically active and are characterised by their low vapour pressures, thus high volatility. They are thus fumigants and are considered to be physical poisons, killing by narcosis rather than biochemical reactions.

The narcotic action of these anaesthetics depends on the concentration achieved in some hypothetical lipid entity, called the biophase.

Shafer (1911) reported that they are rapidly absorbed into the insect, where they reduce the respiratory rate.

The dehydrogenase, which activates the formation of cytochrome, are inhibited by concentrations of narcotics.

**CARBAMATES**

The backbone of all carbamate structures is carbamic acid HO-CO-$NH_2$ the monoamide of carbon dioxide. The acid does not occure in free form, since it decomposes into carbon dioxide and ammonia. Carbamic acid can be stabilized by the formation of simple alkyl ester such as ethyl carbamates. Most carbamates used as insecticides are esters of aromatic and hetetrocyclic hydroxy derivatives of N-methyl and N, N-dimethyl carbamic acids. These structural features are found in a natural product *Physostigma υ-enenosa* which contain physostigmine (1) and prostigmine (2) the active compounds.

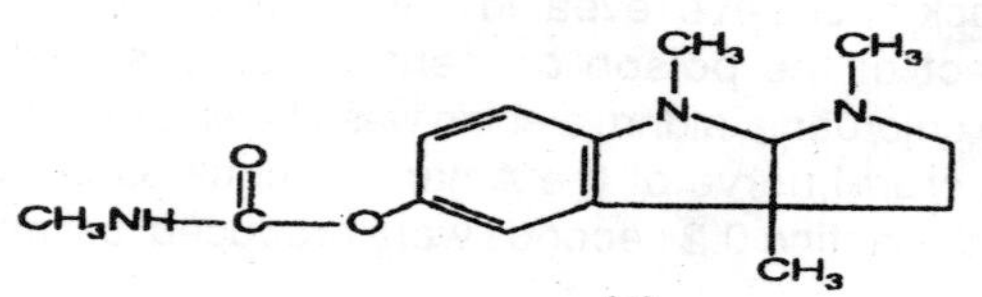

(1)

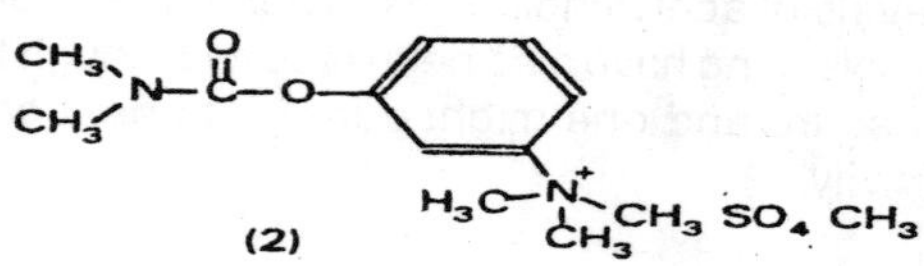

(2)

## Classification of carbamates

Carbamates can be classified into following groups

1. Phenyl carbamates
2. N, N-dimethyl carbamates
3. Oxime carbamates

## PHENYL CARBAMATES

### Carbaryl

(1-Naphthyl-N-methyl carbamate)

Carbaryl is prepared by treating α-naphthol with methyl carbamoyl chloride or phosgene or methyl isocyanate.

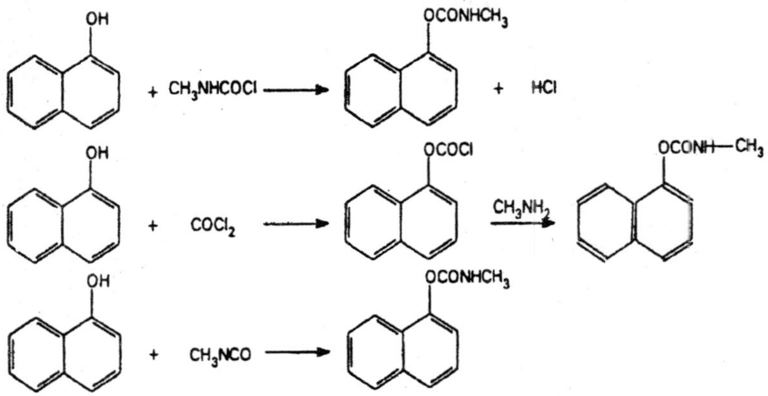


Carbaryl is a potent contact and respiratory poison and is very efficient against chewing pests. Carbaryl is a white crystalline compounds m.p. 150° C It is soluble to less than 0.1% in water but highly soluble in organic solvents. In alkaline medium, it is hydrolysed to α-napthol.

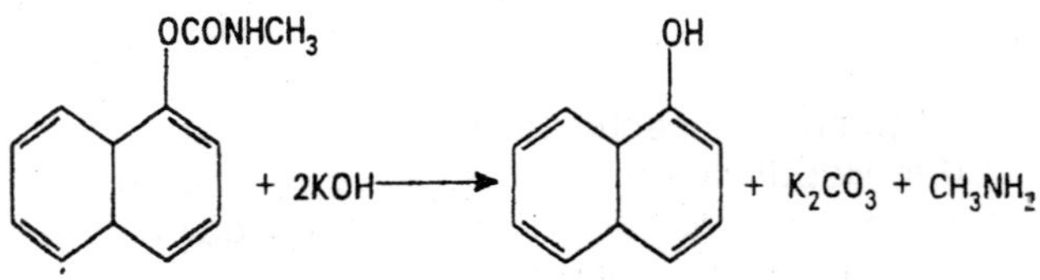

The metabolism of carbaryl on plants is shown below

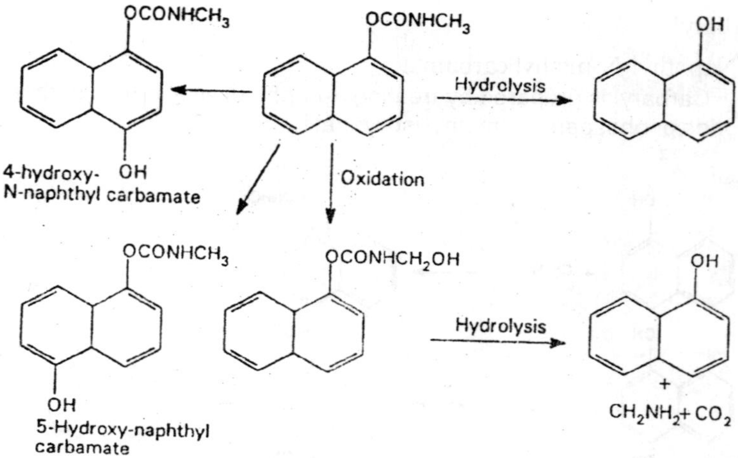


**Bendiocarb**

(2,2-Dimethyl-1,3-benzodioxol-4-yl N-methyl carbamate)

Bendiocarb is synthesied by treating 2,2-dimethyl-1,3-benzodioxol-4-01 with methyl isocyanate.

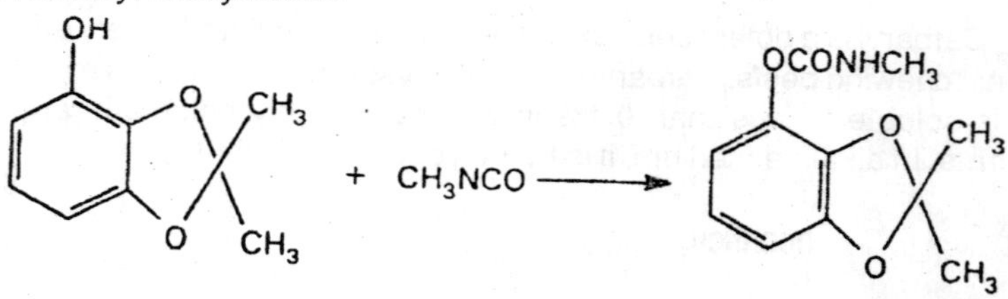


It is a wide spectrum insecticide with good residual activity following soil, foliar, surface application. The chemical has been commercially developed for the control of insects and other arthropod pests in and around buildings where it exhibits quick knowckdown properties.

**Baygon**

(2-Isopropoxy phenyl-N-methyl carbamate)

Baygon is prepared by treating methyl isocyanate with 2-isopropoxyphenol

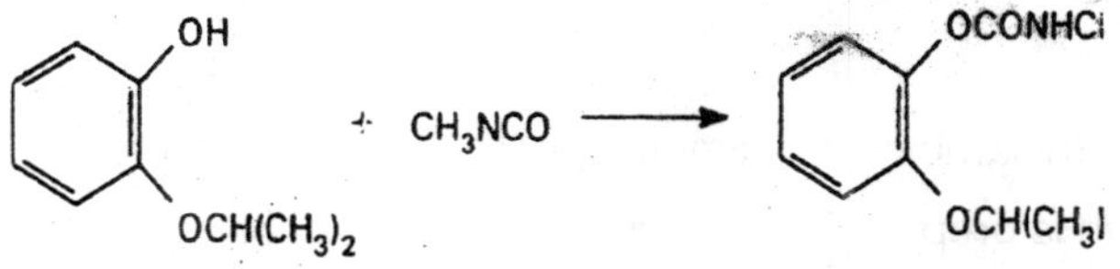

Baygon is a white to cream coloured crystalline compound with mild phenolic odour. Its m.p. is 91.5° C. Its $LD_{50}$ to rats is 100 mg/kg.

Baygon has rapid knockdown properties and long residual action. It is particularly effective against insects affecting man and animals such as cockroaches, flies, mosquitoes. Its rapid knockdown and residual properties are important.

**Carbofuran**

(2,3-dihydro-2,2-dimethyl-7-benzofuranyl N-methyl carbamate)

Carbofuran is prepared by treating 2,3-dihydro-2,2-dimethyl-7-benzofuranol with methyl isocyanate.

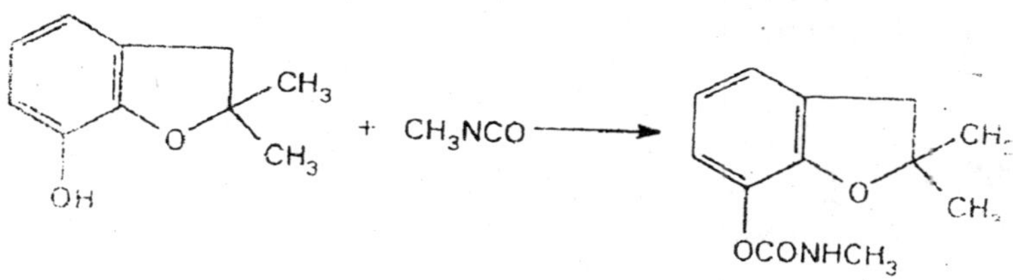

Carbofuran is a systemic carbamate insecticide. It is a white crystalline substance. Its m.p. is 153—54° C.

Carbofuran is a broad spectrum systemic insecticide, acaricide and nematicide which has demonstrated an excellent biological activity on variety of crops. Its $LD_{50}$ value for rats is 11 mg/kg.

Important metabolites of carbofuran on plants are

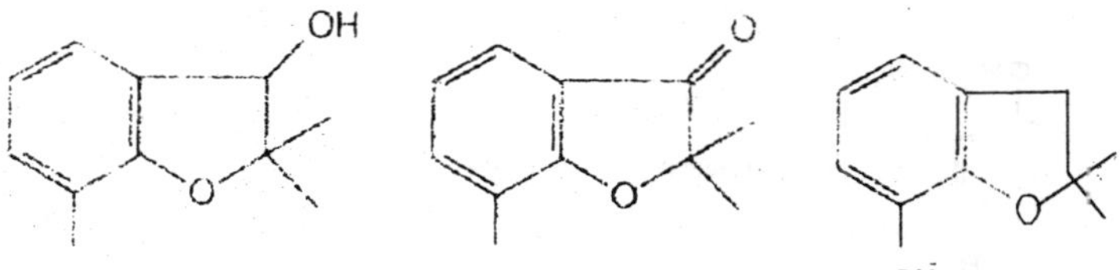

OCONHCH3 OCONHCH3 OH

3-Hydroxy carbofuran 3-keto carbofuran 2,3-dihydro-7-hydroxy-2,3-dimethyl-3-oxobenzofuran

## N,N-DIMETHYLCARBAMATES

### Zectran

(4 (N-N-dimethylamino)-3,5-dimethylphenyl-N-methylcarbamate).

Zectran is prepared by treating 4-dimethylamino-3,5-dimethyl phenol with methyl isocyanate.

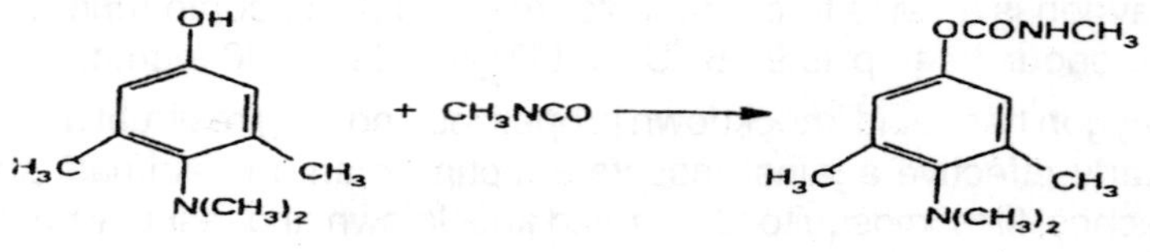


Zectran is a white crystalline substance, m.p. 85° C. Its $LD_{50}$ value is 160—63 mg/kg.

### Dimetan

(5,5-Dimethyl dihydroresorcinyl-N-N-dimethyl carbamate)

Dimetan is prepared by the reaction of monosodium salt of dimetan with dimethyl carbomoyl chloride.

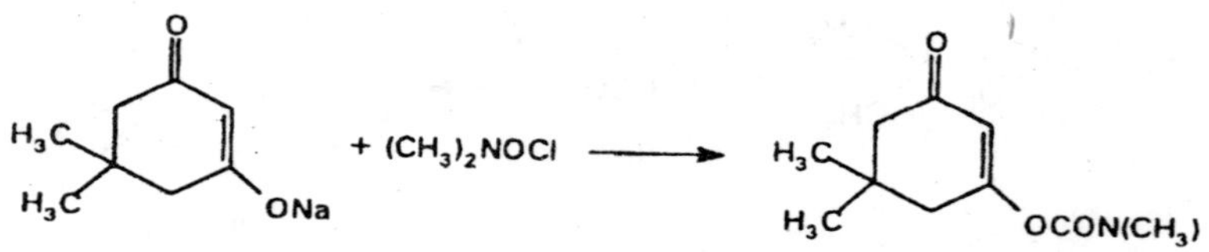


Dimetan is a yellow crystalline substance. The $LD_{50}$ for rats is about 150 mg/kg.

### Mesurol

(4-methyl mercapto-3,5-dimethyl phenyl N-methyl carbamate)

Mesurol is prepared by treating 4-methyl mercapto-3,5-dimethylphenol with methyl isocyanate.

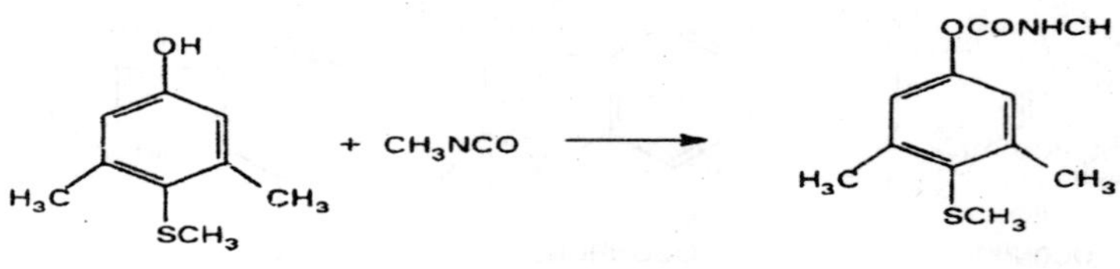


Mesurol is a white crystalline compound. Its m.p. is 121.5° C. Its $LD_{50}$ for rats is 100 mg/kg.

## Isolan

(1-Isopropyl-2-methyl pyrazolyl-5 dimethylcarbamate)

Isolan is prepared by the action of dimethyl carbamoyl chloride on the potassium derivative of enol form of 1-Isopropyl-3-methyl pyrazolone. Its $LD_{50}$ to rats is 11 to 23 mg/kg.

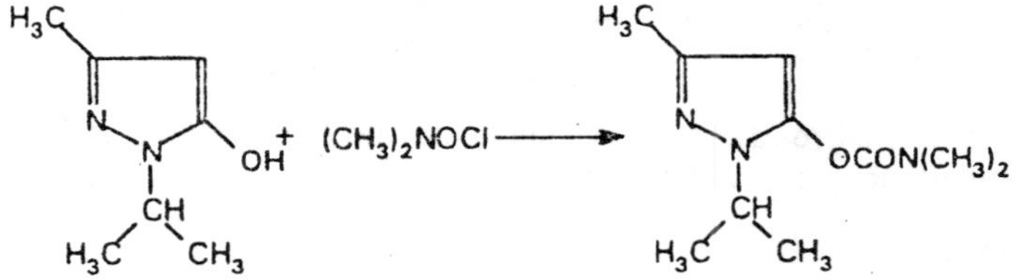

Isolan is a colourless liquid. Its b.p. is 105 to 107° C

## OXIME CARBAMATES

### Temik

(Aldicarb, 2-methyl-2-methylthiopropional-oxime-o, N-methyl carbamates)

Aldicarb is obtained by the reaction of 2-methyl-2 (methylthio) propionaldoxime with methyl isocyanate.

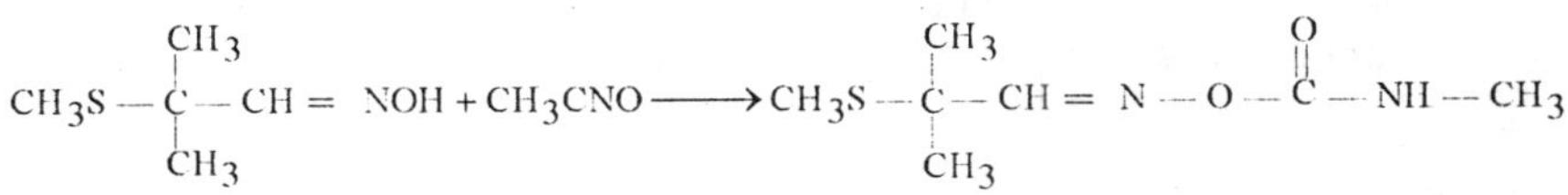

Temik is a white crystalline substance. Its m.p is 100°C. Aldicrab is a broad spectrum soil applied systemic pesticide for the contrcl of insects, mites and nematodes. In moist soil aldicarb is rapidly absorbed by the plant roots and translocated to all parts of the plant. Aldicarb can control many species of aphids, leafhoppers, whiteflies, leafminers, plant bugs, thirps, mealy bugs and mites. Its $LD_{50}$ value for rats is 0.93 mg/kg.

The metabolism of aldicarb on plants is shown below.

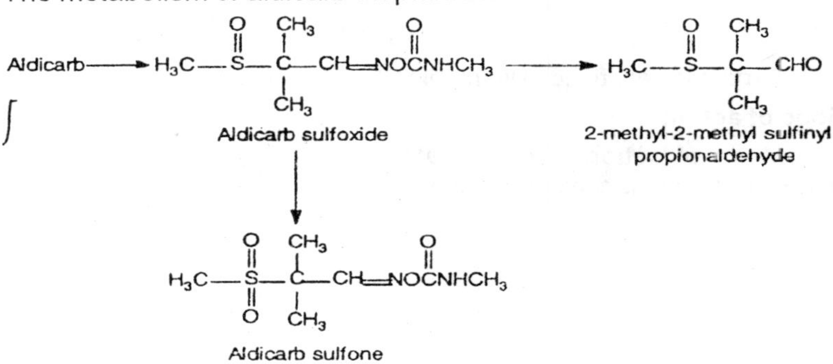

**Oxamil**

S-methyl (1-dimethyl carbamoyl)-N (methyl carbamoyl) oxy) thioformomidate

Oxamil has unique systemic properties and is translocated both upwards and downwards in plants.

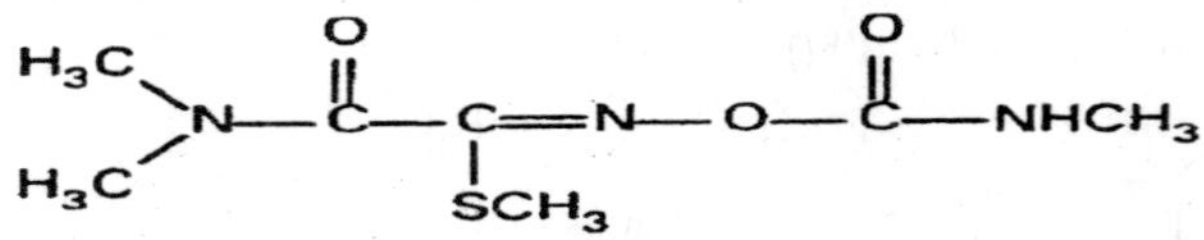

Oxamil is a broad spectrum insecticide and nematicide with excellent biological efficacy on variety of crops. Its $LD_{50}$ to rats is 5.4 mg/kg.

**Methyomyl**

(1-methyl mercaptoacetaldehyde-O-methyl-carbamoyl oxime).

Methomyl is a broad spectrum systemic insecticide and acaricide and is used for the control of cotton pests.

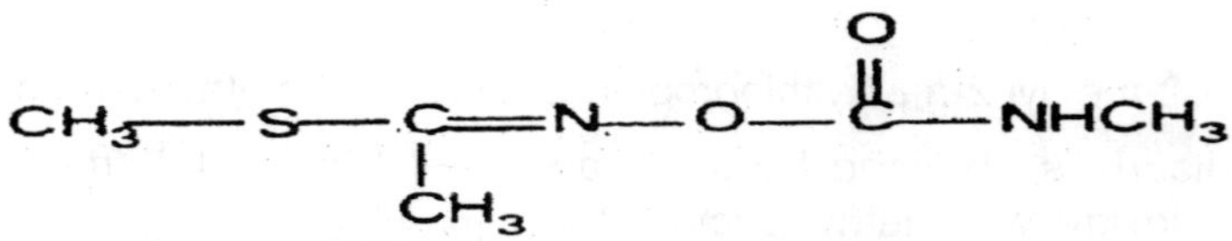

The spectrum of action is similar to aldicarb but it is highly toxic to warm blooded organisms. Its $LD_{50}$ value to rats is 17—24 mg/kg.

**Tirpate**

(2,4-dimethyl-1,3-dithiobanecarboxaldehyde-O-methylcar bamoyl oxime)

Tirpate is prepared by treating mercaptol aldehyde with hydroxylamine and then carbamoylating with methyl isocyanate.

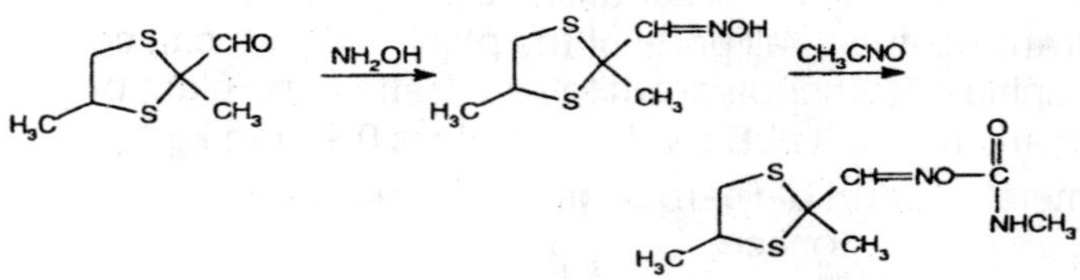

Tirpate is very toxic to warm blooded animals.

**Mode of action**

Mode of action of carbamates is described in the chapter of organophosphorous compounds under mode of action of organophosphorous insecticides.

**Structure Activity relationship of carbamates.**

1. Substitution of carbamate oxygen atoms by sulphur reduces toxicity considerably.
2. If the planer benzene ring is replaced by chair shaped cyclohexane ring, the activity is reduced.
3. Introduction of $CH_2$ group in between aromatic ring and carbamate group reduces toxicity.
4. It $CH_3$ group of -$OCONHCH_3$ replaced by other alkyl groups, then the toxicity is also reduced.

$$CH_3 > C_2H_5 > C_3H_7 > C_4H_9$$

5. Replacement of the second hydrogen atom on the nitrogen by an alkyl radical decreases the activity.

$$(CH_3)_3N > tert\text{-}C_4H_9 > (CH_3)_2N > iso\text{-}C_3H_7 > C_2H_5 > CH_3 > Cl > NO_2$$

6. Phenyl N-methyl carbamates with alkyl substitutent on the aromatic ring are most efficient when the alkyl group is in meta position with respect to carbamate group.

**Organophosphorus insecticides**

Organophosphorous insecticides form an important class of pesticides and about 100 insecticides are registered for use on various crops in the world..

Advantages of organophosphorous insecticides

1. Organophosphorous compounds are used as insecticides, acaricides, fungicides and herbicides.
2. They have broad spectrum of activity against number of pests.
3. They break down into non-toxic metabolites, hence there will be no pollution after their use.
4. Many of the organophosphourous compounds have systemic properties.
5. Due to high pesticidal toxicity, these are very economic and used in smaller dosages.
6. These compounds possess low chronic toxicity.

**Disadvantages**

1. Some of the compounds have bad odours.
2. Some of organophosphorous compounds have high acute toxicity and require special training for application.

Different organic phosphorous compounds can be classified under the following heads. Derivatives of

1. Phosphoric acid

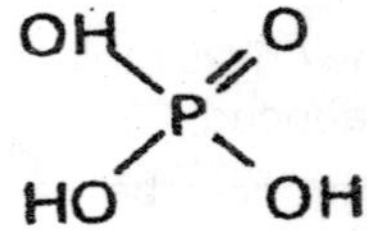

2. Thiophosphoric acid

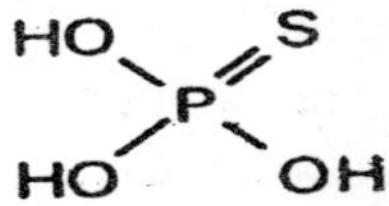

3. Dithiophosphoric acid

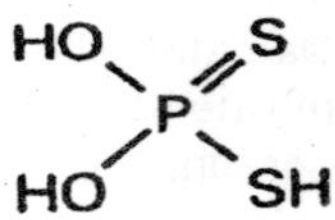

4. Phosphonic acid
5. Esteramides of phosphoric and phosphorothioic acid
6. Cyclic phosphates and phosphorothiolates
7. Pyrophosphoric acid
8. Cyclic phosphates

Reactions involved in the preparation of organophosphorous insecticides

**Michaelis-Arbuzov Reaction**

This reaction is used for the preparation of phosphonate esters. In this reaction phosphonates are formed by the reaction of alkyl phosphites and alkyl halides. The intermediate is a quasiphosphonium salt which stablises by loss of alkyl halide and formation of phosphonate.

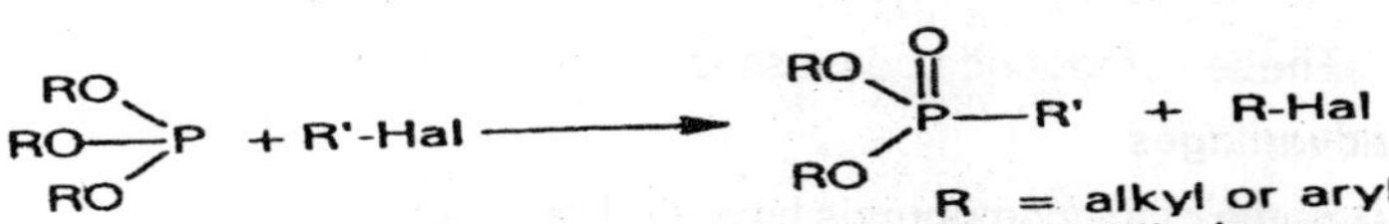

R = alkyl or aryl
R' = alkyl or ary
Hal = Cl, Br, I

### Mechanism of the reaction

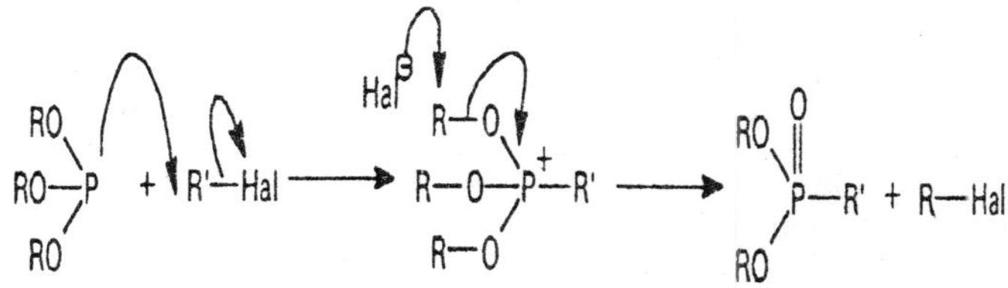

### Perkow reaction

In Perkow reaction, which trialkyl phosphites are treated with a-halocarbonyl compounds, vinyl phosphates are formed.

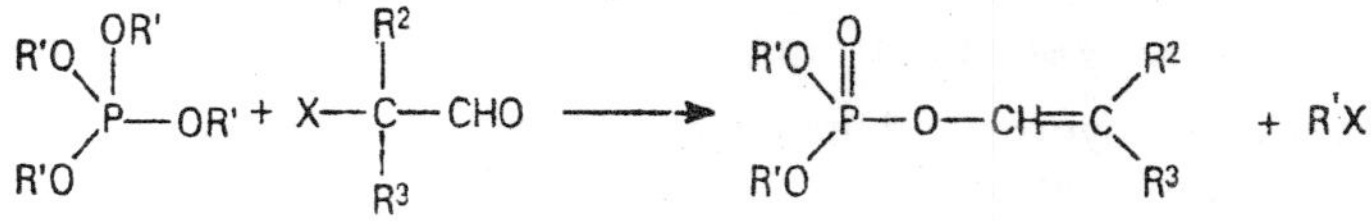

The proposed mechanisms is as follows

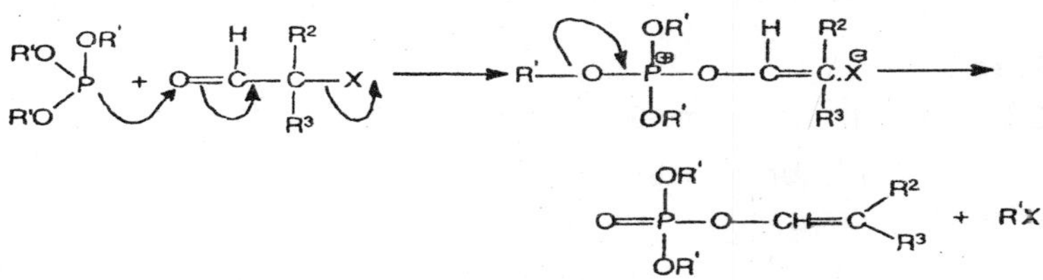

For example, dimethyl dichlorovinyl phosphate is produced from trimethyl phosphite and chloral

$$(CH_3O)P + O{=}CHCCl_3 \longrightarrow (CH_3O)_2\overset{O}{\overset{\|}{P}}{-}OCH{=}CCl_2 + CH_3Cl$$

## DERIVATIVES OF PHOSPHORIC ACID

### Dichlorovos

(O,O-dimethyl O-2,2-dichlorovinyl phosphate, DDVP, Nuvan, vapcroud)

DDVP is prepared by treating chloral with trimethyl phosphite

$$(CH_3O)_3P + CCl_3CHO \longrightarrow CH_3Cl + (CH_3O)_2\overset{O}{\overset{\|}{P}}—OCH{=}CCl_2$$

It is also prepared by treating trichlorofon or diptrex with alkali in aqueous solution at 40—50° C.

$$(CH_3O)_2\overset{O}{\overset{\|}{P}}CH(OH)CCl_3 + KOH \longrightarrow CH_3Cl + (CH_3O)_2\overset{O}{\overset{\|}{P}}—OCH{=}CCl_2 + KCl + H_2O$$

DDVP is a colourless liquid, b.p. 120°C at 14 mm Hg d, 1.425, nD25 1.4543. It is highly soluble in organic solvents. The $LD_{50}$ for rats is 80 mg/kg.

DDVP is hydrolysed in water and forms dichloroacetaldehyde and dimethylphosphoric acid.

$$(CH_3O)_2\overset{O}{\overset{\|}{P}}—OCH{=}CCl_2 + H_2O \longrightarrow (CH_3O)_2\overset{O}{\overset{\|}{P}}—OH + CHCl_2CHO$$

**Naled**

(O,O-dimethyl-1,2-dibromo-2,2-dichloroethyl phosphate, Dibrom)

Dibrom is brominated DDVP and is prepared by brominaming dichlorovos.

$$(CH_3O)_2\overset{O}{\overset{\|}{P}}\text{-}OCH{=}CCl_2 + Br_2 \longrightarrow (CH_3O)_2\overset{O}{\overset{\|}{P}}\text{-}OCH\,Br\,CCl_2\,Br$$

It is a crystalline substance, m.p.25°C, b.p.110°C. It is insoluble in water, soluble in organic solvents. Dibrom is destructively hydrolysed in water in 2 days and provides a short lived insecticides for use in plants. Its $LD_{50}$ for rats is 430 mg/kg.

**Mevinphos**

(O,O-dimethyl O-(1-methyl-2-carbomethoxy vinyl) phosphate, Mevinphos)

Mevinphos is prepared by treating trimethyl phosphite with methyl α-chloroacetoacetate)

$$(CH_3O)_3P + CH_3—CO—\underset{Cl}{\underset{|}{CH}}—CO—OCH_3 \longrightarrow (CH_3O)_2\overset{O}{\overset{\|}{P}}—O—\overset{CH_3}{\overset{|}{C}}{=}CH\,COOCH_3$$

The commercial product is a mixture of cis and trans isomers containing 60% of the cis form and 40% trans. The cis isomer is 100 times more toxic to both insects and mammals than the trans form. It is a colourless liquid, highly soluble in water, b.p. 76°C at 0.2 mm Hg, vapour pressure at 20°C 2.2 x 10 mm of Hg, volatility at 26°c 27 mg/m³. Its $LD_{50}$ to rats is 6.1 mg/kg.

**Phosphamidon**

(O,O-dimethyl-O-(2-chloro-N,N-diethyl carbamoyl) methylvinyl phosphate, Dimecron)

Phosphamidon is prepared by the Arbuzov reaction accompanied by the Perkow rearrangement typical of α-halo carbonyls. Dichloroaceto N,N-diethyl acetamide is reacted with trimethyl phosphite to produce phosphamidon.

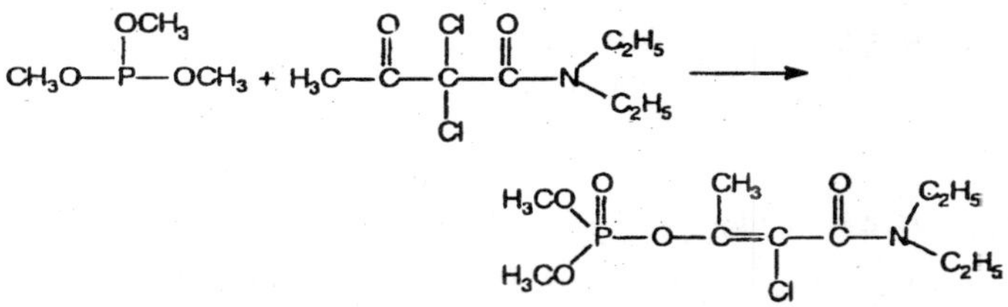

Phosphamidon, when pure, is a colourless, odourless oil. Its boiling point is 1600 °C at 1.5 mm Hg vapour pressure. It is soluble in water, alcohols, ketones and most highly polar oxygenated and halogenated solvents.

**Bidrin**

(O,O-dimethyl-O-(N-N-dimethyl carbamoyl-1-methyl vinyl phosphate)

Bidrin is prepared by Perkow reaction from dimethylamide of monochloroaceto acetic acid and trimethyl phosphite.

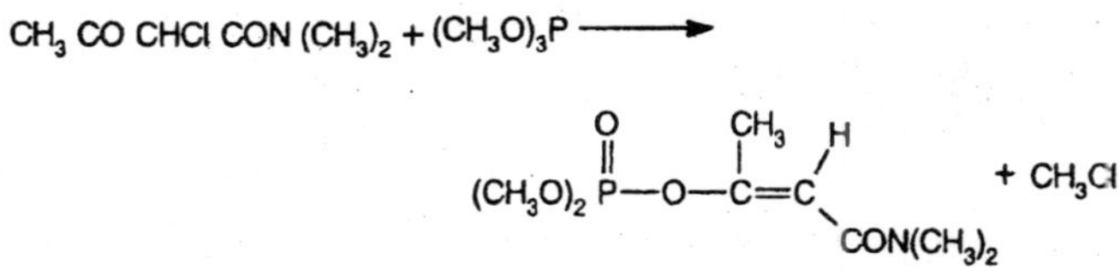

Bidrin is a brown liquid, b.p. 115—120°C at 0.001 mm Hg $d^{23}$ 1.19 soluble in water, ketones and alcohols. The $LD_{50}$ value to rats is 22 mg/kg.

**Birlane**

(2-chloro-(2,4-dichlorophenyl) vinyl diethyl phosphate, Chlorfenvinphos)

Birlane is prepared by the condensation of trethylphosphite with 2,4,1',1'-tetrachloroacetophenone.

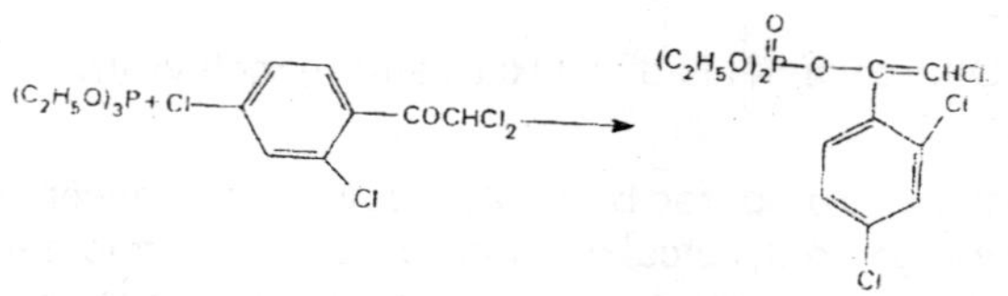

Birlane is an amber coloured liquid. The technical grade product is a mixture of cis and trans isomer in the ratio 8.5:1. the trans isomer is more active.

**Gardona**

(2-chloro-1-(2,4,5-trichlorophenyl) vinyl dimethyl phosphate).

Gardona is prepared by condensation of trimethyl phosphite with 2,4,5,1,8-pentachloroacetophenone.

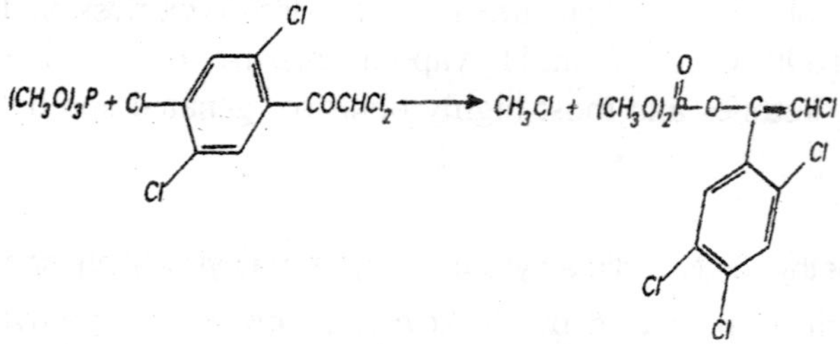

The crude product is a mixture of the geometric isomers; the trans isomer (with the chlorine atoms on opposite sides of the double bond) is obtainted (98%) by recrystallization. Gardona is a white crystalline substance, m.p. 97—98°C. The $LD_{50}$ for rats is 4000 mg/kg.

**Azodrin**

(Monocrotophos, Dimethyl phosphate of 3-hydroxy N -methyl cis-crotonamides)

Monocrotophos is prepared by treating trimethyl phosphite with methyl amide of monochloroacetoacetic acid

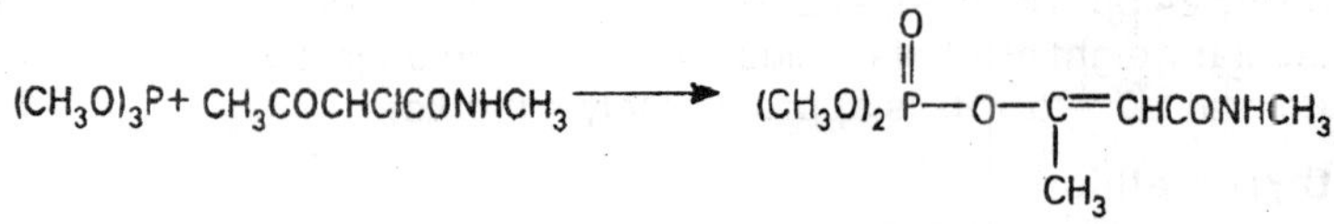

Azodrin is effective against economically important insects which attack on cotton. Pure azodrin is a solid, m.p. 53—55°C. The acute oral $LD_{50}$ for rats is 21 mg/kg.

**Ruelene**

(O-methyl O-(4-tert-butyl-2-chlorophenyl methylphosphoramidate)

Ruelene is prepared by reaction of 2-chloro-4-tertbutyl phenol with O-methyl-N-methyl amidochlorophosphate in the presence of base

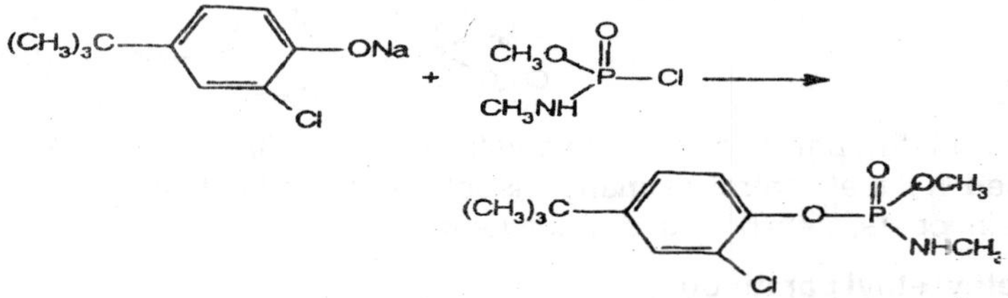

It is insoluble in water but soluble in organic solvents, m.p. 61°C. The $LD_{50}$ for rats is 770—950 mg/kg. Ruelene is used for control of intestina worms. It is also used for the control of ectoparasites of cattle.

## DERIVATIVES OF THIOPHOSPHORIC ACID

**Parathion**

(O,O-Diethyl-O-4-nitrophenylthiophosphate, thiophos, E-605)

Parathion is prepared by reacting diethyl chlorothiophosphate with p-nitrophenol in the presence of potassium carbonate in acetone.

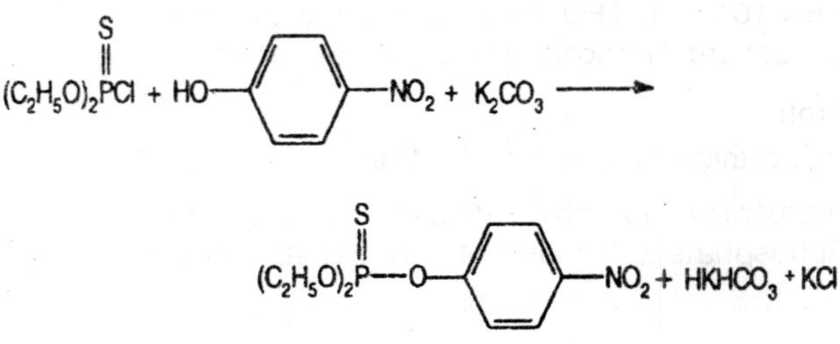

Parathion is a clear liquid, boiling point 157—162°C at 0.6 mm Hg solubility 24 ppm in water at 250°C, miscible with aromatic solvents, lower molecular weight alcohols, acids, esters and chlorinated hydrocarbons. Its acute oral $LD_{50}$ to rats is approximately 4 mg/kg.

**Methyl parathion**

(Folidol, metaphos, O,O-Dimethyl-O-4-nitro phenyl thiosphophate)

Methyl parathion is prepared by reacting dimethyl chlorothiophosphate with sodium p-nitrophenolate in presence of potassium carbonate.

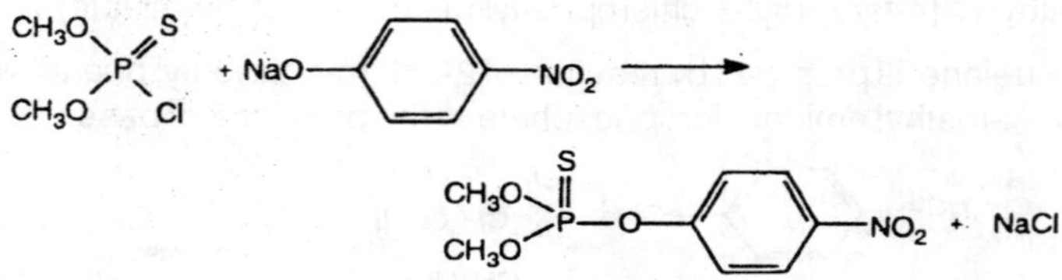

Methyl parathion is white crystalline solid with m.p. 35 to 36°C. It is used for the control of many insects and is effective against green leafhoppers, stem borers, and cutworms.

**Methyl ethyl parathion**

(Thiophos, O-Methyl O-ethyl-4-nitrophenyl thiphosphate)

Methyl ethyl parathion is prepared by condensation of methyl ethyl chlorothiophosphate with p-nitrophenol and hydrochloric acid as acceptor in an organic solvent.

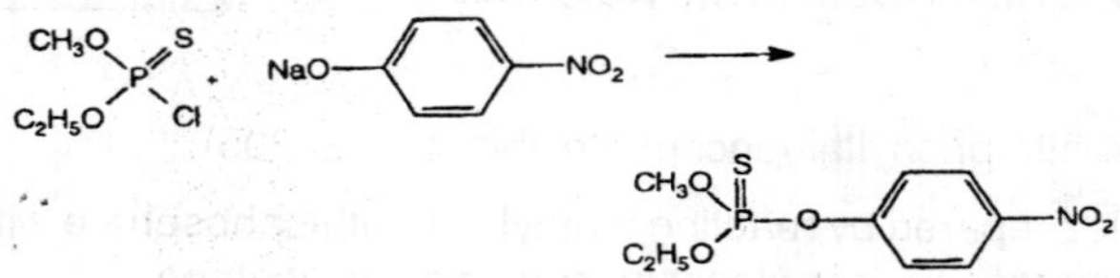

It is a clear liquid, b.p. 116°C at 0.12 mm of Hg vapour pressure at 20°C is 7.6 x $10^{-6}$ mm of Hg. Its solubility in water is about 40 mg/litre. It is soluble in most organic solvents except the paraffin solvents.

**Fenitrothion**

(Sumithion, Folithion, O,O-DimethylO-4-nitro-3-methylphenylthiosphosphate)

Fenitrothion is obtainted by condensation of dimethyl chlorothiophosphate with sodium 4-nitro-3 methylphenolate

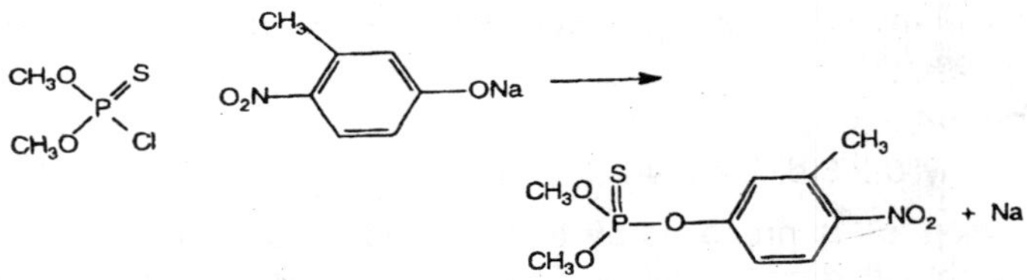

Fenitrothion is a liquid with unpleasant odour b.p. 95°C at 0.01 mm of Hg vapour pressure at 20°C. Fenitrothion is effective to control rice stem borers and is also useful to control flies and mosquitoes in public health programmes. The acute $LD_{50}$ to rats is 1000 mg/kg.

**Chlorothion**

(O,O-Dimethyl O-4-nitro-3-chlorophenyl thiophosphate)

Chlorothion is prepared by the reaction of dimethyl chlorothiophosphate with 3-chloro-4-nitrophenol in methyl ketone in the presence of anhydrous potassium carbonate.

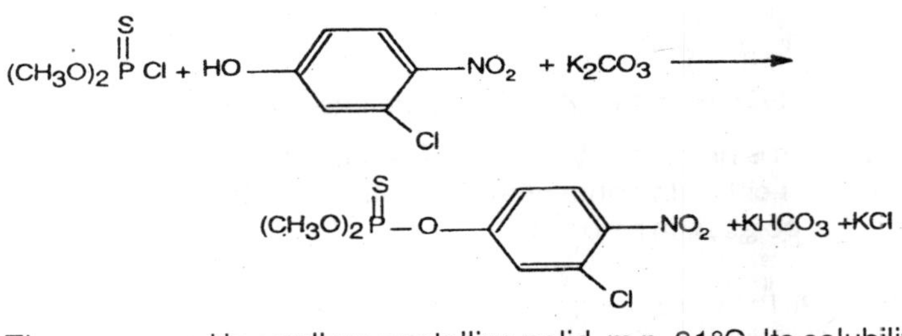

The compound is a yellow crystalline solid, m.p. 21°C. Its solubility in water at 20°C is 40 mg/litre. It is soluble in most organic solvents. The $LD_{50}$ for rats is 850 to 980 mg/kg.

**Ronnel**

(Trolene, O,O-dimethyl 0-2,4,5-trichlorophenylthio phosphate)

Ronnel is prepared by treating sodium 2,4,5-trichlorophenolate with dimethyl chlorothophosphate in aqueous medium in the presence of emulsifiers.

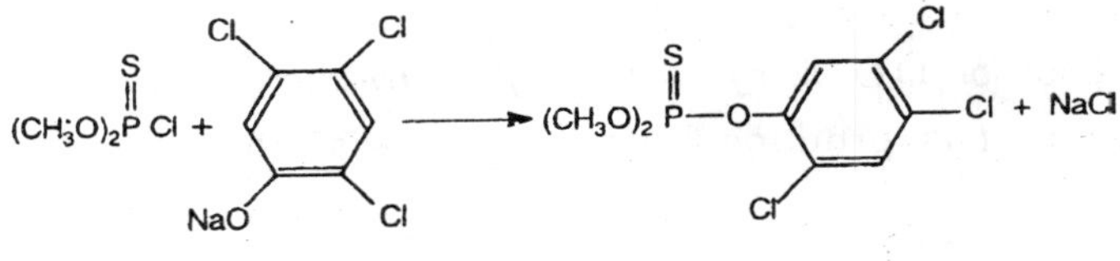

Ronnel is a white non hygroscopic powder with m.p. 36—37°C, soluble in organic solvents. Its solubility in water is 0.01 ppm. The $LD_{50}$ for rats is 1250—1750 mg/kg. It has contact insecticidal activity against flies and cockroaches.

**Bromophos**

(O,O-Dimethyl 0-2,5-dichloro-4-bromophenyl thio phosphate)

Bromophos is prepared by treating sodium salt of 2,5-dichloro-4 bromophenol with dimethyl chlorothiophosphate in aqueous medium in the presence of emulsifiers.

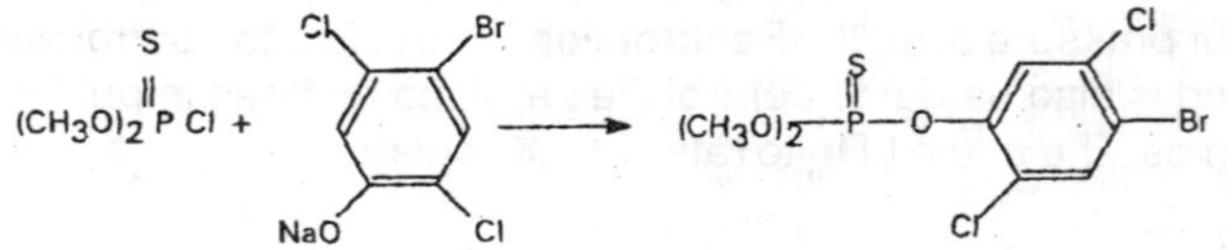

Bromophos is a white crystalline substance m.p. 54°C, solubility in water at 20°C is 40 mg/litre, and is soluble in organic solvents. The $LD_{50}$ for rats is 2000—4000 mg/kg. Bromophos is a nonsystemic insecticide and acaricide and is used on fruits and vegetables. It is useful as public health insecticide.

**Fenthion**

(Lebaycid, O,O-dimethyl-O-(4-methyl mercapto-3-methyl phenyl)

Fenthion is prepared by reaction of 4-methyl mercapto-3-methylphenol with dimethyl chlorothiophosphate in methyl ethylketone at 60°C in the presence of potassium carbonate.

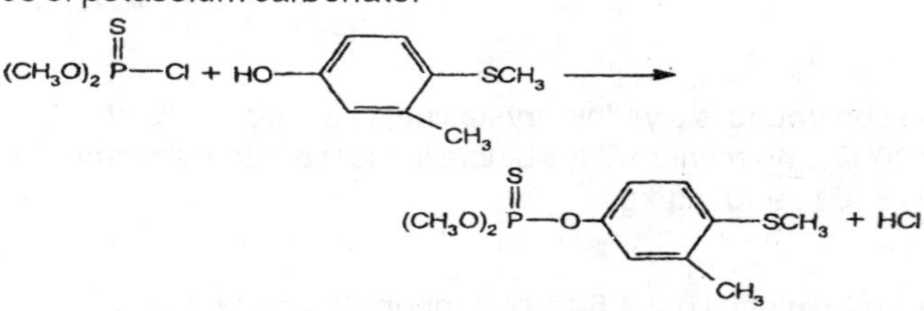

It is a colourless oil, b.p. 87°C. It is effective for the control of mosquitoes, flies, ticks and cockroaches as well as pests on ornamental plants. Its acute oral $LD_{50}$ to rats is 215 mg/kg.

**Dasanit**

(Fensulphothion, O,O-Diethyl-O-[4-methylsulfonyl phenyl] phosphorothiate)

Dasanit is produced by the condensation of o,o-diethyl

chlorothiophosphate with 4-methyl thiophydroxybenzene and oxidation of the resulting ester with hydrogen peroxide.

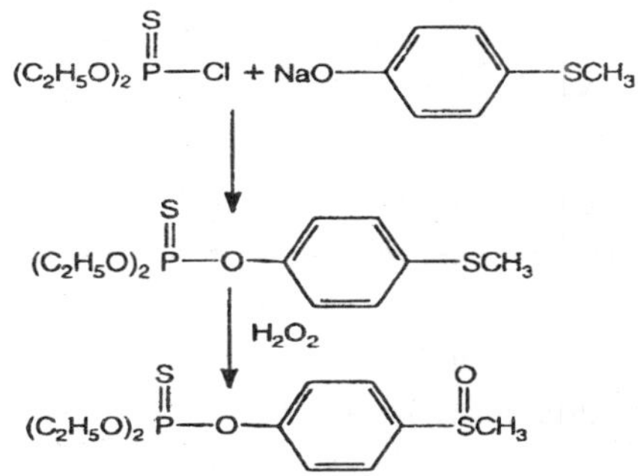


Dasanit is a oily liquid, b.p. 138-141°C. The $LD_{50}$ for rats is 4 to 10.5 mg/kg. Dasanit is effective as soil insecticides with a long residual action. It displays both systemic and contact action.

**Diazinon**

(O,O-Diethyl-O- (2-isopropyl-4-methylpyrimidyl-6) thio phosphate)

Diazinon is prepared by reacting 2-isopropyl -4-methyl-6 hydrcxy pyrimidine with diethyl chlorothiphosphate in the presence of potassium carbonate.

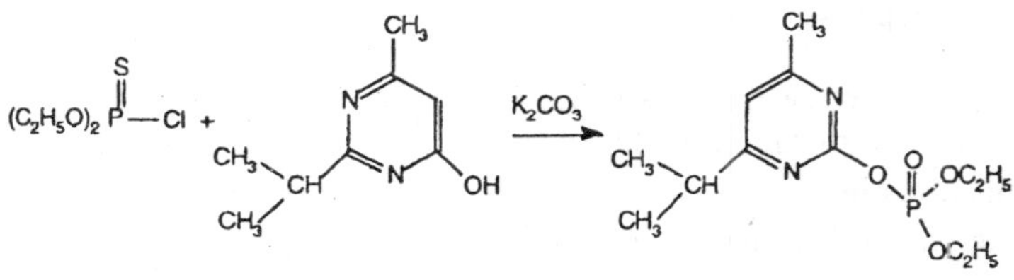


Diazinon is a colourless oil, b.p. 89°C at 0.1 mm of Hg. The $LD_{50}$ value for various experimental animals is 75—320 mg/kg. Diazinon has a long residual action and is effective for control of soil, fruit, vegetables and rice insects. Diazinon is also useful for control of pests of household and livestock.

**Dursban**

(Chlorpyriphos, O,O-diethyl-O-3,5,6 - trichloropyridyl thiophosphate)

Dursban is prepared by the reaction of sodium salt of 3,5,6-trichloro-2-hydroxypyridine with diethyl chlorothiophosphate in dimethyl formamide.

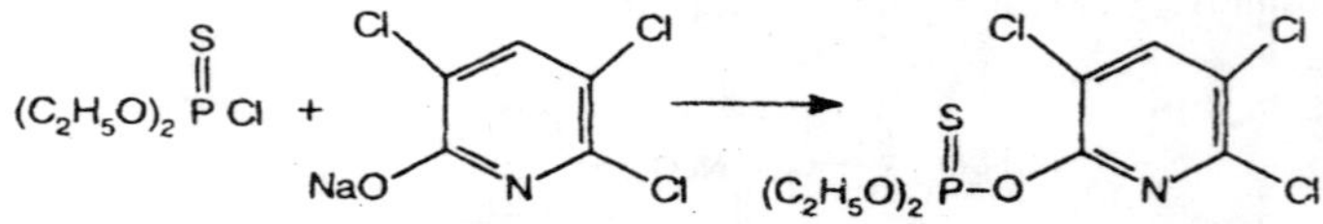

Dursban is a white crystalline solid, m.p. 41.5 to 43°C. The $LD_{50}$ value for rats is 150 mg/kg and for guinea pigs 500 mg/kg. Dursban is used for control of sucking and chewing pests. It is also used for control of termites.

**Quinalphos**

(Ekalux, O,O-diethyl-O-(2-quinoxaline) phosphorothioate)

Quinalphos is prepared by condesantion of O-phenylenediamine with hemiacetel of glyoxylate and then treating it with diethyl chlorothiophosphate.

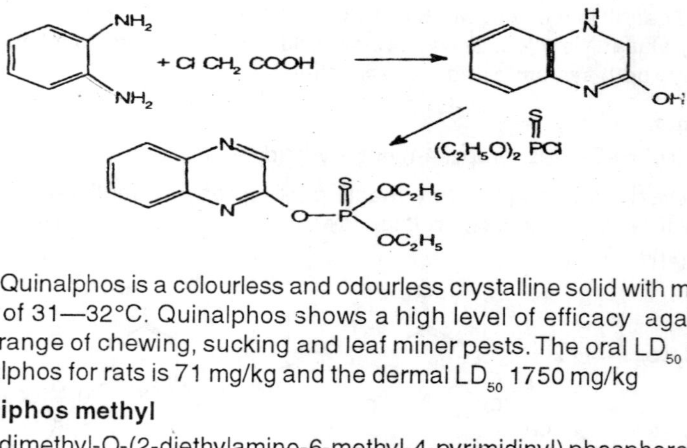

Quinalphos is a colourless and odourless crystalline solid with melting point of 31—32°C. Quinalphos shows a high level of efficacy against a wide range of chewing, sucking and leaf miner pests. The oral $LD_{50}$ of the quinalphos for rats is 71 mg/kg and the dermal $LD_{50}$ 1750 mg/kg

**Pirimiphos methyl**

(O,O-dimethyl-O-(2-diethylamino-6-methyl-4-pyrimidinyl) phosphorothioic acid)

Pirimiphos methyl is prepared by condensation of ethylacetoacetate and N,N-diethyl guanidine.

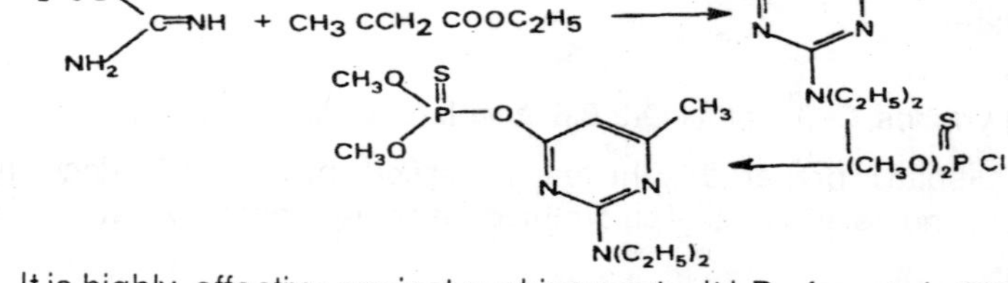

It is highly effective against sucking pests. It $LD_{50}$ for rats is 2000 mg/

kg. Pirimiphos methyl acts as insecticide and acaricide. It is mainly used in stored product protection.

**Phoxim**

(O,O-diethyl phenylglyoxylonitrile phosphorothioate, Voilaton)

Phoxim is prepared by treating α-cyanobenzaldoxime with diethylchlorothiophosphate

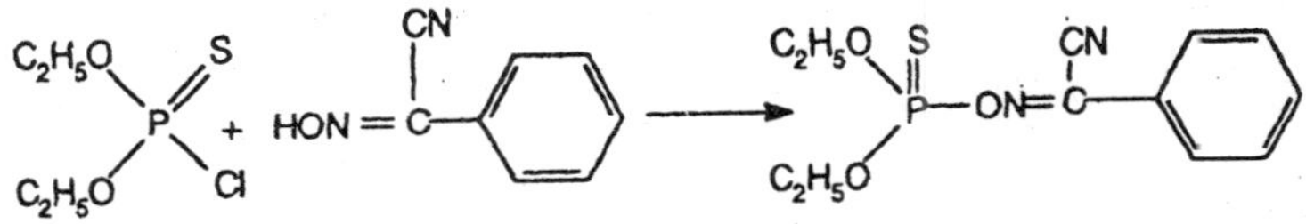

Phoxim is a light yellow liquid, b.p 102°C at 0.01 mm Hg. Phoxim has low toxicity to human and warm blooded animals. The $LD_{50}$ for rats is 2000 mg/kg. Phoxim has broad spectrum insecticidal activity as a contact and stomach poison. It is effective to control leafhoppers, aphids, cut worms and insects of stored products and public health.

**Demeton**

(Systox, O,O-Diethyl-2-ethylmercepto ethyl thiophosphate)

Demeton is prepared by the reaction of ethylmercapton with ethylene oxide, the resulting 2-ethylthio ethanol is treated with diethyl phosphorothionochloridate in the presence of acid binder.

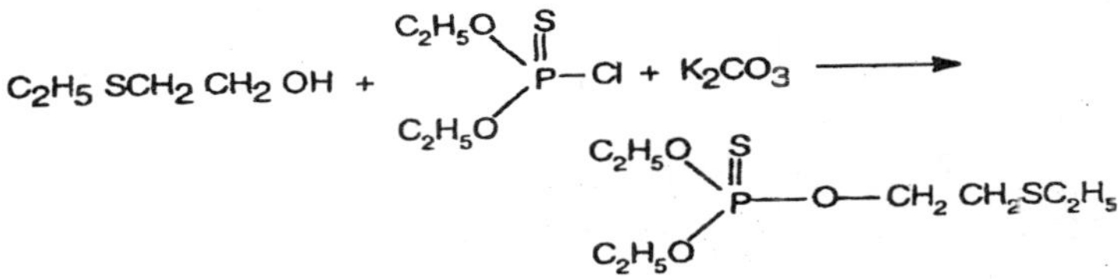

The compound is unstable in this form. It undergoes partial thiono-thiolo isomerization and commercial product (demeton, systox) contains an equilibrium mixture of 30% of the thiolo isomer of (ethylthio) ethyl phosphorothiolate and 70% of the thiono isomer O,O-diethyl-2-ethylmercapto ethyl thiophosphate.

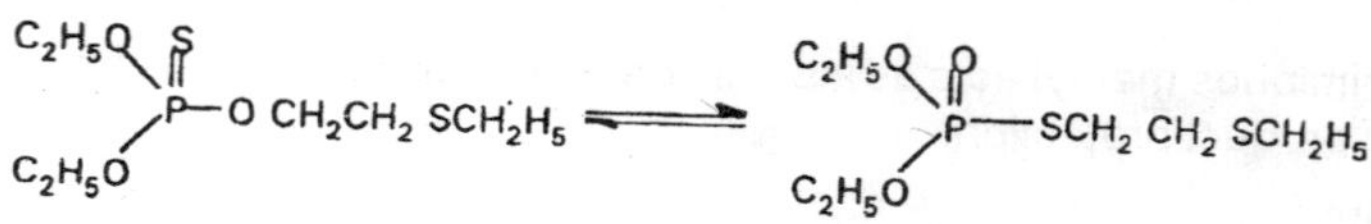

Demeton has powerful systemic effect and is used for the control of many sucking pests. The oral $LD_{50}$ value for rats is approximately 15 mg/kg. In plant tissues both isomers are rapidly oxidised to the sulfoxide and sulfone, derivatives.

**Triazophos**

(O,O-diethyl O-(1-phenyl-1H-1,2,4 triazol-3-yl), phos phorothioate)

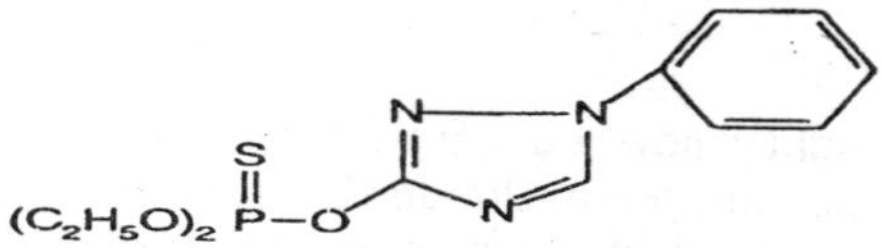

Triazophos is a broad spectrum insecticide effective against insects, mites, and nematodes. Its $LD_{50}$ to rats is 82 mg/kg.

**Methyldemeton**

(Metasystox,O,O-dimethyl-2-ethyl mercaptoethyl thiophosphate)

Methyldemeton is the methyl homolog of demeton. Technical grade methyl demeton is a mixture of thiolo (30%) and thiono (70%) isomers. Methyl demeton is prepared by the reaction of 2-hydroxy diethyl sulfide with dimethylchlorothiophosphate in the presence of HCl acceptor.

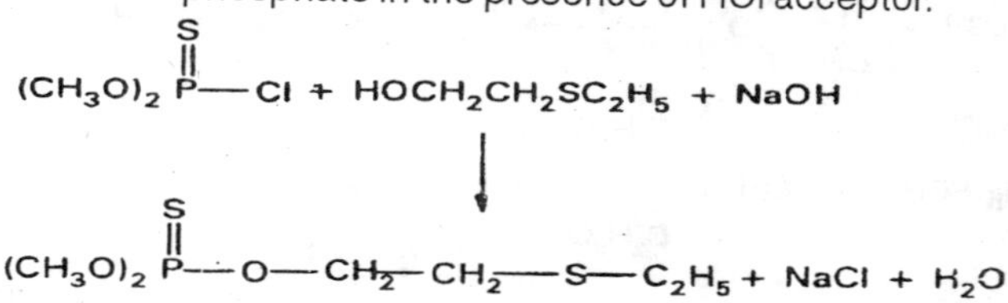

Methyl demeton is less toxic than demeton. Thiono isomer has b.p. 93°C and thiolo isomer b.p. 93°C.

The $LD_{50}$ for thiono isomer of methyldemeton is 180 mg/kg and that of thiolo isomer is 40 mg/kg.

## DERIVATIVES OF DITHIOSPHOSPHORIC ACID

**Malathion**

(O,O-dimethyl-S-(1,2-dicarbethoxyethyl-dithiophosphate)

Malathion is synthesised by reacting dimethyldithiophosphoric acid and maleic acid ester in the presence of basic catalysts.

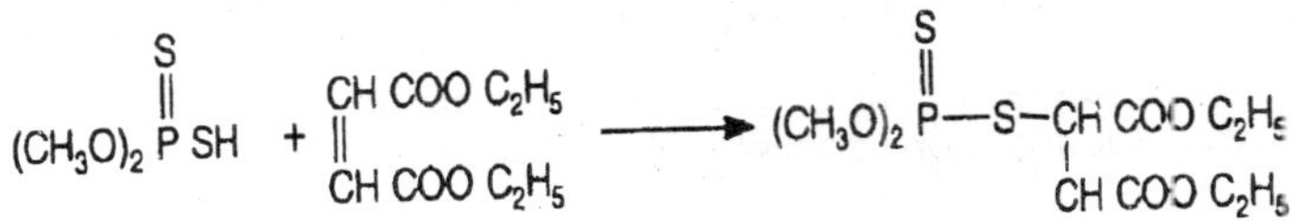

Malathion has a broad spectrum of action and is effective against both sucking and chewing insects on fruits and vegetables. It is also used for the control of flies and mosquitoes. Malathion is least toxic to warm blooded animals and its $LD_{50}$ values for rats is 1200 mg/kg. The metabolism of malathion in plants takes place as per the following scheme.

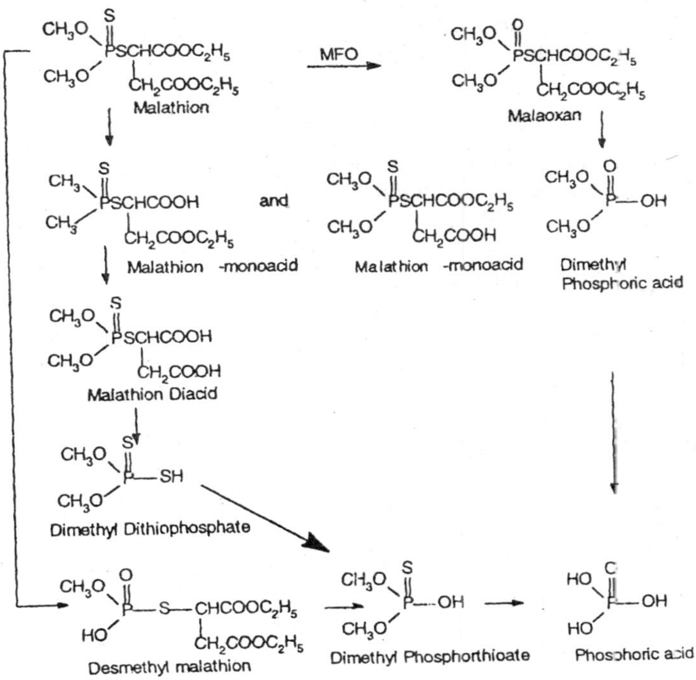


Metabolic pathway of malathion

**Dimethoate**

(Rogor, O,O-Dimethyl-S-(N.methyl-carbamoylmethyl)di-thiophosphate)

Dimethoate is produced by reacting potassium salt of dimethyldithiophosphoric acid with N-methyl chloroacetamide.

$$(CH_3O)_2\overset{\overset{S}{\parallel}}{P}-SK + Cl\,CH_2CONHCH_3 \longrightarrow (CH_3O)_2\overset{\overset{S}{\parallel}}{P}-S-CH_2\cdot CONHCH_3 + KCl$$

Dimethoate is a systemic insecticide. It is used for control of insects on vegetables, cotton, tobacco and sorghum. Dimethoate decomposes slowly in plant tissues. Three processes occur simultaneously namely hydrolysis of the P-X bond, O-dimethylthion with the formation of products having low toxicity, and oxidation to the P=O analogue of dimethoate, a more powerful inhibitor of cholinestrase.

**Thimet**

(Phorate, O-O-Diethyl-S-(ethylthiomethyl) dithiophosphate)

Thimet is prepared by reacitng diethyl dithiophosphoric acid with formaldehyde and ethyl mercaptan.

$$(C_2H_5O)_2\overset{\overset{S}{\parallel}}{P}-SH + CH_2O + C_2H_5SH \longrightarrow (C_2H_5O)_2\overset{\overset{S}{\parallel}}{P}-S-CH_2SC_2H_5 + H_2O$$

Phorate is systemic insecticide and is effective against sucking pests. Phorate is used as granules in soil and has relatively unstable to hydrolysis. However, it protects the plants for a relatively long time because of the greater persistency of the sulphoxide metabolite in plants and soil. Phorate is oxidised to sulphoxide and then to sulphone in plants.

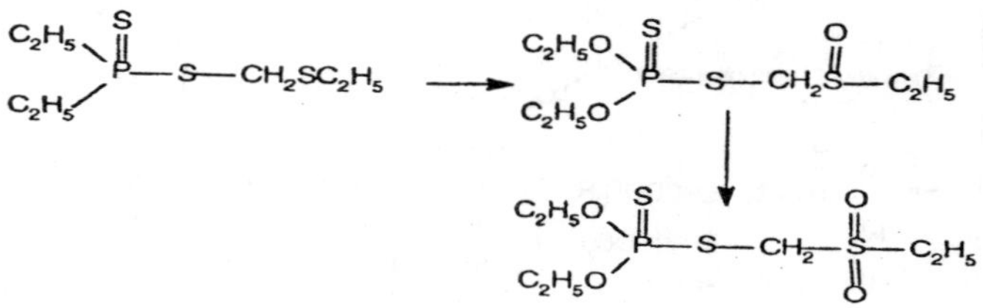

**Disyston**

(Disulfoton, O,O-Diethyl-S-(2-ethylmercaptoethyl) dithio phosphate)

Disyston is prepared by treating salts of diethyldithiophosphoric acid with 2—chlorodiethyl sulphide.

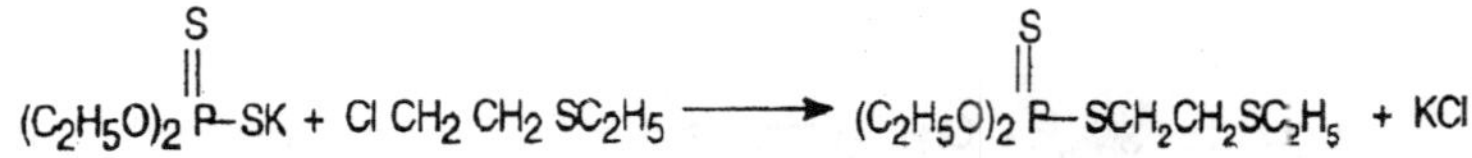

Disyston is a systemic insecticide and is used for control of sucking insects. A disadvantage of disyston is its high toxicity to warmblooded animals. Its $LD_{50}$ for rats 2—12 mg/kg. Disulfoton is oxidised to sulphoxide and then to sulfon.

The sulfoxide of disyston is marketed as oxydesulfoton. Its biological properties are similar to disyston.

**Phosalone**

(O,O-Diethyl-S-(6-chlorohenoxozolinyl-3-methyl) dithio phosphate)

Phosalone is prepared by the condensation of sodium diethyldithiophosphate with 6-chloro-3-chloromethyl benzoxazolone.

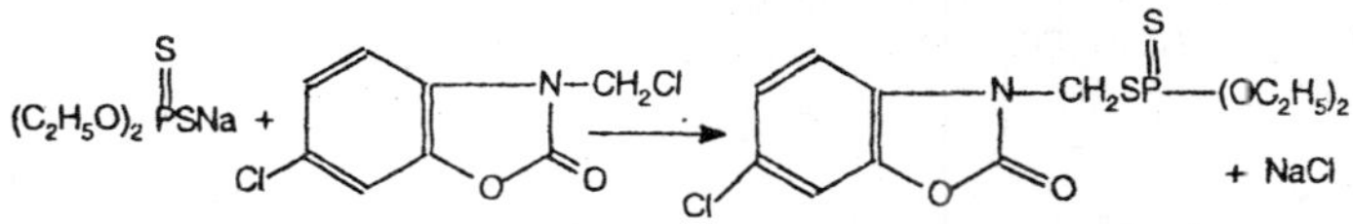

Phosalone is a broad spectrum insecticide and acaricide useful for control of caterpillars, aphids, and mites on apples and field crops. The acute oral $LD_{50}$ value for rats is 120 mg/kg.

**Formothion**

(O,O-Dimethyl-S-(N-methyl-N-formylcarbamoylmethyl phosphorodithioate)

Formothion is prepared by the reaction of potassium salt of dimethyl dithiophosphoric acid with N-formyl N-methyl chloroacetamide.

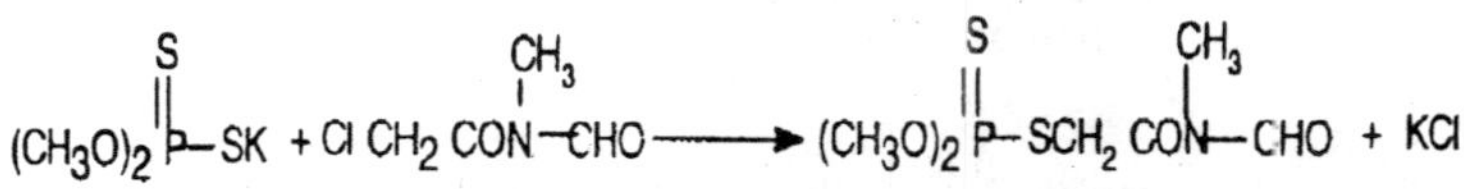

Formothion is yellowish liquid. Formothion has relatively low toxicity to mammals. Its $LD_{50}$ for rats is 330—50 mg/kg and is effective against chewing and sucking pests by systemic and contact action.

**Ethion**

(O,O,O,O-tetraethyl -S,S-methylenebis dithiophosphate)

Ethion is prepared by the condensation of salts of diethyldithiophosphoric acid with dibromomethane.

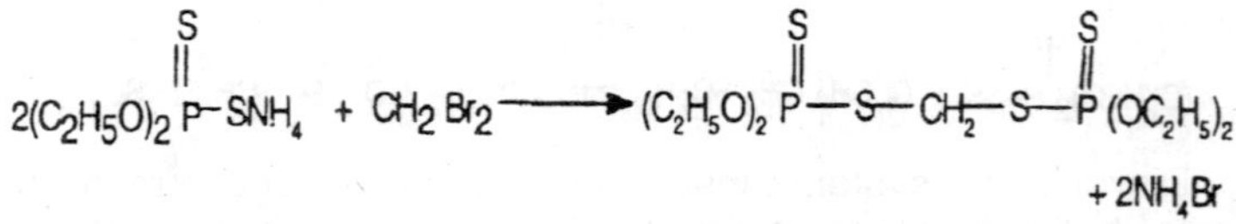

Ethion is a yellow liquid, b.p. 164—165°C. Ethion is used for the control of mites and aphids. The $LD_{50}$ for rats is 55 mg/kg.

**Menazon**

(S-(4,6-Diamino-1,3,5-triazin-2-methyl), O,O dimethyl phosporodithioate,

Menazon is synthesised by the reaction of 2-chloromethyl-4,6-diamino-1,3,5-triazine with sodium salt of O,O-dimethyl S-ethoxycarbonyl methyl phosphorodithioate.

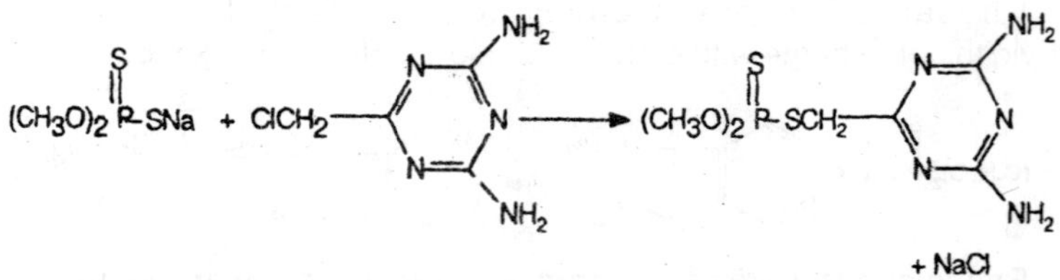

Menazon is a colourless crystalline solid, m.p. 60°C. Menazon is effective against aphids by foliar spray. The $LD_{50}$ for rats is 900—1950 mg/kg.

**Ekatin**

(Thiometon, O,O-Dimethyl-S-2-(ethylmercaptoethyl) dithio phosphate)

Ekatin is produced by reacting 2-hydroxyldiethyl sulphide with dimethyldithiophosphoric acid and p-toluene sulphonyl chloride in the presence of sodium hydroxide.

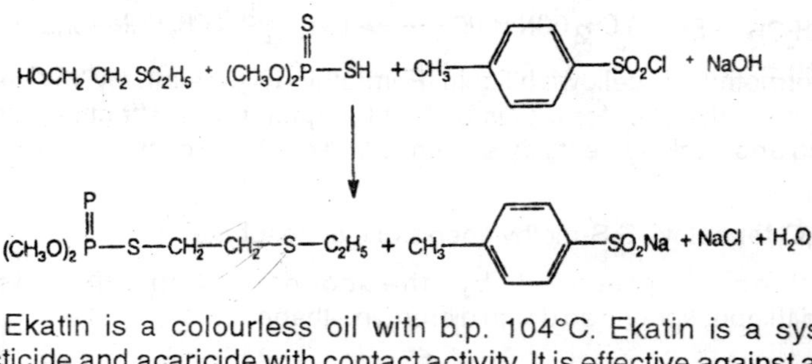

Ekatin is a colourless oil with b.p. 104°C. Ekatin is a systemic insecticide and acaricide with contact activity. It is effective against aphids, thirps and mites. The $LD_{50}$ for rats is 70 to 120 mg/kg.

## Guthion

(Azinphos, O,O-dimethyl-S-(3,4-dichloro-4-keto-1,2,3-benzotriazinyl-3-methyl) dithiophosphate)

Guthion is prepared by treating N-halo methyl derivative of azimidobenzoyl with salts of dimethyl dithiophosphoric acid.

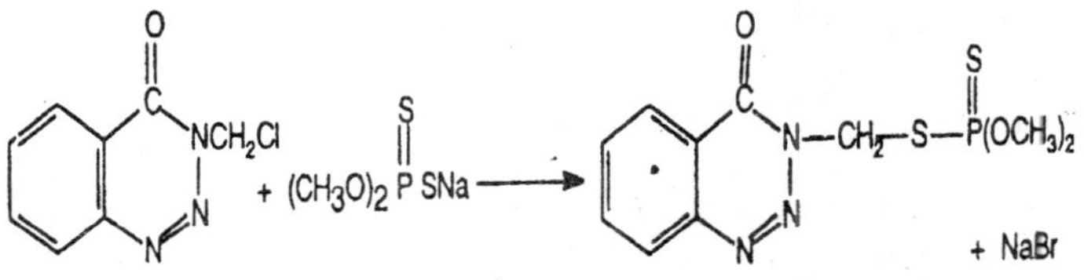

Guthion is white crystalline substance, m.p. 73 to 74°C. It is non sytemic insecticide and acaricide for use in fruit crops, vegetables and cotton. The $LD_{50}$ value for guthion is 15 mg/kg.

## Cidial

(Phenthoate, O,O-dimethyl-S-(1-carboethoxy benzyl) dithio phosphate)

Cidial is prepared by reacting sodium salt of dimethyl dithiophosphate with ethyl α-bromo phenylacetate.

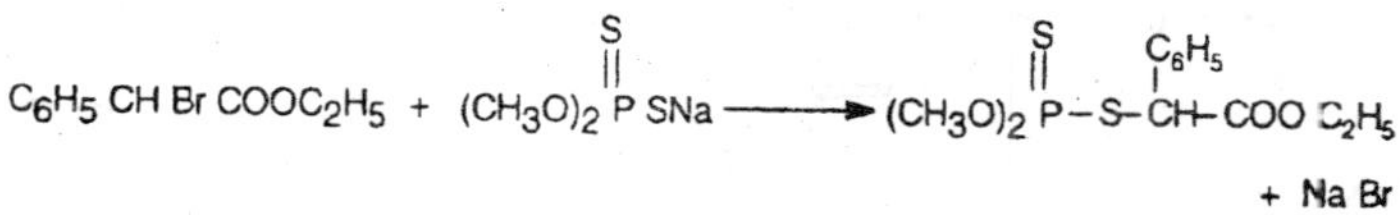

Cidial is a liquid with b.p. 70 to 80°C at 2 x 10-5 mm Hg. Cidial has a broad spectrum of insecticidal and acaricidal activities and is particularly effective against scale insects. The oral $LD_{50}$ value for rats is 4700 mg/kg.

## PHOSPHONIC ACID DERIVATIVES

### EPN

(O,ethyl O-(4-nitrophenyl) phenyl phosphonothioate)

Benzene is reacted with phosphorous trichloride in the presence of aluminium chloride to give benzene phosphonodichloridate. This is reacted with phosphorous thiochloride or elemental sulphur to give benzene-phosphonodichlorothioate, which is reacted with sodium ethoxide followed by sodium salt of p-nitrophenol.

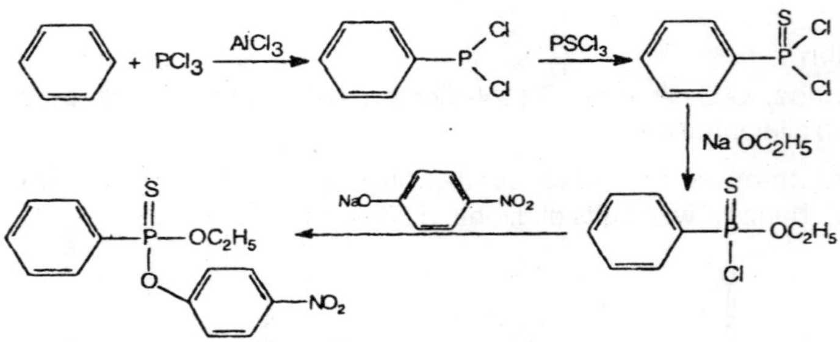

The m.p. of EPN is 36°C . The technical material is a brown liquid. The commercial product has relatively low toxicity against spider mites, grasshoppers and mosquito larvae. The $LD_{50}$ for rats is 36 mg/kg.

**Fonophos**

(O-ethyl-S-phenyl ethane phosponodithioate)

Fenophos is prepared by treating O-ethyl-ethane phosphonothiochloridate and thiphenol in the presence of base.

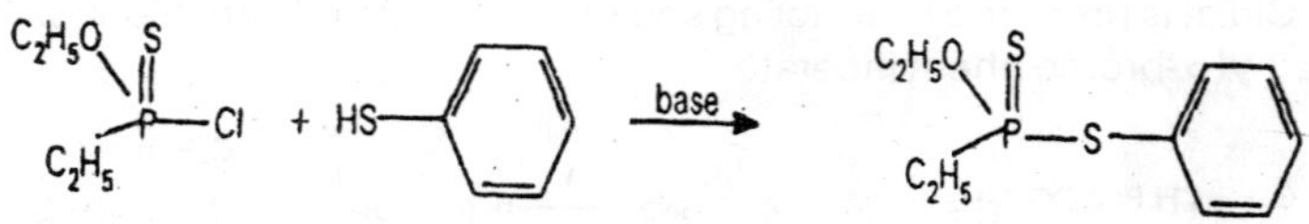

**Diptrex**

(O,O-Dimethyl-(1-hydroxy-2,2,2-trichloro)ethyl phosphonate)

Diptrex is prepared by the addition of dimethylphosphonate to chloral

Diptrex is used aganist chewing pests. Its $LD_{50}$ for rats is 630 mg/kg.

## ESTERAMIDES OF PHOSPHORIC ACID AND PHOSPHOROTHIOIC ACID

**Phospholan**

Phospholan is prepared by the reaction of ethylene 1,2-dithiol with cyanogen chloride, followed by the reaction of 2-imino-1,3-dithiolane with diethyl phosphorochloridate.

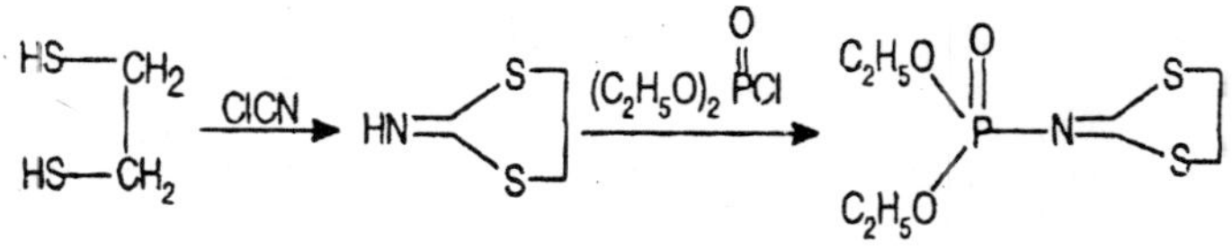

Phospholan has high activity against chewing and sucking insects.

**Methamidophos**

(Tamaron, O,S-Dimethyl phosphorothioamidates)

Methamidophos is prepared by converting dimethyl phosphorothiochloridate with ammonia to O,O-dimethyl phosphorothioamidate which in the presence of methyl iodide undergoes thiono-thiolo isomersation and is converted to O,S-dimethyl analogue.

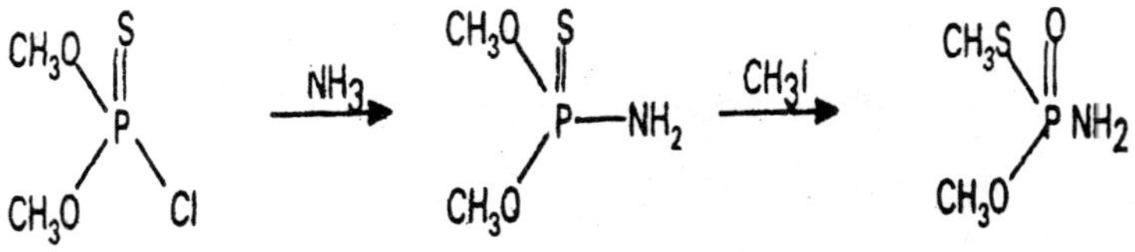

Methamidophos is a colourless crystalline solid, m.p. 44.5°C. Methamidophos is a broad spectrum insecticide particularly effective to control caterpillers and aphids. It has also systemic action against both biting and sucking pests. Its acute oral $LD_{50}$ value for rats is 30 mg/kg.

**Acephate**

(Orthene, O,S-Dimethyl N-acetyl phosphoramidothiolate)

Acephate is N-acetyl derivative of the insecticide methamidophos and is prepared by acetylation of methamidophos with acetic anhydride in the presence of $ZnCl_2$ or $Fecl_3$.

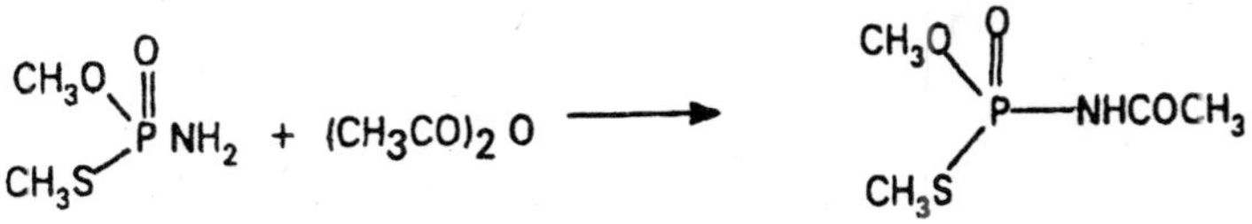

Acephate is a white crystalline solid, m.p.91 to 92°C. Acephate is a systemic insecticide effective against chewing and sucking pests. The $LD_{50}$ value for rats is 945 mg/kg.

## CYCLIC PHOSPHATES AND PHSOPHOROTHIOATES

### Salithion

(2-methoxy-4H-1,3,2-benzodioxophosphorin-2-sulphide) and Salioxon (2-methoxy-4H-1,3,2-benzodioxaphosphoran-2-one)

Among the cyclic phosphates, there are also insecticidal derivatives of Salioxon and its thiono analogue salithion. Salithion is prepared by treating saligenin with methyl phosphorodichlorothioate.

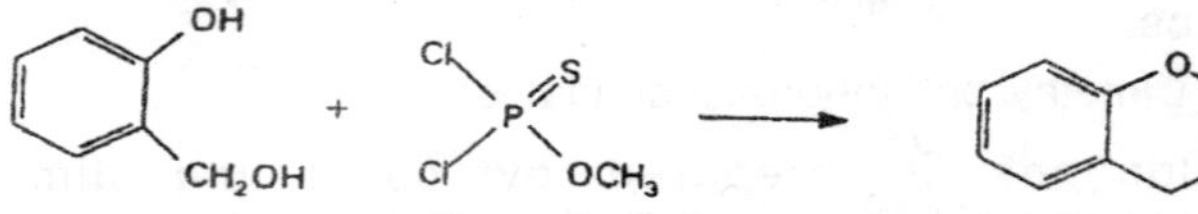

Salithion

The $LD_{50}$ value to rats for salithion is 102 mg/kg and for Salioxon is 0.5 to 1 mg/kg.

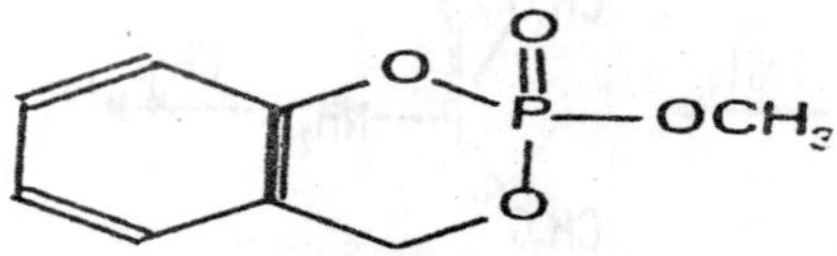

Salioxon

## DERIVATIVES OF PYROPHOSPHORIC ACID

### Tetraethylpyrophosphate

Tetraethylpyrophosphate is synthesised by the reaction of diethyl phosphite with diethyl phosphorochloridate followed by oxidation.

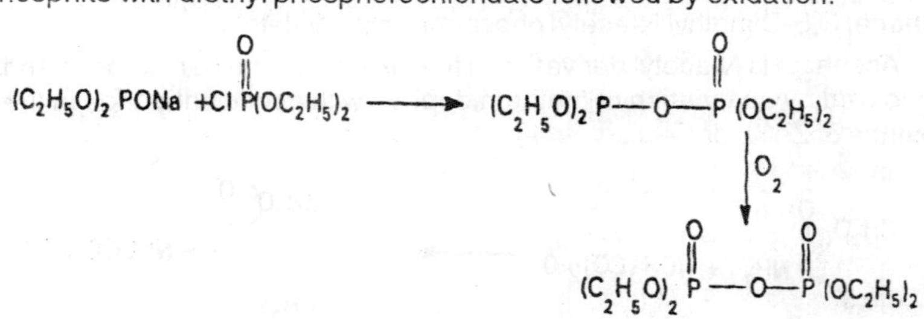

TEPP is colourless, odourless and hygroscopic liquid b.p. 124°C at 1 mm Hg. TEPP is a contact insecticide and acaricide particularly effective to control aphids and mites. The oral $LD_{50}$ for rats is 2.0 mg/kg. Because of high toxicity, the use of TEPP is restricted.

## Schradan

(Octa methyl pyrophosphoamide)

Schradon is prepared by treating dimethylamine with phosphorus oxychloride in the presence of tertiary amine.

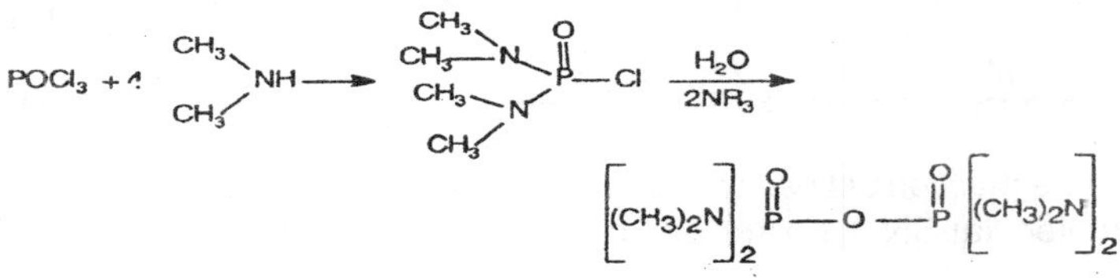


Schradan is a colourless viscous liquid, b.p. 118 to 122°C at 0.3 mm Hg. Schradan is used to control aphids and mites on citrus, apple and hops. The $LD_{50}$ for rats is 35.0 mg/kg.

## MODE OF ACTION OF ORGANOPHOSPHATES AND CARBAMATES

Acetylcholinesterase is an essential components of nervous systems of both insects and mammals and plays an important role in the transmission of nerve impulses. Acetylcholinesterase catalyses the hydrolysis of acetylcholine to choline and acetic acid.

$$(CH_3)_3\overset{+}{N}CH_2\,CH_2\,OCO\,CH_3 \xrightarrow[H_2O]{\text{acetyl cholinesterase}} (CH_3)_3\overset{+}{N}\,CH_2\,CH_2\,OH + CH_3COOH$$

The organophosphorous and carbamate owe their insecticidal properties because they phosphorylate or carbomylate the enzyme acetyl cholinesterase. In the absence of effective cholinesterase, there is an accumulation of acetylcholine which violates the function of the nervous system. This results in giving rise to the typical chlolinergic symptoms associated in insects with poisoning hyper, activity, tremors, convulsions, paralysis and death. The active centres of the enzyme acetyl cholinesterase contains two main active sites, an anionic site which is negetively charged and binds into the cationic part of the substrate (acetylcholine) and the esteratic site containing the primary alcoholic group of the amino acid serine which attacks the carbonyl carbon atom of the substrate. The normal enzymatic hydrolysis of acetylcholine to choline may be illustrated as follows.

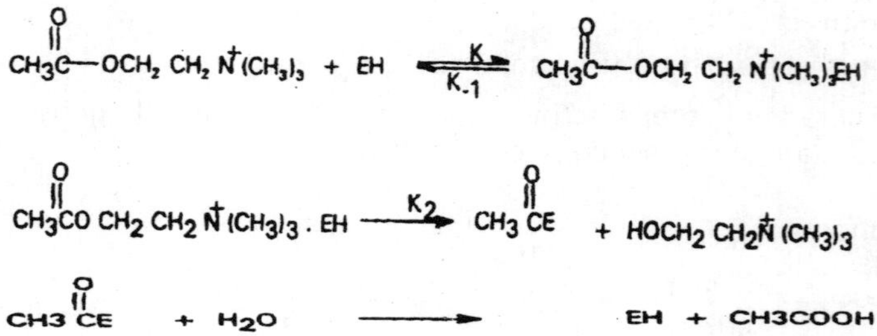

The reaction between esterase and phosphorous or carbamate inhibitor is bimolecular $SN_2$ type and can be illustrated as follows.

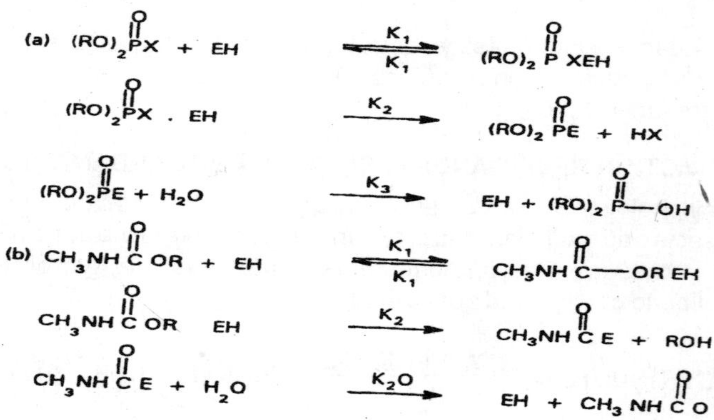

In comparative studies on acetylcholinesterase inhibitors, only the $I_{50}$ value is measured. In the normal process, step 3 occurs very rapidly, while in the inhibition process 'B' and 'C' the step 3 occurs very slowly because the phosphorous oxygen bond is very strong. So the organophosphate and carbamate effectively poisons the enzyme by phosphorylation or carbomylation, and thus blocks the efficient hydrolysis of acetylcholine into choline. The toxicity of different organophosphates and carbamates is different because the toxicity depends on the phosphorylating or carbomylating constant $K_3$. Thus it has been found that constant $K_3$, the rate constant that determines the regeneration of the enzyme is practically equal to zero for organophosphate insecticides, where as value of $K_3$ for carbamates is small but infinite (when the carbamate group is $CONHCH_3$, K=0.01, when the carbamate group is $CON(CH_3)_2$ K=0.003, when the organophosphate group is $PO(OR)_2$ K=0). The difference between the inhibition of cholinesterase by organophosphate and carbamate is that typical organophosphates are about 30 times more phosphorylating than carbomylating but have lesser affinity between the enzyme and inhibitor. The reversion of inhibited acetylcholinesterase enzyme is more in case of carbamates so the enzyme is activated again and in the case of organophosphate insecticides the reversion from the inhibited enzyme is negligible.

## STRUCTURE ACTIVITY RELATIONSHIP

### Phosphates

The organophosphate type of insecticides are vinyl ester derivatives which generally have an electron withdrawing group such as halogens and a carboxylic ester or amide group on the position. Toxicity depends on the development of +ve change on phosphorous which is enhanced by the shift of electrons towards the aryl ring. This depends on the dissociation of substituents. The higher the dissociation constant such as alcohol, phenol or acid, the more toxic is the compound. When the length of alkyl radicals in the esters and amides is increased, the toxicity is decreased. The maximum toxicity for many mixed esters of phosphoric acid occurs as diethyl derivatives. Diethyl phosphates are less toxic to insects and mammals. The activity of arylphosphates substituted in position 1 is higher than in position 2 and 3.

### Thiophosphates

Thiophosphates are safer than phosphates from the mammalian toxicity point of view. In thiophosphates, the toxicity depends on the nature of R. $CH_3$, $C_2H_5$ are more toxic than higher alkyl groups. No toxicity of thiophosphate has been observed when the aryl ring is not substituted by the functional groups. The toxicity of thiophosphates is increased if the substituents are -$SCH_3$, $NO_2$, sulphoxide, sulfone, present in para position. When disubstituent is present in 3 and 4 position, toxicity towards mammals is decreased without change in toxicity to insects.

Thiophosphates having the formula

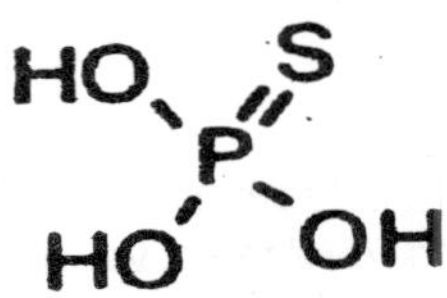

If the carbon atoms in the alkoxy group are more than 4, then activity is decreased. The number of methylene (-$CH_2$-) groups between P and S should not be more than 2, because the activity will be decreased. If more than 3 carbon atoms are present activity is decreased and maximum toxicity is found in 1C. If P is attached to aromatic ring then toxicity is also decreased.

**Dithiophosphates**

All derivatives of dithiophosphoric acid are less toxic to mammals than the corresponding derivatives of thiophosphoric acid. All derivatives of dithiophosphoric acid in

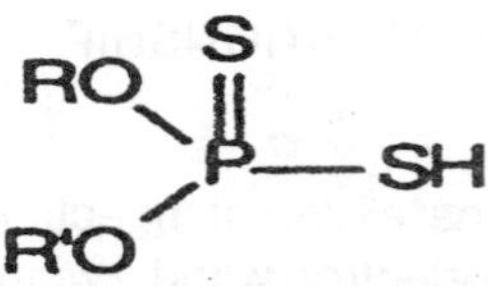


Where R and R` are methyl radicals and are less stable than the corresponding ethyl esters as insecticides. An increase in number of carbon atoms in these radicals increases the toxicity towards mammals without increasing the insecticidal activity. In dialkyl aryl phosphorothionates, maximum activity is obtained, if the substituent group is in the p-position and must be electron attracting. The introduction of a second substituent on the benzene ring such as chlorine or the methyl group reduces mammalian toxicity without any decrease in insecticidal activity. Meta substitution is effective for insecticidal activity. If the aryl group is replaced by aromatic heterocyclics, the insecticidal property is retained but the mammalian toxicity is reduced.

**Pyrophosphoric acids**

The insecticidal activity of pyrophosphoric acid derivative is decreased with increase in size of ester radical. Introduction of second sulphur atom in phosphorous lowers toxicity of the compound of mammals without reducing the insecticidal activity and introduction of a third sulphur on the phosphorous decreased the insecticidal activity.

**Phosphoric acids**

In phosphoric acids, the toxicity of methyl and ethylphosphoric acids to mammals is higher than that of analogues of phosphoric acids. The derivatives of thiophonic acid are less toxic than thiophoric acids. An increase in size of the hydrocarbon radical connected with phosphorous lowers the insecticidal activity.

**Cyclic esters**

In cyclic ester derivatives of phosphates, five membered cyclic phosphate esters are very reactive but these are only poor inhibitors of acetylcholinesterase. On the other hand, five membered cyclic phosphoroamidates have moderate action on anticholinesterase and insecticidal activity. Six membered cyclic phosphate esters are not so unstable and have poor activity. The poor activity may be attributed due to steric effects of the cyclic structures.

### Asymmetry

Toxicity is also affected by the asymmetry. The leavo isomer of O-ethyl S-2 (ethyl thio)-ethyl phosphonatiolate is ten times more toxic than dextro isomer. The leavo isomer of O, S-dimethyl p-nitrophenyl phosphorothiolate is about five times toxic than dextro isomer. Asymmetry in the succinate moiety of malaoxon also affects inhibitors activity on esterases. d-Malaoxon is about 4 to 8 times better than 1-isomer in inhibition of acetylcholinesterase.

## BOTANICAL PESTICIDES

### Nicotine

(3-(1-methyl-2-pyrrolidyl) pyridine)

Nicotine is an alkaloid present in the leaves of *Nicotiana tabacum, Nicotiana glutinosa* and *Nicotiana rustica*.

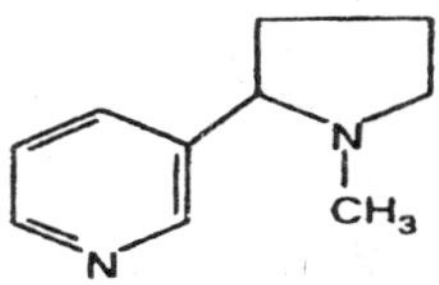


Nicotine occurs in tobacco plants as a salt with citric and malic acid to the extent of 1-8% and may be extracted from leaves and roots of the plants by treatment with aqueous alkali followed by steam distillation. It is converted to nicotine sulphate by treatment with $H_2SO_4$, because it is stable. Nicotine sulphate is being widely used as an insecticide because it is much less toxic to warm blooded animals than free nicotine and is less volatile. Nocotine is commonly formulated as 3.6% dust. Its use is rapidly declining because of its high mammalian toxicity ($LD_{50}$ for rats 50 mg/kg), b.p. 281°C.

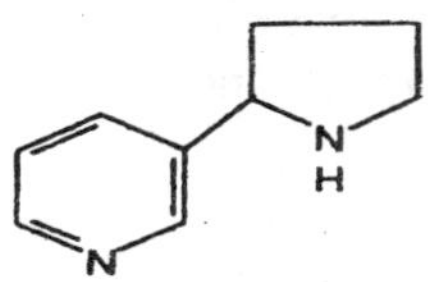


Nornicotine occurs as both d and i forms, the former is present in

*Duboisia hopwoodii* and later predominating in *Nicotiana sylvestris.*

Anabasine occurs in the Tuskestan weed *Anabasis aphylla* and has shown aphicidal activity.

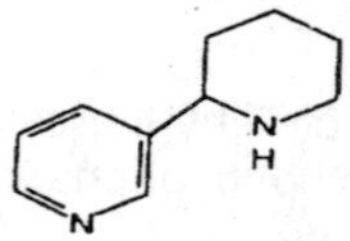

## STRUCTURE ACTIVITY RELATIONSHIP

The essential requirements for toxicity of nicotinoids are a) pyridine ring 2) a highly basic nitrogen c) an unsubstituted a-position of the pyridine ring d) The basicity of the compound is very important, PKa values for the pyridinyl nitrogen moiety (PKa) should be higher than 5.8, preferably 7.4-9.0) The minimum distance between the two nitrogens is about 4.2 A$^0$ and this distance is in approximate agreement with that of the two functional groups of the acetylcholine molecule.

### Rotenone

Rotenone occurs in the roots of *Derris elliptica* (from the East Indies and Malya) and a species of *Lonchocarpus utilis* (from South America). Rotenoids can be extracted from the powdered roots with organic solvents.

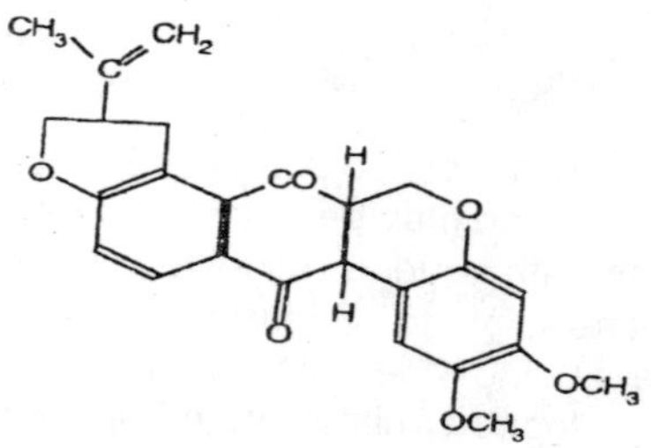

Rotenone is a white to yellowish white crystal, melting point 163°C, and is soluble in polar solvents and insoluble in water. It is readily detoxified by the action of air and light. Almost all toxicity may lost after 2-3 days of summer exposure.

The $LD_{50}$ of rotenone to rats is 150 mg/kg. It is used as fish poison. It is formulated as dusts. With the exception of hydrogenation of the isopropenyl side chain which produces dihydrorotenone of nearly equal toxicity all other chemical alternations greatly decreases the toxicity of the rotenone molecule.

## Mode of Action.

**Nicotine** : Symptoms of poisoning by nicotine follow the general sequence of (1) excitation, (2) convulsion, (3) paralysis and (4) death. Nicotine stimulates the rate of heart beat at low concentration and decrease it at high concentrations. The onset of symptoms from nicotine poisoning in insects is described as (1) period of inactivity, (2) sequence of paralysis begining with hindlegs, then wings and other legs, (3) toppling of the insect on its back, and (4) total paralysis.

Nicotine attacks acetylcholine receptors, which resemble cholinesterases, Inhibition takes place mainly at the anionic site by the competitive binding of the high basic nitrogen atom which is normally ionized at physiological pH. At the same time, the pyridinyl nitrogen assists the action of the high-basic nitrogen by affecting the electronic status of the receptor protein.

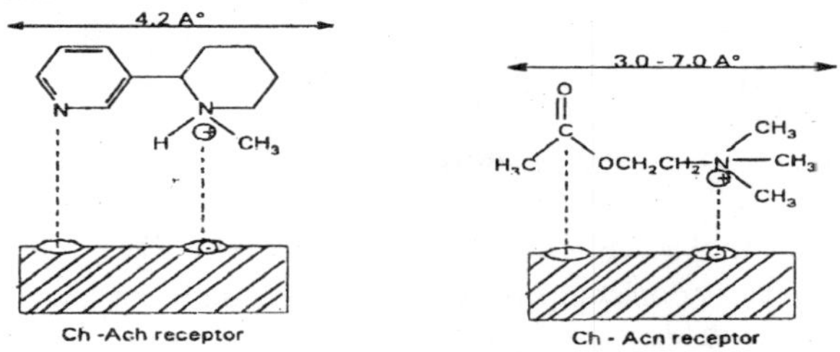


**Fig 4.1:** Similarities between acetylcholine and nicotine binding to the acetylcholine receptor.

**Rotenone :** The poisoning of insects by rotenone is usually a slow process : (1) inactivity, locomotive instability and refusal to eat (2) knockdown (3) paralysis (4) slow death.

Rotenone poisoning mainly derives from the ability of rotenone to inhibit respiratory metabolism. More precisely, rotenone owes its inhibitory potency to its ability to interfere with the electron-transport process between reduced diphosphopyridine nucleotide (DPNH or NADH) and cytochrome b. Inhibition of respiratory metabolism is one of the major causes of nerve conduction block.

### Pyrethrins

Pyrethrum is derived from dried flowers of the plant *Chrysanthemum cinerariaefolium*. The name given to the active insecticidal components of the dried flowers is known as pyrethrins. Chemically "pyrethrins" are organic esters formed by the combination of two carboxylic acids and three keto alcohols. One set of esters is known as the pyrethrin group consisting of pyrethrin I, a combination of chrysanthemic acid with pyrethrolone and pyrethrin II formed by the combination of pyrethric acid with pyrethrolone.

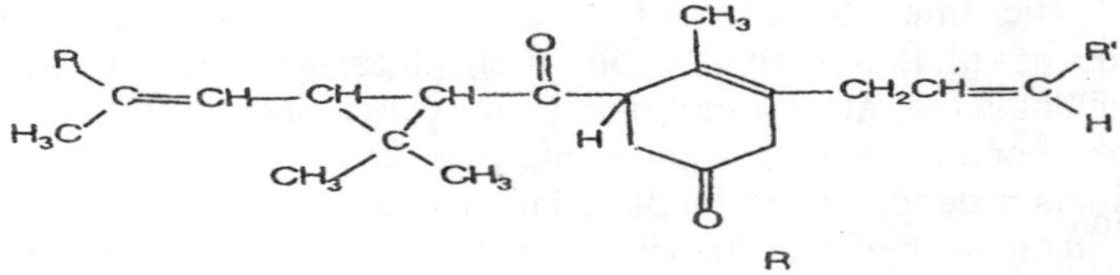

| | R | R' |
|---|---|---|
| Pyrethrin I | $-CH = CH_2$ | $-CH_3$ |
| Pyrethrin II | $-CH = CH_2$ | $-COOCH_3$ |
| Cinerin I | $-CH_3$ | $-CH_3$ |
| Cinerin II | $-CH_3$ | $\cdot COOCH_3$ |
| Jasmolin I | $-CH_2CH_3$ | $-CH_3$ |
| Jasmolin II | $-CH_2CH_3$ | $-COOCH_3$ |

The second group is known as cinerin esters. These consist of cinerin I and Cinerin II and are formed by combination of cineralone with chrysanthemic acid and pyrethric acid respectively. The third group was discovered in 1964 and is known as Jasmoline esters. These consist of Jasmoline I and Jasmoline II and are formed by the combination of jasmalolone with chrysanthemic acid and pyrethric acid respectively.

The active consistuent pyrethrins from pyrethreum flowers are extracted with solvents like kerosene. The solvent is percolated through ground flowers and extract evaporated under vacuum.

The outstanding properties of pyrethrins are

1. **Rapid action:** It is a contact insecticide attacking the nervous system of insects almost immediately and causing knockdown followed by kill.

2. **Low mammalian toxicity:** It has a low mammalian toxicity. It is one of least toxic domestic insecticide available.

3. **Broad spectrum of Insecticides**: Because it consists of a group of related compounds, it has a wider spectrum of activity against insect species than any single insecticide.

4. **Lack of persistence:** Pyrethrum is degraded by the combination of sunlight and air, and therefore presents little of the hazards which are usually associated with certain other classes of persistent insecticides.

5. **Repellency:** Pyrethrum is a powerful insect repellent which in combination with its low mammalian toxicity favours it in many applications.

## STRUCTURE ACTIVITY RELATIONSHIP

The most active isomers are d-trans acid esters of the d-cis alcohols. For biological activity presence of a) isobutylene group b) the dimethyl cyclopropane ring of the acid c) the unsaturated keto group of the keto alcohol d) the ester linkage is essential e) esters derived from chrysanthemic acid is more active than that of pyrethic acid.

### Synthetic Pyrethroids

Advantages of synthetic pyrethroids :

1. They have extremely high insecticidal activity at extremely low doses and are biodegradable in nature.
2. Their activity is most pronounced against lepidopterous pests and are also effective against beetles, leaf miners and bugs.
3. They maintain insecticidal activity over a great extended period of time which helps in controlling overlapping generations of pests.
4. They are effective against eggs, larval and adult stages of insects, particularly so in the case of most lepidoptera insects.
5. They have powerful antifeedant and repellent properties, after contact insects become moribund and stop feeding.
6. They have rainfastness i.e. they are not readily washed off from the plants by rain. The lipophilic character enables ready absorption on waxy layers of plant surface.
7. Synthetic pyrethroid treated crops give increased yields of better quality and in the case of cotton, the crop tends to mature early.
8. The movement from site of application is limited in air due to low volatility and in soil and plants due to low polarity.

**Disadvantages:**

1. Synthetic pyrethroids are not systemic and do not have translamiar action, so they are not effective against sucking pests lime aphids and mealy bugs resulting in the resurgence of these pests.
2. Constant use of synthetic pyrethroids increase incidence of mites in crops like cotton, tea, vegetables etc.
3. With large scale use of synthetic pyrethroids incidence of Alternaria disease increased in cotton mostly in sandy soil.
4. The synthetic pyrethroids are highly toxic to fish. The lipophilicity of pyrethroids indicats, that they will be absorbed strongly by the gills of fish even at very low concentration in water.

5. Some of the synthetic pyrethroids do not have a specific antidote.

**Allethrin**

(2-methyl-4-oxo-3-(2-propenyl)-2 cyclopenten 1-yl)

Allethrin is prepared by esterification of synthetic ± chrysanthemic acid with the alcohol allethrolone.

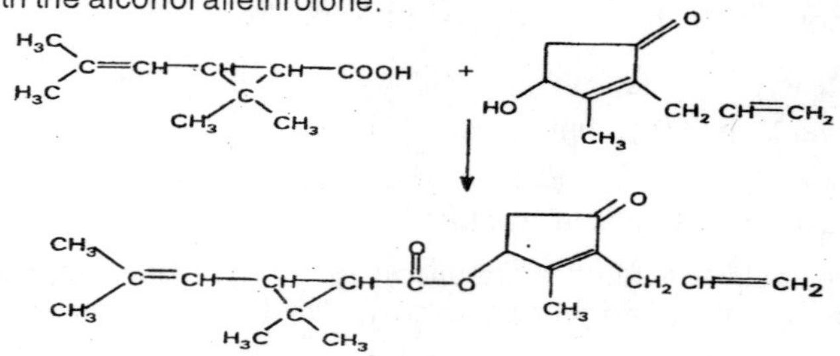

Allethrin is a mixture of four racemic forms or eight optical isomers, four of which are esters of the cis-acid and four are esters of trans acid.

Technical allethrin is a pale yellow liquid b.p. 140°C /0.1 mm Hg. Allethrin is a contact insecticide effective against house hold pests. The acute oral $LD_{50}$ for male rats is 1100 mg/kg and female 685 mg/kg. Bioallethrin is d-trans allethrin. It is amber viscous liquid b.p. 153°C/ 0.4 mm Hg. It is a contact non-systemic insecticide which produces a rapid knockdown and is used against house hold pests. The prefix bio is generally used to indicate the esters of the natural dextrorotatary (1R)-trans-chrysanthemic acid.

## RESMETHRIN AND BIORESMETHRIN

Resmethrin (5 benzyl-3 furanyl methyl (1RS)-cis-trans-2,2-dimethyl-3-(2-methylprop-1-enyl) cyclopropane carboxylate) is prepared by treating chrysanthemic acid with 2-benzyl-4-furylmethyl alcohol.

Resmethrin is a colourless waxy solid m.p. 43-48°C. It is used to control agricultural, horticultural and public health insect pests. The $LD_{50}$ for rats is more than 2500 mg/kg. Bioresmethrin is the ester of the (1R)-trans acid. It is a yellow liquid m.p. 30-35°C, b.p. 181°C/0.1 mm Hg. It is also effective against wide range of agricultural and house hold pests. The acute oral $LD_{50}$ for rats is 7070-8000 mg/kg.

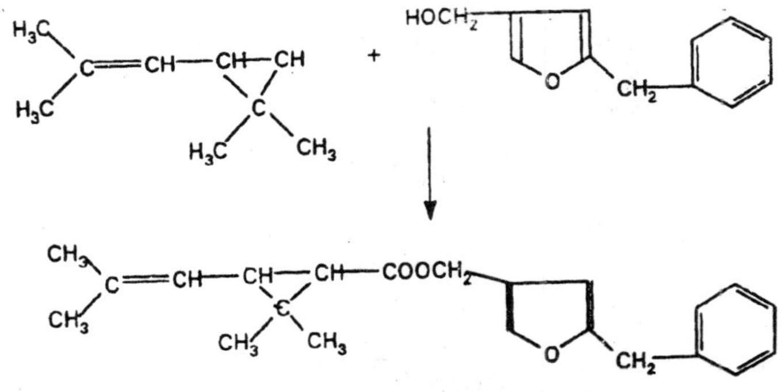

## FENVALERATE

Fenvalerate ((RS)-a-cyano-3-phenoxybenzyl-RS-2(4-chlorophenyl)-3-methylbutrate). Fenvalerate is prepared as follows

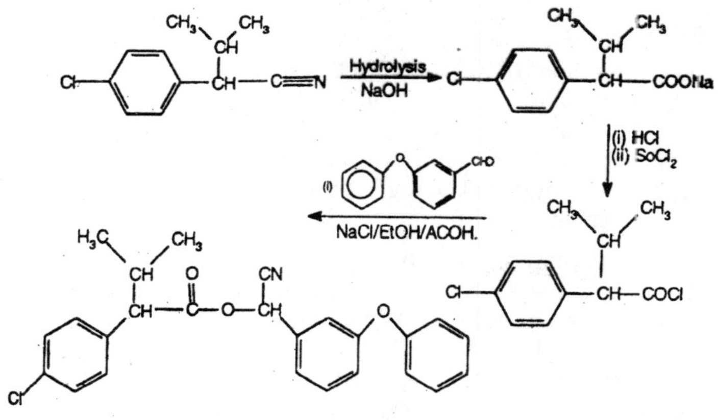

Fenvalerate is a viscous yellow liquid. Fenvalerate acts both as a contact and stomach poison. It controls the pests on crops of cotton, vegetables and fruits. Its $LD_{50}$ for rats is 451 mg/kg.

## PERMETHRIN

Permethrin (3-phenoxy benzyl (1RS) cis, trans-3 (2,2-dichlorovinyl) 2,2-dimethylcyclopropane carboxylate) is prepared by converting methyl (1RS)-cis, trans-3 (2,2 dichlorovinyl)-2,2-dimethyl cyclopropone carboxylate to corresponding acid chloride and then reacting this intermediate with 3-phenoxy benzyl alcohol.

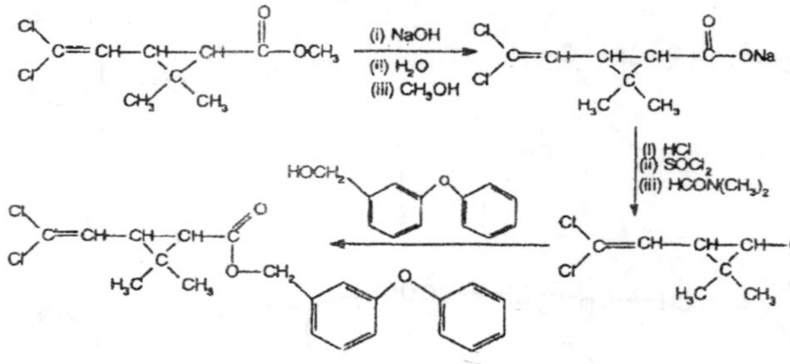

Permethrin is a white, odourless, crystalline solid. The melting point of cis isomer is 54-56°C and trans isomer is 45–46°C. The boiling point of permethrin is 210–220°C at 0.05 mm Hg. Permethrin is a contact insecticide effective against broad range of pests of cotton, fruits, vegetables and tobacco. The acute oral $LD_{50}$ values for cis: trans ratio of about 40:60 are 430 to 4000 mg/kg.

## CYPERMETHRIN

Cypermethrin ((RS) - α-cyano-3-phenoxy benzyl (1RS) - cis, trans-3(2,2-dichlorovinyl)-2,2-dimethylcyclopropane carboxylate) is prepared by converting methyl (1RS)-cis, trans-3-(2,2-dichlorovinyl) 2,2-dimethylcyclopropanecarboxylate to the corresponding acid chloride and then reacting this intermediate with 3-phenoxybenzaldehyde in the presence of sodium cyanide.

Pure cypermethrin is a white, odourless, waxy solid. The m.p. of pure cypermethrin isomers is 81-83°C. Cypermethrin is a stomach and contact insecticide effective against broad range of pests of cotton, fruit and vegetable crops. The chemical is active against eggs and active growth stages particularly larvae and also has antifeeding action. The $LD_{50}$ values of cypermethrin is 303 - 4123 mg/kg for rats.

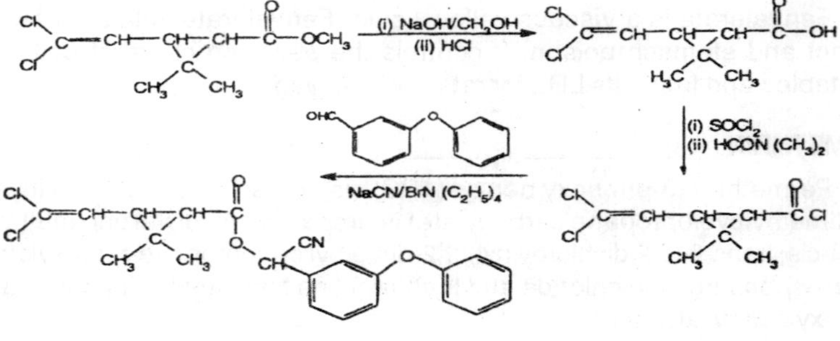

## ALPHAMETHRIN

Alphamethrin is mixture of two isomers out of 8 isomers of cypermethrin. It consists of single most isomer (S) - α-cyano- 3-phenoxybenzyl (1R)-cis- 3(2,2-dichlorovinyl)-2,2 dimethyl cyclo propane carboxylate and its inactive enontiomer in equal proportion. It is used for control of insects of cotton, vegetables, fruits and in storage.

## DELTAMETHRIN

Deltamethrin ((S)- α-cyano-3-phenoxybenzyl (1R, 3R) -3-(2,2-di bromovinyl)-2,2-dimethylcyclopropane carboxylate). Deltamethrin is the single isomer of pair of diastereoisomers (RS)- - α-cyano-3-phenoxybenzyl (1R, 3R)-3-(2,2-dibromovinyl) 2,2-dimethyl cyclopropane carboxylate having 5 configurations at the benzyl ring.

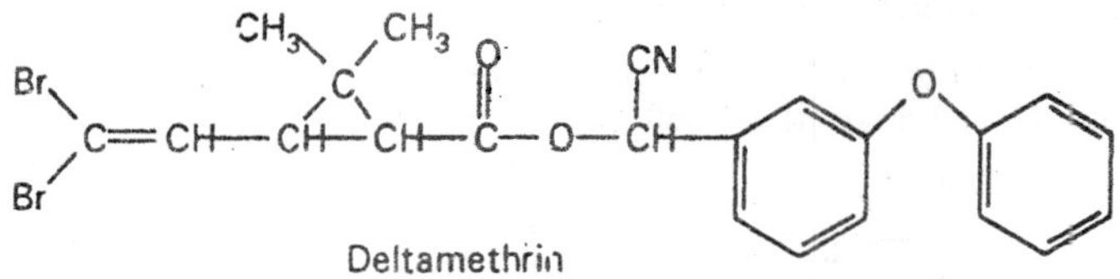

Deltamethrin

Deltamethrin is a colourless crystalline powder m.p. 98-101°C. It s a potent insecticide effective as a contact and stomach poison, against wide range of pests of fruits, vegetables, cotton and of stored products. The acute oral $LD_{50}$ for rats range from 135-5000 mg/kg. It is used at low dosages of 12.0 g/ha for the control of pests.

## CYHALOTHRIN

Cyhalothrin ((RS)-α-cyano-3-phenoxybenzyl (±) cis, trans-(2VE)-2-chloro-3,3,3-trifluoroprop-2-cnyl)-2,2-dimethylcyclopropone-2-carboxylate)

Cyhalothrin is a colourless solid m.p. 49.2°C. It is effective against pests of cotton, vegetables and fruits. Its $LD_{50}$ for male rats is 244 mg/kg.

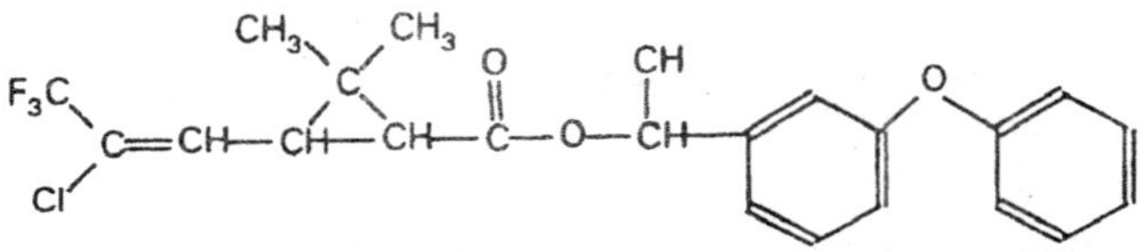

**Cypothrin**

((RS) - α-cyano-3 phenoxy benzyl (RS)-3,3-dimethyl spiro(cyclopropane 1,1-indene)-2 carboxylate)

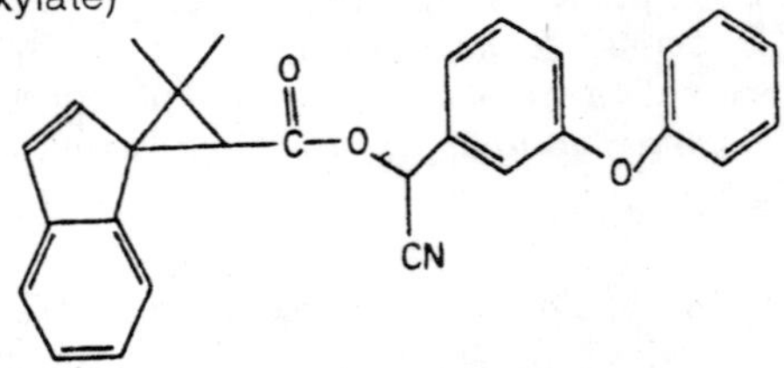

Cypothrin is mainly used in animal health as tickicide.

**Flucythrinate**

(α-cyano-3-phenoxybenzyl (S) -2-(4-fluoromethoxy phenyl)-3-methyl butyrate)

Flucythrinate is effective in suppressing phytophagous mites and is used for control of insects on cotton and vegetables.

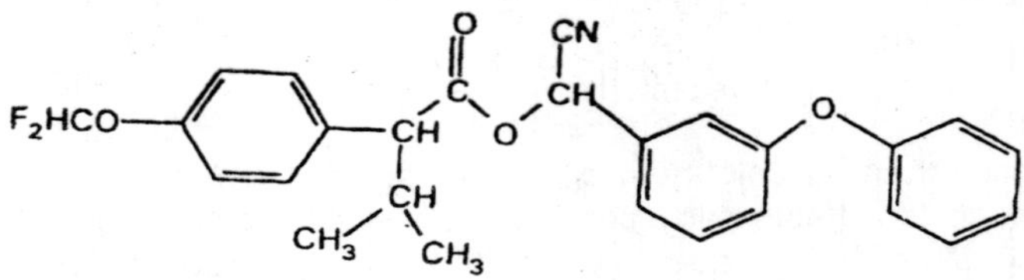

**Fluvalinate**

(RS- α-cyano-3-phenoxy benzyl (R-2-(2-chlorotrifluoromethylanilino)-3-methylbutyrate)

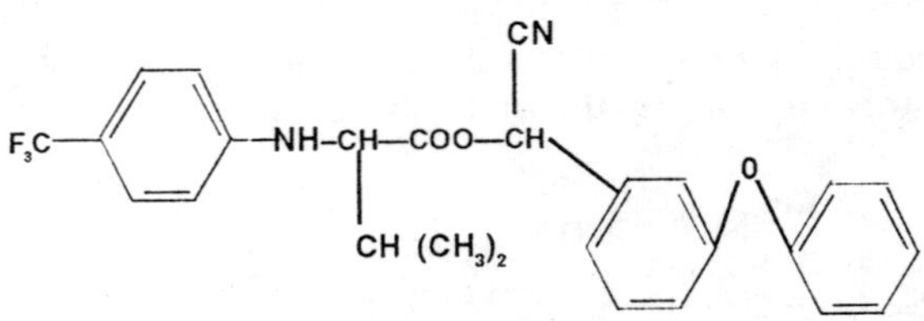

Fluvalinate is viscous yellow oil b.p. 450°C. Fluvalinate is used as a insecticide on cotton, vegetables and ornamental crops. It is also used as **an acaricide and aphicide. Its $LD_{50}$** to rats is 250 mg/kg.

**Cyfluthrin**

(RS)-α-cyano-4-fluorovinyl 2,2-dimethyl cyclopropane carboxylate)

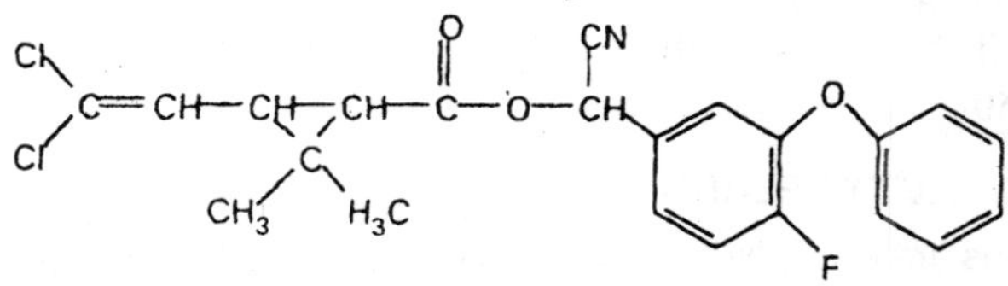

Cyfluthrin is a yellow mass m.p. 60°C. Cyfluthrin is effective against house hold pests. Its $LD_{50}$ value for rats is 500-800 mg/kg.

**Tralomethrin**

((S)- α-cyano-3-phenylbenzyl (1R, 3S) -2-2 dimethyl -3-(RS)-1,2,2,2,-tetrabromoethyl cyclopropane carboxylate)

Tralomethrin is effective in controlling pests of cotton, soybeans, potato and vegetables. Its $LD_{50}$ value to rats is 3000 mg/kg.

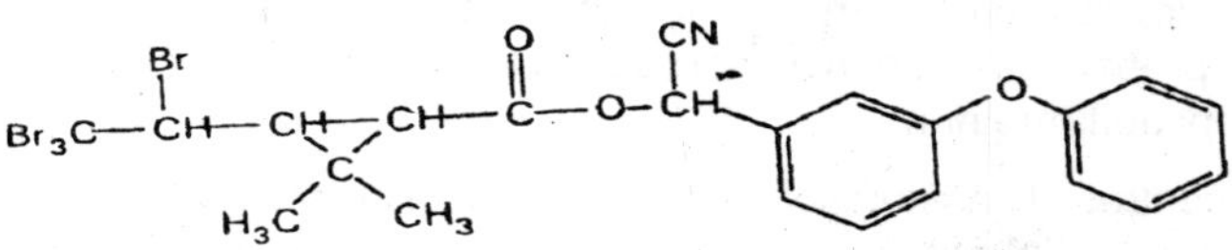

**Fenpropathrin**

((R,S)- α-cyano-3-phenoxybenzyl 2,2,3,3-tetramethylcyclopropane carboxylate)

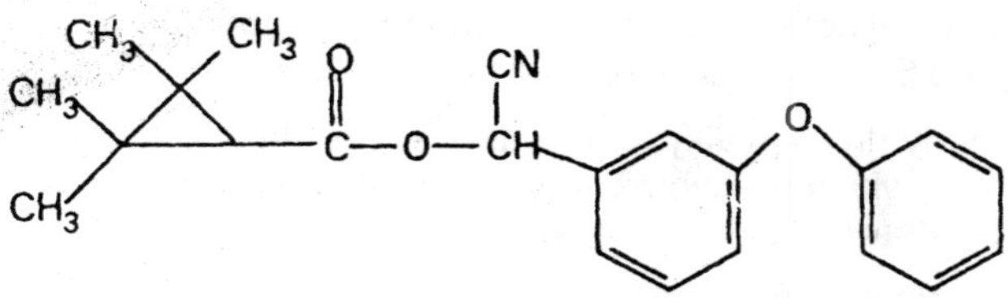

Fenpropathrin is used to control various species of mites and insects on ornamentals, cotton and vegetables. Its $LD_{50}$ value to rats is 164 mg/kg.

**Sumethrin**

(3-phenoxyphenyl) methyl 2,2-dimethyl-3-(2 methyl-1-propenyl) cyclopropane carboxylate

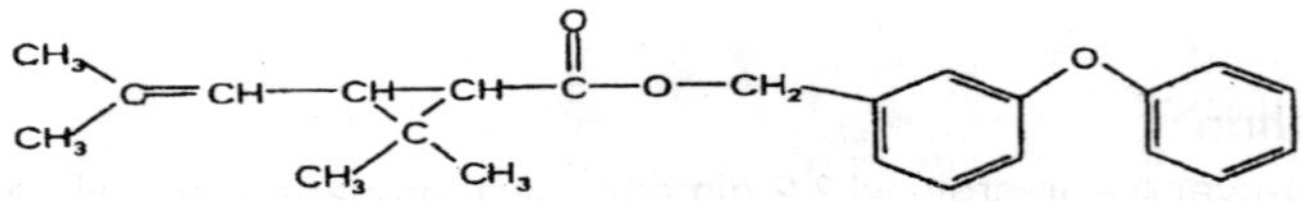

Sumithrin is a pale yellow liquid. It acts on insects of human health importance and shows a powerful lethal effects on them. The $LD_{50}$ values for rats is 5 g/kg.

## STRUCTURE ACTIVITY RELATIONSHIP

1. Pyrethroids are essentially ester compounds. Attempts to replace the ester with other linkages had reduced the insecticidal activity. There is now a single group which falls outside this category. These compounds are ethers of alkyl aryl ketooximes.
2. The presence of cyclopropyl moiety containing gem dimethyl group is crucial for activity. It the gem dimethyl substituent is replaced by spiroalkyl groups even then activity is retained. Synthetic pyrethroids like fenvalerate, cyfluthrin and flucythrinate are active without the cyclopropyl moiety containing gem dimethyl group.
3. Pyrethroids having trans configuration at C-1 and C-3 position of the cyclopropane ring are more active than their corresponding cis isomers except deltamethrin.
4. The centres of unsaturation at the extremes of the molecule are required for insecticidal activity.
5. The configuration at C-2 and C-3 must either 1R, 3S or 1R, 3R.
6. Esters of acids with 3-phenoxybenzyl alcohol have insecticidal activity. Introduction of cyano group (-CHCN)) further produced changes in insecticidal activity. When the absolute configuration of the -CH(CN) group is S, activity is increased to fifteen fold.
7. The derivatives of alkyl or aryl derivatives show activity. The carbon atoms to which the hydroxy group is attached must be $sp^3$ hybridised. Phenyl esters do not show activity.
8. Replacement of isobutenyl to dihalovinyl in the acidic moiety increases toxicity especially with difluoro compounds.

## MODE OF ACTION OF SYNTHETIC PYRETHROIDS

There is a general agreement that synthetic pyrethroids owe their insecticidal activity because of their attack on the insect nervous system. The symptoms of pyrethroid poisoning follow the typical pattern of nerve poisoning, namely excitation, convulsions, paralysis and death. On the basis of the mode of action, synthetic pyrethroids can be grouped into two categories, Type I compounds include pyrethrins allethrins, resmethrin, phenothrin, permethrin and oxime ethers. The type II pyrethrins include cypermethrin fenvalerate, deltamethrin. The type I pyrethroids cause restlessness in cordination, hyper activity followed by paralysis. Type II causes convulsions hyper activity and contractions. It has been established that pyrethroids are good inhibitors of Ca-Mg and Co-ATPase enzyme systems which in turn disturb Na-Ca exchange and calcium pumping which are necessary to maintain gradient across cellular membranes in the nervous system.

# 4

# Fungicides

Chemicals used to kill fungi or control fungi which cause plant diseases are called fungicides. The plant diseases are caused by pathogenic agents known as fungi, viruses and bacteria and parasitic seed plants.

### Fungi

Fungi are plants that lack green colour (chlorophyll). Fungi cannot make their own food. Most fungi reproduce by spores which work about the same way as seeds. Many fungi are capable of penetrating plant tissue directly. Examples of diseases caused by fungi are must on corn, downy mildew on soybeans and red rot of sugarcane etc.

### Bacteria

Bacteria are microscopic and single called organisms. They reproduce by simply dividing in half. Each half becomes a fully developed bacterium. Bacteria must enter through natural openings or through wounded tissue. Blight of pears and scab of potatoes are caused by bacteria.

### Viruses

Virus are ultramicroscopic and are seen by electron microscope. They are studied by their effects on selected indicator plants. Virus diseases are transmitted by from one plant to another by insects, cuttings and by mechanically rubbing leaves of healthy plants with juice from diseased plants. Examples of virus diseases are sugarcane mosaic virus and tomato mosaic virus.

### Parasitic seed plants

The parasite usually attaches itself to the host and deprives the host of nutrients and water. Mosses and dodders are examples of parasitic seed plants.

Fungicides can be classified on the basis of mode of action, use and chemical constitution. Based on the mode of action these are classified as follows:

1. Fungistatics
2. Protectants
3. Eradicant
4. Systemic Fungicides

1. **Fungistatics:** Chemicals which do not kill the fungi but inhibit the growth of the fungi.
2. **Protectants:** These check entry of the fungi into the plant but do not kill the established organisms.
3. **Eradicants:** These destroy, control or kill the established organisms.
4. **Systemic Fungicides:** A systemic fungicide is a compound that is taken up by the plant and is then translocated within the plant thus protecting it by the attack of pathogenic fungi. For a chemical to be effective systemic fungicide:
   - It must itself be fungicide or be converted into active fungitoxicant within the host plant
   - It must have very low toxicity.
   - It must be capable of absorbed by roots, seeds or leaves of the plant and then translocated at least within the plants.

## CHEMICAL CLASSIFICATION

On the basis of their chemical structure fungicides can be grouped into two major groups 1) Inorganics and 2) Organics

### Inorganics

1. Sulphur fungicides
2. Mercury fungicides
3. Copper fungicides

### Organics

These are organic compounds and are subdivided into various groups as below

1. Organotins
2. Organomercurials
3. Organophosphorous
4. Benzene derivatives

5. Diethylthiocarbamates
6. Polyhalogen alkenic sulphonyl group
7. Oxathiins
8. Quinones
9. Carboxyamides
10. Dinitro alkylphenols
11. Azole compounds
12. Benzimidazole derivatives
13. Triazoles
14. Hetrocyclic fungicides
15. Piperazine derivatives
16. Pyrimidines
17. Quinoline derivatives
18. Morpholine derivatives
19. Antibiotics
20. Miscelleneous

Classification based on general use is as follow:

1. **Seed treatments:** These are also called seed protectants. These are chemicals which are used for seed or seedling dips for seed borne diseases.
2. **Seed dressings:** These are chemicals which are used for dressing cuts and treatments of affected stems.
3. **Foliage and flower protectants:** These chemicals are used to avoid damage to leaves and flowers.

## REQUIREMENTS OF AN IDEAL FUNGICIDE

An ideal fungicide should have the following characteristics :

1. **Broad spectrum:** An ideal fungicide should have a broad spectrum of activity and it should kill variety of pathogens during the single spray.
2. **Low mammalian toxicity:** A good fungicide should be safe to mammals and beneficial to predators.
3. **Solubility:** A good fungicide should be sufficiently water soluble to give a cheap hydrophilic spray.
4. **Stability:** A good fungicide should be stable during storage and application.
5. **Low fungitoxicity:** It should not be toxic to plants.

## SULPHUR COMPOUNDS

Sulphur is one of the most important fungicides used for the control of various diseases, particularly powdery mildews. Elemental sulphur occurs both in free state and also in combination. Sulphur is used in a finely ground condition or in colloidal form in dust formulations. Ground sulphur is obtained by grinding coarse sulphur in a micronizers and then fractionating it in with air blasts. As the mechanically ground sulphur tends to aggregate, small amount of inert material like kaolin is added. Most of the sulphur sold for fungicidal use is ground to pass at least a 300 mesh sieve. Sulphur even though finely ground is not wetted by water. Wettable powders of sulphur are made by grinding sulphur with protective colloidal materials such as casein, bentonite clay and flour. Sulphur dusting powders containing materials such as gypsum, bentonite or talc in small amount make the sulphur flow freely and this form is called "conditioned sulphur".

Two forms of sulphur hydrophillic and hydrophobic are also used. Hydrophillic sol is prepared by passing $H_2S$ through a solution of sulphur dioxide in water or by reaction of sodium thiosulphate and sulphuric acid.

$$2H_2S + SO_2 \longrightarrow 3S + 2H_2O$$
$$Na_2S_2O_3 + H_2SO_4 \longrightarrow Na_2SO_4 + SO_2 + S + H_2O$$

Hydrophobic colloidal sulphur is obtained by acidifying lime sulphur solution with mineral acids.

$$CaSx + 2HCl \longrightarrow CaCl_2 + H_2S + Sx_{-1}$$

Lime sulphur or calcium polysulphide (CaSx) is also used as fungicide. Limesulphur is prepared by boiling 1.8 parts of sulphur, 1 part of lime and 10 parts of water for one hour. The solution is filtered and filtered solution is diluted to specific gravity 1.003, for sprays. This is a clear orange coloured liquid consisting mainly of calcium polysulphides which break down on exposure to air to release elemental sulphur. The polysulphide content of a lime sulphur mixture is the best indication of its effectiveness and the official specification contains at least 24% weight/volume of the polysulphide.

Barium polysulphide (BaSx) is also used as fungicide. It is prepared by saturating barium hydroxide solution with hydrogen sulphide or mixing ground sulphur with barium sulphite power. Calcium tetrathionate is also used as fungicide. It is prepared by passing sulphur dioxide into sulphuryl chloride.

$$2SO_2 + 2H_2O + S_2Cl_2 \longrightarrow H_2SO_4 + 2HCl$$
$$H_2SO_4 + CaCl_2 \longrightarrow CaS_4O_6 + 2HCl$$

It is found to be as effective as colloidal sulphur.

**Mode of action of sulphur**

The sulphur compounds act as hydrogen acceptor and thus interferes with the normal redox process of the fungal cells.

## MERCURY FUNGICIDES

Amongst the inorganic mercuric compounds mercuric chloride ($HgCl_2$) and mercurous chloride (HgCl) have been used as fungicides. These have been replaced by organic mercury compounds because of their extreme toxicity to plants and long persistence.

**Copper fungicides**

Copper compounds have wide fungal spectrum and are employed as protective foliar fungicides. Following is list of copper compounds used as fungicides.

Cupric sulphate: $CuSO_4 5H_2O$ for seed treatment

Bordeaux mixture: many fungal diseases.

$CuSo_4$ (4.57 kg) $Ca(OH)_2$ (5.5 kg) in 454 liters of water $[Cu(OH)_2]_x$. $CaSo_4$

Copper dugtdrazubium sulphate: Powdery mildew black spot of roses

$$Cu[N_2H_5]_2\ (SO_4)_2$$

Copper oxychloride : Powdery mildew

$$Cu(OH)_2\ CuCl_2$$

Copper zinc chromate : Diseases of potato, tomato

$$15CuO.10ZnO.6CrO_3.24H_2O$$

Cupric carbonate : Many fungal diseases

$$Cu(OH)_2\ CuCO_3$$

Cuprous oxide : Powdery mildew

$$Cu_2O$$

Burgundy mixture : Powdery mildew

$$CuSO_4 + Na_2CO_3$$

The mode of action of copper fungicides seem to be inhibitors of the variety of -SH containing enzymes. The fungicidal action of copper fungicides is also associated with the adsorptivity of the cytoplasm of cells of fungi.

**ORGANOTIN COMPOUNDS**

**Brestan**

(Triphenyl tin acetate)

It is prepared by treating trialkyl tin hydroxide with acetic acid.

$$(C_6H_5)3\ SnOH + CH_3COOH \rightarrow (C_6H_5)_3\ SnOCOCH_3 + H_2O$$

Its acute oral $LD_{50}$ for rats is 140—298 mg/kg.

**Duter**

(Triphenyl tin hydroxide)

Duter is produced by treating triphenyl stannous chloride with potassium hydroxide.

$$(C_6H_5)_3\,SnCl + KOH \;\; (C_6H_5)_3\,SnOH + KCl$$

The acute oral $LD_{50}$ for rats is 171 mg/kg and is used for control of blights of potato, leaf spot on sugar and blast diseases of rice. Complexes such as chlorotriphenyl (Sulfinyl bis (Methane-O)

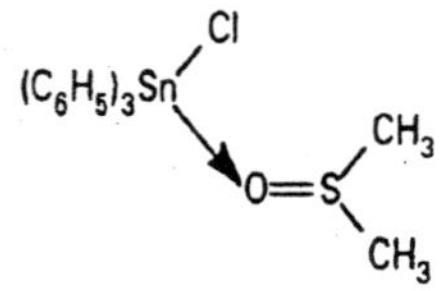

and chlorotriphenyl (quinoline oxide) tin are also fungicides.

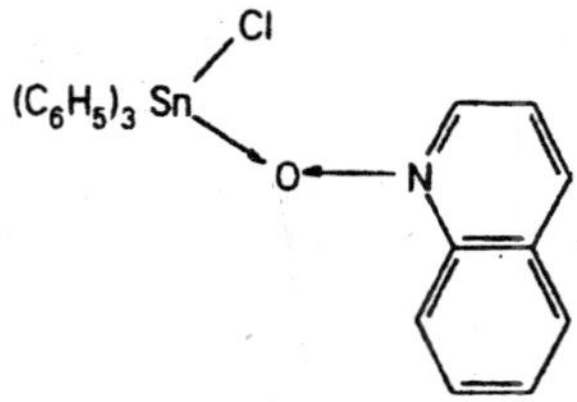

**Mode of action**

The mode of action of tin compounds is due to inhibition of oxidative phosphorylation in the mitochondria. Thus these compounds prevent the incorporation of organic sulphate into highly reactive, high energy ATP or adenosine triphosphate a reaction which typically takes place in mitochondria.

**ORGANOMERCURIALS**

Mercuric chloride ($HgCl_2$) is used as bactericide.

Mercurous chloride (HgCl) is much safer for plants than mercur chloride.

Ethyl mercuric chloride is prepared by treating mercuric chloride and diethyl mercury

$$(C2H_5)_2\,Hg + HgCl \longrightarrow 2Cl_2H_5HgCl$$

Phenyl mercury acetate is obtained by reacting benzene with mercuric acetate in glacial acetic acid

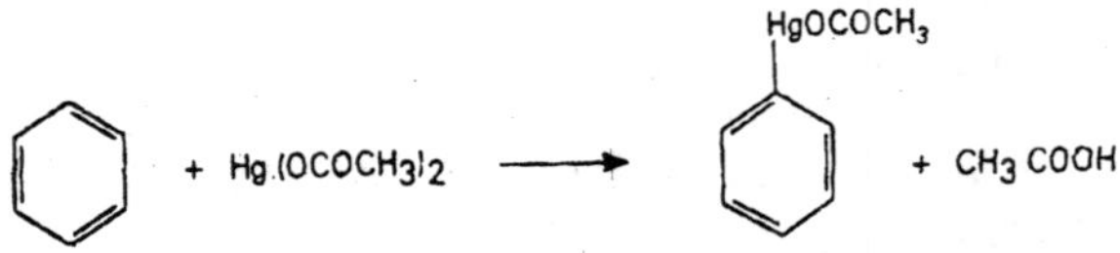

Ceresan-M (N-ethyl mercuric) p-toluene sulphonilide) is produced

by reacting ethylmercuric salts with p-tolune sulphonamide in the presence of NaOH

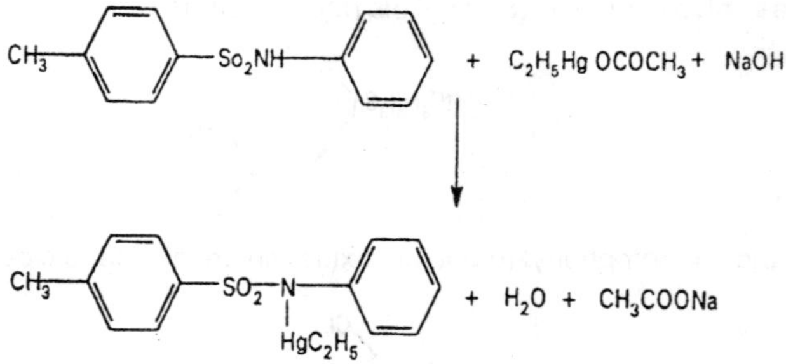

Agallol (methoxy ethyl mercuric chloride) is produced by treating methoxy ethyl mercuric acetate and sodium chloride.

$$CH_3OCH_2CH_2HgOCOCH_3 + NaCl \longrightarrow CH_3OCH_2CH_2HgCl + CH_3COONa$$

Phenylmercury triethanol ammonium lactate is produced by treating phenyl mercuric lactate with triethanol amine.

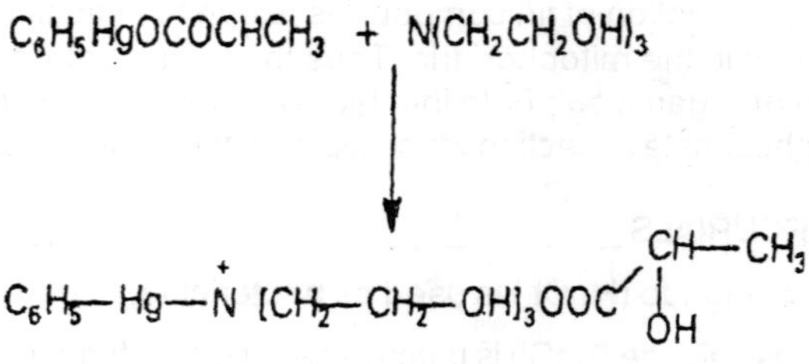

The mercury compounds are used as seed dressing for grains and cereals. The main disadvantage is that they are very poisonous and persistent and there are fears that their continued large scale use may result in serious effects on the ecosystems.

**Mode of action**

The mode of action of the mercury is due to the activity of Hg2+ moiety. The biological action of the mercury fungicides is related to the affinity of Hg2+ for sulfydryl groups of essential respiratory enzymes. Thus mercury treatment decreases the oxygen uptake of the treated fungus spores and poisoned the spores.

## ORGANOPHOSPHOROUS COMPOUNDS
## PHOSPHATES

This group has many important systemic fungicides.

**Wepsyn**

(P-(5-amino-3-phenyl-1H-1,2,4-triazol 1-yl)-N,N,N'N'-tetra methyl phosphonic diamidate)

Wespyn is prepared by the condensation of sodium salt of 3-amino-5-phenyl-1,2,4 triazole with bis (dimethyl amino) phosphoryl chloride

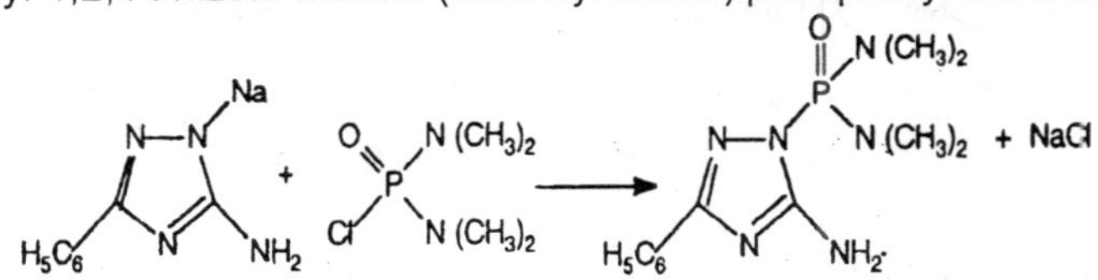

It is used for controlling powdery mildew on apples and ornamentals. The acute oral $LD_{50}$ for rats is 20 mg/kg.

**Kitazin P**

(S-Benzyl O,O'-diisopropyl phosphorothiolate)

Kitazin P is prepared by the condensation of sodium benzylthiolate and O,O'-diisopropyl phosphorochloridate.

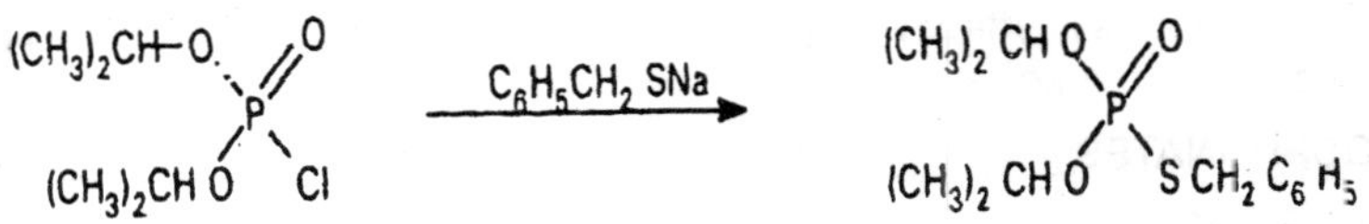

Kitazin P is a systemic fungicide applied as granules to paddy water to control rice blast and it inhibits mycelial growth in the tissue. The acute oral $LD_{50}$ for rats is 660 mg/kg.

**Conen**

(O-butyl-S-ethyl-S-benzyl phosphorodithioate)

Conen is prepared from sodium O-butyl-S-benzylphosphorodithioate and ethyl bromide.

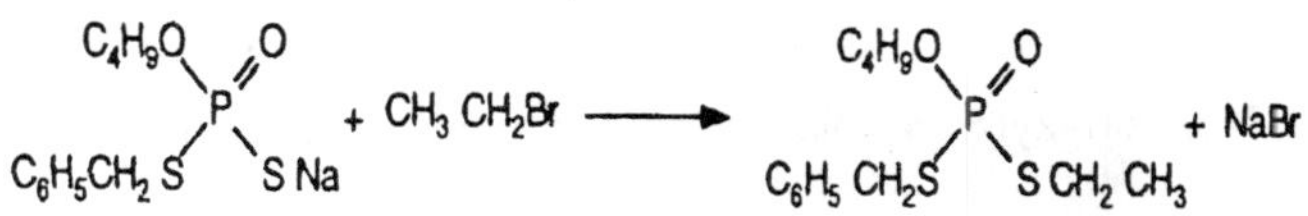

Conen exerts a curative rather than a protective action. The oral $LD_{50}$ for mice is 118 mg/kg.

**Dowco**

(O,O-diethylphthalimidophosphorothioate)

This is obtainted by the condensation of potassium phthalimide with O,O-diethyl phos-phorochloridothioate

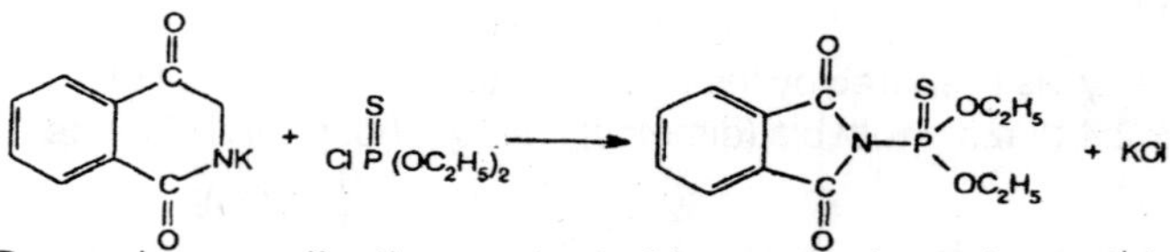

Dowco is very effective against wide range of powdery mildews and has low mammalian toxicity. The oral $LD_{50}$ for rats is 5660 mg/kg.

**Edifenphos**

(O-ethyl S,S-diphenyl phosphorodithioate)

Edifenphos is prepared by treating O-ethyl phosphorodichloridate with thiophenol.

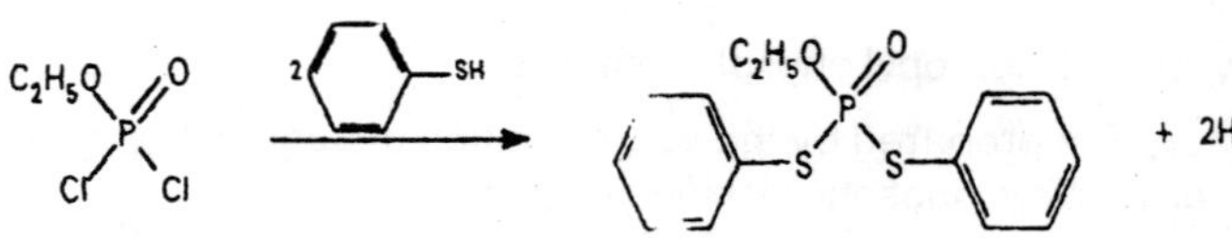

Edifenphos is effective against Pyrca aria oryzaeorice. The oral $LD_{50}$ for rats is 218 mg/kg rat.

**PHOSPHONATES**

**Inejin F 254**

(O-methyl-S-benzyl benzene phosphonothioatoe)

Inejin is used as fungicide to control rice blast and rice eath blight. The oral $LD_{50}$ for mice is 720 mg/kg.

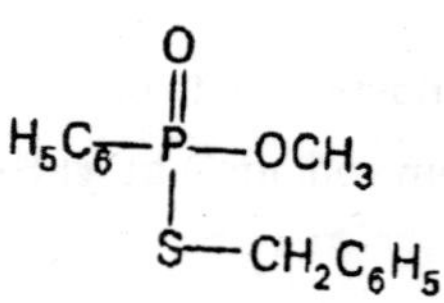

**Cerezin**

(O-methyl O-cyclohexyl S (4-chlorophenyl) phosphorothioate)

It is prepared by reacting O-methyl-O-cyclohexylphosphate in carbon tetrachloride with p-chlorophenylsulphenyl chloride.

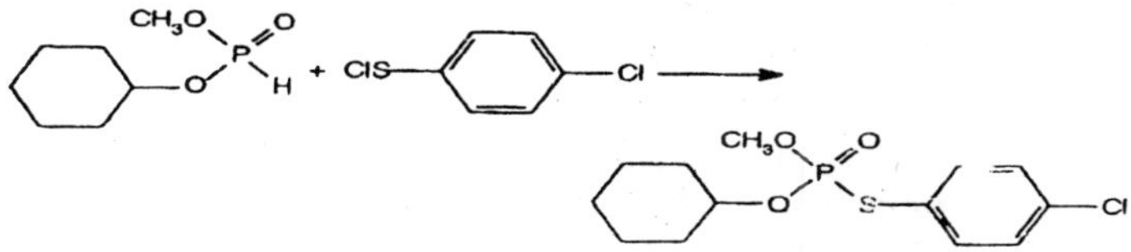

Cerezin has a curative effect on rice blast disease.

**Aliette**

(Aluminum tris (O-ethyl phosphonate))

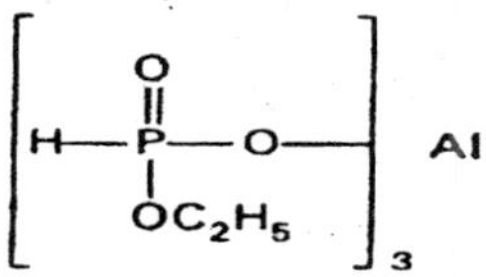

Aliette mainly marketed in combination with a protective fungicide for instance Mikal (50% Aliette, 9.5% Folpel), is active against downy mildews in crops like pineapple, citrus, Avocado, lettuce, vegetables, grapes and ornamentals.

**Mode of action of organophosphate fungicides**

The activity of organo phosphorous compounds is due to the reason that these compound influence fungal metabolism by direct phosphorylation and thereby disturb the vital functions of the cells.

## BENZENE DERIVATIVES

**Quintozene**

(2,3,4,5,6-pentachloro-1-nitrobenzene)

Quintozene is prepared by chlorination of nitrobenzene is the presence of chlorosulfonic acid. Iodine is used as catalyst.

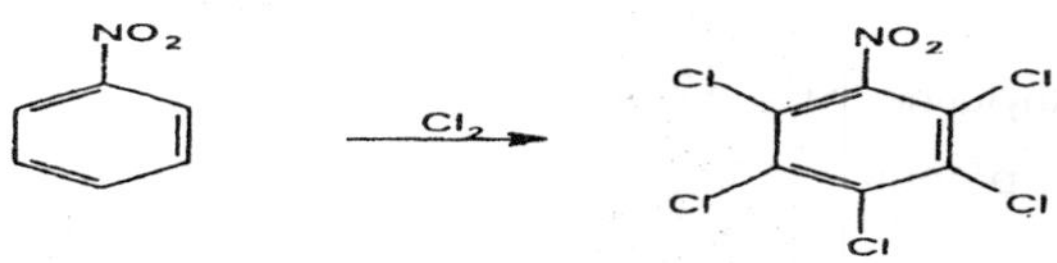

**Chlorothalonil**

(2,4,5,6-tetrachloro-isophthalonitrile)

Chlorothalonil is prepared as follows :

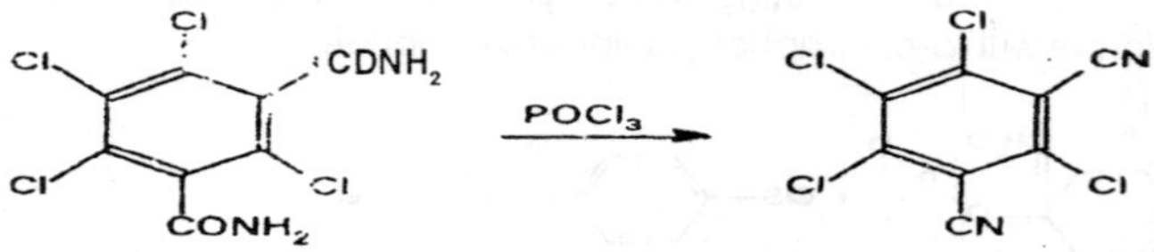

Cholorothalonil is effective against a broad range of plant pathogens on vegetable crops. It is also most effective against blue green algae. Its $LD_{50}$ for rats is 10,000 mg/kg.

**Chloroneb**

(1,4-dichloro-2,5-dimethoxybenzene)

Chloroneb is prepared by the chlorination of p-dimethoxybenzene

Chloroneb is very efficient for treatment of soil and seeds. It is used for protection of cotton, beans and soybeans. Its acute oral $LD_{50}$ for rats is 11,000 mg/kg.

## DITHIOCARBAMATES

Dithiocarbamates can be divided into two groups

1. N-monoalkydithicarbamates
2. N-N'-alkylenedithiocarbamates

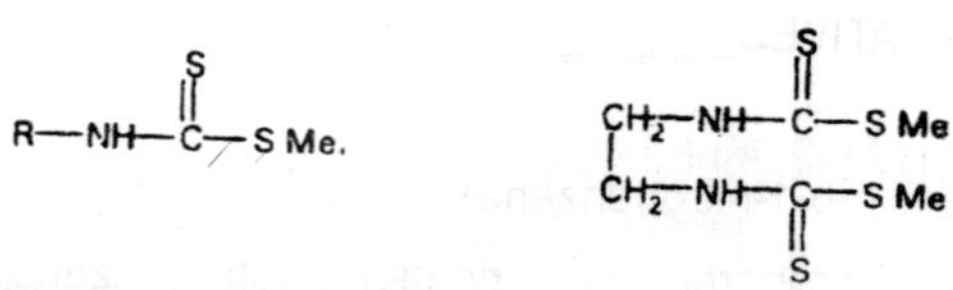

## MONOALKYLDITHIOCARBAMATES

**Metham**

(Sodium N-methyldithiocarbamate)

Metham is prepared by treating carbon disulphide with methyl-amine in the presence of sodium hydroxide.

$$CS_2 + CH_3NH_2 \xrightarrow{NaOH} CH_3NH\overset{S}{\overset{\|}{C}}-SNa + H_2O$$

The fungicidal action of metham is due to liberation of methylisothiocyanate from metham.

Metham is used as a seed dressing and soil treatment purposes.

**Dazomet**

(3,5-dimethyl-tetrahydro-2H-1,3,5-thiadiazine-2thione)

Dazomat is prepared by treating methyl amine with carbon disulphide and formaldehyde

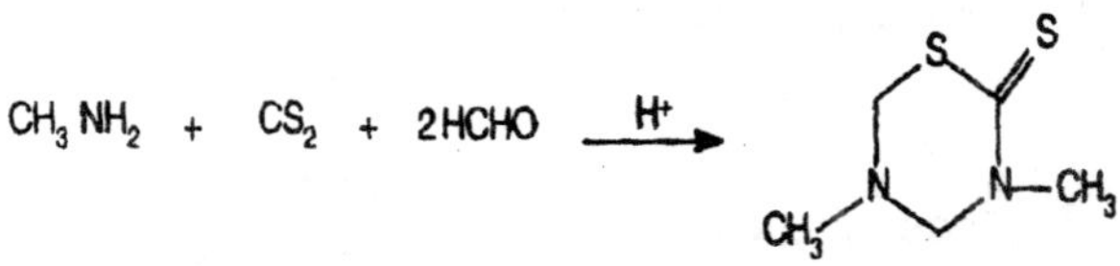


Dazomet on hydrolysis with water liberate formaldehyde and N-methyl dithiocarbamate ester. The later is converted into methyl isothiocyanate which is responsible for fungicidal action.

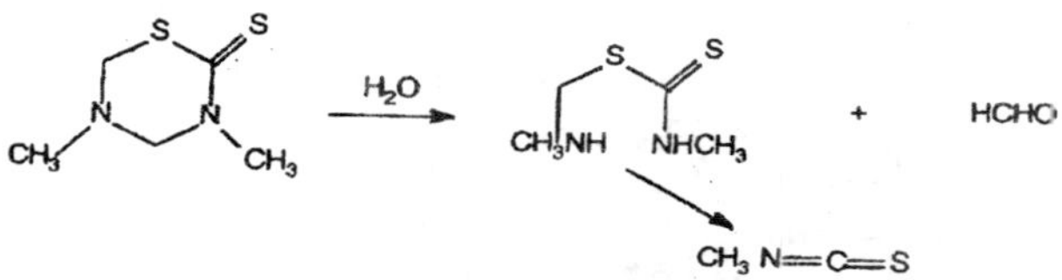


Dazomet is used as soil treatment. It has acute oral $LD_{50}$ of 650 mg/kg to rats.

**Neviram**

(Zinc bisisopropyldithiocrbamate)

Neviram is synthesised by treating isopropylamine, carbon disulphide and ammonium hydroxide. The ammonium isopropyldithiocarbamate thus formed, on treatment with zinc sulphate gives zinc bis isopropyl dithiocarbamate. it is used as a foliage fungicide. it can be used against apple and pear scab.

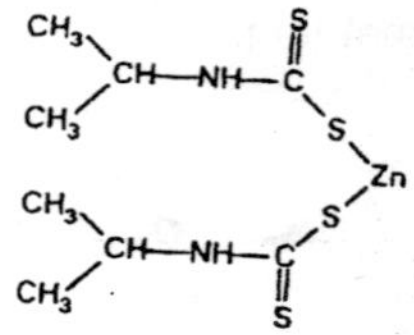

## N,N-ETHYLENE-BISDITHIOCARBAMATES

### Nabam

(Disodium ethylene 1,2-bisdithiocarbamate)

Nabam is prepared by reacting sodium hydroxide, carbon disulphide and ethylene diamine in aqueous medium

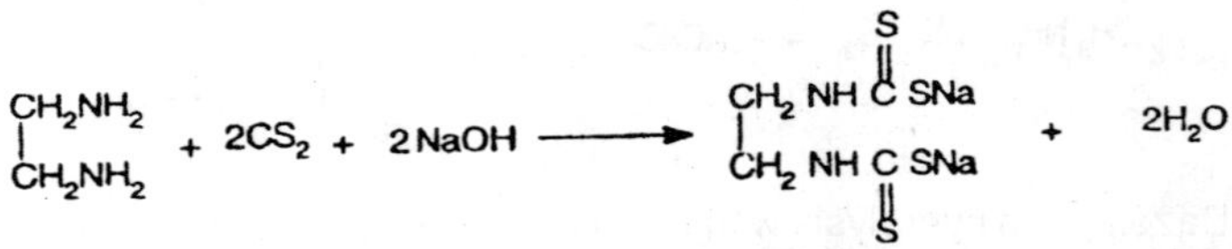

Nabam is converted into either zineb or Maneb by reaction with an aqueous solution of zinc or manganese sulphate.

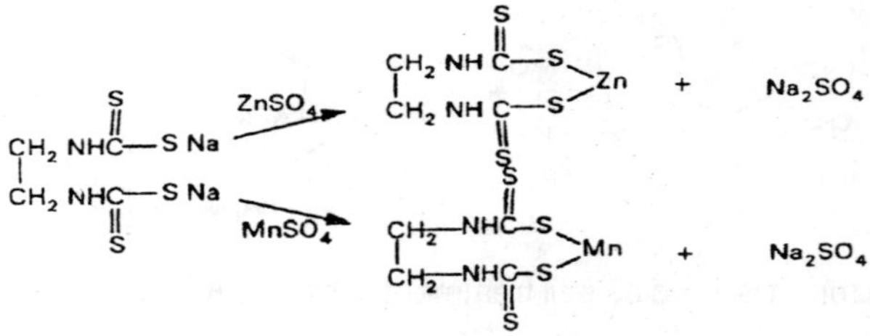

### Mode of action

Nabam is used as soil fungicide. Its acute oral $LD_{50}$ to rats is 395 mg/kg. Zineb and maneb are used to protect foliage and fruits of a wide range of crops against downy mildews and rusts. The acute oral $LD_{50}$ value to rats for zineb is 5000 mg/kg and for maneb is 6750 mg/kg.

### Mancozeb

(Manzate, Dithane M-45)

Mancozeb is the manganese-zinc double salt of N,N-bisdithio-carbamic acid. The active ingredient is a complex zinc ions (2%); manganese (16%) and ethylene bis dithiocarbamates (62%). Mancozeb is prepared as follows:

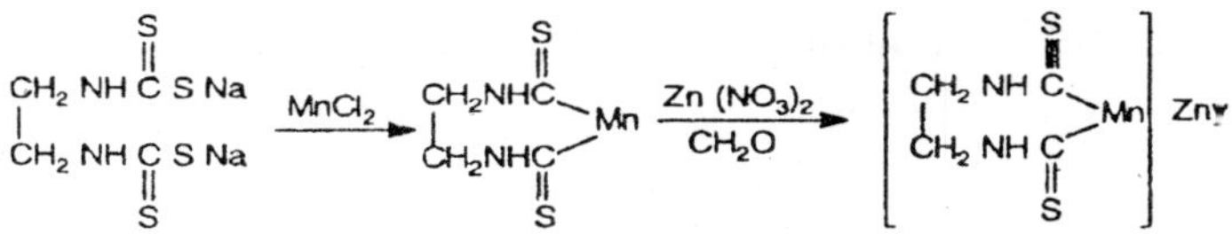

Mancozeb is a protective fungicide and effective against wide range of foliage diseases. It is used in combination with some systemic fungicides to increase the duration of protection given to the crop. Its acute oral $LD_{50}$ value to rats is 8000 mg/kg.

## Mode of action

The ethylenebisdithiocarbamates act by oxidative decomposition of the fungicides on plant surfaces to disothiocyanate.

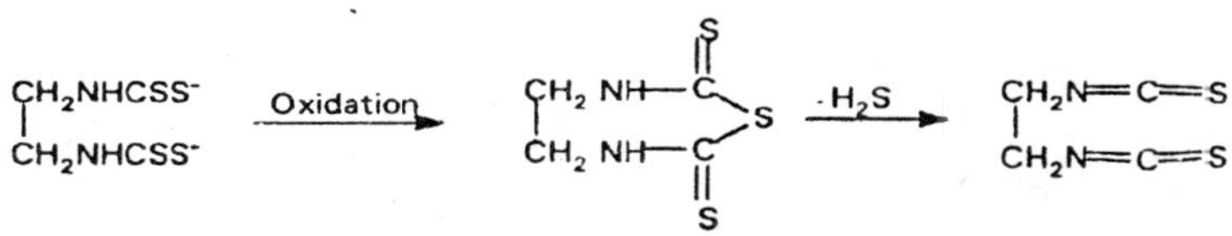

These disothiocynates are fungicidal by virtue of their ability to react with vital compounds present in the fungal cell.

## Dialkyldithocarbamates

Ferbam (ferric dimethyl dithocarbamate), Ziram (zinc bis (dimethyl dithiocarbamate), Thiram (tetramethylthiurum disulphide). These compounds are prepared by the reaction of dimethylamine with carbon disulphide and alkali hydroxide. The individual active substance can be obtainted by the addition of the alkali salt formed.

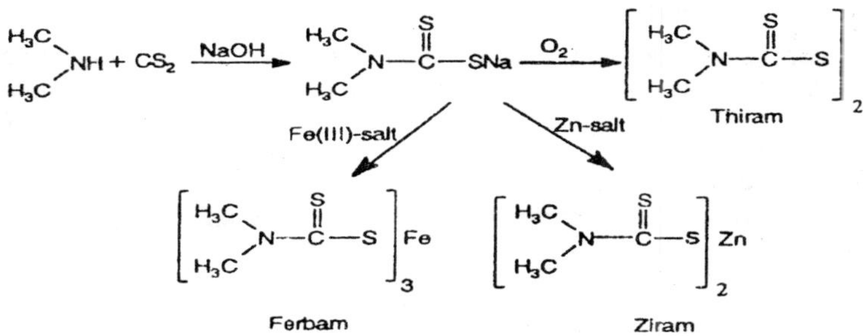

The Ferbam, ziram and thiram are effective against apple scab and blue mold and are also effective against the seedling diseases of vegetables. The mode of action of these dialkyl dithiocarbamates is due to their ability to chelate with metals especially copper.

## COMPOUNDS CONTAINING POLYHALOGEN ALKONOIC SULFENYL GROUP

### Captan

(N-(trichloromethylthio)-cyclohex-4-ene-1,2-dicarboximide)

Captan is a heterocylic nitrogenous compound. It is produced by the condensation of trichloromethylsulphenyl chloride with tetrahydrophthalmide in aqueous alkaline medium.

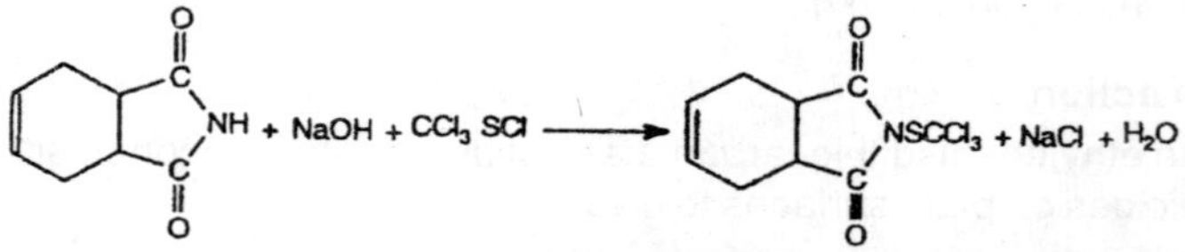


Tetra hydrophthalimide is prepared by Diels-Alder reaction. It is obtained by the condensation of butadiene and maleic anhydride

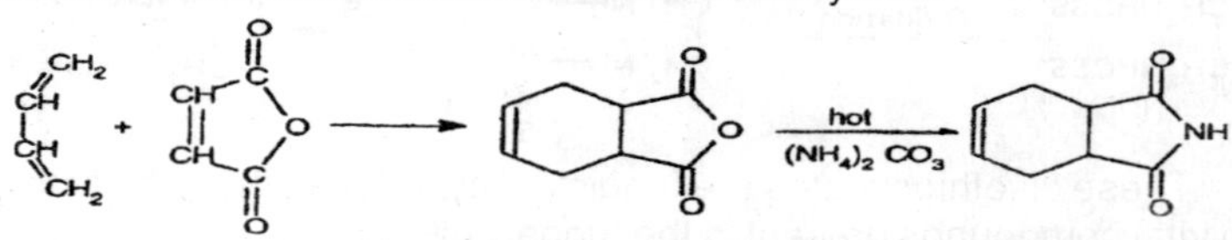


Captan is a fungicide with a very wide range. Captan is foliage fungicide with protective action but is manly used for seed treatment and soil fungici. The acute oralLD$_{50}$ for rats is 900 mg/kg.

### Folpet

(N-(trichloromethyl sulphenyl phthalimide)

Folpet is prepared by treating phthalimide with trichloromethyl-sulphenyl chloride in the presence of NaOH in aqueous medium.

Folpet is a protective fungicide used for leaf spot, downy and powdery mildew diseases of vegetables. The acute oral LD$_{50}$ for rats is10,000 mg/kg.

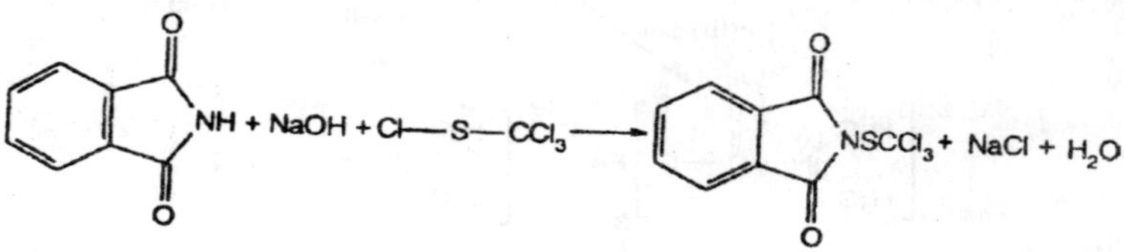


### Captafol

(N-(1,1,2,2-tetrachloroethoyl)thio) 4-cyclohexene-1,2-dicarboximide)

Captafol is produced by the reaction of tetrahydrophthalimide with pentachloroethylmercaptan in the presence of NaOH

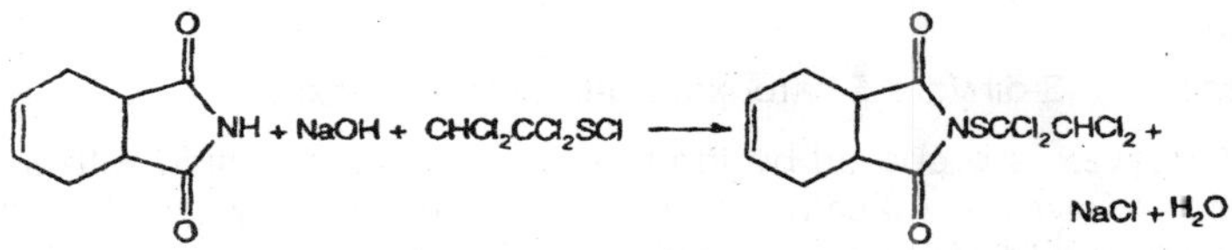

Captafol is protective, wide spectrum foliage and soil fungicide. Its acute oral $LD_{50}$ for rats is 6000 mg/kg.

**Mesulfan**

(N-trichloromethyllthio-4-chloroanilide of methane sulphonic acid)

Mesulfan is produced by reacting trichloromethylsulphenyl chloride with 4-chlorophenylmethane sulphonimide in the presence of NaOH

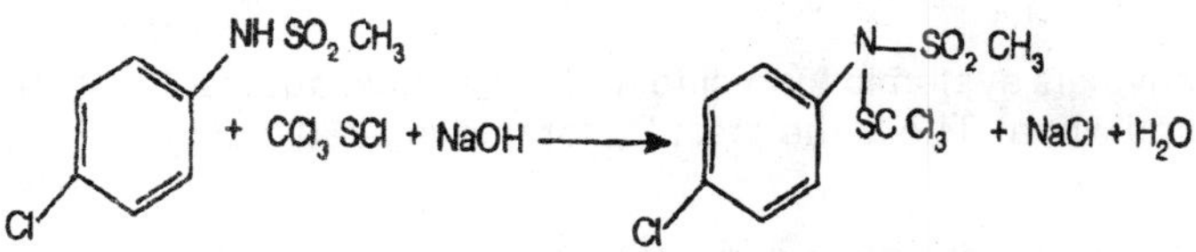

**Dichlofluanid**

N'-dichlorofluoromethylthio-N,N-dimethyl-N'-phenylsulfamide)

Dichlofluanid is prepared by treating sulfuryl chloride with dimethy amine and aniline in turn. N,N-dimethyl-N'-phenyl-sulfamide which is formed as an intermediate product is then coupled with fluorodichloromethanesulfenyl chloride to yield dichlofluanide.

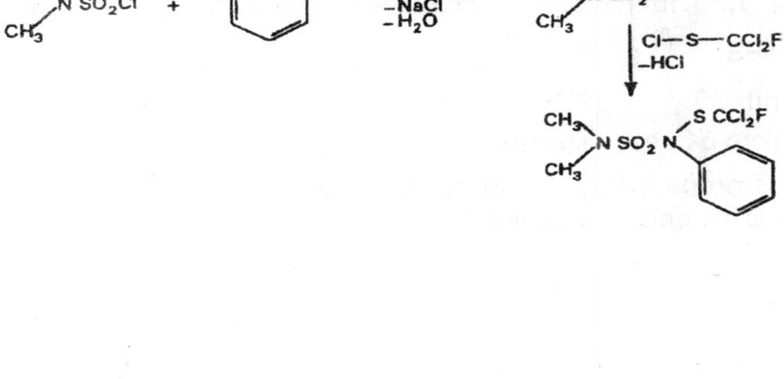

## OXATHIINS

### Vitavax

(Carboxin, 2,3-dihydro-5-carboxanilid-6-methyl-1,4 oxathiin)

Vitavax is prepared by the reaction acetoacetanilide with sulfuryl chloride to give chloroaceto acetanilide. This on reaction with 2- thioethanol followed by cyclization give vitavex.

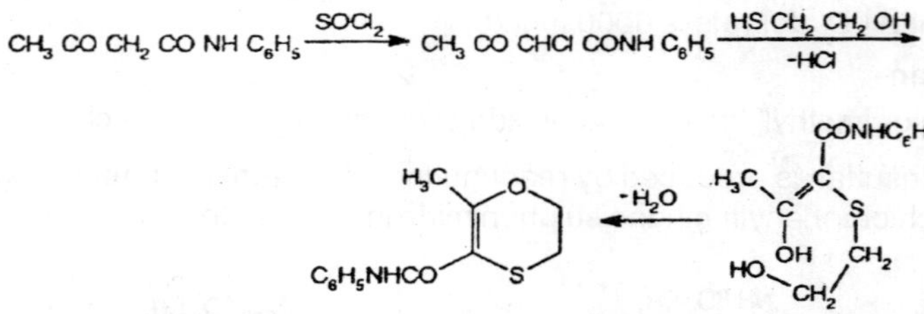

Vitavax is systemic fungicide and is effective against loose smut of barley and wheat. The acute oral $LD_{50}$ for rats is 3820 mg/kg.

### Plantvax

(Oxycarboxin, 2,3-dihydro-5-carboxanido-6-methyl 1,4 oxathiin-4,4-dioxide)

It is prepared by the oxidation of carboxin with hydrogen peroxide.

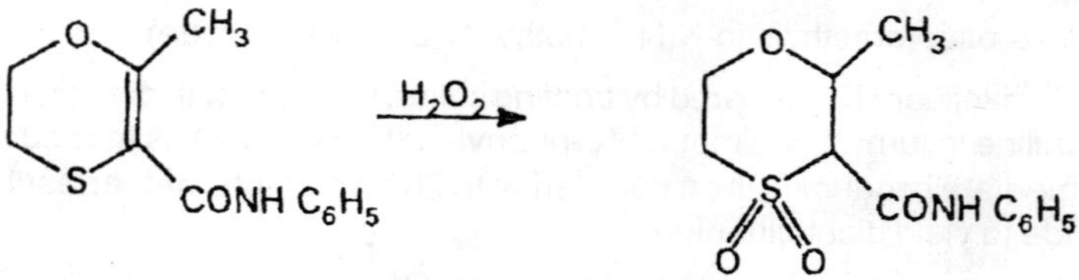

Plantvax is a systemic fungicide and effective against rust diseases of cereals and vegetables. The acute oral $LD_{50}$ for rats is 12000 mg/kg.

### Mode of action

Carboxin and oxycarboxin interfered with succinate oxidation in fungi through inactivation of succinate dehydrogenase. This results in accumulation of succinate in fungal cells and causes fungitoxicity.

## QUINONES

### Chloranil

(Tetrachloro-p-benzoquinone)

It is prepared by oxidative chlorination of phenol or by oxidative hydrolysis of pentchlorophenol

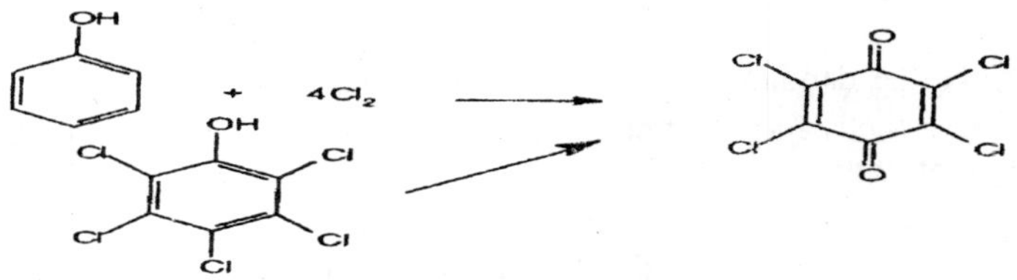

It is used for seed treatment against smut and diseases of vegetable seeds. The acute oral $LD_{50}$ for rats is 4000 mg/kg.

**Dichlone**

(2,3-dichloro-1,4-napthaquinone)

Dichlone is produced by bubbling chlorine gas through a solution of 1,4-aminonaphthalene sulphonic acid in aqueous sulphuric acid.

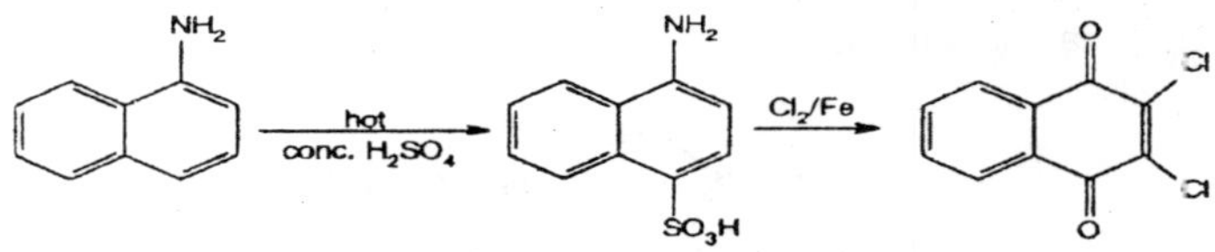

It can be used as foliage fungicide against powdery mildew of apple scab and gay mould.

**Dithianon**

(Delon, 5, 10-dihydro-5, 10-dioxonaphthol [2,3-b] 1,4 dithiin-2,3-dicarbonitrile)

It is prepared by the reaction of dichlone with 2,3-mercapto 2-butenedinitrile

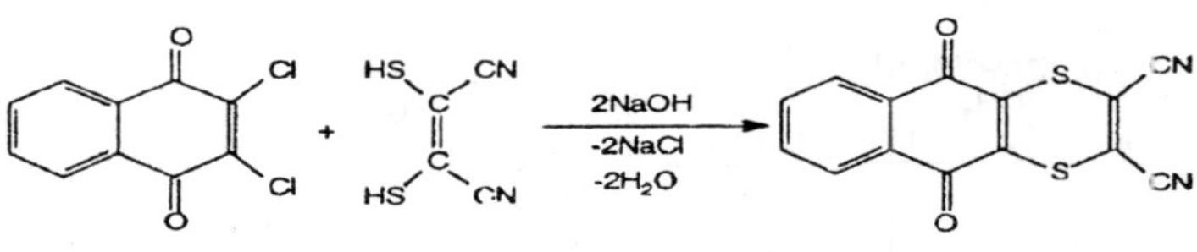

Dithianon is a protective fungicide used mainly against apple and pear scab.

**Mode of action**

The fungicidal properties of quinones are due to an addition reaction with sulphydryl containing respiratory enzymes in the fungal cell. The overall toxic mechanism therefore probably consists in binding the enzyme to the quinone nucleus by substitution or addition to the double bond.

## CARBOXAMIDES

### Metalaxyl

(Methyl-N-(2,6-dimethyl phenyl) N-(2-methoxyacetyl) DL-alaninate)

It is effective against species causing downy mildews, late blight, damping off root, stem and fruit roots.

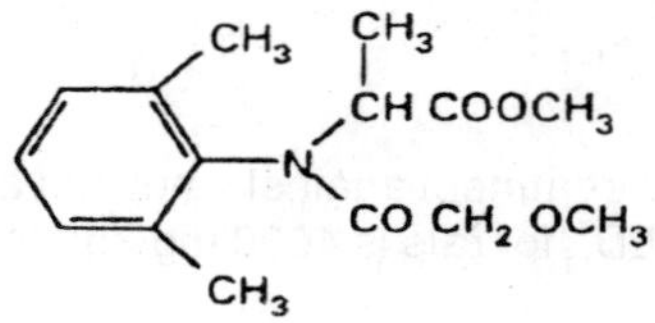

### Fongarid

(Methyl N-(2,6-dimethylphenyl)-N-(2-furanylcarbonyl) DL-alaninate)

Fongarid is a protective fungicide with systemic properties showing high activity against downy mildews of several horticultural crops. It can also be used as protective and curative fungicide as a soil drench. Its acute oral $LD_{50}$ to rats is 940 mg/kg.

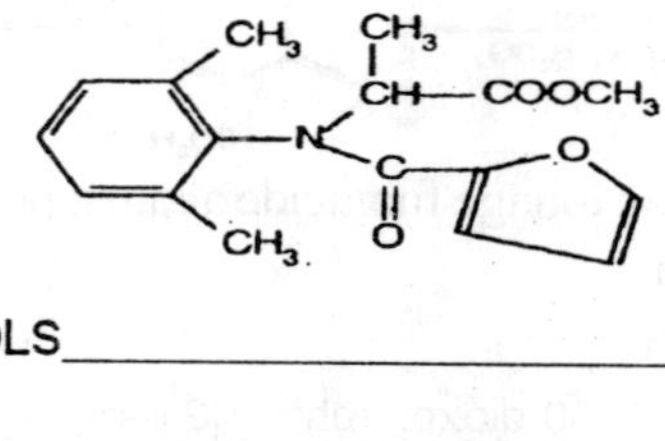

## DINITROALKYLPHENOLS

### Dinocap

(2,4-dinitro-6(1-methyl-n-heptyl) phenyl crotonate

Dinocap is prepared by the nitration of isoocylphenol, dinitro-isooctylphenol so obtained is then reacted in pyridine with crotonyl chloride

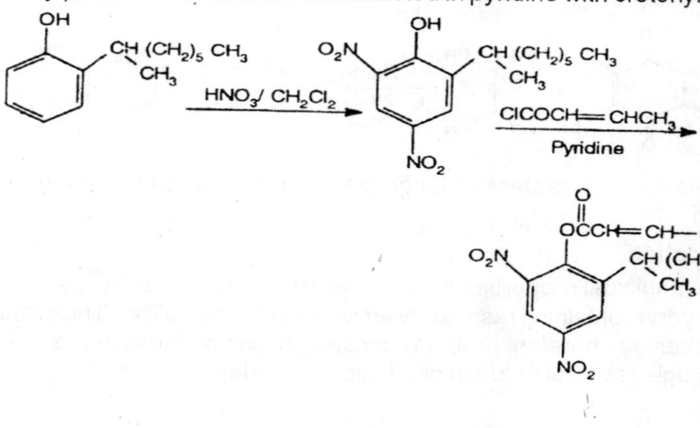

Dinocap is effective only against powdery mildew fungi. It is used mainly in orchards, vine cultures, vegetables and for protection of ornamental crops. Its acute oral $LD_{50}$ to rats is 980 mg/kg.

**Binapacryl**

(4,6-dinitro-2-sex-butyl-phenyl-3-methyl crotonate)

Binapacryl is prepared by esterification of dinoseb with 3-methyl crotonic acid chloride

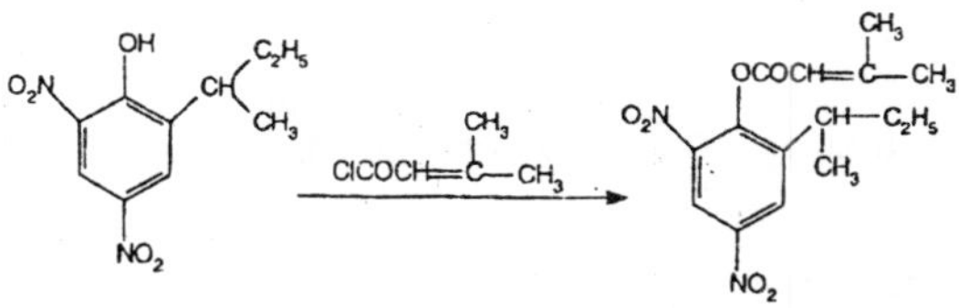

It is mainly used against powdery mildew in orchards.

**Dinobuton**

(2-sec-butyl-4,6-dintrophenyl isopropyl carbonate)

Dinobuton is prepared by treating alkali salt of dinoseb with isopropyl chloroformate

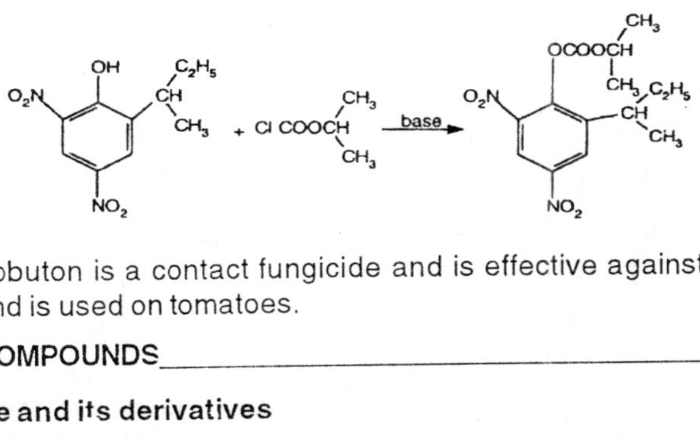

Dinobuton is a contact fungicide and is effective against powdery mildew and is used on tomatoes.

## AZOLE COMPOUNDS

### Imidazole and its derivatives

**Glyodin**

(2-heptadecyl-2-imidazoline acetate)

Glyodin is prepared by treating ethylene diamine and ethyl stearate, forming its acidic amide which on heating is cyclised and forms a salt with acetic acid.

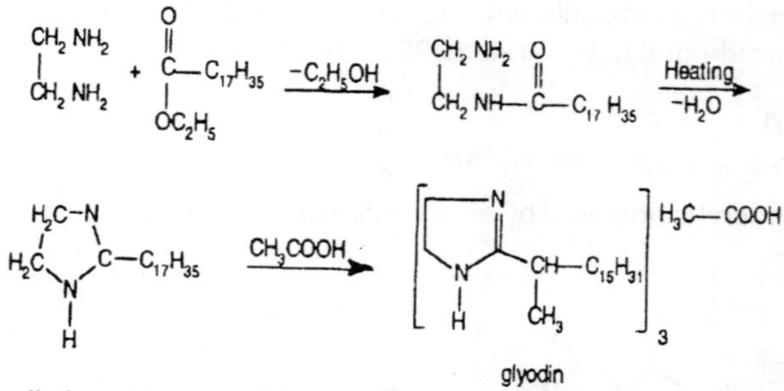

Glyodin is a foliage fungicide with a curative effect against apple scab.

**Imazalil**

(1-β-propenyloxy-2,4-dichlorophenyfl imidazole)

Imazalil can be prepared by reduction of intermediate product formed in the reaction of chlorophenacyl bromide with imidazole and subsequent alkylation with allyl chloride

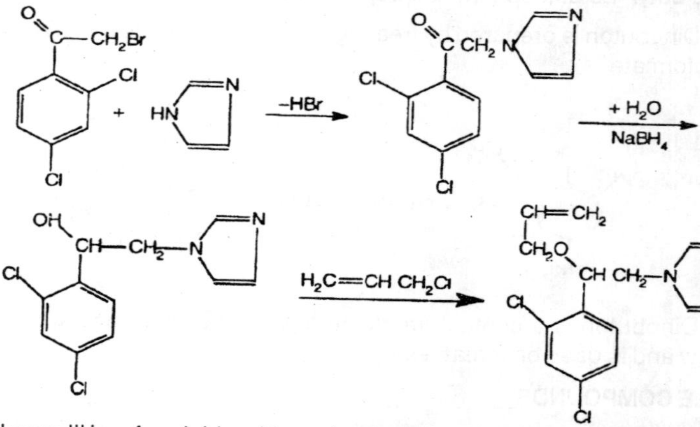

Imazalil is a fungicide with systemic action. It is used as seed dresser against diseases of cereals. It is also used for the protection of fruits and vegetables.

**BENZIMIDAZOLE DERIVATIVES**

**Carbendazim**

(Methyl-N-benzimidazol-2-yl carbamate)

Carbendazim is prepared by methylation of thiourea with dimethyl sulphate and subsequent N-acylation in alkaline medium of the S-methyl-isothiourea formed with methyl ester of chloroformic acid. The N,N'-bis(methoxycarbonyl)-S-methyl isothiourea is condensed with O-phenylene diamine in glacial acetic acid.

Carbendazim is a systemic fungicide controlling a wide range of pathogens of cereals, fruits, grapes, ornamentals and vegetables. It is very efficient against leaf and ear diseases of wheat but it is inactive against rust. The acute oral $LD_{50}$ for rats is 15000 mg/kg.

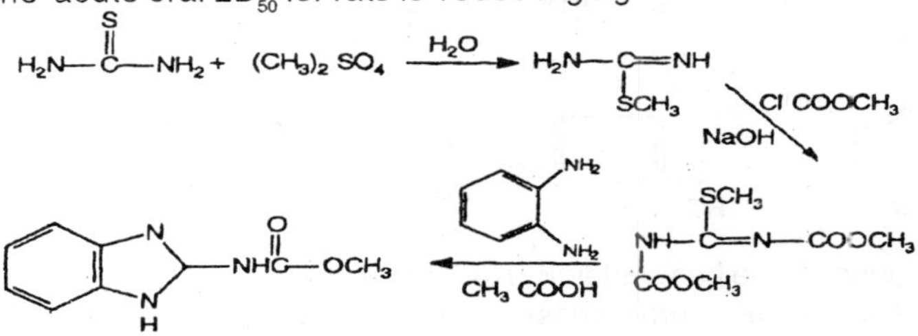

**Benomyl**

(N-(1-butylcarbamoyl-benzimidazole2-yl) methylcarbamate)

It is produced by the reaction of methyl-N-benzimidazol-2-yl-carbamate with butyl isocyanate.

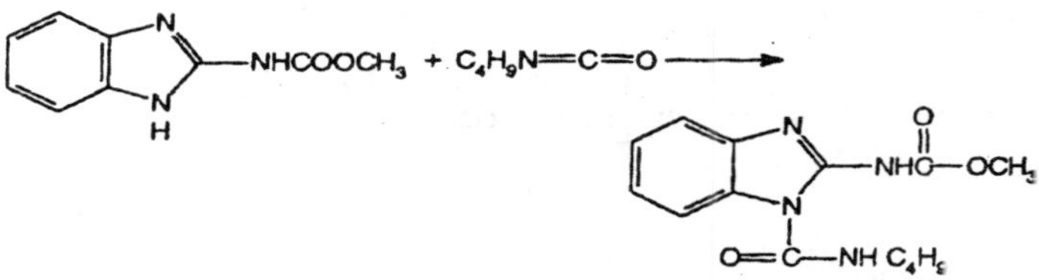

Benomyl has a protective, and eradicant fungicide with systemic activity. Benomylis absorbed by plants and rapidly metabolized into MBC. Benomyl is very effective against a wide range of fungi affecting fruits, nuts and vegetables. It is also a very good seed protectant. The acute oral $LD_{50}$ for rats is 10,000 mg/kg.

**Thiabendazole**

(2-(4'-thiazolyl)-benzimidazole)

It is prepared from O-phenylenediamine and 4-thiazole carboxamide in polyphosphoric acid. Thiabendazole is used in the protection of apples and pears against fungi during storage. It is also very effective as seed treatment against bunt of wheat.

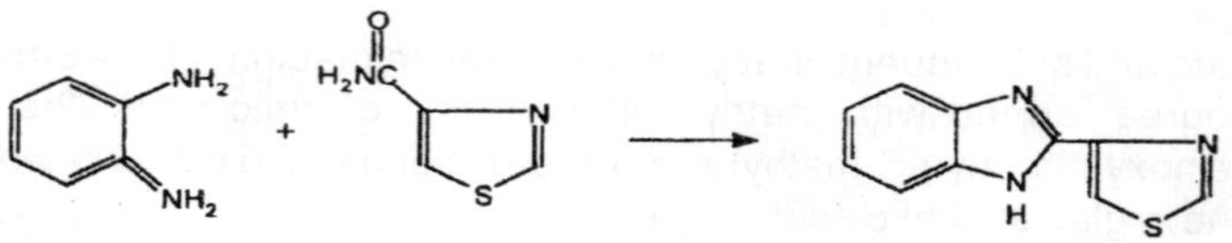

**Fuberidazole**

(2,2'-furyl) benzimidazole)

It is prepared by the reaction of furfural with O-phenylenediamine in the presence of oxidising agent cupric acetate in the medium of methyl alcohol.

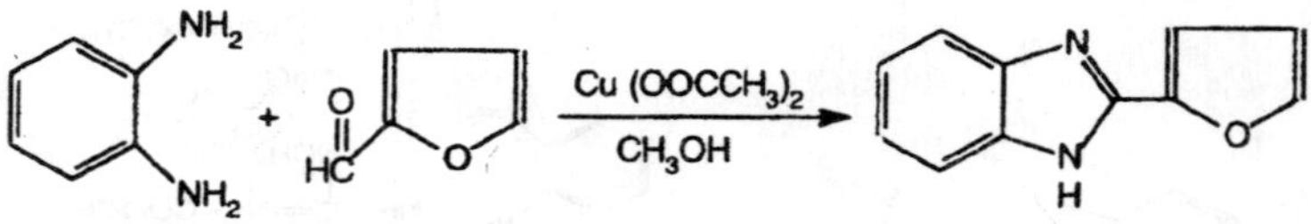

Fuberidazole has systemic used is effective against treatment of seeds mainly against Fusarium diseases leaf rust, and powdery mildew on barley.

**Thiophanate-methyl**

(1,2-bis (3-methoxycarbonyl 1-thiourelido) benzene)

Thiophanate methyl is prepared by the reaction of sodium or potassium thiocyanate with chloroformic acid methyl ester and the intermediate product reacts with O-phenylenediamine to form thiophanate methyl

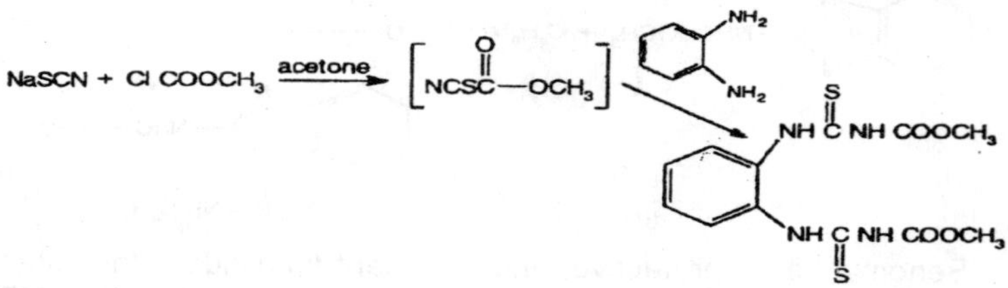

Its ethyl homologue is thiophanate and is commonly known as tapsin. It is prepared by condensation of sodium thiocyanate, ethylchloroformate and phenylenediamine.

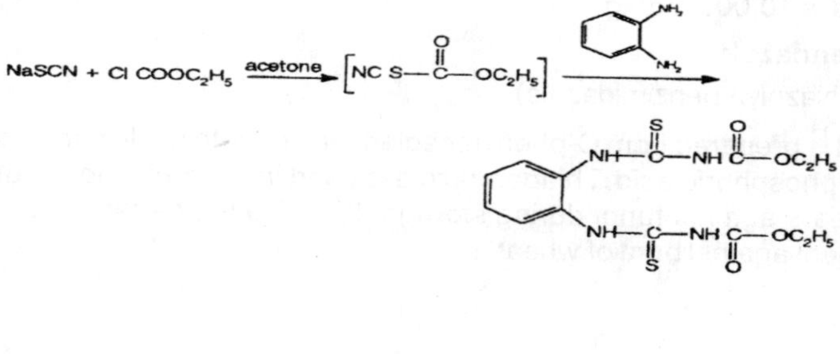

The thiphanates are not themselves fungicidal but are converted into active benzimidazole derivatives. Both methyl and ethylthiophante are effective against such pathogenic fungi as apple powdery mildews, apple scab, sheath blight of rice and leaf spot of sugar beet. The acute oral $LD_{50}$ for thiuphanate ethyl for rats is 15000 mg/kg, for thiophanate methyl it is 2500 mg/kg.

## TRIAZOLES

### Fluotrimazole

(1-(3-trifluoromethyltrityl)-1H-1,2,4-triazole)

Fluotrimazole is prepared by treating m-trifluoromethylphenyl bromide with benzophenone in grignard synthesis. The resulting 3-trifluloromethylphenyl-bis(phenyl) methylcarbinol obtainted is converted to tritylchloride and is treated with triazole in acetone solution to yield fluotrimazole.

Fluotrimazole is effective against all powdery mildew fungi on cereals, apples and roses. The acute oral $LD_{50}$ for rats is higher than 5000 mg/kg.

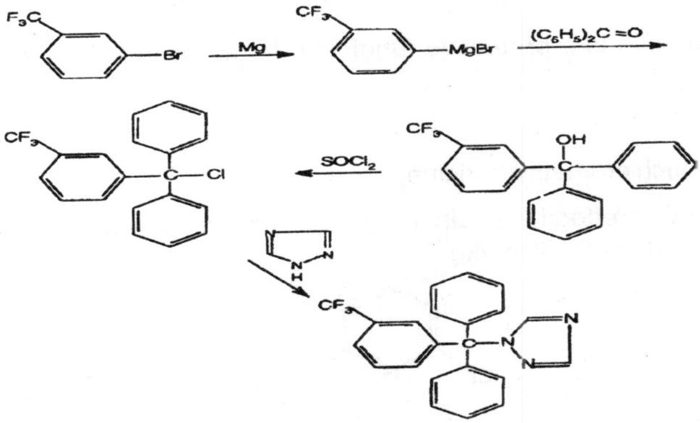


### Triadimefon

(1-(4-chlorophenoxy)-3,3-dimethyl-1-(1,2,4-triazole-1-yl) butan -2-one)

Triadimefon is a fungicide with excellent broad spectrum of action. It is effective against mildews and rusts attacking cereals, coffee, grapes and vegetables. Its acute oral $LD_{50}$ for rats is 5 to 8 mg/kg.

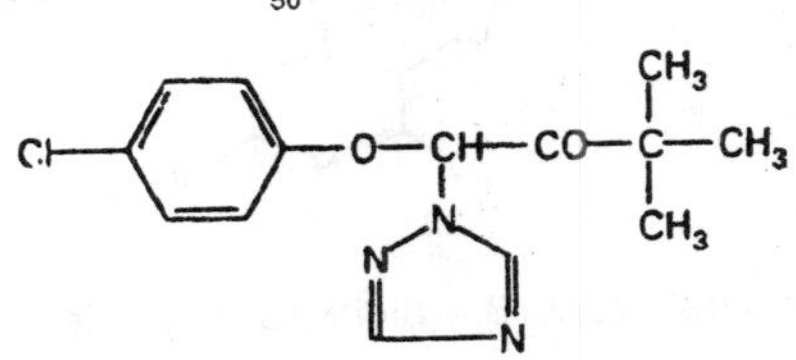

## HETEROCYCLIC FUNGICIDES

### PYRIDINE DERIVATIVES

**Pyridinitrile**

(2-6-dichloro-4-phenylpyyridine-3,5-dicarbonitrile)

Pyridinitrile is prepared by the reaction of cyanoacetic acid ethyl ester with ammonia followed by coupling of two molecules of cyanoacetic amide formed with benzaldehyde and by chlorination of the product, 3,5-dicyano-4-phenyl-6-hydroxyhydro-2-pyridine

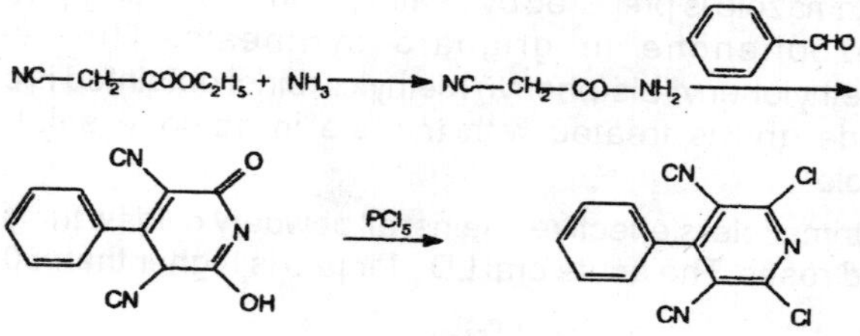

Pyridinitrile is a protective fungicide. Its acute oral $LD_{50}$ for rats is 5000mg/kg.

**Nitrapyrin**

(2-chloro-6-trichloromethyl pyridine)

Nitrpyrin is effective against stem rot of maize and cereals. Its acute oral $LD_{50}$ for rats is 1072 mg/kg.

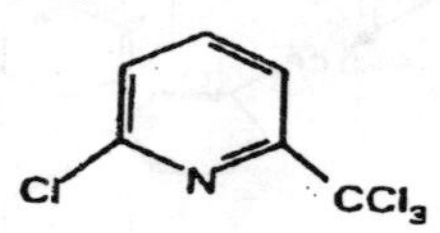

**Dowco 263**

(3,4,5-trichloro-2,6-dicyanopyridine)

Dowco-263 is found to be effective for seed treatment against soil fungi and in cereals and cotton. Its acute oral $LD_{50}$ for rats is 562 mg/kg.

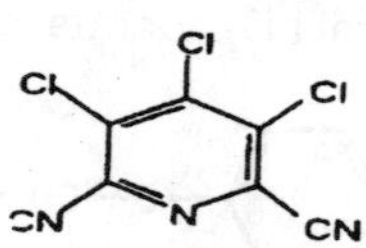

**Piperalin**

(3-(2-methylpiperidino) propyl 3,4-dichlorobenzoate)

Piperalin is protective and eradicant fungicide it is specific fungicide for ornamental plants against powdery mildew fungi. Its acute oral $LD_{50}$ for rats is 2500 mg/kg.

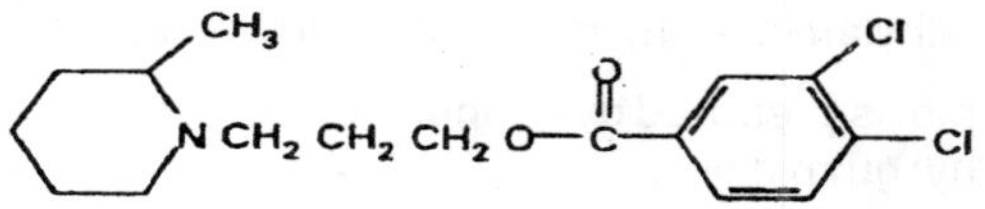

**Parinol**

(3-(hydroxy-bis(4-chlorophenyl) methyl) pyridine)

It is effective against the powdery mildew fungi of ornamental plants. Its oral $LD_{50}$ for rats is 5000 mg/kg.

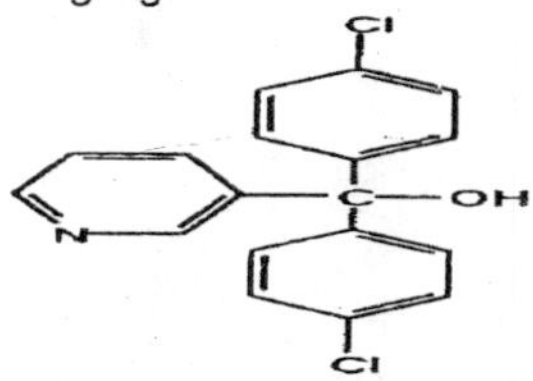

## PIPERAZINE DERIVATIVE

**Triforine**

(N,N'-(1,4-piperazinediyl-bis (2,2,2-trichloroethylidene)) bis formamide)

Triforine is prepared by the reaction of piperazine with 1,2,2,2-tetrachloroethyl formamide.

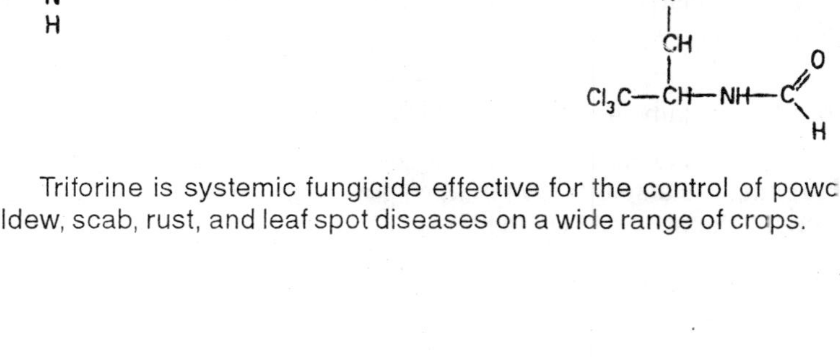

Triforine is systemic fungicide effective for the control of powdery mildew, scab, rust, and leaf spot diseases on a wide range of crops.

## PYRIMIDINES

### Dimethirimol

(5n-butyl-2-dimethylamino-4-hydroxy-6-methyl pyrimidine)

Dimethirimol is prepared by condensation of ethyl butylacetoacetate with N,N-dimethyl guanidine.

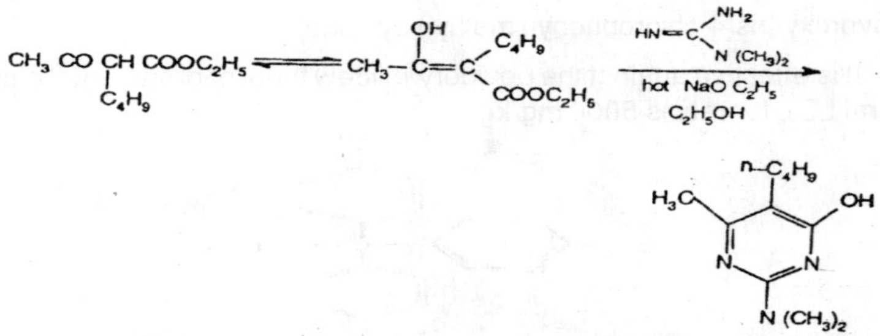

Dimethirimol showed outstanding systemic activity by root application against certain powdery mildews such as those of cucumber, melon and some ornamentals.

**Triarimol** is obtainted by condensation of 5-bromopyrimidine with 2,4-dichlorobenzophenone.

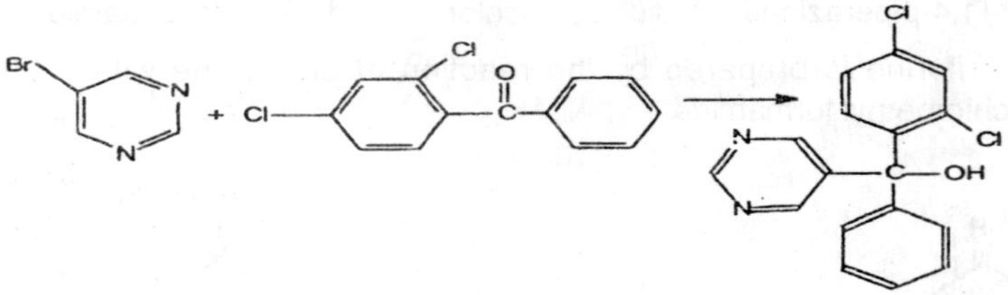

Triarimol is a broad spectrum fungicide showing local systemic action by spraying against phytopathogenic fungi including apple, and barley mildew, apple scab and cherry leaf spot.

### Ethirimol

(5-n-butyl-2-ethylamine-4-hydroxy-6-methylpyrimidine)

Ethirimol is toxic to powdery mildew fungi acting specifically against this parasite. It is also effective against powdery mildew of tobacco, peas and hops, Its acute oral $LD_{50}$ to rat is

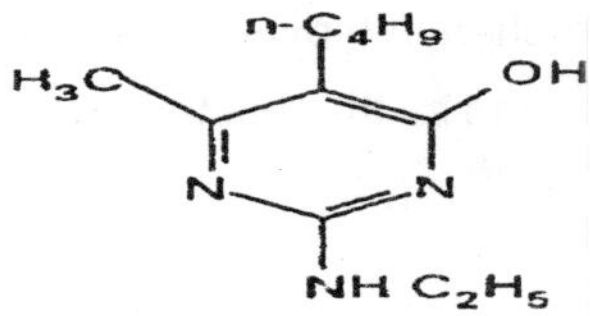

**Bupirimate**

(5-n-butyl-2-ethylamino-6-methyl pyrimidine-4-yl dimethylsulphamate)

Bupirimate is a foliage fungicide. It is effective against apple powdery mildew, cucurbit and rose powdery mildews. Its oral $LD_{50}$ for rats is 4000 mg/kg.

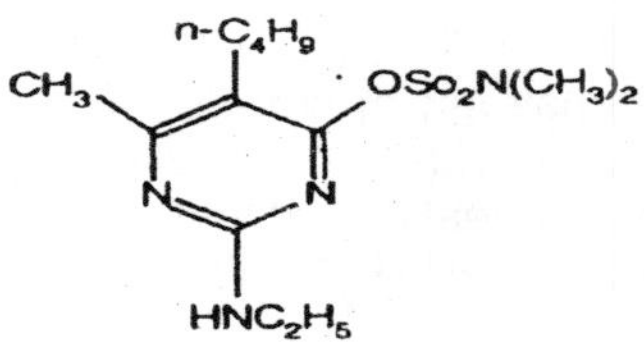

**Fenarimol**

(2,4'-dichloro-pyrimidin-5yl) benzhydryl alcohol)

Fenarimol is prepared by treating 5-bromopyrimidine with 2,4'-dichloro benzophenone

Fenarimol is having a protective, curvative, eradicative activity against powdery mildews and recommended for use on apples, cucurbits, grapes and on roses. It also demonstrates activity against apple scab and against leaf spot diseases of peanut, soybean and sugarbeet. Its $LD_{50}$ for rats is 2500 mg/kg.

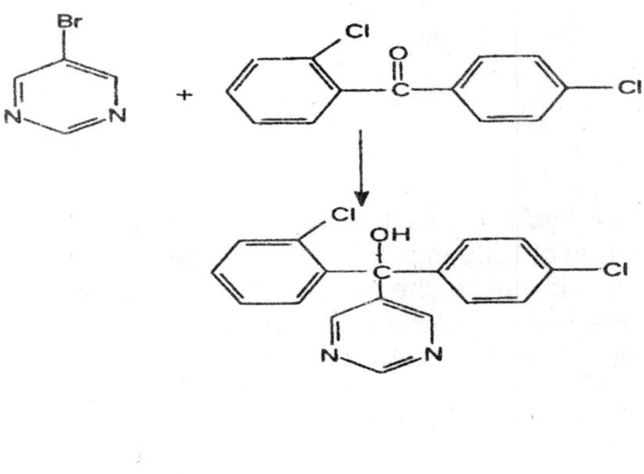

## Nuarimol

((2-chlorophenyl) (4-fluorophenyf)-5-pyrimidinemethanol)

Nuarimol is synthesised by the reaction of 5-bromopyrimidine with 2-chloro-4'-fluorobenzophenone.

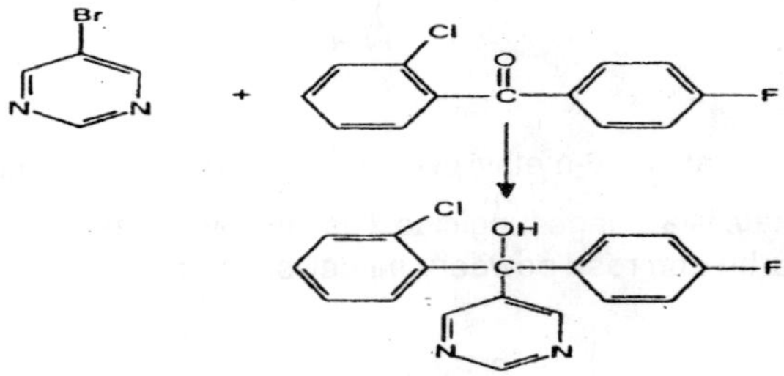


Nuarimol has demonstrated broad spectrum of antifungal activity. As a foliar application, it has provided control of powdery mildews on apple, cherry, cucurbits, grapes, wheat and of leaf spot diseases of strawberry, cherry, soybean. The acute oral $LD_{50}$ for mice and rats are 2700 and 1600 mg/kg respectively.

## QUINOLINE DERIVATIVES

### 8-Hydroxyquinoline

8-Hydroxyquinoline is obtainted from quinoline, which is formed from aniline and acrolein, by treating with fuming sulphuric acid, giving quinoline -8- sulphonic acid, from which 8-hydroxy quinoline can be prepared by decomposition with sodium hydroxide.

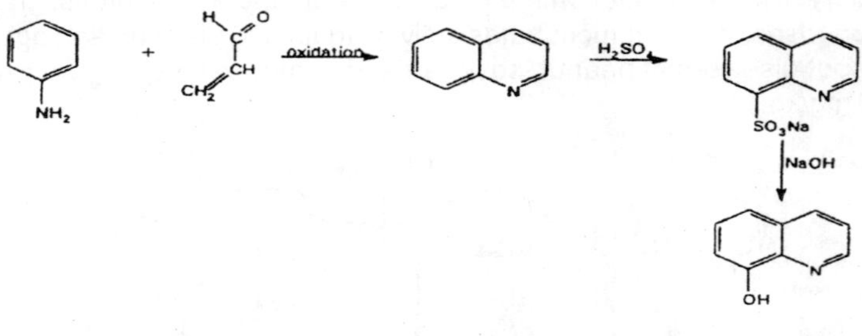


As fungicide 8-hydroxy quinoline does not find wide application. It has acute oral $LD_{50}$ value of 1000 mg/kg for rats. For control of plant diseases, 8-hydroxy quinoline is used in the form of copper -8- quinolinate which is prepared from the aqueous solution of copper (II) salt by precipitation with 8-hydroxy quinoline. Copper-8-quinolinate has the chelate structure.

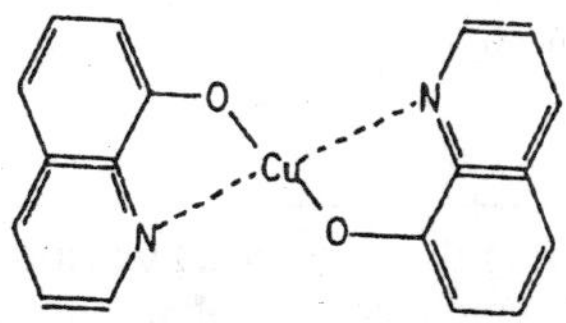

**Quinacetol sulphate**

(bis(5-acetyl-8-hydroxyquinolinium) sulphate)

Title compound is a derivative of 8-hydroxyquinoline and is recommended for seed treatment of wheat, barley and oats. Its acute oral $LD_{50}$ for rats is 2200 mg/kg.

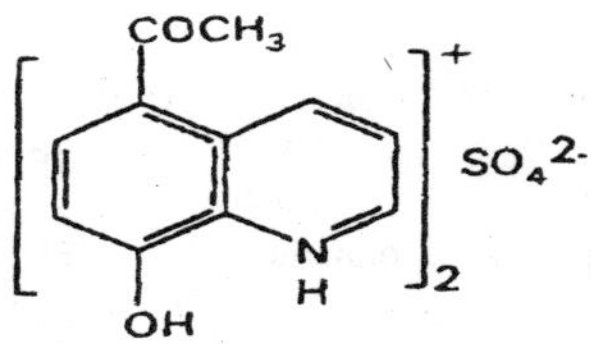

## MORPHOLINE TYPE FUNGICIDES

**Morpholine**

Morpholine can be obtainted in a satisfactory yield by the cyclisation of bis (2-hydroxyethyl) amine with the elimination of water.

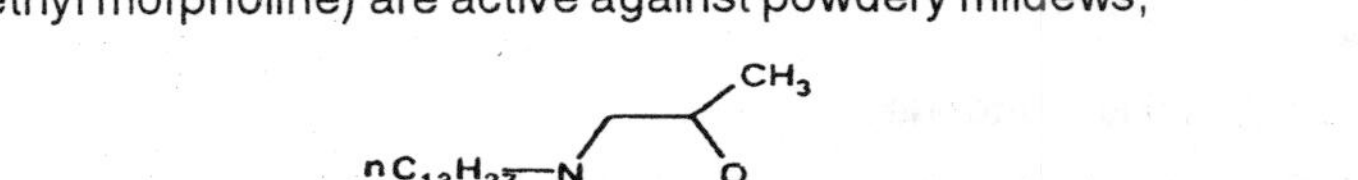

Two morphine fungicides tridemorph (2,6-dimethyl-4-tridecylmorpholine) and cyclododecyl derivative known as dodemorph (4-cyclododecyl 2,6-dimethyl morpholine) are active against powdery mildews,

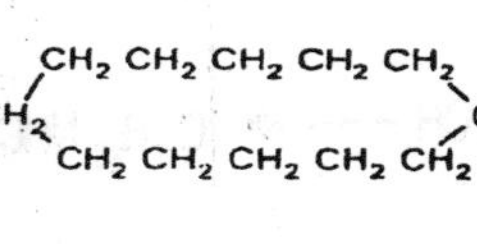

Morpholine type fungicides have an eradicant action when applied on leaves.

## ANTIBIOTICS

Antibiotics are chemicals produced by living organisms, that are toxic to other organisms. Following is the list of antibiotics, their structure, source and uses as the fungicides.

| *Name* | *Source* | *Structure and Uses* |
|---|---|---|
| Gliotoxin | Trichoderma Viride | 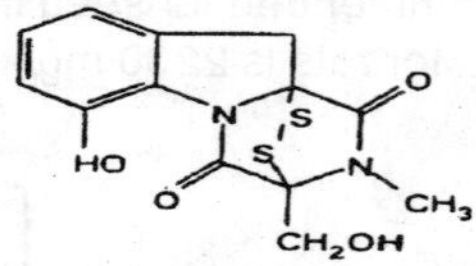 **USE:** Inhibited growth of Botrytis and Fusarium spores |
| Streptomycin | Streptomyces griseus | **USE:** Effective against bacterial pathogens of plants and bacterial disease of stone fruits |

| Name | Source | Structure and Uses |
|---|---|---|
| Blasticidin | Streptomyces griseochromo genes | 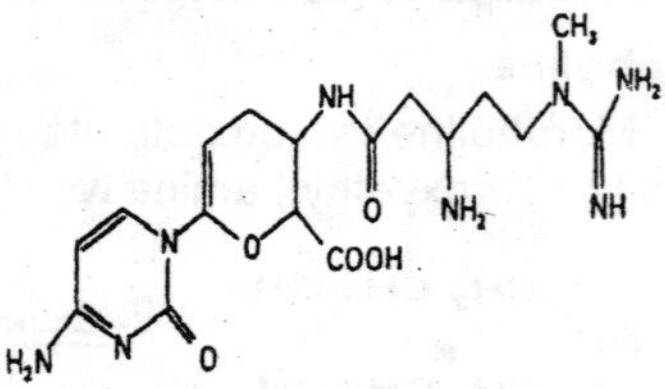 **USE:** Rice blast and inhibits certain bacteria |

## MISCELLANEOUS FUNGICIDES

### Dodine

(N-dodecylguanidine acetate)

Dodine is synthesised by treating dodecyl amine, cyanamide and acetic acid.

$$C_{12}H_{25}NH_2 + NH_2CN + CH_3COOH \longrightarrow \left[C_{12}H_{25}NH\overset{\overset{\displaystyle NH}{\|}}{C}-NH_2\right]^+ CH_3COO^-$$

Dodine has been used as a protective fungicide. It is recommended for the control of a number of major fungal diseases of apple, pear, vegetables and ornamental crops. Its acute oral $LD_{50}$ value for rats is 1000 mg/kg.

**Glyodine** is used as protective and curative fungicide against apple scab. The $LD_{50}$ for glyodine for rats is 3720 mg/kg.

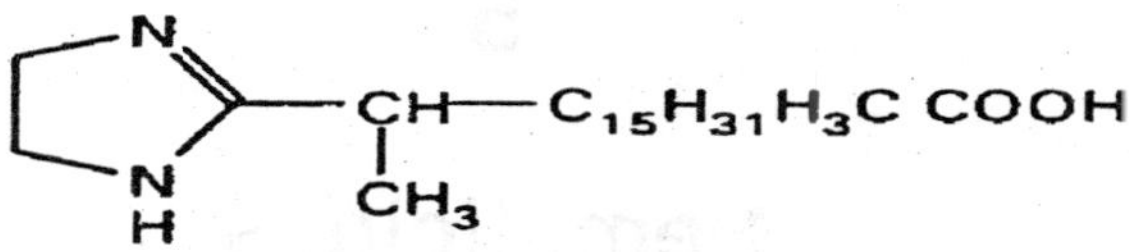

# 5

# Nematicides

Nematicides are chemical which prevent, repel, inhibit or destroy nematodes. Nematodes are multicellular animals and are found in nearly every biological niche that supports life. The nematodes are too small to be seen without the aid of microscope. Nematodes are also called eelworms, nemas, roundworms, threadworms, todes or worms.

## Importance

Nematodes do not kill plants but they cause a reduction in the growth and vitality of the plant leading to an economic loss. Moreover they also serve as vectors for viruses, bacteria and fungi.

Nematodes are spread primarily by man. The most common methods include the movement of infected plants or plant parts and infested soil adhering to implements. In India the plant parasitic nematodes are reported to cause considerable damage to variety of crops like tobacco, potato, vegetable crops, plantation crops, fruit crops, pulses, oilseeds, cereals etc.

The major plant parasitic nematodes in India are:

1. *Heterodera* sp
2. *Meloidogyne* sp
3. *Pratylenchus* sp
4. *Radopholus* sp
5. *Rotylenchus* sp
7. *Helicotylenchus* sp

## PARASITISM

Parasitism of plants by nematodes is of two broad types:

## Ectoparasitism and Endoparasitism

Nematodes that live externally and pierce plant tissues with their stylet or spear or enter with the anterior portion of their body for the purpose of feeding are ectoparasites. Those, which embed their entire body within plant tissues and feed within are endoparasites.

Some genera infect and damage primarily the above ground plant parts and are some times inferred to as aerial parasites. These species may carry out their life cycle in the soil or in the shallow layers, when suitable host plants develop and favourable conditions prevail they attack the growing seedlings. The wheat gall nematode, the stem nematode and chrysanthemum foliar nematode are well known examples.

## Methods of Nematode control

1. **Heat:** Excellent control of plant parasitic nematodes can be achieved through the use of heat in various forms. Temperatures necessary for effective control will depend on
   — 1) other biological agents to be controlled
   — 2) soil conditions whether the soil is wet or dry
   — 3) exposure time.
2. **Hot water treatment :** Plants infected with nematodes are also controlled by hot water.
3. **Sanitation and use of Nematode free planting stock:** Sanitation and use of nematode free planting stock are sure and effective means of nematode control
4. **Time of planting and harvesting :** Certain parasitic nematodes are inactive during winter months, because low temperature inhibit their activities.
5. **Removal or destruction of infected host plants :** The root systems of certain annual crops will continue to live for several weeks after harvest and consequently parasitic nematodes present in the roots continue to reproduce. Populations of some nematodes can be reduced if the stalks are cut and the root systems are turned out soon after harvest.
6. **Following :** Keeping the land free of all vegetation for varying periods by frequently tilling of the soil either by discing, ploughing or harrowing or application of herbicides to prevent plant growth results in starvation and death of nematodes present in soil.

7. **Nutrition and general care of host:** Nematode damage to certain crops can be minimized to some degree, by providing adequate nutrition and moisture and protecting the crop from adverse conditions such as drought or cold which place the plant under stress.

8. **Biological control:** Certain fungi capture and kill nematodes in the soil.

9. **Antagonistic crops:** In recent years considerable interest has been focussed upon plants with roots containing nematicidal substances. These toxic substances reduce the population level of some nematode species. African marigolds (Tagets sp.) and *Asparagus officinalis* L. are examples of such plants.

10. **Use of chemicals:** The chemicals used for control of nematodes, called nematicides are now recognised as an effective method of nematode control Several effective nematicides have been developed and improvements in method of application have been made. In many parts of the world today soil treatment has become an established farm practice.

**Advantages of chemical control**

1. Chemical control reduces population of nematodes to a very low density within a matter of days after chemical is applied.
2. Several nematicides used today are multipurpose. In addition to nematodes, fungi, bacteria and weeds are also controlled.

**Essentials of a good nematicide**

1. Nematicides must have high vapour pressure to spread through the soil and to contact nematodes in the water films surrounding soil particles.
2. Nematodes are covered with an impermeable cuticle which provides them with considerable protection. Chemicals used as nematicides should have ability to penetrate the lipophillic cuticle.
3. Nematicides should have high water solubility.

**Nematicides are classified into five groups**

1. Halogenated hydrocarbons
2. Organophosphates
3. Isothicyanates
4. Carbamates or oxime nematicides
5. Botanicals

## halogenated hydrocarbons

### Methyl bromide

Methyl bromide is prepared as follows:

1. By the reaction of methanol with bromine and hydrogen sulphide

$$2CH_3OH + Br_2 + H_2S \longrightarrow 2CH_3Br + 2H_2O + S$$

2. By reaction of methanol and salts of HBr in the presence of $H_2SO_4$

$$CH_3OH + NaBr + H_2SO_4 \longrightarrow CH_3Br + H_2O + NaHSO_4$$

Methyl bromide is phytotoxic and it must be used as a preplant application, followed by adequate aeration time. It is effective in controlling stem and root knot nematodes.

### Ethylene dibromide

Ethylene dibromide is produced by direct bromination of ethylene

$$CH_2 == CH_2 + Br_2 \longrightarrow BrCH_2CH_2Br$$

EDB is injected into the soil several days before planting to kill nematodes, eggs and soil insects.

### 1,3 Dichloropropane

It is obtainted as by product by chlorination of allyl chloride which is obtained by chlorination of propene

$$CH_3CH == CH_2 + Cl_2 \longrightarrow ClCH_2CH == CH_2 + HCl$$

$$ClCH_2CH == CH_2 + CH_2 \longrightarrow ClCH_2CH == CHCl + HCl$$

### 1,2-dichloropropane

1,2-dichloropropane is prepared by chloriantion of propylene at low temperature

$$CH_3—CH—CH_2 + Cl_2 \longrightarrow CH_3—\underset{Cl}{\underset{|}{CH}}—\underset{Cl}{\underset{|}{CH_2}}$$

### DD

(Nemafene)

The technical product is a clear amber liquid containing at least 50% of cis and trans isomers of 1,3-dichloropropane ($CHCl{=}CH{-}CH_2Cl$) which is the main active ingredient and 50% of 1,2-dichloropropane ($CH_3{-}CHCl{-}CH_2Cl$) and other trichlorides.

DD is extremely toxic nematicide and injection into soil kills both eelworms and their cysts.

**Nemagon**

(1,2-dibromo-3-chloropropane)

Nemagon is prepared by the addition of bromine to allyl chloride

$$CH_2=CHCH_2Cl \xrightarrow{Br_2} BrCH_2CHBrCH_2Cl$$

DBCP is used as post plant treatments and is registered for use on fruits and vegetables and is less toxic than DD. In it was announced that DBCP was found to cause sterility in male workers involved in its manufacture and subsequently it has been removed from the market. It is currently available only as restricted use pesticide for a very few essential needs.

**Isothiocyanates**

**Metham sodium**

(Vapam, sodium N-methyl dithiocarbamate)

Metham -sodium (Vapam) is prepared by the reaction of methylamine with carbon disulphide in presence of sodium hydroxide

$$CH_3NH_2 + CS_2 + NaOH \longrightarrow CH_3NH\overset{\overset{S}{\|}}{C}SNa + H_2O$$

Metham-sodium is a preplant fumigant effective against nematodes, fungi and weeds. The toxic action of metham-sodium is explained by the evolution of methyl isothiocyanate that disrupts the oxidation reduction processes in the cells of organisms.

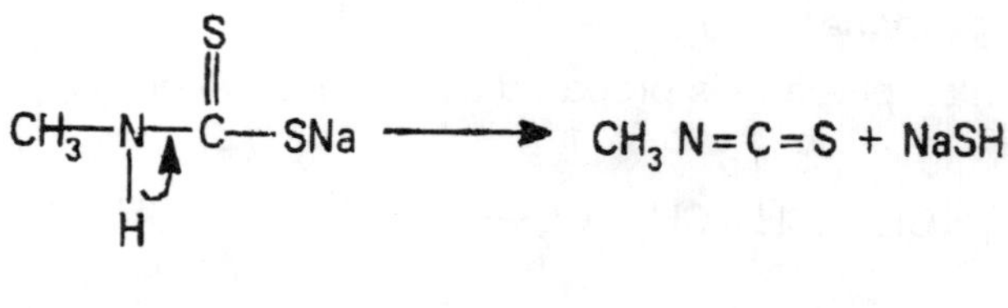

**Dazomet**

(Tetrahydro-3, 5-dimethyl-2H-1,3,5- thiadiazine-2-thione)

Dazomet is prepared by the reaction of carbon disulphide, methylamine and formaldehyde

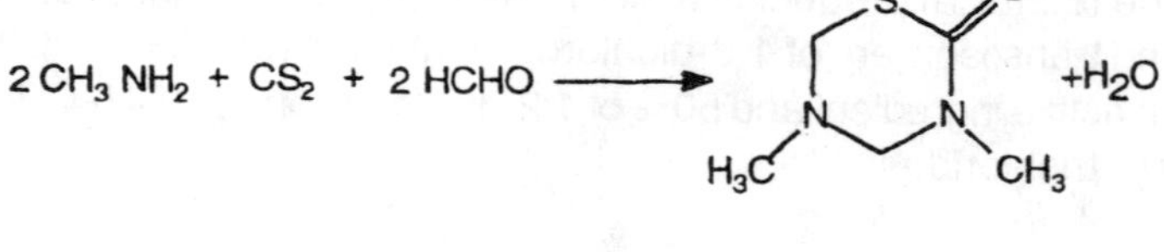

Dazomet like metham-sodium owes its activity due to its decomposition in the soil to give methyl isothiocyanate

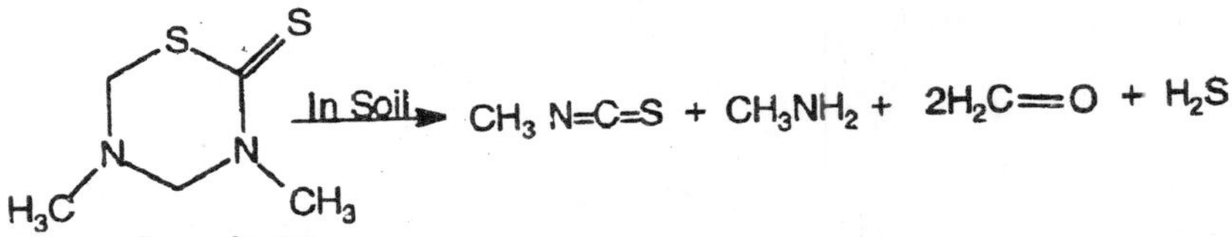


## Organophosphates

Nematodes have nervous system similar to insects. All these organophosphates inhibit the nervous transmitter enzyme, cholinesterase resulting in paralysis and ultimately death of the affected nematode. Following organophosphate nematicides are used for killing nematodes.

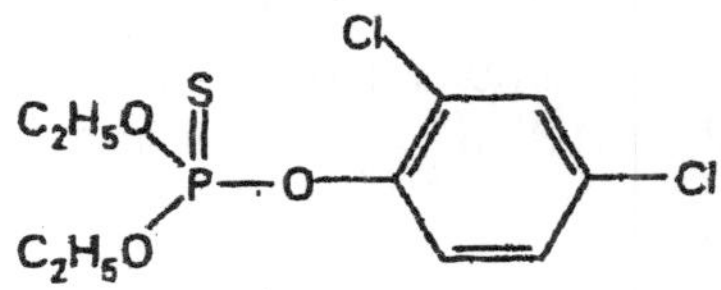

**Dichlofenthion**
**(O,O diethyl dichlorophenyl phosphorothioate)**

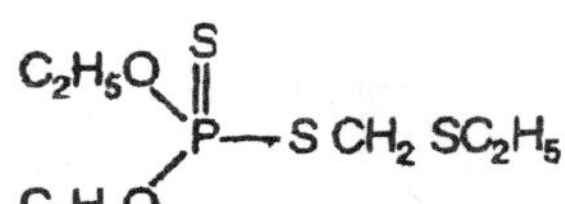

**Phorate**

**(O,O diethyl -S- (ethylthiomethyl) phosphorodithioate)**

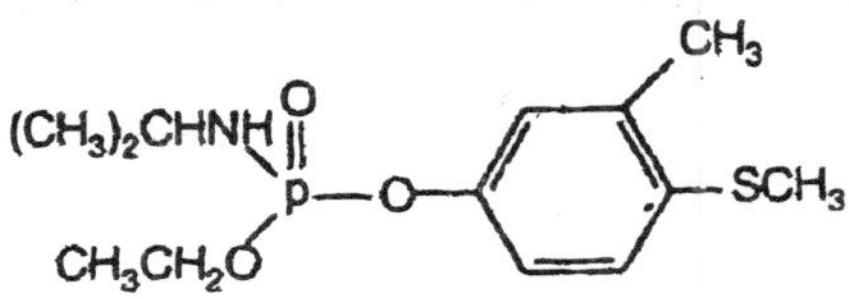

**Fenamiphos**

**(Ethyl -3-methyl -4-(methylthio) phenyl - (1-methyl ethyl) phosphoramidate**

## Carbamates

Several carbamates are also highly nematicidal and examples include carbofuran and aldicarb. These are highly active against soil nematodes but suffer from very high mammalian toxicity.

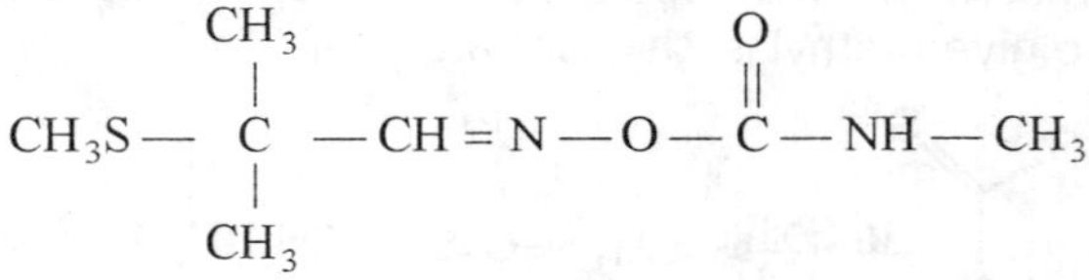

Adicarb (Temil)
(2-methyl-2-(methylthio) propionaldehyde O-(methylcarbamoyl) oxime)

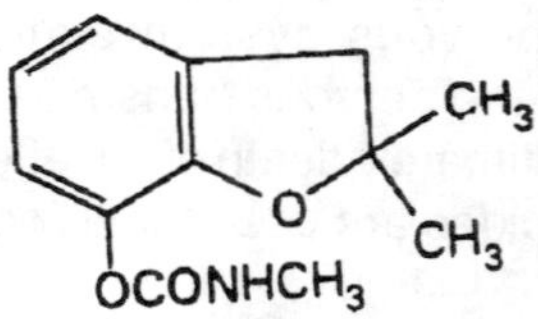

Carbofuran (Furadan)
(2,3 - dihydro - 2,2 - dimethyl - 7 - benzofuranyl methylcarbamate)

**Botanical Nematicides**

Non edible oil cakes like Neem, Mahua and Karanj control nematode population. Marigold (Tagetis *erecta* L) has been found effective in controlling nematodes. The nematicidal principles of root exudates of marigold have been identified as terthienyl(I) and substituted bisthienyl compound (II)

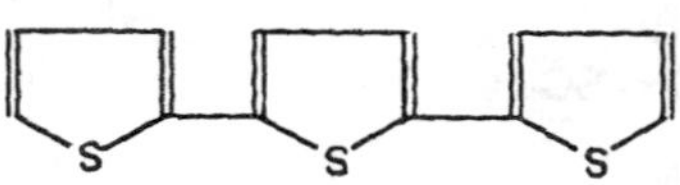

(I)

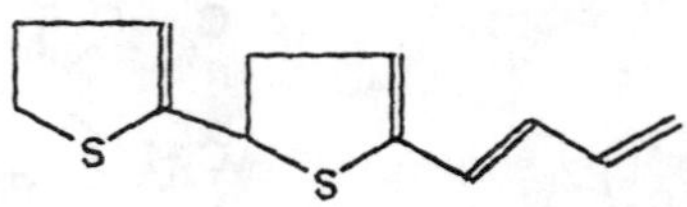

(II)

# 6

# Rodenticides

Rodenticides are chemicals that prevent, inhibit, destroy, kill or mitigate rodents (class-mammalia, order-Rodentia). More than 750 species of rats live throughout the world and their population, estimated to exceed 3 billions, constitutes a permanent menace through diseases and destruction.

The main species of rats found in the world are as follows:

***Rattus norbegicus:*** *Rattus norvegicus* accounts for more than 95% of all the existing rats and is known world wide as the largest species. It lives close to mankind and expels the other species.

**Rattus rattus:** *Rattus rattus* is mainly found in warmer region and in industrial buildings such as mills and warehouses.

**Mus musculus:** *Mus musculus,* the house mouse is less important pest economically but lives in close association with man in his dwellings.

**Rattus alexandrinus:** *Rattus alexandrinus* is mainly found in ponds and near the water front.

Generally rodenticides are applied as baits to control rodent pests. For effective control, the bait must satisfy the following criteria.

1. The bait Should have no repellent action or odour. Bait should be attractive, clean, fresh and hard.
2. It must not induce bait shyness.
3. The poison should make rats go out into the open to die, otherwise the rotting corpses create health hazards.
4. It should have much lower toxicity to domestic animals especially cats and dogs which eat the poisoned rats.

Redenticides can be classified into following groups:

## INORGANIC COMPOUNDS

White arsenic, yellow phosphorous, zinc phosphide, arsenic trioxide have been used as rodenticides.

### Botanicals

Red squill which comes from the powdered bulbs of a plant *Urginea* maritima is used as rodenticide. The active ingredient is an alkaloid scilliroside (1)

Strychnine (2) another alkaloid from *strychnos nuxvomica* is generally converted into strychnine sulphate and is used as rodenticide

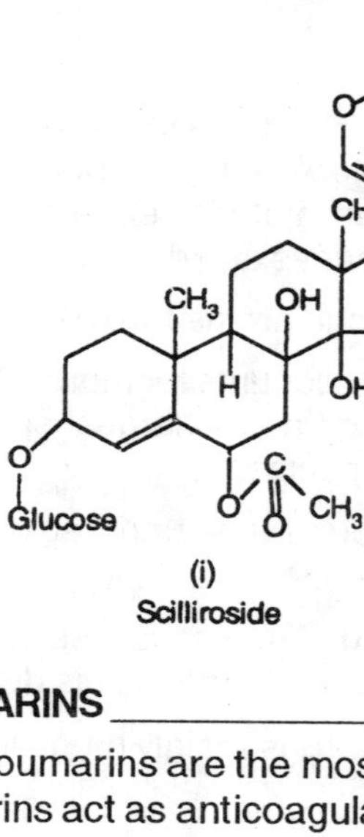

(i)
Scilliroside

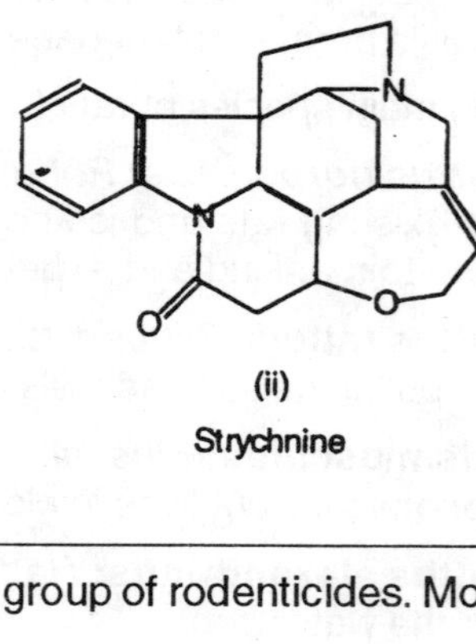

(ii)
Strychnine

## COUMARINS

Coumarins are the most important group of rodenticides. Most of the coumarins act as anticoagulants.

### Warfarin

(3-(1-phenyl-2-acetylethyl)-4-hydroxy coumarin)

WarFarin is prepared by condensation of 4-hydroxycoumarin and benzalacetone.

**Coumatetralyl**

(3-(1,2,3,4-tetrahydro napthyl) 4-hydroxy coumarin)

Coumatetralyl is prepared by condensation of 4-hydroxy coumarin with -hydroxytetraline in acetic acid solution

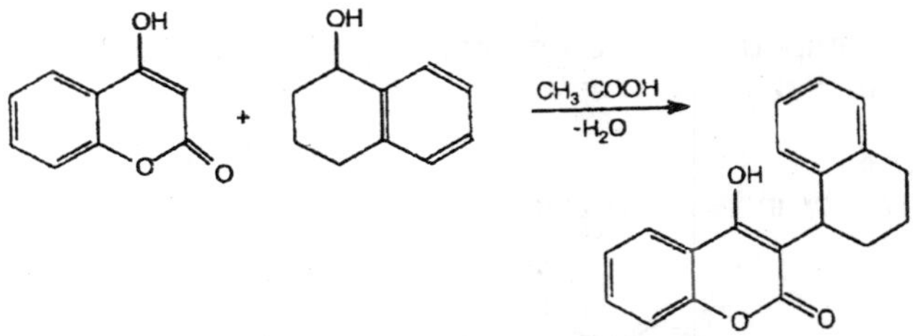


The other rodenticides which contain coumarin group and act as rodenticides are :

**Coumachlor**

3-(2-acetyl-1-chlorophenylethyl)-4-hydroxy coumarin

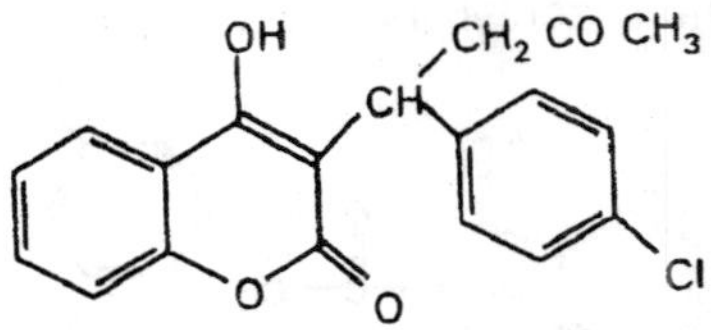


**Coumafuryl**

(3-(2-acetyl 1-furylethyl)-4-hydroxy coumarin)

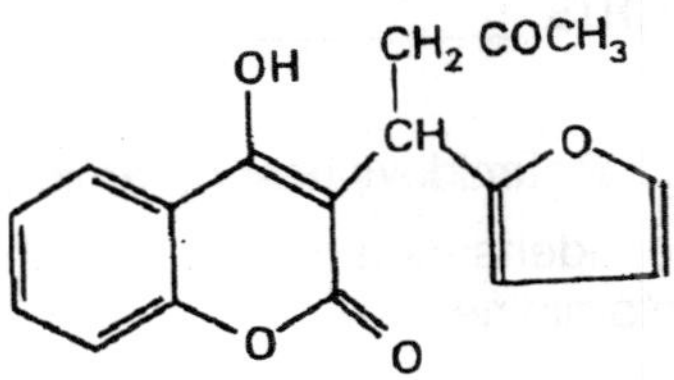


## INDANEDIONES

These substituted indanediones have also remarkable anticoagulant property. Examples of this class of rodenticides are

**Pindone**

(2-pivaloylindane-1,3-dione)

Pindone is prepared by treating diethyl phthalate and pinacolone

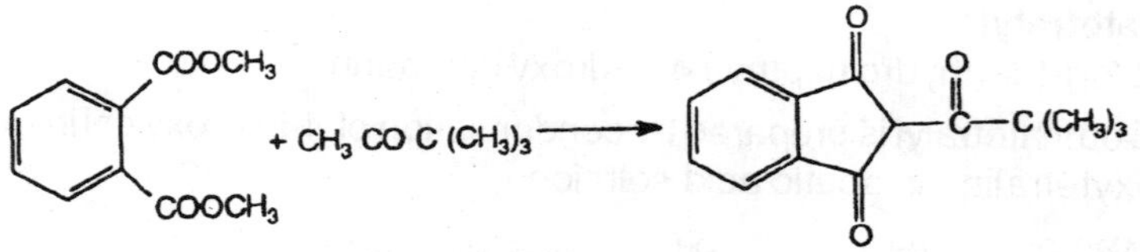

Other compounds which contain Indanedione nucleus and act as rodenticide are :

**Diphacinone**
(2-diphenyl acetyl indane-1,3-dione)

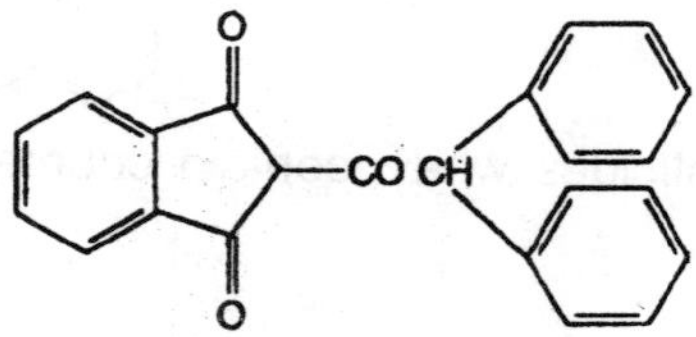

**Chlorophacinone**
(2-p-chlorophenyl-2-phenylacetyl) indane-1,3-dione)

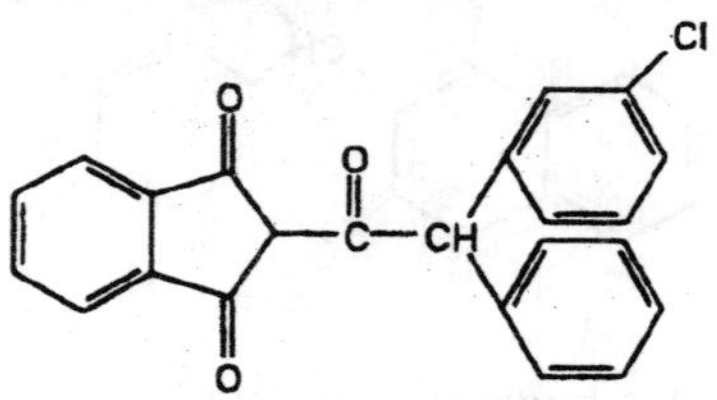

## ORGANOPHOSPHOROUS

**Gophacide**
(O,O-bis(p-chlorophenyl)acetimidoylphosphoramidothioate

It is prepared by condensation of O,O-di-p-chlorophenyl phosphorochloridothioate with acetamidine

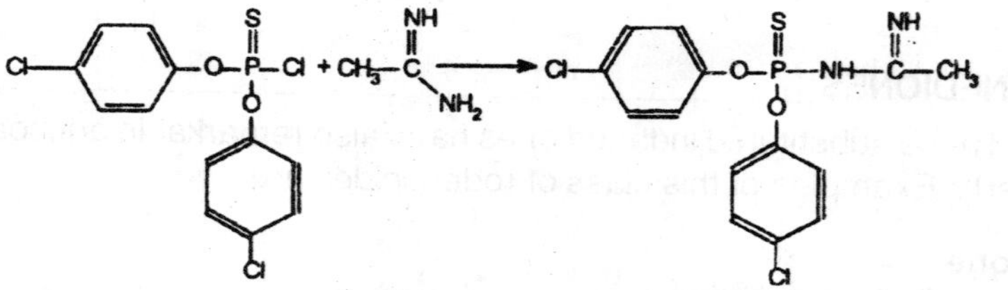

Gophacide is very effective for control of a range of rodent pests, but prove hazarous to non-target species.

## CHLORINATED RODENTICIDES

### Crimidine

(2-chloro-N,N,6-trimethyl-4-pyrimidinamine)

Crimidine is prepared by condensation of urea and ethylacetoacetate followed by chlorination and dimethylation,

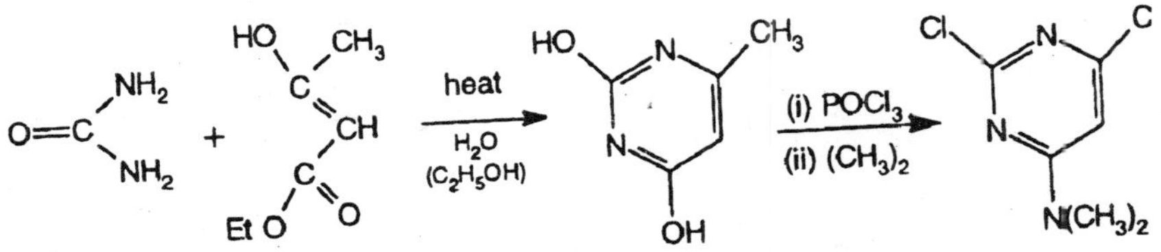

Crimidine is highly toxic to rats and is readily metabolized in the body, therefore poisoned rats are non-toxic to predators.

## MISCELLANEOUS RODENTICIDES

### α-Napthylthiourea or ANTU

α-Napthylthiourea is prepared by the reaction of α-napthylamine and ammonium thiocyanate

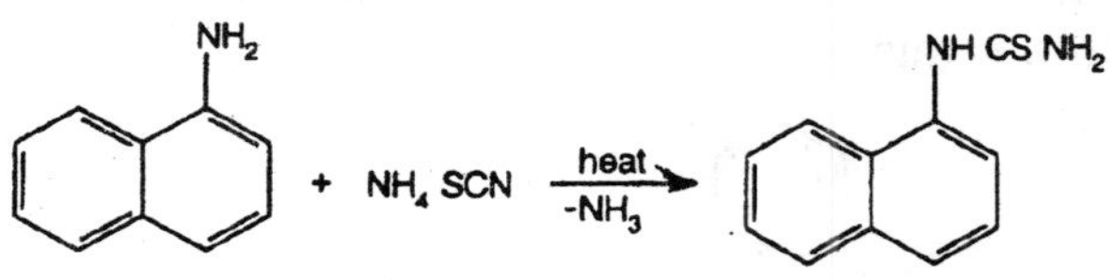

ANTU is a specific poison for adult Norway rats. ANTU is banned in some countries because of carcinogenicity of occasional impurities such as a-napthylamine. As rodents develop a tolerance to ANTU. It has been replaced by other materials.

### Vacor

(1-(3-pyridylmethyl)-3-(4-nitrophenyl)urea)

Another important rodenticide is Vacor. It is effective against rats that have developed resistance to warfArin.

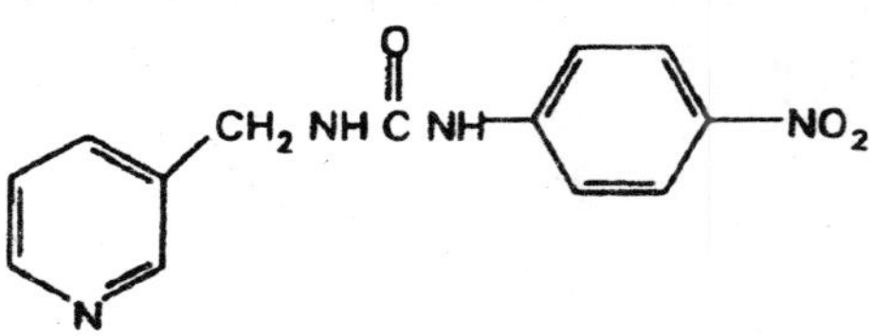

**Brodifacoum**

(3-(3-(4'-bromobiphenyl-4-yl)-1,2,3,4-tetrahydronapth-1-yl)-4-hydroxy coumarin)

Brodifacoum is effective against resistant rodents and its effectiveness against Norway rats and root rats is more than that of any other rodenticide.

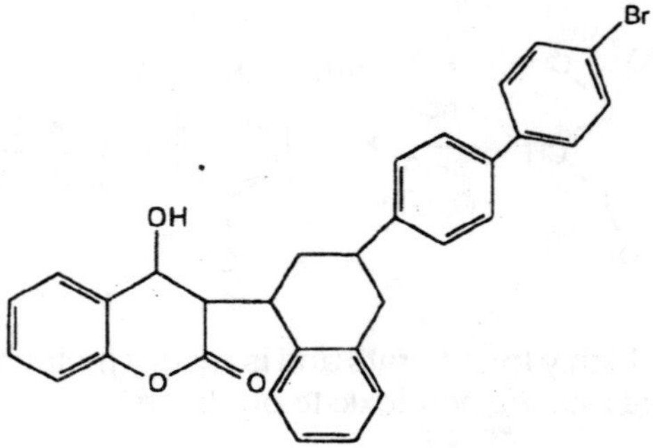


**Bromadiolone**

(3(3-(4'-bromo-1,1'-biphenyl-4-yl)-3-hydroxy-1-phenyl propyl)-4-hydroxy coumarin)

Bromadiolone is highly palatable anticoagulant and capable of controlling Norway rats

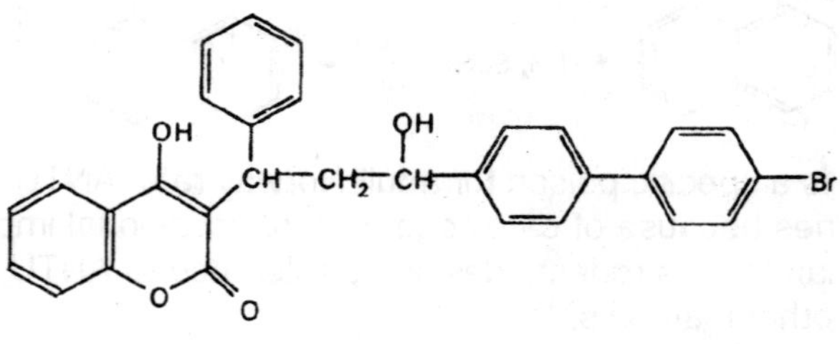


**Norbromide**

(Raticate, (5-(α-hydroxy-α-2-Pyridylbenzyl)-(7-(α-2-pyridylbenzylidene)-5-norbornene-2,3-dicarboximide)

It is highly selective rodenticide and is non toxic to other animals.

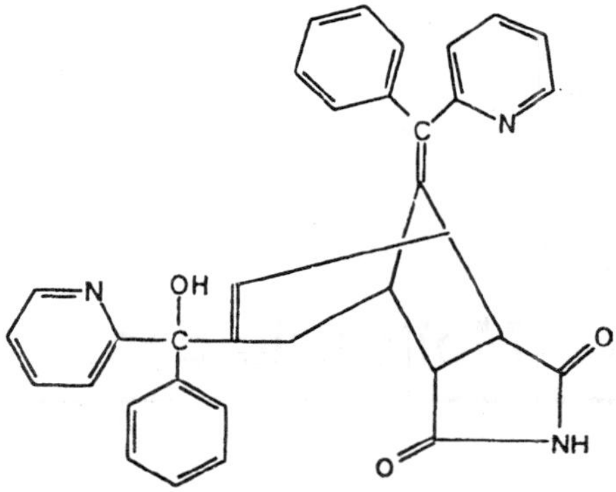


## PROBLEMS IN RODENT CONTROL

Both in the field as well as in the building, a number of rodent species live in association with each other in India as against single species composition in Europe and in other countries. The toxicities of rodenticides differ from species to species with the result that the predominant species is soon controlled but the others survive unaffected, so the choice and evaluation of rodenticides should be therefore of wide spectrum nature, highly cost effective, safe to non-target species, easy to handle and which is effective under diferent ecological situations. In India the main hinderances to rodent control are the religious and social taboos of the peace loving farmers. Therefore there is need for creating awareness of rodent control in a large number of farm families to cómbat rodent menance. Huge losses are caused by rodents every year to cereals, millets, pulses, sugarcane, cotton, vegetables, fruits, cocca, coconut, eggs and to almost all agricultural products.

# 7

# Molluscicides

Molluscs include land slugs and snails which do a considerable amount of damage by eating vegetable seedlings and green vegetables. Molluscs do not directly harm mammals, but are alternate hosts for some species of parasites. Mulluscicides are chemicals which prevent, repel, inhibit or destroy members of the Phyllum Mollusca.

Important molluscicides are :

**Metaldehyde** Metaldehyde is obtainted by the polymerization of an ethanolic solution of acetaldehyde in the presence of sulphuric acid.

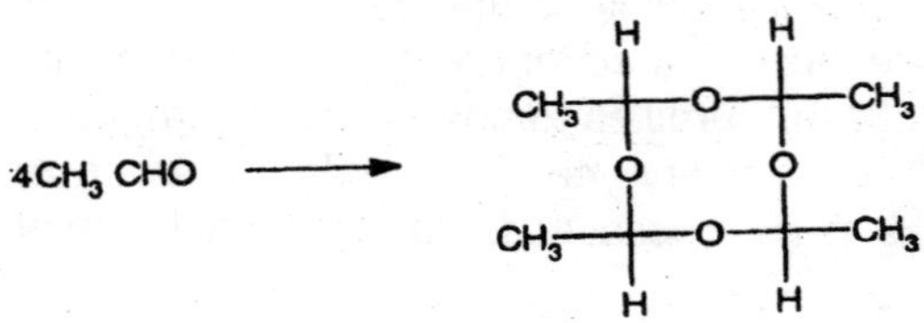

Metaldehyde has been used as baits for the control of slugs and snails. Its continued used can be attribute4d to its attractant and toxicant qualities.

**Methiocarb**

(3,5-dimethyl-4-(methylthio) phenyl methyl carbamate)

It is prepared by the reaction of 4-methyl thio-3, 5-xylenol and methyl isocyanate

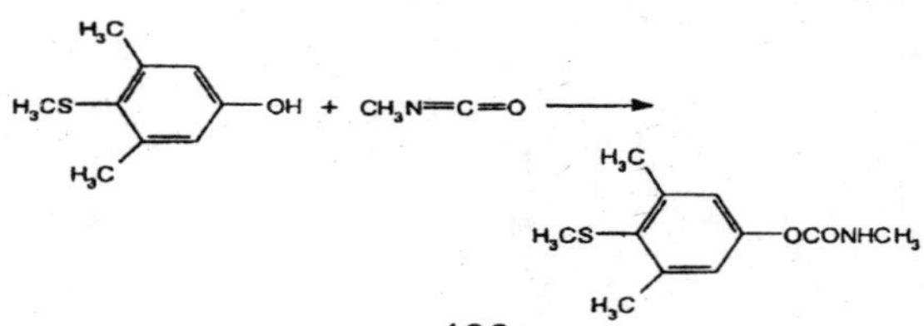

Methiocarb is registered for use against snails and slugs on ornamental plants.

**Trifenmorph**
4-(triphenyl methyl) morpholine

Trifenmorph is obtainted by the condensation of triphenyl methyl chloride with morpholine

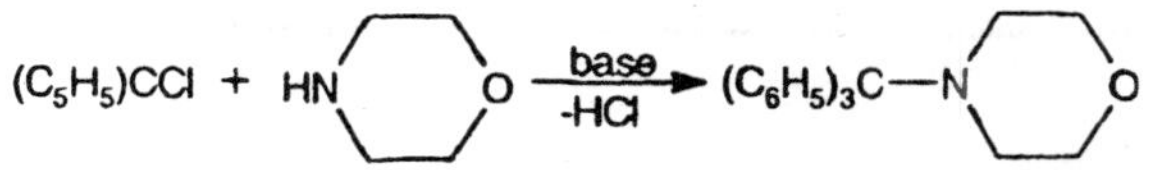


Trifenmorph is used against aquatic snails.

**Bayluscid**
(5-chloro-N-(2-chloro-4-nitrophenyl)-2-hydroxybenzamide)

Bayluscid is prepared by condensation of 5-chlorosalicylic acid and 2-chloro-4-nitroaniline

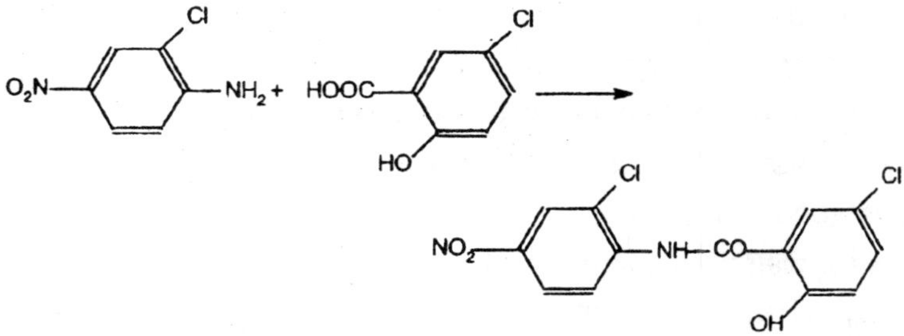


Bayluscid is formulated as the water soluble ethanol amine salt and is used against snails.

**TRIPHENYLTINACETATE**

Triphenyltinacetate is prepared by treating triphenyltinhydroxide with acetic acid.

$$(C_6H_5)_3\,SnOH + CH_3COOH \longrightarrow (C_6H_5)_3\,SnOCOCH_3$$

Triphenyltinacetate is used as a fungicide, algicide and moulluscicide.

**Copper sulphate** ($CuSO_4$) has also been used to kill the snail, liver fluke vectors.

# 8

# Fumigants

A fumigant is a chemical which at the required temperature and pressure exists in a gaseous state in sufficient concentration to be lethal to a given pest or organism.

Important characteristics of an ideal fumigant :

It should be

1. Highly toxic to all stages of insects
2. Have high vapour pressure
3. Have no adverse reaction with the fumigant commodity.
4. Have least of absorption with the treated commodity.
5. Desorbed easily
6. Able to distribute uniformly without settling down
7. Easy to handle and transport
8. Non-inflammable
9. Able to treat seeds without affecting viability
10. Be economical and indigenously manufactured.

## FACTORS INFLUENCING FUMIGATION

Through respiration insects directly develop susceptibility to fumigants since a lethal dose is absorbed by their tissues in a shorter or longer period. The rate of respiratory metabolism is increased by increase in temperature, increase in carbon dioxide content of fumigated space, decrease in oxygen content of fumigated space and also increase in the action on pests. Some other factors like density or insect population, pre and post fumigation effects, starvation effects, relative humidity, sub-lethal fumigation length or exposure period, fumigation interval and relative susceptibility of deferent stages of insects also play important role in fumigation.

Important fumigants are:

Ethylene dichloride carbon tetrachloride mixture (3:1 by volume)

$$Cl\,CH_2\,CH_2\,Cl\,CCl_4$$

The EDCT mixture is a popular fumigant due to least hazards involved in its use, inspite of many drawbacks. Being heavy, gas diffusion is slow and requires prolonged ventilation after fumigation. The carbon tetrachloride is feared to induce cancer and therefore not favoured in some countries.

## ETHYLENE DIBROMIDE

It has high boiling point 131.6°C and is sorbed by many fumigated commodities resulting in poor penetration. It is a nerve poison and a narcotic. It causes serious injury to the central nervous system and needs careful handling.

## METHYL BROMIDE

This is a very effective fumigant with a gas tight structure for controlling most insects. Because of its low boiling point and high volatile nature, it is readily converted into gas, rendering it for fumigation. In pure form it is a colourless liquid boiling at 3.6°C with a density of 1.732 g/cm$^3$. It is non-explosive and non-inflammable. It is a difficult fumigant to handle.

Methyl bromide decomposes in mammals to form methyl alcohol and subsequently formaldehyde which increases the toxic action of the fumigant.

$$CH_3Br + H_2O \longrightarrow CH_3OH + HBr$$

$$CH_3OH + O \longrightarrow HCHO + H_2O$$

### Methallyl chloride

(1-chloro-2-methylprop-2-ene)

Methallyl chloride is a fumigating insecticide and acaricide. It is highly toxic to a broad range of stored grain pests. The fumigant in the form of vapour readily penetrates into a pile of grain to depth of two meters. It is a colourless oily liquid boiling point 72°C and is highly toxic to human and warm blooded animals.

$$CH_2 = \underset{\substack{|\\ CH_3}}{C} - CH_2Cl$$

Methallyl chloride does not corrode metals and does not destroy rubber and other materials.

**Chloropicrin**
(trichloronitromethane)

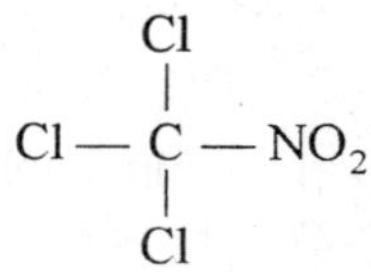

In pure form it is colourless heavy liquid boiling at 112.4°C. it s volatility at 20°C is 16 mg/litre. Chloropicrin is sorbed to a great extent by grains and is slowly desorbed.

**Aluminium Phosphide**

It is a solid fumigant in compressed tablet or pellet forms. The round tablet is dark brown in colour and yellowish tinge. It is composed of pure aluminium phosphide and ammonium carbamate. The tablet consists of a minimum 56% w/w aluminium phosphide (active ingredient) and maximum 44% w/w inert ingredients. The tablet weights three gram and releases about one gramme of phosphine on exposure to moisture. In addition, carbondioxide and ammonia are also evolved, thus preventing self inflammation of phosphine gas. It is indigenously manufactured with indigenous raw materials and the cost of fumigation is less.

**Ethylene oxide** $[(CH_2)_2O]$

It is a gas and is marketed as a liquid in pressure cylinders. It is mainly employed in grain stores and for plant disinfection.

**Formaldehyde** (HCHO)

Formaldehyde is used as 40% aqueous solution and is mostly used as surface dressing for seed beds to combat soil fungi.

Other fumigants include methyl isocyanate, hydrocyanic acid and sodium N-methyl dithiocarbamate dihydrate.

# 9

# Acaricides

Acaricides are chemicals used for control of mites that damage plants.

## CHLORINATED COMPOUNDS

### Dicofol

(1,1-bis(chlorophenyl)-2,2,2-trichloroethanol)

Dicofol is prepared by chlorination of (chlorfenethol)

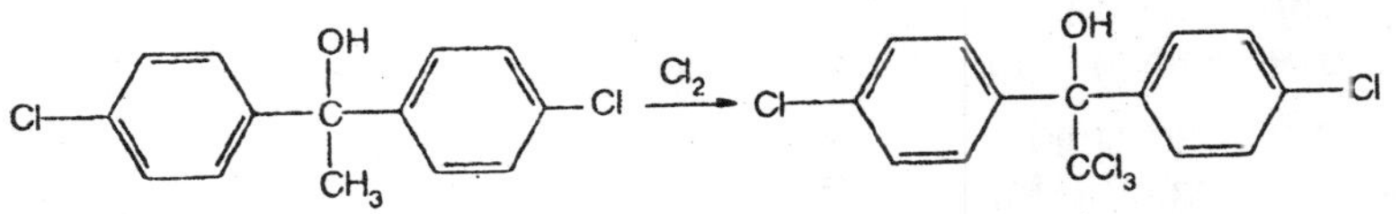

Dicofol is a contact acaricide with a high initial toxicity to phytophagus mites. Its acute $LD_{50}$ for rats is 430 mg/kg.

### Dienochlor

(bis(pentachloro-2,4-cyclopentadien-1-yl)

Dienochlor is obtainted by catalytic hydrogenation of hexachloro-cyclopentadiene

Dienochlor is used for control of mites and its acute oral $LD_{50}$ for rats is 316 mg/kg.

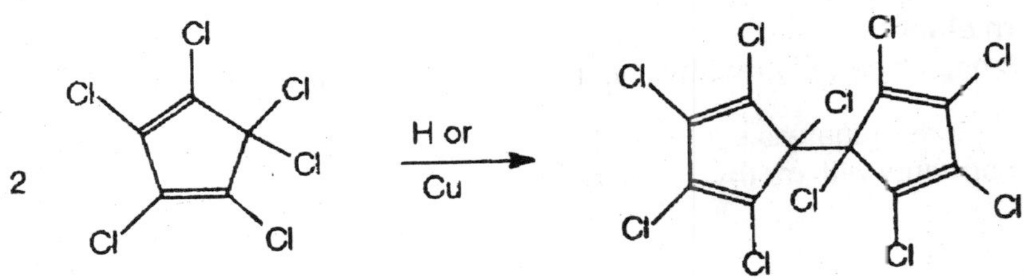

**Chlorfenethol**

(1,1-bis(4-chlorophenyl)ethenol)

Chlorfenethol is prepared by treating 4,4'-dichlorobenzophenone and methyl magnesium bromide.

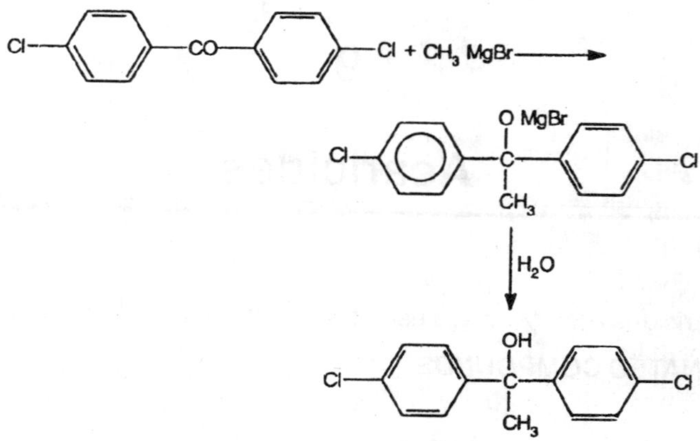

## DERIVATIVES CONTAINING A C=N OR N=N DOUBLE BOND

**Chlorphenamidine**

(N,N-dimethyl-N(4-chloro 2-methylphenyl) formamidine)

Chlorphenamidine is prepared by the reaction of 4-chloro-2-methyl-aniline and dimethyl formamide.

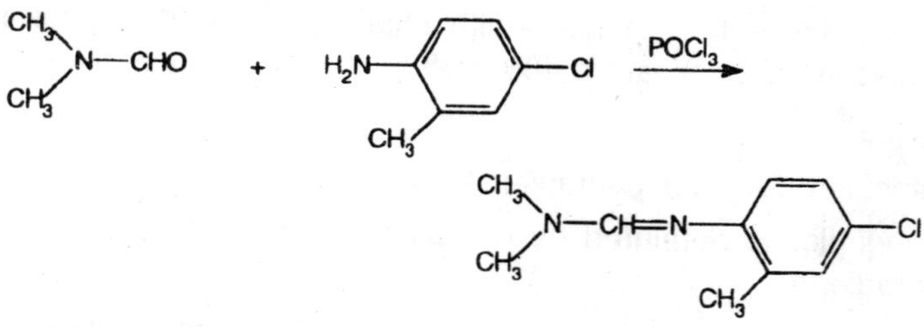

Chlorphenamidine has strong ovicidal properties. Its acute oral toxicity to rats is 335 mg/kg.

**Formetanate**

(3,3-dimethylamino-(methyleneiminophenyl) N-methyl carbamate)

Formetanate is synthesied by treating 3,3-dimethyl aminomethyllene-iminophenol with methyl isocyanate

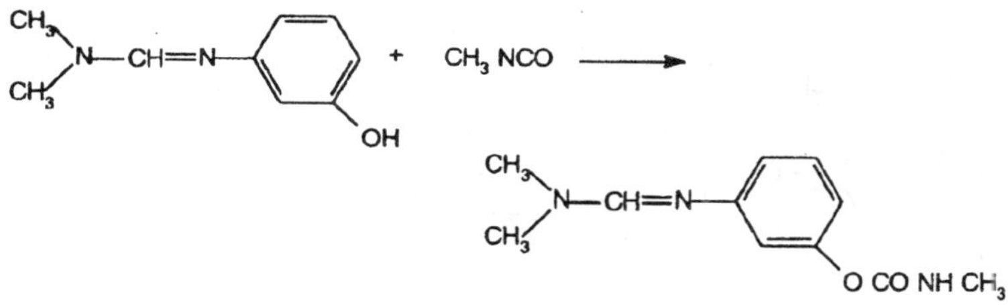

Formetanate is effective against spider mites. The acute oral $LD_{50}$ of formetanate for rats is 24 mg/kg.

## COMPOUNDS CONTAINING SULPHUR

### Chlorfensulfide

(4-chlorophenyl-2,4,5-trichlorophenylazosulphide)

Chlorfensulfide is prepared by reaction of 2,4,5-trichlorobenzene-diazonium chloride with 4-chlorothiophenol

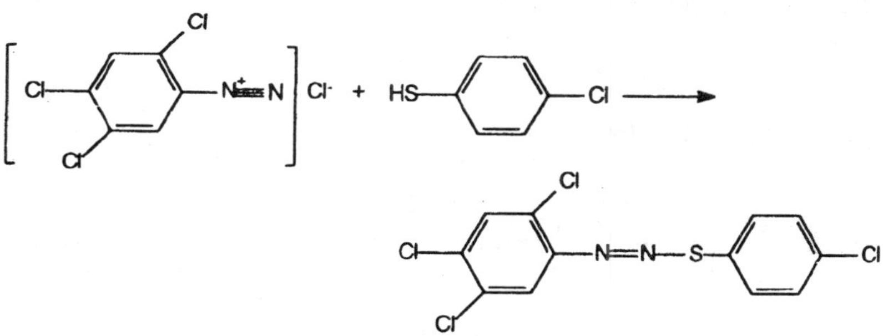

Its acute oral $LD_{50}$ for mice is 3000 mg/kg.

### Tetrasul

(4-chlorobenzyl-2,4,5-tri-chlorophenyl sulphide)

Tetrasul is prepared by treating 4-chlorothiophenol with 1,2,4,5-tetra-chlorobenzene

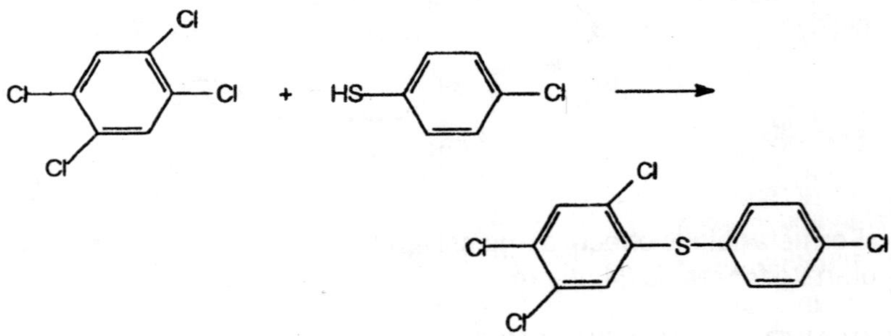

Tetrasul is toxic to tetranychis mites. Its acute oral $LD_{50}$ for female rats is 6800 mg/kg.

**Tetradifon**

(1,2,4-trichloro-5(4-chlorophenyl sulfonyl) benzene)

Tetradifon is prepared by friedel-crafts reaction between 2,4,5-tri-chloro benzenesulfonyl chloride and chlorobenzene.

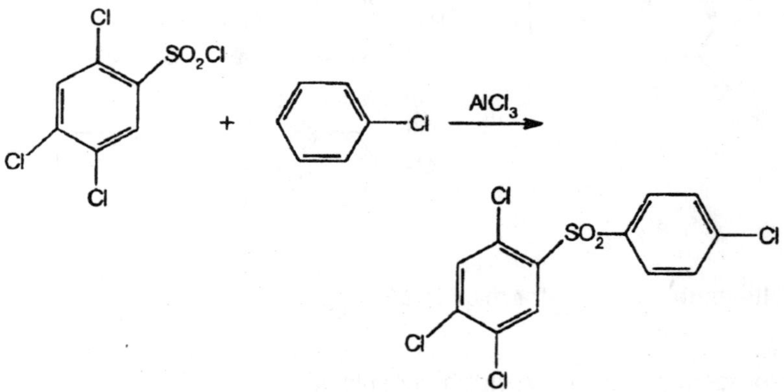

Tetradifon is used for protection of fruit trees and is active against phytophagus mites. Its $LD_{50}$ for rats is 15 mg/kg.

**Aramite**

(2-chloroethyl 2-(p-1,1-dimethylethyl) phenoxy) 1-methylethyl sulfite)

It is used as acaricide.

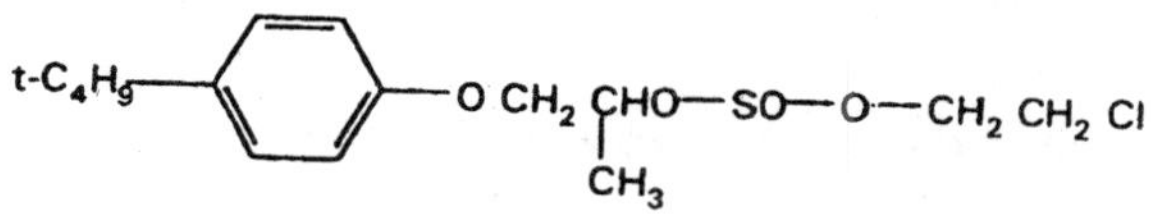

## ORGANOPHOSPHOROUS COMPOUNDS

### Carbophenethion

(S-((4-chlorophenylthio) methyl) O,O-diethyl phos phorodithioate)

Carbophenethion is prepared by reaction of p-chloro thiophenol with formaldehyde and hydrochloric acid followed by the reaction of the substituted chloromethyl phenyl sulphide with sodium diethyl phosphorodithioate.

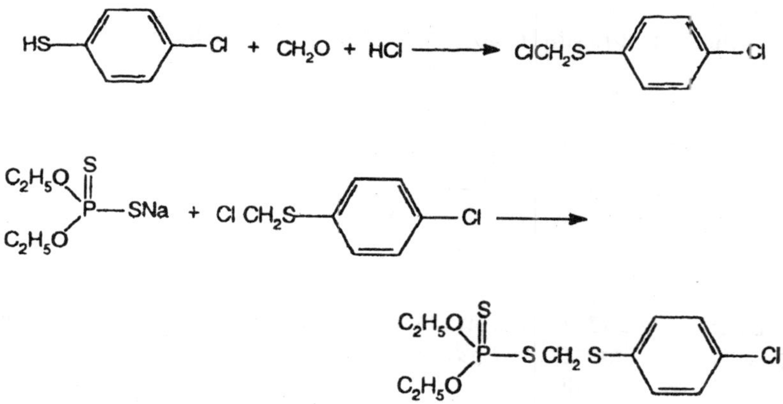

Its $LD_{50}$ value for rats is 28—100 mg/kg.

## ORGANOMETALLIC COMPOUNDS

### Fentin hydroxide

(Triphenyltin hydroxide)

It is used against plant feeding mites. Its acute oral $LD_{50}$ for rats is 540 mg/kg.

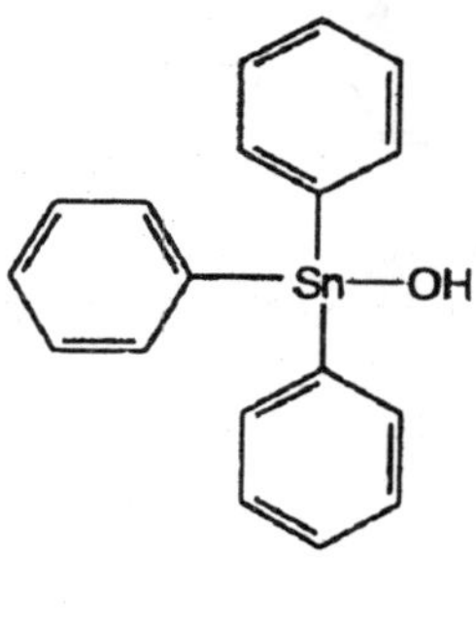

## ITROPHENOL DERIVATIVES

**Binapacryl**

(2-1-methylpropyl)-4,6-dinitrophenyl-2-methyl-2-crotonate)

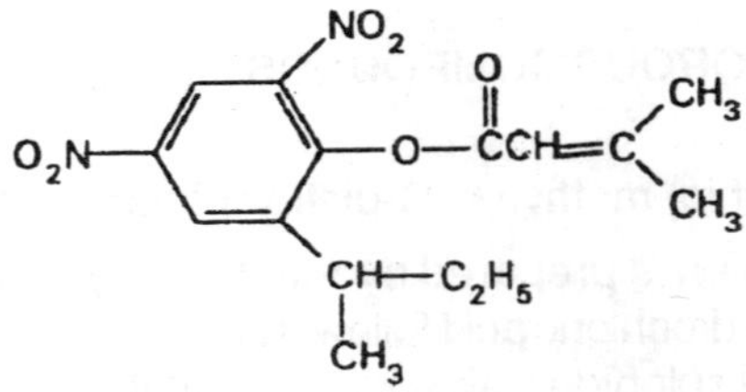

**Dinobuton**

(1-methylethyl 2-(l-methyl propyl) 4,6-dinitrophenyl carbonate)

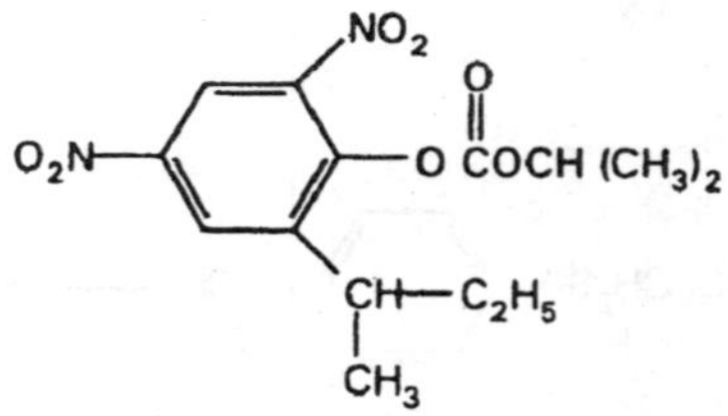

Binapacryl and Dinobuton are mainly effective against mobile stages of spider mites. The $LD_{50}$ of binapacryl and dinobuton to rats are 165 and 140 mg/kg respectively.

## FORMAMIDINES

**Chlordimeform**

(N'-(4-chloro-2-methylphenyl) N,N-dimethylmethanimidamide)

Its acute oral $LD_{50}$ value to rats is 340 mg/kg rats.

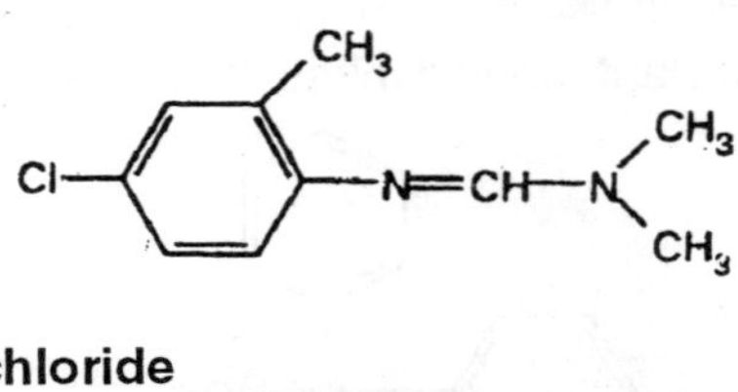

**Fometanate hydrochloride**

(N,N-dimethyl-N'-3 (methylamino carbonyl)oxy) phenyl methanimidamide) monohydrochloride

Its acute oral $LD_{50}$ to rats is 21 mg/kg.

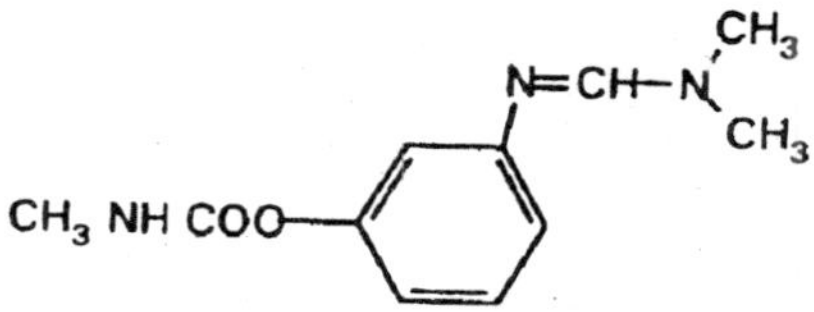

HCl

## HETEROCYCLICS

### Oxythioquinox

(6-methyl-2,3-quionoxalinedithiol cyclic dithiocar-bonate) and thioquinox (2,3-quinoxalinedithiol cyclic trithiocarbo-nate)

They are important examples of heterocyclic which act as acaricides.

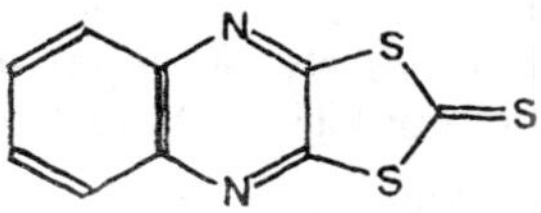

Thioquinox

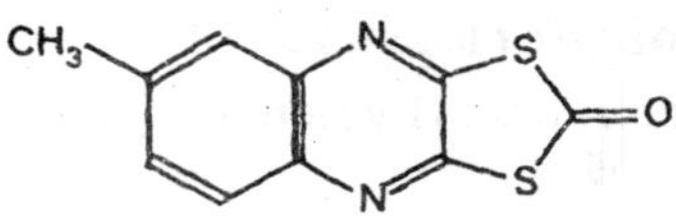

Oxythioquinox

# 10

# Herbicides

A herbicides in the broadest sense of the word, is any compound that is capable of either killing or severely injuring plants and may thus be used for elimination of plant growth or killing of plant parts.

The designation weed covers a variety of meanings accordings to a particular situation. According to the general definition weed is any plant either a wild or cultivated variety that is undesired in that particular place.

**How weeds cause damage or losses :**

1. Weeds decrease crop yields by removing a vast amount of water and nutrients from the soil.
2. They also compete with crops for space and sunlight.
3. Weed material in agricultural seed, in grain and hay reduce the value and quality of these products.
4. Many weeds cause loss to farmers by acting as host to insect pests and to other organisms which cause plant diseases.
5. Livestock may be poisoned by certain poisonous weeds that grow in the field or get into harvested crops. Poison milkweed, poison hemlock, pigweed are just a few examples.
6. Weeds may cause many other problems for man and animals. Plants such as sandbur, three-owned grass and wild barley have spines and harbed awns which may cause physical injury to the feet, mouths and eyes of animals.
7. The presence of weeds in crop increases wear on machinery.
8. The weeds compete for carbon dioxide required for photosynthesis.

**How weeds are introduced and spread to new areas :**

1. Weeds may be distributed by nature and man.

2. Nature, animals and birds help spread of weeds. The seeds of many plants have hooks, barbs or become sticky wet so they are made to cling to the wool or hair of animals. Both animals and birds eat many weed seed which can pass through their digestive tracts without being damaged. Seeds can thus be spread through the manure or drcpings over large distances.

3. A strong wind can spread almost all kind of weed seeds.

4. Rains or melting snows are natural ways by which weeds may be spread to long distances

5. Runners, rhizomes, and creeper type of weed roots are capable of spreading weeds over large areas regardless of their seed production and disperse.

6. Impure farm seed is the important way by which man has aided in the introduction and spread of weeds.

7. Modern irrigation systems are able to collect and distribute water over large areas of land. This system also aids weed seeds to spread throughout this large area.

8. Farm machinery spreads weed seeds specialy in wet weather, when the seeds attach to implements and vehicles in mud or by their natural stickness.

## WEED CLASSIFICATION

Based on life span, weed species are classified into three broad groups annuals, biennials and perennials.

1. **Annuals :** Plants with a one year life cycle are annuals. They propagate through seeds. They produce a crop of seed and die. There are two types of annuals a ) Summer annual b) Winter annual. Summer annual are plants that result from seeds which germinate in the spring, grow, mature, produce seed and die before winter of each year. Examples are crabgrass, foxtail, pig weed.

   Winter annuals are plants that grow from seeds which germinate in the winter, produce flowers and ripens seeds in the following spring or early summer and then die. The seeds of winter annuals remain dormant in the soil during summer. Examples are annual blue grass and winter galic.

2. **Biennials :** Plants with a two year life cycle are biennials. These plants require two years to complete their life cycle. They grow from seeds which germinates in the spring. They develop a heavy root and a

compact rosette to cluster of leaves in the first summer. Biennials remain dormant through the first winter and in the second summer they mature, produce seed and die before winter. Examples *Cyanadon dactylon.*

3. **Perennials :** Plants which live more than two years and may live indefinitely are perennials. These plants may grow from seed, but many produce tubers, bulbs, rhizomes and stolons. The above ground parts of these plants may die back each winter but develop new above ground parts each spring. Examples Johnson grass, field bindweed, donoletion, and plantain. Perennial plants can be further grouped as follows :

   Simple perennials reproduce mostly by seeds but in some instances root pieces may produce new plants following mechanical injury during cultivation. Bulbous perennials propagate through the underground parts like bulbs, and tubers as well as by seeds e.g. wild onions and wild garlic. Creeping perennials spread by lateral extensions of the creepers above ground stems (rhizomes) either by roots or by seeds. Examples are Bermuda grass, Johnson grass.

## METHODS OF WEED CONTROL

### Prevention

Prevention of the introduction of the weeds to new areas deals mainly with attempts to cut down the steps of spread of weeds caused by man.

1. Stopping the use of impure farm seed. There are laws regulating the quality of farm seed used.
2. Keep hay and grain as pure as possible so that animals do not further spread weeds from the seeds still alive in manure and droppings.
3. Keeping the farm machinery and other equipments used in farming free of weed seeds.
4. Limiting the introduction of weed seeds through irrigation seeds.

### Cultural and Mechanical control

1. **Crop rotation :** A carefully planned rotation of crops involving hay, grain and intertilled crops is a practical and efficient method. Many weeds that are known to associate with certain crops are destroyed in this manner.
2. **Cultivation :** This is the oldest and most effective mechanical method of controlling weeds. However all weeds are mostly easily and economically killed when they are seedlings.

3. **Mowing :** This is a most effective method of preventing the maturation of annual and biennial seeds. Mowing is used often in places where cultivation is impossible. Flowering should not be permitted before mowing because man weeds are able to mature seeds after the flowers have been grown even if they are cut.

4. **Grazing :** this method serves the same purpose as does the method of mowing.

**Biological control**

In biological weed control a 'natural energy' of the pest plant is used which is harmless to all other plants.

Parasitic plants or highly competitive plants are used as biological control. The risk of introducing new insect plant or disease into a new area is great. Much time must be spent on testing of the proposed control organisms to see of all if it can survive in a new environment and secondly it destroy only the noxious weed in field.

**Chemical weed control**

Employing chemicals for weed control constitutes chemical method. These chemicals, commonly referred to as weedicides or herbicides, are being used for over 85 years.

Benefits of chemical weed control :

1. Herbicides can be applied for weed control in crop rows where cultivation is impossible.
2. Preemergence herbicides provide early season weed control. This is very beneficial as crop-weed competition during early stages of crop growth is maximum than at later stages.
3. Cultivation and manual method of weed control may injure the root system in plantation crops like tea and coffee which grow for several decades.
4. Herbicides can control many perennial weed and brush species which cannot be controlled by other methods.

## CLASSIFICATION OF HERBICIDES

The herbicides are classified on the basis of

1. method of application
2. mode of action
3. chemical affinity and structural similarity

### Classification based on method of application

Classification on the basis of method of application divides herbicides into two main groups. Soil applied or preemergence and foliage applied or post emergent herbicides.

Preemergence are applied to soil before crops and weeds emergence. It may also refer to applications after crops emergence but before the weeds emerge. Presence of adequate soil moisture is essential for the success of pre-emergence herbicides.

Post emergence are applied after the emergence of crop and weeds.

Preplant herbicides are generally applied before planting of crops.

### Classification based on mode of action

The classification on the basis of mode of action of herbicides takes into account differences in the physiological and biochemical action of herbicides. On this basis they are categorized as systemic or translocated herbicides and no systemic or contact herbicides.

1. **Contact herbicides-** Herbicides that kill plant parts when come in contact are known as contact herbicides. They must be directly toxic to living cells and the effects are usually rapid. Contact herbicides are effective against annual weeds, but usually only 'burn off' perennial plants. Selective contact herbicides kill or stunt some plants with little or no injury to other.

2. **Translocated Herbicides-** Herbicides that can be absorbed by either the roots or above ground parts and move or are translocated through the plant systems. These herbicides upset the plant's growth and metabolic processes particularly enzyme systems. Full effects may not be evident until a month or more after application.

3. **Residual-** A chemical which provides weed control for a period of time even after the application as soil applied herbicide. Residual chemicals may be selective or non-selective. A selective herbicide is a herbicide that is more toxic to some kinds of plants than to other. The degree of selectivity is affected by plant age, rate of growth, form of plant and physiological differences. Non selective herbicide is toxic to all plants.

### Classification based on chemical affinity and structural similarity

The herbicides which originate from one chemical nucleus have structural and chemical similarities and affinities and thus provides the basis for chemical classification. The two major classifications are inorganic and organic herbicides.

Inorganic Herbicides- Inorganic herbicides include copper sulphate ($CuSO_4.5H_2O$), copper nitrate ($CuNO_3$), ammonium sulphate ($(NH_4)_2SO_4$), ammonium sulfamate ($NH_4$-$SO_3$-$NH_2$), sodium tetraborate ($Na_2B_4O_7.10H_2O$), sodium metaborate ($Na_2B_2O4.4H_2O$), amorphous sodium borate ($Na_2B_4O_{13}.4H_2O$), sodium chlorate ($NaClO_3$),ammonium thiccyanate ($NH_4SCN$) and sulphuric acid ($H_2So_4$). These were used between 1896 and 1930's. Intensive EPA restrictions have been placed on some inorganic herbicides because of their persistence in soil. The inorganic herbicides are not wise choice for use except aiming to remove all vegetation from an area.

## The Organic Herbicides

**Petroleum oils -** The earliest organic herbicides were the petroleum oils which are a complex mixture of long chain hydrocarbons containing traces or nitrogen and sulphur linked compounds. These mixtures contain alkanes and often alicyclics and aromatics. The petroleum oils are effective herbicides for all vegetation. The petroleum oils exert their lethal effect by penetrating and disrupting plasma membranes.

**Organic arsenicals -** Organoarsenicals are widely used as agricultural herbicides. They are the organic arsenicals namely arsenic and arsenic acid derivatives. The following arsenic herbicides are used in agriculture

1. Methanearsenic acid is used for control of grasses in cotton and turf.

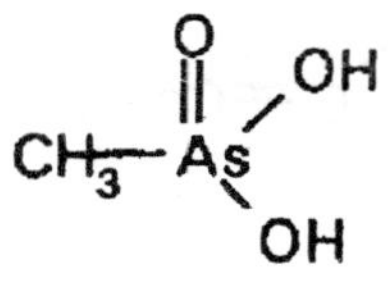

2. Disodium methane arsonate is used for control of grass weeds in cotton and rubber plantations

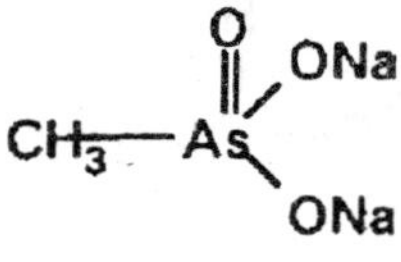

3. Monosodium methanearsonate is used in tea and rubber plantation.

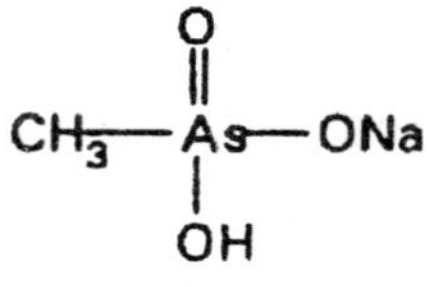

4. Cacodylic acid (dimethyl arsenic acid)

Cacodylic acid is used as postemergence contact herbicide for controlling weeds in non cropped areas. It is also used as defoliant and desiccants for cotton.

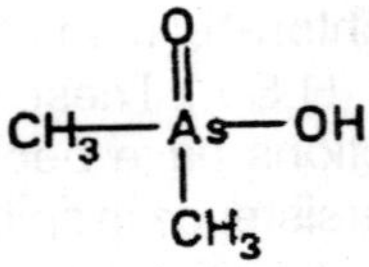

5. Hexaflurate (Potassium hexafluoro-arsenate)

Hexaflurate is a selective post-emergence herbicide for the control of prickly pear in non cropped areas

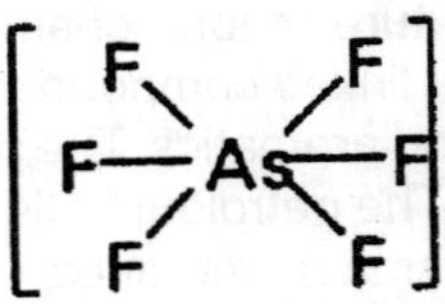

Aliphatic

1. Acrolein is used as aquatic herbicide on submerged and floating weeds mainly in irrigation canals, detacher drains and ponds.

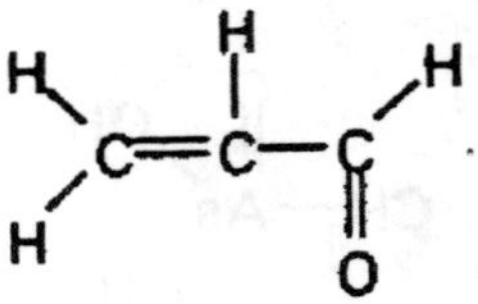

2. Allyl alcohol used as a preplant treatment to kill weed seeds in tree nurseries, tobacco seed beds, and ornamental plantings.

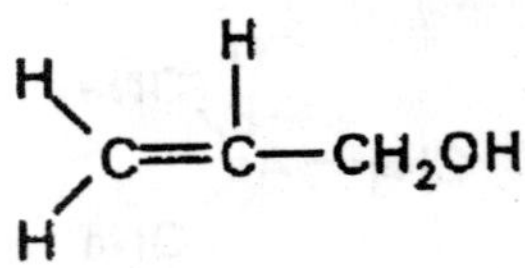

3. Trichloroacetic acid controls wild oat and is effective against perennial grasses.

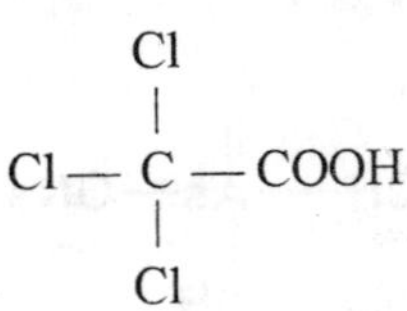

4. Dalapon is applied as post emergence on foliage and used for control of weeds in sugarcane, grapes, coffee, tea and orchard crops

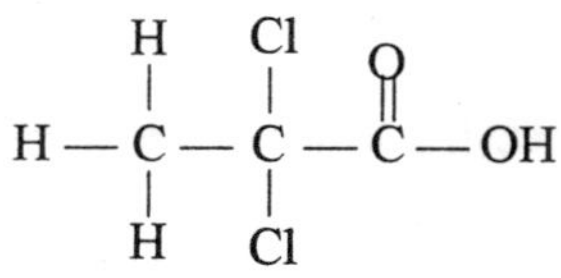

## PHENOXYALIPHATIC ACIDS

These herbicides are highly selective for broad leaf weeds and are translocated through the plant system.

### 2,4-D

(2,4-dichlorophenoxyacetic acid)

2,4-D is a selective systemic postemergence herbicides in used for the control of many annual broadleaf weeds in cereals, sugarcane and plantation crops. It is available in salt and ester formulations. Ester formulations are volatile. 2,4-D is prepared by the following methods :

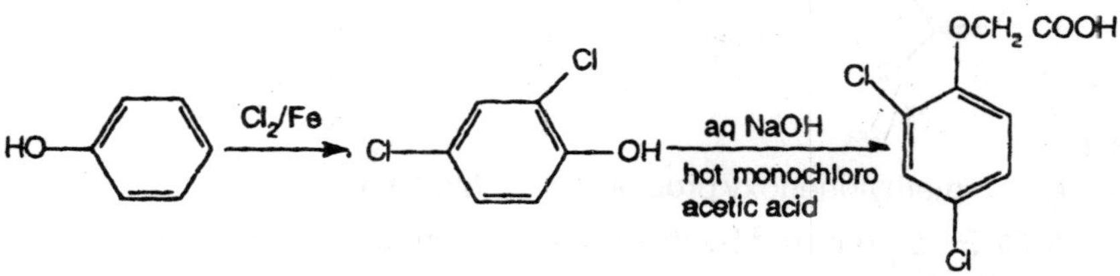


2. Chlorination of phenoxy acetic acid

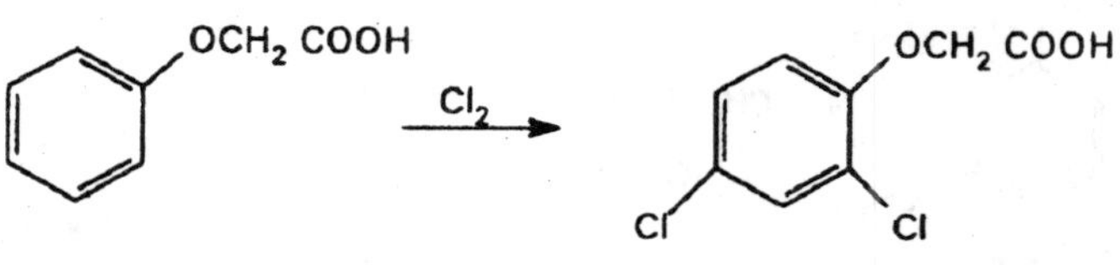


The esters are formed from 2,4-D with respective alcohols in the presence of catalyst. Isopropylester is most widely used.

### MCPA

(4-Chloro-2-methylphenoxyacetic acid)

MCPA is more selective than 2,4-D at equal rates. It is widely used in cereals legumes and aquatic areas. It is available as amines, esters and sodium or potassium salts.

It is prepared by treating 4-chloro-2-methyl phenol with monochloroacetic acid in alkaline medium by heating the reaction mixture to 103—105°C.

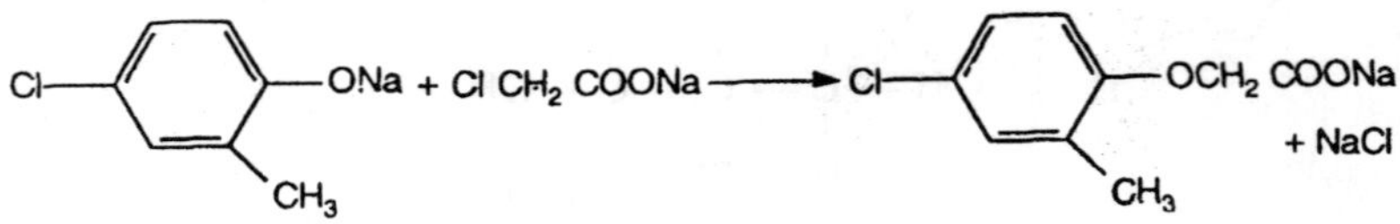


**2,4,5-T**

(2,4,5-trichlorophenoxy acetic acid)

It is widely used for weed control in rice and sugarcane. It is also available as amine salt and ester formulations. It is prepared by treating 2,4,5-trichloro-phenolates with alkali monochloroacetate in aqueous solution at pH 10—12 and at 103—107°C.

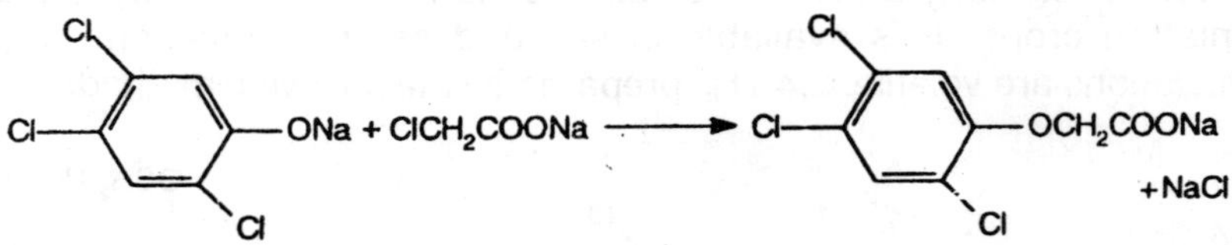


**MCPP**

(4-chloro-2-methylphenoxy propionic acid, Mecoprop)

MCPP is prepared by the condensation of p-chloro-O-cresol with - chloro propionic acid.

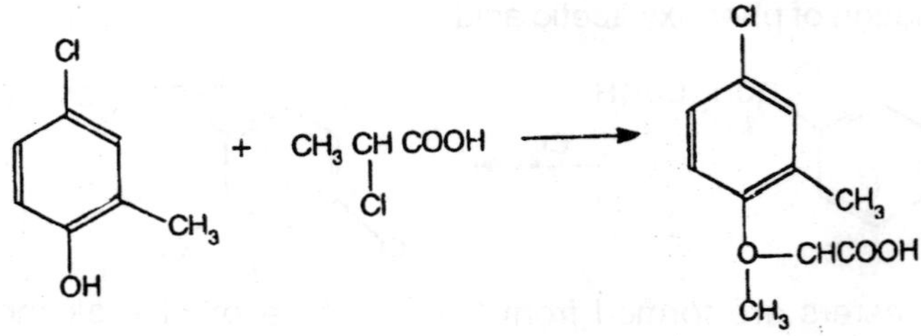


**2,4,5-TP**

(2,4,5-trichlorophenoxy propionic acid, Fenoprop)

Fenoprop is used for aquatic weeds.

Fenoprop is produced by treated 2,4,5-trichlorophenolate with chloropropionic acid.

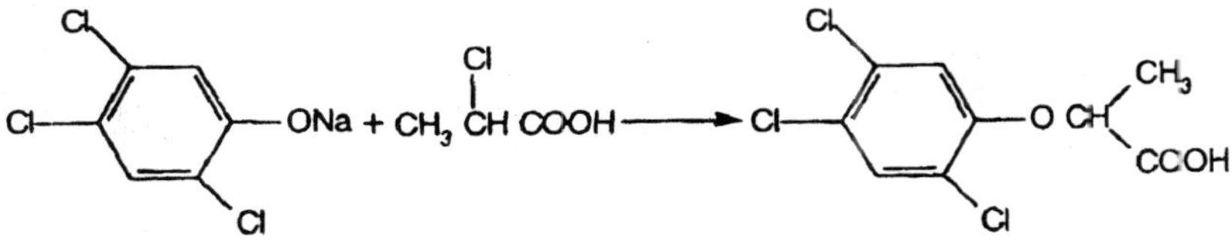

**MCPB**

(2-methyl-4-chlorophenoxy butyric acid)

MCBP is prepared by reacting sodium 4-chloro-2-methylphenolate with 1,3-chlorobromopropane

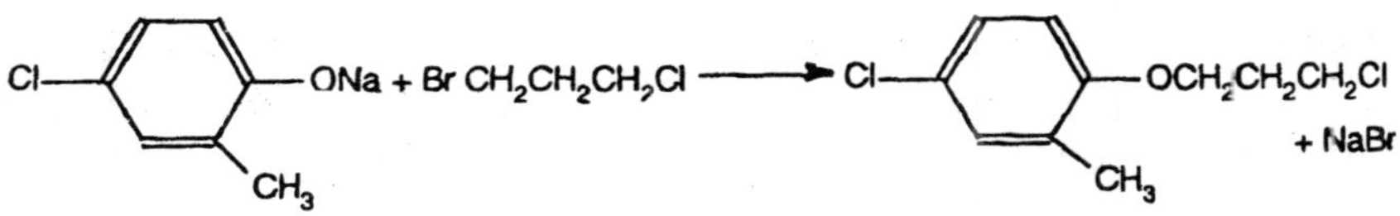

MCPB is used for control of weeds in legume crops.

**2,4-Des**

(Sesone, sodium-2-(2,4-dichlorophenoxy ethyl sulphate)

2,4-Des is prepared by the reaction of 2,4-dichloro phenoxy-ethanol with chlorosulphonic acid

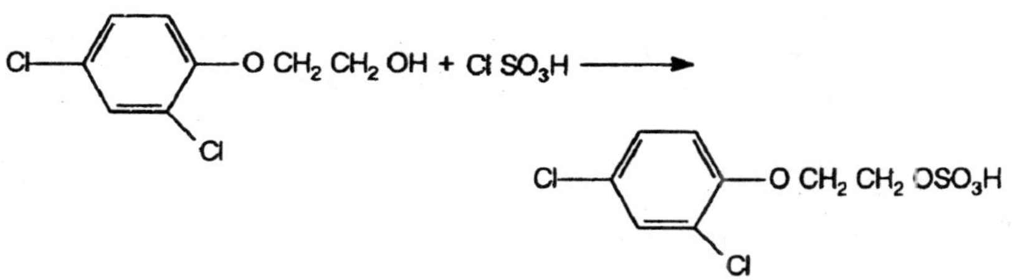

2,4-Des is used in the form of sodium or ammonium salt for the control of broad leaved and grassy weeds.

**Erbon**

{2-(2,4,5-Trichlorophenoxy) ethyl 2,2-dichloropropanoate)

Erbon prepared by the esterification of 2,4,5-trichlorophenoxyethanol with 2,2-dichloro propionic acid in the presence of sulphuric acid.

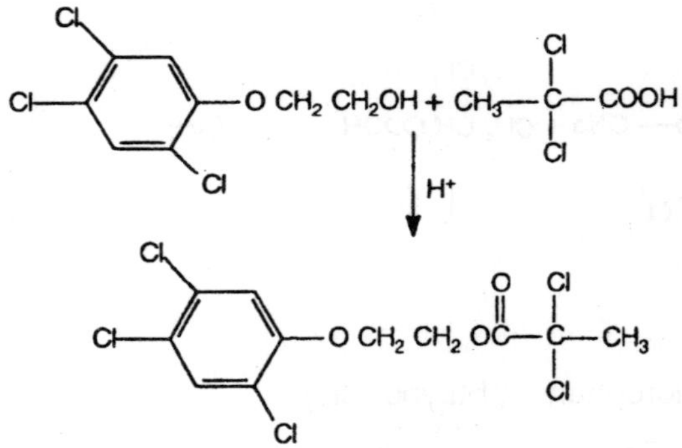

Erbon is a non-selective herbicide used for killing vegetation in noncropped areas.

**2,4-DEP**

(tris[2(2,4-dichlorophenoxy) ethyl] phosphite and bis [2-(2,4-dichlorophenoxyethyl)] phosphite)

It is prepared by reacting phosphorous trichloride and 2,4-dichlorophenoxyethanol in the presence of pyridine.

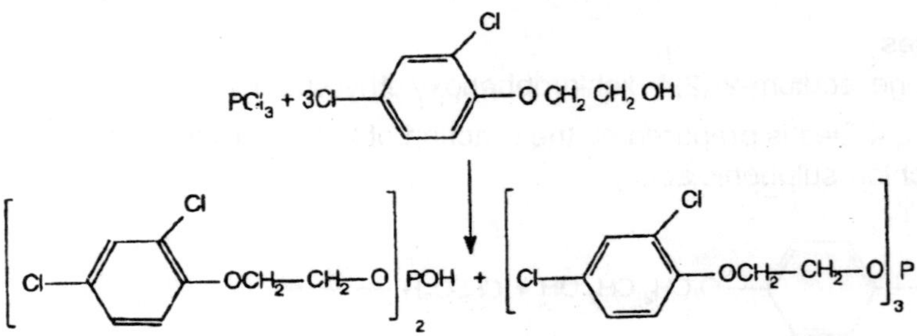

It is a selective herbicide effective for the control of mono-and dicotyledonous weeds in maize, potato and peanut. It is hydrolysed in soil to 2,4-dichlorophenoxyethanol.

These herbicides are mainly used for annual and perennial grass weeds in broad leaved crops.

## DERIVATIVES OF BENZOIC ACID

**2,3,6-TBA**

(2,3,6-trichlorobenzoic acid)

Trichlorobenzoic acid is obtained by chlorination of benzyl chloride in the presence of a catalyst

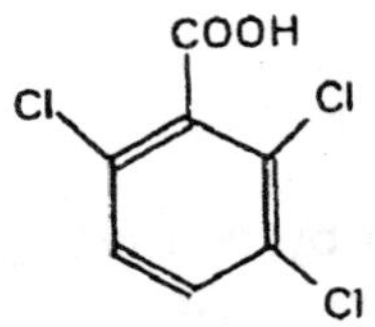

It is used as postemergence application against broad-leaved annual and perennial weeds including deep rooted weeds.

**Dicamba**
(2-methoxy-3,6-dichlorobenzoic acid)

Dicamba is synthesised from benzene hexachloride.

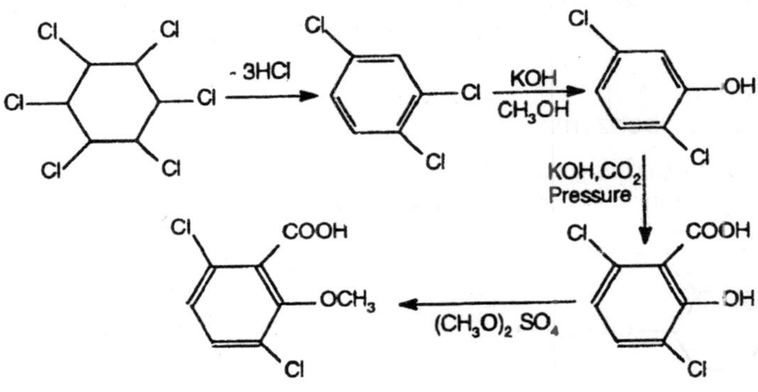

Dicamba, in the form of its dimethylamine salt is used for control of grasses, broad leaved weeds and several shrubs.

**Dinoben**
(2,5-dichloro-3-nitrobenzoic acid)

It is synthesised by the nitration of 2,5-dichlorobenzoic acid.

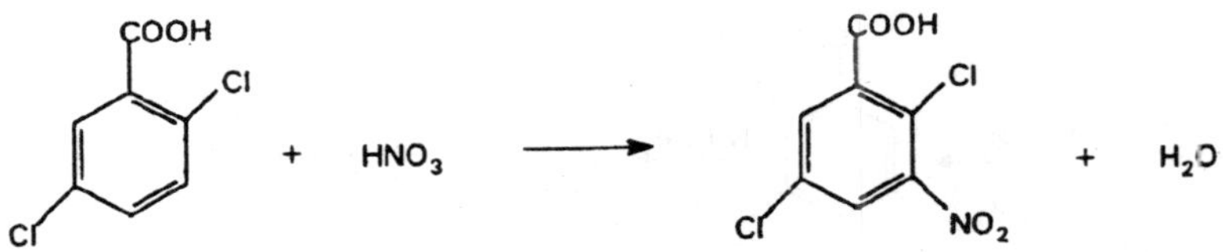

Its water solution, sodium and trimethyl amine salts are preemergence selective weed killers against annual and broad-leaved weeds in maize, soybean and horticultural crops.

## BENZONITRILES

### Dichlobenil

(2,6-dichlorobenzonitrile)

Dichlobenil is obtained by converting 2,6-dichlorotoluene in the presence of catalyst vanadium pentaoxide with mixture of ammonia and oxygen.

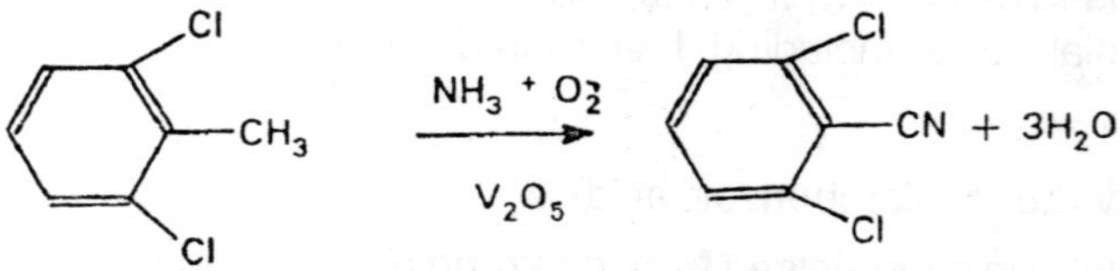

Dichlobenil is effective against several annual and perennial weeds. Dichlobenil can be used for the control of aquatic weeds.

### Chlorthiamid

(2,6-dichlorothiobenzamide)

Chlorthiamid is prepared by the action of hydrogen sulphide on 2,6-dichlorobenzonitrile in the presence of pyridine.

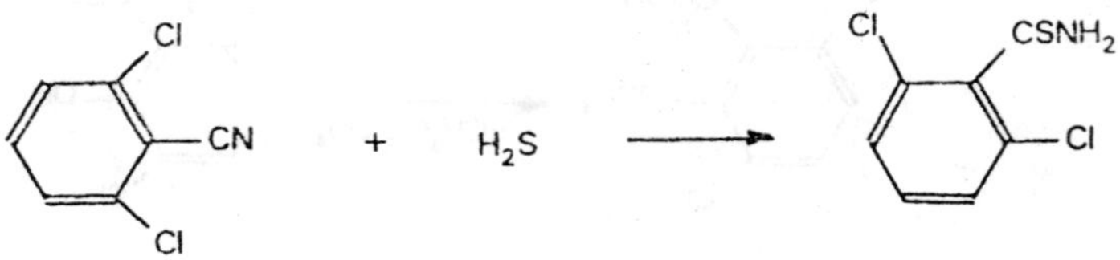

It is used for the control of weeds in rice and in orchards.

### Loxynil

(3,5-Diiodo-4-hydroxybenzonitrile)

Ioxynil is produced by the direct iodination of 4-hydroxybenzaldehyde followed by conversion to the oxime and subsequent dehydration to nitrile.

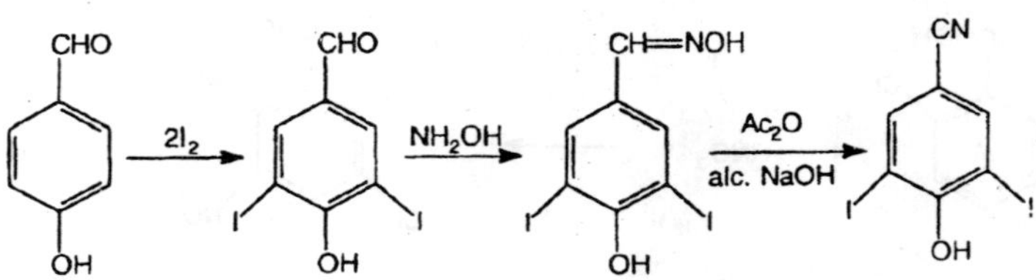

Ioxynil is post emergence contact herbicide and is used for control of broad leaved weeds in cereals and monocot crops.

**Bromoxynil**

(3,5-dibromo-4-hydroxybenzonitrile)

Bromoxynil is produced by reacting 4-hydroxybenzonitrile with sodium hypobromite.

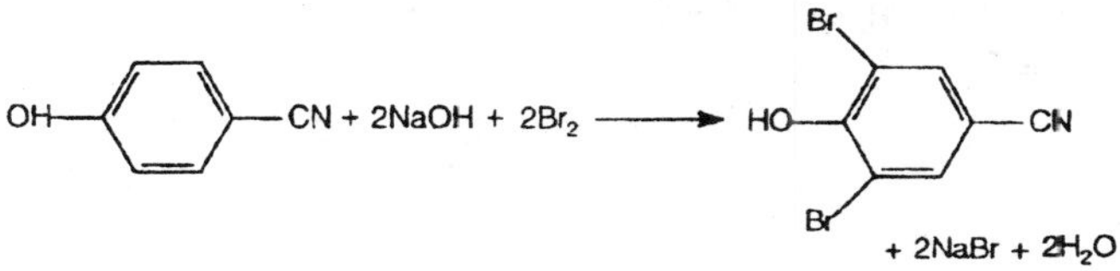


Bromoxynil is a post emergence contact herbicide and is used for control of broad leaved weeds in cereals and grass crops.

## CARBAMATE HERBICIDES

Carbamates are esters of carbamic acid ($NH_2COOH$). The alkyl esters of N-aryl carbamic acids are powerful herbicides.

**Propham**

(Isopropyl-N-phenylcarbamate)

Propham is produced by the reaction of phenyl isocyanate with isopropyl alcohol

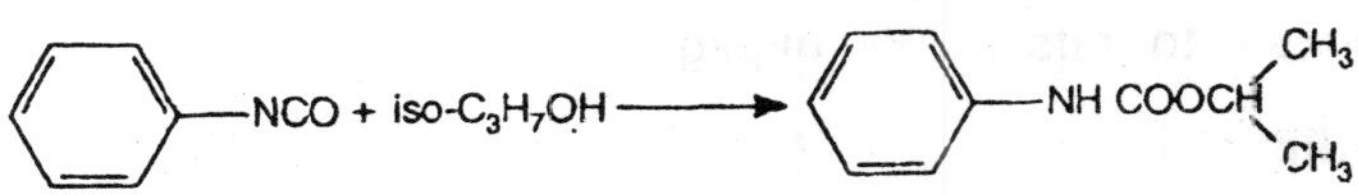


Propham is a preemergent selective herbicide used for the control of grass weeds in beet, cabbage, peas and lettuce.

**Chloropropham**

(Isopropyl-N-3(chlorophenyl) carbamate)

Chloropropham is prepared by reacting m-chlorophenylisocyanate with isopropyl alcohol

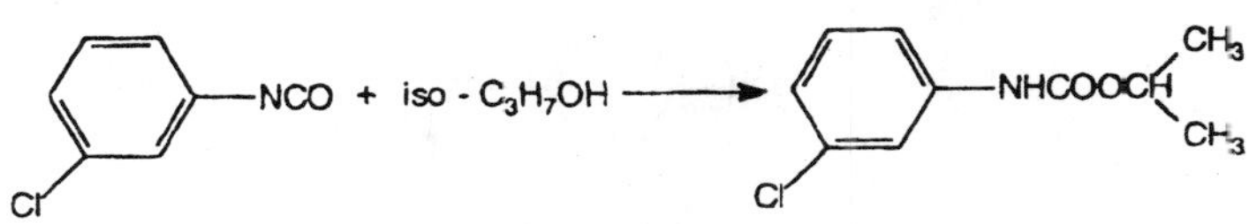


Chloropropham is used in soybean, onion, cotton and garlic for control of several grass weeds.

**Proximpham**

(O-(N-phenylcarbamoyl) propanon oxime)

Proximpham is prepared by the following reaction

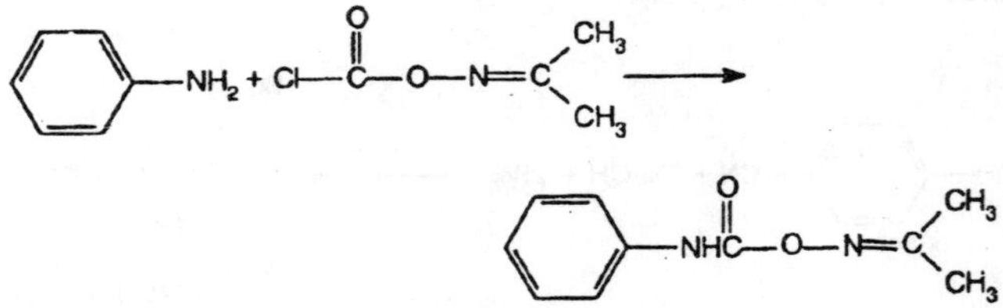

Proximpham is a selective soil herbicide. It is used for the control of weeds in beet, onion and vegetables.

**Asulam**

(methyl 4-aminophenylsulfonyl carbamate)

Asulam is prepared by treating 4-aminobenzenesulfonamide and methyl chloroformate in the presence of acid binding agent.

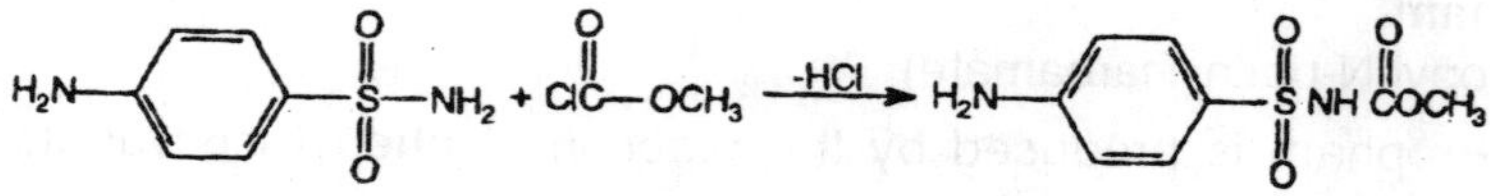

It is effective against weed grasses. The acute oral $LD_{50}$ of its potassium salt for rats is 2000 mg/kg.

**Phenmedipham**

(3-methoxycarbonylaminophenyl-N(3'-methylphenyl) carbamate)

Phenmedipham is prepared by treating m-amino phenol with methvlchloroformate to give 3-methoxycarbonyl aminophenol which on reacting with m-tolyl isocyanate gives phenmedipham.

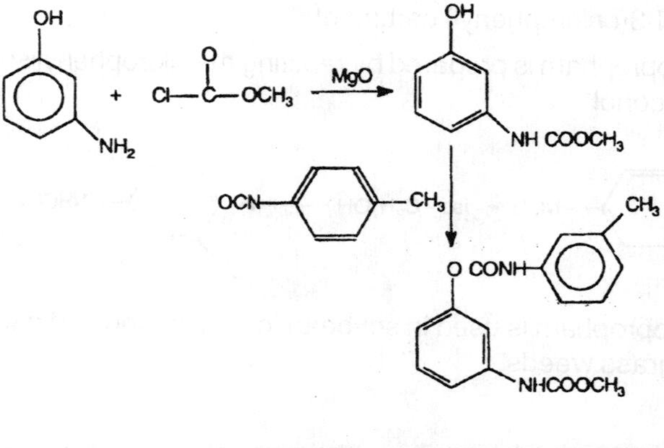

Phenmedipham is a selective post emergence herbicide effective in sugar beet. The acute oral $LD_{50}$ for rats is 8000 mg/kg.

**Bi-PC**

(1-Methylprop 2-yn yl-N-(m-chlorophenyl) carbamate)

Bi-PC is prepared by treating m-chloro-phenylisocyanate with methyl ethyl carbinol or methyl propenyl chlorocarbonate with m-chloroaniline in the presence of base.

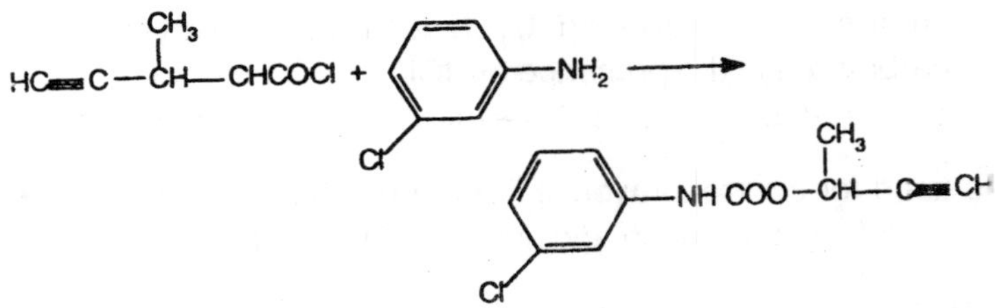

**Barban**

(4-chlorobut-2-yn yl-N-(m-chlorophenyl) carbamate)

It is prepared by reacting m-chlorophenyl isocyanate with butyndiol and thionyl chloride in the presence of pyridine

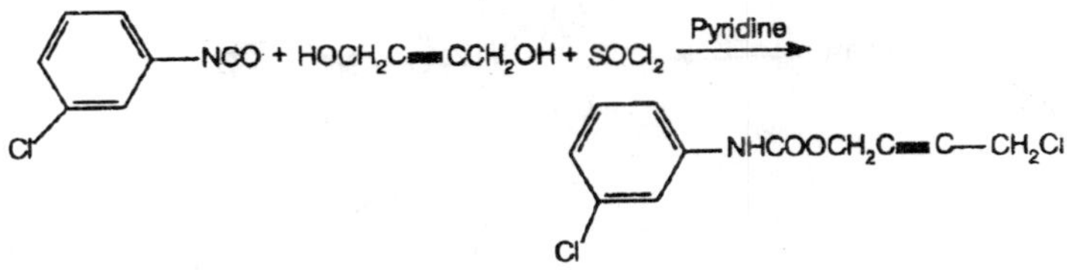

Barban is used to control wild oats.

## THIOCARBAMATES

This group of herbicides is characterised by the general formula

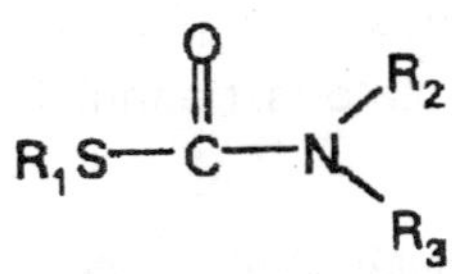

where $R_1$ is an alkyl, dichloro, trichloroalkyl or 4-chlorobenzyl group, $R_2$ and $R_3$ and the same or different alkyl, methyl cyclohexyl or azepino groups.

## Eptam

(S-ethyl N, N-di-n-propylthiocarbamate)

Eptam is produced by reacting dipropyl carbamoyl chloride with sodium ehtyl mercoptides.

$$(nC_3H_7)_2NCOCl + C_2H_5SH + NaOH \longrightarrow (nC_3H_7)_2N\overset{O}{\overset{||}{C}}SC_2H_5 + NaCl + H_2O$$

It can also be prepared by treating di-propyl amine with thiochlorocarbamate in the presence of HCl.

$$(n-C_3H_7)_2NH + C_2H_5\ SCOCl + NaOH \longrightarrow (n-C_3H_7)_2\ N\overset{||}{C}S\ C_2H_5 + NaCl + H_2O$$

It is used for control of weeds in potato, alfalfa, beans, carrot, corn, sugarbeet, sunflower, tobacco and number of vegetable crops.

## Benthiocarb

(S-(4-chlorobenzyl) dithiocarbamate)

Benthiocarb is prepared by the reaction of carbonyl sulfide with diethylamine and the condensation of the diethylthiocarbamic acid obtained with 4- chlorotoluene.

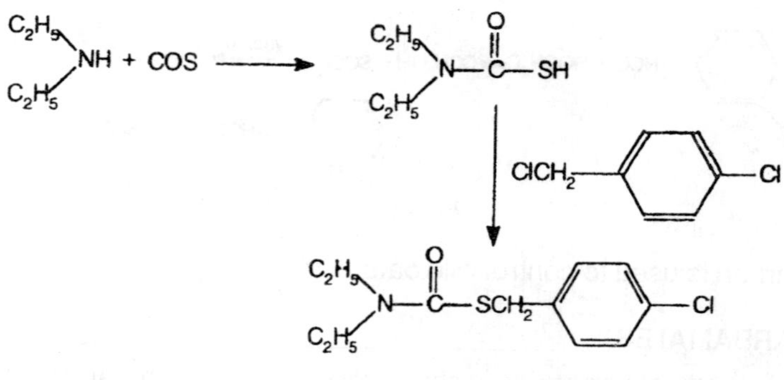

Benthiocarb is a selective herbicide in rice but is also used for weed control in cotton, soybean, potatoes, peanut, beet and beans.

## Diallate

(S-2-3,-dichloroallyl diisopropylthiocarbamate)

Diallate is prepared by treating disopropylamine, carbonyl sulfide and 1,2,3-trichloropropene in the presence of base.

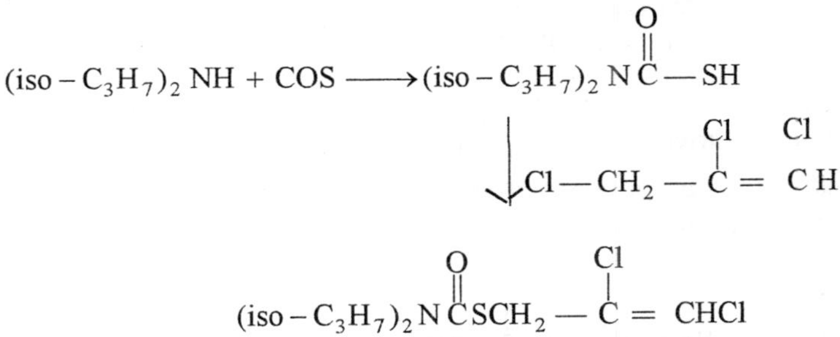

Diallate is used for the control of wild oat and block grass.

**Triallate**

(S-2,3,3-trichloroallyl diisopropyl thiocarbamate)

Triallate is prepared by treating diisopropylamine, carbonyl sulfide and 1,1,2,3-tetrachloroprop-1-ene in the presence of a base.

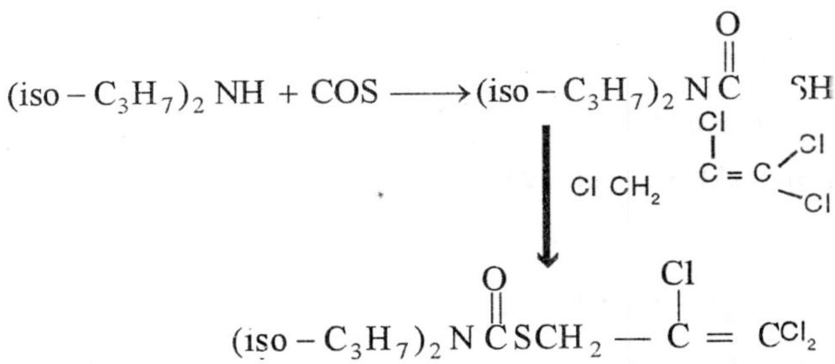

Triallate is selective in cereals, wheat and barley.

## DITHIOCARBAMATES

Dithiocarbamates are derivatives of dithiocarbamic acid

$$H_2N-\overset{\overset{\displaystyle S}{\|}}{C}-SH$$

**Metham-Sodium**

(Sodium-N-methyl dithiocarbamate)

Metham is prepared by treating methylamine, carbondisulphide and sodium hydroxide.

$$CH_3NH_2 + CS_2 + NaOH + H_2O \longrightarrow CH_3NH\overset{\overset{\displaystyle S}{\|}}{C}SNa + 2H_2O$$

During the decomposition of metham, methylisothiocyanate is formed and this exerts the biological action.

### Sulfallate

(2-chloroallyl diethyl dithiocarbamate)

Sulfallate is prepared by treating sodium diethyldithiocarbamate with 2,3-dichloropropene.

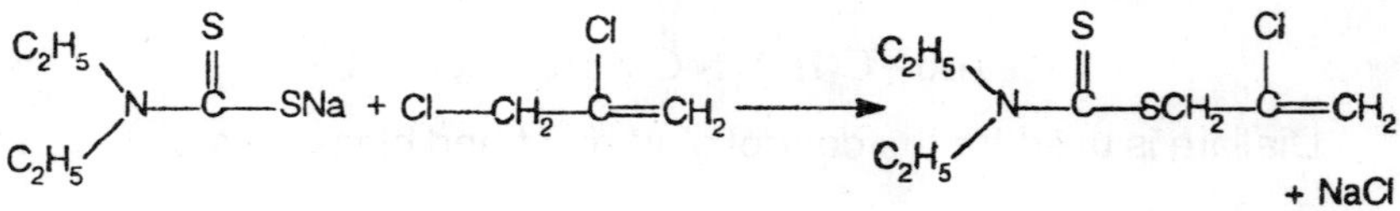

Sulfallate is used as a preemergence soil applied herbicide against grass weeds in vegetable crops such as brassica, celery, spinach, beans, corn and in ornamentals.

## AMIDES

### Allidochlor

(N,N-diallyl-2-chloroacetamide)

Allidochlor is prepared by the reaction of diallylamine and chloroacetyl chloride.

$$(CH_2 = CHCH_2)_2NH + ClCH_2COCl \xrightarrow{\text{base}} (CH_2 = CHCH_2)_2NCOCH_2Cl$$

Allidochlor inhibit the germination of grass weeds and growth of roots and shoots and is particularly effective against annual grasses in corn, sorghum, beans, sugarcane and ornamentals.

### Propachlor

(2-chloro-N-isopropylacetanilide)

Propachlor is prepared by treating N-isopropylaniline with chloroacetylchloride in the presence of sodium hydroxide.

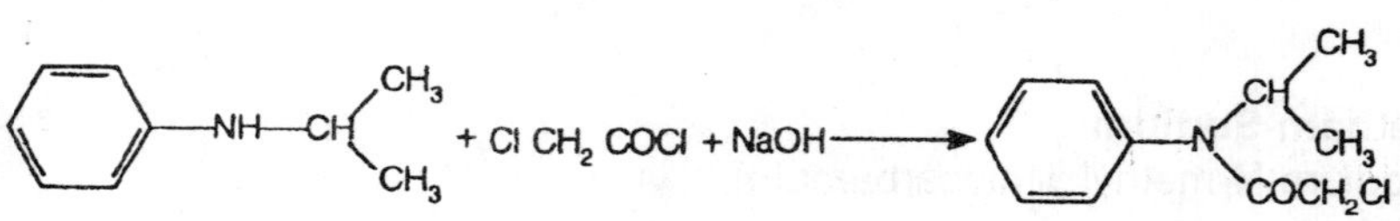

Propachlor is a preemergence selective herbicide effective against annual grass weeds and several broad-leaved weeds in maize, cotton, sugarcane, soybean and several vegetable crops. The acute oral $LD_{50}$ of propachlor to rats is 710 mg/kg.

## rynachlor

-chloro-N-(1-methyl-2-propynyl) acetanilide)

Prynachlor is prepared by treating butynyl chloride with aniline to give -(1-methyl-2-propynyl) aniline which is then reacted with chloroacetyl chloride give prynachlor.

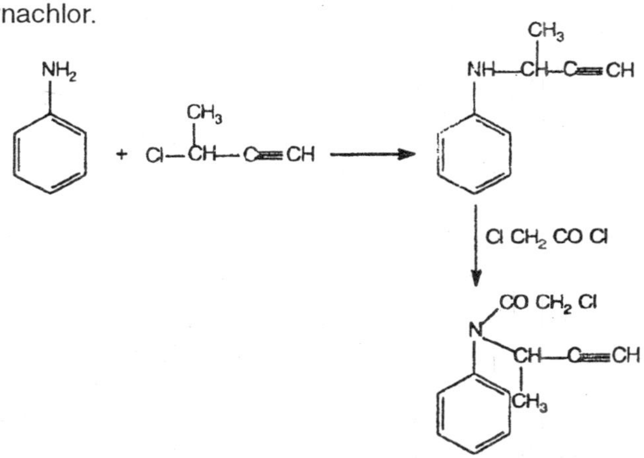

Prynachlor is a preemergence selective herbicide effective in maize ybean and onion against annual grass weeds and several broad leaved eeds.

## lachlor

-chloro-2'-6'-diethyl-N-methoxymethylacetanilide)

Alachlor is prepared from azomethine substituted at the phenyl groups reaction first with chloroacetyl chloride and then with methyl alcohol.

Alachlor is a selective preemergence soil herbicide and is effective gainst annual grass weeds and several broad leaved weeds in maize ybean, peanut, cotton and fruit trees.

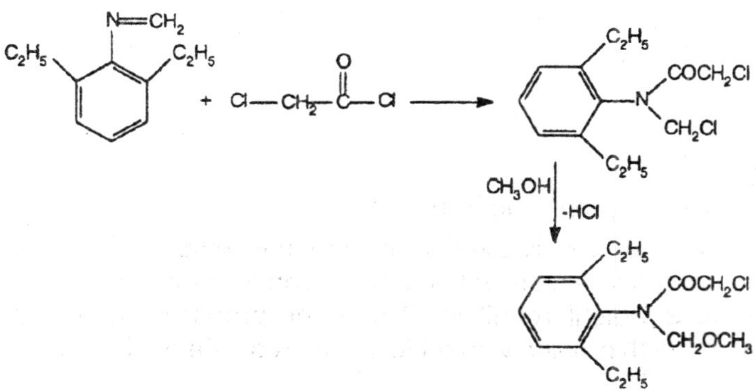

**Butachlor**

(2-chloro-2',6'-diethyl-N-butoxymethyl acetanilide)

Butachlor is prepared by treating azomethine first with chloroacetylchloride and then with butyl alcohol

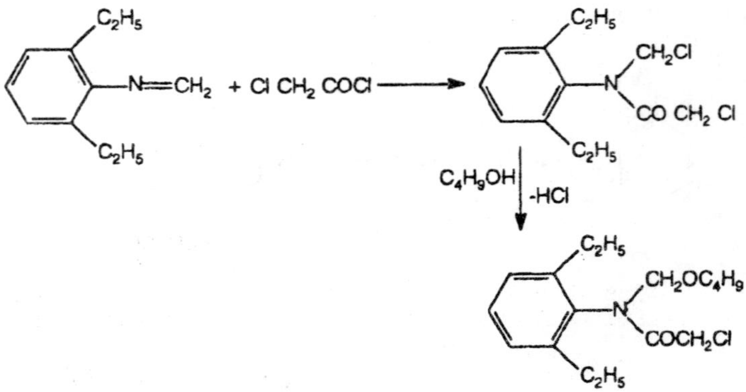

Butachlor controls most of the annual grasses and some broad leaved weeds in transplant and direct seed rice. It is applied as preemergence in EC formulations and as early post emergence in the form of granules. Its acute oral $LD_{50}$ for rats is 1740 mg/kg.

**Diphenamid**

(N,N-dimethyl-2,2-diphenyl acetamide)

Diphenamid is used as pre-emergence soil herbicide against annual grasses and certain broad leaved weeds. It is prepared by the condensation of sodium salt of diphenyl methane and dimethyl carbamoyl chloride.

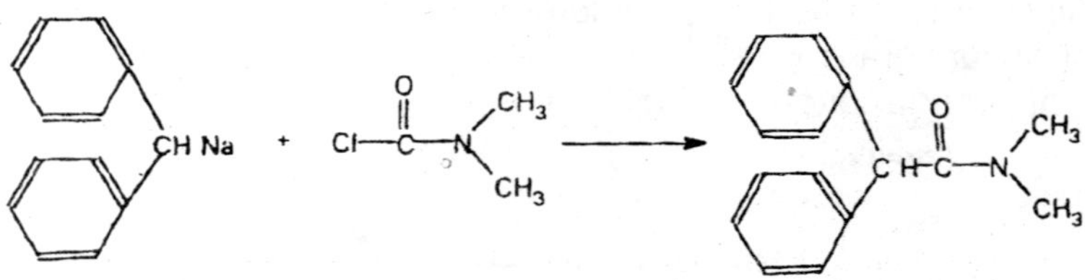

**Propanil**

(3'4'-dichlorophenyl propionanilide)

Propanil is extensively used for selective post-emergence weed control in rice fields. The rice is resistant because it can deactivate the chemical by hydrolysis to 3,4-dichloroaniline. It can be prepared by treating 3,4 dichloroaniline with propionly chloride in the presence of triethylamine.

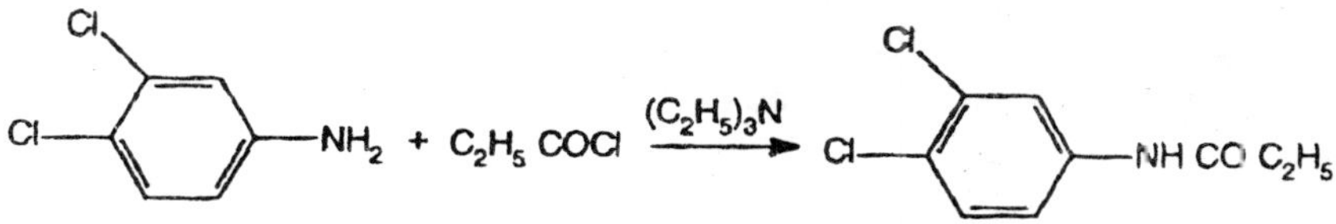

## BIPYRIDYLIUM HERBICIDE

### Paraquat

(1, 1, Dimethyl-4,4, dipyridybium chloride)

It is synthesied by treating 4,4'-dipyridyl with methyl chloride at high temperature and pressure.

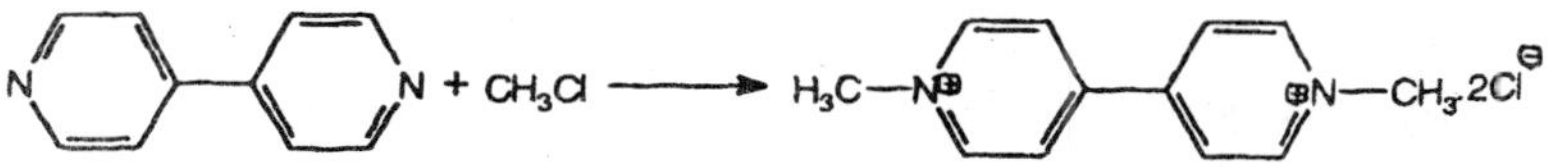

### Diquat

(1, 1, ethylene-2,3-dipyridybium bromide)

It is prepared by reacting 2,2' dipyridyl with 1,2, dibromoethane

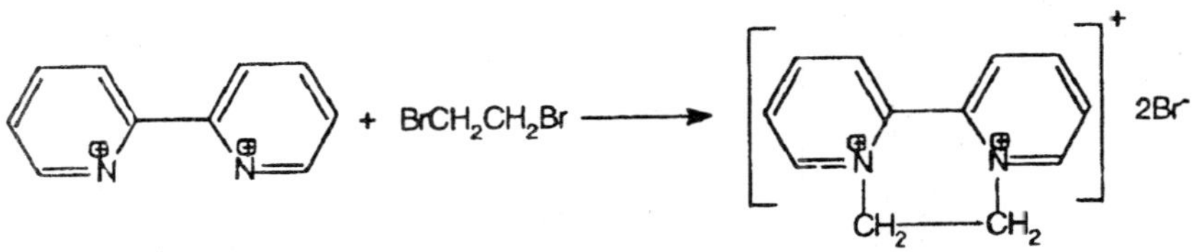

Diquat is used for general aquatic weed control as noncropweed killer and for defoliation. Paraquat is used for stubble cleaning and total weed control in non areas.

## DINITROPHENOLS

### DNOC

(2,4-Dinitro-6-methylphenol)

DNOC is produced by the direct nitration of o-cresol with a nitrating mixture at low temperature.

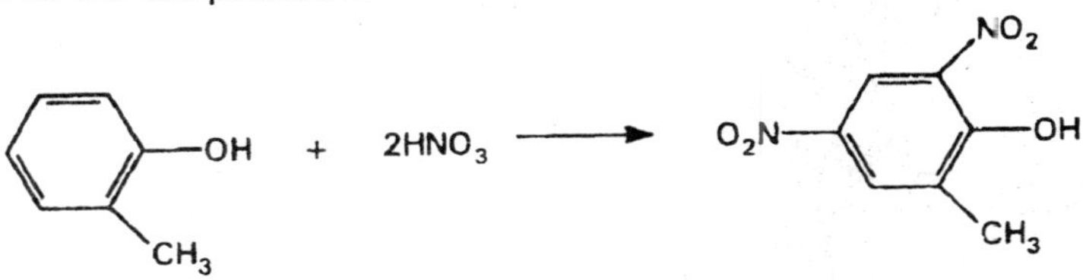

It is used for control of annual broad-leaf weeds in cereals, dessicant for potatoes and leguminous seed crops.

**Dinoseb**

(2,4-dinitro-6-sec-butyl phenol)

Dinoseb is prepared by direct nitration of 2-sec-butyl phenol with nitric acid in the presence of sulphuric acid.

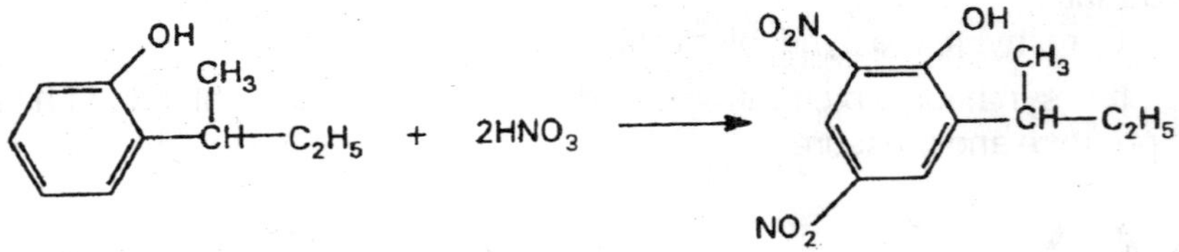


It is used for control of weeds in cereals, pea, alfalfa (post emergence), bean and potato (pre-emergence).

## TRIAZINES

The triazines are six membered ring compounds containing three heterocyclic nitrogens (the prefix tri means three and azine means nitrogen containing). The fundamental triazine nucleus is shown as

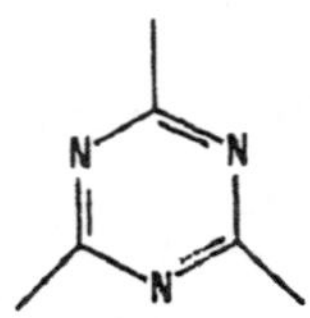


**Simazine**

(2-chloro-4,6-bis(ethyl amino)-s-triazine)

Simazine is widely used as a selective preemergence herbicide for the control of weeds in maize, sugarcane, coffee, tea, aquatic weeds and algae in ponds and at higher application rates as total herbicide on noncrop land. Simazine is prepared by reaction with cyanuric chloride with ethylamine and NaOH in aqueous medium or in organic solvents.

$$Cl_2 + NaCN \longrightarrow CNCl + NaCl$$

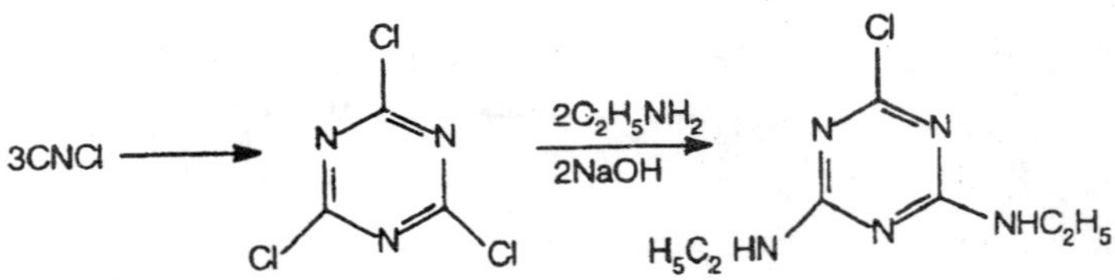

**Atrazine**

(2-chloro-4-(ethylamino)-6-(isopropylamino)-s-triazine)

Atrazine is a selective preemergence herbicide for the control of broad leaf weeds in maize, sorghum, sugarcane, pine apple, and orchards. It is also used as nonselective herbicide in non crop areas. It is prepared by treating cyanuric chloride with ethyl amine and NaOH which produces 2,4-dichloro-6-ethylamine-s-triazine and by further reaction with a molecule of isopropylamine and NaOH gives atrazine.

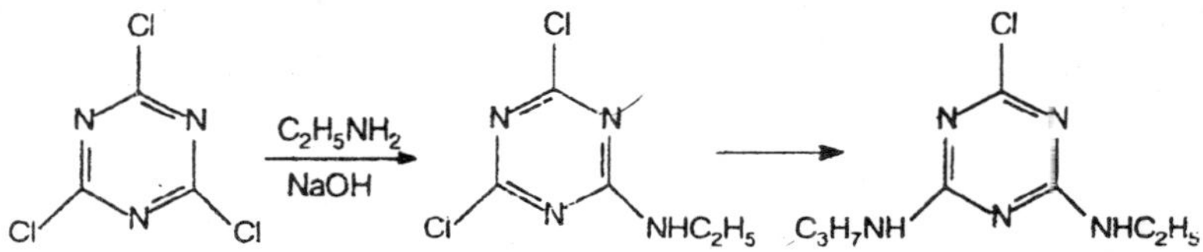

**Prometryne**

(2,4 bis (isopropylamine(-6-(methylthio)-s-triazine)

Prometryne is used for control of weeds in cotton. It is prepared by reacting 2-chloro-4,6-bis(isopropyl amino)-S-triazine with sodium mercaptide.

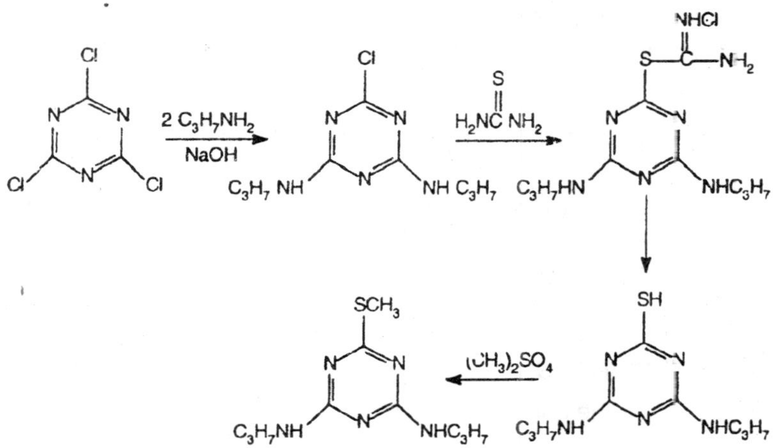

## ORGANOPHOSPHOROUS COMPOUND

A wide range of different types of organophosphoros compounds show some herbicide properties and the major groups are phosphorothiolates, phosphoroamidates and phosphonates.

## PHOSPHOROTHIOLATES

### Bensulide

(O,O-disopropyl-S-(2-phenyl sulfonylamino) ethyl phosphorodithioate)

Bensulide is prepared by the condensation of sodium O,O-diisopropylphosphorodithioate with N-(2-chloroethyl) benzene sulfonamide

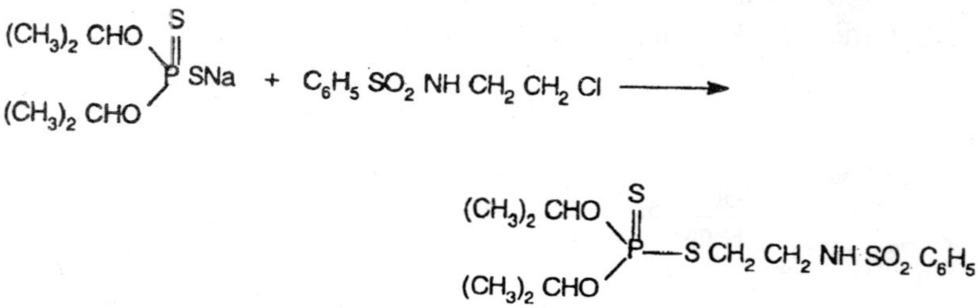

Bensulide is used as preplant and premergence herbicide on cotton, brassicos and lettuce.

## PHOSPHONATES

### Glyphosate

(N-phosphonomethyl glycine)

It is obtained from glycine and chloromethyl phosphonic acid.

$$(HO)_2\overset{O}{\overset{\|}{P}}CH_2Cl + NH_2CH_2COOH \xrightarrow{OH} (HO)_2P\overset{O}{\overset{\|}{C}}H_2NHCH_2COOH$$

Glyphosate is a non selective pre-emergence herbicide. It is very effective on deep rooted perennial species, and annual and biennial species of grasses and broad leaved weeds. The acute oral $LD_{50}$ for rats is 4320 mg/kg.

## SUBSTITUTED UREAS

Ureas have the following structure

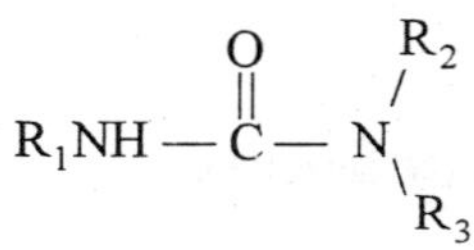

In this $F_1$ represents a non-halogenated or halogenated aromatic hydrocarbon moiety while $R_2$ and $R_3$ represent alkyl groups.

### Monuron

(N,N-dimethyl N'(p-chlorophenyl) urea)

Monuron the first urea herbicide developed for commercial use, introduced as a pre-emergence, broad spectrum herbicide for control of all weeds in non-crop land areas. When applied at low rates, monuron show selectivity for use in cotton, sugarcane, pineapple and citrus. It is prepared by follow :

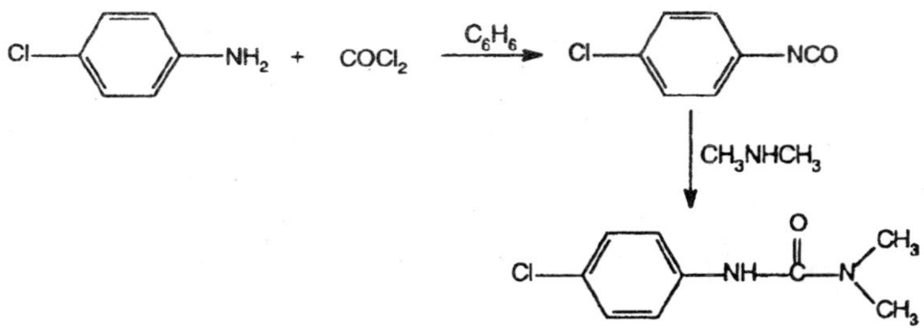


### Linuron

(3(3,4-dichlorophenyl)-1-methoxy-1-methyl urea)

It is prepared as follows :

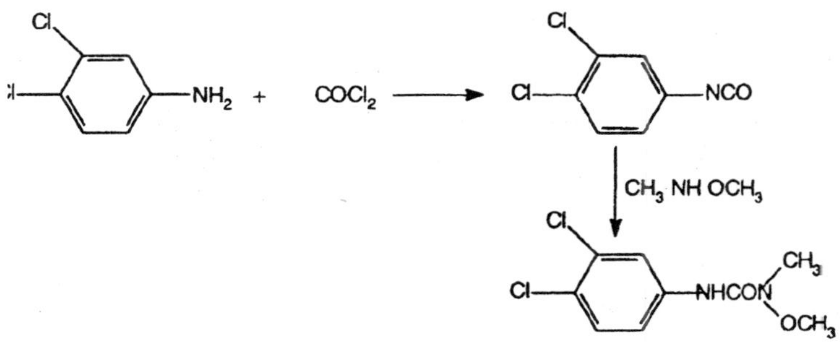


It is used as pre-emergence for selective control of germinating and newly established broadleaf weeds and grasses in soybean, cotton, corn, sorghum, wheat and potato.

### Diuron

(3(3,4-dichlorophenyl) 1,1-dimethyl urea)

It is preemergence selective herbicide for controlling emerging grass and broadleaf weed seedlings in cotton, tea, coffee, grapes, apples, pears and citrus etc. It is prepared as:

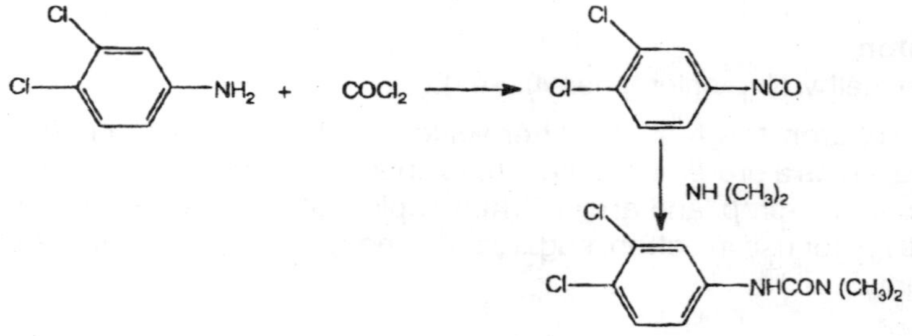

**Neburon**

(N-Butyl N'-(3,4-dichlorophenyl) N-methyl urea)

It is used as selective root absorbed herbicide for control of annua broad leaf and grass weeds. It is prepared as follows :

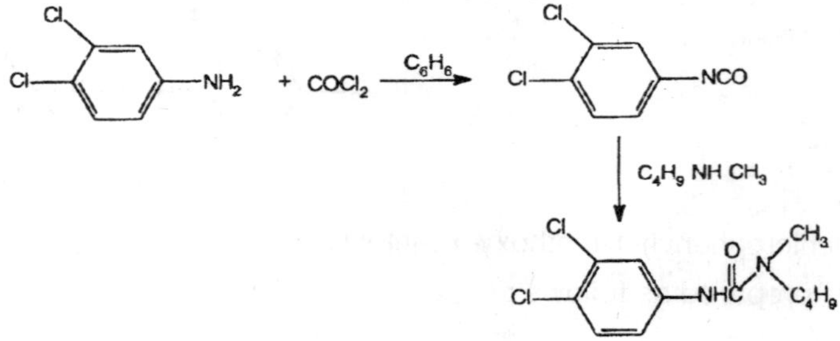

**Trimeturon**

(N-(4-chlorophenyl) O,N,3-trimethylisourea)

Timeturon is prepared by chlorinating phenyl isocyanate in chloroform to give p-chlorophenyl carbonim idoyl dichloride, which is reacted with dimethylamine to give p-chlorophenylimino chlorocarbonic acid dimethy amide. This is treated with sodium methoxide solution in benzene to yield trimeturon.

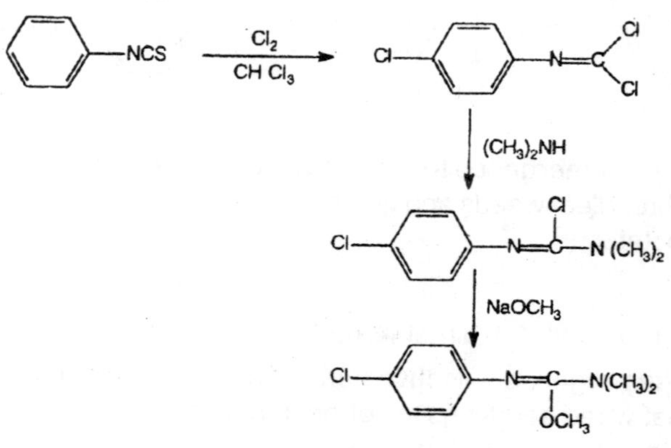

### Meturin

(1-phenyl-1-hydroxy-3-methyl urea)

Meturin is prepared by reaction of phenylhydroxylamine with methyl isocyanate.

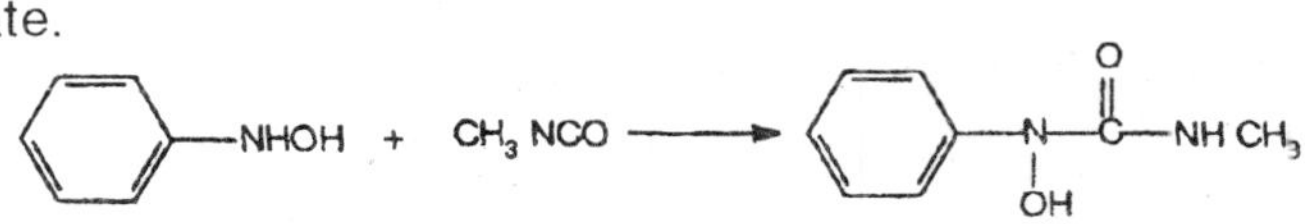


Meturin is used as a pre-emergence herbicide for the control of annual weeds in cotton and potatoes. Its acute oral $LD_{50}$ for rats is 5000 mg/kg.

### Dichloral urea

(N,N-di-(2,2,2-trichloro-1-hydroxyethyl) urea)

Dichlorol urea is prepared by the condensation of chloral and urea in the presence of HCl

$$2CCl_3CHO + NH_2CONH_2 \longrightarrow CCl_3-\underset{\displaystyle OH}{\underset{|}{C}}H-NH-\underset{\displaystyle O}{\underset{||}{C}}-NH-\underset{\displaystyle OH}{\underset{|}{C}}H-CCl_3$$

Dichloral urea is a soil herbicide for pre-emergence treatment in sugar beet, cotton, potato and carrots.

### Cycluron

(3-cyclooctyl-1,1 dimethyl urea)

Cycluron is prepared by treating cyclooctyl isocyanate with dimethyl amine.

Cycluron is used for pre-emergence weed control in sugar beet and spinach.

### Noruron

(3-(hexahydro-4,7-methanoindan-5-yl) 1,1-dimethyl urea)

Noruron is prepared by the condensation of tetrahydrodicyclopentadienyl isocyanate with dimethylamine

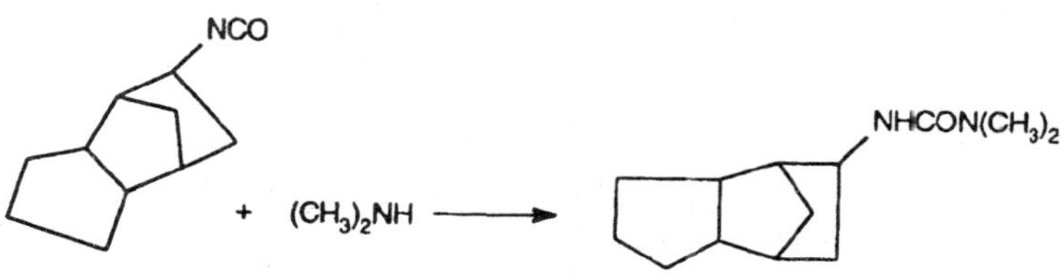

Noruron is a selective pre-emergence herbicide on cotton, sugarcane soybeans and potato.

### Monolinuron

(3-(4-chlorophenyl)-1-methoxy-1-methyl urea)

Monolinuron is prepared by treating aryl isocyanate and hydroxylamine to give 3-aryl-11-hydroxy urea, which is then treated with dimethyl sulphate.

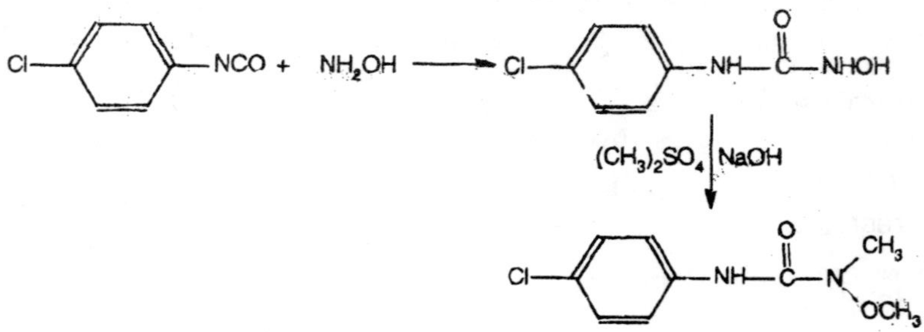

It is used as a pre emergence herbicide for the control of weeds in potatoes, medicinal plants, vineyards and orchards. Its acute oral $LD_{50}$ for rats is 2250 mg/kg.

### Isoproturon

(3,(4-isopropylphenyl) 1,1-dimethyl urea)

Isoproturon is prepared as :

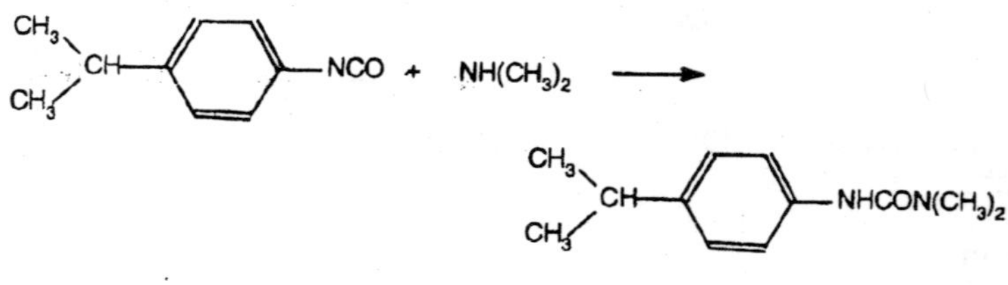

Isoproturon is used to control annual grass weeds in wheat, rye and barley. The acute oral $LD_{50}$ for rats in 2000 to 3600 mg/kg,

## DINTROANILINES

### Nitralin

(2,6-dinitro 4-methyl sulphonyl N, N-dipropylaniline)

Nitraline is prepared by nitration of 4-chlorophenyl methyl sulphone and coupling of 4-chloro-3,5-dinitrophenyl methyl sulfone obtained with dipropylamine.

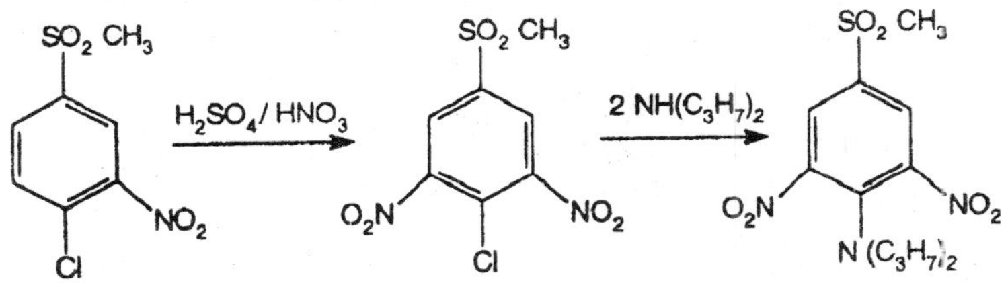


**Dipropalin**

(N,N-di-n-propyl-2,6-dinitro-4-methyl aniline)

Dipropalin is prepared by converting p-cresol; into dinitrocresol which is then treated with thionyl chloride. The 4-chloro-3,5-dinitrotoluene so obtained is reacted with di-n-propylamine to give dipropalin.

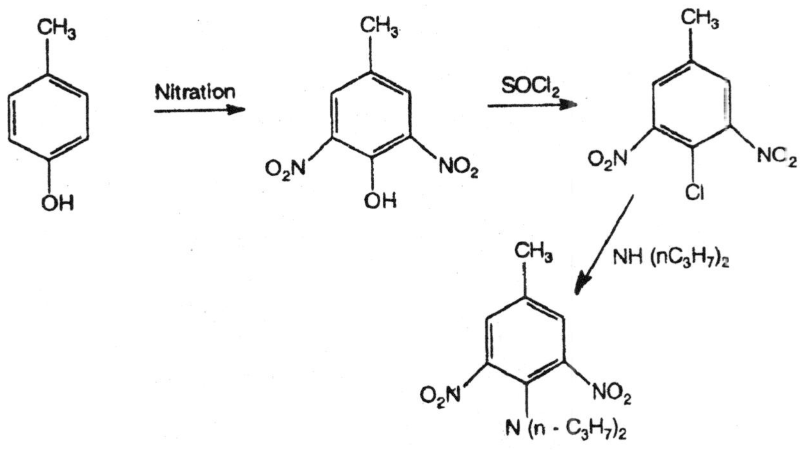


**Butralin**

(N-sec-butyl-4-t-butyl 2, 6-dinitroaniline)

Butralin is prepared by nitration of 4-t-butylphenol with a mixture of nitric acid and sulphuric acid to give 4-t-butyl-2,6-dinitrophenol. The dinitrophenol is reacted with phophorous oxychloride to give 1-t-butyl-4-chloro-2-dinitrobenzene. The reaction of the later with sec-butylamine give butralin.

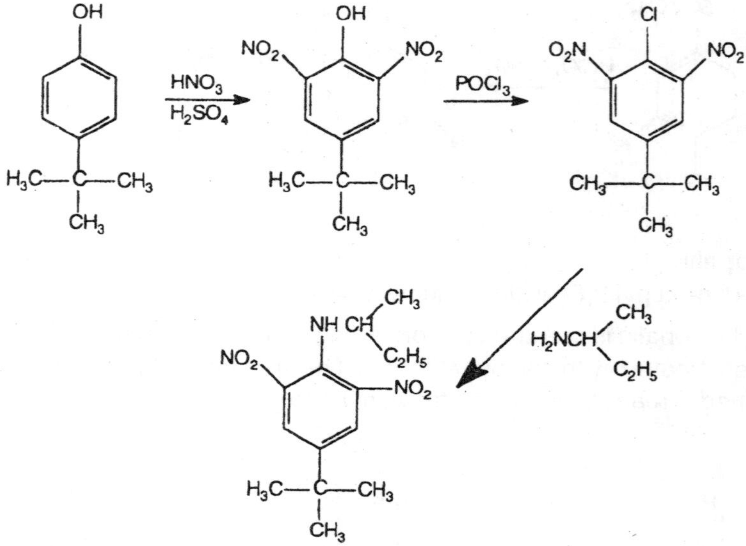

**Chlorinidin**

(N,N-bis(2-chloroethyl)-4-methyl-2,6-dinitroaniline)

Chlorinidin is prepared by treating 4-chloro-3,5-dinitro toluene with diethanolamine and the resulting compound is treated with thionyl chloride.

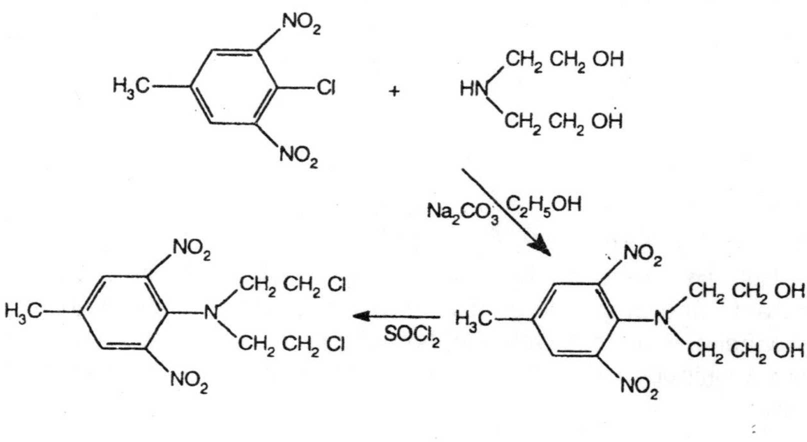

## Isopropalin

(4-isopropyl-2,6-dinitro-N,N-dipropylaniline)

Isopropalin is prepared by nitration of cumene to give 2,4-dinitrocumene which is then converted with phosphorous oxychloride into 1-chloro-2,6-dinitro-4-isopropylbenzene, the later giving isopropalin with di-n-propylamine. The later giving isopropalin with di-n-propylamine.

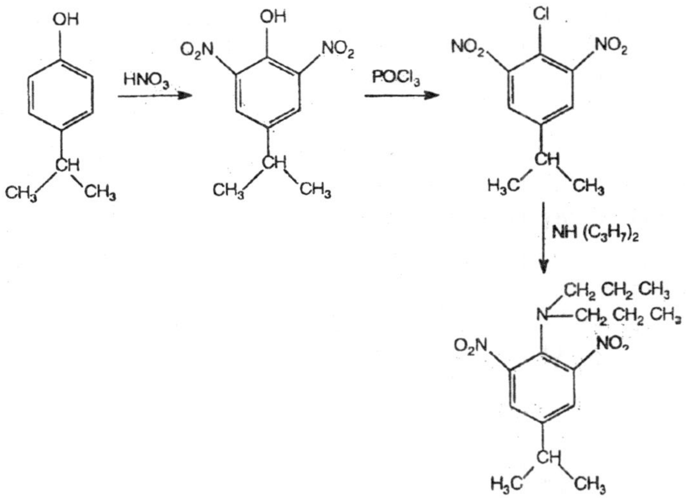


## Fluchloralin

(N-2-chloroethyl)-N-propyl-2,6-dinitro-4-trifluoromethylamine)

Fluchloralin is used as pre planting herbicide against annual grasses and broad leaf weeds in cotton and soybean.

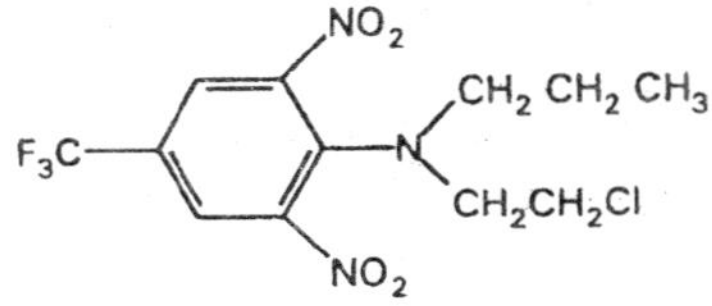


## Pendimethalin

(Stomp, N-(1-ethyl propyl) 3,4-dimethyl-2,6-dinitro aniline)

Pendemethalin is the first N-monoalkyl 2,6-dinitroaniline and is mainly used for control of grasses in maize, cereals, rice, cotton and soybeans. Its $LD_{50}$ value to rats is 1050 mg/kg.

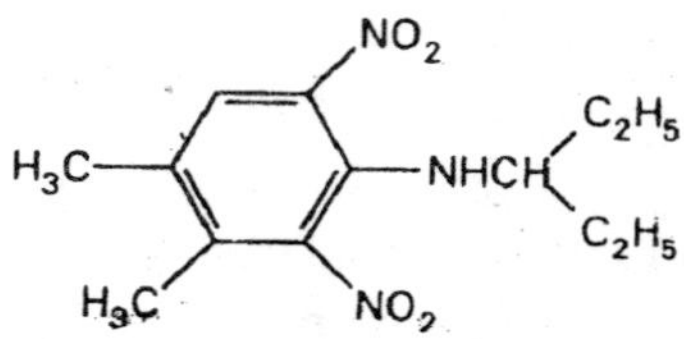


The main uses of dinotroaniline herbicides is the control of annual grass weeds. Some annual dicotyledonous weeds are also sensitive to dintroaniline herbicides. All herbicides of this group are fairly volatile and hence are sprayed to moist soil surface.

## PYRIDINES

### Pyrichlor

(2,3,5-trichloro-4-pyridinol)

Pyrichlor is prepared by the alkaline saponification of 2,3,4,5-tetrachloropyridine

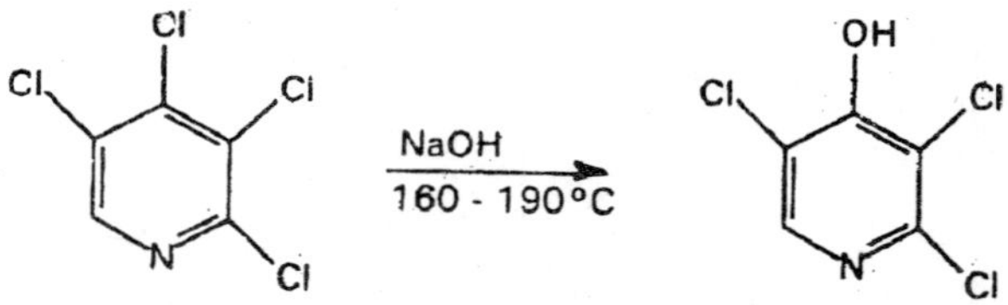


Pyrichlor is used as preemergence herbicide for the control of annual grass weeds and broad leaved weeds. It is also used for selective weed control in sugar cane, banana and rubber plantations.

Other important herbicide of the pyridine groups are:

— Picloram (4-amino-3,5,6-trichloropicolinic acid)

— Trichlopyr (3,5,6-trichloro-2-pyridinyloxyacetic acid)

— DPA (3,6-dichloropicolinic acid)

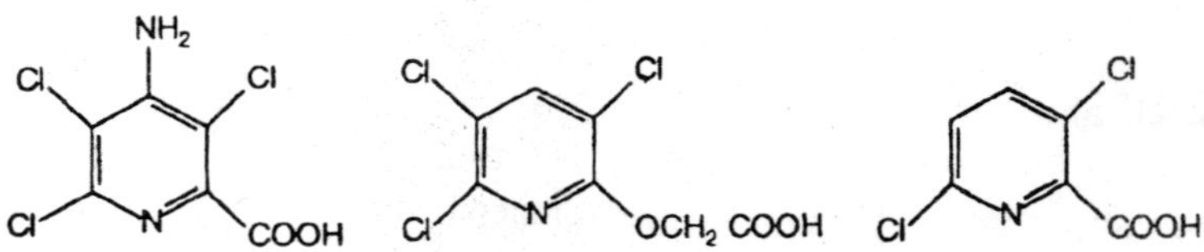


Picloram Triclopyr DPA

## AZOLES

### Amitrole

(3-amino-1,2,4-triazole)

Amitrole is prepared by condensation of aminoguanidine and formic acid.

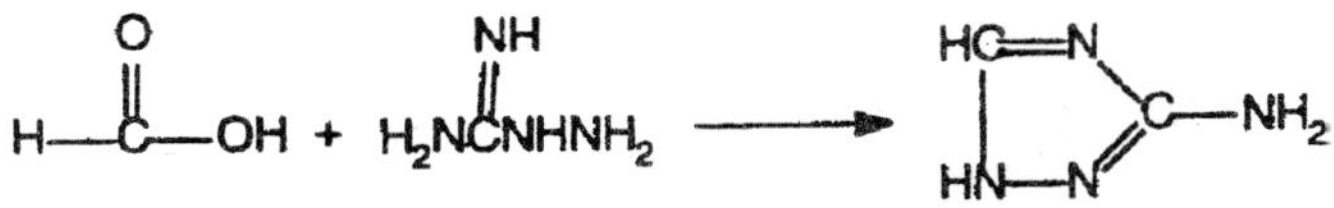

Amitrole is a non-selective herbicide and is used for control of deep rooted weeds.

### Methazole

(2-(3,4-dichlorophenyl)-4-methyl-1,2,4-oxadiAzolidine-3,5-dicne)

Methazole is prepared by the reaction of N-(3,4-dichlorophenyl)-hydroxylamine with methyl isocyanate to give 1-(3,4-dichlorophenyl)-1-hydroxy-3-methyl urea which is cyclised with methyl chloroformate to give methazole

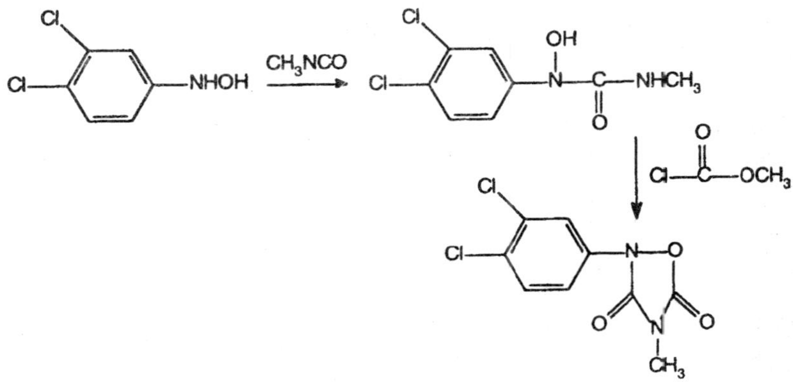

Methazole is a selective herbicide and can be used for control of certain grasses and many broad leaved weeds.

### Oxadiazon

(5-t-butyl-3-(2,4-dichloro-5-isopropoxyphenyl)1,3,4-oxadiazol-2-one)

Oxadiazon is obtaioned by condensing trimethyl acetylchloride with 2,4-dichloro-5-isopropoxyphenyl hydrazine and the product is cyclised with phosgene to give oxadiazon.

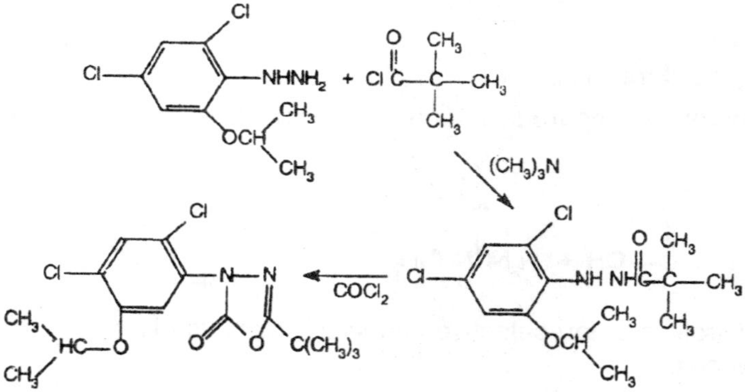

Oxadiazon is selective herbicide, effective against mono- and dicotylednous weeds in rice, orchards and vine yards. The acute oral $LD_{50}$ for rat is 8000 mg/kg.

## SULFONYL UREA HERBICIDES

Sulfonylurea herbicides are new group of selective herbicides and are used for the control of broad-leaved weeds. These herbicides are applied at very low dosage of 10—40 g $ha^{-1}$. Important sulfonyl urea herbicides are :

— chloruslfuron (1-(2-chlorophenylsulfonyl)-3-(4-methoxy-6-methyl-1,3,5-triazin-2-yl) urea

— metasulfuron-methyl 2-(3-(4-methoxy-6 methyl-1,3,5-triazin-2-yl) ureido sulfonyl) benzoate)

— sulfometuron (2-[3-(4-dimethyl-1,3-pyrimidin-2-yl)-ureidosulfonyl]-benzoate)

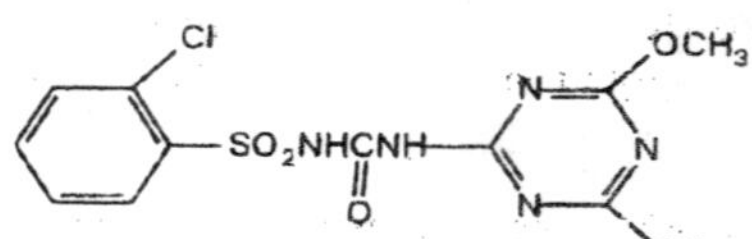

Chlorsulfuron

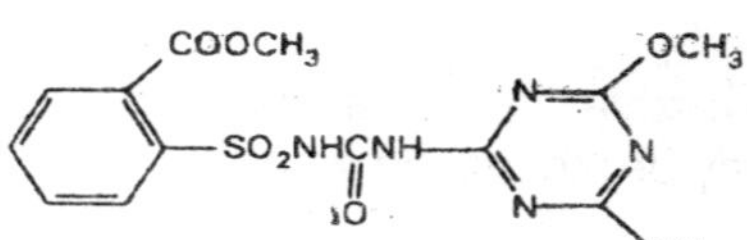

Metsulfuron -- methyl

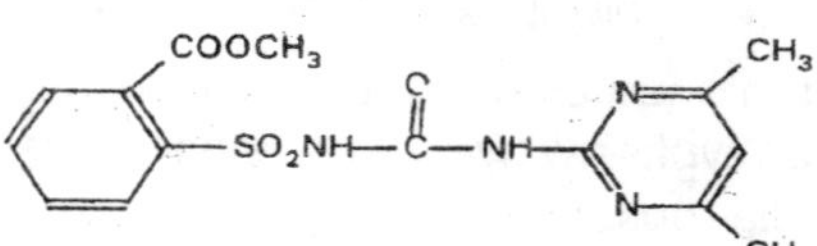

Sulfometuron

The high activity of the sulfonyl urea herbicides suggests that they act by a very specific biochemical mode of action. The herbicidal action of sulfonyl urea arises from inhibition of cell division, because this was demonstrated to be most sensitive process. Genetic and biochemical studies indicated that sulfonyl ureas inhibit the action of enzymes acetolactate synthase (ALS) which catalyses the first stage in the biosynthesis of the essential amino acids valine and isoleucine. The primary biochemical target of the sulfonyl urea herbicides is therefore concluded to be enzyme ALS. The proposed biochemical mode of action is supported by the studies that showed that the addition of amino acids valine and isoleucine completely reversed the herbicidal action of sulfonyl ureas towards sensitive plants.

## IMDAZOLINONES

The imidazolinones represent a new class of herbicide developed by the American Cyanamid Company in 1983 for control of mono and dicotyledonous weeds. The imidazolinones have a primary role in weed control in many crops. Imazaquin is widely used to control many broad leaved weeds in soybeans. Imazethapyr is also highly effective herbicide for difficult control grass and broad leaved weeds in soybean as well as other legumes including beans, alfalfa and peanuts. Imazamethabenz-methyl is used to kill lusters and deciduous trees.

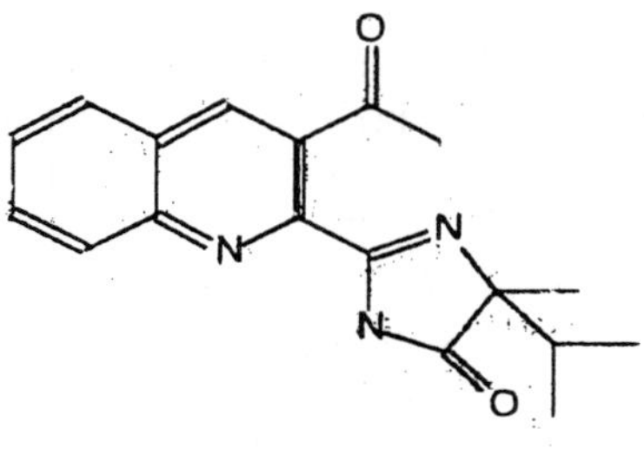

Imazaquin

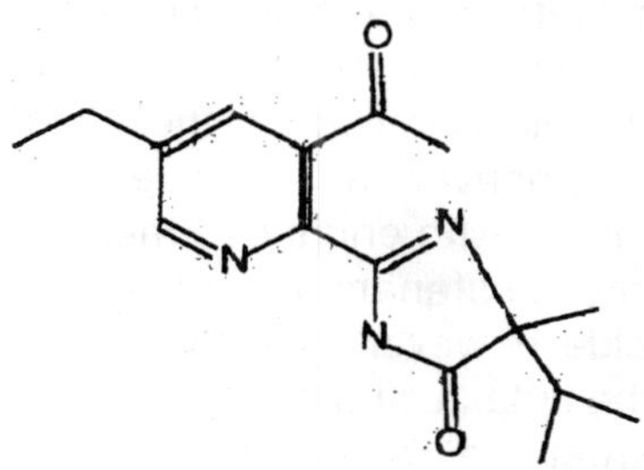

Imazethapyr

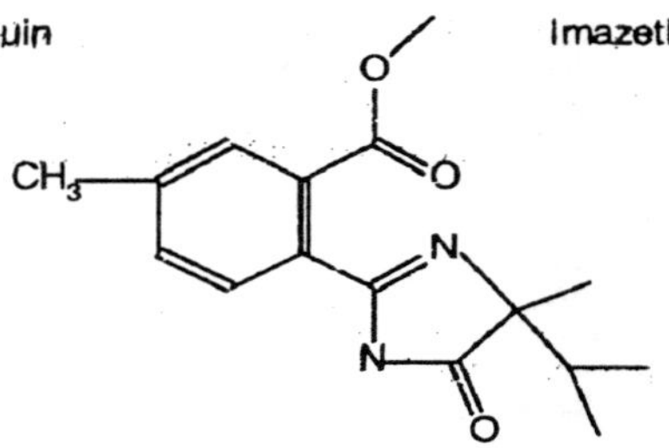

Imazamethabenz-methyl

## HERBICIDE EXTENDERS

There is an increasing interest in compounds that protect crops from the action of herbicides that would otherwise be toxic to them. These compounds have been termed 'safeners', protectants or with semantic accuracy 'antidotes'. They are used to treat the crops, before or along with the herbicide application. Compounds like diallyl dichloroacetamide, used in combination with EPTC, and cyometrinile, (dichlonaid). applied to sorghum seed to protect it from chloroacetamide herbicide injury. Napthalic anhydride and phathalic anhydride protected crops like sorghum and rice from injury by chlorosulfuron are already instituted and others are at various stages of development.

The introduction of crop safeners for herbicide have opened a new era in chemical weed control. They permit chemicals to be safely applied in higher doses and may allow the use of more potent herbicides, so giving a wider spectrum of weed control. To date, there has been little success in discovery of safener to protect crops against damage caused by photosynthesis inhibiting herbicides, paraquat or glyphosate. The majority of safeners are effective against soil herbicides especially thiocarbamates and chloroacetanilides.

The precise knowledge of mode of action of safeners remains incomlplete, however the dichloroacetanilides owe their specific safening action towards thiocarbamates and dichloroacetamides to their structural and chemical similarity to these herbicides. The mode of action of safeners with sulphonylurea herbicides in wheat and maize also appears to be associated with enhanced metabolism to herbicidal active products. The majority of safeners appear to act by increasing the rate of metabolism of herbicide, however other possible mechanisms of action include interference with the uptake and translocation of the herbicide or effecting sensitivity of the target site.

# 11

# Plant Growth Regulators

Plant growth regulators are chemicals used for causing acceleration or retardation of the rate of growth or rate of maturation of the plants and are legally considered as pesticides. Hormones are natural substances produced by the plants that control growth, initiate flowering, cause blossoms to fall, set fruit, cause fruit and leaves to fall, control initiation and termination of dormancy and stimulate root development. The plant growth regulators are classified into following groups:

1. auxins
2. gibberelins
3. cytokinins,
4. inhibitors and retardants
5. ethylene generators.

## AUXINS

Auxins are compounds that include elongation in shoot cells. The only naturally occurring auxin is indole acetic acid which probably occurs in all plant tissues. Important examples of auxins are :

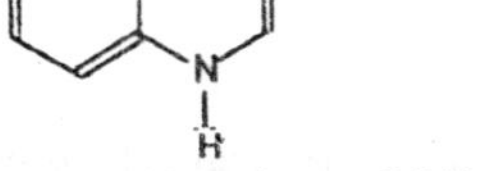

Indole acetic acid

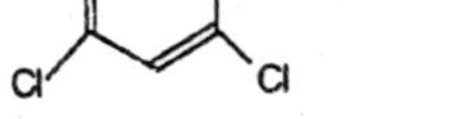

2,4-Dichlorophenoxy acetic acid

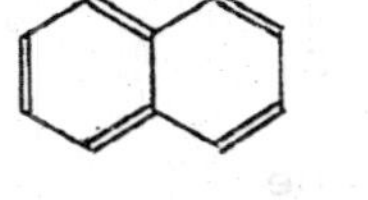

1-Naphthyl acetic acid

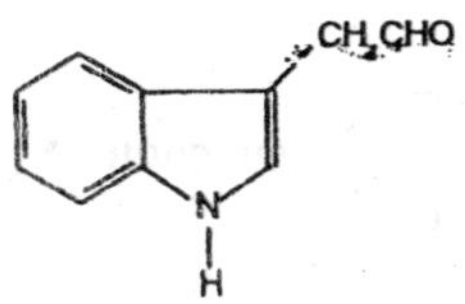

Indole acetaldehyde

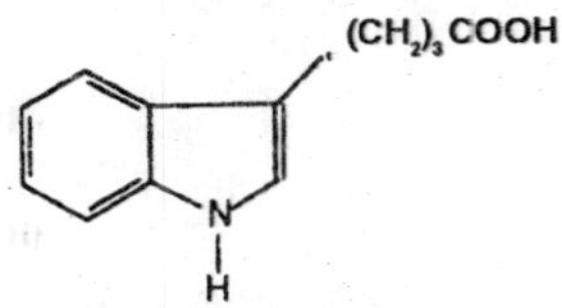

3-Indole butyric acid

## SYNTHETIC GROWTH INHIBITORS

### Maleic hydrazide

It was the first synthetic plant growth regulator and it is used as a stunting agent to reduce rate of growth of grapes and some weeds on ranches to support root and sucker growth on tomatoes, tobacco and certain trees and to prevent sprouting of potatoes and onions in storage. Maleic hydrazide is prepared by maleic anhydride and hydrazine

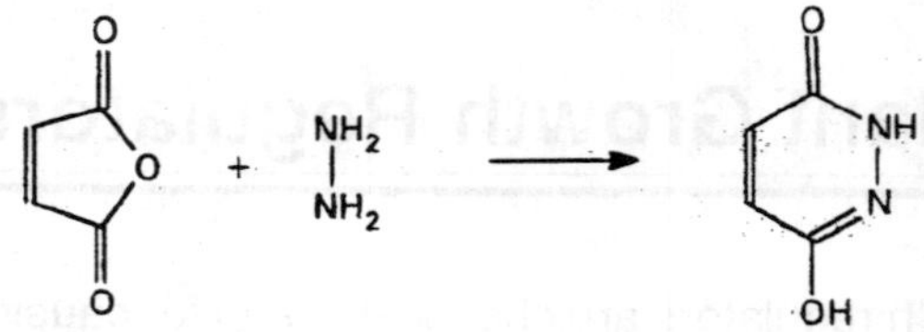


### Chlormequat

Chlormequat reduced stem length and lodging and produces compact plants with reduced internodes. It is used commercially in fruit trees and for reducing the height of cereals. It is prepared by treating ethylene chloride and trimethyl amine

$$ClCH_2CH_2Cl + N(CH_3)_3 \longrightarrow ClCH_2CH_2N^+(CH_3)_3Cl$$

### Daminozide

Daminozide is used to control the growth of fruit trees and shape and height of ornamentals. Daminozide is prepared by reaction of succinic anhydride and N,N-dimethyl hydrazine.

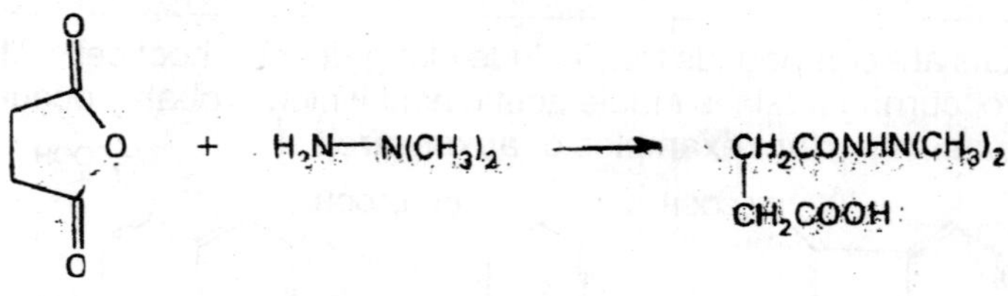


### Glyphosine

Glyphosine is used to increase the yield of sugar and hasten ripening

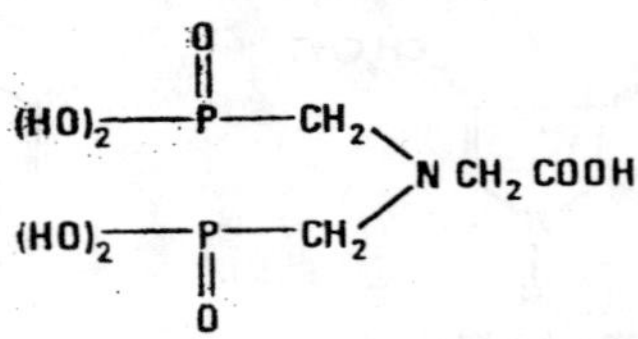

## GIBBERELLINS

Gibberellins are compounds that stimulate cell division or cell elongation and have a gibbane skeleton. Gibberellic acid was isolated from fungus Gibberella fujikuroi. Gibberellins were found to be natural constituents in all plants. More than 33 gibberellins have been isolated and are identified as GA1, GA2 etc. The gibberellic acid is the commonly used as GA3. The use of gibberellins are :

1. increase stalk length
2. yields of celery
3. to break down dormancy of potatoes seed
4. to delay fruit maturity
5. to improve fruit quality

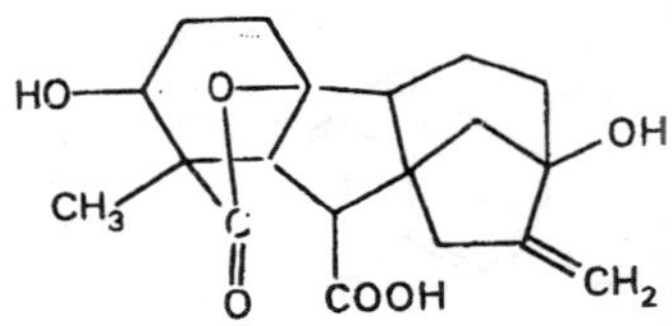


Gibberelic acid

## CYTOKININS

Cytokinin are compounds that induce cell division in plant and are used for prolonging the storage life of green vegetables, cut flowers, and mushrooms.

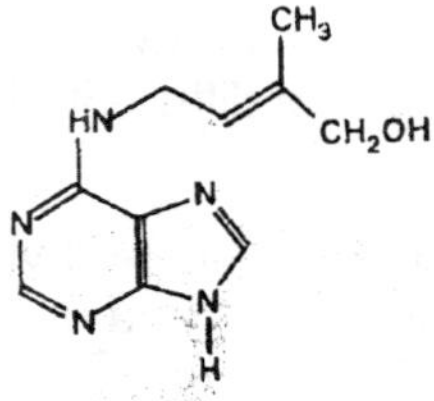


Zeatin

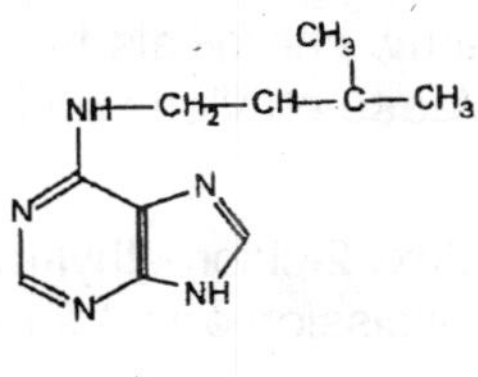


6 - isopentyl amino purine

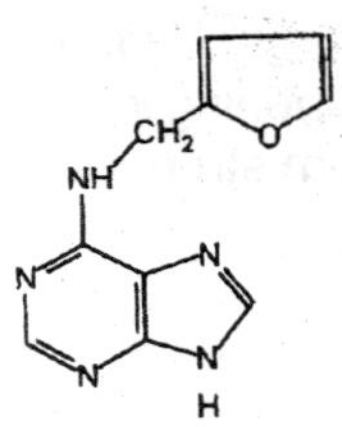


6- Furfuryl amino purine
Kinetin

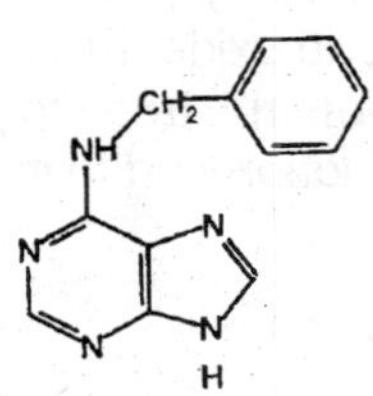


6 - benzyl amino purine

## INHIBITORS AND RETARDANTS

These are group of substances that inhibit a physiological process in plants. The use of inhibitors are :

1. They prevent sprouting of stored onions, potatoes and other root crops.
2. They induce shortening of stems
3. They prevent lodging of grain and
4. They permit controlled growth of flower crops and ornaments.

Natural growth inhibitors exist in cotton, sycamore and yellow lupin. The cotton growth inhibitor abscisic acid also occurs in other plants.

Abscisic acid is a natural growth regulator one used to induce dormancy in cotton leaves, plum twigs and reduced germination in rose tips.

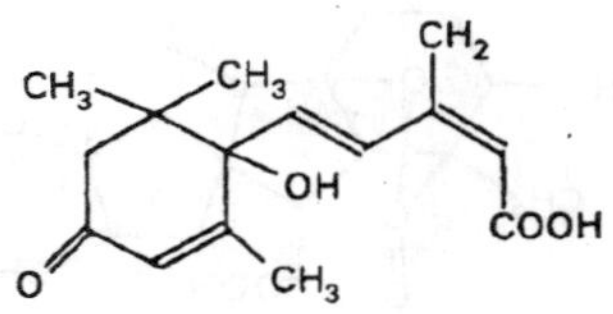


Abscisic acid

## ETHYLENE GENERATORS

Ethylene can inhibit growth, accelerate leaf and flower drop (abscission), the ripening of fruit and flowering depending upon the stage on which it is applied. Recently, chemicals have been developed which when sprayed onto plants release ethylene and hence control different phases of plants development.

Bisbenzoloxy 2-chloroethyl-methylsilane produces ethylene and is used as chemical abscission agent for apples, peaches and oranges and other fruits.

Ethepon (2-chloroethyl phosphonic acid) is prepared from phosphorous trichloride and ethylene oxide. Ethepon generates ethylene in solutions with pH > 4. It is sprayed on fruit trees to promote ripening in rubber plantation to stimulate latex production and to improve stem strength in cereals.

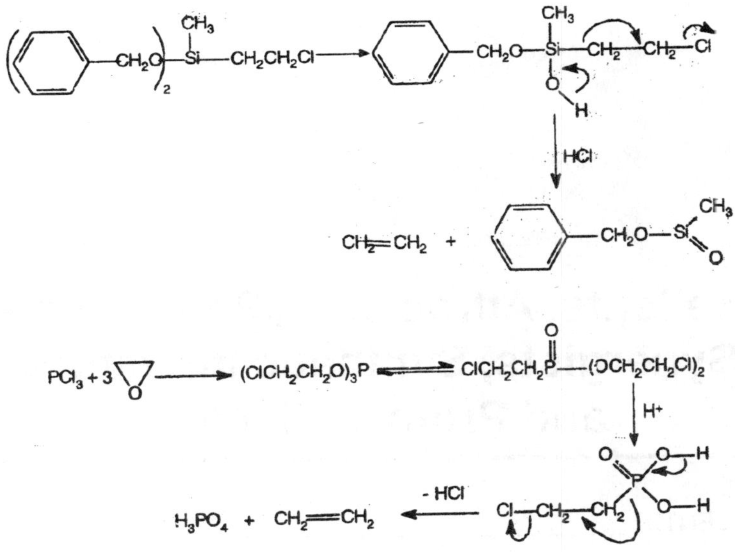

The plant growth regulator (PGR) market is currently dominated by six chemicals chlormequat, daminozide, maleic hydrazide, ethephon, gibberellic acid and glyphosine and it is estimated that one million hectares of crops are annually treated with PGRs. Little is known about mode of action of many PGRs and a better understanding of the mechanism of the structure activity relationships should permit introduction of more effective compounds.

# 12

# Repellents, Attractants, Pheromones, Synergists, Synthetic Inhibitors and Proinsecticides

## REPELLENTS

Repellents are chemicals which cause insects to make oriented movements away from its source. The first chemical repellent was discovered soon after man became acquainted with fire. When he found that fire was a fairly efficient method of repelling insects. Plant extracts of citronella, which is extracted from *Andropogm nardus* (L.), which contains gerniol, cintronellol, cintronellal, borneol, and terpenes are considered to be the principal mosquito repellents. Now more effective, synthetic repellents are in use.

### Dimethyl Phthalate

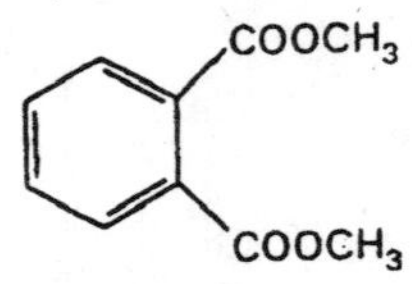


Dimethylphthalate is used as effective mosquito repellent. The disadvantage of this repellent is that it causes irritation to the eyes and mucous membranes. Its $LD_{50}$ value is 8200 mg/kg.

### N,N-Diethyl-m-toluamide (Deet)

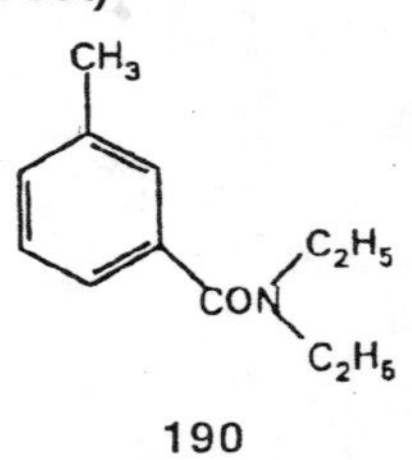

Deet is used as repellent for various insects particularly to mosquitoes. Its $LD_{50}$ value is 200 mg/kg.

**Benzyl Benzoate**

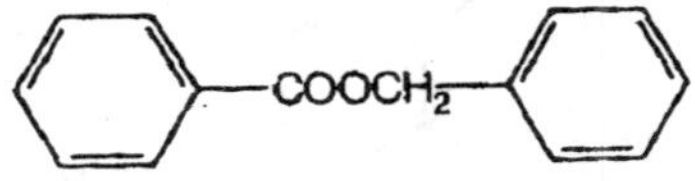

Benzyl benzoate is used as repellent for clothing treatment against chiggers and mites. Its $LD_{50}$ value is 7900 mg/kg.

**Butoxypolyproplene Glycol**

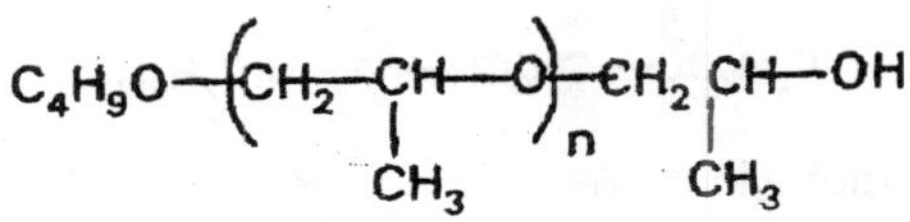

Butoxypolyproplene glycol is used as repellent for flies against cattle.

**1,5a, 6, 9, 9a, 9b-hexahydro-4a (4H) dibenzofuran-carboxaldehyde (MGK, Repellent 11)**

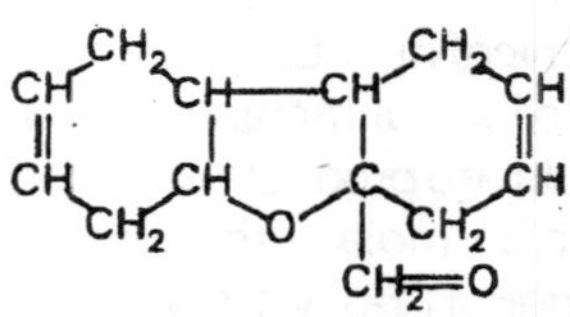

MGK repellent used as repellent for cockroaches and for biting flies on cattle. Its $LD_{50}$ value is 2500 mg/kg.

**2-Ethyl-1,3-hexanediol (Rutgers 612)**

$$CH_3\,CH_2\,CH_2\,CH(OH)-CH(C_2H_5)-CH_2OH$$

Ruters 612 is used as repellent against flies and mosquitoes.

**Butyl 3,4-dihydro-2,2-dimethyl-4-oxo-2H-pyran-6-carboxylate (Indalone)**

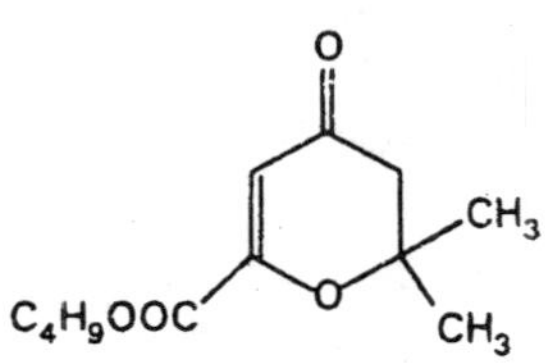

Indalone is used as repellent against mosquitoes and bitting insects. Its $LD_{50}$ value is 7800 mg/kg.

**Di-n-propyl 2,5-pyridine dicarboxylate (MGK 326)**

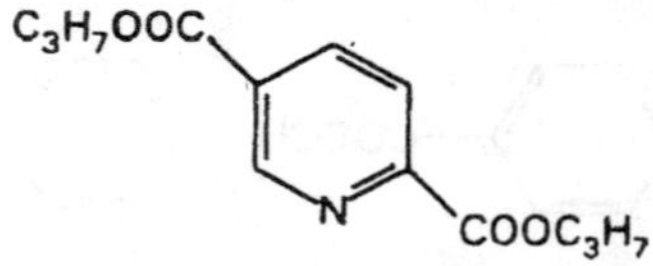

MGK 326 is used as repellent against housefly.

**n-Propyl-N-N-diethylsuccinamate**

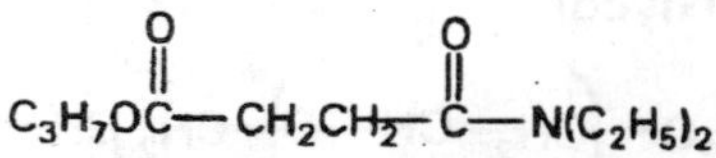

n-propyl-N-N-diethylcuscinamate is used as a repellent for mosquitoes.

Repellents are used in the forms of ointments, pastes, solutions, emulsions and acrosols.

**Atractants and Pheromones**

Attractants are chemical substances whose vapours attract insects. They are mostly divided into food attractants and sexual attractants. Important examples of food attractants are products of decomposition of food products, proteins, enzymatic and also molasses. Some of the important synthetic attractants are methyl eugenol (1-ally 13, 4-dimethoxybenzene),

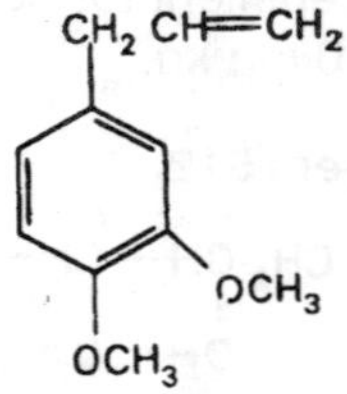

attracting estern fly and trimedlure (1, 1-dimethyl, Ethyl 4 (or 5) choloro-2- methyl (cyclohexane) carboxylate, an attractant for melon fly.

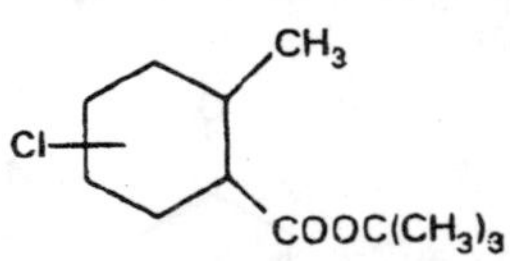

Trimedlure

There are few examples of synthetic attractants that are effective for using over fruit flies. Butyl sorbate is an effective for base for European cockroches and methyl linolenate for bark beetle.

## PHEROMONES (SEX ATTRACTANTS)

Pheromones are defined as those chemicals that are secreted into the external environment by an animal and that elicit a specific reaction in a receiving individual of the same species.

Sex pheromones are those pheromones which are released by one sex only and trigger behaviour patters in other sex that facilitate mating. Sex pheromones are produced by males of certain insect species. In most cases they serve as short-range mating stimulants after the individuals have come into close proximity.

**Chemistry** The identified sex phermones are

Silkworm : trans-10-cis-12-hexadecadienol,

$$CH_3\,(CH_2)\,2\,CH = CHCHCH = (CH_2)_8\,CH_2OH$$

Gypsy moth, Lymantria obfuscata : 10-acetoxy-cis-7-hexadecenol

$$CH_3(C_2H_5)_2\underset{\displaystyle |\atop \displaystyle OCOCH_3}{CH} - CH_2CH = CH(CH_2)_5CH_2OH$$

Pink boll worm, *Pectinophera gossypiella :* 10-propyl-trans 5, 9-tridicadienly acetate.

$$(CH_3(CH_2)_2)_2Cl = CH(CH_2)CH = CHO(CH_2)_3(CH_2)_6O\overset{\displaystyle O\atop \displaystyle \|}{C} - CH_3$$

Cabbage looper, *Trichloplusia ni* (Huubner) - Cis-7- dodecenyl acetate

$$(CH_3(CH_2)_3CH = CH(CH_2)_5CH_2O\underset{\displaystyle \|\atop \displaystyle O}{C} - CH_3$$

Honey bee Queen, *Aphis mellifera* L. 9-keto-trans-2-decenoic acid

$$CH_3 - \underset{\displaystyle \|\atop \displaystyle O}{C} - (CH_2)_5CH = CH - COOH$$

Aggregation pheromones, are those pheromones which may be released only by one sex but cause approach responses by individual of both sexes of the species.

## Uses of pheromones

1. Pheromones can be used to attract insects to a site where they are then destroyed by treatment with insecticides
2. The use of pheromones enables pests to be controlled specifically. The minute application quantities avoid contamination of food and fodder as well as environment.
3. Pheromones have great potential usefulness in surveys to determien the presence of abundance of species in question, so that other measures can be excercised.

## Synergists

Synergist may be defined as any chemical which itself is not toxic to insects at dosages used but when combined with an insecticide greatly enhance the toxicity of the insecticide. Synergism differs from poteniation which occurs when two toxic materials applied together elicit a response greater than that expected from the sum of the individual toxicants.

Advantages of using synergists

1. It reduces the amount of pesticide required for insect kill, much smaller application of pesticides would be required for field application.
2. It reduces the environmental pollution.
3. It broadens the spectrum of the insecticide. Of the several different groups of chemicals able to synergise insecticides, the most widely studied are methylenedioxyphenyl derivatives. Important examples are piperonyl butoxide, safrole, sulfoxide, tropitol and thanite.

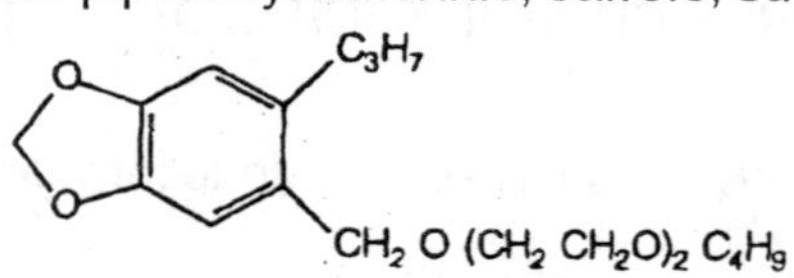


Piperonyl butoxide

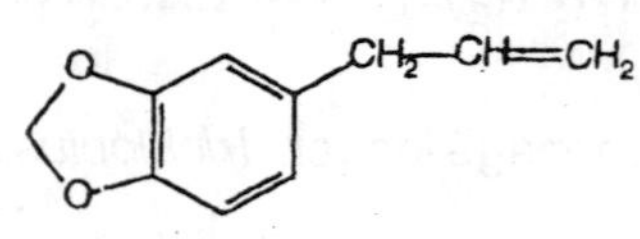


Safrole

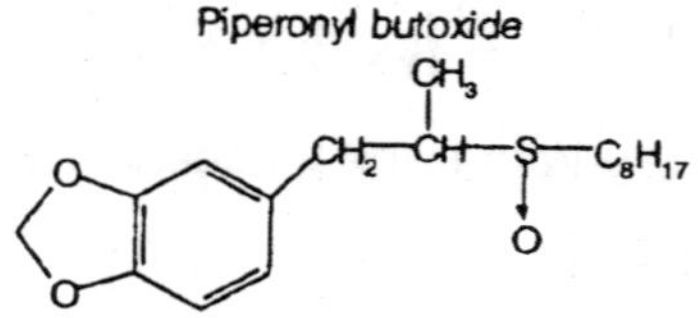


Sulfoxide

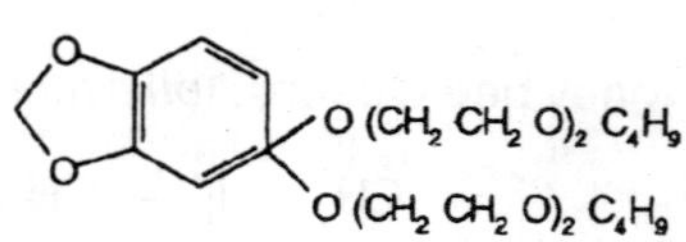


Tropitol

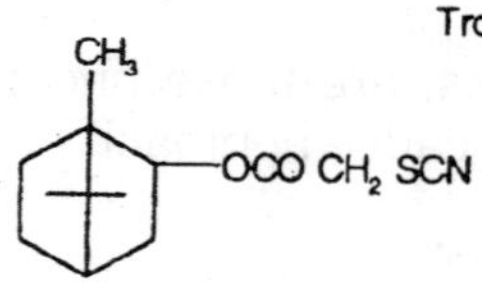


Thanite

### Autosynergism

Autosynergist is a compound which synergises its own toxicity. This would involve forging a synergophore and toxophore into the same molecule in such a way that the former does not interfere with the action of the latter. Important example of auto synergism in 3,4-methylenedioxy phenyl N-methyl carbamate

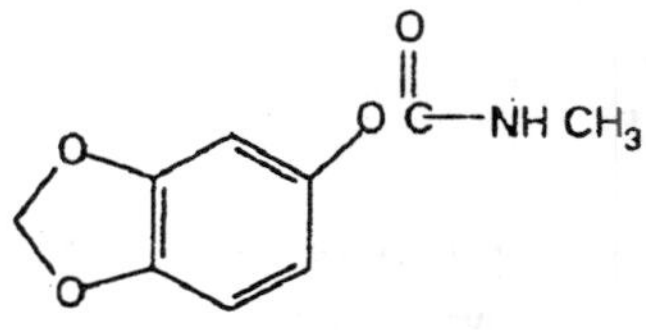


## SYNTHETIC INHIBITORS

Inhibitors are organic or inorganic substances of a varied chemical nature, and also the products of metabolism of a cell, that cause the partial or complete suppression of the activity of enzymes or metabolism in a living organism.

Chitin, essentially a polymer of N-acetyl-glucosamine, is a structural feature of the insect cuticule and fungal cell walls, hence its biosynthesis is an attractive target for selective fungicides. Important example of chitin inhibitor is diflubenzuron. Diflubenzuron is highly active against mosquitoes, livestock fly pests, cabbage white butterfly caterpillars, moths and other larval fly pests at low dosages. The biochemical basis of action is considered to be disruption of the moulting process by inhibition of the normal insect cuticle formation. Diflubenzuron is prepared by the reaction of 2,6-dichlorobenzamide with p-chlorophenylisocyanate.

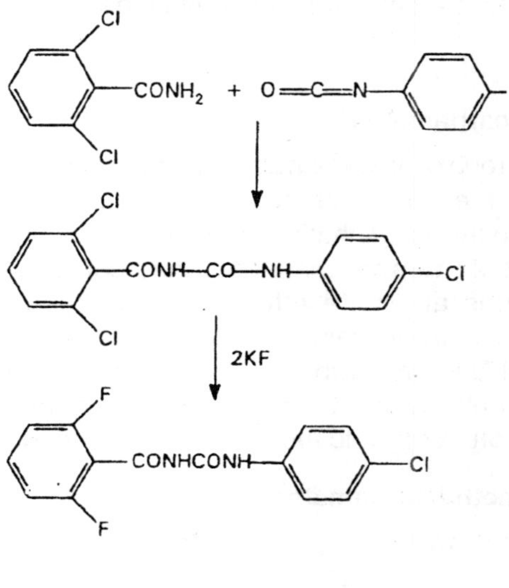

The benzoylphenylureas (BPUs) are important developing class of chitin inhibitors. Flufenoxuron and flucycloxuron are important insecticides belonging to the form and are active against mites as well as insects. The benzoylphenylureas, all act by the interference with chitin synthesis in immature insects and are highly selective insecticide with low toxicity to target organisms.

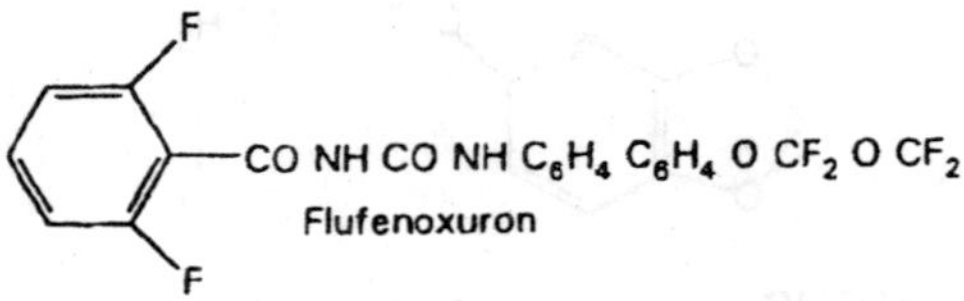


Flufenoxuron

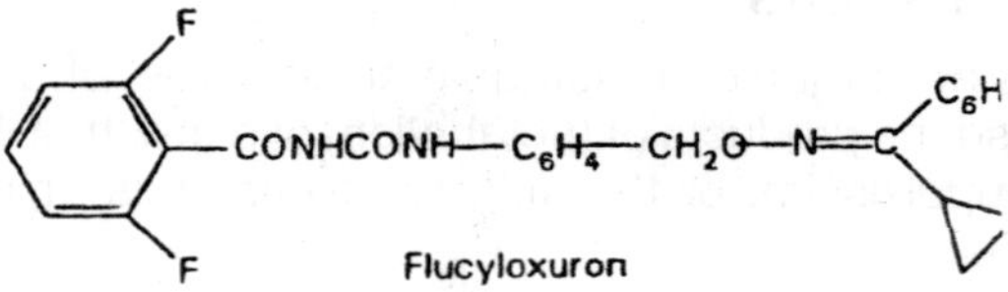


Flucyloxuron

## PROINSECTICIDES

In 1958, Albert introduced the term prodrug, a substance which has to be modified to become a true drug. By analogy, substance which have to be transformed in order to show or to enhance their insecticidal activity are known as pro-insecticides. Such compounds can be activated in various ways. The process can be non catalytic such as hydrolysis, thiolysis, elimination, cyclization, rearrangement etc. or by enzymatic catalysis, catalysed by oxidases, carboxylases, amidases, peptidases etc.

### Procarbamates

### N-acyl-N-methylcarbamates

The oldest group of procarbamates are the N-acyl-N-methylcarbamates. Derivatistion of N-methylcarbamates insecticides such as carbaryl, landrin and propxur with different aliphatic acyl moieties produced compounds that were much less toxic to mice than the parent carbamates. The N-acyl-N-methyl carbamates are quite effective insecticides than their parent compounds in their activity against insects. Despite their insecticidal activity, none of the N-acyl-N-methyl carbamate have been developed as commercial insecticides. Recently, Union Carbide examined a new compound N-acyl derivative of carbofuran in field tests under the code No. UC54229.

### N-sulphenyl-N-methylcarbamates

In comparison with their parent compounds, N-sulphenyl-N-methyl carbamates show lower mammalian toxicity, better insecticidal activity and lower phytotoxicity. From the group of N-sulphenyl-N-methyl carbamates, carbosulfan, thiodicarb, and furathiocarb have been developed to commercial insecticides.

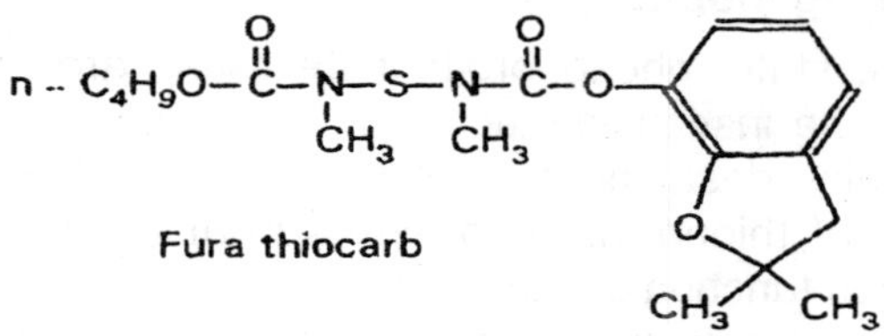

Fura thiocarb

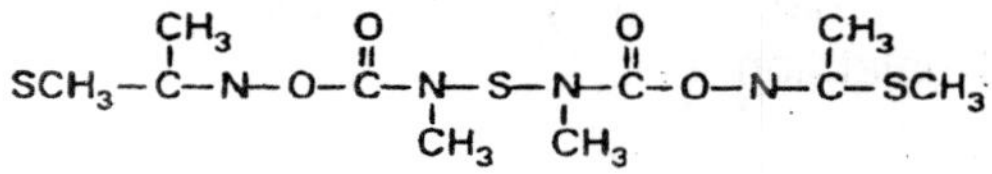

Thiodicarb

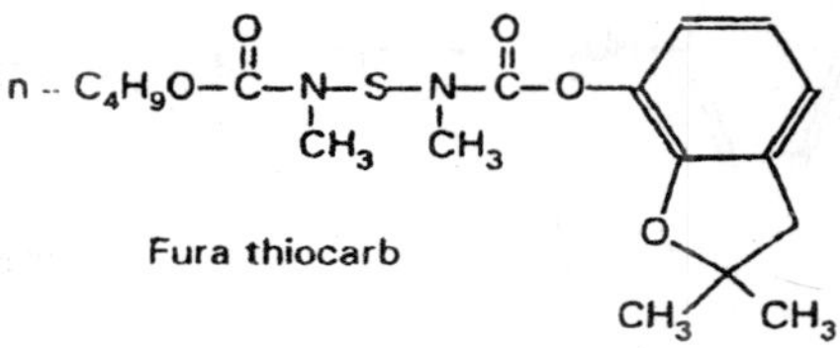

Fura thiocarb

## Propyrethroids

On the vinyl side chain of the acid moiety brominated derivatives of permethrin, cypermethrinand deltamethrin, show insecticidal activity which on molecular basis is comparable to that of the corresponding dihalovinyl analogues. This activity is hardly compatible with the structure because the presence of the vinyl group in the acid moiety determined to a great extent the biological activity of such esters.

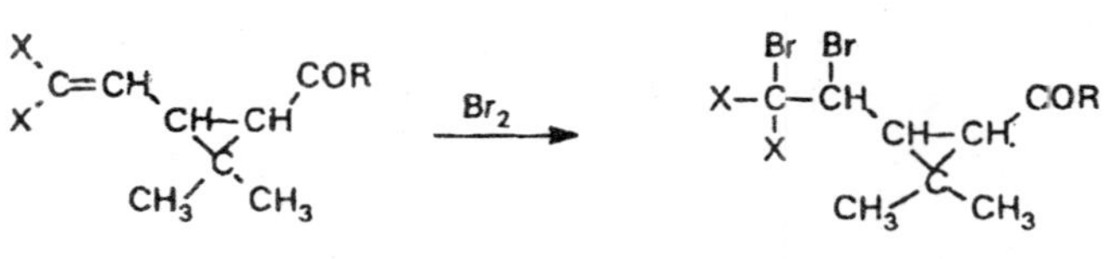

X = Cl,Br R = OH,Cl or ester group

It is known that the organophosphorus insecticides is transformed in the presence of metals, SH groups or other reducing groups to dichlorovos, which is the actual toxicant. It was expected that similar debromination which leads to the vinyl esters could be responsible for the high insecticidal activity of brominated pyrethroids. *In vitro* brominated cypermethrin and deltamethrin can be debrominated to cypermethrin and deltamethrin by cystein or $H_2S$

**Proinsecticidal organophosphates**

In the pure state, phosphorothionate esters are poor inhibitors of cholinestrases. The insecticidal activity of the thiono compounds is the result of the oxdative desulphuration of the thionophosphoryl group *in vitro.* The conversion of thiono into oxo esters in animals is caused by the microsomal mixed function oxidase systems. Inplants, per-oxidases and / or light may play a role in the thiono-oxo-transformation or oxidative desulphoration of the thioplosphoryl sulphur has been demonstrated such as parathion and malathion.

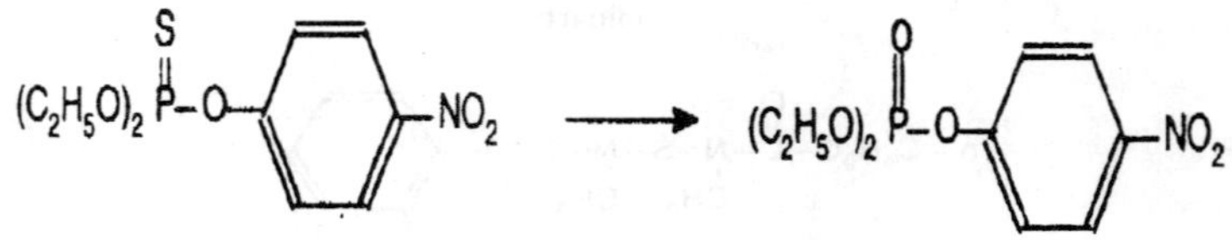

Parathion Paraoxon

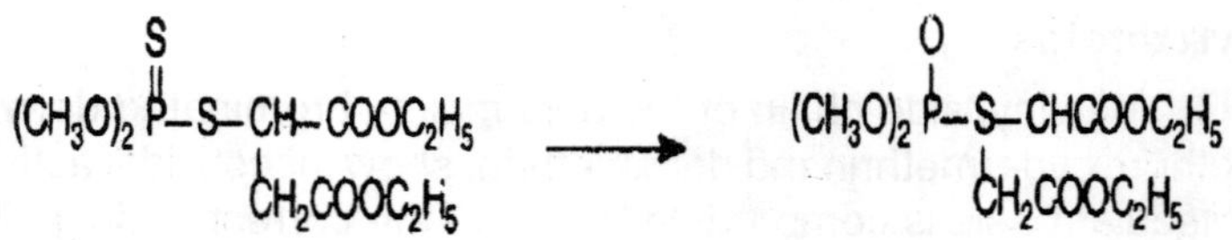

Malathion Malaoxon

Chapter-13

# Toxicology and Safe Use of Pesticides

## FUNDAMENTALS OF TOXICOLOGY

Toxicology is a branch of the science studying the properties of the pesticides used in agriculture, their action on warm blooded animals, insects, bacteria, fungi, plants and ecological systems.

### Toxicity and Hazards

There is a marked distinction between toxicity and hazard. These two terms are not synonymous. The word toxicity refers to the inherent toxicity of a compound, in other how toxic it is to animals under experimental conditions. The word hazard refers to the risk or danger of poisoning when a chemical is used or applied. Hazard depends not only on toxicity but also on the chance of exposure to toxic amount of the material.

1. **Acute Toxicity :** Acute toxicity of an organisms by a pesticide occurs when the pesticide acts at once. It manifests itself in upsetting of the vital activity of the organism with a possible lethal outcome. The acute toxicity is obviously of paramount interest to people engaged in manufacturing and preparing formulation of pesticides and to those responsible for application.

2. **Chronic Toxicity :** Chronic toxicity of an organism is the result of the repeated action of relatively small amounts of pesticide and manifests itself in slowly developing malfunction of normal, vital activity. The toxicity of pesticides varies, depends on their amount, the ways of penetration, the duration of action, the state of organism and the environment etc. In the early stages of developing a pesticide for further experiments and exploration, toxicity data are collected on the pure toxicant. These tests are conducted on test animals that are easy to work with and whose physiology, in some instances, is like that of human e.g. white mice, white rats, white rabbits, guinea pigs, and beagle dogs.

3. **Acute oral Toxicity :** Acute Dermal toxicity is that property of a substance which causes adverse effects in an organism by swallowing of that substance.

4. **Acute Dermal Toxicity :** Acute Dermal toxicity is that property of a substance which causes adverse effects in an organism if the substance being absorbed through the intact skin of the organism.

5. **Inhalation Toxicity :** Inhalation toxicity is that property of a substance which causes adverse effects in an organism by the substance being absorbed during respiration of the organism.

6. **Mutagenicity :** Mutagenicity is that property of a substance which induces changes in the genetic complement of somatic or germinal tissue in subsequent generations. Objectives for umtagenicity assessment is to detect the capacity of a chemical to alter the genetic material in the cell.

7. **Teratogenicity :** Teratogenicity is that property of a substance which produces or induces functional deviation of developmental anomalies in an animal embryo of foetus. This study is designed to examine the potential of test substance to induce permanent malformation and function disorder of the foetus as a result of exposure of the mother during pregnancy. Data of this study provide information on the safety for the applicator, particularly for woman in pregnancy.

8. **Oncogenicity :** Oncogenicity is the property of a substance which produces or induces either benign or malignant tumors in living animals. The purpose of this study is to examine whether, the test substance has the potential to cause carcinogenicity.

9. **Carcinogenicity :** Carcinogenicity is a specific form of oncogenicity characterised by malignant tumors.

10. **Delayed Nueropathy :** Delayed nueropathy is that property of a substance which causes acetyl chloinesterase depression or has the ability to cause it. Hens are used for this study.

11. **Reproduction Study :** Two generations reproduction test is designed to provide information concerning the general effects of the test substance on gonadal function , uterus cycle, mating behaviour, conception, parturition, lactation, weaning and growth and development of the offspring. The test species is rat.

12. **Primary Eye and Dermal Irritation Studies :** These studies serve to identify possible hazards due to exposure of the eyes and skin. These studies serve for the direction on the wearing of protective goggle and clothing. Rabbits are used for these studies.

## Measurement of Toxicity

Chronic toxicity studies are conducted on two species for extended period and the compound is usually incorporated in animals daily diet. Inhalation studies may involve any of the test animals, but rats, guinea pigs and rabbits are most commonly used. Before pesticide is released for public use, the manufacturer must declare toxicity to the rats under laboratory conditions. This toxicity is defined by the $LD_{50}$, expressed as milligram (mg) of toxicant per kilogram (kg) of body weight, the dose that kills 50 per cent of the test animals to which it is administered under experimental conditions. The $LD_{50}$ value is measured in terms of oral (feed or placed directly in the stomach of rats), dermal (applied to skin of rats) and respiratory toxicity inhaled.

The $LC_{50}$ is somewhat similar concept to $LD_{50}$. It is the concentration usually in the air or water surrounding experimental animals which causes 50 percent mortality. It is therefore a convenient index for studying vapours inhaled by mammals or water soluble pesticides in context with fish. Related terms are $ED_{50}$ and $EC_{50}$ which are respectively, the 50 percent effective dose and 50 percent effective concentration and are applicable, when some criterion of toxicity other than death is adopted. The $I_{50}$ is similarly the concentration which inhibits by 50 percent of an in vitro enzyme systems.

To determine $LD_{50}$ of a substances, batch of animals are exposed to a range of doses and the percentage of killed organisms in each batch is recorded. The results can usually be represented by the sigmoid curve (a). The curve is steepest in the region of 50 percent response so that a small change in concentration in this region of the curve causes a large change in percentage kill. The does which kills half the organism is thus a more sensitive index of toxicity than any other dose and that is why $LD_{50}$ is usually adopted as a standard for comparing the relative toxicity of the substances.

## Estimation of Toxicity to Humans

In order to assess the potential chronic toxic hazard of a pesticide, individuals of a suitable animal species are fed with varying amounts of the substances and the highest concentration having no effect on any organism in that batches of animals is determined. This is known as threshold daily dose. Numerous observations are made during the longer duration feeding trial by autopsy examination when animals are eventually sacrificed. The data includes change in body weight, activities of enzymes in serum, liver and behaviour changes, (after death) histological examination of liver, kidney, lung and brain. In order to arrive at a figure for acceptable daily intake (ADI) for man, threshold daily dose (mg/kg/day) is determined using an appropriate animal species and this is divided by safety factor. The later is often 100.

## CLASSIFICATION OF PESTICIDES BY HAZARDS

WHO (1975) has given the following criteria for classification of pesticides.

WHO criteria for classification of pesticides :

| LD50 for rat (mg/kg body weight) | | | | |
|---|---|---|---|---|
| | *Oral* | | *Dermal* | |
| | *solid* | *liquid* | *solid* | *liquid* |
| Extremely toxic | 5 or less | 20 or less | 40 or less | 10 or less |
| Highly hazardous | 5-50 | 30-200 | 10-100 | 40-400 |
| Hazardous Moderately | 50-500 | 200-2000 | 100-1000 | 400-4000 |
| Slightly hazardous | over 500 | over 2000 | over 1000 | over 4000 |

The terms solids and liquids refer to the physical state of the product or formulation being classified.

### Pesticide Toxicity and Its Leble

All pesticide lables must contain 'signal words' in bold print' to attract the attention of the buyer/user; Danger-Poison-warning-caution.

— **Category I:** The word Danger-poison and the skull and crossbones symbol are required on the labels for highly toxic compounds. Pesticides having $LD_{50}$ range 0—50 mg/kg are grouped into this category.

— **Category II:** Warning is required on labels for all moderately toxic compounds. Pesticides having $LD_{50}$ of 50 to 500 are grouped into this category.

— **Category III:** The caution is required on labels for pesticides having $LD_{50}$ of 500 to 5000 mg/kg.

Besides, important information about the name of the pesticide, its concentration, type of formulation, date of manufacture, expiry date and Registration number of the pesticide, antidotes is provided on label. The label contains a diamond shaped warning symbol. It is divided into two triangles by a horizontal line. The colour of the lower triangle gives on idea about the degree of toxicity or potential hazards of the pesticides.

| Colour of the lower triangle | Category | Single word in upper triangle |
|---|---|---|
| Red | Extremely toxic | Poison |
| Yellow | Highly toxic | Poison |
| Blue | Moderately toxic | Danger |
| Green | Slightly toxic | Caution |

**Information on the leaflet:** Due to limitation of space on the pesticide container, detailed information on the use of pesticide is given on the leaflet. The following information is normally available on the leaflet:

— Particular of application of pesticide on various pests

— Directions of use

— Warning and cautionary statement

— Container disposal and

— Storage information.

## SAFETY WITH PESTICIDES

### Safe storage

1. Store pesticides in their original containers.
2. Do not store pesticides near food, feed, or a source of portable water.
3. The storage area should be well ventilated. Ventilators should be located near floor level.
4. Floors should be of impervious material such as cement or stone.
5. Keep pesticides away from the reach of the children
6. Dampness from the soil should not rise into walls or floor.
7. Warning signs should be placed on the outside of all walls of the store.
8. The store should have an adequate size.
9. Check periodically the stored pesticides for signs of damage and leaks.
10. The storages site should be accessible preferably from all sides.

## SAFETY IN APPLICATION OF PESTICIDES

### Before Application

1. Read label and leaflet carefully and follow instructions there in.
2. Make sure that the application equipment is in working order.

3. Never spray pesticide alone while handling highly toxic pesticide.
4. Ensure that water, soap, and towels are available at the site of operation.
5. Ensure that goggles, shoes and gloves are available before application of pesticides.

**During Spraying**

1. Wear personal protective clothings.
2. Spray crops with the wind. In other words, spray with the wind coming from back.
3. Ensure that there are no animals, people, food or animal feed down wind to the area i.e. in the direction in which the wind is blowing.
4. Check the sprayer and sprayer equipment for leaks.
5. Do not blow out blocked spray nozzles with the mouth.
6. Apply pesticide when needed.
7. Take care to prevent the applied pesticide from contaminating nearly streams, ponds, lakes or wells.
8. If during spraying the person feels ill or notices any irregular body symptoms, work should be stopped and medical care should be sought immediately.
9. Spray pesticides in the morning or evening. Don't spray pesticides during the noon.

**After Spraying**

1. Empty the spray tank completely during spraying.
2. Never empty the spray tank into the irrigation canals water ways, ponds or wells.
3. Do not leave dirty spray equipment unattended. Immediately clean up and decontaminate.
4. Decontaminate or destroy all devices such as buckets, sticks, measuring cups etc. used in preparation of spray solution..
5. Take a bath with plenty of clean water and soap.
6. Wash clothes separately
7. Mark the sprayed field and prevent unauthorized entry into the treated area.
8. Decontaminate all protective clothing and footwear.

## EMERGENCIES

Accidents, while using pesticides may occur inspite of taking all precautions. The symptoms of mild poisoning include headache, giddiness, weakness, nervousness, bulrred vision, excess perspiration and eye irritation. If severe poisoning occur, high fever, stroke and loss of consciousness may also take place.

## FIRST AID

### Inhaled poisons

1. If victim is in an enclosed space, do not go in after him, without an air supplied respirator.
2. Carry patient (do not let him walk) to fresh air immediately.
3. Open all doors and windows.
4. Loosen all tight clothing.
5. Apply artificial respiration if breathing has stopped or is irregular.
6. Keep patient as quiet as possible.
7. If patient is convulsing, watch his breathing and protect him from falling and striking his head. Keep his chin up so his air pasage will remain free for breathing.
8. Prevent chilling (wrap patient in blankets, but don't overheat) Do not give alcohol in any form.

### Swallowed Poisons

1. The most important choice you must make when aiding a person who has swallowed a pesticide is whether, you should make the victim vomit. The decision must be made quickly and accurately, the victim's may depend on it. Usually, it is best to get rid of the swallowed poison fast. But, there are exceptions.
2. Never induce vomiting in the victim if unconscious or in convulsions The victim could choke to death.
3. Never induce vomiting if the victim has swallowed a corrosive poison. A corrosive poison will burn the throat and mouth severely while coming up as it did going down.
4. Never induce vomiting if the person has swallowed petroleum products (Kerosene, gasoline, oil, lighter fluid)

### How to Induce vomiting

Do not waste a lot of time in inducing vomiting. Use it only as first aid until you can get the victim to a hospital. Make sure the victim is lying face down or kneeling forward while resting. Do not let him lie on his back because vomited matter could enter the lungs and do more damage. First give the patient large amounts of milk or water one to two cups for victims up to five years old; up to 0.9 litre for victims of five years and older.

Induce vomiting by using syrup of ipeac (use only on physician's orders) or by putting your finger or the blunt end of a spoon at the back of victim's throat. Do not use anything that is sharp or pointed. A glass of soapy water or salt water will also cause the victim to vomit.

### Dilute Poison Quickly

The best first aid for a person who has swallowed a poison is to dilute the poison as quickly as possible and to neutralise the acid or alkali causing the burns. Also, get the victim to a hospital without delay.

For acid or alkaline based pesticides, give the victim water or preferably milk-240 ml. to 480 ml., for victims under five years; up to 0.9 litre for patients over five years. Milk is better than water because it dilutes and helps neutralizes the poison. Water only dilutes the poison.

— If you are sure the poison is an acid, give the victim milk of magnesia ( 15 ml to 24 ml of water), baking soda or chalk in water.

— If you are sure the poison is an alkali, give the patient lemon juice or vinegar.

1. **Universal Sponge:** Use these sponges to absorb excess poisons only after first aid. Suggestions for the corrosive or noncorrosive poisons are followed.
2. **Activated charcoal:** It absorbs many poisons at a high rate. Mix it with water into a thick soup for the victim to drink. Activated charcoal is found in aquarium filters or is available from a drug store.
3. **Home made absorber:** A home-made 'universal sponge' for poison is a mixture of four tablespoons of toast (burnt black), two table-spoon of strong tea (instant ice tea mix will do), and two tablespoons of milk of magnesia. This is used to absorb and neutralize most poisons.

### Shock

Sometimes poisoned victims go into shock. If untreated or ignored, shock can kill victim even if, the poisoning injuries would not have been fatal.

**Table 17.1** : Antidotes for the treatment of pesticide poisoning

| *Pesticide* | *Symtoms of Poisoning* | *Antidotes* |
|---|---|---|
| Aldrin, chlordane, Heptachlor, DDT, HCH, Lindane Dicofol endosulfan | Nervousness, headache, dizziness, nausea, vomiting, tremors, and diarrhoea | i) Phenobarbital 0.7 per day or phenobarbital 0.5 g per day<br>ii) Do not give morpholine, theophyline or aminophyline |
| Carbamates Aldicarb, carbaryl, carbofuron, | giddiness headche and nausea, diarrhoea blurred vision | i) Inject atropine sulphate 2-4 mg for an adult respectively for 24—48 hours. |
| Propoxur | muscular twitching, convulsion | ii) Convulsions and anxiety can be treated by 5—10 mg of diazepam injected intramuscular<br>iii) While keeping the patient fully atropinised administer also an oximeif available e.g. 2—PAM 100—200 mg IM or IV for adults or 155 mg/kg after 1—2 hours. |
| Organophosphates (Malathion, Parathion, Acephate, Monocrotophos, Oxydemeton, phorate Phosalone, Quinalphos Oxydemeton, temephos, Phosphamidon, | Same as carbamates | Same as carbamates |
| Synthetic Pyrethroids (cypermethrin, n,-deltamethrin, Fenvalerate Fluvalinate, Fenpropathrin) | Irritation of oral/nasal mucosae salivation, convulsive seizurs, facial sensations | i) Perform gastric lavage followed by saline cathartic with sodium sulphate solution<br>ii) Control seizurs with injectable diazepam or barbi-turates. |
| Mercury compounds | Tingling of figure, tongue, tips may occour, Headache, loss of peripheral vision, contact with skin may cause blisters or dermatitis | i) Inject freshly prepared 100 to 200 ml of sodium formaldehyde sulphoxylate solution intervariously<br>ii) give 100 ml of 10 per cent calcium gluconate solution introvenously for muscular spasm |
| Fumigants, (Ethylene bromide, MethyL bromide Ethylene dibromide Carbon tetrachloride mixture | Cause respiratory irritation and itching , dermatitis blistering of skin and carneal, ulceration, dizziness, convulsions and respiratory failure | i) Administer artificial respiration<br>ii) Administer amino phylline 1 mg/kg slowley I.V. as a loading dose, followed by 0.6 mg/kg per hour as a maintenance regime.<br>iii) Furosamide Adults 40 mg slowly I.V Children 0.5 to 1.5 mg/kg slowly I.V. |

| | | |
|---|---|---|
| Dinitro compounds (Bina pacryl, Dinitrophenol | i) Yellow staining skin (ii) Tremors increased respiratory | Adequate emptying of stomach and the use of activated charcoal |
| Dinoseb | rate, sweating, nausea restlessness, rapid heart beat | followed by saline, cathortic with sodium sulphate solution |
| Copper compounds | Gastrointestinal and renal manifestations. | BAL (Dimercaprol) 3—5 mg/kg body weight |
| Anticoagulants Rodenticides (brodifacoum ,Warfarin, Bromadiolone, Coumochlor, Chlorophocinone) | Nausea, Vomiting diarrhoea, bleeding from mose, gums | i) give vitamin K1 Phytonadione 15—25 mg in mild cases. In severe cases give Agnamephyton 5—10 mg to adults, 1—5 mg to children, !M or IV |
| Bipuridyllium (Diquat, Paraquat) | Irritation of mouth and throat with nausea, diarrhoea, abdominal pain | i)Large doses of vitamin C and E as antioxidants. ii) Avoid oxygen therapy for first 48 hours iii) Give charcoal 50 g in 150 ml of water or 8 beaten eggs whites. |
| Zinc and Aluminium Phosphides | Vomiting, cough, liver and kidney failure | i) Give morphine for relief of abdominal pain ii) High doses of corticosteroids and blood transfusion for treatment of shock and haemorrage |
| Nicotine sulphate Arsenic compounds | Neurological manifestations Severe gastrointerinal | Phenobarbital 0.7 g daily BAL (Dimercaprol) 3—5 mg/kg body weight |

Where no antidote is recommended or none is available, use some general measures to prevent absorption of the poison. Give activated charcoal as an absorbent in a dose of 50 g in 400 ml of water by mouth for pesticides remaining in intestinal tract. More can be given if needed. Repeat administration, if necessary. For elimination of toxic substance from the intestinal tract, use cathartic such as sodium sulphate (30 g of sodium sulphate dissolved in 250 ml of water. The quality of liquid given should not exceed 5 ml/10 kg body weight.

# 14

# Insecticide Act

## WHY INSECTICIDE ACT

For sustaining productivity of agricultural, horticultural, and plantation crops, adopting plant protection measures against weeds, rodents, nematodes etc. assume greater importance. It is in this context that the use of plant protection chemicals popularly called pesticides have become an essential part of production technology. These pesticides are toxic substances and required to be used judiciously and with great care to safeguard the users, animals and wild life, birds and environment from hazards. It is in this background that Government of India passed in 1968 a comprehensive legislation called the Insecticide Act.

## INSECTICIDE ACT

The main objective of the Insecticide Act is to regulate the import, manufacture, safe transport, distribution and use of insecticides with a view to prevent risk to human beings, animals and for matters connected herewith. The enforcement of the Act was transferred to the Ministry of Agriculture in the year 1970 by Ministry of Health and Family Planning. All the provisions of the Insecticide Act were brought into force with effect from 1st August, 1971.

It should be noted that due to legal reasons, the Act was called **Insecticide Act** and not the **Pesticide Act** and therefore, under Section 93 (c) of the Act the word insecticide means

1. Any substance specified in the schedule
2. Any other such substances including fungicides and the weedicides may be included after consultation with the board and central Government.
3. Any preparation containing one or more of such substances.

## Salient Features of the Insecticide Act

The Salient features of the Insecticide Act are:

1. Compulsory registration of the product at the central level and licenses for manufacture, formulation and safe use at state level.
2. The inter departmental/ministerial/organization coordination is achieved by a high-level advisory board, the Central Insecticides Board with 24 members which has now been raised to 28 members, drawn from various fields having expert knowledge of the subject.
3. Registration Committee to attend to the task of compulsory registration of all pesticides and their formulations before the state grant manufacture/formulation and sale licenses.
4. Establishment of the enforcement machinery like the Insecticides Analysts and Central or State governments.
5. Establishment of Central Insecticides Laboratory
6. Power to prohibit the import, manufacture and also to confiscate the stocks.

## Functions of Central Insecticides Board

1. to advise the Central Government on the manufacture of insecticides under the (Industries Development Regulation) Act, 1951.
2. to specify the use or classification of insecticides on the basis of their toxicity as well as their being suitable for aerial application.
3. to advice on tolerance limits of insecticides residues and establishment of minimum intervals between the application of insecticides and harvest in respect of various commodities.
4. to specify the shelf life of insecticides;
5. to carry out such other functions as a re-supplemental, incidental and consequential.

## Registration Committee

The registration committee consists of a chairman and not more than 5 members including the Drug Controller of India and the Plant Protection Adviser to the Government of India. The main functions of this committee are as under:

1. to register insecticides after scrutinizing their formulae and verify their claims made by the importers/manufacturers as regards their efficacy and safety to human beings and animals.

2. to specify the precautions to be taken against poisoning through the use of handling insecticides.
3. to carry out other incidental and consequential matters.

**Registration Procedure**

Any person who desires to import or manufacture any insecticide has to obtain a registration certificate from the registration committee. However, the entire registration procedure may be classified into four steps as enumerated below:

Inclusion of pesticide in the schedule of the act:

Any pesticide which is to be imported or manufactured in India for use has to be first included in the schedule of the act by the central insecticides board. Any person desiring any chemical to be included in the schedule is to furnish information to the central insecticides board on the following parameters:

1. Chemical identity and physicochemical properties of the insecticide, along with technical bulletin from the principal manufacturer;
2. Bioefficacy data on the product to prove that it is a potential insecticide;
3. The registration status of the product in other countries including the country of its origin;
4. The status of the insecticide as per Pesticide Manual, Pesticide Index or in any other standard pesticide bibliographical book;
5. Detailed information on mammalian toxicity of the insecticide;
6. Any supporting evidence to illustrate, if the need of the product has been substantiated by the Central/State Agricultural Research Organisation/Agricultural University.

After an insecticide has been included in the schedule, any body can make an application for registration of the same for import or for manufacture.

**Provisional Registration under Section 9(3B)**

The provisional registration under section 9(3B) is granted for a period of two years only for data generation under Indian conditions. These are as under:

Data requirement for consideration of provisional registration under section 9(3B)]

(A) Technical : (Import)

1. Source
2. Chemical composition with complete impurity profile
3. Chemical identity of the technical
4. Physicochemical properties of the technical
5. Specifications
6. Methods of analysis
7. Analytical report from principal
8. Shelf life claim
9. Chemical composition on lebels.

(B) Formulation (Indigenous manufacturers):

1. Chemical composition
2. Chemical identity of the technical and other ingredients
3. Physicochemical properties of the other ingredients
4. Specification as per ISI format
5. Methods of analysis
6. Analytical test report from independent pesticide testing laboratory.
7. Shelf life claim
8. Chemical composition of lebels.

II. Packaging and labelling

1. Proposed labels
2. Proposed leaflets
3. Manner of packaging:

   a) specification for primary package

   b) specification for secondary package

   c) specification for transportation packaging
4. Instructions for storage and use, including first aid and precautionary measures proposed for labelling
5. Information regarding disposal of used packages, surplus material and washing of insecticides.

III. Efficacy

1. Effectiveness:
2. International data on Bioeffectiveness

3. Results from some trials under different agroclimatic conditions of India

4. International data on translocation within the plant or animal.

IV. Residues

1. Metabolism of the pesticide in the plants, animals, soil and water, conducted under foreign conditions with the nature of metabolities and their toxicities.

2. Residues data on crops under foreign conditions.

V. Toxicity; (Both for Technical & formulations)

1. Acute toxicity studies
   - Oral
   - Dermal
   - Inhalation
   - Primary skin irritation
   - Irritation of mucous membrane

2. Subacute toxicity studies:
   - Oral
   - Dermal
   - Inhalation

3. Information on the following:
   - Toxicity to birds
   - Toxicity to fish
   - Toxicity to other beneficial insects
   - Toxicity to livestock
   - Human toxicity data from foreign countries
   - Registration status in the country of origin and also in other countries of the world with information on the commercialisation of chemicals

**Regular Registration under Section 9(3) of the Act:**

During the period of the provisional registration or after the expiry of provisional registration, the application is supposed to come for regular registration under Section 9(3) of the Act.

Data requirement for regular registration under Section 9(3)

I. Chemistry

1. Source of supply
2. Chemical composition
3. Specifications
4. Analytical test report
5. Shelf life data
6. Methods of analysis

II. Packaging and labelling

1. Type of packaging
2. Manner of packaging
3. Specifications for primary package
4. Specifications for secondary package
5. Specifications for transportation package
6. Manner of labelling
7. Instructions for storage and use etc.
8. Information regarding disposal of used packages.

III. Bioefficacy and residues data:

1. Effectiveness
2. Phytotoxicity
3. Translocation within the plant or animal being treated
4. Persistence in soil
5. Persistence in water
6. Persistence in plants
7. Compatibility with other chemicals
8. Direction concerning the dosage
9. Time of application
10. Type of application
11. Equipment
12. Manner in which the insecticide is to be used
13. Methods of sampling for residue tests
14. Residue analysis in food and feeding stuffs.
15. Residue analysis in water
16. Residue analysis in soil
17. Residue analysis in wild life
18. Expected residue level in edible crom and soil

19. Workers hazards after treatment

IV. Safety/toxicity data requirements

1. Acute oral toxicity studies
2. Acute dermal toxicity studies
3. Acute inhalation toxicity studies
4. Primary skin irritation
5. Irritation of mucous membrane
6. Sub-acute oral toxicity studies
7. Sub-acute dermal toxicity studies
8. Sub-acute inhalation toxicity studies
9. Neurotoxicity
10. Effects of reproduction
11. Terratogenicity
12. Carcinogenicity
13. Synergism and potentiation
14. Metabolism
15. Mutagenicity
16. Toxicity to birds
17. Toxicity to fish
18. Toxicity to other beneficial insects
19. Toxicity to livestock
20. Signs of poisoning, diagnosis of poisoning, chemical
21. Tests and records on poisoning cases
22. Treatment of poisoning
23. First aid measures
24. Medical treatment
25. Human Cattle Exposure studies

**Data Requirement for Repeat Registration under Section 9(4)**

Under Section 9(4) of the Insecticides Act, where an insecticide has already been registered on the application of any person, any other person desiring to import or manufacture thereof shall make an application and on payment of a prescribed fee be allotted a registration number and grant a certificate of registration in respect thereof on the same conditions on which the insecticide was originally registered. In this case, the applicant neec not submit all the data on biological parameters, if he has already established the chemical equivalence with the earlier registered product. However, the following normal information have to be supplied to the Registration Committee for its satisfaction that the chemical applied for is identical with that of the earlier registered one:

I. Import of technical grade material

1. Minimum purity and the source of principal supplier alongwith associated manufacturing information.
2. Specification
3. Analytical test report (from principal)
4. Method of analysis
5. Shelf life claim
6. Packaging and labelling
   - proposed labels
   - proposed leaflets and
   - manner of packaging

II. Import of formulators

1. Complete chemical composition
2. Specification
3. Analytical test report (from principal)
4. Shelf life claim
5. Method of analysis
6. Information regarding manner of packaging and lebels and leaflets

III. Indigenous manufacture of technical grade material

1. Chemical composition, both purity and impurities
2. Specification
3. Method of analysis
4. Analytical test report
5. Raw material used, their source of supply and the reaction steps involved during the process of manufacture
6. Shelf life claim
7. Packaging and labelling

# 15

# Pesticide Formulations

Pesticide formulation is the process of transforming pesticide chemical into a product, which can be applied by practical methods to permit its effective, safe and economic use. Alternatively, it can be defined as a physical mixture of one or more biological active chemicals with inert ingredients, which provides effective and economic control of pests.

Reasons for formulations:

1. Ease of application and handling
2. Greater effectiveness
3. Good and uniform distribution pesticide
4. More surface area of the pesticide will be exposed if mixed with the diluent than if applied in lumps
5. Overdosing of material may prove to be phyotoxic
6. Hazardous to human beings if concentrated pesticide is applied
7. Safety to forms of life other than target organizms

## TYPES OF FORMULATIONS

### Dusting powders

Dusts are very finely powdered dry formulation. Pesticides are formulated to field strength which may vary from 1 to 10 percent active ingredient depending upon the potency of the pesticide and rate of application.

These essentially contain a toxicant mixed intimately with an inert diluent or a carrier. A distinction must be made between diluent and carrier.

### Diluent

A diluent is one with low sorptivity, which is used to extend dust concentrate or a toxicant to a low field strength dust.

### Carrier

A carrier is a material of high sorptivity and low bulk density which is used to make dust concentrate of above 10%

## METHODS OF PREPARATION OF DUST

Dusts are made by two methods:

Straight mix:

Pesticides and dust carriers are ground together in Raymond Kiln or micronizer mill.

Impregnated dust

(i) Moving column of carrier and over it insecticidal liquid is poured.

(ii) Insecticide is dissolved in solvent and carrier is saturated in it and solvent is then evaporated.

Impregnated dust is better than straight dust. From toxicological point of view, 3% impregnated dust is roughly equal to the 5% straight dust.

## CHARACTERISTICS FOR SUITABILITY OF CARRIERS AND DILUENT

The most important dry carrier and diluents used in pesticide formulations are inorganic materials principally of natural origin. They are processed for use in pesticide fomulations by many techniques ranging from simple drying, pulverizing to washing, and air floating and calcining. The properties of powdered carriers and diluent, are described below.

### Specific Gravity

The material used for dust formulation should have low specific gravity.

### Bulk density

Desirable bulk density of 20 to 40 (lbs cft) should be used.

### Particle Size

Particle size has a tremendous effect upon the performance of dust formulations. Particle of 10μ exhibit poor performance and particles of 5μ exhibit very good performance. Adherence increases by decreasing particle size but, below 2μ size the particle adhere each other to form aggregates. Usually, dust formulations involve particle size from 10 to 100μ.

### Particle Shape

The shape of the dust particles may be spherical, polyhedral, tublar, irregular or otherwise and is responsible for many differences in dust performance. Highly irregular material tend to flow poor.

Materials made up of widely different shapes may not mix up evenly and may aggregate during application.

The finer dusts having less toxicant but more specific surface are more effective.

## Hardness

The hardness of solid particles is dependent upon the composition of sand particles and may cause serious abrassion of shaping and dusting equipment.

## Electrostatic Charge

Electrostatic charges are produced by friction between the particles themselves and between the particles and dusting equipment. The magnitude of charge depends upon the composition of the dust, the material of which the equipment is made of, the amount of agitation of pesticides, the temperature and humidity. Arsenicals, fluorides and sulphur compounds gen negatively charged when injected from the equipment made of steel, iron or aluminium, which get positively charged. Gypsum and pyrophyllite also get positively charged while talc, silica etc get negatively charged.

Normally the plant surfaces are negatively charged and positively charged particles get quickly adheres to plant surfaces.

## pH

Insecticides like chlorinated hydrocarbons etc. are susceptible to alkaline pH and cannot be formulated with alkaline dusts.

## Surface Density and Sorption

Absorption and adsorption by dusts are dependent upon the nature of the surface, number of active centres per unit area, the size and the shape. Oil absorptivity is of practical importance in the field of diluents for the production of deterioration of oil containing dusts in storage, owing to caking. It is expressed as lbs of raw linseed oil for 100 lbs of powder required to produce a stiff like paste.

## Surface Acidity

Surface acidity may be defined as a disproportionate distribution of electric charges in the mineral to produce a surface with positively chargred centres. These charged centres are referred to as acid sites or electrophillic centres. The acidity will in turn affect reaction with other chemicals. The strength of the acid centres may be measured by certain dyestuffs known as Hammett Indicators, which change colours at very specific acid strengths. These dyes form conjugated bases with the nucleophillic centres at different surface acidities which are defined as pK with a numerical system ranging from +7 to -8.

Consequently $pK_a$ is a measure of acid strength (i.e. the affinity for electrons) of the average acid site. Indicators used for determining surface acidity are given in Table

**Table 19.1:** Indicators for determining surface acidity

| Indicator | $pK_a$ of the indicator | Colour of natural base | Colour of conjugate acid | Weight % sulphuric acid |
|---|---|---|---|---|
| Natural red | +6.8 | Yellow | Red | $8.19^{-8}$ |
| 4-Phenylazo-1-naphthyl amine | +4.5<br>+4.0 | Yellow | Red | $5.10^{-5}$ |
| 4-Dimethyl- amino azobenzene | +3.3 | Yellow | Red | $3.10^{-4}$ |
| 4-Phenylazo-diphenylamine | +1.5 | Yellow | Purple | 0.002 |
| 4-Nitro-4'-nitrophenylazo-diphenylamine | +0.4 | Orange | Violet | 0.3 |
| 1,8-Diphenyl-1,3,6,8-nona-tetraen 5-one | -2.2 | Yellow | Red | 50 |
| Chalcone | -5.6 | Colourless | Yellow | 70 |
| Anthraquinone | -8.2 | Colourless | Yellow | 90 |

Pesticidal chemicals vary greatly in their susceptibility to decomposition as result of catalytic activity of acid sites. These acid sites can be deactivated with certain organic chemicals such as urea, hexamethylenetetramine, diethylglycol which preferentially share their electrons with the mineral to form a covalent bond, which is stronger than bonds formed between the pesticidal chemicals and acid centres.

## Flowability

The flowability of a powdered carrier is the rate at which the material can be poured, moved or displaced. Its significance in the formulation process is that as flowability increases, the power requirement for blending or working material decreases. This is a significant factor in field application because, as flowability increases, the flow through the dusting hopper imprcves, and the rate is more easily controlled.

**Dustability**

Dustability is a characteristic of powdered diluents relating to the ability to flow through the air, to be transported by air currents within a limited area of application and to cling to the surface of the crop after application. There are no precise laboratory methods for testing the dustability other than practical application under actual or stimulated conditions of use.

**Abrasiveness**

Abrasiveness is the property of the certain carriers and diluents to cause wear of processing equipment, metering devices and orifices of application equipment. This action significantly changes the flow characteristics of the nozzles thereby, increasing dusting volume rates. The dusting pattern is changed and resulting applications are inacurrate.

Good criteria for the selection of carrier and diluent is sorptivity and surface activity followed by bulk density flowability, and capacity to absorb less moisture. The following are the main diluents used for the manufacture of insecticidal dusts in India.

- **Talc:** Talc also known as soap stone or steatite in its solid form is essentially metasilicate of magnesium ($MgSO_4.SiO_2$). Mostly talcs are of alkaline pH 8-10 and bulk density 20-40 lbs cft.
- **Prophyllite:** This is chemically a hydrous aluminium silicate ($Al_2O_3.4SiO_2H_2O$).
- **White shale:** The mineral of unknown geological class and is also used for formulation in India.

**Driftless Dust**

Driftless dust was developed to resolve the drift problem of conventional dusts. It differs from the conventional dusts the mean diameter in driftless dust is 20-30 μm as compared to 10 μm of regular dust other properties are compared as follows:

| *Property* | *DL dust* | *Regular dust* |
|---|---|---|
| Fitness | Above 300 mesh | Above 300 mesh |
| mean diameter | 20-30 μm | 10-12 μm |
| % of particle, | | |
| under 10μm | Blow 30% | About 50% |
| Bulk density | 0.7-1.1 | 0.45-0.65 |
| Floatability | Below 20 | 40-60 |

## Advantages

Dusts are easy to apply, less phytotoxic, require no sophisticated equipment and are useful where there is scarcity of water.

## Disadvantages

Transport or handling is costly, highly susceptibility to drift, less deposits due to wash of by rain, wind or gravity, Dermal toxicity is less but inhalation hazards are more, residual life is less and to control pests repeated application is necessary.

## WATER DISPERSIBLE POWDER AND WETTABLE POWDERS

Water dispersible powders are finely divided pesticidal dust concentrates blended with a wetting agent plus a dispersible agent, that will yield stable, sprayable, homogenous suspensions when diluted with water to field strength. Where as a wettable powder consists of finely ground powder of pesticide a wetting agent. The wettable powders are generally used for making paste. Normally 50% of the active ingredient present in WDP should remain suspended in water for half an hour after mixing in water. The inert material used in the manufacture of WDP is generally china clay which is hydrous aluminum silicate. A good clay has pH from 4.5 to 6.0 and iron should not more than 1% by weight.

## Criteria for WDP

1. Particle size should be less than 5 μm and all the particle should pass through 44 μm sieve.
2. It should be free flowing.
3. It should wet and disperse readily without forming lumps when diluted with water or during storage.

## Wetting agents

The wettability and spreadiability of water dispersible powders is achieved by adding wetting and or spreading agent, which help to reduce the surface tension in water and thus aid the spray droplets to wet and then spread over the leaf surface. It is flattened on a leaf surface. The attractive force (surface tension) of the leaf tends to resist the tendency of the droplets to return to a spherical shape. It is is sufficiently large, it will overcome the cohension of the molecules of the liquid so that the later will spread. The addition of wetting agent reduces the surface tension of the spray droplet and thus aids in wetting and the spreading of the application in the pesticide formulations because of high wetting property. The wetting agents indigenously manufactured are available under various trade names such as Idet 20, Idet 10, surgaol- 0.5, Dispersol, Sarcol DNL and DNC. Wetting agents upto 2 to 3% are commonly used for WDP formulations.

**Spreadability**

The angle o contact (Cos θ) of the droplet with the plant surface gives the picture of the spreading concept. The three forces namely the surface tensions of the solid (Plant surface- TVS) and liquid (drop-TLV) and interfacial tension between solid and liquid (TSI) exert force in three directions. The relationship between these three forces can be put in following equation.

$$TSV = TLV \cos(\theta) + TSI$$

$$TLV \cos(\theta) + TSI = TSV$$

$$TLV \cos(\theta) = TSV - TSI$$

$$\cos(\theta) = \frac{TSV - TSI}{TLV}$$

The angle of contact is the measure of all the three forces and lesser the angle, greater the area covered by liquid. The angle of contact is never aimed at zero nor at 180$^0$, because of fear of dripping due to infinite spread where the coverage will be nil. An ideal angle of contact is between 20-30$^o$.

**Dispersibility**

The ability of the powdered concentrate to be suspended in water as a fine solid particle in termed as dipersibility. A fine particle size and wettability are not usually sufficient to keep the particles in suspension. The cohesive forces between the particles cause their aggregation flococulticn after dispersion. To overcome this tendency to floculate, water dispersible powders contain dispersing agents which ensure that the dispersed particles will remain in suspension for a reasonable period of time. Some of materials used for dispersing agent are sodium carboxymethyl cellulose (CMC), polysaccharide gums. (eg guor gum), proteins, like animal glue, and also sodium lignin sulphonates.

**Chemical Stability**

Addition of decomposition inhibitors or 'deactivators' as they are called, play a substantial role in enhancing stability of WDP. Glycols are reported to be effective stabilizers for chlorinated hydrocarbons and organophosphates. Metallic impurities like iron, catalyse decomposition of organophosphates.

**Emulsifiable concentrates**

Pesticide emulsifiable concentrates (ECs) are blends of the pesticides, solvent and emulsifier. The function of the solvent is to help in dissolving the pesticide in desired quantities and emulsifier disperses the toxicant and carrier solvent in water prior to application.

Charateristics of good solvent

1. The pesticide should be highly soluble in it.
2. It should have no phytotoxicity
3. It should have no toxicity
4. It should be easily available
5. It should have high flash point

Characteristics of good emulsifier

The emulsifying agent should

1. dissolve completely in the solution of pesticide and should not adversely affect its solubility in the solvent.
2. should confer the desired emulsification characteristics to the EC.
3. should not cause chemical decomposition of the toxicant
4. should be neutral or mildly acidic
5. be free from impurities likely to have a deleterious effect on the toxicant
6. should not contain carrier solvent which will interfere with the stability of EC.

**Types of Emulsions**

Two types of emulsions are possible. Either the i) Oil in water or OW type, water is external or continuous phase and oil is the internal or disperse phase ii) water in oil or WO type, oil is the external and water is internal. The type of emulsion generally required in spraying practice in agriculture are the OW emulsion where water in continuous phase is readily diluted with water. Inverted emulsion are not yet made in India, but their use and needs are yet to be explored.

## Function of the Emulsifier

The function of the emulsifier is to prevent separation of the pesticide dissolved in solvent from the diluent water so as to give stable emulsion. Normally when two liquids of different specific gravity such as oil and water are mixed together, they tend to form distinct layers but after agitating with emulsifier, oil breaks into small droplets that floats in water phase to give a homogenous emulsion. Each oil breaks into small droplets that floats in water phase to give a homogenous emulsion. Each droplet is surrounded by water and the emulsifying agents reduce interfacial surface tension between oil and water and thus oil droplets are prevented from coalescing. It is very necessary not to use hard water for diluting emulsifiable concentrates, since the electrolites present in water disturb the balance of forces maintaining the equilibrium between oil and water and break the emulsion into separate components from which they are prepared.

## Emulsions

An emulsion is a heterogenous systems consisting of a least one immiscible liquid intimately dispersed in another in the form of droplets, whose diameters generally exceed 0.1μ. Emulsions essentially are unstable heterogenous systems, their stability is accentuated in suitable additives which are surface active agents.

Instability of an emulsion is first indicated by creaming, this manifests in the form of separation of the dispersed phase as a top layer containing a higher proportion of the inner phase (and consequently toxicant) then the rest of the system. As the dispersed phase progressively coaleseas, the oil droplets increase in sixe leading to re-aggregation of an oily layer and the breakdown of emulsion in complete.

**Emulsion concentrate** (E.W. also called emulsion oil in water)

In emulsion concentrate the use of solvents has been dispersed with and it only contains an active ingredient blend of surfactant to regulate hydrophilic/lipophilic characteristics. The EW is utilized as new formulation substitutes for the emulsifiable concentrate and has the following advantages.

1. Decreased acute toxicity: As EW formulation does not contain organic solvents, the skin permeability, inhalation, skin and occular irritation are reduced and are confined to the characteristics of the active ingredient.
2. Decreased vapour pressure: In the absence of petroleum solvents, the other ingredient being less volatile vapour pressure is decreased.
3. Higher Flash Point: There is no ingredient in the formulation which gives off inflammable vapours. The water diluents viz., water and emulsifier does not fall in this hazardous category.

4. Less manufacturing hazard: The inflammable solvents are not involved in formulation and manufacture of the product becomes much safer and the contamination of the skin, if any, will be of less concern.
5. Cleaner working environment: Less vapour pressure, decreased odour, decreased spillage of solvent system involved in the manufacture of the product, all o which contribute to maintain a clean ambient working environment in the formulation premises.
6. Nonphytotoxic : The EW products are not phytotoxic in nature because they do not contain the solvents.

## GRANULAR FORMULATIONS

Granular formulation is one in which the pesticide is impregnated in suitable carrier and then converted into granules.

Types of granules: There are two types of granules.

Extruded granules and Non Extruded granules. The extruded granules disintegrate when comes in contact with water. Non extruded granules will disintegrate after a certain lapse of time. These two types are further subdivided according to volatile matter content. LVM indicates low volatile material content and RVM indicates regular volatile material content.

Typical physical properties of these two subgranules are be as follows:

| | *LVM* | *RVM* |
|---|---|---|
| Moisture | 1% | 6% |
| Volatile matter | 5% | 15% |
| Oil absorption | 120% | 95% |
| Water retention | 180% | 135% |
| Bulk density | 30-35 lbs | 40-45 lbs |
| Specific heat | 0.25 | 0.25 |
| pH | 7-9 | 5-6.5 |

**Mean size:** Granules are available in several sizes as per requirements 10/20, 20/40, 30/60. Size 30/60 means that most of the granules will pass through a 30 mesh sieve but will be retained on 60 mesh sieve. The selection of meshing for a given application is only influenced by area requirements, application method, drift problems. Absorption increases with decreasing particle mesh size. By and large, the dominant criterion is the toxicant doses to be applied per acre and number of granules required per square feet. The approximate number of granules required per square feet resulting from application of 100 lb per acre of pesticidal granules is as follows:

| *Mesh size* | *Particle size* |
|---|---|
| 10/20 | 750 |
| 20/40 | 15,200 |
| 10/60 | 20,800 |

## SELECTION OF INERT CARRIERS

The carriers for granules are minerals like attapulgite, kaolin, alumina, bentonite etc. It may, however, be noted that efficacy of granules of some pesticide concentration on different basis differs greatly in the control of pests. For each application, choice of the carrier has to be first tested for its efficacy by biological assay. Mineral clays from which either the granules are made have acid sites in their molecules. These acid sites act as catalyst for the rapid decomposition of the pesticidal ingredients.

## TECHNIQUES OF FORMULATION

### Impregation of unextruded granules

A known quantity of unextruded granules is placed in a Ribbon blender so that loses by attrition are reduced to the minimum. First these granules are deactivated by a suitable deactivator. Thereafter, a solution of the active ingredient is sprayed by suitable nozzles on the granules and tumbling continued for, at least for half an hour. The granules so formed should be left for aging to enable the solvent to evaporate, otherwise it may cause caking or prove phytotoxic to the crop because of the excessive solvent adhering to it.

### Extruded Pesticidal Granules

For extruded granules, the clays are first ground with a suitable deactivator and after it is determined that the deactivation is complete, the active ingredient is added and the result of the required strength is made. The dust is then mixed with water into a kneading machine from where it is passed into a granulator, which turns the material into granules. The granules are then passed over a conveyor where hot filled gases are being let in, to enable the material to contain the minimum moisture before it is packed into drums.

### The Quality Control

The following tests must be carried out for each batch by following standard sampling methods.

- Active ingredient content
- **Bulk density:** The weight per cft determined for any mesh size, must be constant.
- **Deactivation:** Neutralization of catalytic activity is tested so that $pK_a$ value is higher than 1.5.
- **Moisture content:** Same is tested for deterring the loss in weight after 24 hours placement in an oven at 100°C. The percentage should not exceed 6%.
- **Attrition Quality:** The attrition should not be more than 2%
- **Grain size:** The sieve shaker fitted with the size of the specified sieves is used to test for the required grain sizes.

**Advantages**

1. These can be directly applied in soil.
2. No costly equipment is needed
3. No drift problem.

**Encapsulated granules**

The principal objective of this new approach is to provide a controlled released rate of toxicant for specific pesticidal action. Microencapsulation is a process designed to apply thin, continuous, polymeric coatings on to small particulate solids, droplets of pure liquids. The factors to be considered in selecting coating material are

The chemical inertness of the material towards active ingradient.

The ability of the material o dissolve or disintegrate at a controlled rate by the action of certain environmental factors such as soil and microorganisms.

The advantages claimed to be derived from controlled release of pesiticides are:

1. Lower mammalian toxicity of the formulation.
2. Substantially extended duration of activity at equal level of active ingredient, hence better cost benefit ratio.
3. Reduction of evaporative losses.
4. Decreased phytotoxicity.
5. Reduced leaching into soil and water.
6. Regulates release of active ingredient.

## Floating Granules

Floating granules are formed from divided solid materials that are compressed into granules during compounding and manufacturing process. When floating granules are applied to field, they sink once to the bottom of the water and soon come up to the water surface and the carriers gradually dissolve into the water releasing effective ingredients from the granules. In 24 hours after application, 80% of the applied granules will be dispersed in water. Active ingredient partially comes up to the water surface in the form of oil film and when these granules are applied in paddy field the pesticide partially adheres to columns of paddy rice and partially comes in contact with rice water weevil. The ingredients spreading over the water surface gradually sink o the bottom, forming an active layer on the surface of the soil of paddy field and passing through the soil to reach the larvae of the weevil. Such floating granule is suitable for control of rice water weevil and is now attracting public attention as a new granular formulation. The articular advantages of floating of granules include a high pesticide concentration per unit weight of the product, relatively dust free formulation and a comparatively safe package.

## Water Dispersible Granules

Water dispersible granules are granules which disperse or dissolve readily and completely in water. They provide spray slurries atleast equivalent to slurries from WP. A WDG formulation consists of hard, uniform in size, free flowing, low dust granules which readily disintergrate in water and under minimal agitation, forms a homogenous sprayable suspension. To the user they provide advantages of safety and convenience.

1. Free flowing and packages are easily, quickly and completely emptied into the spray tank.
2. There is insignificant dusting during handling and preparation of spray slurries, so that sprays can be prepared without hazard to workers or nearby areas, even when there is appreciable wind.
3. The granules are generally spheroidal, so they do not cling to dry skin or clothing in case of spill.
4. Spilled material can be readily swept up.
5. Emptied containers contain insignificant residues, thus minimising waste or hazards during container disposal.
6. Package contents can usually be measured volumetrically. The bulk density of dry WDG is not much affected by handling i.e. the loose and bulk density are very closely the same.

7. They provide rapid wetting and dispersion in the spray tank which is often better, faster and more complete than can be achieved by WP.
8. Reduced transport and warehousing cost
9. Eliminates physical problems of flowables i.e. setting, thickening etc.
10. Novel, generates consumer interest.

## Water Miscible Liquids

The technical grade material may be initially water miscible or it may be alcohol miscible which is formulated with an alcohol to become water miscible. These formulation resemble the emulsifiable concentrates in viscosity and colour, but do not become milky when diluted with water.

## Fogging Concentrates

Fogging concentrates are the formulations sold for public health purposes. Fogging machines generate droplets, whose diameters are usually less than 10 microns, but usually greater than 1 micron. The thermal fogging device utilizes a flash heating of the oil solvent to 0produce a visible vapour or smoke. The eluent fogger atomizes a tiny jet of liquid in a venturi tube, through which passes an ultra high velocity air stream. The materials used in fogging machines depend on the type of fogger. Thermal devices use oil only, whereas ambient generators use water, emulsions or oils.

## Baits

Baits consist o the technical pesticide compound with suitable diluent such as corn, starch, or sugar. Local baits may incorporate attractant substance or colour in a manner found to be attractive to the pest. The disadvantages of baits are that

1. It can be eaten by domestic animals.
2. It leads to the development of bait shyness, especially when dead animals are left near a bait.

## Aerosols

It is possible by suitable means, to produce suspensions of solids and liquid in air, the individual particles of which are of colloidals dimensions. Such colloidal suspensions are called aerosols. The most common method of producing aerosols is by means of release of compressed gas, with which the toxicant is mixed. The drops of aerosols are in the range 10-50μ diameter. Fluorocarbons such as diflurodichloromethane (Feron 12) and 1,1 and 1,2-dichloroetetrafluroethanes are most common propellents.

### Smokes

Pesticide is mixed with an oxidant e.g. (sodium chlcrate) and combustible material (solid carbohydrate) with a retarding agent ($NH_4Cl$) in the generator and ignited, when a large amount of hot gases with high velocity are emitted from the generator causing the pesticide to vapourise and mix in air to produce a fine smoke. The period of high temperature is os short that breakdown of the active ingredient is minimised. These are used in isolated places. A special form of smoke generator is mosquito coil made from wood dust, starch, various additives and green colour and pesticide (natural pyrethrin/allethrin etc.). Effects of smokes from a mosquito coil in sequence are deterency, repellency, interference with host location, knockdown and eventually death.

## ULTRA LOW VOLUME FORMULATION (LOW VOLUME SPRAYS)

This type of formulation is concentrated solution of the toxicant in a suitable solvent. an ideal ULV solvent is that which has good disselving power, low volatility low viscosity, no phytotoxicity and compatible with a range of chemicals. In addition, the solvent should not cause any deterimental effect. The solvents used are Riselle oil, a mixture of heavy aromation naptha, dutrex, vegetable oils, aromatic hydrocarbonds, glycols and mineral oils. This technique has proved extremely useful where insect control is observed over vast areas.

## CONTROLLED RELEASE FORMULATIONS

Controlled release technolgy can be defined as a technique or method in which the active ingredient is made available to a specified target, at concentration and duration designed to accomplish an intended effect. Controlled release formulations have several advantages over conventional formulations.

1. Satisfactory effect for longer period of time
2. Small dosage
3. Longer application interval
4. Decrease in mammalian toxicity
5. Decrease in phytotoxicity
6. Decrease in environmental degradation
7. Decrease in environmental pollution

8. Decrease in leaching and evaporation
9. Decrease in reactivity
10. Changing liquid into solid
11. Masking of odour
12. Easier handling

**Kind of controlled release technology**

Controlled release technology is mainly attained by interacting pesticides with polymers. Several methods have been developed and are classified according to the mechanism or material used as follows:

Diffusion of pesticides in polymeric medium

**Monolithic system:**

Pesticides are dissolved or dispersed uniformly in polymeric or elastomeric materials

1. **Reservoir system:** pesticides are covered by membranes. Reservoir layer is mainly made of flexible PVC
2. **Polymeric pesticide:** Pesticide is bound via covalent bond to polymers. Pesticides, that contain very reactive functional groups such as carboxyl, hydroxyl, sulphydryl and amino groups can react with monomers or polymers directly. If pesticides do not have any functional groups, some bridging agents are needed in order to bind pesticides to monomers or polymers. pesticide is released from the polymeric pesticide by hydrolysis of the polymer pesticide bond in the environment.

## MATERIALS USED FOR CONTROLLED RELEASE FORMULATION

Various kinds of polymers are used for controlled release formulations. They should satisfy the following conditions in general.

1. The polymer should have proper molecular weight and molecular structure in order to get proper diffusion and release rates of the pesticides.
2. The polymer should not be reactive with pesticides.
3. The polymer and its degradation products must not cause any environmental impact.
4. The polymer should be stable during storage and usages.
5. The polymer should not be expensive
6. For agricultural application, it should be biodegradable to avoid environmental pollution.

Examples of polymers used for controlled release formulations are:

1) Cellulose 2)starch, 3) sawdust 4) bark 5) starch xanthate 6) starch borate 7) polyacetic acid 8) polyglycolic acid.

## ADJUVANTS

Adjuvant are materials that are added to a pesticide mixture to improve mixing and application or enhance pesticide performance. An adjuvant customizes the formulation to meet specific needs or compensate for local conditions.

Adjuvant can be used to improved the wetting ability of a spray solution, control evaporation of spray droplets, improve whether inability of pesticides, increase the penetration of pesticide through the plant adjust the pH of the spray solution, imporve spray droplet deposition, increase safety of the spray to target plants, correct in compatibility problems and reduce spray drift. A few of the more important types, their usage are described below.

### Penetrant aids

There are two significant factors that affect the biological activity of a pesticide formulation, namely the penetration of the formulation through an outer protecting lipid memberance of the pest and rate of reaction of the pesticide with a vital reactive site. Penetration may be enhanced or reduced by the addition of nonionic surface active agents to the formulations. Penetrant additives should be present at a sufficient concentration that the final spray solution will contain greater han 0.5 percent by weight of the penetrant aid.

### Stabilizers and deactivators

Many of the clays, minerals and inorganic substances used as carriers and diluents for dry formulation have the property of surface acidity which catalyses the decomposition of many pesticides. The surface acidity must be neutralized to overcome catalytic activity. Alcohols, glycols, hexamethyleneteytramine (HMT) can be used deactivators.

PH-Regulators such as organic acids and bases prevent decomposition reactions that are favoured in certain pH ranges. Certain exponidised compounds are suitable as proton traps.

### Anticaping agents

When dust concentrates, water dispersible powders and granular formulations are prepared at the saturation point of carriers, capping occurs in storage Diatomaccous earth, and microfine silica, and attapulgite are often used as anticaping agents.

### Dry Lubricants

Dry lubricants improve the flow or the slip characteristics of the formulations. Materials useful as drylubricants in pesticide formulation are powdered graphite, soapstone talcs and certain metal stearates.

### Stickers

Stickers prevent the run off spray solutions when applied to crops. Many protective colloids, and gelling agents such as blood albumin and polyethylene polysulphide are used as stickers.

### Antidusting agents

Antidusting agents are generally liquid substances, which cause extremely fine particles of dry materials to adhere to each other, thus making them less susceptible to drift water soluble materials such as glycerine, peteroleum oils (desel oil, motor oil viscosity SAE 30) may be used as antidusting agents.

### Antifoaming agents

Antifoaming agents are surfactants which suppress the tendency to foam fomulation by other surfactants used as emulsifiers or wetting agents when the formulation is diluted with water. Silicones are the first choice because of their chemical inertness and alliphatic alcohols of eight to ten carbon atoms in length are also used.

### Viscosity regulators

Viscosity plays a leading role ULV formulations, viscosity may be raised by addition of clays such as bentonite or of water soluble polymers, or it may be lowered by certain dispersing agents. Synthetic silica can cause a drastic increase in viscosity.

### Surfactants

Surfactants are chemicals which reduce the interfacial tension between immiscible liquids or between and solid surfaces. A surfactant is used for management of systems containing two immisible solvents. In pesticide formulations, the surfactant characteristics of greatest interest are wetting and dispensing for water dispersible powders and emulsifying for emulsifiable concentrates. Surfactants are classfied depending on the charge of the surface active moiety, usually the lengthger part of the molecule. In anionic surfactants this moiety carries a negative charges as in soap.

$$C_{17}H_{3}CO^{-}_{2}Na^{+}$$

In cationic surfactants the charge is positive

$$(C_{18}H_{37})_2N^+ (CH_3)_2 (CH_3)_2Cl^-$$

In nonionic surfactants there is no charge on the molelcule

$$C_{15}H_{31} (-OC_2H_4-)_7OH$$

In amphoteric surfactants, solubilization is provided by the presence of positive and negative charges in the molecule.

$$C_{12}H_{25}N^+ (CH_3)_2 CH_2 CO_2^-$$

In general, the hydrophobic group consists of hydrocarbon chain containing approximatiely 10-20 carbon atoms. This chain may be interrupted by oxygen atoms, a benzene ring, amide ester and other functional groups. Hydrophic, solubizing groups, for anionic sufactants include carhcxylates, sulfonates, sulfates and phosphates. Cationics are solubilized by amine and ammonium groups. Ethylene oxide chains and hydroxyl groups are the solubiizing groups in nonionic surfactants. Amphoteric sufactants are solubilized by combinations of aniomic and cathonic solubilizing groups.

**Anionic Surfactants**

Carboxylates : Soaps represent the most of the commercial carboxylates. The general of soaps is RCOO-M+ where R is a straight hydrocarbon chain in the $C_9$-$C_{21}$ range and $M^+$ is a metal or ammonium ion.

$$C_{12}H_{25}\text{-O-Na}^+$$

Sulphated alcohol (Dreft)

$$R_2 CH - O- SO_2 - O - Na^+$$

Sulphated alcohol (Teepol)

$$C_2H_{25} - C_6H_4- SO_2O^-Na^+$$

Sulphonated hydrocarbon (Dispersols)

$$RR' CH C_6H_4 - SO^-_3Na^+$$

Alkyl benzenesulfonate

$$C_{13}H_{33} CON (CH_3) CH_3 CH_2SO_3^- Na^+$$

Amidosulfonate (Sodium N-olcoyl - N - methyl phosphate ester aurate)

$$C_{12} H_{25} (-OCH_2 CH_2 CH_2^-)_4 OPO (OH) ONa^+$$

**Cationic Surfactants**

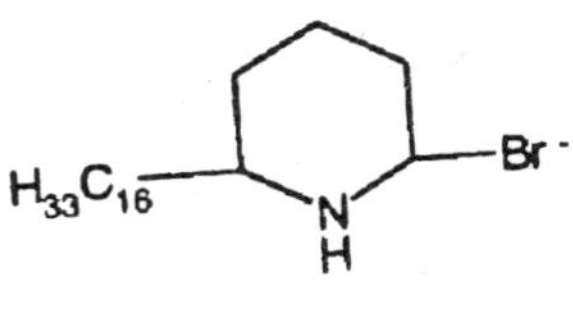

Quatenary ammonium salts (cetyl trimethyl ammonium bromide and pyridinium salts (cetyl pryridinium bromide)

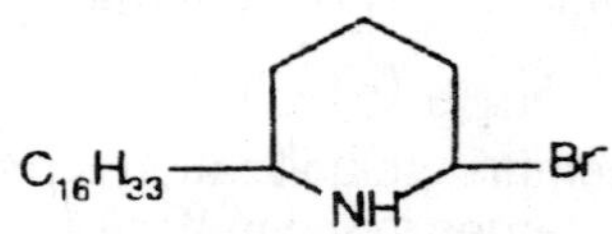

**Nonionic Suractants :** Many non-ionics surfactants are polyethylene oxide derivatives formally derived as follows:

For example Tween 40 contains isomers of polyoxyethy sorbition monopalmiate

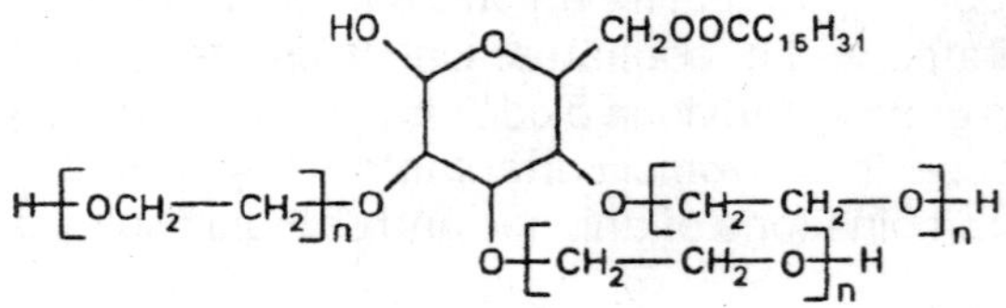

The mean value of n veries in different marketed products.

# 16

# Pesticide Mixtures

## 1. Introduction

The use of pesticide mixtures is common, and their application will be growing in the near future for a number of reasons, which include improved biological performance and decreased costs of application. But there are other economic and environmental factors that are of critical importance.

By simultaneously applying more than one pesticide in a mixture, the applicator saves time, fuel costs and labour. At the same time he also reduces equipment wear and losses caused by mechanical damage to the crops and soil.

Using pesticide mixtures, one can combat a broad spectrum of pests. Different species of insects, pathogens of plant diseases and weeds can be controlled in a single application. Frequently the economic and effective control of an undesirable species can be achieved by using a mixture prepared from one relatively inexpensive component and one more expensive one as opposed to exclusive use of only the latter component.

Another important aspect of the usage of pesticide mixtures is synergism of two or components in a mixture. In such a case the observed joint action of a multicomponent mixture is greater than the expected response calculated by adding the effects induced by individual components of the mixture.

An additional reason for using pesticide mixtures is the necessity to minimize the selection pressure, which may cause an increase in the population of resistant strains of pests and to delay the dominance of resistant strains as a result of the long-term use of some particular pesticides.

## 2. PESTICIDE INTERACTION TERMS

### 2.1 Compatibility and Incompatibility of Mixture Components

The basic prerequisite for high effectiveness of pesticide mixtures is the compatibility of their components. The term "compatibility" means that all components of the mixture are in harmony with one another (1) There is no disadvantageous interaction between them which could decrease the expected efficacy of the mixture or cause phytotoxicity and/or toxicity to warm-blooded organisms, including man.

Reduced mixture performance can result from chemical or physical interactions as well as from biological incompatibility. Chemical incompatibility results from hydrolytic and photochemical degradations and interaction with pesticide components including solvents, surfactants, fillers and other types of mixtures ingredients. The physical properties such as melting and boiling points, volatility, solubility and other less clearly defined physical parameters may adversely affect the handling properties and performances of mixtures if the ingredients are not compatible.

Physical incompatibility is evidenced by formation of agglomerates, crystals, phase separation of emulsions or suspensions and thickening of spray liquids such that the spray application cannot be performed accurately or effectively.

The chemical and physical compatibility of the components of a mixture will be inadequate for high performance of the mixture if, at the same time, the components are not biologically compatible. Such incompatibility can happen if one component of a mixture is able to block the biological activity of the other. In such a case a mixture can be less effective or even completely inactive.

Two other kinds of incompatibility are phytotoxic incompatibility and toxicological incompatility. The former is used to describe the case when desirable plants are injured by pesticide mixtures and the latter, when the toxicity to warm-blooded organisms is higher than had been expected from the toxicity of individual components of the mixtures. Phytotoxic and toxicological incompatibilities may be induced by the chemical or physical incompatibilities may be induced by the chemical or physical incompatibility of the components as well as biological incompatibility.

## 2.2 Synergism, Antagonism and Additivity

The efficacy of a pesticide can be increased by a totally inactive component or by another pesticide. Such a phenomenon is termed the "synergistic" action of the second component. Synergism is more precisely defined by the Weed Science Society of America (2) as an interaction of two or more pesticide components of a mixture such that the combined effect is greater than the predicted one based on the response to each component separately. This synergism is generally interpreted as a biological summation and not as an arithmetic addition of the biological effects of individual components.

A phenomenon opposite to synergism is antagonism, which is defined as a response to the joint application of two or more pesticides that is less than the response anticipated.

The third term, additivity, is defined as the combined action of two biologically active components, that turns out to be equal to the response predicted by adding the responses of each pesticide component if applied separately (3).

The above three definitions can be pictured graphically by the isobol method, which is illustrated for herbicides in Figure 2.1 (4). The term isobol designates a line passing through points of equal action or injury, e.g. a series of $ID_{50}$ values resulting from administering two compounds in different ratios. The solid straight line is the isobol of a precisely additive performance at all dosage ratios. The line above this straight solid one represents some degree of antagonism and the line below the straight line represents some degree of potentiation.

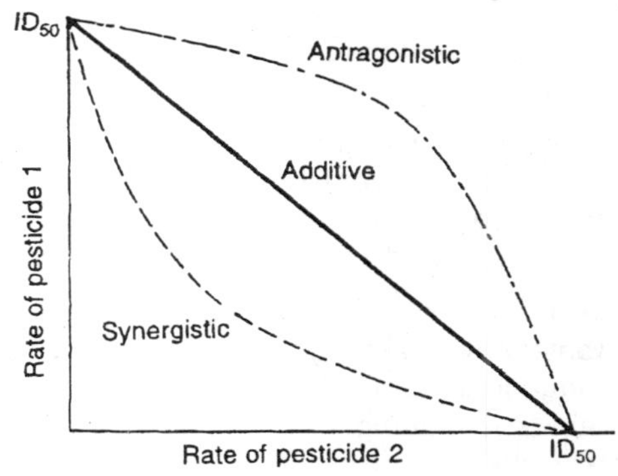


**Figure 2.1** Types of plant responses to mixture of pesticides expressed graphically

From the practical standpoint, synergism is the most desirable response because it enhances the activity of pesticides. By analogy, one can say that antagonism is the only response which is undesirable because it would reduce the efficacy of pesticides.

## 2.3 Pesticide Resistance

Pesticide resistance is the phenomenon of the loss of potency of a pesticide within a few years, sometimes even sooner, due to the development of a resistance gene in the pest (5). Resistance, in this context, refers to the loss of or decreased control over a pest population resulting from the use of chemicals for its control. Resistance of insects and mites to insecticides and acaricides, resistance of pathogens to fungicides and resistance of weeds to herbicides constitute the most serious and widespread aspects of the resistance phenomenon (6). It is the same sort of natural response shown by any life form in the face of an applied selection pressure. The pesticide kills the susceptible strains of pests or pathogens and if resistant individuals exist in the population, they survive. If the pesticide is used too intensively, the resistant strain becomes predominant, leaving the grower with a problem because he is unable to protect crops effectively by using a particular class of products. The rate at which resistant strains are likely to developed depends on the intensity and frequency of application of the pesticides and on the pesticide's specificity and mode of action. The more nonspecific a pesticide, the less chance that an organism can become resistant to it. However, even older products that act on many metabolic sites may induce resistance after intensive and prolonged use.

Modern, more specific pesticides, on the other hand, act only on one or two metabolic sites of the organism and resistance appears at an earlier time. The ability to develop resistant strains and the rate at which this happens vary enormously with different species of pests, pathogens and weeds to be destroyed.

A common phenomenon is cross-resistance. This term denotes the resistance of an organism to several pesticides of related structure acting on the same metabolic site. Cross-resistance can be induced after prolonged usage of only one of the related pesticides.

The relative abundance of insecticides in the 1950s and 1960s encouraged the wasteful, sequential usage of different insecticides to control resistance. This induced a multiplicity of resistance mechanisms within a given insect species, resulting in broad cross resistance covering insecticides of many chemical groups (7).

From what has already been said, it follows that the key method of avoiding of delaying resistance is to minimize the selection pressure exerted by pesticides, thereby prolonging their useful life. The most effective way to do this is to establish an acceptable level of pest control (perhaps less than 100% control) and then apply the required amount of pesticides in a most efficient manner. If, however, resistance is detected, another pesticide (not related to the previous one or an effective mixture of pesticides should be used.

The desirability of using pesticide mixtures to delay resistance is generally accepted in the case of fungicides and herbicides. However, in the case of insecticides the opinions of entomologists vary. There is a body of opinion that if a pest is controlled strongly with a combination of two insecticides, It is apt to develop resistance simultaneously against both insecticides. Persons who support this opinion do not recommend usage of mixed formulations for insect control.

## 3. KINDS OF PESTICIDE MIXTURES AND SOME OF THEIR PROBLEMS

Pesticide mixture may be prepared by growers in the spray tank in the form of so-called tank mixtures or, alternatively, prepared by producers in the form of so-called prepacked mixtures or multi pesticide formulations (MPFs).

The tank mixture is an aqueous dilution, brought to a specific use concentration suitable for application, utilizing two formulations of the individual compounds designed to be diluted with water. However individual formulations may not be compatible. Each of them should be accurately adjusted to match physical and chemical properties. This requires, with respect to each active component, a special selection of the solvents and the systems of auxiliaries such as emulsifiers, dispersing agents, wetting agents and thickeners. The incompatibility of individual formulations to be employed may cause several difficulties, including separation, flocculation, agglomerate formation (resulting in the spray nozzles becoming blocked) or coagulation.

All of the mentioned drawbacks of tank mixtures can be eliminated by the use of MPFs comprising two or more individually active compounds and use of compatible auxiliaries and formulation ingredients.

The advantages of MPFs are the following:

(a) All components are compatible and there is no anxiety of bad behaviour of spray liquids prepared from MPFs.

(b) The proportion of active components is precisely chosen to gain the best biological result;

(c) The preparation of liquid sprays from MPFs is much easier and less troublesome than the preparation of tank mixtures;

(d) The producer of MPFs is better able to prepare different mixtures of good standards than are farmers, who prepare tank mixtures.

It is relatively simple to prepare MPFs of such formulations as wettable powders (WP), emulsifiable concentrates (EC) or water dispersible granules (WG); more complicated to prepare are suspension concentrates (SC) and emulsion concentrates (EW). The most difficult to prepare are MPFs of the suspo-emulsion type. (Abbreviations are in accordance with *The Pesticide Manual,* 8th edition, 1987.)

Examples of some of MPFs are as follows :

| | **Solubility characteristics of pesticide component** | | **Possible MPFs** |
|---|---|---|---|
| (i) | Solid pesticide (SP) insoluble in water ($P_1$) | ia) | ECs of $P_1$ and $P_3$ |
| | SP insoluble in organic solvents ($P_2$) | ib) | SC of $P_2$ in EC of $P_3$ |
| | SP soluble in organic solvents ($P_3$) | ic) | SC of $P_1$ in EW of $P_3$ |
| (ii) | SP insoluble in water ($P_1$) | iia) | SC of $P_1$ in SL of $P_2$ |
| | SP soluble in water ($P_2$) | iib) | $P_1$ solublized in SL of $P_2$ |
| (iii) | Liquid pesticide (LP) insoluble in water ($P_2$) | iiia) | Emulsion of $P_1$ in SL of $P_2$ |
| | SP soluble in water ($P_1$) | iiib) | SC of $P_2$ in EC of $P_1$ |
| (iv) | SP insoluble in water ($P_1$) | iva) | SC of $P_1$ and EW of $P_3$ in SL of $P_2$ |
| | SP soluble in water ($P_2$) | | |
| | LP insoluble in water ($P_3$) | | |

It is apparent from the above list that some MPFs are multiphase systems in which at least one phase is a liquid. In such systems critical attention must be given to the method of manufacture, formulation approach, component materials selection and the effect of environmental factors (temperature and holding-time). These factors profoundly affect the variability in the product's performance, stability characteristics and a host of other properties.

There are many theories and experimental works dealing with disperse systems. Unfortunately most of them do not have a direct relation to the practical problems met in the production or usage of such systems. But, there is a large body of knowledge that, on proper use, enables the formulator to prepare better products more efficiently and evaluate them in a more systematic and realistic manner.

Problems associated with dispersed liquid pesticide formulations are primarily related to their nonequilibrium state. Each phase of such a system continuously seeks to reach thermodynamic equilibrium. In the case of an emulsion, equilibrium is represented by a completely coalesced emulsion.

In the case of a suspension, equilibrium is synonymous with a settled, non-redispersible suspension. If both systems attain thermodynamic equilibrium, the products, for the most part, are of no value. Since, however, the final state of equilibrium is inevitable, the task of pesticide formulator is merely to delay its occurrence. Basically he must attempt to make the product as independent of processing variables as possible and to introduce the necessary energy barriers to delay thermodynamic equilibrium to achieve the desired shelf-life of the product. The concept of thermodynamic equilibrium, coupled with an under standing of free energy, constitutes a framework for design of the disperse systems of interest.

## 4. MPFS ANALYSIS

It is obvious that chemical analysis of MPFs is more complicated than the analysis of a formulation containing a single pesticide. The additional difficulties appear when the MPFs are multiphase formulations, e.g. in the case of SCs, EWs and suspo-emulsions. The most critical chemical analysis concerns the quantitative determination of the active ingredients of a composition of MPF to see if they are in accordance with the nominal composition given by the producer.

In order to determine what pesticide components are mixed together, their separation from the mixture is most often required. This can be performed using conventional techniques, especially in the case of multiphase MPFs.

Depending on the physical and chemical properties of the pesticide components, several methods of analysis must be considered. For example, in the case of three-component MPFs, the analytical methods should involve titration, an ultraviolet (UV) spectrophotometric method and a chromatographic method (either gas liquid chromatography (GLC) or high-pressure liquid chromatography (HPLC). For the GLC method the components must be volatile and stable at the relatively high temperature of the determination. Nonvolatile compounds may be transformed into volatile derivatives, and the reaction must be quantitative, relatively fast, repeatable and reproducible. The modern or-column derivatization using N-methyl-N-trimethylsilyl trifluoracetamide or trimethyl anilinium hydroxide may be carried out, as well as classical silylation or methylation. For the low-volatility pesticides (such as pyrethroids) or nonvolatile (such as phosphonomethyl glycine) and temperature-labile pesticides (majority of substituted ureas), HPLC is a more commonly used technique (8).

The lack of modern analytical equipment in local analytical laboratories, particularly in proximity to manufacturing operations in developing countries, is the main obstacle to performing quantitative chemical analyses of MPFs.

For that reason, such formulations are seldom used in these countries.

**5.Toxicological Aspects of Multicomponent Pesticides**

When combining pesticides, one must be concerned about a possible potentiation of the toxicity of the pesticides to warm-blooded organisms. The toxic effects of the pesticides may be additive, synergistic or antagonistic. For that reason, apart from the hygienictoxicological investigations which are carried out on individual pesticides, several additional experiments should be conducted.

The fundamental test is the determination of an $LD_{50}$ from measurements of the acute oral toxicity. From this value, the coergistic coefficient (J) is calculated for both individual pesticides and mixtures using the following formula:

$$J = \frac{LD_{50} \text{ predicted}}{LD_{50} \text{ experimental determination}}$$

where $LD_{50}$ predicted is

$$\frac{\sum_{n=1}^{n} LD_{50}}{n}$$

and n is the number of pesticide components. In the same way one can determine the acute inhalation toxicity $LD_{50}$ and also its coergistic coefficient J.

When coefficient J indicates an additive or antagonistic action of a mixture, further investigations are unnecessary. In the case of a synergistic effect, however, further tests are necessary. Measurements should be made of the subacute or subchronic toxicity of the mixture paying special attention to the toxicological profile and the mechanism of action. The results obtained on the mixture are compared with the summarized effects of the individual components.

The objective of the above tests is not only to discover the possible coergistic effect but also to determine the ineffective dose (NOEL = no effect level) and the minimum dose value corres-ponding to a visible effect (MEL = minimum effect level).

The toxicological results obtained from the mixture of half NOEL doses of pesticide A and B, as well as from the mixture of full MEL doses of these pesticides, are next compared with the corresponding results for the individual components.

If no enhancement of toxicological effects is found, it should be concluded that no extra additive action exists. This concentration can be accepted as a joint NOEL. If toxic effects are found, it should be concluded that this is the outcome of the mutual influence of the components on toxic effects.

If no NOEL is obtained for a mixture in this test, further investigations should be conducted to explain the coergistic effect (9).

## 6. EXAMPLES OF PESTICIDE MIXTURES

The numbers of individual formulations and MPFs available on the European market in 1989 are given in Table 2.1. The data show that the use of pesticide mixtures is often more advantageous than the use of single ones.

**Table 2.1** Indvidual and MPFs available on the European market in 1989 (10)

| *Kind of pesticides* | *Number of all formulations* | *Number of formulations containing the following number of pesticides* | | | | | |
|---|---|---|---|---|---|---|---|
| | | 1 | 2 | 3 | 4 | 5 | 6 |
| Insecticides and acaricides | 584 | 183 | 270 | 101 | 24 | 3 | 3 |
| Fungicides | 730 | 163 | 358 | 172 | 30 | 3 | 4 |
| Herbicides | 728 | 193 | 313 | 166 | 47 | 6 | 3 |

Mixtures of pesticides can lower the required combined doses if the mode of action of the pesticides components is additive. Furthermore, when a chemical mixture exhibits synergism, an even lower dose of the chemicals may be considered.

In spite of the apparent advantages of pesticide mixtures, their ultimate value must be measured in terms of a derived economic advantages to their user.

Examples of recommended MPFs of particular kinds of pesticides are given below.

### 6.1 Insecticides

Most of the organophosphates and carbamate insecticides that have been commonly used are ineffective against some insects, e.g. against green rice leafhopper. However, it has been observed that some organophosphate like malathion and diazinon have synergistic insecticidal activity in combination with carbamate insecticides such as metolcarb (MTMC), fenbucarb (BPMC), xylylcarb (MPMC) and isoprocarb (MIPC) resistant green rice leafhopper (11). Some of these mixed insecticides have been put on the market in Japan and are widely used for controlling resistant strains (12). The synergism found is believed to be due to inhibition by the carbamate of enzymes that decompose the organophosphate insecticide.

The other MPFs recommended by various producers against green leafhopper are chlorpyrifos methyl + dimethoate, chlorpyrifos ethyl + cypermethrin and malathion + fenitrothion + cypermethrin.

### 6.2 Fungicides

Fungicide mixtures are used to broaden the spectrum of activity of a product or to minimize the selection pressure inducing the formation of resistant strains. Examples for the enlargement of the spectrum are (a) triadimefon + carbendazim for controlling powdery mildews, rust and eyespot in cereals and (b) metalaxyl + mancozeb for activity against *Phytophthora* and *Alternaria* in potatoes To delay the build-up of resistance, mixtures of fungicides with different modes of action are used, for example (a) benlate + captan against apple scab, (b) dicarboximides + folpet against *Botrytis* in grapes and (c) mixtures of phenylamide fungicides with suitable partners against patato late blight (13)

Demethylation inhibitors (DMIs) in combination with non-DMI fungicides are recommended for the control of apple scab (*Venturia inaequalis*), vine powder mildew (*Uncinula necator*) and cucurbit powdery mildew (*Sphaerotheca fuliginea*) (14).

Seed dressing against pathogens may be based on mixtures of thiram + carboxin for wheat, barley, oats, rice, cotton, soybeans and dry beans.

### 6.3 Insecticide/fungicide

There are numerous seed dressing formulations containing a combination of insecticides and fungicides. One example of such a combination used against wheat bulb fly and *Anthracnose* on beans is based on thiram + dichlofenthion.

### 6.4 Herbicides

The simultaneous application of more than one herbicide in a mixture is a standard practice in most weed control strategies. Historically the first cases of synergism were with hormone herbicides. Examples include combinations such as (a) 2, 4–D or 2, 4–DB and atrazine, which have been reported to be synergistic on yellow nutsedge and on bean and (b) chlorpham, which is active against grass weeds, and picloram, which is active against field bindweed etc. (15).

When the action of components is additive then the dosage level of each herbicide component can be reduced. This is particularly true in the commonly used mixture of 2, 4-D + dicamba commonly used for weed control on maize, Reduction in the rate of use of the individual components results in reduced costs of application as well as an increase in crop safety (15).

Mixture of a large number of highly active grass herbicides with selective broadleaf herbicides offer the potential for total post emergence weed control in certain crops. A mixture of two sulfonylureas, chlorosulfuron and metsulfuron methyl, is a recent commercial mixture used on wheat. It utilizes the complementary strategy of components singly as well as their additive action on the more difficult-to-control broadleaf weeds.

A problem associated with a number of post-emergence herbicides, especially the wild oat herbicides, is that they must be applied at a particular growth stage. Mixtures of herbicides that are effective at different growth stages offer a way to reduce this growth stage specificity. A combination of barban and benzylprop or the methyl ester of flamprop were shown to have this effect (15). Fast-acting herbicides like paraquat are often used with long residual soilsterilant heribicides to provide both rapid and long-term weed control (15).

# 17

# Modern Equipment for a Pesticide Formulation Laboratory and Pilot Plant

## 1. Introduction

A large array of modern equipment is available for processing, testing and analsing of pesticide formulations. When establishing a formulation laboratory, the purpose and function of the laboratory should determine the choice of equipment. The laboratory can have any of the following three basic objectives:

(a) To support general production activities, including quality control;

(b) To carry out formulation development, including specification and development of the required ingredients;

(c) To undertake basic researching pesticide formulation and formulation ingredients.

In practice, each of these may be combined with any or all of the others (1). The role of formulation laboratory can also evolve: from initially supporting production activities may subsequently undertake formation research and development. This can be achieved by gradually adding equipment to meet a required need and degree of sophistication. However, if a clear objective is known in the beginning, it would be better to plan the laboratory layout and provide the requisite support facilities and utilities.

Formulation laboratory equipment may be broadly classified as either processing equipment or analytical equipment. Processing equipment includes equipments that carries out various unit operations such as size reduction, blendig, agglomeration and granulation, Analytical equipment can be further divided into two classes: measurement of physical characteristics and chemical assays. Methods for chemical assay are covered in detail in chapter 5. Equipment commonly employed for processing and formulating at an intermediate level as well as for physical testing will be discussed here.

## 2. Formulation Laboratory To Support General Production and Quality Control Activities

The functions of such a laboratory would normally be to provide support to production in the areas of physical testing, including (a) assessment of the suitability of alternative fillers or emulsifiers, (b) determination of the quality of incoming raw materials and (c) maintenance of the quality of day-to-day production. The laboratory functions as an integrated component of the production system leading to fewer lost batches and hence a better output rate. It needs to be suitably equipped to carry out basic quality control tests and storage stability tests on formulations such as (d) dusts and wettable powders, (e) emulsifiable concentrates and emulsion concentrates and (f) suspension concentrates.

Tests to assess the performance of dusts, wettable powders and emulsifiable concentrates can all be carried out in simple glassware using suitable balance, a stopwatch and a set of sieves. Tests such as dry sieve test, flowability, wettability, suspensibility and foaming do not need elaborate equipment. Similarly, the performance of both wettable powders and emulsifiable concentrates can be assessed using simple glassware.

A simple volumetric assessment of settling, using a graduated measuring cylinder to measure the volume of compacted sediment, comparing it with that of a good quality sample, would give a very good indication of whether a formulation will meet specifications. The effect of changing surfactants or fillers in a wettable powder can be assessed in similar way. For emulsifiable concentrates and emulsion concentrates, a comparison of the volume of settled cream with that of a standard, using a graduated conical cylinder, will provide emulsion stability information.

It would be obvious that a new formulation or changes in adjusvants in formulations can be usefuly assessed without carrying out a special chemical determination in expensive analytical equipment. In many cases, a chemical assay can also be carried out by a volumetric method. Here, an autotitrator (ex Mettler, Switzerland) is very handy and eliminates the possibility of manual errors in repeat analysis. A Brookfield viscometer is another handy device to check the stability of suspension concentrates by measuring the non-Newtonian flow characteristics of the composition at different spindle speeds.

It would be desirable to include in the processing equipment a small hammer mill, or equivalent. However, if this not available, a simple coffee mill or a kitchen grinder can be equally effective provided the material to be ground is not too hard.

### 3. Formulation Development Laboratory

For a laboratory designed to develop new formulations, the equipment requirements are basically the same except that more sophisticated and specialized equipment is needed. In particular, more sophisticated powder mills are required which can be used to yield variable particle sizes. Air mills are best when it is desired to obtain the smallest particles. Additionally, equipment for wet grinding and for granulation would also be necessary.

### 3.1 Processing Equipment

At its simplest, a small hammer mill with exchangeable screens is required, together with a pin mill and, if possible, an air jet mill. Pin and hammer mills produce materials in a particle size range from 5 to 30 μm in diameter, with the majority of the particles being between 10 and 20 μm. air mills bring the particle size down to 2–5 μm. These three mills produce a range of particle sizes suitable for the study of wettable powders and their physical properties.

Suspension concentrates, on the other hand, are generally prepared by wet milling the pesticide down to 1-2 μm (2). Thus, a laboratory size wet process bead mill such as a Dynomill (ex W. Bachofen, Switzerland) or a Molinex PE 075 vertical mill (ex Gebr. Netzsch, Germany) is essential if any serious work is too be carried out on suspension concentrates. This is often complemented by a Silverson-type high shear homogenizer (ex Silverson Machines, England) to provide a lump-free slurry for feeding into the Dynomill. High speed homogenizers are also useful for the preparation of emulsifiable concentrates and emulsion concentrates.

The Dynomill is an agitated-type horizontal bead mill and produces a fine (below 5μm in diameter) and narrow particle spectrum. It consists of a short horizontal shaft with an agitator disc assembly that turns the beads used as the grinding media. These beads are distributed along the shaft in a stationary chamber (Figure. 6.1).

**Figure 6.1** Laboratory Dynomill type KDL-Special (by courtesy of W.A. Bachofen AG, Basel, Switzerland)

The high sheer rate chances media action for particle size distribution (impact action) and agglomerate separation (shear action) (3). This is a closed-type mill, which eliminates air entrapment and foaming during milling. Laboratory models with 0.8 litre and 0.6 litre capacities are available. However, for processing smaller quantities (as small as 75 ml), an Eiger mini motor mill (Ex Eiger Engineering England), which functions on a similar principle, can be used. One of the advantages of a Dynomill is that a laboratory process can be scaled up to production batches without going through intermediate pilot plant studies, because Dnomills and Silverson high sheer mixers (Figure 6.2) of varying processing capacities are available.

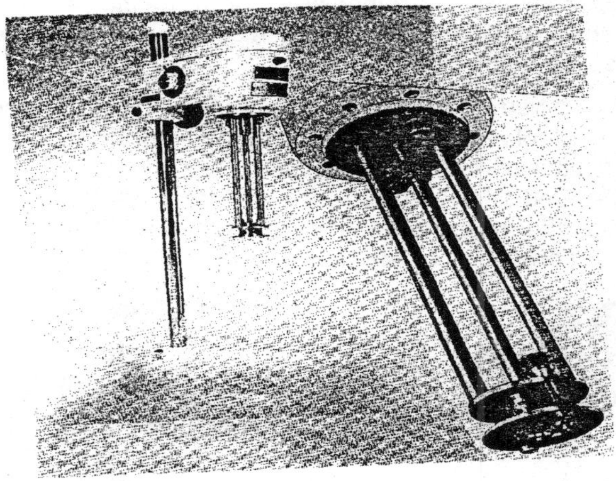

**Figure 6.2** Silverson Laboratory Mixer (by courtesy of Silverson Machines Ltd., Chesom, Bucks, England)

For the development of granular formulations, including water dispersible granules (WGs), compositions can be formed using tumbling, compacting (4) and fluid-bed granulating techniques. If the base material is a liquid, a spray-drying aggomeration technique is applicable.

Pan granulation is a well known technique and is currently used for many agrochemical WGs. The process works on a tumbling and granulating principle. In a broad description of the process, a micronized mixture of the pesticide and additives is placed in an inclined rotating pan. Liquid (acting as a binder solution) is sprayed upon the powder in such a quantity that the powder balls up and produces granules. This technique can be made to work as a continuous process relying on the fact that larger particles migrate to the top of the pan and overflow when additional powder is added to the pan.

Compacting granulation is exemplified by an extrusion process. The most sophisticated machines are twin-screw extruders in which the finely divided dry base is kneaded with water or a binder solution. The resulting dough is forced through a screen perforated with small holes. The spaghetti-type extrusions are dried, comminuted to the desired size and screened. This technique seems to have been most commonly used for granules that are totally or mainly water soluble. A multiplicity of machines is available for the above-described operations. However for a pesticide formulation process laboratory, the most desirable equipment is an Erweka multi-purpose processor (ex Erweka Apparatebau, Germany). This apparatus is similar to a food processor, with attachments such as a coating pan, ribbon blender, extruder and a palettizer. (Figure 6.3). It offers an ideal choice in terms of cost and space requirements.

Fluidized-bed granulation is a versatile technique to form agglomerated granules. Granulation is effected by spraying a binder solution on the pulverized material, which has been brought to a fluidized state. A laboratory-size fluidized-bed piece of equipment suitable for preparing water-dispersible granules is offered by Aeromatic, Switzerland. This apparatus has a transparent covering useful for monitoring the process during the

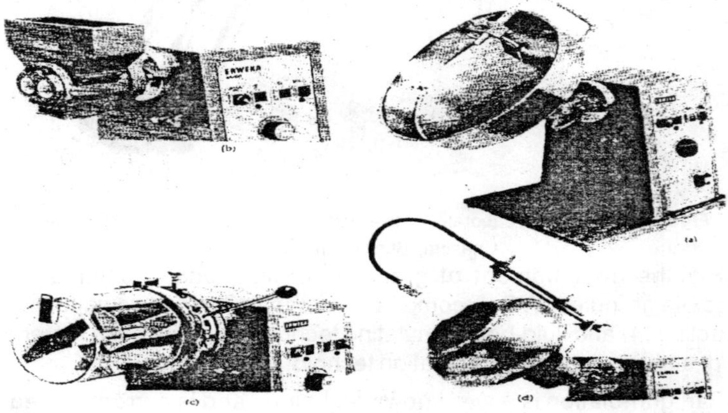

**Figure 6.3** Erweka multi-purpose processor: (a) coating pan, (b) grinder(c) ribbon blender (d) tumbling and spray granulation (by courtesy of Erweka Apparatebau GmbH Heusenstamm, Germany).

development of a formulation (Figure. 6.4). The equipment offers the advantage that, in addition to agglomeration and drying, operations involving impregnation, coating etc. can also be carried out in the equipment.

Similarly, spray drying is a well-known and well-tried technique for the preparation of agglomerated granules. It is used for a wide variety of food products such as soluble coffee and milk. The technique involves spraying a solution or a concentrated water suspension of the pesticide, with or without binder agent, into a conical cylinder in which hot air is circulated. Solid particles form from the spray droplets and agglomerate during the drying process, forming

**Figure 6.4** Aeromatic fluid-bed granulator, laboratory unit Strea-1 (by courtesy of Aeromatic AG; Bubendorf, Switzerland)

microgranules. These particles collect in the bottom of the cone and are removed. A mini spray dryer for laboratory use is available from Buchi, Switzerland.

It is generally difficult to distinguish between fluid-bed and spray-dried granules, but they are clearly distinguishable from extrusion and pan granulation products. Other devices employed for granulation include the inclined rotating cylinder, used in making fertilizers, and Lodige mixers, which are used in food mixing.

At the development phase it is desirable to have a variety of laboratory equipment available to evaluate different techniques of granulation. However, selection of a process will depend upon the type of product required and the availability of the plant-size equipment for manufacture. The process equipment described for granulation is also useful for the development of slow-release and controlled-release formulations, which employ much the same techniques. A list of some of te more important laboratory process equipment for formulation development, along with the identity of their manufacturers/suppliers, is given in Appendix A.

### 3.2 Physical Testing Equipment

Formulation chemists have to employ a number of test methods for the evaluation of the physical characteristics of processed formulations. These methods can be classified into two categories. The first category constitutes methods used to correlate different parameters in order to improve certain properties of the compound that is to be fromulated. The second category consists of methods used to test the products for their conformity to certain quality requirements and the selection of specification limit values (5).

Under the first category, a gamut of techniques is available for testing the wide range of physical characteristics that occur in formulation development. Examples range from light or electron microscopic methods through techniques for the measurement of rheological characteristics, interfacial tension, absorption isotherms etc. Equipment useful in these tests includes biological and stereo microscopes, supporting photographic facilities, a rotational viscometer and a tensiometer.

An extremely important property of most solid formulations and suspension concentrates is particle size. Critical sizes are in the range of 0.1 and 10μm. The measurement of particle size generally requires sophisticated equipment, although some simple qualitative tests are available. The Hegman gauge is one such. However, more sophisticated means of measuring particle size such as the Malvern, are desirable.

Although most of this laboratory equipment would be considered important for developmental purposes, procurement of the highest level of sophistication and sensitivity may be impeded by budgetary constraints. Unfortunately the more sophisticated and more sensitive equipment is usually more costly. In industrial research one must weigh the relationship between the data obtainable and the price of obtaining it. The formulation chemist will need to make a decision concerning the trade-off between the cost of the equipment and the quality of the data that will be obtained. In this connection, one can always concentrate on the most important properties of the formulation and first try to optimize them.

The second category consists of equipment that measures properties described in the specifications. The principle characteristics of the quality of a pesticide formulation are its biological activity, its tolerance by the crop and its ease of use. However as biological activities and crop tolerances are difficult to determine quantitatively in the laboratory, other parameters that can be measured readily by physical and chemical methods are specified in a specification. Often the method used has been tested in a collaborative study and has been widely approved. This includes equipment suitable for carrying out an assy of the active ingredient in a formulation and equipment able to assess both the chemical and physical stability of new formulations. Generally speaking, this involves, at its simplest, a UV spectrophotometer and chromatography equipment, i.e. a GC and/or HPLC. A tropical climate tester is desirable to study the stability of a formulation under conditions of accelerated storage and to check its compatibility with the packaging.

A suggested list of physical and analytical testing equipment, along with some of the identified sources, is given in Appendix B.

## 4. LABORATORY FOR BASIC FORMULATION RESEARCH

To set up a laboratory to carry out basic research on formulations and formulation adjuvants requires considerable expenditure of funds. In addition to the equipment cited earlier, it is essential to have available very sophisticated means of measuring particle size with a Malvern c a Coulter counter. The Malvern master sizer can measure particles in the range 0.1-600 µm; the Coulter counter covers the range 0.6–800 µm in diameter. One should note, however, that these two machines may produce different results if the particle shape differs substantially from the spherical.

Additional desirable equipment would include equipment to measure surface tension, zeta potential, absolute density etc.

Desirable mechanical equipment would include a pray graulator, a spray drier, a pan granulator, a colloid mill, a high-energy disperser and a drum blender. Such an array of equipment would give a good variety of approaches for the preparation of different formulations.

On the analytical side, equipment such as thermal analyses, including differential thermal analysis (DTA), differential scanning calorimetry (DSC) and thermal gravimetric analysis (TGA), and an atomic absorption spectrophotometer are particularly useful in evaluating the suitability of a mineral carrier as a pesticide diluent. These instruments yield information on the mineral characterization of clays, their crystallinity and the type of associated water (structural, bound or unbound), which may affect the stability of a formulated pesticide.

DTA is an excellent method for an accelerated evaluation of the compatibility of clays with an active ingredient. Here one compares the thermal curve when heating an active ingredient with the curve obtained when heating a mixture of the active ingredient with a potential carrier (6). Atomic absorption spectroscopy can generate information on heavy metal impurities present in the clay that may catalyse chemical decomposition of the active substance.

Equipment for GLC and HPLC, with standard detectors, is essential for a chemical assay of active ingredients. Some equipment is now available with an interface with a mass spectral detector (MSD). This detector offers an economical way to enable one to identify and analyse breakdown products of pesticides in the formulations and to analyses pesticide residues. However, equipment with an MSD is quite expensive and its acquisition has to be rationalized with the available budget.

Supercritical fluid chromatography (SFC), permits analysis of complex, high molecular weight or thermally liable mixtures that are difficult to separate by other techniques. It supplements the capabilities of gas and liquid chromatography, combining the solubility behaviour of liquids and the diffusion and viscosity properties of gases. The equipment can be coupled with an SFE, which rapidly extracts the components of interest from a complex mixture selectively and quantitatively for subsequent analysis. The technique is particularly useful fro pesticide residue analysis.

Among the various spectrophotometric techniques, UV-visible and IR spectrophotometers are regularly employed for assaying pesticides in the formulations. A Fourier Transform Infra Red (FTIR) system provides a high resolution spectrum by means of a signal averaging of repeated scans at a desired signal-noise ratio. A photo diode-array UV-visible spectrophotometer offers the advantage of measuring full spectra (from 190 to 820 mm) very rapidly. Both devices can be interfaced with GC and HPLC to function as detectors. Modern analytical equipment, by and large, is microprocessor controlled, and often possesses its own dedicated computer. It is possible to network the dedicated computers of different pieces of equipment by ensuring their mutual compatibility at the time the equipment is ordered. This can facilitate the task of data storage and handling.

### 5. Pilot Plant Equipment for the processing of Formulations

Ideally, pilot plant equipment for the processing of fomulations will effectively simulate, on a larger scale, the processes observed in the laboratory. However, it does not always succeed in this. The situation becomes particularly complex when the equipment employed for laboratory-scale process development is not available in larger capacity models or when the larger equipments functions on a different principle. In such a situation, the laboratory process needs to be revalidated by changing process parameters such as temperature, time, feed rate, size, and number of recyclings.

Frequently the same pilot plant equipment will be used for processing different pesticides, such as herbicides, fungicides, and insecticides. Contamination problems may arise. Thus, versatile equipment should be selected which has easy clean-up and decontamination (7).

Many types of processing equipments, such as the size reduction mills, mixers and blenders and granulating systems described in Section 3.1, are available in larger models and are suitable for the pilot plant. There may be, however, scale-up problems. For examples, in the size reduction process, the choice of the type of size reduction mill is dependent upon the physical properties of the feed material and the desired size distribution of the output. In some mills, such as a high-speed hammer mill or a pin mill, a temperature rise in the grinding chamber occurs due to heat generated during their operation. This temperature rise may cause the formation of sticky materials that will agglomerate or it may cause heat-sensitive materials to decompose. And of course, sticky agglomerated materials do not grind well. Some of these problems may be alleviated by processing the formulation in an air jet mill. On the other hand, a relatively efficient size reduction mill known as an air-swept ultra-fine vortex mill is widely used in Europe for the production of wettable powder formulations. The mill may provide a finely ground product (below 10μm) at a much higher rate than a hammer mill and more economically than an air jet mill (7). The equipment is available in a pilot-plant size model from Ultrafine, France. However, sticky and heat-sensitive materials cannot be processed in it under normal conditions. For a wet grinding process, dynomills are available in several large-size models. Similarly, larger versions of Silverson mixers are also available. Both of these machines are commonly used in the pesticide industry for the processing of suspension concentrate formulations.

The availability of different types of size reduction mills in the pilot plant provides the flexibility to tailor operations with consideration of such factors as functionality, economy and safety.

For different granulation processes, a variety of equipment is available for pilot-plant scale operations, including sigma mixers, or kneaders, for dough making and screw extruders for making extrusion-type granules. Similarly, fluid-bed systems are offered by Aeromatic, Switzerland, and Alpine, Germany. The Aeromatic systems are available either as multi-processors or as a building block system that can be assembled to suit the required use. Spray-drying equipment is available from manufacturers like Anhydro, Stork Friesland and Niro Atomizer. It comes in a wide variety of dryer shapes to suit different products and processing conditions. To improve the control of product dryness and raise the overall energy efficiency, it is possible to add a fluid-bed dryer to a basic spray dryer. Such spray dryer-fluid bed combinations are particularly suitable for heat-sensitive materials.

## 6. Conslusion

As rapid advances in technology and newer developments in highly sophisticated processes and analytical equipment have a symbiotic relationship, it is only to be expected that state-of-the-art equipment is soon superseded by even more versatile or sophisticated equipment. However, it is not necessary to have an extremely elaborate and fully equipped laboratory to do useful work on formulations and formulation development. As important to a good formulation laboratory as sophisticated equipment are innovative ideas drawn from day to-day observations. Besides, many of the techniques used in pesticide formulations are drawn, either directly or indirectly, from food processing techniques. It is often possible to develop new formulations with very simple equipment. In this context, an appropriate approach for equipping a pesticide formulation laboratory might be the gradual addition of equipment as needed. Let the laboratory evolve in conformity with the exposure and training of the formulation chemists and in relation to the level of sophistication foreseen for various planned projects. In addition, the financial support available would have a significant influence on the development of the laboratory.

## APPENDIX A

List of processing equipment for a pesticide formulation laboratory and some of the source for their supply.

| | *Equipment* | *Source* |
|---|---|---|
| 1. | Hammer mill (Condux type) | F.G. Bode & Co., GmbH |
| 2. | Laboratory grinding mill (Condux type) | SchlossmÜhlendamm 11<br>P.O. Box 900167<br>D-20457 Hamburg, Germany |
| 3. | Pin mill (Laboratory Universal Mill) | Alpine AG<br>D-86199 Augsburg, Germany |
| 4. | Air Jet mill (Micronizer) | Sturtevant International Sales Corp.<br>103 Clayton St. Drochester<br>Boston, MA 02122, U.S.A.<br>Fluid Energy International Sales Corp.<br>153 Penn Avenue<br>Hatfield, PA 19440, U.S.A. |
| 5. | Air-swept micro vortex mill | Societe Ultrafine Usine de Villeneure sur Verberie 60410 Verberie, France |

| | | |
|---|---|---|
| 6. | Agitated-type-horizonal Bead mill Dynomill) | Willy A. Bachofen AG Machinenfabrik, 17 Utengasse Strasse CH-4005 Basel, Switzerland |
| 7. | Agitated bead/sand mill (Eiger minimotor mill) | Eiger Engineering Ltd. 40 Hardwick Grange, Woolstone Warington - Cheshire WA 1 4RF, England. |
| 8. | High-sheer homogenizer (Silverson laboratory mixer) | Silverson Machines Ltd., Wateside, Chesham, Bucks HP5 1 PQ, England |
| 9. | Multipurpose processor with (a) palletizer, (b) coating pan (c) extruder and (d) ribbon blender attachments | Erwek Apparatebu GmbH P.O. Box 1253 Ottostrasse 20-22 D-63150 Heusenstamm, Germany |
| 10. | Fluid-bed granulator with Wurster accessory (Aeromatic Laboratory unit STREA-1) | Aeromatic AG Hauptstrasse 145 CH-4416 Bubendrof, Switzerland or Aeromatic Inc., Towaco, NJ 07082, U.S.A. |
| 11. | Mini spray dryer | Buchi laboratoriums Technik AG Flawil, Switzerland |
| 12. | Ploughshare mixer (Lodige mixer) | Gebruder lodige Machinenbau GmbH Postfach 2050 Elsener Srasse 7-9 D-33102 Paderborn, Germany. |

## APPENDIX B

List of physical testing and analytical equipment and some of the sources for their supply

| | *Equipment* | *Source* |
|---|---|---|
| 1. | Sieving apparatus (Alpine Luftsrahlsieb) | Alpine AG, Postfach 629, D-86199 Augsburg Germany |
| 2. | Tropic Climate Tester (fro accelerated storage studies) | Hereus-Votsch GmbH. Beethovenstrasse 34 D-72334 Balingen-Frommern, Germany |
| 3. | Biological and stereo microscopes | Olympus Optical Co. Ltd. San-Ei Building, 22-2 Nishi-Shinjuku 1-Chome Shinjuku-ku, Tokyo, Japan |

| | | |
|---|---|---|
| | | Nikon Corporation, Fuji Building,<br>2-3 Marunouchi 3-Chome,<br>Chiyoda-ku, Tokyo 100, Japan |
| 4. | Particle size analyser (Malvern Master sizer to measure 0.1-600 μm particle sizes) | Malvern Instrument Ltd.<br>Springlane South, Malvern,<br>Worcestershire, WR14 1 AQ, England. |
| 5. | Malvern Zeta Sizer IIc | |
| 6. | Eectronic particle counter<br>(Coulter Counter TA-II) | CoulterElectronics Inc.<br>Hialeah, FL, U.S.A. |
| 7. | Brookfield LVT Viscometer | Brookfield Engineering Lab<br>240 Cushing Street<br>Stoughton, MA 02072, U.S.A. |
| 8. | Haake Rotovisko | MSE Scientfic instruments.<br>Crawley, Sussex, England. |
| 9. | Deer rheometer | Integrated Petronic Systems<br>London, England |
| 10. | True denser | Sheshin Enterprises Co. Ltd.<br>5-27-7 Sadagaya<br>Shivaya Ku, Tokyo, Japan |
| 11. | analytical balances | Satorious Instruments<br>1430 Wankegan Road<br>McGaw Park, IL 60085, U.S.A. |
| 12. | Autotitrator/memotitrator | Mettler Instrumente AG<br>CH-8606 Griefensee, Switzerland |
| 13. | Gas-liquid chromatograph | Hewlett Packard Co.<br>3495 Deer Greek Road,<br>Palo Alto, CA 94304, U.S.A.<br>Perkin-Elmer Corporation<br>761 Main Ave.<br>Norwalk, CT 06859-0012, U.S.A.<br>Shimadzu Corporation<br>3, kanda-Nishikicho 1-Chome<br>Chiyoda-ku, Tokyo 101, Japan. |

| | | |
|---|---|---|
| 14. | High-pressure liquid chromatograph | Waters, Divisions of Millipore,<br>Maple Street<br>Milfor, MA 01757, U.S.A. |
| 15. | Supercritical fluid chromatograph | Suprex Corporation<br>SFC Research Centre<br>125 William Pitt Way<br>Pittsurgh, PA 15238, U.S.A.<br>Computer Chemical Systems<br>Rt. 41 & Newark Road, P.O.Box 683,<br>Avondale, PA 19311, U.S.A. |
| 16. | Infra-red spectrophotometer and Fourier Transform IR spectrophotometer | Perkin-Elmer Ltd.,<br>Norwalk, CT, U.S.A.<br>Shimadzu Corporation, Tokyo, Japan<br>Mattson Instruments Inc.<br>1001 Fourier Drive<br>Madison, WI 53717, U.S.A. |
| 17. | Photodioded-array UV-visible spectrophotometer | Hewlett-Packard Co.,<br>Palo Alto, CA CA 94304, U.S.A.<br>Backman Instruments Inc.<br>Alex Division, 23050 Camino Ramon,<br>P.O. Box 5101<br>San Ramon, CA 9458, U.S.A. |
| 18. | Atomic absorption Spectrophotometer | Perkin-Elmer Corporation<br>Norwalk, CT 06859, U.S.A.<br>Pye Unicam Ltd., York Street,<br>Cambridge, CB1 2 PX, England. |
| 19. | Thermal analyser | DuPont Company<br>Instrument Systems<br>Concord Plaza, Quillen Bldg.,<br>Wilmington, DE 19898, U.S.A.<br>Mettler Instrumente AG,<br>Greifensee, Switzerland. |

# 18

# Aerosol Formulations

## 1. Introduction

Approximately eitht billion aerosol units were produced worldwide in 1990, including almost three billion in the United States, three billion in Western Europe and two billion in the remainder of the world (1). Aerosol insect sprays account for over 190 million units, or 6.5% of the total in the United States. The United Kingdom contributes an additional 50 million insecticide aerosol units and Australia produces a substantial 20 million units. Based on per capita consumption in Argentina, Brazil and Mexico, over 150 million aerosol insect sprays are produced in those three countries (2). Worldwide, insecticide aerosols account for over 600 million units, and it appears that the advantages offered by aerosol packaging will maintain this production trend well into the future.

### 1.1 Advantages and Disadvantages

Aerosol insect sprays have many advantages over other types of delivery systems. The aerosol package is safe and convenient for the consumer. The sealed package minimizes deterioration of the contents and shelf-lives of 5-10 years are not uncommon. The contents of the aerosol units are unavailable unless activated by the dispensing system, which controls the delivery rate. In actual usage, only a few seconds of spray are needed to provide the performance desired. Aerosols also provide for a variety of delivery systems,which allows dispensing the product in a form that is optimum. The forms includes a fine particle spray for spraying a space, a coarse wet spray for surface treatment and any degree of foaming for either a crack and crevice treatment or a foam tracer. All these parameters combined result in a product form that is most efficient and effective for insect control.

There are very few disadvantages of aerosol insect sprays from a technical standpoint. However, price, lack of visibility of the product, little differentiation between products and confusion concerning use of the actuator function are some disadvantages that inhibit market growth. The major technical disadvantages of aerosols are their flammability (for hydrocarbon-propelled systems) and ozone depletion (for fluorocarbon-propelled systems). Flammability concerns are more important in shipping and storage since very few consumer problems have occurred in relation to the number of units used. The ozone depletion problem is a worldwide concern. Fluorocarbons are known to deplete the ozone layer, which protects the earth from ultraviolet radiation. Depletion of the ozone layer results in more exposure to UV rays and a correspondignly increased risk of skin cancer. This potential problem has resulted in a ban on the use of fluorocarbons in aerosol products in the United State as well as in many other countries. The fluorocarbon propellants have been replaced by hydrocarbons, which are the propellants of choice at present time.

The removal of the fluorocarbons did not, however, ease consumer concerns regarding aerosols. The Roper Organization was commissioned to do a study in the United States on consumer perception of aerosols (3). A majority of the people who knew about ozone thought that aerosols were the main contributor to the problem and 78.0% would support regulations to ensure the use of safer propellants. They were unaware that regulations had been in place since 1978 in the United States and that present-day aerosols did not contribute to the ozone depletion problem. Similar regulations will phase out fluorocarbon propellants by the year 2000 in developed nations and by 2010 in developing nations. This negative consumer perception about aerosols is the major disadvantage for the aerosol industry and needs to be addressed by a programme now in place that will provide accurate information to environmental groups, lawmakers, the media and consumers.

## 1.2 Definition

The word "aerosol" was first used in colloid chemistry to describe a suspension, in air or gas, of solid or liquid particles having a diameter less than 50 µm. Using this definition as a baseline,the United States Department of Agriculture defined a pressurized aerosol insecticide product as a system where 80% of the particles, by weight, must be less than 30 µm in diameter and all particles must be less than 50 µm (4).

In 1955, the Chemical Specialties Manufactures Association (CSMA) adopted the following definition for aerosol products (5). "a self-contained sprayable product in which the propellant force is supplied by a liquefied gas. "This definition includes space, residual, surface coating, foam and various other types of products but does not include gas-pressurized products such as whipping cream.

At the present time, the word aerosol is understood by the general public to mean any product that is dispensed with the aid of a propellant.

### 1.3 Aerosol Operation and Theory

The aerosol package consists of a sealable container equipped with a valve and containing a liquefied gas propellant, solvents, active ingredients and other miscellaneous materials packaged under pressure.

The aerosol container is never completely filled so that the propellant can exist in a gaseous form in the head space, thereby maintaining a constant pressure in the container.

When the valve is opened, the internal pressure forces the product up the dip tube and out the valve. As soon as the product leaves the container, some of the propellant molecules vapourize and fly off into space. In doing so, they collide with solvent molecules and cause collisions between the solvent molecules themselves thereby disrupting the attractive forces between them. As the propellant vapourizes in air, the solvent molecules are left almost isolated in relatively small groups of particles. The liquefied gas propellant, therefore, not only provides the pressure to force the product out of the container when the valve is opened, but also breaks up the concentrate into small droplets or particles once the aerosol has reached the atmosphere.

## 2. TYPES OF AEROSOL FORMULATIONS

Aerosol formulations can be classified as homogeneous or heterogeneous systems, based on the solubility of the components in the system.

### 2.1 Homogeneous Systems

All components of homogeneous systems are mutually soluble or miscible, forming a two-phase system consisting of a single liquid phase and a vapour phase. These systems do not require shaking before used and are used for some insecticide as well as insect repellent products.

The liquid phase of these solution-type systems can be liquid solvents or a combination of a liquid solvent and a liquid propellant, with all components soluble in the liquid phase. The liquid phase can consist of only liquid solvents (mineral spirits, methylene chloride, alcohol), alcohol-water solutions or water-dimethyl ether propellant solutions. The vapour-propellant phase can consist of various propellants, including hydrocarbons, fluorocarbons or dimethyl ether.

## 2.2 Heterogeneous Systems

Heterogeneous systems are not mutually soluble are result in a three-phase system consisting of two liquid phases or a liquid and a solid phase in combination with a vapour phase. These systems require shaking before use and are used for some insecticide products as well as numerous personal care products.

Heterogeneous systems can be further classified as emulsion or suspension systems. Emulsion systems are aqueous systems using emulsifiers to incorporate the non-soluble components. Suspension systems contain material that is insoluble in the mixture of the propellant and solvent or insoluble in an emulsion system. These systems usually contain solid material (talcs, powders, clays) suspended in the liquid phase. Since the solid material settles, shaking is necessary before use.

Insecticide aerosol formulations can also be classified as solvent-based systems, oil-out emulsion systems or water-out emulsion systems.

## 2.3 Solvent-Based Systems

Solvent-based systems are non-aqueous systems consisting of an organic solvent as a carrier and any one of several propellants to expel the product from the container. These are usually two-phase homogeneous systems but can also be heterogeneous systems if powder is added to serve as in insecticide carrier. The powder will settle upon standing and the container will need shaking before using the product. Non-powder solvent systems do not require shaking. Mineral spirits, or non-deodorized kerosene blends, are commonly used solvents due to availability and economics. Most insecticides are readily soluble in kerosene, but a co-solvent (methylene chloride, trichloroethane, isopropanol) may be needed for some compounds. Other components, such as fragrances, synergists and inhibitors, can also be added to solvent systems. Most solvents are quite compatible with most of these materials and the propellants now used in insect control products.

Solvent-based insect control aerosol products are marketed throughout the world as surface, space and multi-purpose sprays.

## 2.4 Oil-out Emulsion Systems

Oil-out emulsions contain a fairly large amount of propellant miscible with the oil of the formulation, which forms the external phase of the emulsion. This external phase encloses the internal aqueous phase. These systems are quite stable, but may also separate over time and require shaking before use. Many of the space spray insecticide products are formulated as oil-out emulsions. Performance comparable to that of all solvent-based systems against flies and mosquitoes can be obtained with properly formulated oil-out emulsions. Against larger insects such as cockroaches, oil-out emulsions are also effective. However, there is a longer time period between direct spray treatment and mortality than with solvent based systems. Formulated as a residual preventative treatment, aqueous-based systems can be just as effective as solvent-based system, and they offer the advantage of using less organic solvent.

### 2.5 Water-Out Emulsions

Water-out emulsion systems, or foam emulsions, have a reduced level of propellant. The propellant and solvent of the system creates the internal phase of the emulsion, while the aqueous intermediate creates the external phase. The propellant travels through the emulsion when exposed to the atmosphere and creates a foam as it expands the external phase. Various formulation techniques can be used to create stable or quick-breaking foams for various applications in insect control. However, since the aqueous external phase provides performance characteristics that are insufficient for direct spray application against insects, the systems have been little used worldwide. Some water-out emulsion products are available as crack and crevice foam treatments and provide excellent performance in this application.

## 3. COMPONENTS OF AEROSOL SYSTEMS

The complete aerosol system consists not only of the chemical formulation, which includes the intermediate and the propellant, but also the valve and actuator, which influence the performance obtained from the formulation. These three important components of all aerosol insecticide systems will be discussed here.

### 3.1 Aerosol Intermediates

The intermediate of an aerosol system consists of all the chemical components in the formula with the exception of the propellant. The intermediate can contain various chemicals necessary or desired for specific functions in the formulation. Depending on the type of insecticide formulation, the intermediate may include:

(a) Active ingredients:

(b) Solvents;

(c) Water;

(d) Emulsifiers;

(e) Inhibtitors;

(f) Fragrances.

### 3.1.1 Active ingredients

For our discussion,active ingredients will include conventional insecticides as well as synergistis, insectgrowth regulators, repellents and attractants, as all these chemicals must be registered with EPA.

Table 12.1 provides a classification of active ingredients by function as well as by aerosol product application. It provides a good guideline for selecting active ingredients for a specific purpose. For each product type, active ingredients were ranked to indicate preference based on present usage as well as consumer acceptance and worldwide availability

### 3.1.2 Solvents

Hundreds of solvents are available but only a few are commonly used in aerosol insecticide formulations. The choice of a solvent is to a degree based on that it must dissolve, using "like dissolves like" as a guideline. Fo rinstance, if an organic chemical must be dissolved,an aromatic solvent would be the best choice. However, this will depend on the total properties necessary for developing an acceptable product.

**3.1.2***(a) Solvent properties :* In general, the following solvent properties should be reviewed when developing an aerosol product : solvent power, flash point, toxicity, speed of evaporation, cost, aniline point, distillation range, specific gravity, weight per gallon and solubility parameter.

Solvent power may be defined as a lilquid's ability to dissolve a given substance. It is usually expressed as so many grams of a particular substance in 100 cc of solvent. For instance, 100 cc water dissolves 36 g salt, while 100 cc alcohol dissolves 3 g. This solvent power is usually expressed as the kauri-butanol value(k.b.value) for the solvent. This value is the millilitres of that solvent that will produce turbidity when added to 20 g of a solution of kauri gum resin in butyl alcohol at 25°C. For toluence, 105 ml are required, showing toluene to have excellent solvent power, which is used as the standard. The k.b. value is only used in describing hydrocarbon sovents since alcohols are better solvents than toluene and a measure of relative solvent power would be less meaningful when using k.b. values.

The flash point of a liquids is the temperature at which the saturated vapour will ignite in the presence of a spark or flame, or the temperature that must be reached before the material will give off sufficient vapour to form an explosive mixture with air when exposed to a test flame. The standard method of measurement is called theTag Closed Cup as defined by ASTM (6). Flash points determined in a closed cup are always lower than determined in an open cup.

**Table 12.1** Classification of active ingredients for use in aerosol formulations

| *Product type* | *Functions of active ingredients* | | | | | |
|---|---|---|---|---|---|---|
| | *Knockdown agent* | *Synergist* | *Kill agent* | *Residual kill agent* | *Insect growth regulator* | *Repellent* |
| Space spray aerosol | Pyrethrin<br>Tetramethrin<br>Pynamin forte<br>Bioallethrin<br>Neopynamin forte | PBO | Sumithrin<br>Resmethrin<br>Permethrin<br>DDVP | | | |
| Surface aerosol | Pyrethrin<br>Tetramethrin<br>Neopynamin forte<br>DDVP | PBO<br>MGK 264 | | Permethrin<br>Cypermehrin<br>Deltamethrin<br>Cyfluthrin<br>Propoxun<br>Dursban<br>Malathion<br>Sumithion | Hydroprene<br>Fenoxycarb<br>Dimilin | MGK 874 |
| Multi-purpose aerosol | Pyrethrin<br>Tetramethrin<br>Neopynaminforte<br>Pynamin forte<br>Bioallethrin<br>Esbiothrin<br>Prallethrin | | DDVP | Propoxur<br>Cyphenothrin<br>Permethrin | | |
| Aerosol fogger | Pyrethrin<br>Tetramethrin | | DDVP | Permethrin<br>Cyphenothrin | Hydroprene<br>Fenoxycarb | |
| Aerosol repellent | | | | | Deet | |
| Aerosol mothproofer | | | Permethrin<br>Vaporthrin | | | |

Toxicity of the solvent is important since it makes a significant contribution to the toxicity of the finished product. Methylene chloride is a commonly used solvent in aerosol systems but is now under question and should not be considered for aerosol formulas. The threshold limit value (TLV) is the maximum airborne concentration of the solvent that a person could be repeatedly exposed to day after day without adverse effects. The flammability rating is a relative number, i.e.the lower the number, the less flammable the solvent. Carbon tetrachloride, which is non-flammable, is rated 0 and benzene rated 100.

Speed of Evaporation is expressed in relation to the evaporation rate of toluence, which is standardized at 1. All products with evaporation rates greater than 1 evaporate faster than toluene and conversely, numbers lower than 1 indicate a slower evaporation rate.

Cost is always a consideration in attempting to develop a cost effective formulation.

Aniline point is the temperature at which a volume of hydrocarbon will dissolve an equal volume of aniline oil. 5 ml of the solvent and aniline oil are heated in a test tube until the mixture becomes homogeneous.

Distillation range is a series of temperatures recorded while boiling a solvent sample. The initial boiling point (IBP) occurs when the boiling starts and the dry end point occurs when the sample has just boiled away. The IBP gives an indication of flash point, i.e. a solvent with a higher IBP will have a higher flash point and the dry end point will show which solvent will be completely evaporated first. The distillation range also indicates chemical impurities: the shorter the range, the fewer constituent products.

Specific gravity is the ratio of the weight of a given volume of liquid to the weight of an equal volume of distilled water at a specific temperature. This is important when comparing costs of different liquids sold by weight and if the final product is sold by volume.

The weight per gallon of any liquid is determined by multiplying the weight of a gallon of distilled water (3.78 kg) by the specific gravity of the liquid.

The solubility parameter is a physical constant for a compound and provides a means of predicting (a) whether mixtures of liquids will be miscible, (b) whether an amorphous solid will dissolve in a solvent or a mixture of solvents and (c) whether a valve gasket will be affected by an aerosol propellant, solvent or co-solvent of the formulation. If two compounds have similar solubility parameters, the chances are that they will be miscible.

**3.1.2** ***(b)*** *Solvent Types :* Insecticide aerosol solvents fall into three chemically distinct groups :

(a) Hydrocarbons;

(b) Chlorinates solvents;

(c) Alcohols.

Hydrocarbon solvents consists of only carbon and hydrogen and include petroleum naphthas, benzene, toluene, xylene, aromatic petroleum solvents and turpentine. The petroleum naphthas, aromatic petroleum solvents and turpentine are mixtures of several chemical hydrocarbons (7). Aliphatic or straight-chain hydrocarbons, also commonly known as paraffins, make up over 85% of the petroleum naphthas. Aromatic hydrocarbons have stronger solvent power than the aliphatics and include benzene, toluene an xylene. Cyclic hydrocarbon solvents are somewhat of a compromise between the aliphatics and aromatics and include the naphthenes, which are formed to small extent in petroleum naphthas and to a larger extent in aromatic petroleum naphthas. Terpenes are also included in this group and include pinene, the main constituent of turpentine.

Chlorinated solvents consist of carbon, hydrogen and chlorine or carbon and chlorine. Most chlorinated solvents are quite pure and therefore have a narrow boiling range. They also have excellent solvent properties and are commonly used for dissolving oils and fats. Methylene chloride is a fast-evaporating chlorinated solvent with excellent lifting power suitable for paint stripping applications. It is also used in insecticide products but is now banned in many countries. 1,1,1-trichloroethane is also widely used in aerosol formulations, including insecticides, and is sold under various trade names. Chlorothene NU contains a corrosion inhibitor. Chlorothene VG is 1, 1, 1-trichloroethane proprietary grade to replace trichloroethylene where restrictions on solvent vapour emissions have been legislated.

Alcohols vary greatly in their solvent properties when compared to hydrocarbons. The low-boiling alcohols, methyl, ethyl and isopropyl, are all miscible with water, while the hydrocarbons are not. Alcohols dissolve various compounds that cannot be dissolved by hydrocarbons, including shellac, vanilla gum, natural kauri resin and synthetic resins. The alcohols also differ from hydrocarbons in having oxygen in addition to carbon and hydrogen. Primary and secondary alcohols of the same name have the same formula but a different isomeric structure and, therefore, different chemical properties. Ethanol, or ethyl alcohol, can be produced by fermentation, but most industrial grades are produced by less expensive synthetic routes using petroleum gases. Isopropyl alcohol is produced from natural gas and is widely used because it is non-poisonous. It can be marketed as anhydrous or as an over 90% grade, the remaining portion being water.

### 3.1.3 Water

Water has many properties that make it desirable for use in aerosol systems. Itis an excellent solvent,non-flammaable, readily available, inexpensive and low in toxicity. Its major disadvantage is its immiscibility with liquefied gas propellants. This immiscibility can be overcome using coupling solvents such as ethyl alcohol or using a dimethyl ether propellant systems. The most common method is to use surface-active agents to produce stable emulsion systems that can be dispensed as a foam or spray.

### 3.1.4 Emulsifiers

Surface-active agents are commonly used in water-based aerosol systems to produce stable water-out (foam product) or oil-out (spray product) emulsions, as described previously.

### 3.1.5 Inhibitors

Inhibitors can be used in aerosol products as stabilizers for the active ingredients or to prevent corrosion of metal containers used for aqueous-based formulations.

### 3.1.6 Fragrances

Fragrances are commonly chosen to provide a preferred odour for the product or to mask the odour of the solvent used in the formulation.

## 3.2 Aerosol Propellants

An aerosol propellant can be defined as a material that is capable of expelling the contents of an aerosol container. They are usually classified as follows (8):

(a) Fluorocarbons, either true fluorocarbons containing carbon, hydrogen and fluorine (FC-152a) or chlorofluorocarbons containing carbon, hydrogen, fluorine and chlorine (FC-11, FC-12, FC-114, FC-22, FC-142b);

(b) Hydrocarbons containing carbon and hydrogen;

(c) Dimethyl ether containing carbon and hydrogen; and oxygen;

(d) Compressed gases consisting of carbon dioxide, nitrogen and nitrous oxide.

### 3.2.1 General properties

The general properties of the more commonly used propellants in insect control products will be emphasized in the discussion.

**3.2.1** *(a) Fluorocarbons* The term fluorocarbon is used for all organo-fluorine compounds, while the non-flammable fluorocarbons bear the Freon trade mark of DuPont, including Freon 11,12, 22 and 114. Fluorocarbons 11 and 12 were once the most widely used materials in aerosol insect control products due to their nonflammable nature. Their present use in insect control is diminishing, however, due to their contribution to the depletion of the protective ozone layer in the upper atmosphere. This has led to the widespread use of hydrocarbon propellants.

**3.2.1** *(b) Hydrocarbons:* The major hydrocarbons propellants are propane and isobutane, with n-butane being used to some extent. The hydrocarbons are stable, noncorrosive and essentially odourless liquefied gases with low toxicity and good environmental acceptance. They are also considerably cheaper than fluorocarbons. Their major disadvantage is their flammability.

Aerosol-grade hydrocarbons are designated by the letter "A" followed by a number that indicates the propellant vapour pressure in psi at 70°F. Cosmetic-grade hydrocarbons use the letter "C" in the same manner.

Specific properties of the most commonly used hydrocarbons are described below.

(a) Propane is a high-pressure propellant that can be used alone or in blends with other hydrocarbons or fluorocarbons. It is nonpolar and has poor overall solubility and is essentially insoluble in water. Water can be used in a propane system if alcohols are used as a co-solvent to form a homogeneous solution system;

(b) Isobutane has many properties similar to those of propane as regards solubility, but it has a lower vapour pressure and can easily be used in many applications in blended form. It is slightly heavier than propane and also slightly more flammable. It is commonly blended with propane when higher pressure propellants are needed;

(c) N-butane is rarely used alone due to its low vapour pressure and is usually blended with propane or isobutane;

(d) Dimethyl ether (DME) is not widely used in the United State but is commonly used in Japan and Europe. The propellant has a slight ethereal odour that is sometimes considered disagreeable. It is unique among propellants in having a high solubility in water and also functions as an excellent solvent for many substances. DME is highly flammable but produces less flame extension than to hydrocarbons. With DME, higher air concentrations are tolerated, compared to hydrocarbons, before a mixture becomes flammable.

**3.2.1** *(c) Compressed gases :* A compressed gas is generally defined as a high-pressure propellant that must be injected into containers in the gaseous form instead of as a liquid under pressure. These gases comprise of carbon dioxide, nitrous oxide and nitrogen. The solubility of the compressed gas in the liquid concentrate is one of its most important properties since a higher solubility will result in (a) a better initial spray and (b) during use, fewer changes in pressure and spray characteristics. Nitrogen has extremely low solubility and for that reason is not used to any significant degree as a propellant. Carbon dioxide, on the other hand, is considerably more soluble and is more widely used in insecticide aerosol products.

Compressed gases offer many advantages since they are basically odourless, colourless, ono-toxic, non-flammable, inexpensive and environmentally acceptable. Temperature variations do not result in pressure changes to any significant degree when compared to liquefied gas propellants.

Their disadvantages include an inferior spray (wetter and less forceful). In addition, the spray becomes coarser during product use as the pressure is decreased. There is also more potential that the product will no longer discharge if it is misused. The presence of moisture can result in the formation of carbonic acid, which may lead to corrosion. Finally, filling equipment is usually slower with carbon dioxide than with other propellants.

### 3.3 Valves and Actuators

As the valve and actuator of an aerosol system play a significant role in the performance and quality of the final product they are included in our discussion. The variety of valves available from numerous manufacturers worldwide allows for the flexibility to use an appropriate valve for any type of aerosol product in steel, aluminium, glass or plastic containers. The purpose of the valve is to control the flow of product from the container and allow dispensing the contents in desired amounts as needed.

The valve also greatly influences the characteristics of the product dispended, which may be a foam, a coarse spray or a fine spray. All valves work in a similar fashion and consist of basically the same components.

#### *3.3.1 Mounting Cups and Corresponding Gaskets*

Mounting cups and corresponding gaskets are used to clamp the valve stem, stem gasket, spring and body together and to provide a seal to the opening of the container.

#### *3.3.2 Valve Steam Gaskets*

Valvestem gaskets are crucial for the proper operation of the aerosol product. The stem gasket provides the seal to prevent leakage of product and unacceptable weight loss. A proper selection of gasket material is also necessary (a) to deter interaction with the product and (b) to provide proper gasket swell to close the opening in the stem when the valve is not in operation. Optimum swell is between 2 and 9% depending on the product and valve system used. Gaskets can be checked for compatibility with the product by immersing them gasket in the intermediate for 48 hours. Measurements of diameter, hardening or softening of gasket material and deterioration can be compared before and after immresion in the product.

### 3.3.3 *Valve Stems*

Valve stems contain the metering orifices that determine the spray rate. The stem also contains an expansion chamber to provide a smaller particle size in the spray.

### 3.3.4 *Springs*

Springs control the upward and downward movement of the valve stem and are usually made from stainless steel.

### 3.3.5 *The Valve Body (Housing)*

The valve body provides a base for the spring and also serves to make a connection with the dip tube. When the body orifice is less than the stem orifice, the valve body orifice becomes the metering orifice. The valve body can also contain a vapour tap orifice, which allows additional vapour phase propellant to mix with the product and provide a finer particle size. Vapour taps are commonly used for space spray products.

### 3.3.6 *Dip Tubes*

Dip tubes function (a) to transfer the product to valve body, (b) to serve as a metering device in some systems and (c) to be used as a product reservoir for the inverted spraying of products. Inverted spraying is common with insect repellent sprays.

### *3.3.7 Valve Actuators*

Valve actuators may be simple spray buttons or an integral part of various spouts or spray domes. The actuator not only allows operation of the valve but can also be important in determining whether the product will be dispensed as a foam, spray or stream pattern. It will also influence the spray rate and the particle size of the spray.

Actuators come in tremendous variety of sizes and shapes. The actuator orifice is usually chosen larger than the metering orifice to obtain a more uniform particle size in the spray. The terminal orifice may be straight or tapered to produce moderate width sprays or wider sprays, respectively.

Actuators can also contain a swirl chamber and are referred to as mechanical break-up actuators. They function by imparting a swirling motion to the discharged product, resulting in an improved spray pattern.

## 4 PROPERTIES OF AEROSOL FORMULATIONS

In addition to understanding the ingredients and proper valve selection to provide desired attribute, formulated products should also be evaluated for specific characteristics that influence product performance.

### 4.1 Spray Properties

One of the most important characteristics of an aerosol product is a satisfactory spray. This is especially true of space spray insecticides, where a correlation exists between particle size and biological activity.

The spray is formed when an aerosol is discharged and the propellant changes from a liquid to a gas at atmospheric pressure. Some flash evaporation occurs in the expansion chamber of the valve,which is at lower pressure than the container. Additional flash evaporation occurs when the vapour-liquid phase exists the outer orifice. After these initial flash evaporations, additional evaporation takes place depending on various factors (9).

The flash evaporizations are primarily responsible for the initial breakup of the liquid product and the resulting spray characteristics, which will also depend on the type of propellant, valve, actuator or intermediate.

There are many ways to evaluate the spray pattern, which can then be classified as follows :

(a) *Fine spray :* Spray disappears at a distance of approximately there to four feet ater it leaves the actuator and gives only slight wetting of paper sprayed from a distance of 18 in.

(b) *Medium.* The spray pathway is more horizontal and wetting of paper occurs at a distance of 18 in. The particle size is noticeably larger than a fine spray.

(c) *Coarse.* Particle fallout is very evident and significant wetting of paper occurs at a distance of 18 in.

The fine spray would be appropriate for a space spray application, the coarse spray for a surface application and the medium spray for a multi-purpose application.

The two most important propellant variables that affect the spray are vapour pressure and the concentration of the propellant in the product. An increase in propellant concentration decreases particle size. Also, a high-vapour-pressure propellant provides a finer spray than a low-vapour-pressure propellent at the same concentration. This is a result of the increased flash vapourization of a propellant with a high vapour pressure. More important is the vapour pressure of the total formulation. The use of a high-vapour-pressure propellant may produce a coarser spray than a low-vapour-pressure propellant if a pressure-depressing solvent is included in the formulation.

Valving parameters also have a significant effect on spray characteristics. This is a especially important when using a vapour tap valve in combination with a propellant that has a low vapour pressure. Using a vapour tap, the vapour pressure and discharge rate are decreased, resulting in a change in spray during the discharge of the container. These results emphasize the importance of testing spray characteristic initially and after discharging 70-90% of the container.

The actuator, as well as the valving can have a big influence on spray characteristics. This is especially so when comparing mechanical and non-mechanical breakup actuators.

Depending on the construction of the actuator orifice this same shift in spray pattern can occur with other types of actuators. A study was conducted comparing a twenty-thousandths mechanical breakup button actuator to five alternate actuators. These six actuators were tested with an aqueous oil-out emulsion system with three valve variables. The valving variables included a standard, the standard with a thirteen-thousandths vapour tap and a high discharge valve. Overall, the use of three valving variables with any one actuator hardly changed the spray pattern, but a significant difference in spray pattern could be distinguished when the various actuators with the same valving were compared.

### 4.2 Particle Size Characteristics

Particle size can be an important characteristic for an aerosol product, especially in insecticidal aerosols. As described earlier, an aerosol was technically defined as having no particles greater than 50μm and 80%, by weight, smaller than 30μm. However, many products may not fit this particle size defenition but still be classified as aerosols for the purpose of our discussion (10). In general, particles under 50μm should be effective in a space spray, with 20-30 μm diameter particles being optimum.

The relationship between particle side and biological activity was studied with various propellant levels, as shown in Table 12.2. As the propellant level is increased the particle size is decreased and the number of particles per gram of product is increased. However, biological performance reaches an optimum at approximately 60% propellant, which provides particles having a mean diameters of 20μm.

**Table - 12.2**

**Effect of propellant levels on particle size and biological activity**

| | *Sample No.* | | | | |
|---|---|---|---|---|---|
| *Product composition (%)* | 1 | 2 | 3 | 4 | 5 |
| Synergized pyrethrin | 1.8 | 1.8 | 1.8 | 1.8 | 1.8 |
| Mineral spirits | 78.2 | 58.2 | 38.2 | 18.2 | 8.2 |
| Propellant(46 PSI) | 20.0 | 40.0 | 60.0 | 80.0 | 90.0 |
| **Total** | **100.0** | **100.0** | **100.0** | **100.0** | **100.0** |
| Mean Particle Size (μm) | 65.0 | 38.5 | 21.5 | 12.0 | 9.0 |
| Fly knockdown KD 75(min) | 40.8 | 23.3 | 14.1 | 12.0 | 14.8 |
| Fly mortality (%) | 4.2 | 32.2 | 67.1 | 63.9 | 43.7 |

The effect of valving on particle size was also determined and it was again confirmed that the most imprtant contributing factor is the actuator. When the actuator was kept the same but the valve stem orifice was increased, the particle size remained the same. This was most evident with a large orifice actuator. These results correlate with those of our previcus discussion, indicating that the stem orifice is the influencing orifice unless the actuator orifice is larger.

To compare particle size and spray characteristics, a standard set of samples can be prepared for comparison. The test sample spray can then be compared to the standard samples. This will provide a good basis for making a judgement on a valve change that may or may not affect performance.

## 4.3 Discharge Rate

The discharge rate or delivery rate of an aerosol product is the quantity of material '*q*' expelled through the valve in a given period of time at a specific temperature. The typical aerosol valve is made up of a series of channels, orifices and expansion chambers, all of which may influence delivery rate. The prime metering points available for manipulation of the discharge rate, in order of flow, are as follows.

(a) *Dip tube.* The use of a capillary dip tube can be important in metering and influencing the discharge rate;

(b) *Valve body orifice.* This can become tne metering orific when the diameter of the orifice is less then tha diameter of the valve stem orifice;

(c) *Vapour tap orifice.* The use of a vapour tap in the valve body will usually produce a softer, warmer and drier spray with a fine particle size and a reduced delivery rate;

(d) *Stem orifice.* This orifice usually detemines the spray rate and is thus called the metering orifice;

(e) *Actuator orifice.* Actuator orifices have a great effect on many delivery characteristics of the spray. An orifice of some what larger diameter than the metering orific is often chosen for a more uniform spray.

The effect of valving orifices on the discharge rate is presented in Table 12.3 Samples 1-3 illustrate that a decreasing body orifice will decrease the delivery rate when other parameters are constant. A larger actuators (samples 4–6) provides a higher discharge rate, but the same trend in decreased discharge rate is evident. Addition of a vapour tap decreases the discharge rate, as shown for samples 7-9. As illustrated, the vapour tap can significant by decrease the discharge rate of the product. Increasing the stem orifice increases the discharge rate, as shown for samples 10-13. The discharge rate will also decrease as the contents of the containers are dispensed. This decrease can be significant when using compressed gas aerosol systems.

Varying the discharge rate can also affect the biological activity of insecticide aerosols. Three aerosols that differ significantly in discharge rate but that have similar mean particle size ranges were compared. The data show a trend to improved activity using a higher discharge product that required less time to total fly knockdown. These differences are not great but do indicate that some improvement can be made in biological activity without any major changes in the system.

**Table - 12.3**

**The effect of valving orifices on discharges rates**

| *Sample number* | *Actuator* | *Stem* | *Body* | *Vapour tap* | *Discharge rate* |
|---|---|---|---|---|---|
| | | *(in)* | | | *(q/sec.)* |
| 1. | 0.018 | 0.018 | 0.080 | none | 0.88 |
| 2. | 0.018 | 0.018 | 0.040 | none | 0.80 |
| 3. | 0.018 | 0.018 | 0.020 | none | 0.71 |

Contd.....

| | | | | | |
|---|---|---|---|---|---|
| 4. | 0.040 | 0.018 | 0.080 | none | 1.34 |
| 5. | 0.040 | 0.018 | 0.040 | none | 1.23 |
| 6. | 0.040 | 0.080 | 0.020 | none | C.92 |
| 7. | 0.040 | 0.018 | 0.080 | 0.013 | 1.15 |
| 8. | 0.040 | 0.018 | 0.080 | 0.025 | 1.07 |
| 9. | 0.040 | 0.018 | 0.080 | 0.040 | C.33 |
| 10. | 0.018 | 0.024 | 0.080 | none | 1.17 |
| 11. | 0.018 | 0.018 | 0.080 | none | 1.28 |
| 12. | 0.018 | 0.040 | 0.080 | none | 1.77 |
| 13. | 0.018 | 0.025 | 0.080 | none | 1.85 |

## 4.4 Vapour Pressure

The vapour pressure of a liquid is defined as the pressure of the vapour in equilibrium with the liquid and is constant at a given temperature. Vapour pressure is an important characteristic of aerosol products, not only as it relates to product performance but also due to pressure limitations that regulations place on aerosol containers. The vapour pressure of any aerosol formulation depends upon the vapour pressure of the propellant and the effect the other components in the formulation have upon the vapour pressure of the propellant.

Pressure in aerosol containers are commonly expressed as pounds per square inch guage (psi). Although air pressure is 14.7 psi, the gauges are set to read zero, so 14.7 would need to be added to the gauge pressure to obtain the absolute pressure.

These measurements of vapour pressure consider only the vapour pressure of the solution of propellant and concentrate, but the concentration of air in the container also has an effect on pressure. The amount of air in the container can be determined by gas chromatography to determine its contribution to total pressure. The amount of air can be controlled to some degree depending on the method of aerosol filling.

Using Raoult's law and Dalton's law, the vapour pressure of any solution can be determined if the cmposition of the solution and the molecular weights and vapour pressure of the pure components are known. This involves determining the partial pressure of each component by mutiplying the mole fraction of each component by its vapour pressure. The total pressure of the solution is obtained by adding together the partial pressures of the components.

Conversely, if the vapour pressure of a blend of isobutane and propane is specified, we can calculate the weight % of each propellant in the blend.

These calculations will allow determining the vapour pressure of any known propellant blend or the propellant blend ratio if the vapour pressure of the blend is known.

### 4.5 Density and Fill Weight

There is often confusion between density and specific gravity, so we must differentiate between the two. Density has the dimensions of mass over volume, usually expressed as g/cc, and is important in determining the weight of an aerosol product that can be packaged in an aerosol container. Specific gravity is a pure number without dimension: it is the ratio of the weight of a given valume of substance at one temperature to the weight of the same volume of a reference substance, usually water, at the same or a diffferent temperature.

The density of propellant blends can be calculated using the known densities of each propellant in the blends can be calculated using the known densities of each propellant in the blend. The density of a formulated product can be calculated in a similar manner. However, in many cases, the concentrate consists of many ingredients, and it is difficult to calculate the density of the concentrate itself. In these cases, a weight determination of the concentrate in a certain volume will provide an acceptable experimentally determined density.

In many instances, ingredients contained in the concentrate at low levels can be combined with an ingredient of known density. Knowing the density of specific formulas, we can now calculate the fill weight for any size container.

Using a 202 × 509 container (290 ml brimful capacity) we can calculate the amount of product for fill weight. The brimful capacity is reduced by 5 ml for the valve, resulting in a 285 ml capacity is container. Using 85% fill volume, the fill capacity can be calculated (285 ml × 85%) as (242.25 ml). The density of a theoretical aqueous formula is 0.737 g/cc, so the fill weight would be 242.25 cc × 0.737 g/cc = 178.54 g. Taking the density of a theoretical solvent formula as 0.626 g/cc, the fill weight would be 242.25 cc × 0.626 g/cc = 151.65 g.

It is clear that, more aqueous product is needed to fill lthe same volume of container. This need for more product may sometimes offset the other advantages of an aqueous-based system. In the theoratical case presented above, the aqueous system required 17% more product to provide a filled unit than the solvent system. If the cost of raw materials for an aqueous formula showed a saving of 15%, the end result would be a slight cost increase per unit fill for the aqueous formula. The above example shows the importance of calculating not only the cost of raw materials used in the formula but also the cost based on fill.

## 5. APPLICATION OF AEROSOL FORMULATIONS

Aerosol insect control products can be classified in three general categories by type of application: surface sprays, space sprays and multi-purpose sprays. Basic solvent-based formulations for these applications are provided in Table 12.4. The insecticide concentration can vary considerably depending on the active used and the level of performance desired while the solvent and propellant level can be maintained at levels similar to what has been suggested. The valve chosen can also vary considerably but the recommendation provided can serve as an excellent base from which to experiment. Details of these formulations will be addressed individually.

**Table - 12.4**

**Basic insect control aerosol formulations**

| *Composition (%)* | *Surface spray* | *Space spray* | *Multi-purpose spray* |
|---|---|---|---|
| Insecticides | 0.5 | 0.5 | 0.5 |
| Solvents | 69.5 | 29.5 | 49.5 |
| Propellant (46 psi) | 30.0 | 70.0 | 50.0 |
| | 100.0 | 100.0 | 100.0 |
| *Dimensions of valving orifice (in.)* | | | |
| Stem | 0.024 | 0.024 | 0.024 |
| Body | 0.080 | 0.080 | 0.080 |
| Vapour tap | – | 0.018 | 0.018 |
| Actuator | 0.02 | 0.024 | 0.024 |
| Spray pattern | Coarse | Fine | Medium |

### 5.1 Surface Sprays

Surface sprays, also known as, crawling insect killers (CIK), are designed to be sprayed onto a surface, providing a residual deposit, or to be sprayed directly on an insect for fast activity. Insecticide actives utilized usually include a knockdown agent in combination with a residual kill agent (Table 12.1). Common knockdown agents for a CIK are pyrethrin, neopynamin or DDVP in combination with one of several residual kill agents, including propoxur, permethrin, cypermethrin or cyfluthrin. Commonly available mineral spirits or kerosene can be used as the solvent carrier for most of the actives.

A co-solvent is necessary for propoxur-based systems. Methylene chloride trichloriethane have been used, but anhydro isopropanol is the preferred substitute due to toxicity and environmental concerns with the chlorinated solvents.

The use of a hydrocarbon propellant at 30% will produce a coarse, wet spray suitable for this type of application. Valving parameters are also provided that will deliver a discharge of over 1 g product/sec. Many valve selections could be made for a CIK product since the particle size is less important and valves with delivery rates of 1-3 g producing a coarse wet spray are quite common. Similar levels of fluorocarbon propellants could also be used with similar results but the hydrocarbons are preferred due to the ozone depeletion hazard associated with the fluorocarbons. Compressed gas propellants are also compatible with the solvent CIK formulations. Carbon dioxide at a 2-3% level would produce a coarser, wetter spray but one that is still acceptable for controlling crawling insects.

### 5.2 Space Sprays

A space spray can also be used for direct sprayng of insects, although it actually is intended for delivering a spray into the air and thereby controlling insect moving through the space. Therefore, a space spray (or flying insect killer) is designed to deliver particles in a range that will remain airborne for a sufficient period of time to allow flying insects to be exposed to a lethal dose. Target insects usually include various flies and mosquitoes as well as moths. The insecticides used for a space spray should include knockdown and kill agents as described in Table 12.1 Pyrethrin, or tertamethrin are used worldwide in combination with resmethrin, sumithrin or a synergist to provide adequate killing power. As with surface sprays, the availability of mineral spirits or kerosene make them the solvent of choice, although a specific solvent can have a significant influence on the performance of the product (11). Hydrocarbon propellants are the most suitable for space sprays at this time. Although they may pose a flammability hazard, they are not responsible for ozone depletion like the fluorocabons and they can provide the continuous, proper pressure necessary in a space spray but not yet possible with compressed gas technology. The level of propellant and the valve selection are extremely important to achieve a space spray with particles under 50μm land preferably in the 20-30 μm range. A 60-70% level of propellant with a pressure of 46 psi in combination with a suitable valve will provide this preferred particle size. The valving provided in the basic system (Table 12.4) is appropriate for providing a discharge of over 1 g/ sec and a particle size in the range of 20 μm. Depending on the propellant pressure and propellant concentration, other valving options may be required to provide similar properties. Overall, the selection of valves is more limited than for surface sprays, but many appropriate valving systems can be developed with some basic understanding of what is required to produce a good space spray.

### 5.3 Multi-purpose Spray

Multi-purpose spray is designed to be effective as a space spray for flying insects as well as a surface spray for crawling insects. It requ res that the formula be modified to incorporate properties of surface and space sprays and limits the options that are available for these specific formulations. As illustrated in Table 12.4, multipurpose spray is a hybrid of surface and space sprays. The propellant level is greater than for a surface spray to provide a finer spray to control flying insectsbut it must also serve similar to that for a surface spray to provide a residual deposit. Valving, a space spray can be used to achieve a break-up of particles. Insecticides similar to those residual agent should be reduced or replaced by kills agents, as described in Table 12.1. This will provide some residual activity when the product is used as a surface spray but minimize residual activity when the product is as a space spray.

There are many parameters to consider in developing an aerosol formulation that will deliver the characteristics desired. The above information can serve as an appropriate starting point in potimizing aerosol formulations using local materials and obtaining the desired results.

# 19

# Advances in Pesticides Formulations Packaging

## 1. REQUIREMENTS PROFILE

When developing packaging for a crop protection product, 10 basic ruls are to be observed. Matters relating to the presentation of the package are not included in these rules.

### 1.1 Statutory Demands

Very specific legal requirements apply in the following situations:

(a) *Agrochemical legislation :* Country-specific regulations on safety in the workplace, protection of health and the environment and packaging must be satisfied to gain registration. The FAO Code of Conduct (1) provides valuable assistance;

(b) *Directives on quantity accuracy :* National laws are based on two principles. The mean value requirement is the fundamental idea of the directive of the European Community (2), which has been adopted as national law in European and many other countries. This statistically logical concept influenced the development of more accurate dynamically controlled filling and weighing machines.

The alternative concept is the minimum quantity requirement, which does not so strictly demand the economy of product;

(c) *Hazardous goods transport regulations:* United Nations recommendations on the transport of dangerous goods (3) cover the classification of products, packaging requirements, conditions for performance tests and the official registration of package. They serve as a framework for more specific national and international laws;

(d) *Waste disposal legislation :* Governments in places such as Germany, the Netherlands and several states in the United States have already introduced laws on disposal. The common philosophy is based on a hierarchy of demands.

(i) Avoidance of packaging material,

(ii) Reduction of the quantity of packaging material.

(iii) Re-use of packages and packaging material

Deposition in landfills or burying is least desirable alternative.

(e) *Laws on product liability :* Responsibility, in the event of damage is governed by such legislation. The tendency in many countries is that, in case of a defect, the manufacturer of the packaging product must prove it made serious efforts to prevent any damage.

### 1.2 Product Compatibility

The essential prerequisite is that there should be no interaction between the packaging material and contents. A pesticide formulation is said to be stable when the changes in its properties and characteristics over a given period of time vary only within predetermined, acceptable limits (4). Further details will be given in Section 3.

### 1.3 Pack Size

The packs should contain either the right amount for one use, e g. the quantity for one hectare (taking into account active ingredient content and concentration) or a multiple of such amounts.

Solid products (WP, WG) have different bulk volumes and hence will require different size packages. When liquids are packaged, a certain space must be left empty (prescribed in the transport regulations).

### 1.4 Closure Concept

Basic requirements call for a hermetic seal and the possibility of opening the pack without tools and with a gloved hand. If the closure consists of two devices, one of them must be of the screw-type.

Tamper-proof seals are of increasing importance. The aperture must be large enough to allow glug-free pouring and easy rinsing (the minimum internal diameter should be 38 mm). For liquids the recommended design is a neck with a buttress-type thread as per DIN 6063 KS 50 mm, or as per GIFAP Industrial Standard 63 mm, using appropriate caps.

### 1.5 Design

Packages for liquid and solid products must be designed in order to allow a safe and economical filling process. They must be easy to handle and completely rinseable. Packages for liquid products must not have hollow handles, while those for solids must not have any hidden pockets.

Graduations can facilitate the removal of partial quantities. GIFAP will publish detailed design criteria for packaging for crop protection products.

### 1.6 Filling Process

Packages are filled in semi-or fully automated processes. It is advisable to carry out trial runs before drawing up the definite specifications. Symmetrical packages for liquids, such as cylindrical containers with a concentric opening, facilitate filling. Form-fill and sealing machines and bag-in-box systems are common for powders and granules. Two-stage filling processes (first bulk and then controlled metering) improve accuracy and safety.

### 1.7 Information on the label

The package has to convey information from the manufacturer to the consumer. It is important also that containers for crop protection products should not be confused with edible packs and, above all, that the empty packs are not re-used to preserve foodstuffs.

Embossed pictorial information is useful. Quick and precise identification is essential. The following need to be included: product name, manufacturer, quantity, registration marking, statements on risk and safety, hazard symbols, recommendations for application and first aid measures. The FAO Code of Conduct (1) provides valuable assistance in this regard.

### 1.8 Labelling

Labels must stick firmly to the packaging material; the glue must fulfil its function even under unfavourable conditions. It must not cause corrosion on metal packs. Overlapping paper labels are advisable. If the prescribed texts are too long to be accommodated, folded multiple (double, triple) labels could be used.

### 1.9 Transportation and Storage

The packs are mainly transported and stored on pallets. Consequently the shipping units must be designed for pallets, i.e. they must allow stacking on pallets without projecting. The material used to secure the load on the pallets must be strong and durable; shrink-wrapping or stretch films must not relax due to temperature or time.

Standard rules for palletization are as follows :

(a) Maximum load on one pallet, 1 tonne;

(b) Maximum height of the unit load, 2 m;

(c) If the individual packs are too small to form a safe load, half height, i.e. 1m, is recommended.

The compression strength of the shipping cartons must comply with these rules and with customer specifications.

### 1.10 Disposal

The final task in developing packaging is to guarantee safe disposal. Quantities of packaging materials should be minimized. The selected material should not absorb the chemical. It should, however, allow the recovery of energy or be reusable after having been properly rinsed according to good agricultural practice.

## 2. SELECTION OF PACKAGING MATERIALS

### 2.1 Solid Products

There are four typical solid products :

(a) Wettable powders (WP);

(b) Water dispersible granules (WG);

(c) Dusting powders (DP);

(d) Granules (GR).

The universal material of construction is polyethylene. It is thermoplastic, therefore an ideal sealing medium, and it offers very good moisture barrier properties. To preserve the agrochemicals in a humid atmosphere is the main requirement. In monolayer constructions, a thickness of 0.1 mm will be sufficient in most applications.

If the product is highly hygroscopic (which fact would have been established in an accelerated storage test), the only suitable package would be of an aluminium composite foil. Depending on the weight of the product, a thickness of 0.009 mm (up to approx 1 kg) and of 0.012 mm for greater weights should be sufficient. Aluminium foil requires a sealable layer on the inside and, on the outside, protection against environmental influences, a strengthening layer and a pre-treated surface that can be printed on. Ideally the shape should be symmetrical.

A typical composite foil would consist of 40 g/m$^2$ low-density polyethylene (LDPE) as the sealing medium, 0.012 mm aluminium, 20 g/m$^2$ LDPE and one of the following : 30 g/m$^2$ polypropylene (PP), or 0.012 mm polyester (PET), or 0.015 mm polyamide (PA).

Products with certain properties, e.g. a strong odour or volatile toxic by-products, require a composite film consisting of LDPE and an additional barrier, which should be PET or PA rather than aluminium. These are also an ideal reinforcement for larger packages. e.g. those containing 10-20 kg GR.

A typical construction would be 0.015 mm PA (external, to form the gas-barrier and to give physical strength) and 0.05-0.1 mm LDPE (internal, responsible for moisture protection and for sealing).

The principle in designing multi-layer films is that of additive properties. A comparison of the permeation rates of LDPE and PA in Table 16.1 illustrates this principle.

**Table 16.1** Permeation rates of films[a]

| | $O_2$ *permeation/ transmission* | *Water vapour* |
|---|---|---|
| | *(cm³/m² x day x bar)* | *(g/m² x day)* |
| LDPE, 0.1 mm | 800 | 0.7 |
| PA, 0.015 mm biaxially oriented | 15 | 40 |
| LDPE/PA biaxially oriented, 0.05 mm/0.15 mm | 25 | 1.9 |

(a) 23°C and 75% relative humidity (DIN 53 122).

There are numerous alternative barrier plastics, of which only films based on vinyl might be used for crop protection products. In the author's opinion, the agrochemical industry should concentrate on the four most common films, mentioned above, which are available in almost all countries, as their demand is usually not as high as in other industries. This will result in economical solutions.

Film or composite foil packages for powders or granules, are usually tubular pouches made on form-, fill- and sealing (FFS)- machines. They can also be gusseted square-bottom bags or cartons with an internal lining.

Beside considering the protective properties, any decision will also consider costs. It is essential to calculate the cost not only of the material but also of the filling operation. More expensive packaging material can easily be offset by more economical filling costs.

### *2.1.1* Water-soluble film

A special packaging option for WP is water-soluble bags of polyvinyl alcohol (PVA). These packages do not protect the product in the usual sense, but they do protect the operator when applying the product. They contain premeasured doses and leave behind uncontaminated outer packages. The packaging material becomes part of the spray liquid, whose properties it could influence.

Tubular pouches made on FFS-machines or pre-fabricated bags for quantities from 0.1 to 25 kg have been introduced to the market. Of course, water-soluble packages have to carry water-soluble or at least water-degradable printing for identification and they need suitable outer protection, which adds to the packing costs. Cartoons lined with outer protection, which adds to the packing costs. Cartons lined with almunium-compos te foil are the usual choice.

Although water-soluble film is ideal for WPs, WGs and gels (GLs) (see Chapter 4), even liquid herbicide have also been packed in PVA bags.

## 2.2 Liquid Products

Liquid agrochemicals always contain an active ingredient and may also contain solvents and emulsifiers. As all these component chemicals influence the packaging choice, it is almost impossible to make a decision based on the literature alone. Usually compatibility studies have to be performed to prove the suitability of a packaging system. The tests should be carried out on the packaging in which the pesticide is to be sold, with original closing systems.

From the point of view of packaging engineer, the most important types of formulations are the following:

(a) Emulsifiable concentrates (EC) and soluble liquids (SL), which are usually not compatible with high-density poly-ethylene (HDPE);

(b) Suspension concentrates (SC) and emulsion concentrates (EW), usually HDPE-compatible.

The most common packaging materials are glass, metal (Alum num or tin sheet), plastics and lined corrugated cartons.

### *2.2.1* Glass

In spite of its universal product compatibility, glass is not recommended for chemicals because of its fragility.

### *2.2.2* Metal

Usually, containers are made from aluminium or tin sheet with or without internal lacquer linings. Aluminium has the advantage that it can be converted in mono-or biblock containers, if a suitable alloy is used. Although its purity should be min. 99.5% (as per DIN 1712.3) an internal protective lin ng is required for many products. However, because the lacquer has to be applied in a discontinuous spray process, it is not very economical. The latest aluminium containers have standard closures (DIN 6063/KS 50), using seamed lids diminishing the disadvantage of previous designs, which had small apertures and internal threads.

All tin sheet containers have to be three-piece constructions, which means the seams must be precise and uniform to prevent leaks. The seaming compound also has to be tested for chemical compatibility.

Internal lacquer linings are generally required. They are applied by roller, which result in a rather uniform coating. Disadvantages include the possibility of pore formation and the resulting effect on adhesion. The longitudinal seam requires a separate protection. Due to limited construction possibilities, it may be difficult to remove product quantitatively.

Closures for metal packages must also have good barrier properties.

### *2.2.3 Plastics*

Blow-moulded containers made of HDPE offer a wide flexibility in construction and good moisture barrier properties. However, they are suitable mainly for water-based products.

Chemical compatibility can be improved by fluorination, which is done either during the blow-moulding of the container or, off-line, after blow moulding in a vacuum chamber, resulting in the treatment of the internal and external surfaces of the containers.

Another means of modifying HDPE to improve its barrier properties, is to blend the resin with, for example, polyamide. The resulting laminar structure (SelarRB) will allow its use for products where HDPE normally is unsuitable.

The best possibilities are offered by coextruded, multi-layer plastic containers, which are available in sizes up to 10 litres. Here, plastics with different properties can be combined to produce multi-layer packaging tailored to the product requirements in the same way as has long been done with laminated films.

A typical 1-litre bottle (weight 85 g) is made of HDPE at least 0.7 mm thick, a bonding agent at least 0.01 mm thick and an internal EVOH or PA layer at least 0.02 mm thick. Reground material from the manufacturing process could be blended with virgin HDPE and used as a fourth layer between the external PE and the bonding agent without increasing the container weight.

Although the initial investment is higher and the process control has to be very strict, coextruded bottles are the most advanced solution for all products for which HDPE is not sufficient.

PET is widely used for the packaging of liquid products. However, its water vapour transmission rate is approximately six times greater than that of HDPE. This deficiency is often offset by its rather good compatibility with many chemicals.

The investment cost for the manufacturer of stretch blow-moulded containers is very high. As the resin is expensive, there is a constraint on bottle weight. For example, a 1-litre bottle is competitive with alternatives only if its weight is not more than 50 g.

There are signs that combination packs (film liners in corrugated cardboard boxes) may find application in the agrochemical industry. They will undoubtedly be successful if the problem of quantitative removal of liquid can be satisfactorily solved. Their advantage is the possibility of removing the contaminated lightweight liner for the clean outer carton and disposing of them separately.

### 2.2.4 Biodegradable Plastics

In view of the limited availability of landfills and the problem of disposing of packaging, biodegradable plastics are gaining attention. In fact it would be a splendid idea to design packages that just fade away.

We are not as optimistic as some about photo- or biodegradable packaging material, because when they are disposed of in a landfill, they will require as much space as other materials and they will take a long time to degrade. Moreover, they cannot be re-used as packaging material. Despite these reservations, an overview of the state of the art is provided in Table 16.2 (5).

**Table 16.2** Photo- and biodegradable plastics

| *Source* | *Product* | *Degradation type* | *Current/ potential use* | *Technology* |
|---|---|---|---|---|
| Ideamasters Miami, FL | Plastigone proprietary resin | Photodegradable additive system | Used in Israel in mulch film. Wider uses expected | Additives absorb UV, releasing metal ions in anti-oxidant to act as catalysts for the breakdown of chains. |
| ICI Americas Wilmimington, DE | Biopol resin | Biodegradable aliphatic/ polyester copolymer | Production of bottles in Europe. | Polyhydroxybutyrate polyesters are produced by soil bacteria during fermentation of sugars to produce a natural polymer. |

| | | | | |
|---|---|---|---|---|
| U.S. Dept. of Agriculture, Washington, DC | Technology available for licensing | Biodegradable starch additive | Agri-Tech Industries, Gibson City, IL, plans pilot plant for blown film | Starch is used to fill ethylene-acrylic acid or PE film, after which microorganisms attack the natural polymer causing film to degrade. |
| St. Lawrence Starch, Mississauga, Ontario | Ecostar master batch | Biodegradable starch additive | Used in trash bags and bottles. | Starch is silane treated for compatiblity with polymer; when consumed by fungi, the starch leaves porous structures that disintegrate. |
| Ecoplastics Willowdale, Ontario | Ecolyte master batch | Photodegradable ketone copolymer | Used in mulch film and has potential in bags. | Molecules are altered by interspersing ketone carbonyl groups on polymer chains during synthesis |
| Dow Chemical Six-pack, Midland, MI<br>DuPont Wilmington, DE<br>Union Carbide Danbury, CT | Resin | Photodegradable ethylene/carbon monoxide comonomer | Currently used in 11 states requiring degradable six-pack yokes, Dow has applied for permission in food use. | Incorporates carbonyl groups by copolymerizing ethylene and carbon monoxide so that UV-absorbing carbonyls snap to form shorter, weaker chains. |
| Ampacet Mt. Vernon, NY | Poly-grade master batch | Photodegradable additive system | Used in Bespac trash bags made by Webster Industries. | A proprietary additive susceptible to UV light absorption degrades liner LDPE. |
| Princeton Polymer Labs Princeton, NJ | Additive system for licensing | Photodegradable additive system | No current commercial use. Suited for use in polyolefins and polystyrene. | Combines a photo activtor and prooxidant synergistically to break polymer chains. |

### 2.3 Large Returnable Containers

Intermediate between primary packs (Sections 2.1 and 2.2) and transportation packs (Section 2.4) are large multiway containers. n countries where the farms are very large, there is an increasing usage of minibulk multi-way (approx 500 1) and of small volume (approx 50 1) returnable containers.

Multi-way receptacles would be suitable for products required in large quantities, products applied over a long period of time and products that need quick refilling. In addition, the products (EW and SC) must remain homogeneous and should allow volumetric dosing. The advantage, which are primarily for the consumer, are obvious:

(a) Application in closed transfer systems, which reduces the risk of contamination to the operator;

(b) No need to dispose of empty containers;

(c) The containers can be used for the same product without cleaning them;

(d) Tampering with products can be avoided more easily.

However, the disadvantages cannot be overlooked:

(a) High initial investment costs;

(b) Higher requirement profile for the development of formulations.

The marketing conditions have to be adapted to special conditions of logistics and financing. It is recommended to use stainless steel kegs, as is common for beer. A chemical-specific coupling system for the transfer of material could prevent unauthorised re-filling of the container thereby avoiding contamination due to interchanging containers.

### 2.4 Transportation Packaging

The fundamental task is to protect product and environment by means of primary containers. Individual receptacles are conventionally collected in shipping cartons for dispatch from the formulation and packaging plant to warehouses and customers.

Attention must be paid to the quality of these cartons, since loads are often transported over long distances on bad roads. Faulty or unsuitable packaging can lead to accidental leakage of the product during transport and present a safety hazard. All packages should meet recognized performance standards (3), be able to withstand the conditions normally experienced in transport and provide the desirable level of safety (6).

The main concern is with corrugated cartons, which should have double nodulation and kraft paper at least on the external layer. One set of guidelines gives the very simple Cobb test (3). The moisture absorption should not exceed 155 g/m$^2$. In humid climats, the stacking stability of corrugated cartons can be up to 50 % less if paper of poor quality has been used.

The more recycled fibres are used, the more important proper specification and stringent testing of the corrugated carton. Corrugated boxes should be safely closed by means of suitable tapes. Staples are not recommended as there is always a risk that irregular hooks will puncture the bottom of the internally packed containers.

It improved safety and economics if the shipping boxes are stacked on pallets and protected by shrink film (min. thickness 0.1 mm) or stretch wrapping. The preferably interlocking arrangement of the boxes on pallets needs thorough planning. when developing primary packages (bottles, folded cartons), the arrangement of the shipping cartons and the utilization of the surface of the pallets must be considered at a very early stage.

Protection of the load with shrink film or with stretch wrapping should take care of the safety requirements in the plant. However, since it is more difficult to operate shrinking equipment in a packaging plant that has to observe explosion-proof conditions, spirally wound wrapping may be the best method. During storage, pallets have to be separately covered with a film hood.

## 3 Measures of Quality Control

### 3.1 Storage Stability Test (4)

The stability of a pesticide formulation depends on the intrinsic stability of the active ingredient(s), the formulation itself and the protective function of the packaging material.

The quality of a pesticide formulation is not only that quality which the manufacturer measures before the product is released for sale but, more importantly, it is also that quality which is present when the end-user finally applies the product. The end-user therefore expects that the manufacturer will have carried out tests to determine whether the product will be fit for use at its final point-of-use. As the manufacturer cannot follow on a real-time basis all the potential transportation, storage and environmental conditions that a product may be subjected to, tests need to be devised that will simulate such conditions as closely as possible. Such tests are called stability tests.

Based on the knowledge gained from studies of the formulation, important conclusions can be drawn from the stability tests in the selection of the primary packaging configuration. Specifically, stability tests will yield the following information to the formulator:

(a) Whether the commercial pack provides adequate protection from the climatic influences to which the formulation may be subjected;

(b) Whether there is a catalytic reaction between packaging material and the formulation;

(c) Whether the function of the package is unaffected by the product it is supposed to protect (cap impossible to open, stress cracking of the container etc.)

Before initiating any stability study it is essential to plan this carefully. In the planning of stability studies the following points must be considered:

(a) *Storage conditions*: It is essential that the storage conditions selected for stability studies are identical and standardized;

(b) *Test intervals*: Typical time intervals for removing samples for testing are 4 weeks, 8 weeks, 3 months, 6 months, 12 months and 24 months. Table 16.3 shows recommended storage conditions and time intervals for both accelerated and real time studies;

(c) *Tests required*: It must be pointed out that not every recommended test needs to be carried out at every recommended test point and once the stability profile has been established and the stability indicating parameters are known, the more selective one can be in the choice of tests to be carried out. Depending on the type of the formulation, the testing for indicator parameters (Table 16.4) should be carried out. Table 16.5 gives an overview of tests that should be carried out on important types of containers. Irrespective of the type of the final container, the tests in Table 165 should always be carred out as the minimum requirement: weight loss or gain, appearance of the container (including internal surface) and appearance of the container/closure system;

**Table 16.3 Storage conditions and test intervals**

| *Time* | *-10°C* | *0°C* | *25°C* | *30°C 85% RH* | *40°C 85% RH* | *54°C* |
|---|---|---|---|---|---|---|
| Initial | | | A | | | |
| 4 Weeks | | C | C | C | B | C |
| 8 Weeks | | | | | B | |
| 3 months | D | | B | B | B | |

Contd....

| | | | | |
|---|---|---|---|---|
| 6 months | | B | B | C |
| 12 months | | B | B | |
| 18 months | | B | B | |
| 24 months | D | B | B | |
| 30 months | | C | C | |
| 36 months | | C | C | |

A = Initial tests are carried out at prevalent laboratory temperature and humidity.

B = Recommended test intervals.

C = Optional test intervals

D = Reconfirm "initial" if necessary

**Table 16.4 Recommended tests to be carried out on formulations**

| *Formulation* | *Test required* | |
|---|---|---|
| EC | Acidity/alkalinity<br>Water content<br>Specific gravity | Emulsion stability<br>Oxygen content/head space |
| SC | pH<br>Specific gravity<br>Sieve test (wet) | Particle size<br>Suspendablity<br>Viscosity |
| SL | Acidity/alkalinity<br>Water content<br>Specific gravity | Emulsion stability<br>Spontaneity |
| WP | pH<br>Water content<br>Sieve test (wet) | Wettability<br>Suspendability |
| WG | pH<br>Water content<br>Sieve test (wet) | Wettability<br>Suspendability<br>Dust content |
| Dusts | pH<br>Water content | Sieve test (dry) |

**Table 16.5 Recommended tests of final packs**

| *Packaging* | *Test required* | |
|---|---|---|
| **Containers** | | |
| Tin sheet | Tin layer thickness<br>Quality of seams | Corrosion |

Contd.....

| | | |
|---|---|---|
| Tin sheet with | Porosity | Elasticity |
| Protective lining | Adhesion | |
| Aluminium | Corrosion | |
| Aluminium with | Porosity | Elasticity |
| protective lining | Adhesion | |
| HDPE | Deformation/wall thickness | Colour changes |
| | Odour barrier properties | Drop stability |
| PET | Internal pressure (head space) | Stress cracks |
| | Oxygen content | |
| Coextruded plastics | As for HDPE; additionally | |
| (multi-layer) | thickness of single layers, | |
| | homogeneity and porosity of the barrier | |
| **Closure sustems** | | |
| Caps | Torque | Leaks |
| | Differences in dimensions | Stress cracks |
| Gaskets | Weitht differences | |
| | Differences in dimensions | |
| Sealing disks | Corrosion | |
| | Adhesion of | |
| | laminates/ delamination | |
| **Films** | | |
| Laminated films/foils | Odour barrier properties | Deformation |
| | Tightness of seals | Corrosion |
| | Brittleness | Porosity |
| | Adhesion of laminates/ | |
| | delamination | |
| Water-soluble films | Water solubility | Brittleness |
| | Tear resistance | Elongation |
| | Total penetration | Spray properties |
| | Energy (free-falling dart) | (with product) |

(d) *Test methods*: An absolute prerequisite in the choice of the best test method is that it should be stability-indicating. Secondly, it must be capable of giving a true and accurate initial value. Thirdly, all the parameters that might possibly be affected by a change in quality with time/storage conditions must be determined as an initial value at t = 0. Fourthly, one should not rely solely on recognized international methods, e.g. CIPAC methods, for stability testing. These methods should be supplemented with in-house methods if these are better in detecting changes in product characteristics with time/storage conditions. Fifthly, one should not change the test method without due cause and certainly not in the middle of a stability test programme, without running both methods in parallel;

(e) *Major review points*: After each check-point the results should be reviewed to determine whether the product is behaving as expected. For accelerated studies, a mojor review should be conducted after four weeks and no later than the third month, at which time a graphical presentation of the data is very valuable;

(f) *Presentation of stability data*: As the purpose of stability testing is to determine change with time, it is important to present the stability data in such a way that such changes are immediately visible. A recommendation is to present the results of each test at each individual storage condition in vertical sequence, from the initial value up to the value measured at the longest time. Major changes in stability indicating parameters should be presented graphically;

Apart from the obvious use of determining whether the product will have an acceptable use life under various climatic conditions in the selected containers, the results of stability studies can be used for the following:

(a) Fixing specification limits;

(b) Evaluating changes in the manufacture of the active ingredient, a change in the synthetic route for making it or a new source for it;

(c) Testing the influence of a changed formulation.

If the commercial pack is changed, e.g. if the manufacturing process of the primary packaging configuration is altered substantially or another supplier is selected, it is necessary to investigate, under accelerated conditions, critical parameters of the formulation and package.

### 3.2 Continuous Quality Checks

As with all manufacturing processes in the chemical industry, it is important for packaging processes to have a continuous and well-organized documentation of quality measurements. Therefore, a system of in-process control has to be established. The minimum requirement would be to identify the product and all elements of the final package configuration and to control the product quantity on a statistical basis, the function of the closing system and the completeness of the labelling.

The regular inspection of ready goods in warehouses, prior to their dispatch, allows making a detached judgement to the packaging development engineer.

### 3.3 Control of Incoming Material

All incoming packing material must be tested as to whether or not it meets the specifications. This requires the use of statistical analysis techniques such as statistical sampling, test methods for the important properties, designed experiments and control charts (7).

Elements common to many effective quality assurance programmes are outlined in ANSI/ASQC Q 94 (8). The control of dimensions and weights is the minimum requirement. Other important tests were summarized in Table 16.5.

The test programme and the test methods have to be worked out in agreement with the suppliers. These negotiations should take place in an atmosphere when no problems with the quality of the supplied material or the design criteria are disturbing the peace between the organizations. Harmonized specifications, test programmes and test methods are especially needed in critical, controversial situations for an independent evaluation of the quality of a product.

Periodic audits of the suppliers should create a climate of confidence. This is a prerequisite for the acceptance of certificates. But there should be no misunderstanding: certificates do not replace the receiver's own well-organized control of incoming material and the systematic documentation of results. Certificates may help to minimize the need for in-house control measures.

## 4 Specifications

A correct specification is the first step necessary to ensure the consistent performance of the completed package. It is important that all packaging material components are precisely specified in package specifications ("raw material specifications"), but it is also important to give clear instructions to the refilling plant. the latter task, packaging instructions, should be independent of the first one.

### 4.1 Package Specifications

The package specification is the main means of communication between the packaging plant and the supplier. It must define all critical types of raw materials, dimensions and physical and chemical properties. Drawings are self-explanatory. specifications have to be accepted by the supplier as well as the receiver of the material and must be continuously updated to reflect the latest technology.

Typical package specifications are shown in Table 16.6 and in Figure 16.1

## 4.2 Packaging Instructions

The instruction for the refilling and packaging plant has to be as precise as any other specification as it is the plant's main source of information. It also is useful for planning and logistics, for quality assurance (in-process and final goods control) and for accountability. The packaging instruction contains information for the warehouse and for marketing.

The kinds of information that might be included in packaging instructions are shown in Table 16.7.

**Table 16.6 Package specification example**

| *Requirement* | *Package specification* |
|---|---|
| Definition of the item | HDPE bottle |
| Nominal volume | 1 litre |
| Code no. | 7 123 456 |
| Prescription | Cylindrical bottle, extrusion blow-moulded, neck KS 50/DIN 6063 |
| Raw material | Lupolen .... Hostalen<br>virgin material reground only from the same process (closed system recommended) |
| Colour | Natural transparent |
| Print | Neutral |
| Total volume | 1.1 litre |
| Weight | 85±3.4 g |
| For further technical details refer to drawing no. | 3353 g |
| Test instruction | 03, dated 1.5.1995 |
| Test instruction (programme, AQL, procedures) | |
| Delivery instruction | Palletized 1.2 m x 1.0 m x 1.8 m, each layer packed on trays, securely wrapped |
| Date/signatures | |

**Table 16.7 Packaging instruction**

| *Category* | *Details* |
|---|---|
| Parts list | Code number of bottle, closure, label, shipping box, tape, pallet, shring film |
| Instruction for the packaging plant | Torque, type of glue, type and width of tape |
| Weight accuracy | Mean weight, tolerance limits |
| Marking and labels | Numbers and positions of hazard label (3), batch number, date of manufacture, method of application |
| Stacking plan | Position, size of pallet, arrangement of boxes and number of layers per pallet, means of securing, gross volume and weight per pallet, warehouse instruction on max. height for stacking of pallets |
| Annual colour code | Annual colour (first in/first out) |
| Pallet label | Identification of the pallet load |

## 5. DISPOSAL

The agrochemical industry has taken responsibility for the safe, environment-friendly disposal of post-consumer packages. Early in the development stage, this task has to be taken into consideration. The duties of the various parties may be seen as follows:

(a) Industry selects materials of construction, that do not allow intolerable rates of permeation and that allow at least the recovery of energy. Containers are designed so that rinsing is easy; this requires:

   (i) Wide apertures, min.40 mm diameter;

   (ii) No hollow handles in cans or no hidden pocket in bags;

   (iii) The product can be removed completely (max. 0.01% product residue) after rinsing as per standardized methods with integrated rinsing equipment on the spray rig.

(b) Farmers are committed to rinsing as per the above mentioned procedure and are willing to return the empty packages to the point of sale;

(c) Dealers are prepared to collect the post-consumer packs after controlling for correct rinsing. This makes them responsible for buying goods that can be easily disposed of;

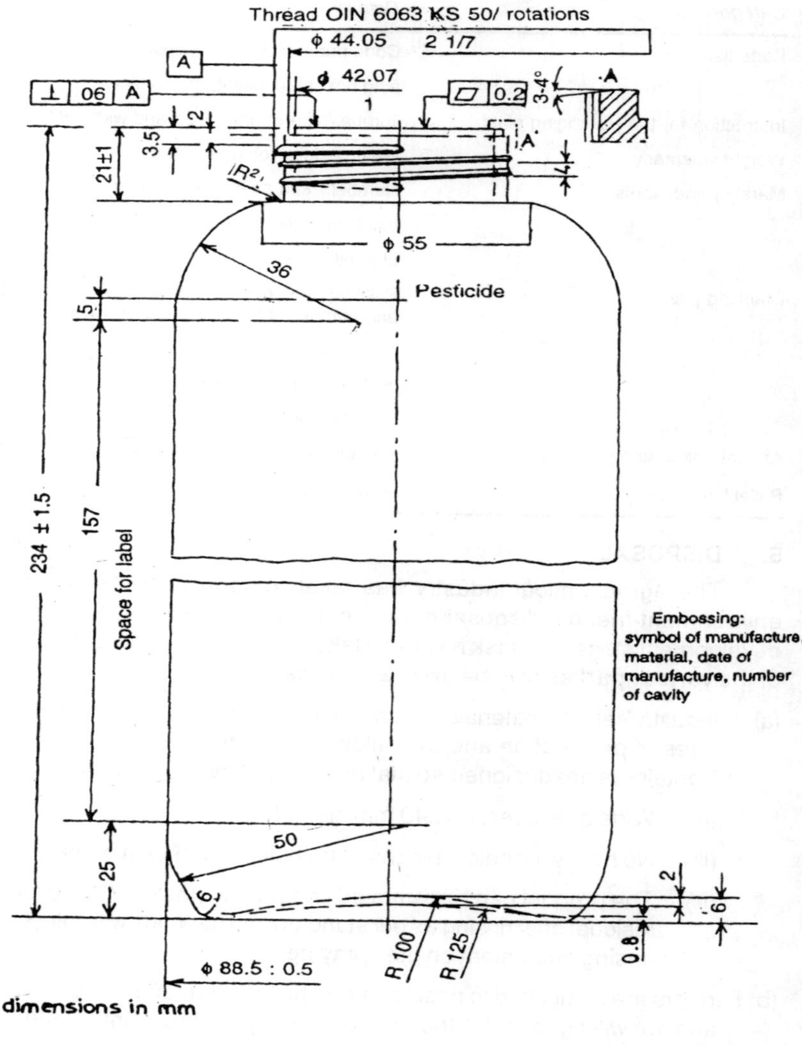


Figure 16.1 Diagrammatical specification

(d) Disposal companies with professional qualifications, take care of the rinsed and clean containers. In a cascade flow they recover the energy content, preferably in cement works or in controlled incineration p ants, or re-use the material if possible.

The empty containers must not litter the environment. Farmers should assume that responsibility when they decide to apply crop protection products.

# 20

# Aerosol Packaging Technology

## Introduction

An aerosol pack is designed to deliver conveniently a vast array of products under pressure. The aerosol pack is made up of four basic components, the can the valve, the product and the propellant.

## Working Principle of Aerosol

The propellant (e.g. liquified gas propellant) possesses a liquid and a gaseous phase. To achieve uniform spraying of active substances by means of the propellent, the active substances and the propellant in the container must form either a homogenous solution or a suspension/emulsion. The active substance and the liquid propellant phase should be considered as a single phase. The headspace above the liquid phase is always filled with the gaseous propellant. This vapour phase exerts its pressure not only against the wall of the container but also against the liquid phase, thereby forcing the latter through the dip tube towards the valve orifice. When the actuator is depressed, the liquid phase passes through the valve orifice and then into the atmosphere. As soon as it gets into the atmosphere, the liquid propoellant expands and evaporates, simultaneously breaking the active ingredient which is dissolved in the propellant into fine particles. The magnitude of this dispersion depends upon the nature of the propellant and its concentration within the preparation i.e. the ratio of propellant to active ingredient solution. As the level of liquid content withing the container drops, the headspace available on account of this is occupied by gaseous phase of the propellant.

Products which are to be dispensed in the atmosphere and left air borne are called 'Space Sprays' e.g. Room Deodorants and Insecticides etc. Here the product concentrate is relatively small, and does not normally exceed 20:80 ratio of the product to propellant. The particle size will be in the order of 50 microns. Products which are sprayed on to surfaces at close ranges are called 'Surface Sprays' e.g. Hairsprays, Suntan Lotions, Paints etc. The ratio of product to propellant in surface sprays could be as high as 72:25 and since the particles are not required to remain air borne, the particle size is in the order of 100-200 microns.

## Pack Contents (Product and Propellant)

Little need be said about the products contained in an aerosol pack, except that they may range from liquids such as solvent or water based insecticides, through wax–containing polishes, up to highly viscous fluid such as hand cream.

## Propellants Fall into Two General Groups

(a) *Liquefied Gases*

These are gases easily liquefiable at normal temperatures and pressures permissible for aerosol containers. The most commonly used liquefied gases are of the halogenated hydrocarbon type such as the Freons, Arctons, Mafrons etc. The range of such propellants is large, and the choice of propellant or propellant blend is made on the grounds of the saturated vapour pressure required, and also on considerations of product/propellant compatibility. The three halogenated hydrocarbon propellants in most common use are : Propellant 11, Propellants 12 and Propellant 114. Blends from these three propellents generally provided the required vapour pressure.

Alternatively, liquefied gases may be of the hydrocarbon type. Hydrocarbon propellants are commonly classified as Butane 30, 40 and 48, the figure referring to the saturated vapour pressure of the blend at a temperature of 21°C. Unlike halogenated hydrocarbons, these are inflammable.

(b) *Compressed Gases*

These propellants are gases which have critical temperatures and pressures such that they do not liquefy under the conditions at which they are used in aerosol packaging. Gases normally used as propellants include carbon dioxide and nitrous oxide, or a mixture of the two.

Whereas a liquefied gas propellant provides a virtually constant vapour pressure throughout the life of an aerosol pack, this is not so for a compressed gas system, where expulsion of product results in an increased gaseous volume and a corresponding dropo in pack pressure. Consequently, compressed gas systems usually operate at higher initial pressure than liquefied gas systems. A typical initial pressure of a compressed gas package may be as high as 90 p.s.i.g., whereas liquefied gas systems seldom operate at pressure above 50 p.s.i.g. The disadvantage with compressed gas systems is that at the end of the service life of a pack, some quantity of the product may be left in the can which cannot be expelled.

## AEROSOL CANS

### (a) 3–piece tinplate aerosol cans

These cnas are by far the most widely used type of aerosol containers. They are manufactured by seaming together three components – the cylinder, the cone and the dome made from tinplate.

(I) *The Cylinder*

The cylinder is formed from a flat sheet of tinplate by curling it into a cylinder and attaching the two ends together by:

1. Hooking the two ends together and soldering.
2. Direct lap resistance welding.

(ii) *The Dome*

The dome forms the bottom of the aerosol can and is a tinplate stamping.

(iii) *The Cone*

It forms the top of an aerosol can and is again a stamping, but of a more complex nature than the dome since it has a 1" aperture into which the valve fits.

This 1" profile (the curl) is added to the cone after the press operations.

### (b) 2–piece aerosol containers

These containers do not have a separate cone, cone/cylinder as a one piece aluminium extrusion. The dome is tinplate, and is double – seamed to the bottom flange of the body in the same way as it is done for 3–piece containers.

### (c) Single-piece Aluminium Cans

These containers are generally referred to as monoblocs, since they are made entirely from one piece of aluminium.

Nearly all types of aerosol can incorporate a 1" aperture to accommodate the aerosol valve. Exceptions include very small diameter aluminium extrusions for pharmaceutical products or hand bag size cosmetics.

All types of container may be lacquered internally or may be plain, depending on the pack contents.

Apart from the above there are glass and plastic containers also with 13, 15 and 20 mm open aperture which cna be crimped with suitable aluminium valves.

**Aerosol Valve**

The aerosol valve influence the explusion of product in three ways:-

1. It determines the discharge rate, that is the quantity of product expelled per second.
2. It may influence the distribution of the spray, i.e. the spray pattern.
3. It may affect the particle size of the spray.

(1) *The dip tube*

(a) **Standard dip tube**

– usually extruded in low density polythene – used for majority of products. In India, mostly nylon is used to achieve better dimensional control.

(b) **Visco tubing**

– extruded in low density Polypropylene – used for viscous products – wider internal bore than standard.

(c) **Capillary tubing**

– Polypropylene – smaller internal bore than standard tubing – used to reduce discharge rate.

(ii) **The Mounting Cup**

The cup forms the support for the valve system, and is swaged into the 1" aperture of the can, a tight cup/can seal being made by the lining compound.

Cups are nearly all stamped from tinplate, but a small number of aluminium cups are also manufactured. Tinplate cups may be supplied lined or a grommet may be used alternatively.

(III) **The Housing**

The Housing forms the main body of the valve, and provides a seat for the inner valve sub-assembly of spring, stem, and gasket. It also provides a link between the dip tube, which is fitted over the housing spigot, and the valve assembly internal to the housing. The seal (crimp) of the housing into the cup completes the overall valve assembly.

After the product has been filled into the can, the cup is then swaged on to the latter. Propellant may be filled either before the cup is swaged on to the can (under-cup filling), or afterwards injected through the valve (pressure filling).

All the housing are manufactured from Nylon.

(iv) **The Stem**

This is the most important valve component in determining the discharge rate of the pack. The discharge rate will depend on the pack pressure and on the area of channels through which product flows. Orifice size from 0.013" to 0.040" are used for different packs.

(v) **The Spring**

The springs are usually formed from passivated stainless steel.

(vi) **The Gasket**

Gasket are normally made of Nitrile or Neoprene rubber. Where an improved seal is essential, for instance in compressed gas packs, or packs containing solids, such as antiperspirants, then the softer Nitrile gasket gives increased sealing efficiency.

Some products, for example those containing large quantities of ketones or methylene chloride, would cause excessive swelling of a Nitrile gasket, which would in turn lead to high leakage rates from the pack. For these particular products a Neoprene gasket is recommended.

(vii) **The Actuator**

The actuator, serves the job of spraying the final product. Depending on the geometry of the actuator section, it could give a mechanicalbreak up of the jet or non-breakup sprays.

**Methods of Filling Aerosol Containers**

The process of filling aerosol containers involves four separate operations –

1. Product filling
2. Removal of air in the headspace
3. Swaging
4. Propellant filling

1. **Product filling**

The product is filled into the aerosol can before valve insertion, and is a simple process of metering out a definite volume of product from a reservoir by means of pneumatically operated cylinder and piston arrangement.

2. **Removal of air in the headspace**

This may be performed in three ways – .

(a) The headspace above the product is evacuated. This may not be possible if the product contains highly volatile components.

(b) A few drops of volatile propellant may be added after the product has been filled. Rapid evaporation of this propellant will drive out air from the headspace. This technique is known as purging.

(c) Additionally inert gas may be blown through the product. This gas may be nitrogen or carbon dioxide. This process known as sparging is employed for highly critical products such as oven cleaners.

The removal of air is often necessary to prevent excessive corrosion within the enclosed container. Moreover, if propellant is injected after the valve has been closed on to the can, the presence of gas in the headspace may lead to high internal pressures.

3. **Swaging**

The valve is inserted into the can, and the side-walls of te cup are forced outwards underneath the can curl by a number of chives in the swaging head.

4. **Propellant filling**

The method of filling propellant will depend on whether the material is a liquefied or compressed gas.

(i) *Cold filling*

In this method, the product is chilled and refrigerated liquid propellant is introduced through the 1" aperture of the can, prior to swaging. This automatically removes air from the headspace. Cold filling is little used because certain product categories, in particular the water based products, cannot be chilled without detrimental effects to the emulsion system.

(ii) *Pressure filling*

Although there are three classes of pressure filling, all methods consist of injecting high pressure propellant through the valve after swaging and purging operations. Pressure filling may take place without a button in position ('button off'), with a non-skirted button in position ('around button] or button on'), and with a skirted button in position, when the propellant is injected through two holes in the button itself.

(iii) *Under-cup filling*

After product filling, the valve is placed in position. The under-cup filling machine then lifts the valve cup slightly, simultaneously evacuating the can headspace. Propellant is then injected between the cup and the can, the valve is re-inserted and swaged into position.

(b) **Compressed Gases**

There are two important methods of filling compressed gas packs –

1. The product concentrate is saturated with the gas under pressure. This gas is usually carbon dioxide or nitrous oxide, or a mixture of the two. The saturated product is then injected into the can using one of the methods discussed above.
2. The product is first filled and the valve swaged into position. Compressed gas is then injected throough the valve, and the can shaken vigorously for a fixed time period to cause solution of the gas in the product.

## GROWTH POTENTIAL (Productwise)

(a) *Toiletries*

Expansion of the toiletry market is hindered by the high tax levels but nevertheless, there seems to be a strong future for shaving foam and room deodorants. Another product range of significance is antiperspirants. A rough standard of at least 20% reduction of perspiration must be achieved to classify this as an antiperspirant. Such formulations have good potential in India.

(b) *Insecticides*

This is the most important product group today where a substantial market expansion can be expected. At present, there are no aerosol insecticides sold in India and the market is supplied by 'Spray Guns'. These are rather ineffective due to coarse spray particle size and generate more waste. Aerosol in this area should be expected to have a fair change to penetrate the market because it can offer least wastage, more effectiveness and acceptable odour. All the products of this category have to be approved by the Central Insecticide Board who are concerned about the product's toxicity.

(c) *Pharmaceuticals*

Very little activity in the area of pharmaceuticals at present, but this has a fair potential especially with the unique advantage that the product can remain sterile 'during use' and be applied if necessary as a metered dose.

(d) *Household products*

With the strong cost effective benefits of some household products – (most notably furniture polishes) – the aerosol should be successful on grounds of economy.

(e) Industrial products

A number of existing fillers are producing industrial products with a strong emphasis on silicones and dye penetrants.

From these bases more expansion of this group of products could be expected.

It can be seen that although insecticides are likely to lead the early growth of aerosols many other products already exist or have good potential. Increased production efficiencies and cost reduction brought about by volume will encourage more growth.

It is difficult to forecast how quickly market growth in India will occur but it would depend mainly on how soon deodorised liquid petroleum gas (LPG) would be available in place of costly fluorocarbon around Rs. 40/- kg LPG mainly consists of hydrocarbons e.g. n–butane and iso–butane together with Mercaptans which are intentionally mixed with the gas at the time of filling as a safety measure (Mercaptans, by virtue of their strong smell alarms people in case of possible leakage of LPG which is, as pointed out earlier, highly inflammable).

## LEGISLATION

### Chlorofluorocarbons (CFCs)

The so called 'CFC ozone hypothesis' that CFCs destroy the ozone layer around the earth was mainly responsible for current disturbances in the growth potential of aerosol market in the world. A few schools of Scientists identified CFCs as one of the group of solvents which might harm human skin which are normally protected from ultra violet radiation by a layer of ozone around the earth. Although till date there is no concrete evidence the CFCs are leading to a reduction in ozone, it might take another decade to provide real evidence. This led to different legislations which are in force in different countries concerning elimination or reduction of use of CFCs as aerosol propellants. In India, however, no such legislation exists.

### Flammability

In view of the current legal position affecting limited use of CFCs in aerosol formulations technologists concentrated more on use of higher levels of flammable products e.g. deodorised butane in the formulation. Proper precautions were recommended to handle such flammable products during storage, aerosol filling and transport of filled cans.

### Developments

*New Formulations*

In USA, UK and Europoean countries development effort in the last decade has been centred around new formulations to adapt hydrocarbons as propellant. In these works considerations have been given on avoidance of corrosion of the pack in the market by formulating water in oil emulsions.

Water was incorporated to limit the flammability of the pack due to butane propellant. Controlling of odour in the formulation was also being done by using masking agents and chemical stabilisers. In India, pilot scale plants have been developed to produce deodarised LPG. Some has been initiated locally to develop different formulations based on deodorised butane as propellant.

### New products

Personal deodarants, perfumes, room fresheners, hairsprays and silicone mould release agents were being marketed in India in the last ten years. Of late, interests have been shown on development of aerosol domestic insecticides and shaving foam. In general, fillers have been more market acceptability of industrial products inlarge size cans than cosmetic products in small size cans. At present, silicone spray and dye penetrants, for non-destructive testing constitute a major share of market in India.

Some of the relatively new products which have appeared in Europe and USA are Frying Pan Sprays, Edible Cream, Antistatic Sprays for carpets and clothes. Polyurethane Sprays, water based domestic pains and fire extinguishers.

### Alternative Propellants

Europe and USA had the following propellants available for many years – Carbon dioxide, Nitrous oxide, Ether, Dimethyl ether, Flurocarbon 11 and 114 mixture and Hydrocarbons.

The trend in Europe is to reduce the level of fluorocarbon by replacing upto 30% with hydrocarbon – essentially this allows the basic character of the formulation to be maintained – although flammability is increased.

### Cans

No major development work could be seen in glass and aluminium containers.

In Europe, tinplate cans were given a trimline shape in 45 mm, 52 mm, 57 mm and 65 mm based diameter cans by introducing WIMA welding on the side seam and necking – in the body. This had resulted in better can appeal, material savings (cones and domes), cheaper cover cap and cheaper carriage of filled packs.

### Valves

Faster filling valves have generally been developed abroad. This has given food performance in terms of gassing speed, minimising propellant loss and filling reliability.

Further improvement in such valves has resulted in 30% increase in filling efficiency, lower gas loss at the filling head, reduced filling pressure etc.

## Conclusion

The convenience and cost effective application aspects of aerosols will catch in the India with increase in purchasing power of the society. The packaging costs of aerosols will come down once deodorised butane is established as a propellant and increase in volume of aerosol filling takes place. One can therefore assume a reasonable growth potential for this sophisticated package in India.

**AEROSOL PACKAGE CROSS SECTION**

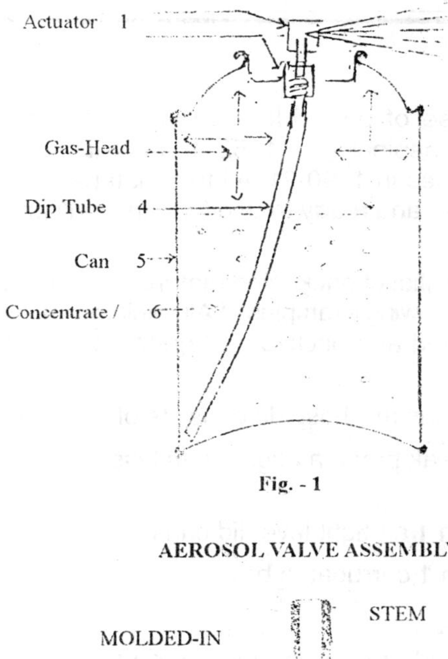


**Fig. - 1**

**AEROSOL VALVE ASSEMBLY**

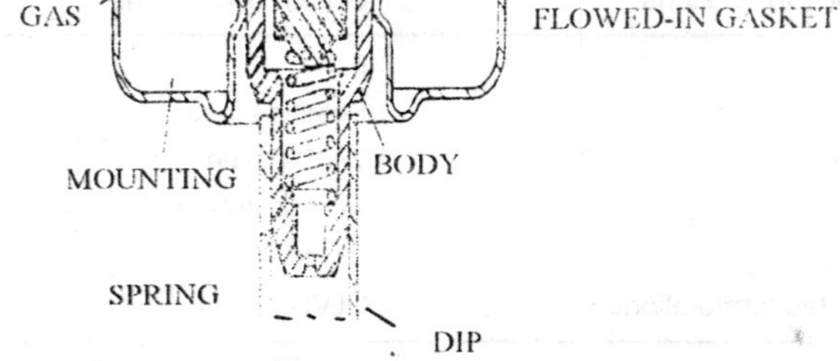


**Fig. - 2**

# 21

# Packaging in Pesticides Industry

Production and use of pesticides in our country has increased tremendously. Making a beginning in 1952, the production of pesticides has reached 80,000 tonnes in 1990-91. All this material reaches the end user in diluted, formulated and ready to use form in small packing from 10 grams upwards.

The enormous potential of packaging materials in pesticides industry can by gauged from the following examples of Aluminium Phosphide packing. It is a fumigant, formulated and packed in 3 gram tablet form, the active ingredient being 50%.

A unit pack of Aluminium Phospide consists of :

(a) 10 tablets in 1 leak proof, air tight seamless, extruded rigid aluminium tube.

(b) 16 such tubes in 1 air tight lever lid cans.

(c) 24 such cans in 1 corrugated box.

**Formulation types**

However, the method of packing and packing cost vary depending upon the type of formulation.

All formulations fall under any of the following categories :

| Dry/solid formulations | Liquid formulations | Gaseous |
|---|---|---|
| WDP | EC | Aerosols |
| Dusts | Soluble liquids | |
| Granules | WSC (Water Coluble Concentrates) | |
| Tablets | Liquid Aerosols | |
| Capsulated formulations | ULVS | |

## MAJOR FEATURES

### (a) Packaging

The proposed package should be approved by the Registration Committee. This committee has adopted INDIAN STANDARDS IS: 8190 which specifies 'Requirements of packaging of Pesticides'. If the proposed package complies with the specifications given in IS: 8190, the committee generally approves the package.

This standard is published in 4 parts.

**Part I** – Requirements for packaging of SOLID PESTICIDES

**Part II** – Requirements for packaging of LIQUID PESTICIDES

**Part III** – Requirements for packaging of HOUSEHOLD PESTICIDES

**Part IV** – Requirements for packaging of FUMIGANTS

Each part vividly gives the requirements for individual pesticides. It is practically impossible here to give all the details. However, as an example the general requirements for liquid pesticides are given.

- The liquid pesticides, technical or their formulations, shall be packed in containers in quantities of 100 ml, 250 ml, 500 ml, 1 litre, 5 litres, 20 litres and 50 litres. Only technical grade liquid pesticides may be packed in quantities of up to 200 litres in a container.
- Retail packs shall be further packed in corrugated fibreboard boxes or wooden cases where they require transportation.
- HDPE used in the fabrication of containers shall be of designation HDPE 43 BA having melt flow index not more than 1.8 g/10 minutes.
- Aluminium used in the fabrication of containers shall be of minimum 99.5% purity.
- Containers of mild steel and tin plate shall also be lacquered externally to prevent rusting from outside.
- Closures shall be leakproof and pilferproof.
- Containers holding 5 litres or more of liquid pesticides shall be provided with a suitable pouring and measuring device with each container.

## MAJOR FACTORS GOVERNING THE SELECTION OF PACKAGING MATERIALS AND PACKAGES

1. Chemical compatibility of the product and the proposed packaging materials.

2. Requirements of transport, storage, market and end use.
3. Economics.
4. Legal obligations.

1. **Chemical Compatibility**

Packaging materials having known chemical reactions rule out themselves. e.g. Mild Steel for acidic compounds.

Some others are eliminated by the physical form of the product under consideration e.g. Woven bags and liquid products.

In most cases, any action of the product on the packaging material or vice versa is actually studied.

Initially a test piece of known weight of the proposed packaging material is kept immersed in the product for several weeks. later on it is removed and cleaned and inspected for any visual signs of attack, rigidity, flexibility, weight increase or weight decrease, etc. The product is also checked visually and chemically.

After the initial approval a few test containers are filled with the materials and again above observations are made.

**2. Requirements of Transport and Storage**

During loading, unloading, transportation and storage the packages are bound to undergo mechanical vibrations, jerks, falls and compression. The package should be good enough to protect and retain the contents intact under all such occasions. This is confirmed by laboratory conditions and actual field trial before the package is approved.

***Requirements of Market and End Use***

Retail packs of formulated material are planned keeping in all levels of users i.e. small, medium, and big. Hence the same material will be packed in different sizes like 250ml, 500ml, etc.

Technical material going to formulators will be normally packed in larger quantities say 50 kgs to 200 kgs.

3. **Economics**

The material selected should be competitive in cost to other possible materials. Both tangible and intangible benefits are taken into account in calculating cost effectiveness e.g. Drum packing v/s Woven Bags or Wooden crates v/s corrugated boxes.

4. **Legal Obligations**

An insecticide for sale has to be PACKED and LABELLED in

accordance with the provisions described in Chapter 5 of the Insecticides Rules, 1971.

## MOC OF PACKAGING MATERIALS

Availability of newer packaging materials has pushed many of the conventional packages like carbuoys, wooden casks, crates etc. into the bottom rung. Metals and plastics occupied their place. Now do only metals but some of the plastics like LDPE and HDPE are facing stiff competition from improved versions of their family viz. Linear low Density Poly Ethylene and High Molecular HDPE (LLDPE AND HMHDPE)

Both LLDPE AND HM HDPE have for superior film properties compared to LDPE.

*A Great Cost Saver*– Both are twice as strong as LDPE. Where a 200 gauge LDPE bag is used, a 100 gauge HM HDPE bag can safely replaced it.

e.g. At the prevailing market rates, a gag of 12" x 12" will cost around 16 paise with LDPE. A 9 paise HM HDPE can replaced it.

*Time Saver*– LLDPE is non sticky in nature and hence easily operable vis-a-vis LDPE which sticks together. Thus the time wastage while packing with LDPE is avoided.

Other important characteristics are tabulated below for comparison.

| | *Property* | *Units* | *LDPE* | *HMHDPE* | *LLDPE* |
|---|---|---|---|---|---|
| 1. | Tensile Strength | Kg/cm2 | 200 | 600 | 350 |
| 2. | Elongation | 40% | 400 | 500 | 800 |
| 3. | Elmendorf Tear Resistance | gms/ micron | 4 | 10 | 12 |
| 4. | Puncture Resistance | gms–cm/ micron | 200 | 50 | 1500 |
| 5. | Haze | % | 6 | 80 | 14 |

# 22

# Emulsifier for Pesticides

Emulisifier is a surface active agents. In other words two or more immiscible liquids held in suspension by small percentage form a stable mixture is called **"EMULSIFIERS"**.

1. Proteins or carbohydrate polymers, which act by cooling the surfaces of the dispensed fat or oil particles, thus preventing them from coalescing (eg. albumin in milk, egg yolk in mayonnaise), these are sometimes called protective colloids.
2. Long chain alcohols and fatty acids, which are able to reduce the surface tension at the interface of the suspended particles because of the solubility properties of their molecules.

Soap behave in this manner, they exert cleaning action by emulsifying the only components of soils. All such substances both natural and synthetic, are known collectively as detergent (q.v.).

Polymerisation reaction are often form, a wide variety of food and industrial of are kind or another, e.g. floor and glass waxes, drugs, paints, shortenings, textile and lather dressing etc.

### Uses & Applications

Any attempt at preventing the use of sparious or sub-standard pesticides should be greatly welcomed. Otherwise what is likely to happen is that the farmors may be dissuaded to go in for even quality products. Already the general feeling is that the farming community is not sufficiently aware of the role of pesticides in preventing crope damage something which is very essential of agricultural production is to be stepped up. Perhaps it is the lack of sufficient awareness about the adequate use of pesticides that is responsible for the pestidies industry failing to catch up with the fertilizer industry. Farmers have to be educated on the use of pesticides and the truth must be deriven home that the use of such inputs as water, seeds and fertilizer will not produce to the desired result in the absence of plant portaction measurers since the crops are subject to attacks by pests and diseases.

It is in this context that the efforts being made to consolidate the guidelines and different aspects of technical data requirement for consideration of registration of insectidides under the insecticides act 1963, acquire importance. It is not the duty of the several associations connected with the pesticides industry in fulfilling the actual data requirement. It would appear that there are at present several deficiencies in the fulfilment of data requirement. The guidelines finalised by the Registration committee cover broadly the data requirement on:

1. Chemcial composition and allied requirement.
2. Packaging and labelling requirements.
3. Data requirements on bioefficency and residues and
4. Data requirement on Safety/ to - cology.

**Applications**

In the applications of both sprays and dusts, it is obviously desirable to distribute the active chemical in mouh away that the pests will ingest or be exposed to its quickly as possible after they appear and regardless of the part of the plant they inhabit.

With the development of Insecticides which singly posses the action of stomach, poisons, contact poisons and fumigans, combined with increased knowledge of the biology and habits of the major insect and mite pests, adequate control may often to be obtained. With economical and rapid methods of applications. As the newly hatched codling moth larvae roam over the plant surface before making their entrance holes, for example, the contact affect of DDT or other newer insecticides may result in satisfactory mortability even through small untreated islands are available for entrance of the larae into the fruit.

The efficienty of a pest control application therefore lies in its ability to kill the maximum number of insects with the minimum amount of insecticide and minimum cost of application. To obtain this efficiency the insecticides must be tailored to the application or vice versa and both should be selected according to the hiology and habits of the pest as well as the weather conditions prevailing at time of treatment.

## NON - IONICE EMULSIFIER OTHER FORMULATION

**Chlordane Formulation**

1. 85% Emulsifier Concentrate (Non Ionice)

| | |
|---|---|
| Tech. Chlordane | 85 parts. |
| Polyoxy Ethylene Fatty Acids | 15 parts. |

**Formulation Emulsifier Concentrate**

| | |
|---|---|
| Polyoxy Ethylene Fatty Acids | 2.5 Kg. |
| Amyl Trimethyl Chloride | 25 Kg. |
| Kerosen | 45 kg. |
| | 100 kg. |

## PLANT ECONOMICS

| | | |
|---|---|---|
| **Rated Plant capacity** | = | 200.00 Lts/day |
| **Land & Building** | Rs. | 4,40,000.00 |
| (Area 500 Sq. Mt.) | | |

## PLANT & MACHINERY

1. Stainless Vessels
2. Cooking Kettle
3. Cooling Tower
4. Other Accessories viz; Baby Boiler

## FIXED CAPITAL

| | | | |
|---|---|---|---|
| 1. | LAND & BUILDING | Rs. | 4,40,000.00 |
| 2. | PLANT & MACHINERY | Rs. | 5,30,000.00 |
| 3. | OTHER FIXED ASSETS | Rs. | 5,000.00 |
| | TOTAL | Rs. | 9,75,000.00 |

## RAW MATERIALS

1. Instead of Ethylene Oxide Also Use Ethylene Glycol but preferance will be Ethylene Oxide.

2. Carbon Dioxide
3. Propylene Oxide Solution
4. Other Chemicals
5. For Packaging, Transporting etc.

## TOTAL WORKING CAPITAL/MONTH

| | | |
|---|---|---|
| 1. Raw Material | Rs. | 44,000.00 |
| 2. Salary & Wages | Rs. | 18,125.00 |
| 3. Utilities & Overheads | Rs. | 11,900.00 |
| TOTAL | Rs. | 74,025.00 |

## TOTAL CAPITAL INVESTMENT

| | | |
|---|---|---|
| Total Fixed Capital | Rs. | 9,75,000.00 |
| Total Working Capital for 2 Months | Rs. | 1,48,050.00 |
| TOTAL | Rs. | 11,23,050.00 |

## TURN OVER/ANNUM

| | | |
|---|---|---|
| Through Sale of 60000 LT. Emulsifier | Rs. | 16,80,000.00 |

PROFIT SALES RATIO = PROFIT / SALES X 100 = 23.35 %

RATE OF RETURN = OPERATING PROFIT / T.C.I X 100 = 34.93 %

BREAK EVEN POINT (B.E.P) = 58.08 %

# 23

# Pesticides

1. Malathion 500 MT/Annum
2. Mancozeb 500 MT/Annum
3. CopperOxy Chloride 200 MT/Annum
4. WettableSulphur300 MT/Annum
5. Zinc Phosphide 100 MT/Annum

Malathion

Malathion was the first example of a wide-spectrum organophosphorus insecticide introduced in 1950 by the American Cyanide company. Combined with a very low mammalian toxicity. and more recently other safe compounds such as the selective aphicide menazon (1961) have been developed an important advantage of organo phosphorous insecticide is that they are generally rapidly degraded after application (with 2 to 4 weeks of application) to non toxic materials, consequently they are not persistent, like oroganochlorine insecticides, and, therefore, do not tend to accumulate in the environment and long food chain.

**Copper Oxy Chloride**

Copper oxychloride uses as fungicides is a bluish green powder which is highly toxic by injection. It is an excellent pesticide uses mainly in potato and tomato crops. It also abundantly uses as fungicidal pigment in paints and as a good preservative.

Chemical formula of copper oxy chloride is $3CuO. CuCl_2\ 3/2\ H_2O$ also known as cupric oxychloride. it is soluble in acids and ammonia but in-soluble in water.

Copper fungicides uses in India in bordeaux mixture and proprictary compounds containing copper oxy chloride and cuprous oxide.

## Wettable Sulphur

Wettable sulphur is an insecticide which comes under the category of fungicide as in 1803, elemental sulfur was first recommended for this use by Royal Gardends Forsyth in the nineteenth century sulphur was increasingly employed against powdery meldew on fruit and lates for control of powdery meldew on grapes sulphur exists in nature both in free state and combined forms.

Sulphur is one of the most important basic raw materials in chemical industries. the main use of sulphur one as fungicide and in sulphuric acid manufacture.

# 24

# Pesticide Preparation Using Neem Fruits and Seeds (Margosa)

The use of neem seed kernel extracts for controlling insect infestation has been known in rural communities in India for a long time.

The credit of arousing world-wide interest in the use of neem kernel extract should go to Robert Larson of Vikwood Botanicals, U.S.A., who during his many business trips to India, had observed the use of neem extractives in rural areas for saving crops from insects and the multifarious uses of the products of neem in villages.

With the advice of assistance of USDA, Baltimore, Maryland, USA, he developed a neem kernel formulation, named Margosan-O, standardised to certain 3000 ppm azadirachtin. When diluted 150-fold this would afford a spray solution with 20 ppm azadirachtin adequate to control many pests. Extensive toxocological studies were carried out on Margosan-O, which was finally cleared for use in horticulture by EPA in the U.S.

Neem oil contains only traces of azadirachtin but compounds like salomnin, meliantriol, etc. are present, which may be useful in the control of some insects.

We in India are favourably placed in regard to the availability of neem kernel for the manufacture of an effective and non-toxic product for use in agriculture.

Neem formulations can in specific cases prove more effective and in general reduce harm to the environment and hazards in agricultural operations. Neem has been subjected to worldwide scrutiny to a degree not accord by any other plant and a fund of information exists which attests to its usefulness for insect control.

This is a medium sized tree, with a clear bole of 10-25' and a girth of 6-8'. Although described as evergreen, in drier areas it become decidious. Its bark is moderately thick with longitudinal or oblique furrows on the outer surface. It is dark-grey outside and reddish inside. The flowers appear from March-May and the fruits ripen during June-August. They are greenish yellow when ripe and usually contain only one seed.

## MANUFACTURING PROCESS OF PESTICIDE USING NEEM FRUITS & SEEDS

The manufacturing process involves extraction from selected neem seed kernel & fruits with solvent extraction under controlled conditions, which enables extraction of neem pesticides.

Direct extraction from the seeds after proper preparation with total quality control (TQC) at the selection stage of the seeds itself only can ensure the product of required efficacy and other qualities. The plant and machinery includes :

(a) Preparatory section
(b) Critical plant (solvent extraction distillation and recovery section)
(c) Offsites (steam generators, electricals, etc.)
(d) Control system
(e) Purification equipment
(f) Rectification columns
(g) Liquid - liquid extractors
(h) Vacuum drying system.

### Preparatory Steps

Neem seeds are dried in controlled temperature, stones, debris and iron particles removed, decorticated, husk is removed by cyclone separators, kernels pulverised. Likewise, fruits are dried, pulverized etc. by pulverizer, likewise neem fruits are subjected to sorting & grading, peeling, drying, pulverizing.

### Extraction

The prepared material is fed into an extractor and the feed is extracted by solvent or multi solvent.

Neem seeds & fruits which are in powdered form are introduced into an extractor/mixer (stainless steel steam jacketed) and a sufficient amount of alcohol is added into the reactor. It is heated slowly by passing steam into the jacket of the reactor.

After sometimes, when all the extract from seeds and fruits has been recovered, then, it is filtered which is a mixture of alcohol e.g. ethyl alcohol and neem extract.

The neem extract is fed into the distillation column, while the oil extract is fed into solvent recovery section and oil and solvent are separated.

**Distillation**

The above neem extract is fed into the distillation column and thus alcohol (ethyl alcohol, colorless volatile liquid, b.p. 78.3°C) and neem extract (which has b.p. 90-95°C) are being separated by means of the distillation columns.

The alcohol recovered from the distillation column is recycled back into the mixer.

The operation of the distillation depends on the fact that liquids have different vapour pressure at a given temperature. When a liquid mixture is volatilized, the vapour produced is richer in the more volatile component and the liquid remaining in the boiler is richer in the less volatile component. On this basis, the separation of liquids is achieved.

The distillation column is filled with packing materials such as Raschig rings, bearl saddles, etc. or they may contain a series of perforated bubble, cap plates or sieve plates.

During the process, a continuous distillation is achieved by returning the liquid condensate to a point approximately mid-way up the fractionating column where the liquid in the column has about the same composition as the returning liquid (reflux). Generally, the higher the reflux ratio, the greater the efficiency of operation. The relatively pure vapour leaving the top of the column may be taken off continuously.

**Concentration**

Neem extract is concentrated. The entire operation is done in controlled temperature, flow and pressure.

The neem extract is further concentrated in a fall-in-film evaporator.

The concentrate is treated further with two solvents (liquid/liquid extraction) to get the neem pesticide.

The product may be dried to remove all moisture and solvents (vacuum, low temperature drying).

Desolventising and rectification are the other sections where the solvents are recovered and purified.

The entire process is done under controlled conditions and there is no relevance with conventional solvent extraction plant.

All the product contact parts are stainless steel make.

**Neem Formulations**

If neem formulations are desired, then the technical concentrate is dissolved in suitable solvents, emulsifiers, wetting agents, antioxidants and other stabilizers and mixed suitably to get microemulsion emulsifiable concentrate.

Apart from the preparatory and solvent extraction techniques, the technology adopted for the formulations of neem pesticides is based on micro-emulsion technology, which ensures the stability of the product through homogenous mixing of stabilizers and anti-oxidants, which are responsible for increase in shelf-life.

## PLANT ECONOMICS

| | | |
|---|---|---|
| Rated Plant capacity | = | 1 Mt./Day |
| Land & Buildings (Land 800 Sq.Mts) | Rs. | 19,07,500.00 |

## PLANT & MACHINERY

1. Extractor/reactor mixer of S.S (steam jacketed) fitted with agitator
2. Distillation column with packing of raschig's rings/bearl saddles with accessories
3. Filter press
4. Decorticator
5. Cyclone separator for removal of husk of neem seeds
6. Solvent recovery unit for separating of oil & solvent
7. Pulverizer for pulverizing of kernels
8. Evaporator (fall-in-film type) for concentration of neem extract
9. Vacuum drying system with all accessories
10. Baby boiler
11. D.G. set
12. Lab testing equipments
13. Storage tanks
14. Instrumentation & process control equipments
15. Miscellaneous viz. pipe fittings, valves, motors, etc.

## FIXED CAPITAL

| | | | |
|---|---|---|---|
| 1. | Land & Building | Rs. | 19,07,500.00 |
| 2. | Plant & Machinery | Rs. | 6,50,000.00 |
| 3. | Other Fixed Assets | Rs. | 1,70,000.00 |
| | TOTAL | Rs. | 67,27,500.00 |

## RAW MATERIALS

1. Neem seeds/fruits
2. Alcohol (ethyl alcohol)
3. Miscellaneous

## TOTAL WORKING CAPITAL/MONTH

| | | |
|---|---|---|
| 1. | Raw Material | 13,30,000.00 |
| 2. | Salary & Wages | 81,500.00 |
| 3. | Utilities & Overheads | 69,400.00 |

## TOTAL CAPITAL INVESTMENT

| | | |
|---|---|---|
| Total Fixed Capital | Rs. | 67,27,500.00 |
| Total Working Capital for 2 Months | Rs. | 29,61,800.00 |
| TOTAL | Rs. | 96,89,300.00 |

## TURN OVER/ANNUM

| | | |
|---|---|---|
| By sale of 300 MTs of Pesticide from neem fruits & seeds | Rs. | 2,55,00,000.00 |

**RATE OF RETURN = OPERATING PROFIT/T.C.I X 100 = 44.60 %**

**BREAK EVEN POINT (B.E.P) = 48.87 %**

# 25

# Insecticides for Rats, Termites, Rodents, Mouses, Cockroahes, Monthicide

Insecticides are used to kill or to repel various domestic insects such as termite, rodents, mouse , month, cockroaches, flies, bats, mosquitoes etc. Which are causing huge loss to domestic items, furnitures, living as well as non - living bodies.

So everybody needs strict productions against this insects. So insecticides are highly consumed all over the world.

## FORMULATIONS OF VARIOUS INSECTICIDES

### Termite Control

| Formulation - 1 | | % by wt. |
|---|---|---|
| Copper Naphthenates | | 5 |
| Fuel Oil No: 1 {Kerosene} | | 95 |
| | Total = | 100 |

**PROCESS**

Mix the above compounds well with homogenization. Treat wood and infested soil with liberal amounts.

| Formulation - 2 | | % by wt. |
|---|---|---|
| Pentachloro Phenol | | 5 |
| Ortho-dichloro Benzene | | 95 |
| | Total = | 100 |

**PROCESS**

Dilute this concentrate with 4 gallon fuel oil {Kerosene} to 1 gallon concentrate used 1 gallon of this to each lineal foot of the soil surface.

| Formulation - 3 | % By Wt. |
|---|---|
| Pentachloro Phenol | 30 |
| Ortho - Dichloro Benzene | 70 |
| Total = | 100 |

**Commercial Product**

" Wood Guard " liquid chemical can be used directly or by mixing with Kerosene oil to desined dilution. It can be sprayed by sprayer or by injection over the wood which is affected by termites.

## RAT REPELLENT

**Formulation - 1**

2,3,5,6 - Tetracchloronitrophenol butyl ether. It can be used to rappel rats.

| Formulation - 2 | % by wt. |
|---|---|
| Fluoroacetamide | 0.1 - 1 |
| Brans, Oats and Starch to make | 100 |
| Total = | 100 |

**PROCESS**

Mix all the ingredients together and prepare cakes to the desired sizes 1" X 1" size.

## MOTHICIDE

**Formulation**

| Ingredients | % by wt. |
|---|---|
| Hexachloroethane | 94 |
| Sodium Bicarbonate | 5 |
| Chloretone | 1 |
| Total = | 100 |

## COCKROACH REPELLENT (LIKE LAXMAN REKHA)

| Formulation | % wt. by wt. |
|---|---|
| Delta - Methrine | 0.50 |
| Talc Powder | 10.00 |

| | |
|---|---|
| Wax ( Paraffin Wax ) | 2.00 |
| Gum | 5.00 |
| Dye (C1 Natural Dye 7 based) | 0.50 |
| Plaster of Paris Powder | 82.00 |
| Total = | 100.00 % w/w. |

**PROCESS**

Melt the wax in a Stainless Steel vessel then to it add the Delta - methrine, Gum, Dye and mix well. Then to it add the plaster of paris anc talc powder and feed into the high speed mixer. The product is now casted into tablet form or capsule form by automatic casting machine into desired shapes.

## PLANT ECONOMICS

| | | |
|---|---|---|
| Land & Building (Land 1000 Sq.Mts.) | Rs. | 18,25,000.00 |

## PLANT & MACHINERY

1. Mixer
2. Liquid Mixing Unit
3. Hydraulic Press
4. Moulds
5. Automatic Weighing filling, Pouch Sealing Machine for Powders, Cakes
6. Liquid Filling Tank (S.S)
7. Hot Air Gun
8. Laboratory Equipments

## FIXED CAPITAL

| | | | |
|---|---|---|---|
| 1. | Land & Building | Rs. | 18,25,000.00 |
| 2. | Plant & Machinery | Rs. | 7,77,500.00 |
| 3. | Other Fixed Assets | Rs. | 4,75,000.00 |
| | TOTAL | Rs. | 30,77,500.00 |

## RAW MATERIALS

1. Pentachloro Phenol
2. Ortho-Dichloro Benzene
3. Rat Control Agent : Fluoroacetamide
4. Bran, Oats, Starch
5. Mothicide : Nitro Benzene
6. Sulphur
7. Naphthalene
8. Cockroach Repellent : Delta-Methrine
9. Talc Powder
10. Wax (Paraffin Wax)
11. Gum
12. Dye (CI Natural Dye 7)
13. Plaster of Paris Powder
14. Packaging Materials Cartons, Bottles, Laminated Paper, Adhesive Tapes

## TOTAL WORKING CAPITAL/MONTH

| | | | |
|---|---|---|---|
| 1. Raw Material | | Rs. | 9,61,275.00 |
| 2. Salary & Wages | | Rs. | 1,32,335.00 |
| 3. Utilities & Overheads | | Rs. | 1,42,000.00 |
| | TOTAL | Rs. | 12,35,610.00 |

## TOTAL CAPITAL INVESTMENT

| | | | |
|---|---|---|---|
| Total Fixed Capital | | Rs. | 30,77,500.00 |
| Total Working Capital for 2 Months | | Rs. | 24,71,220.00 |
| | TOTAL | Rs. | 55,48,720.00 |

## TURN OVER/ANNUM

| | | |
|---|---|---|
| 1. | By SaLe of Termite Control Agent | 75,000 Kgs. |
| 2. | By Sale of Mouse/Rat insecticide | 75,000 Kgs. |
| 3. | By Sale of Cockroach Insecticides | 75,000 Kgs. |
| 4. | By Sale of Mothicides | 75,000 Kgs. |
| | TOTAL | Rs. 1,87,50,000.00 |

**PROFIT SALES RATIO = PROFIT / SALES X 100 = 14.49 %**

**RATE OF RETURN = OPERATING PROFIT / T.C.I X 100 = 48.96 %**

**BREAK EVEN POINT (B.E.P) = 48.15 %**

# 26

# Mosquito Larva Destroyer

Mosquito Larva Destroyer is a very conspicuous larvicide for the destruction of mosquitoes. Primarily this constitutes Formaldehyde phenol 23 essential oils viz. eucalyptus cinnmon oil, ginger oil, coconut oil, lemon grass oil, basil oil, clove oil, pine oil, clove oil, citronella oil, etc., besides camphor. The mosquito larva destroyer exhibits excellent properties for killing mosquito larva.

## Uses & Applications

Mosquito Larva killer finds great use for killing the larva of mosquitoes in the initial stage which thereby checks the outspread of disease which otherwise might have inflicted open the health of people.

## Manufacturing Process of Mosquito Larva Killer

As per the formulation for Mosquito Larva Destroyer, various ingredients viz. Formaldehyde (Formalin Solution 37 %), Phenol, Essential oils (23 Nos) viz. cidar oil, Eucalyptus oil, Cassia oil, Ginger oil, Coconut oil, Lemon Grass oil, Basil oil, Spikenard oil, Jatamansi oil, Charilla oil, Lichen oil, Clove oil, Pine oil, Citronella oil, Lavender oil, Rose oil, Linalool oil, Cinnamon oil, Ajowan oil, Flennel oil, Chilli oil, Cumin oil, Lily oil, etc. besides, camphor oil and water all in requisite quantities are taken in reaction vessel M.S. (FRP lined) fitted with an agitator. The there is a provision for Fan Belt for rotation of oil with agitator in the tanks. The duration of 14 days is intended for oil fermentation with yeast as ferment in storage tanks made of M.S. (FRP/Polypropylene lined) camphor is added into the contents of the reation vessel and the entire mass is well stirred till a complete homogenous solution is made. It is then passed through a rotary vacuum filter for removal of any entrainment material of impurities coming along with it. Then the stuff is passed into a distillation colum. After that, it is checked for quality. Then the product viz. Mosquito Larva Killer is packed in suitable plastic 1 kg. containers and then despatched for marketing.

## PLANT ECONOMICS

Rated Plant capacity = 100000.00 Ltrs../day

(All figures in Thousand Rupees)

## LAND & BUILDING

(Land Area 5.50 acres (22,548 sq.mtrs) Rs. 26,320.00

## PLANT & MACHINERY

1. Storage tank M.S.
2. Reaction Vessel M.S.
3. Distillation Column with condenser & accessories
4. Filter Press (Vacuum Rotary filter) with accessories
5. Automatic Bottle Weighing, Filling
& Sealing machine for packing the product in plastic containers
6. Lab Testing Equipments
7. Boiler
8. D.G. Set
9. Miscellaneous Equipments viz. pipe fittings, valves, motors etc.
10. Fan belt for Rotation of oil with agitator in the Tank
11. Drop mixing cooler
12. Camphor cooler
13. Air Vacuum Sealer
14. Spray Type Sealer
15. Water Storage Tank (M.S.)

## FIXED CAPITAL

| | | | |
|---|---|---|---|
| 1. Land & Building | | Rs. | 26,320.00 |
| 2. Plant & Machinery | | Rs. | 32,200.01 |
| 3. Other Fixed Assets | | Rs. | 7,000.00 |
| | TOTAL | Rs. | 65,520.01 |

## RAW MATERIALS

1. Formaldehyde (Formalin Soln. 37%)
2. Phenol
3. Essential oils
4. Camphor
5. Packing Material Polythene containers

## TOTAL WORKING CAPITAL/MONTH

| | | |
|---|---|---|
| 1. Raw Material | Rs. | 1,29,625.00 |
| 2. Salary & Wages | Rs. | 543.97.00 |
| 3. Utilities & Overheads | Rs. | 485.90.00 |
| TOTAL | Rs. | 1,30,654.87 |

## TOTAL CAPITAL INVESTMENT

| | | |
|---|---|---|
| Total Fixed Capital | Rs. | 65,520.01 |
| Total Working Capital for 3 Months | Rs. | 3,91,964.61 |
| TOTAL | Rs. | 4,57,484.62 |

## TURN OVER/ANNUM

| | | |
|---|---|---|
| By Sale of 3,00,000 litres | Rs. | 17,40,000.00 |

**PROFIT SALES RATIO = PROFIT / SALES X 100 = 5.91 %**

**RATE OF RETURN = OPERATING PROFIT / T.C.I X 100 = 22.47 %**

**BREAK EVEN POINT (B.E.P) = 41.96 %**

# 27

# Pesticides

Monocrotophos was introduced in 1965 by CIBA. It is produced by the Perkow reaction from trimethyl phosphite and N-methyl-2-Chloroacetosceta-made. The pure compound is a crystalline substance, mp=52 to 55°C. The technical product mexix at 25 to 30°C. It is soluble in water, and polar organic solvents, but only slightly soluble in alkalies. It is stable to heat but rather readily decomposed by absorbents.

Monocrotophos is effective against variety of foilage insects, particularly against bollworms on cotton, and has a good systemic activity. It may also be used for soil insect control. The acute oral $LD_{50}$ for rats is 21 mg/kg.

(Metaphos, dimethyl parathion, metacide, folidol-80, wofattex, O-O-dimethyl O-4- nitro-phenyl thiophosphate)

Methyl parathion is industrially prepared by reacting dimethyl chlorothiophospahte with p-nitrophenol in the presence of HCl accepts like potassium carbonate in acetate or with sodium p-nitrophenol-late. Reaction is carried out in the presence of emulsifiers like ammonium or amine naphthenates, and in water.

### COMMON NAME - BUTACHLOR

**Chemical Names**

N-(Butoxymethyl)-2-Chloro-2/6'-diethyl acetannilide (IUPAC)

N-(butoxymethyl)-2-Chloro

N-(2,6, diethylphenyl)-acctamide

2-chloro-2" diethyl-N-(butoxymethyl acetannilide.

Trade Names-Machete, Butanex, Lambast, Pillar sete.

Molecular formula $C_{17}H_{26}CL\ No_2$

Molecular Weight = 311.9

Manufacture - Monsanto,

GNEP International,

Makhateshim Agan

Shiming Pilar International

Physical form - Light ambeliquid

Melting Point - Less than, -5°C

Boiling Point - 156°C at 0.66 mbar (decomposes at 165°C)

Vap. pressure = 6.0 x $10^{-6}$mbar at 25°C

Density = 1.070 at 25 ° C

Stability = Very stable for long term storage.

Solubility- In water at 20°C

20 mg/1. soluble in ether, acetone, benzene alcohol, ethyl Acetate & hexane at room temperature.

Analysis of products- By gas chromatography mode of action-absorption primarily via germinating shoots, and secondary wia roots, followed by transolocation: Acts by inhibition of protein synthesis.

**Uses**

Selective pre-emergence herbicidal control of most animal grasses, certain broad leaf weeds and certain aquatic weeds in both seeded and transplanted rice and barely.

Formulation types-Granules, emulisificable concentrate.

PH range between 7-10

Compatibility with other products-no compatibility known.

*Toxing to mammals-* Acture oral LD 50 form rats 3000-3630 mg/kg (emulsifiable concentrate) and 7,10,000 mg/kg (granules). Acute derminal LD 50 mg/kg (emulsifiable concentrate0 10,000 mg/kg (granules) slight eye irritant, non-irritating to skin toxicity to Birds-non-toxic birds. Toxicity to fish LC 50 forrrainbow trout 0.52 cp. 0.76 mg/1 (96 hours).

Degradation and metabolism- In soil primarily by microbial activity. Rapidly converted to soil or rate to water-soluble derivates with a slow evolution of $CO_2$. Actively many persist to 6-10 weeks.

*Precaution-* Avoid contact with mouth skin and eyes stoe in a cool dry place away from feed and foodstuffs and out of the reach of children.

**Pyrethriods**

Pesticide synergist is a term usually used for compounds that are non toxic or negligible toxic at the dosage employed but which serve to enhance the toxicity of a pesticide chemical when combined with it. Synergism in a wide sense, is related to greater than-additive toxicity, but the additive toxicity is somewhat difficult to assess when both compound involved are toxic.

**Metabolism of Pyrethriods in Insects**

For many years it was considered that the major detoxication mechanism for pyrethrins, involved hydrolysis of the ester linkage, based on the following criteria; the ester nature of pyrethrins the insecticide inactivity of the components acids alcohol; the production often unspecified acid from incubation of pyrethrins in nitro with cockroach lipase preparation; dub ous characterization of chrysanthemic acid and the alcohol from ion vivo metabolism of. The first definitive demonstration of nonhydrohyytic mechanism for metabolism of O-labeled pyrethrins I, allethrin, dimethrin, and tetremethrin involved the use of an in nitro enzyme system, consisting of housefly abdomen homogeneities fortified with reduced nictornamide-ademine dinulecticd phosphate (NADPH) and living houseflied; R' Baygon.

**Synthetic Phyrothriods**

Pyrethrum is a contact insecticide obtained from the flower heads of chrysanthemum cineraries-folium and since ancient times it has been used as an insecticide. The varieties grown in the high lands insecticide. The varieties grown in the high lands of Kenya yield the highest proportions of active ingredients; it is also grown commercially in the caucuses, Iran, Japan, Ecuvador and new Guinea. The production of pyrethrum as an insecticides dates from about 1850 and, unlike nicetine and derris, the use of pyrethrum has increased despite the large scale introduction of synthetic insecticides. Pyrethrum owns its importance to the outstanding rapid knowdown action (a few seconds) on flying insects combined with a very low mamalian toxicity due to its ready metabolism to non-toxic products. So unlike DDT, pyrethrum is not persistent and leaves no toxic residues which may be why this insecticide does not tend to induce the development of resistant insect population. Pyrethrum is used to control posts instead foods and against household and industrial pests. Pyrethrum aerosol sprays are excellent home insecticides because of their safety and rapid action.

Disadvantages of the Pyrethrum- A major disadvantage of the pyrethrum, especially for use against agricultural pests lies in its lack of persistence due to its instability in the presence of air and light.

Pyrethrum is obtained from the dried chrysanthemum flowers by extraction with kerosene or ethylene dichloride and the extract concentrated by vacuum distillation. It contains four main insecticidal components which are collectively termed pyrethrums. These are the esters of two chyclopentenolonnes (6; R'= CH = $CH_2$ or $CH_3$) and two cyclopropanecarboxylic acids. (7;R=$CH_3$ or $CO_2CH_3$). The structure of the main pyrethrime are shown in formula 1.

## PROCESS OF MANUFACTURE

### Formulation

Methyl Parathion 2% D.P.

| | | |
|---|---|---|
| 1. Methyl Parathion | = | 50% |
| Noigen M.P. - 22 | = | 8% |
| Aromax | = | 42% |
| 2. Parathion | = | 50% |
| Emulsifier UP - 3 | = | 5-8% |
| Aromax | = | 42-45% |

3. 2% Methyl Parathion field

Strength Dust

25% Methyl Parathion Dust

| | | |
|---|---|---|
| Concentrate | = | 8% - 9% |
| Soap stone | = | 50% |
| Kaolin | = | 37.3% - 38-10 |

Deactivator (dipropylene glycol) 2.7% - 3.7%

## MONOCROTOPHOS

### Manufacture

Reaction of trimethyl phosphite with methyl N-methyl-2-Chloroactamide.

### Formulations

5 Water-soluble concentrates containing 200 kg/1, 400 kg/1 active ingredient, also 250 g a.i. IULV, mixtures with DDT-Nuvacron combi.

### Endosulfan

6,7,8,9,10, 10- Hexachloro-1,5,5a 6,9,9a-hexahydro- 6,9- methano-2,4,3-benzodioxathiepin- 3- oxide.

### Manufacture

For its manufacture, the diels-Alde adduct of hexachlorocyclopentadiene and cis-1, 4-di-acetoxybutena is hydrolyzed to the diol which is reacted with thionyl chloride.

### Formulations

Thiodan-wettable powder 17.5, 35 & 50% active; emulsifiable concentrate 17.5% & 35% active, emulsion 2L6/gallon, dust 1,L,3 & 4% active granule 3 and 5% active, ULV-concentrates, combination products with other pesticides.

## METHYL PARATHION

### Manufacture

It is made by the reaction of dimethyl phosphroochlorideothionate with sodium 4-nitrophenate.

### Formulation

Spray concentrate, dusts, Nitrox 80 =80% in aromatic petroleum solvent. Metacide 50 (chemagro 40% plus 119% parathion as emulsifiable concentrate. Nitrate 6-3 combination of parathion and methyl parathion (Monsante).

## Butachlor

N- (Butaxymethyl) - 2- Chloro-N- 2,6 - diethylphenyl) acetamide.

### Manufactures

It is produced by the reaction of chloroacetyl chloride with the azomethine of 2,6-diethylaniline and formadehyde followed by treatment with 1- butanol.

### Formulation

The l.c. is 516 a.i/U.S. gallon and granules 50 g.a.i./kg.

| | | |
|---|---|---|
| Butachlor | - | 50% |
| Butachlor | - | 50% |
| Unimul B P T | - | 5-6% |
| Aromax | - | Balance. |

Isopoturon

N,N - Diemethyl -N' (4- (i-methyl-ethyl) phenyl) ures.

**Manufactures**

It is made by the reaction of 4-isopropylphenyl isocyanate with dimethylamine.

**Formulations**

Formulated alone or in association with the hydrobenonitriles or dinoterb for post-emergence application or with neburon for pre-embergence application. Aralon 75 Wp: Aralon 50 DP.

**Solutions of *Pesticides Esticides* Pesticides in water and organic solvents**

Next to dusting powders, liquid formulations are the most popular or all types of formulations for agricultural use, particularly because of versatility of their use as high, low and ultra low volume sprays. The accuracy and ease of dilution to field strength, the cheapness of water as the main dispersant and parctically no clogging of nozzles and ease of application by a variety of spraying devices are added advantages. These can also be used for fogging an as larvicides in public health.

In general, these formulations present less hazard by drift that dusting powders and are not only more persistently held on sprayed surface but also the liquid phase helps in their absorption within the plant tissue through the outside. At the same time because of the same characteristic emulsifiable concentrates and solutions pose greater toxic hazards to operators through deermal absorption. Regardless of type of formulation, all have on requirement in common, that is the solvent or the fluid diluent be physically stable under all conditions of storage with the toxicant.

Only compounds that are rather soluble in water can be used in the form of aqueous solution. The main pesticides used in the aqueous solutions are herbisides whichare salts of organic acids with different bases, and some organophosphorous insecticides and fungicides.

Disinfection of seeds with aqueous solutions of formalin. Organic mercury compounds, and also some other fungicides and bactericides is widely practiced.

Aqueous solutions of compounds are also used to control some diseases and pests or growing plants, various solutions of pesticides in organic solvents are widely used for so-called low volume, findy dispersed spraying of plants.

Solutions of pesticides in organic solvents also find use in controlling various insect pests parasites of man and animals, for protecting non-metallic materials from damage by insects and micro-organisms. In choosing solvents for pesticides or mixtures of pesticides, it is necessary to take into account not only the solubility of the pesticides but also other properties of the solutions and the solvents. In practice, the most frequently used solvents for the preparation of dearomatized kerosene white spirit, mineral cils and diesel full. Intermediate solvents for the preparation of concentrated sclutions of pesticides in mineral oils are cyclohexanone, methylchyclohexanones, mesitylo oxide, tetrahydro furan, thiopheneisophhorone, methyl ethyl ketone, dimethyl formamidethyl carbonate, alkyl acetates, xylenes, and chlorobenzene.

In the formulation of pesticides dists, powders etc. chemical engineering operations like mixing, grinding, blending, dust collection etc., are used and for this different equipments are required. These will be described is detail below :

**Mixing and Blending**

Before grinding or milling the various ingredients are to be first mixec properly. The mixing equipment may be called a blender. Peoper kneading of the mixture of inerts and technical toxicants which may be waxlike in nature can be thus accomplished. Impregnation of inerts with liquids is also possible at this stage. These liquids may be toxicants in pure form or may be their solutions. Solutions are pumped and sprayed under pressure over the solids which are mixed in the mixer through.

There are several types of solids-mixing machines. In some machines the container moves. In others a device rotates within a stationary container.

In some cases, acombination of rotating container and rotating internal baffles or blades are present in the mixer.

Tumbler type blenders are suitable for gentle blending, capable of handling large volume. These can be cleaned easily, suitable for dense powders and abrasive materials. Double gone type blender is equipped with an agglomerate breaking device. Spray nozzle is blown dotted line. These two applications. Twin shell or vee type tumble consists of shell in the form or letter V. Agglomerate breaking and liquid feeding device are shown in the broken line. Where no liquid feeding is necessary a pin-type agglomerate breaking device is used. Tumblers of this type area available plain or with any of the above features.

The selection of mixing or blending machine is important. Ribbon blender can be used both as primary and final mixer. Ribbon mixers are capable of primary mixing most formulations in less than 15 minutes. The mixing of finished fine products can be carried out in corresponding less time. A further consideration in selection of mixing and blending equipment is the frequently at which formulations are going to be thoroughly and the to this reason various parts of the mixer should be easily accessible for such jobs. Ribbon blender can be cleaned because of its simple construction.

Methods of minimizing dust formation during mixing are 1) proper venting so as to enable filtering of displaced air rather than unregularted loss of dust laden ari 2) Dust light arrangements for loading and unloading the mixer. Care should be taken to avoid powerful suction on the mixer feed into the mixture. If the dust-collection suction on the mixture is too strong, vital ingredients may be sucked out. If the dust collection system on the weighing system is too strong error in weighing may result.

## MILLING OF WETTABLE POWDERS

### Micronizer

In consists of shallow-circular grinding chamber in which the material is acted upon by a number of gaseous fluid jets, issuing through orifices spaced around the periphery of the chamber. Jet orifices are drilled through the peripheral wall of the grinding chamber and vary in number from 3 to 16, equally spaced around the chamber the orifices vary in diameter upto 1/4. They are generally placed in atangential position (the streams coming in a tangential fashion on an imaginary circle inside the chamber. so that entering steam or air will promote the rotation of the material to be pulverized in one direction. The fluid pressure is covered into velocity head due to expansion to near atmospheric pressure. This causes a high-speed rotation of the contents of the grinding chamber. Centrifugal force of rotation causes the material to concentrate at the periphery where the jets is are introduced. Since most of the energy of the fluid jestsis dissipated near the point of entry, intense local velocity gradients and intense interactions are set up within the circulating material. A great reduction in size of the material takes place by impinging of the particles upon one another, this also be reduce the wear of the pulveriser housing.

## PLANT ECONOMICS

| | | |
|---|---|---|
| Rated Plant capacity | = | 1333.34 LTR/day |
| Land & Building (Land 800 sq.mts) | Rs. | 19,50,000.00 |

## PLANT & MACHINERY

1. Mixer
2. Stainless steel tanks
3. Storage tank

4. Filter press
5. Ribbon Blender
6. Weighing Balance
7. Packaging Machine
8. Mixing tanks
9. Safety gloves & equipments
10. Laboratory equipments
11. Miscellaneous (Milling equipments & Cyclone collector)

## FIXED CAPITAL

| | | | |
|---|---|---|---|
| 1. Land & Building | | Rs. | 19,50,000.00 |
| 2. Plant & Machinery | | Rs. | 14,00,000.00 |
| 3. Other Fixed Assets | | Rs. | 3,30,000.00 |
| | TOTAL | Rs. | 36,80,000.00 |

## TOTAL WORKING CAPITAL/MONTH

| | | | |
|---|---|---|---|
| 1. Raw Material | | Rs. | 14,00,000.00 |
| 2. Salary & Wages | | Rs. | 79,000.00 |
| 3. Utilities & Overheads | | Rs. | 1,83,000.00 |
| | TOTAL | Rs. | 16,62,000.00 |

## TOTAL CAPITAL INVESTMENT

| | | | |
|---|---|---|---|
| Total Fixed Capital | | Rs. | 36,80,000.00 |
| Total Working Capital for 3 Months | | Rs. | 49,86,000.00 |
| | TOTAL | Rs. | 86,66,000.00 |

## TURN OVER/ANNUM

**BY SALE OF 4 LAKH LITRES OF PESTICIDES RS. 2,80,00,000.00**

**PROFIT SALES RATIO = PROFIT / SALES X 100 = 20.23 %**

**RATE OF RETURN = OPERATING PROFIT / T.C.I X 100 = 65.35 %**

**BREAK EVEN POINT (B.E.P) = 39.19 %**

# 28

# Mosquito Coils and Mats

Mosquito coil is used for repelling and killing of household insects like mosquitoes, files and garden insects. Because of the pyrethrine contained in it, the mosquitoes usually die in its vicinity.

The good night king type of mosquito repellents are used during right for protection against biting/disturbances of blood sucking mosquitoes. The equipment is simple. The body is made of plastics in two pieces with in which heating coil and connection places are assembled safely. Conductor lead is plugged in the electric supply switch board. The coil gets heated which in turn heats up the steel plate on which the repellent mat is placed securely. This evaporates and liberates invisible gas with an effect which makes it unfavourable for the mosquitoes in the surrounding. But, it gives off no smoke. no fume and no harmful pollution in the atmosphere which could cause discomforts to human beings at any stage. Rather a mild aromatic fragrance gives a fueling of case. It has no toxicity to poisonous behavior and also available economical for the whole night. Since it does not burn, it does not leave any ash etc. on the heating plate. The remenant is the same mat which gets white after heating hours together. This spent in then thrown away with out a possibility for creasing any harmful effects in its presence ever. Thus, it is easy to use and provided the highest possible protection from mosquitoes whose bites invite inevitable malaria.

The mat remains on the table in the room, It protects human bodies from mosquitoes without coming into direct contact of humanbody except while placing the mat on the heating plate. Thus, there is no question of skin or other harms by it to human beings animals. It does not certainly knock down the mosquitoes either. It simply expels them from the area making them unable to sit on animal bodies and suck blood there by injecting some diseases works in the bodies.

**Formulation**

| | | |
|---|---|---|
| 1. | Pyrethrum Marc. | 40 - 50 parts by weight |
| 2. | Bark of Litrea Sabifera (Maida Wood) | 35 - 45 parts by weight |
| 3. | Deodar Saw Dust | 8 - 12 parts by weight |
| 4. | Pyrethrun Oleoresin | 1 - 3 parts by weight |
| 5. | Oil of Citronella | 1 - 3 parts by weight |
| 6. | Benzoic Acid | 0.1 - 0.3 part by weight |

## Mosquito Repellents

Travis Morton an Sitt have drawn attention to the fact that chemical used as repellents vary greatly in their effectiveness against different insects. Laboratory and field tests indicated that the the following mixtures were effective against a wide range of species.

**Formula No.1**

| | |
|---|---|
| Dimethyl Phthalate | 4 parts |
| Dimethyl Carbonate | 3 parts |
| 2-Ethyl 1,3 hexanedial | 3 parts |

## Pyrethrum

Although the discovery of the insecticidal properties of pyrethrum is unknown it is probable that the incrushed flowers of the plant were used for this purpose for several centuries by the cavcassian natives. Up to 1918 the firmly ground flower heads were used as an insect powder but more recently the greater part of the pyrethrum used in this country has been extracted with solvents and used as the van's for house hold insecticide sprays as much as 13000000 lb. of dried pyrethrum flowers were used in one year in this country consumption today is lower due to the wide use of synthetic organic insecticides and estimate indicate that 4200000 lb. were used in the US in 1948.

Commercial pyrethrum consists of the dried flower heads of a daisy like plant two species of which are recognized as commercial sources. These are chrysantheman accineum and c.cinerasial folium. The latter is the more important commercial source. The plant itself is a wide range of climatic conditions. When the flower heads appear they are harvested normally by hand and dried. Pyrethrum has been grown commercially in Dalmatia, Japan, Brazil, Kenya and Belgium cargo and small scale in other areas. Kenya now produces the largest part of the commercial pyrethium crop. Although pyrethrum has been cultivated successfully in the US, the high cost of hand labour involved in this vast operations has made commercial production economically impossible.

The active insecticidal principles of pyrethrum were first isolated and identified by standinger and Ruzicka Laprage and Associali have modified the chemical structure as originally proposed and have identified two other active principles which they have named cinerius. Both the pyrethrum and the cinerius are isters and the oily liquids under normal conditions. The formula are given below:

**Formulation**

| | | | |
|---|---|---|---|
| (a) | N.N-diethyl-meta-toluomide (DEET) | - | 25 % |
| (b) | Di-methyl phthalate | - | 30 % |
| (c) | 2-ethyl-1,3-hexanedial | - | 30 % |
| (d) | Solvent, hexane | - | 15 % |
| (e) | Pigments (1%) Dyes | - | as required |
| (f) | Perfumes (0.5%) | - | as required |

## PROCESS OF MANUFACTURE

The manufacturing of Mosquito Repellent Coil involves the following operations.

1. Grinding the pyrethrum or pyrethrine or pyrethrum marc.
2. Grinding separately the deodar saw dust, the bark of litrea sabifera, (Maida wood) and leaves/roots.
3. Mixing all the ingredients in the mixer.
4. Kneaded with hot water into a stuff dough.
5. Crushing the dough with into smaller sizes.
6. Dough are put into the hopper of the extruding machine to form strip of fixed thickness.
7. Cutting the extruded strip.
8. Moulding
9. Drying
10. Packing.

## MOSQUITO REPELLENT MATS MANUFACTURING

The main chemicals used in mfg. of mosquito repellent are :

(a) Sandalwood powder or Aromatics,

(b) Pigments and

(c) Pyrethrine which are invariable used in all formulations. But, depending upon other requirements we can adopt any formulation comprising of chemical compounds in accepted proper actions like.

(i) Dimethyl phthalate

(ii) Indolone,

(iii) 2-ethyl-1, 3-hexandediol

or

(i) Demethyl phthalate,

(ii) 2-ethyl-1, 3-hexanediol

(iii) Dimethyl carbat.

Well any other suitable formulation can also be adopted depending upon experimental results.

## PLANT ECONOMICS

Rated Plant capacity = 10,50,000 Packets coils & 3 Lakh Packets Repellent Mats/year

**Land & Building** (Land 500 sq.mts) Rs. 5,47,500.00

## PLANT & MACHINERY

1. Grinder
2. Mixer (SS) with mixing tank
3. Kneading M/C
4. Crushing Machine
5. Extruding Machine with all accessories
6. Cutting Machine
7. Mould extracting Machine
8. Dryer
9. Screen printing equipments viz rack board, screen etc.
10. Semi automatic mats packing M/C.
11. Miscellaneous.

## FIXED CAPITAL

| | | |
|---|---|---|
| 1. Land & Building | Rs. | 5,47,500.00 |
| 2. Plant & Machinery | Rs. | 7,95,000.00 |
| 3. Other Fixed Assets | Rs. | 1,80,000.00 |
| TOTAL | Rs. | 15,22,500.00 |

## RAW MATERIALS

1. **I.FOR COILS**
   Pyrethrum mark
2. Pyrethrum Gleasrin
3. Dedar Saw dust
4. Maida Wood
5. Oil of Citronella
6. Benzoic acid
7. Other Dye, Fungicides,Packaging etc.
8. **II. MOSQUITO MATS**
   Dimethyl Phthalate
9. 2-Ethyl 1,3-Hexane coil
10. N.N. Diethyl Meta toluamide
11. Solvent Hezane
12. Miscellaneous like pigments & perfume
13. Packaging materials.

## TOTAL WORKING CAPITAL/MONTH

| | | |
|---|---|---|
| 1. Raw Material | Rs. | 3,14,417.50 |
| 2. Salary & Wages | Rs. | 77,520.00 |
| TOTAL | Rs. | 3,91,937.50 |

## TOTAL CAPITAL INVESTMENT

| | | |
|---|---|---|
| Total Fixed Capital | Rs. | 15,22,500.00 |
| Total Working Capital for 3 Months | Rs. | 11,75,812.50 |
| TOTAL | Rs. | 26,98,312.50 |

## TURN OVER/ANNUM

1. By sale of 10,50,000 Packets coils.
2. 3 Lakh packets Repellent Mats

**PROFIT SALES RATIO = PROFIT / SALES X 100 = 32.12 %**

**RATE OF RETURN = OPERATING PROFIT / T.C.I X 100 = 95.52 %**

**BREAK EVEN POINT (B.E.P) = 30.22 %**

# 29

# Insecticides from Neem Seeds, Neem Oils & Neem Leaves

(1) Insecticides are used to control the insects.

(2) They kill insects by poisoning the body fluids choking the breathing apparatus or paralyzing nerve centers.

(3) Insecticides are suitable for use in domestic premises, Air craft cabins, Amatsur glass house and small gardens.

(4) In recent years a large number of different kinds of insecticides and their numerous formulations are being put into the market. It is sometime problem to choose the right type or kind to meet a particular need.

The paint that must be taken into account while selecting the insecticides are:

(i) Selective action in killing insects.

(ii) Quick toxic action i.e. (knock down effect)

(iii) High toxicity to insects

(iv) Stability on treated surface (Residual effect).

(v) Harmlessness to higher. Animals including human being.

(vi) Compatibility with other pesticides.

(vii) Effectiveness in small balks per unit of surface are or material covered.

(viii) Reasonable stability under ordinary conditions of storage.

(ix) Freedom from obnoxious odours and from irritating action of human skin and system.

(x) Non inflammability

(xi) Non corrosive action on metal and rubber parts of appliances.

Insecticides kill insects because they affect a life process ike respiration, desestion; circulations and nerve reactions. A person also might experience some effect on his life process if enough of the chemicals should get into the body by mouth with or without food, through more, by breathing vapour or particles of dust or liquids or through the skin by absorption.

The insecticides, fungicide, and Radenticides act requires that insecticides entering interstate commerce by registered and that lables on them carry information to safeguard and user and the public. Insecticides differ in degree of toxity the amount that would harm man. These materials should be stored in a place where children cannot touch them and where they cannot contaminate food. Commercial operators who are exposed to inhalation of spray mists or dusts day after that should use a simple and respirator. It the insecticide might harm the eyes goggles should be worm.

Most insecticides are poisonous and good care should be taken to store them in a well ventilated room free from dampress. All the containers and packages of insecticides should be properly labeled and kept in an orderly manner.

Operators who have to fill plant protection appliances with sprays and dusts and work with them in the field should also observe these precaution strictly. A list of general precautions which are should follow while handling insecticides is given below :

(1) The instructions given on the lables of packages or containers should be strictly followed.

(2) The breathing in of insecticidal dusts or inhaling of the spray must during operation or preparation of dusts or sprays should be avoided.

(3) Contact with the skin should be avoided but if this happened accidentally, the material should be washed off with soap immediately.

(4) While using the insecticides smoking and eating should be strictly avoided.

(5) To avoid exposure to spray or dust drifts protective clothing and respirators should be worn.

(6) The material should not be handled with bare hands.

(7) Excessive or noticeable residues on any products ready for consumption should be avoided.

## MANUFACTURING PROCESS

Neem seeds which are in powder form and neem leaves are taken in a mixer (Stainless steel steam Jacketed) and a sufficient amount of alcohol is added into reactor. It is being heated slowly for a sufficient time.

After sometimes when all the Juice from seeds and leaves have been extracted then it is being filtered and thus a Juice concentrated of Neem solution is obtained which is a mixture of now alcohol i.e. ethyl alcohol ($C_2H_5$ OH) and neem Juice.

Now neem concentrated solution is being taken into a distillation column and thus alcohol (ethyl alcohol which is colorless, limpid, volatile liquid b.p 78.3°c f.p. -117.3°C ethereal, vinous odour pungent taste & miscible with water.) and neem juice (which have b.p 90-95°C) are being separated with means of the distillation column. Hence Neem Juice solution is extracted & diluted.

**Details of distillation Process**

The term simple distillation generally refers to the separation of a mixture of two or more liquids by boiling to produce a vapour more volatile (lower boiling point) component and the condensation of this vapour back to a liquid which is collected in a receiving vessel.

This unit operation depends on the fact that liquid have different vapour pressure at a given temperature. When a liquid mixture is volatilized the vapour produced in richer is the more

volatile component and the liquid remaining in the boiler is richer in the less volatile component. Hence a particle separation of the liquids is achieved.

If the condensed vapour - the distillate is heated again the vapour produced will be even richer in the more volatile component. This process of redistillation can be repeated many times until the separation of the liquids is nearly complete but this is a lengthy operation and may be achieved more conveniently by fractional distillation.

Fractional distillation or rectification is a combination of redistillation and particle distillation of the vapour and employs a fractionating column part of the condensed vapour is returned to the boiler down the fractionating column where the liquid is brought into contact with the vapour rising up the column on its way to the condenser. This results in the less volatile component of the liquid mixture in the column becoming enriched whilst the vapour leaving the top of the column is enriched in the more volatile components. The liquid condensate being returned to the boiler is called reflux and the reflux ratio is the number of gallons of the liquid collected in the receiver. Generally the higher the reflux ratio the greater the efficiency of operation. Columns may be filled with a packing materials such as rasching rings, bers saddles or small glass cylinders or they may contain a series of perforated bubble cap plates or sieve plates.

Continuous distillation is achieved by returning the liquid condensate to a point approximately midway up the fractionating column where the liquid in the column is about the some composition as the returning liquid (reflux). The relatively pure vapour leaving the top of the column may be taken off continuously, leaving. Only the unwanted i.e. still bottom in the boilers, the section of the column above the inlet is called the rectifying section and that below is called the stripping section.

Steam distillation is a special method employed for distillating liquids with a higher boiling point or those that decompose when heated to their boiling point, this is carried by heating the liquid in the presence of water or injecting live steam into it through a pipe. The operation usually involves two unmiscible liquids (for exp aniline & water). In this case the vapour mixture condenses to give two liquid layers which may be separated in the receiver. Another method employed for distilling heat sensitive compounds is vacuum distillation. The pressure in the system is reduced to the boiling point of the liquid to be distilled.

From distillation column whatever amount of alcohol is being collected it is being reused in the mixer.

## PLANT ECONOMICS

| | | |
|---|---|---|
| **Rated Plant capacity** | = | 1.00 MT./day |
| **Land & Building** (Land required 600 sq. mts.) | Rs. | 6,00,000.00 |

## PLANT & MACHINERY

1. Reactor mixer
2. Filter
3. Storage tanks
4. Baby Boiler
5. Distillation Column
6. Seeds crushers

## FIXED CAPITAL

| | | | |
|---|---|---|---|
| 1. Land & Building | | Rs. | 6,00,000.00 |
| 2. Plant & Machinery | | Rs. | 7,50,000.00 |
| 3. Other Fixed Assets | | Rs. | 2,10,000.00 |
| | TOTAL | Rs. | 15,60,000.00 |

## RAW MATERIALS

1. Neem Leaves
2. Neem seeds in crushed form
3. Alcohol ethyl alcohol

## TOTAL WORKING CAPITAL/MONTH

| | | | |
|---|---|---|---|
| 1. Raw Material | | Rs. | 1,55,000.00 |
| 2. Salary & Wages | | Rs. | 31,500.00 |
| 3. Utilities & Overheads | | Rs. | 46,300.00 |
| | TOTAL | Rs. | 2,32,800.00 |

## TOTAL CAPITAL INVESTMENT

| | | |
|---|---|---|
| Total Fixed Capital | Rs. | 15,60,000.00 |
| Total Working Capital for 3 Months | Rs. | 6,98,400.00 |

## TURN OVER/ANNUM

By sale of 300 MT. Rs. 52,50,000.00

**PROFIT SALES RATIO = PROFIT / SALES X 100 = 33.10 %**

**RATE OF RETURN = OPERATING PROFIT / T.C.I X 100 = 76.95 %**

**BREAK EVEN POINT (B.E.P) = 38.59 %**

# 30

# Air Fresher (Odonil Type)

The importance of the process is its usefulness as a method of odor control. Air freshners, perfumes and industrial deodourants are examples of odor modifiers. Perfumers employ the principles of odor modification in creating fragrances. Functional fragrances are odor modifier; thus, odor modification refer specifically to use of fragrance materials for odor control. Aerosol is one of the odor modifiers which is manufactured by some definite company. Most aerosol products contain three major components : propellents, Solvents and active gradients. Depending on the manner in which these components are combined in the product, aerosols can be divided into two broad classes : homogeneous or heterogeneous. Products are homogeneous or have been formulated as homogeneous systems when all the components are mutually soluble. Homogeneous products are two phase systems, consisting of a single liquid phase in equilibrium with a vapour phase, an example of common homogeneous aerosols are hair sprays, personnal deodorants and products formulated as homogeneous systems is that they do not need to be shaken before use. Heterogeneous systems contain at least three phases suspension systems consist of a solid phase and liquid phase in equilibrium with a vapour phase Emulsion systems contain two liquid phase in equilibrium with a vapour phase.

Air freshner (odonil type ) also have a heavy demand for the export market as well as in India.

## MANUFACTURING OF AIR FRESHNER (ODONIL TYPE)

### Formulation

| | |
|---|---|
| Ethyl alcohol (95%) | 81.0% |
| Carbitol | 3 |
| Glycerol | 3 |

| | |
|---|---|
| Water (Distilled) | 5 |
| Sodium Stearate | 6 |
| Perfume | 2 |
| Colour Soln. | Q.S |

Place the ingredients, except the perfume oil, into a closed stainless steel kettle and heat with constant stirring to reflux temperature. Considerable time is required to dissolve complete Sodium stearate. When the sodium Stearate is completely dissolved add the perfume and color and pour into moulds at 65°C . ( Aluminium moulds have been found satisfactory for this purpose ). Allow to cool slowly at room temperature. Rapid cooling may cover a hollow core to form in the centre due to excessively rapid concentration. It may also Stimulate rather crystallisation resulting in more opadue mass.

## PLANT ECONOMICS

**Rated Plant Capacity** = 150000 Pkt of 75 Gm per year

Land & Building (Land 500 sq.mt.) Rs. 4,30,000.00

## PLANT & MACHINERY

1. Jacketed stainless steel kettle
2. Aluminium Moulds
3. Closed stainless steel tank
4. Manual Impulse Sealing machine

## FIXED CAPITAL

| | | | |
|---|---|---|---|
| 1. Land & Building | | Rs. | 4,30,000.00 |
| 2. Plant & Machinery | | Rs. | 85,000.00 |
| 3. Other Fixed Assets | | Rs. | 40,000.00 |
| | TOTAL | Rs. | 5,55,000.00 |

## RAW MATERIALS

1. Ethyl Alcohol
2. Carbitol
3. Glycerol

4. Distilled water
5. Sodium Stearate
6. Perfumes
7. Colour

## TOTAL WORKING CAPITAL/MONTH

| | | |
|---|---|---|
| 1. Raw Material | Rs. | 43,430.00 |
| 2. Salary & Wages | Rs. | 13,560.00 |
| 3. Utilities & Overheads | Rs. | 23,280.00 |
| TOTAL | Rs. | 80,270.00 |

## TOTAL CAPITAL INVESTMENT

| | | |
|---|---|---|
| Total Fixed Capital | Rs. | 5,55,000.00 |
| Total Working Capital for 2 Months | Rs. | 1,60,540.00 |
| TOTAL | Rs. | 7,15,540.00 |

## TURN OVER/ANNUM

| | | |
|---|---|---|
| By selling 150000 packets of 75 gm capacity each (Air-freshner odonil type) | Rs. | 15,00,000.00 |

**PROFIT SALES RATIO = PROFIT / SALES X 100 = 24.63 %**

**RATE OF RETURN = OPERATING PROFIT / T.C.I X 100 = 51.62 %**

**BREAK EVEN POINT (B.E.P) = 48.23 %**

# 31

# Phenyl (Black and White)

A disinfectant is basically an agent which destroys pathogenic organism. A good disinfectant should also be a deodorant possessing good keeping qualities. And it would be effective against microorganism of widely varying types.

Phenyl type disinfectants fall in the category of black oil disinfectants and are extensively used for sanitation purposes, for drains, floor, stables etc. and are prepared from coal tar distillates containing high boiling tar acids. These are, however, less, affected in contact with organic matter.

Phenyl is being used since very beginning for killing insects grown in nallahas, lavatory and kooradan. Most of the diseases causes due to insects.

The black coal tar disinfectants are intimate mixture of coaltar oils and phenols with water and a suitable soap in such a physical state that it is optically clear. Rosin and liquid rosin; fixed oils such as castar palm, kernel, coconut and fish oil or any of their fatty acid or naphthenic acid can be used, usually as mixture in the black fluids. These fluids dilute only with moderately hard water.

The white coal tar disinfectants are readily made concentrated emulsion in water and stabilized by some suitable protective colloid certain protective colloids such as gelatin and suitable cesein well permit the dilution of the conc emulsion with any water hard or saline.

By varying the amount and type of the phenolic homologues and the tar oils (Carbolic acid or Crysylic Creosotes) these disinfectantscan be produce to cover a wide range, both for phenol content and germicidal value.

Because the special dispersing agents (the protective colloids) are used in small quantities as compared to the soaps used in the manufacture of dark fluids, the white fluids are generally cheaper on the basis of expenses per germicidal unit of rideal walker value than the black fluid. White fluids seldom contain less than 45 percent water and often considerably more while the black fluids contain water only up to 10 percent although some of the cheaper household fluids many contain up to 20 percent water. However the black fluids rae more suitable than the white fluid and if properly stored the black variety well remain in good usable condition for years together while the white fluid deteriorates on prolonged storage. It is always better to use the white fluids within a few months of its preparation.

## MANUFACTURING PROCESS

### High Boiling Tar Acid Black Fluids (Phenyl)

**Formulation**

| | | (%) |
|---|---|---|
| H.B.T.A (Boiling range 90% between | | 220°C% - 310%C) - 40 |
| Creosote Oil (5- 7% Tar acids) | - | 25 |
| W.W. Rosin | - | 12 |
| Castor Oil (Commercial grade) | - | 7 |
| Linseed oil | - | 3 |
| Soybean Oil | - | 2 |
| Caustic Soda | - | 3.4 |
| Soft Water | - | 7.6 |

**Process**

The castor oil and linseed oil are mixed together in a saponif cation vessels and heated slowly to 90°C. A pre-prepared 33% Caustic soda solution in water is then slowly added with stirring. After the complete addition the mixture is boiled for a few minutes for the complete saponification of the fats. The castor oil accelerates and assists the saponification of otherwise slowly reacting linseed oil and soybean oil. After the complete saponif cation of the fats rosin's is added and again the mixture kept in boiling stage for the saponification of rosin.

During the saponification process whatever water is lost by it evaporation is compensated by adding water.

When the saponification is over heated, is stopped and sufficient quantities of water added to get a soap solution. To this soap solution, is added with stirring the high boiling tar acid and Creosote oil followed by the remaining quantities of water. The disinfectant thus formed is stirred for a period of 15 minutes to get a stable emulsion in water which can be packed and put into the market.

## METHODS OF MANUFACTURING OF BLACK PHENYL

Coal tar disinfectant are generally manufactured in a steam Jacketed kettle fitted with a stirring equipment commercially various methods are in practice. The rosin may be first heated and saponified with caustic soda solution after which the tar acid oil are stirred in. Heating is continued for several hours at about 90°C until the mixture is uniform.

During final mixing test should that the product in the kettle gives a definite emulsion when added to water. If the product gives more of a solution then an emulsion when added to water mixing & heating should continue with occasional testing. If it is still facts to give an emulsion adjustments are needed. There may be in sufficient tar acids oils present or the alkalinity of the soap may be too high. Maximum water content of the finished product should be between 8 - 10%. The caustic soda should be governed by the saponification values of the rosin, tall oil or other material used while the total soap contained will depend on the character of the tar acid oil.

Tar acid distiller's have found it profitable to extract as much phenol as possible from tar acid oil. This producing a product better adopted to the manufacture of disinfectant.

The boiling range of the tar acid is another determining factor. Higher Coefficient may result with 25% tar acids of the higher boiling range than with 60% tar acids in the low boiling range. A correctly made coal tar disinfectant should form a milky emulsion when mixed in 220 parts of distilled water at 25°C. The emulsion should show no appreciate separation on standing for five hour at 25°C, other than possible traces of only float sediment. The disinfectant should be made from chilled tar acid so that no napthlane precipitates when subjected to a temperature of 0°C for 12 hours. Germicidal strength should remain constant or nearly so without any appreciable variation.

Higher coefficient disinfectants are made commercially using "high boiling tar acid". In preparing such high coefficient disinfectant, one third or more of a castor oil or a castor oil fatty acid soap is preferable to a soap made wholly from-tall acid or from rosin because it gives a better emulsion and hence a higher coefficient.

About one third of the castor oil may be replaced by some other vegetable oil such as Castor oil. The alkali may be potash or a combination of potash and 20% Caustic soda. A mixture of 15% tar acids and higher boiling acid will yield a finished disinfectant having a coefficient somewhere between 3 and 20 depending upon how much of each in employed, although there is no definite relation.

## (FORMULATION (WHITE PHENYL)

### Formulation - 1

| | | |
|---|---|---|
| H.B. T. A (Boiling range 220-310°C) | | |
| (High boiling tar acid) | - | 4% |
| Cresylic Creosote (20-30% phenol) | - | 30% |
| Casein (fine powders) | - | 4% |
| Borax | - | 2% |
| Sodium dodecyl benzene sulphonate (SDBA) | - | 0.1% |
| Water | - | 59.9% |

### Process

Firstly Casein and borax are mixed in water at 30°C and stirred well for 1 hour to get a homogeneous fluid this is then filtered through a 100 mesh gauge. To the filtered solution a sodium dodecyl benzene sulphonate is added, and with vigorous stirring is then added the mixture of high boiling tar acid and Cresylic Creosate at a slow rate. The final solution is then homogenised in a shearing colloid mill.

In these preparation care should be taken to use a freshly prepared solution of casein and it should not be allowed to stand for any length of time.

## PLANT ECONOMICS

| | | |
|---|---|---|
| **Rated Plant capacity** | = | 1000.00 KGS/day |
| **Land & Building** (Land 600 sq. mts.) | Rs. | 8,10,000.00 |

## PLANT & MACHINERY

1. Steam Jacketed kettle fitted with a stirring equipment
2. M.S. tank
3. Emulsifier, storage tanks,
4. Liquid disinfectant (Phenyl)storage tank
5. Bottle filling & sealing M/c

6. Pumps, valves, motors, starters & other ancillaries
7. Boiler
8. Caustic soda Preparation tank
9. Lab testing Equipments
10. Raw Material storage tank

## FIXED CAPITAL

| | | |
|---|---|---|
| 1. Land & Building | Rs. | 8,10,000.00 |
| 2. Plant & Machinery | Rs. | 6,86,000.00 |
| 3. Other Fixed Assets | Rs. | 2,00,000.00 |
| TOTAL | Rs. | 16,96,000.00 |

## RAW MATERIALS

1. **FOR BLACK PHENYL**
   High Boiling Tar Acid (H.B.T.A.)
2. Creosote Oil
3. Rosin
4. Castor Oil
5. Linseed Oil
6. Soybean Oil
7. Caustic Soda
8. **FOR WHITE PHENYL**
   High Boiling Tar Acid
9. Cresylic Creosote
10. Casein (fine powder)
11. Borax
12. Sodium Dodecyl Benzene Sulphonate
13. Packaging Material Glass Bottles,

## TOTAL WORKING CAPITAL/MONTH

| | | | |
|---|---|---|---|
| 1. Raw Material | | Rs. | 5,28,135.00 |
| 2. Salary & Wages | | Rs. | 71,372.00 |
| 3. Utilities & Overheads | | Rs. | 88,100.00 |
| | TOTAL | Rs. | 6,87,607.00 |

## TOTAL CAPITAL INVESTMENT

| | | | |
|---|---|---|---|
| Total Fixed Capital | | Rs. | 16,96,000.00 |
| Total Working Capital for 3 Months | | Rs. | 20,62,821.00 |
| | TOTAL | Rs. | 37,58,821.00 |

## TURN OVER/ANNUM

1. By sale of 1,50,000 Kgs of Black Phenyl.
2. By sale of 1,50,000 Kgs. of white Phenyl.

| | | |
|---|---|---|
| TOTAL | Rs. | 1,00,50,000.00 |

**PROFIT SALES RATIO = PROFIT / SALES X 100 = 9.63 %**

**RATE OF RETURN = OPERATING PROFIT / T.C.I X 100 = 25.74 %**

**BREAK EVEN POINT (B.E.P) = 63.09 %**

# 32

# Benzene Hexachloride

BHC Technical Grade BHC contains I-isomer 65-70% B isomer 6-8% gamma-isomer 8-15% and isomer 2-5% and isomer 3-7%, off white to brown in colour with persistent must odour stable to light, air and heat, resistant to strong acids but decomposed by alkali, almost as toxic to man and livestock as DDT.

BHC is stomach poison and persistent contact insecticides with fumigant action; BHC more is toxic that DDT it is used in the control of field and garden insects e.g. wireworks, sphids, boll worms, leaf worms, plant bugs, also houseflies and mosquito larva.

The fields of uses includes field crops, vegetable crops, fruit crops, fruit cops viticulture ornamentals, pasture and forage crops, forestry, soil treatment seed treatment, to curt control, timber protection, stored materials and products agricultural and industrial stores, public health and vatinery hygiene.

## PROCESS OF MANUFACTURE

### From Benzene and Chlorine

Reaction

$C_6H_6 + 3\ cl_2$ ------> $C_6H_6Cl_6$

Material RequirementsBasis - 1 ton benzene hexa chloride (24% gamma-isomer)Benzene - 477 Kgs.Chlorine - 1340 Kgs.

### PROCESS

Benzene hexachloride, commonly called BHC, is manufactured by reacting chlorine and benzene in the presence of actinic light. Only one of the several isomers formed, the gamma isomer, is highly toxic to insects, processes vary in the purification stage, depending upon the purity of gamma-isomer desired.

Chlorine s contacted with benzene continuously in a reactor fitted with a mercury - vapour lamp. Chlorine is readily dissoviated by ultraviolet light at a wave length of 3050 Angstrom units, well within the range supplied by the mercury arc. Further the rays may be directed with aluminum reflectors and transmitted though special glass/quartz transmitters to minimize loss of light.

Collulated quantities of the reactants are charged to the vessel. Reaction is continued in the presence of ultraviolet light and operated at or slightly above atmospheric pressure and a temperature of 20 to 60°C. Higher temperatures and pressures favour the formation of an undesirable amount of monochloro benzene the BHC concentration in the reactor is controlled at 12 to 15 percent to prevent precipitation of the less soluble isomers. The reactor product is then concentrated is an evaporator where unreacted benzene is liberated and recycled.

The concentrated solution which is liquefied BHC (10 to 15 per cent gamma isomer) from the evaporator is then pumped to a crystallizer where it is cooled to a tempt of 35° to 40°, where some of the gamma and beta isomers crystallize. These are filtered out and the filtrate is further steam distilled to remove entrained benzene. the molten HBC from the bottom of the still is cast in metal pans, cooled and grand to desired size. The product ( about 24 percent gamma-isomer) is generally packed in fibre drums of shipment to an insecticide mixing plant. Further fractional crystallization yields lindane (99% gamma-isomer).

# 33

# Aerosol & Mosquito Repellant Spray (Baygon, Hit, Mortein Type)

The word "aerosol" was first employed in the field of colloid chemistry to describe a suspension of small particles in air or gas in which radium of the particles was less than 50 micron. The suspended particles could be either solid or liquid. Dust, smoke and fog are examples of this class of aerosol. The particles in dusts may have diameter as small as 0.1 micron or less. The suspensions produce haze smoke is an aerosol consisting of solid particles, usually carbon, in air. Carbon smoke is composed of small particles with a radius of about 0.01 micron. The particle sizes in fogs are longer and range from about 4-50 micron in diameter. The first aerosol of any commercial significance, the aerosol insecticide, was defined in 1949 as a system of particles suspended in air where 80 % of the particles were less than 30 microns in diameter and no particles were larger than 50 micron.

## AEROSOL INSECTICIDE FORMULATION

**Formulation**

Brand : Hit (Aerosol mosquito and flies repellent)

Size : (320 ml) = 200 gms.

**Formulation**

| | | |
|---|---|---|
| d-Allethrine technical | = | 0.55 % w/w |
| Piperonyl Butoxide | = | 0.5 % w/w |
| Perfume | = | 0.2 % w/w |
| Solvent deodorized kerosene | = | 58.75 % w/w |
| Liquified petroleum gas (LPG) | = | 40 % |

## MANUFACTURING PROCESS

First of all take the suitable solvent of little quantity and mix with the emulsifying agent . Mix homogeneously and pump into the mixing tank in which solution of the required amount of propoxur and little amount of solvent is previously present. Then mix homogeneously the whole solution for approximately for 1 to 1.5 hour. After complete mixing of the solvent, emulsifier and propoxur, add the suitable masking agent and again mix homogenously then add the rest solvent into the mixing tank to dilute the product. The product after completely homogenization is passed on to the automatic filling and sealing machine. Where the automatically weighed amount will be filled, in the tin container and then it will be automatically sealed by sealing machine. Before filling the product into container, it should be analytically tested in the laboratory then it is filled after satisfactory laboratory test.

## METHOD OF FILLING OF CANS

### (I) Pressure Filling

**STEP 1**

Empty aerosol containers are removed from their shipping cartons and placed in the unscrambler. The unscrambler separates the containers and sends them into the line at predetermined intervals.

**STEP 2**

After the cans leave the unscrambler, they are inverted and cleaned by an air blast which removes dirt and other foreign matter. In some cases, air cleaning is carried out in the presence of a continuous vacuum.

**STEP 3**

The concentrate, at room temperature, is added to the aerosol container.

**STEP 4**

Air is removed from the vapour phase in the container either by purging with propellant or byevacuation. If air is removed by evacuation, the valve is placed on the container and crimped in the same operation.

**STEP 5**

If air is removed by purging, the valve is placed on the container and crimped as soon as the purging operation is completed.

**STEP 6**

Propellant is pressure filled through the valve. The total pressure in the system for filling propellant is generally about 50 psig higher than the vapour pressure of the propellant.

**STEP 7**

Filled containers are heated to a temperature of 130°F in the water bath.

**STEP 8**

Containers may be weighed at this point to be certain that product fill is correct.

**STEP 9**

Actuators are placed on valves if necessary and the product may be spray tested. Other tests such as those for foam products, may be carried out at this point.

**STEP 10**

Protective caps or overcaps are placed on the containers.

**STEP 11**

For the purpose of identification, the cans are labelled and coded if this has not been done previously.

**STEP 12**

The complete aerosol products are packed in shipping cartons.

## PLANT ECONOMICS (Amount in Rs.)

| | | |
|---|---|---|
| **Rated Plant capacity** | = | 90,00,000 CANS/ANNUM |
| **Land & Building (Land 2000 Sq.Mts.)** | Rs. | 53,00,000.00 |

## PLANT & MACHINERY

1. Stainless steel (closed top) mixing tank with stirrer
2. S.S.Lined storage tank (m.s)
3. LPG gas storage tank (S.S)
4. Automatic aerosol 9-head imported filling, sealing, packaging machine
5. Automatic shrink wrap machine.
6. Carton sealing machine.
7. Laboratory equipment.
8. Compressor.
9. Pumps.
10. Genset

## FIXED CAPITAL

| | | |
|---|---|---|
| 1. Land & Building | Rs. | 53,00,000.00 |
| 2. Plant & Machinery | Rs. | 84,60,000.00 |
| 3. Other Fixed Assets | Rs. | 5,00,000.00 |
| TOTAL | Rs. | 1,42,60,000.00 |

## RAW MATERIALS

1. D-allethrine technical
2. Piperonyl butoxide
3. Perfume
4. Deodorized kerosene solvent
5. LPG gas
6. Aluminium cans(seamless) printed
7. Valves
8. Plastic caps
9. Shrinkable film
10. Corrugated cardboard boxes

## TOTAL WORKING CAPITAL/MONTH

| | | |
|---|---|---|
| 1. Raw Material | Rs. | 1,17,29,375.00 |
| 2. Salary & Wages | Rs. | 2,08,560.00 |
| 3. Utilities & Overheads | Rs. | 40,000.00 |
| TOTAL | Rs. | 1,19,77,935.00 |

## TOTAL CAPITAL INVESTMENT

| | | |
|---|---|---|
| Total Fixed Capital | Rs. | 1,42,60,000.00 |
| Total Working Capital for 2 Months | Rs. | 2,39,55,870.00 |
| TOTAL | Rs. | 3,82,15,870.00 |

**TURN OVER/ANNUM**

By sale of 90,00,000 Cans of aeros-ol insecticides
(size 320 ml = 200 gms.) Rs. 22,50,00,000.00

**PROFIT SALES RATIO = PROFIT / SALES X 100 = 31.32 %**

**RATE OF RETURN = OPERATING PROFIT / T.C.I X 100 = 184.38 %**

**BREAK EVEN POINT (B.E.P) = 14.55 %**

# 34

# Mosquito Repellant Agarbatti (Incense Sticks)

Agarbatti is a well known product amongst every children, men and women. The word Agarbatti reminds an Indian mind of a temple, a shrine, its sacred perfume and the holy atmosphere of the place of worship. It has for ages been an inevitable element in the performance of religious rites in this country. From this immemorials marriages in thread ceremonies and other rites and religious functions have needed aggarbattis to give an auscipicious touch to the occasion. The perfume spread by agarbatti which it burns makes it more sacred to a religious mind. Aggarbattis also known as udbathies, similar to Joss-sticks, are a development of dhcop agarbatti industry, is a cottage type industry and this industry is very simple. The principal form in which incense is burnt in this country is on sticks. They are principally made of sandalwood dust, but the incense burnt in the western countries in mainly made of olibanum, some specimens contains a little charcoal, benzion and storax of the incense sticks available in the market.

## TYPICAL COMPOSITION OF AGARBATTI OF MEDIUM QUALITY

| | |
|---|---|
| Sandal wood | 30 |
| Black Agar | 20 |
| Vetiver | 5 |
| Kapur Kachri | 5 |
| Leaves and flowers | 10 |
| Olibanum or myrrh | 20 |
| Charcoal and other ingredients | 10 |

Agarbattis are used by many communities in India, Ceylon, Burma, and by Indians residing in Africa, Malay states, Dutch East Indies, etc. Before the war, there was also a small demand for them in the U.K., the USA and Canada.

## MOSQUITO REPELLANT BATTI

**Formulation**

| | | |
|---|---|---|
| White sandal (Powder) | : | 150 gm. |
| Loban | : | 50 gm. |
| Wood coke (Powder) | : | 50 gm. |
| Guggal (Powder) | : | 50 gm. |
| Citronella oil | : | 30 gm. |
| D - Allethrine | : | 0.20 gm. |

## MANUFACTURING PROCESS

Manufacturing of Agarbatti is not a very complicated process if theproper composition is used. The addition of synthetic perfumery compound to the other ingredients like fillers, wood powder charcoal etc. is done with extra case in the composition because a very small amount of this compound is required for a large quantity of Agarbatti compound production. ie about 0.05 to 2% of synthetic compound is used according to the nature of the perfumery compound and also considering the economic view point.

The manufacturing process of perfumery compound includes mainly the mixing of ingredience and packing of the compound, in suitable containers in varying quantities. Various types of containers made up of glass, plastics and Tin coated metal vessels.

First of all, the particular formulation is decided for the manufacture of synthetic perfumery compound. each ingredient is weighed accurately as per the composition. If the solid ingredients are not in the fine powder form, they should grind in a grindes. In a mixer, fitted with agitator and having proper closing arrangements during mixing (otherwise vapour volatile of oils will as cage from the mixer resulting, in the reduction of quality of the compound), all the oil ingredients of the formula are added. Mixing is carried out with the help of agitator. Then other powdered ingredients are added one by one. Mixing process is continued. After the proper mixing of all the ingredients, the mixture is taken out of the mixer.

Packing in suitable containers, according to the nature of compound, is done with the help of automatic packing machine or it is done manually.

If the product is intended to sell to the agarbatti manufacturing units, it is packed containers of 1 kg or more capacity. It is also packed in small bottles of 100 g., 200 gms and 500 gms. The products are then stored in the products are then stored in the products store prior to the market.

## PLANT ECONOMICS

**Rated Plant capacity** = 100.00 KGS/day

Land & Building (Rented - Covered area 200 sq. mts.)

## PLANT & MACHINERY

1. Incense powder dabbing machine
2. Screw type paste mixing machine
3. Pulveriser or grinder

## FIXED CAPITAL

| | | | |
|---|---|---|---|
| 1. Plant & Machinery | | Rs. | 1,00,000.00 |
| 2. Other Fixed Assets | | Rs. | 20,000.00 |
| | TOTAL | Rs. | 1,20,000.01 |

## RAW MATERIALS

1. Bamboo sticks
2. Wood powder
3. Jigat powder
4. Perfumery compounds (rose, lavender jasmine, kewra, mogra, etc )
5. Packaging materials (Printed cardboard packs, adhesive tapes, BOPP wrapping films, inside butter paper, cartons etc.)
6. D-Allethrine,
7. Piperonyl butoxide,

## TOTAL WORKING CAPITAL/MONTH

| | | | |
|---|---|---|---|
| 1. Raw Material | | Rs. | 5,72,625.01 |
| 2. Salary & Wages | | Rs. | 1,66 500.00 |
| 3. Utilities & Overheads | | Rs. | 1,15 500.00 |
| | TOTAL | Rs. | 8,54 625.01 |

## TOTAL CAPITAL INVESTMENT

| | | |
|---|---|---|
| Total Fixed Capital | Rs. | 1,20,000.01 |
| Total Working Capital for 3 Months | Rs. | 25,63,875.03 |
| TOTAL | Rs. | 26,83,875.04 |

## TURN OVER/ANNUM

**By sale of 30000 Kgs. of incense sticks**

| | | |
|---|---|---|
| (15,00,000 packets of 10 sticks each) | Rs. | 1,20,00,000.00 |

**PROFIT SALES RATIO = PROFIT / SALES X 100 = 10.05 %**

**RATE OF RETURN = OPERATING PROFIT / T.C.I X 100 = 44.92 %**

**BREAK EVEN POINT (B.E.P) = 61.09 %**

# 35

# Allethrin Mosquito Repellant Oil

Allethrin is the name given to the allyl homolog of cinerin I, a component of Pyrethrum, with almost identical insecticidal properties. It was discovered in 1949 by the U.S. Department of Agriculture and within a year was in commercial production. Flowers of the Pyrethrum plant which is a type of chrysanthemum contain toxic, nonnitrogenous organic esters 'Pyrethrins. The principal source of flowers of Pyrethrum plant are Kenya, Japan, Belgium, Congo and Brazil. The insecticidal properties of pyrethrum from the ground flowers of chrysanthemum cinerariaefolium and C Coccineum result from six esters the pyrethrons I and II, the Jasmolins I & II which are present in the flowers mostly in the achenes, from 0.7 - 3% in selected strains. The pyrethroid esters differ considerably in potency as shown by the topical LD 50 values (micro gram/g) to the housefly.

**LD 50 VALUES TO HOUSEFLY**

| | |
|---|---|
| Pyrethrin I | 0.59 |
| Pyrethrin II | 0.38 |
| Cinerin I | 1.42 |
| Cinerin II | 1.14 |

The naturally occurring form are the D-trans acid esters of the D-cis alcohols. The active principles are extracted from the ground flowers by petroleum ether, ethylene dichloride or other organic solvent and freed from wax by adsorption on carbon to produce 90-100% pyrethrins. These insecticides are highly unstable to the action of light, air, moisture, and alkali and residues diteriorate rapidly after application. Knowledge of the structure of the pyrethrins and their high cost stimulated the structural optimization of synthetic derivatives.

## PROCESS OF MANUFACTURE

Allethrin is a constituent of pesticide pyrethrum obtained from flowers of pyrethrum plant which is a type of Chrysanthemum containing toxic non nitrogenous organic esters (Pyrethrins). Bales of compressed flowers are broken up, ground to a fine powder and extracted several times with kerosene or other organic solvent. The extract is concentrated by removing the solvent in a vacuum still below 60°C and the resulting oleoresin is employed to prepare the finished insecticide chemically Allethrin is dl-2-allyl-3-methyl-cyclopentene-1-one ester of dle-cis-trans-2,2-dimethyl-3-(2-methyl propenyl) Cyclo-propane Carboxylic acid. The commercial process is very complicated requiring 12 steps, 11 different intermediates and approximately 200 lb. of chemicals to produces 1 lb. of Allethrin. Synthetically glycerin, acetylene and ethyl acetoacetate are the major raw materials utilized in manufacture of Allethrin. The chemical is preferably being impated to make various formulation effective as mosquito replants and refill of mosquito mats as required.

Formulation for Allethrin based mosquito repellent oil.

| I | | 334II | |
|---|---|---|---|
| Allethrin | 15 parts | Allethrin | 20 parts |
| Sesame oil | 5 parts | Deodorised | |
| Kerosene oil | 75 parts | | |
| Deodorised | | Piperonyl | |
| Kerosene oil | 80 parts | butoxide | 5 parts |
| Total | 100 parts | Total | 100 parts |

The preparation of mosquito mats refill as per formulations is a simple process requiring only weighing of various ingredients and mixing in mixing vessel till homogenised. The prepared Allethrin mix is packed in glass bottles for sales and marketing. For each mat 4 mg. of solution is soaked last for one night only.

### PLANT ECONOMICS

| | | |
|---|---|---|
| **Rated Plant capacity** | = | 100.00 Kgs/day |
| **Land & Building** (Land 300 sq.mts.) | Rs. | 2,70,000.00 |

## PLANT & MACHINERY

1. Mixing Vessel S.S. with stirrer
2. Weighing Scale
3. Miscellaneous Utensil S.S.
4. Bottling equipment automatic
5. Lab Testing equipments
6. Miscellaneous fittings

## FIXED CAPITAL

| | | |
|---|---|---|
| 1. Land & Building | Rs. | 2,70,000.00 |
| 2. Plant & Machinery | Rs. | 97,000.00 |
| 3. Other Fixed Assets | Rs. | 45,000.00 |
| TOTAL | Rs. | 4,12,000.00 |

## RAW MATERIALS

1. Allethrin
2. Sesame Oil
3. Deodorised Kerosene Oil
4. Miscellaneous

## TOTAL WORKING CAPITAL/MONTH

| | | |
|---|---|---|
| 1. Raw Material | Rs. | 72,000.00 |
| 2. Salary & Wages | Rs. | 17,760.00 |
| 3. Utilities & Overheads | Rs. | 8,460.00 |
| TOTAL | Rs. | 98,220.00 |

## TOTAL CAPITAL INVESTMENT

| | | |
|---|---|---|
| Total Fixed Capital | Rs. | 4,12 000.00 |
| Total Working Capital for 2 Months | Rs. | 1,96 440.00 |
| TOTAL | Rs. | 6,08 440.00 |

**TURN OVER/ANNUM**

| | |
|---|---|
| **Return by sale 30,000 kg. Allethrin mosquito mat/repellent Refill** | Rs. 18,00,000.00 |

**PROFIT SALES RATIO = PROFIT / SALES X 100 = 26.06 %**

**RATE OF RETURN = OPERATING PROFIT / T.C.I X 100 = 77.08 %**

**BREAK EVEN POINT (B.E.P) = 37.23 %**

# 36

# Aerosol Insecticide Spray (Baygon, Hit, Mortein, Hesit Type)

Aerosols are dispersions of liquid droplets or small solid particles in gases. Gaseous dispersions can be produced from atomizers, nebulizers, or insufflators. Pressurized containers utilizing various propellent gases for delivering chemical products through appropriately designed valve systems and actuator devices have been available. These propellent include liquefied gases or gas mixturers. Non-liquefied compressed gases are also used. The products can be produced in the form of suspensions, emulsion, gel, solutions, foam depending on the formulation, valve system, dip-tube, propellant, actuator and container.

The word "aerosol" was first employed in the field of colloid chemistry to describe a suspension of small particles in air or gas in which radius of the particles was less than 50 micron. The suspended particles could be either solid or liquid. Dust, smoke and fog are examples of this class of aerosol. The particles in dusts may have diameter as small as 0.1 micron or less. The suspensions produce haze smoke is an aerosol consisting of solid particles, usually carbon, in air. Carbon smoke is composed of small particles with a radius of about 0.01 micron. The particle sizes in fogs are longer and range from about 4-50 micron in diameter. The first aerosol of any commercial significance, the aerosol insecticide, was defined in 1949 as a system of particles suspended in air where 80 % of the particles were less than 30 microns in diameter and no particles were larger than 50 micron.

## AEROSOL COMPONENTS

### Propellants

Propellants provide the pressure that forces the product out of the container when the valve is opened. They also influence the form in which the product is discharged foam, stream, or spray. Variations in the type and concentration of a propellant can change a corase, wet spray to a fine, dry spray.

There are two general types of aerosol propellants : liquefied gases and compressed gases. In the pressure greater than atmospheric pressure (14.7 psia) at 105°F. The purpose of the particular pressure and temperature limitations of the definition was to include liquids such as fluorocarbon 11 (trichloromonofluoromethane) and methylene chloride. Neither of these compounds can function alone as a propellant because they have too low a vapor pressure at room temperature. However, they give satisfactory propellant blends when mixed with other liquefied gases having higher vapor pressures. Methylene chloride has a vapor pressure of 14.7 psia at 103.6°F and just falls within the definition. The two major classes of liquefied gas propellants are fluorinated hydrocarbons (fluorocarbons) and hydrocarbons.

The distinction between liqufied and compressed gases is somewhat artifical. Gases such as carbon dioxide and nitrous oxide can be liquefied at very low temperatures. They are excluded from the definition of liquefied gases, however, because they have pressures in excess of 700 psig at 70°F in the liquefied state. These pressure are far too high for any practical consideration of these compounds as liquefied gas propellants for aerosol products. Therefore, they are used only in the compressed state in aerosol systems, generally at pressures less than 100 psig.

## General Properties

Some general properties of liquefied gas propellants are summarized below.

## Boiling Point and Vapor Pressure

A liquefied gas propellant (or propellant blend) must boil enough below room temperature so that the pressure in the aerosol container is sufficient to expel the contents when the valve is opened. The pressure cannot exceed certain limits, however.

## Cost

The manufacturing cost of a propellant has to be low so that the ultimate price of the aerosol product is within reach of the general public.

## Flammability

Nonflammability is not a necessity. It is, however, an extremely desirable property for an aerosol propellant. This is particularly true for the propellant manufacturer and aerosol filler who must store and handle large qunatities of the propellants. Flammable propellants require explosion-proof filling equipment. The flammability of an aerosol product is important to marketers because of regulations.

### Odor

The odor of aerosol products such as sprays, deodorants, perfumes, etc. is important to the consumer. Therefore, propellants with very low odor levels are desirable. Propellants for aerosol perfumes and colognes must have essentially no odor.

### Purity

Propellants must be very pure and their quality must be consistent. Variable amounts of impurities could result in change in perfumer odor, inoperable valves, and container corrosion. These adverse effects could lead to withdrawal of the product from the market.

### Stability

Propellants must be stable in the aerosol formulation in which they are used. Any reaction with other components of the formulation, or propellant decomposition alone, could lead to product deterioration, change in perfume odor, and container corrosion.

### Toxicity

Low toxicity is essential. Inhalation of many aerosol products, such as sprays, deodorants, perfumes, etc., is difficult to avoid.

Since liquefied gas propellants are liquids, they are part of the solvent system in homogenous products. Therefore, they influence the solvent properties of the liquid phase. The solvent characteristics of propellants in the liquid state must be taken into consideration in formulating products.

### Solvents

Typical solvents, such as ethyl alcohol, isopropyl alcohol, methylene chloride, methyl chloroform, or odorless mineral spirits, are present in many aerosols. Like the prpopellants, solvents generally perform a number of functions. One of the major uses of solvents is to bring active ingredients into solution with the propellants. Most propellants have poor solvent characteristics, in many cases, active ingredients are not soluble in propellants. In order to obtain a homogenous mixture, it is necessary to add liquid with the necessary solvent properties. It is sometimes desirable to have another liquid present which is not miscible with the propellant, for example, water or propylene glycol. In these cases, a co-solvent such as ethyl alcohol is added to obtain a homogenous system.

Another function of solvents is to help produce a spray with a particle size that is most effective for the particular application involved. Aerosol insecticides, for example, are most efficient when the particle size is neither too large not too small. If no solvents were present, the propellants would evaporate completely in air shortly after discharge, leaving extremely small particles. High boiling solvents evaporate only slowly in the air once the propellant has vaporized, therfore, droplets of a specified size can be obtained by proper formulation.

Still another use of solvents is to reduce the vapor pressure of the propellant. There are various pressure regulations governing the packaging of aerosol products. Some propellants, such as fluorocarbon 12, have too high a vapor pressure to be used alone. In such a case, a vapor pressure depressant is added to reduce the vapor pressure to an acceptable level. The vapor pressure depressant may be a solvent such as ethyl alcohol or odorless mineral spirits, or it may be a high boiling propellant like fluorocarbon 11, which can be considered both a solvent and a propellant.

### Active Ingredients

Active ingredinets are the materials (perfumes, isecticides, deodorants, etc.) essential for the specific application for which the aerosol was designed. It is the job of the aerosol chemist to combine the active ingredients, solvents, and propellants so that an efficient, attractive and acceptable product is obtained.

In addition to the three major components (propellants, solvents, and active ingredients), aerosols usually contain a number of other materials that have been added to improve the product. Some of these, such as perfumes, enhance the aesthetic appeal, while others increase the performance or efficiency of the product. Typical additives in this group include moisturizers, emollients, plasticizers, stabilizers, surfactants and skin penetrants.

### Operation of an Aerosol

Basically, a homogenous aerosol is an intimate mixture of liquefied gas propellant, solvents, and active ingredients packaged under pressure in a suitable container equipped with a valve. When the valve is opened, the internal pressure forces the aerosol up the dip tube and out the valve. As soon as the aerosol leaves the container and enters the atmosphere, part of the propellant vaporizes and the propellant molecules fly off into space. In doing so, they collide with solvent molecules and cause collisions among the solvent molecules themselves, disrupting the attractive forces between them. As the propellant vaporizes in air, the solvent molecules are left almost isolated in relatively small groups of particles. The liquefied gas propellant, therefore, not only provides the pressure to force the aerosol out of the container when the valve is opened, but also breaks up the concentrate into small droplets or particles once the aerosol has reached the atmosphere.

## AEROSOL INSECTICIDE FORMULATIONS

(To be Specificed in the application form while Applying for household Aerosol)

1. **Aerosol Insecticide Spary (Baygon Type)**

For mosquitoes, Cockroaches & flies.

| | | |
|---|---|---|
| Net contents | - | 201.8 gm (320 ml). |
| Propoxur Technical | - | 2.06% w/w. |
| Isopropyl Alcohol | - | 15.00% w/w. |
| Mineral Turpentine | - | 12.5% w/w. |
| Kerosene | - | 12.5% w/w. |
| Liquefied Petroleum gas | - | 57.94% w/w. |
| Total | - | 100.00 w/w. |

2. **Aerosol Insecticide Spray (Hit Type)**

For mosquitoes & Flies,

| | | |
|---|---|---|
| Net contents | - | 200 gms (320 mls) |
| Allethrin Tech (90% purity) | - | 0.55% w/w. |
| Synergist (PBO) | | |
| Piperonyl Butoxide | - | 0.50% w/w |
| Perfume | - | 0.2% w/w. |
| Solvent Deodorised Kerosene | - | 48.75% w/w. |
| Liquefied Petroleum gas | - | 50.00% w/w. |
| Total | - | 100.00 w/w. |

## OTHER FORMULATIONS OF HOUSE HOLD AEROSOLS

**I. Aerosol Insecticide Spray for mosquitoes, Cockroaches & flies (Baygon Types) wet contents 200 gms (320 ml)**

| | | |
|---|---|---|
| Propoxur Technical | - | 2.10% w/w |
| Isopropyl alcohol | - | 17.00% w/w |
| Mineral Turpentine | - | 11.50% w/w |

| | | |
|---|---|---|
| Kerosene | - | 11.50% w/w |
| Liquefied Petroleum Gas | - | 57.9% w/w |
| Total | - | 100.00% ww |

## DETAILED MANUFACTURING PROCESS

### 1. For Aerosol Insecticide Spray (Baygon Type)

For the preparation of aerosol insecticide spray for mosquitoes, cockroaches & flies (Baygon type), as per the following formulation (with propoxur tech as the basic insecticide).

| | | |
|---|---|---|
| Net Contents | - | 201.8 gms (320 ml) |
| Propoxur Technical | - | 2.06% w/w. |
| Isopropyl Alcohol | - | 15.00% w/w |
| Mineral Turpantine | - | 12.50% w/w |
| Kerosene | - | 12.50% w/w |
| Liquefied Petroleum gas | - | 57.94% w/w |
| Total | - | 100.00% w/w |

## PLANT ECONOMICS

### 1. FOR AEROSOL INSECTICIDE SPRAY - (BAYGON TYPE)

**Land & Building (Land area 1300 sq.yds.)** Rs. 5,00,000.00

### PLANT & MACHINERY

1. Stainless steel (closed top) mixing tank with stirrer
2. S. S. lined storage tank (SS)
3. L.P.G. Gas storage tank (S.S.)
4. Automatic aerosol ahead imported filling,sealing & packaging m/c.
5. Automatic sprink wrap machine
6. Carton Sealing m/cs.
7. Laboratory equipments
8. Compressor
9. Pumps
10. Gen Set
11. Instrumentation & process control
12. Automatic stretch wrap sealing m/c.

13. Air Pollution control equipment.
14. Misc equipments Viz. Fire fighting eqpts. pumps,valves,pipe fittings valves, etc.

## FIXED CAPITAL

| | | | |
|---|---|---|---|
| 1. Land & Building | | Rs. | 75,00,000.00 |
| 2. Plant & Machinery | | Rs. | 1,86,10,000.00 |
| 3. Other Fixed Assets | | Rs. | 24,10,000.00 |
| | TOTAL | Rs. | 2,85,20,000.00 |

## RAW MATERIALS

1. **FOR AEROSOL INSECTICIDE SPRAY - (BAYGON TYPE)**

   **Prepoxur Tech.**

2. Isopropyl alcohol
3. Mineral Turpentine
4. Kerosene
5. Liquefied Petroleum Gas
6. **II.AEROSOL INSECTICIDE SPRAY-(HIT TYPE)**

   **For mosquitoes; Allethrin Tech (90%purity)**

7. Piperonyl Butoxide
8. Perfume
9. Solvent Deodorized Kerosene -
10. Liquefied Petroleum Gas
11. **III. AEROSOL INSECTICIDE SPRAY-(MORTEIN TYPE)**

    **d-Allethrin Tech.**

12. Piperonyl Butoxide
13. Petroleum distillate(light Naphtha)
14. Propellant Gas
15. **IV. FOR AEROSOL INSECTICIDE SPRAY(HEXIT TYPE)**

    **Deltrram ethrin**

16. Allethrin
17. Dichloromethane (methylene chloride)

18. Odour Masking Agent
19. Deodorized Kerosene
20. Liquefied Petroleum Gas
21. **V. FOR AEROSOL INSECTICIDE SPRAY (HIT TYPE) for Cockroaches) Propoxur**
22. Isopropyl Alcohol
23. Petroleum distillate(light Naphtha)
24. L. P. G.
25. Aluminium Cans
26. Plastic cap
27. Shrinkable film
28. Corrugated Card board boxes

### TOTAL WORKING CAPITAL/MONTH

| | | | |
|---|---|---|---|
| 1. Raw Material | | Rs. | 1,83,06,103.92 |
| 2. Salary & Wages | | Rs. | 1,76,250.00 |
| 3. Utilities & Overheads | | Rs. | 1,24,000.00 |
| | TOTAL | Rs. | 1,86,06,353.92 |

### TOTAL CAPITAL INVESTMENT

| | | | |
|---|---|---|---|
| Total Fixed Capital | | Rs. | 2,85,20,000.00 |
| Total Working Capital for 1 Months | | Rs. | 1,86,06,353.92 |
| | TOTAL | Rs. | 4,71,26,353.92 |

### TURN OVER/ANNUM

1. By sale of 1800000 Cans of Aerosol insecticides spray (Baygon Type)
2. 1800000 Cans of Aerosol Insecticide spray (Hit Type) for mosquitoes [200 gms (320 ml)]

3. 1800000 Cans of Aerosol Insecticide Spray (Mortein Type) [170 gms - (250 ml)]
4. 1800000 Cans of Aerosol Insecticide Spray (Hexit Type) [204 gms(320 ml)]
5. 1800000 Cans of Aerosol Insecticide Spray (Hit Type) for cockroaches [208 gms (320 ml)]

**TOTAL** **Rs. 25,92,00,000.00**

**PROFIT SALES RATIO = PROFIT / SALES X 100 = 8.73 %**

**RATE OF RETURN = OPERATING PROFIT / T.C.I X 100 = 48.00 %**

**BREAK EVEN POINT (B.E.P) = 39.46%**

# 37

# Recent Development in Pesticide Formulations

## Introduction

In India, liquid formulations are preferred over dust formulations because of their increased bioefficacy and easiness in use. Due to awareness in environmental hazard and workers' safety, water-based formulations are still popular. But new techniques made it possible to reduce the particle size of the dispersed solids in suspension concetrates. Similarly, more and more structuring agents are incorporated to reduce the cost of formulation. However, the recent trend is to formulate granules, and emulsifiable concentrates. Wettable powders are also advocated but the cost of manufacturing includings search for appropriate surfactants, adjuvants, solvents etc. is high. Therefore, efforts are being made to improve the performance of the existing EC to provide better emulsion stability at high temperatures. The granular formulations are generally employed on cereals due to easiness in application and water dispersal granules may be accepted for agricultural use in future. The recent technology of formulating the thermodynamically stable toxicants has proved to be applicable, effective and economical as they do not need the energy to disperse hydrophobic toxicants in water. The microemulsions are now being formulated by adding minimum surfactants and cosurfactants with reasonalbe stability in the formulations for wider range of temperature.

It is always ceconomical to load maximum toxicant on cheap solid carriers but the dust being hazardous during manufacturing and application due to fine particles, safer formulations are needed. Most of the technical materials used in agriculture are based on hydrophobic complex organic compounds. The water-based formulation with maximum a.i. is possible with minimum possible adjuvants with minimum energy consumption. When a formulated material is poured into water before spraying, it should form a spontaneous collodial dispersion which can uniformly cover a large surface area of the target without sedimentation or aggregation.

Day by day, toxic a.i. and solvents (e.g. xylene, cyclothexancne, isophorone used in EC) are facing regulatory pressure from some developing countries. The consciousness of environmental pollution and safety to human has compelled the industrialists to formulate pesticides which are less toxic, effective and stable (chemical stability of a.i- in the concentrate in a solvent-based formulation on prolonged storage, stability of droplets in emulsions and that of particles in dispersions). Emulsion droplets and dispersed particles will cluster together causing flocculation leading to coalescence and eventual separation unless they are stibilized by adding emulsifiers and polymers which form a protective film around the droplets/particles and provide repulsive forces between the protected droplets/particles. This film can be formed due to adsorption of a suitable surfactant (in monolayer or multilayer). Similarly, the electrostatic stabilization can be provided by using anionic surfactants which act as a charge barrier. The creation of energy barrier arising from either stearic or electrical stabilization is responsible for stability in the formulation because total potential energy of attractive components is much higher than the repulsive forces.

The development in formulation technology resulted in more effective and safer formulations and packings, viz. water dispersible granules, suspension concentrates, suspoemulsions, gels, microencapsulation, ultra violet protection, leaching inhibition and water-soluble bags etc. The worldwide data indicate that EC, WP, DP, and water solubles predominate in the market (60-75%) compared to other formulations (25-40%).

The major problem in developing new formulations is the registration with CIB. It is easier to obtain a registration for any product based on already registered pesticide than a new formulation for which a lengthy official procedure is to be followed. Also, development of new molecules requires huge finance and continuous R & D activities.

Certain criteria in any formulation are to be considered, *viz.*, cost, effectiveness (application, packing, storage, transportation), better coverage of targeted area, longer shelf life and environment friendliness at all stages of manufacturing till application by which maximum possible bioefficacy can be achieved. A thorough knowledge of kinetics of decomposition and evaluation of activation energy for the process as a function of temperature should be used in computation of storage stability.

A correct choice of emulsifiers, stabilizing polymers and a combination of solvents is important. The molecules of surfactants initially adsorb on air/water, particle/water or oil/water interface and when conc. of surfactant approaches the critical micelle conc., agglomeration takes place. The stabilization of solid particle in dispersion is possible because of adsorption of surfactant or film forming polymer. In case of emulsion, large quantity of emulsifier is needed for the stabilization or solubilization of droplets. In the modern world, the computer-aided optimization techniques are being applied to screen several compositions for better formulations of any pesticide.

Some changes in formulation technology are expected in India and other Asian countries some of these changes are enumerated below:

1. Water soluble packaging for WP and WDG to avoid container disposal and to reduce direct contact.
2. More use of CS formulations to reduce pesticide application level, extend residual effect and to lower mammalian toxicity.
3. From single a.i. to multiple component packages (e.g. SC, SE and WDG) because of certain advantages : Convenient to use by the farmer as tank mixing is avoided and proper dosage is assured. It will reduce the liability for the manufacturer from overdose or insufficient dose of a.i.
4. WDG may replace WP and SC as they are dust free and handling is easier. The problem of container disposal is also minimized.
5. An increasing use of EW or ME in place of EC to avoid or at least to minimize the use of toxic flammable solvents.
6. SC is preferred over WP to provide dust free and user friendly formulations.

**Water Dispersible Granules (WDG)**

This formulation is the latest development and is in great demand in developing countries but the prohibitive manufacturing cost may hinder its introduction into India. Also, it is unsafe to manufacturing personnel due to drift of fine powder. Major advantages of WDG include :

(a) Higher a.i. in the formulation.

(b) Formulation is free from dust and spray is uniform.

(c) Measuring and handling is easy due to free flowability.

(d) No spillage because WDG can be emptied completely from the containers.

(e) Easiness in cleaning of containers and also in packing and therefore better storage stability and disposal can be practised. Water soluble packages can be used for packaging because they are less dangerous to environment, safer to worker and precis on in the dose of insecticide is maintained.

In formulating WDG, same ingredients as for WP are used except suitable binders and disintegrants which are used additionally. They can replace WP or SC because they are hard free-flowing dustless grains of uniform particles (size of 1-2 mm). The granules disintegrate read ly in water and form a homogeneous sprayable suspension with minimum agitation. Generally, WDG are based on solid or liquid a.i. (60-90%). In case of liquid a.i., it is converted into granules after absorbing it onto inert material (e.g. highly absorptive clays, carbonates, micronized silica etc.) or by coprecipitation or coextrusion of the melt with polyhydroxy polymers. Depending up on the properties and conditions of coextrusion, plasticizers and surfactants (anionic/nonionic) are sometimes needed to make WDG formulation by pan, spray drying and fluid-bed granulation involving low pressure and extrusion, dry compaction and high shear agglomeration. Less moisture is needed in the pan granulation process when pyrrolidone-based polymers are employed because of the capacity to imbibe water.

## Suspension Concentrate (SC)

Three types of SC formulations can be manufactured : water-based, oil-based and aqueous form.

The suspension concentrate which is also known as flowable concentrate is a stable dispersion in a liquid medium (e.g. water or oil) of the micronized solid technical material of particle size about 2. In suspension concentrate or emulsion in water, water is already present in the external phase and only dilution is required to create fine particles. A poorly formulated SC may not be different from WP if coarser particles are produced and their distribution is not uniform. The physical stability on storage of SC formulations needs to be maintained because solid particles have tendency to settle down due to gravity which leads to caking or claying. The prolonged stability of the dispersion in water is the most important requirement of SC formulation which is attained if polymeric surfactants, "comb" type surfactants and polymeric film forming polyelectrolytes are used. Use of flocculating agents, such as, nonionic surface active polymer, may be necessary to enable easy redispersion on dilution or for formulating an aqueous SC. An aqueous flowable formulation can also be manufactured if the pesticide is chemically stable in water, its melting point is >80°C and its solubility in water is <200 ppm. In the formulation process, the technical material is wet grinded in the colloidal mills with different sized grinding media (e.g. ceramics, steal or glass beads) and thoroughly mixed in a solution of dispersing agent in water containing antifrezing chemical. (e.g. glycols) so that slurry is formed. Then this slurry is wet milled to obtain required particle size (0.1-5μ). The additives (most common are those based on polysaccharides) are incorporated into dispersion in order to avoid any settling in the prepared concentrate. For oil-based formulation, ingredients are similar to aqueous form but a.i. should be stable and insoluble in oil. Therefore, the nature of dispersing agent, the wetting agent and agents responsible for forming the film should have low hydrophilic-lipophilic balance (HLB) compared to water-based SC.

The major advantages of SC are : no hazard to user (as it is solvent free) and low formulation cost. However, SC requires additional use of activactors like oil type spreader or adjuvants like polymeric spreader/sticker. The stickiness of the concentrated makes difficult to transfer it in containers. SC is not compatible with other formulations and drying of the formulation occurs due to evaporation of water. Also, the instability during storage is due to extreme temperature variation.

**Concentrate Emulsion (CE)**

These emulsions are being introduced and will be marketed in India. The concentrated is generally based on liquid technical material. However, solid material (particle size of 0.5-2μ) having lower melting point can be used by dissolving it in minimum amount of water. The liquid a.i. and emulsifier are mixed and later both are added to water. Air should not be allowed to enter while mixing. In case of 'oil in water' emulsion some polysaccharides are added to attain a desired thickness. The speciality of CE is that they are made only kinetically soluble (and not thermodynamically stable) in the colloidal form by formulating in an appropriate manner. This process also helps to augment the shelf life of formulation up to two years without any sedimentation or phase separation and without a major change in its viscocity.

CE produces less mammalian dermal toxicity, phytotoxicity and ecotoxicity because water is used and hazardous flammable solvents are eliminated. Having high flash point, it is safe in handling, requires less packing and transportation cost is reduced considerably.

It is difficult to develop these formulations because of difficulty in stabilization and requirement for special surfactants. Also, formulation is possible with liquid and water insoluble toxicants only.

**Susposuspension (SS)**

The formulations contain <50% a.i. in water to which anionic/nonionic surfactants are added and emulsions are thickened by proper agents. Both solid and liquid toxicants can be used in combination and hazardous flammable solvents are eliminated. At present, physical stability of susposuspension is not yet proved and marketing chances are rare in India.

### Water soluble concentrate/soluble liquid

This formulation contains about 85% a.i.. Solvents and stabilizer are added to make the mixture with desired spray qualities.

### Concentrated Solution (CS)

These formulations are being introduced in India because they are most environment friendly. The concentrated solution or solution concentrate are suited to a.i. which are water soluble.

The formulation consists of a.i. in water or water soluble solvents, wetting agents and antifreezing agents (optional). The CS contains <75% a.i. which is dissolved in water, surfactants and structuring agents make the formulation applicable. So, hazardous flammable solvents are eliminated. Low dosages are applied due to fine particles and excellent spray tank properties are achieved. CS are user friendly as they are dust free. Easy handling, less packing volume and low transportation cost are other advantages.

Before spraying, CS is further diluted in water in a spray tank up to the desired concentration. Certain adjuvants can be employed for faster wetting and rainfastness, if desired. It is possible for some a.i. to derivatize them as water soluble salts (e.g. isoprophylamine salt of phosphonomethyl glycine) before mixing with water. However, the stability of such soluble salts must be ascertained otherwise, a super water soluble solvent like N-methyl pyrrolidone or gamma butyrolactone should be used; the former acts as synertist with chloroethyl phosphonic acid.

Being easy to formulate, the cost of manufacturing is comparatively low. There are no risks involved in its use but only a few a.i. can be formulated. Corrosion of the storage system takes place because of high anionic strength of the formulation.

The disadvantages are : Potential hydrolysis, cold temperature instability, crystallization forming the concentrate, poor wettability and rainfastness. These formulations are limited to solids and toxicants compatible with water.

### Microemulsion (ME)

Microemulsions still need more R & D efforts before their introduction in India. This is a colloidal system which produces thermodynamically stable emulsions containing <50% a.i. which is combined with water and anionic and nonionic surfactants so that a concentrate is formulated. From this conc., emulsions can be prepared as follows :

a. oil in water.
b. water in oil (which becomes oil in water type after dilution in water)
c. concentrated solution of a.i. (which forms emulsion after dilution in water)

ME consists of essentially a.i., water, oil, surfactant, coemulsifier and cosolvent.

The formulation largely depends upon the chemical constitution of the micellar surface with optimized composition of the droplets.

Micromulsions are formulated for a.i. which are required to apply at low application rates. These formulations are more effective than macroemulsions because of the small particle size of hydrophobic/ hydrophilic domains (about 10 nanometers) and low dynamic surface tension which facilitates wetting and spreading of pesticide on the plant leaf or insect cuticle. Also, ME being transparent are preferred to treat wood and furnishers.

Formulation is a spontaneous process and therefore it is thermodynamically stable but certain factors are important such as, low interfacial tension, largefree energy of adsorption of the surface active components (e.g. emulsifiers, polymmers, cosolvents, hydrotropes).

Th most important requirement is the ultra low interfacial tension with least amount of surfactant. A proper selection of surfactant and an appropriate ratio of nonionic and anionic surfactants and cosurfactants reduces the cost of manufacturing and formulation becomes cost effective.

Some secondary surfactants (e.g. amines, alcohols such as, isopropanol, butanol, cyclohexanone, ether etc.) are needed to improve the solubility of the primary surfactant. They are stable over a wide range of temperature (2.50°C) and the physical stability is not at all affected by the process if chemical degradation does not take place. Highly concentrated ME can be formulated if their stability on dilution is ascertained because ME is spontaneous and resulting emulsion is not dependent on the preparation technique. It is recommended that organic phase should be blend with surfactants particularly those which are nonionic and anionic emulsifiers. Then only emulsion should be added to water are mixed at a slow speed.

ME are water-based and thrmodynamically stable. Though the process of formulation is easy and ME have enhanced biological activity, but very high requirement of surfactants increases the cost of formulations.

These formulations contain <50% a.i. in water to which anionic/non-ionic surfactants are added and emulsions are thickened by proper agents. The emulsifiers are added upto 15-20% only. They are formulated for a.i. which are required to apply at low application rates.

Microemulsions are more effective than macroemulsions because of the small particle size of hydrophobic/hydrophilic domains (10 nano metres) and low dynamic surface tension which facilitate wetting and spreading on a plant leaf or an insect cuticle. Also, microemulsions being transparent are preferred to treat boards and wood.

In agriculture, water-based microemulsions are mostly used. Several compositions and their behaviour are to be well studied. Mixed N-alkylpyrrolidones and optimized surfactants based on tri-styryl phenol, tri-styryl phenyl ethoxylate, phosphate ester neutralized with TEA and cyclohexanol /isobutanol are successfully used in the formation of stable mixed pyrethroids and synergists as microemulsions in water.

Permethrin and cypermethrin have been microemulsified in water by using poly-alkylphenol ethoxylate, (tristyryl phenol ethoxylate) dodecyl benzene sulphonate and isobutanol/octanol as cosolvent. Use of fatty acid methyl esters as solvents, vegetable oil ethoxlate, EO/PO blocks as non-ionic surfactants and Calcium dodecyl benezene sulphonate as anionic surfactant has been demonstrated for microemulsion concentrate.

Both solid and liquid toxicants can be used in combination and hazardous flammable solvents are eliminated from the process. Other major advantages of ME are as follows :

- can be prepared from MEC by dilution with water or can be presented as a stable, prediluted formulation.
- ingredients can be added at random
- transparent and low turbidity
- isotropic, for the most part
- particle size of micelle (0.01-0.1μ)
- high tolerance for electrolytes
- infinitely stable
- high emulsifier level
- low application rates
- low a.i. content.

### Microemulsion Concentrate (MEC)

These formulations are similar to EC in composition. All the ingredients are mixed together. Although they are easy to prepare, MEC are more expensive than ME as higher amount of emulsifiers is required.

The surfactants help in bending of the micelle and in avoiding lamellar or liquid crystal matrix otherwise solubilization may not occur. Similarly, strong adsorption of the emulsifier/coemulsifier can induce formation of liquid crystals. The stabilizing factor of the liquid crystals protects against coalescence. The liquid crystal network reduce the mobility of the dispersed droplets. Even small changes in the emulsifier conc. can bring considerable changes in the relative proportion of the oil, water and liquid crystalline phases. The stabilizing phase is a part of the emulsion itself. The liquid crystals play a role of transient state in enhancing biological activity.

### Microencapsulation

It is the recent technology very well appreciated though comparatively expensive. Pesticide is wrapped in a very tiny cylinders of thin polyvinyl plastic which releases the toxicant at varying rates resulting in delayed or slow release. This formulation enhances the life of highly volatile material. The main advantages of these formulations are : low mammalian toxicity, rare phytotoxicity (as evaporation is controlled), less degradation by environmental factors, reduced leaching, negligible residues.

### Methods of Encapsulation

In general, toxicant is encapsuled in non-volatile envelope of a cross-linked gelatine in such a way that it is non-toxic by contact but toxic to target pest by ingestion. Stickers are added to prevent weathering of capsules. It has also been possible to formulated leaking capsules which release the toxicant for a prolonged period. The capsules are small and handy to carry, and safe to beneficial organisms as contact is avoided.

The encapsulation is achieved by the following techniques.

1. Interfacial polymerization
2. *In-situ* polymrization
3. Solvent evaporation
4. Cation exchange
5. Spray drying
6. Complex coacervation

First SC is prepared and suspension of encapsulated a.i. is obtained. Emulsification of the microcapsule is performed by using polymeric surfactants which are also employed during interfacial polymerization. Thus, the technique is based on interfacial condensation polymerization reactions resulting in nylon or polyurea type wall formation. Then this aqueous dispersion is stabilized by adding suspending or structuring agents. The suspension can be diluted with water before spraying.

The advantages of these suspension are as follows :

— prolonged persistence of biological activity
— reduced phytotoxicity
— less environmental pollution
— low mammalian toxicity
— low dermal and ocular irritation
— better packaging compatibility
— easier to transfer between containers.

The disadvantages of these suspensions are as follows :

— long development time
— expensive and complicated processing
— potential hydrolysis of active and inert ingredients
— leakage of the core due to wall breaking or wall collapse
— irreproducible release of a.i.
— involvement of multiple process parameters
— wall sensitivity towards changes in pH.

**Microencapsulated Suspension**

The recent development in formulation technology is the microencapsulation. The liquid a.i. (generally 10-30%) is encapsulated in a polymeric membrane or wall.

**Suspoemulsion or Suspension Emulsion (SE)**

In reality, it is a combination of emulsifiable concentrate and suspension concentrate. This formulation is based on both solid and liquid a.i. which has low melting point and is insoluble in water.

In aqueous phase, a.i. is insoluble in water or oil and has higher melting point. But when it is in the emulsion/oil phase, it has low melting point and is water insoluble but oil soluble. Therefore, it is dissolved firstly in a minimum quantity of solvent and dispersed in an aqueous medium. In case of solid a.i. it is insoluble in liquid so that a stable formulation is obtained. Physical stability of SE being an important criterion, the combination of emulsifiers, dispersants, rheology modifiers and properties like flowability, dispersability, should be carefully studied. When SE consists of a combination of more than one biologically complementary a.i., it has a broad-spectrum activity and also tank mixing is not necessary. But stability of mixed phase is essential due to difference in compatibility.

In SE a.i. is coated in a polymeric film which is advantageous by the way of reduced toxicity, reduced degradation for unstable a.i., reduced volatility and reduced leaching, capability of formulation potentiality, incompatible a.i., modified sustained release biological activity.

**Low Volume (LV) and Ultra Low Volume (ULV) Type**

These formulations need to be sprayed by using low volume sprayers (mist blower, micronizer) and ultra low volume sprayers with concentrated material. In case of LV formulations, the application rate can be 100-200 1/ha for ground operation and 15-75 1/ha for aerial application for LV, the carrier liquids are mostly organic solvents although water is used sometimes whereas the toxicant is used without dilution in water in ULV preparations (e.g. 1-5 1/ha compared with 500 1/ha for HV formulations). They are well suited for aerial spraying because a.i. is dissolved in non-volatile and non-toxic solvent. Fine droplets (about 70µ) ensure adequate coverage of target area in less time. The drift of fine particles and evaporation in hot weather are some of the problems remain unsolved.

The UV protection and leaching inhibition are important criteria for filed application of any formulated pesticide. The polymeric materials containing UV chromophores and UV blockers (e.g. Titanic oxide, Zinc oxide) are employed as UV protectants.

Leaching of pesticides can be prevented by adding polymeric materials, such as, pyrrolidone copolymers containing positively charged pendant groups.

**Gel Type**

These formulations are thickened EC formulations packed in water soluble bags. These bags are ecofriendly and safer to applicator than EC. Polymers are extensively used in this formulation. Formulation disperses slowly in water and rheological changes and consequent instability during long term storage are other inconveniences. Microgels can be formed on dilution so precautions are necessary.

# 38

# Classification of Pesticides

By definition, a pesticide is a pest-killing agent (the Latin word *cida* means to cut or kill). The term usually refers to one or more materials developed and used to destroy a board range of specific pests. In legal terminology, pesticides may be defined as "any substance used for controlling, preventing, destroying, repelling, or mitigating any pest." Hence, even chemicals that do not actually kill pests may, for practical and legal reasons, be considered pesticides. Included under the term are compounds used as repellents, attractants, antifeedants etc.

A great many pesticides are available today for the control of unwanted organisms. The insecticides, fungicides, herbicides and microbial agents given below are classified by chemical nature, which stresses the relationship in chemical structure; this shows the principle involved for these well-known compounds. Some information is provided too on the type of activity, spectrum of pests to be controlled, persistency in the soil and toxicity. However, one should refer to the product label for details on each separate pesticide. Also shown are various ways of classifying these main groups of pesticides by their mode of action.

**Classification of Pesticides according to the type of pests they control. (terms bearing the suffix-cide)**

Acaricide ..................... mites, ticks and spiders

Adulticide ..................... adult insects

Algicide ....................... algae

Arboricide ..................... trees, brush, shrubs

Avicide ......................... birds

Bactericide ................... bacteria

Fungicide ..................... fungi

Insecticide .................. insects and sometimes related

.................................... pest such as ticks and mites

Ixodicide ...................... ticks

Larvicide ...................... larvae

Miticide ........................ mites, ticks and spiders

Molluscicide ................ molluses such as slugs and snails

Nematicide .................. nematodes

Ovicide ........................ eggs

Piscicide ...................... fish

Predacide .................... vertebrate pests

Rodenticide ................ rodents such as rats, mice, gerbils

Silvicide ...................... trees, brush, shrubs

Termiticide .................. termites, ants.

For more detailed information on pesticides specifically suited to control certain kinds of animal pests such as rodents, snails and nematodes, and plant pests such as weeds and pathogens, or pesticides suited for treatment of seeds and fumigation, the reader should refer to the specialized chapters in the second half of this manual.

The newly generated term "biocide' is a nondescript word, commonly associated with the adverse effects of pesticides and frequently used as a synonym for pesticide. It has no exact scientific meaning, but is increasingly being used in writings on environmental issues to describe substances that kill living organisms.

**Classification by effect on pests**

**(Terms bearing the suffix-cide)**

Anti-feedant ............ inhibits feeding while insects remain on the treated plant; the insects eventually starve to death

Anti-transpirant ....... reduces transpiration

Attractant .............. lures pests to treated location, e.g. sex attractants

Chemosterilant ....... destroys a pest's ability to reproduce

Defoliant ............... removes unwanted plant growth without immediately killing the whole plant.

Desiccant ............. dries up plant parts and insects

Disinfectant .......... destroys or inactivates harmful organisms

Feeding stimulant ... causes insects to feed more vigorously

Growth regulator ..... stops, speeds up or retards growth processes of plants or insects

Repellent .............. drives pests away from treated object without killing them

Semiochemicals ..... pheromones, allomones and kairomones; substances emitted by plants or animals which stimulate or inhibit certain behavioural activities of insects

Synergist .............. enhances the effectiveness of an active agent.

**Classification of Insecticides**

The term "insecticide" refers to chemicals which are capable of destroying, mitigating or repelling insects, but they usually also exert a certain efficacy against mites, ticks or even nematodes.

**Classification by Chemical Nature**

Most common insecticides can be classified into main chemical groups consisting of inorganic or organic, natural or synthesized compounds.

Inorganic Compounds **are derived from naturally occuring elements and do not contain carbon. They are stable, non-volatile chemicals frequently soluble in water. Many of them are persistent; those containing arsenic, cyanide, mercury and thallium are cumulative poisons. Because of their residual persistence and high mammalian toxicity, the use of almost all inorganic chemicals has been discontinued in favour of less hazardous synthetic organic ones. Examples of inorganic chemicals are :**

boric acid
copper hydroxide
copper oxychloride
copper sulphate
mercuric oxide
mercurous chloride
sodium fluoaluminate (cryolite)
sodium arsenite
sodium chlorate
sodium fluoride
sodium fluoroacetate
thallium sulphate
silica aerogel

The elements copper and sulphate formulated as dusts or sprays are still widely used as fungicides (see below). Cryolite is regaining a place as a selective insecticide in integrated pest control. Boric acid and silica gels affect the waxes of an insect's cuticle, which becomes permeable to water from the insect's body. Consequently, the insect dies from dehydration. Both boric acid ands silica gets are used in baits for controlling household insects such as cockroaches and ants.

**Organic compounds are man-made or extracted pesticides consisting of carbon, hydrogen and one or more other elements such as chlorine, oxygen, sulphur, phosphorus and nitrogen. The main groups are described hereafter.**

**Botanicals,** also known as "natural insecticides", are toxicants that have been derived from plant materials. These may be produced in the form of powder made from finely ground plant parts or extracts which are used in sprays.

Neem extracts obtained from the neem tree (*Azadirachta indica*) have an insecticidal, repellent, anti-feedant and growth inhibiting effect on many insects belonging to six taxonomic orders. Neem seed oil, admixed at 3-5 ppm concentration, protects stored beans against bruchid bean beetles for a period of up to six months. Watery extracts from neem leaves and fruit can be sprayed at weekly intervals against leaf-feeding caterpillars on vegetables. Neem is non-hazardous to man and other mammals, and there are no harmful side-effects on natural enemies.

Nicotine is an alkaloid extracted from tobacco leaves (Nicotiana tabacum) that has long been used as an insecticide, but since it is also a strong neuro-muscular poison in man and animals, its use is discouraged.

Pyrethrum is extracted from chrysanthemum flowers (*C. cinerariaefolium*). Pyrethrum is a powerful degradable contact insecticide causing a rapid knock-down action, but insects may recover. Insecticidal activity is markedly increased by the addition of synergists, e.g. piperonyl butoxide. Pyrethrum is very safe to man and mammals. As dusts or sprays, pyrethrum is used in animal husbandry, in stored food protection and in households.

Scilliroside is a very toxic glucoside with stomach action, which is extracted from ground bulbs of the red squill, *Urginea (Scilla) maritima.* Mixed with bait, it controls most species of rats and mice.

Rotenone is extracted from the roots of bean legumes, i.e. *Derris* spp. in South-east Asia and *Lonchocarpus* spp. in South America. It has long been used as an insecticide and is still used as a piscide. Because of its toxicity to fish and its relatively short residual effect, it can be employed in fish farming to clean unwanted fish from ponds prior to restocking.

Ryania is obtained from the stem of Ryania speciosa, a shrub from South America. It has a high mammalian toxicity with symptoms resembling those evoked by strychnine, an intense mammalian poison extracted from *Strychnos* spp. seeds. Its use should be discouraged.

Sabadilla is an alkaloid extracted from seeds of *Schoenocaulon officinale* (Liliaceae). It too is a superseded compound.

**Organochlorine compounds** are synthetic organic insecticides that contain carbon, chlorine, hydrogen and sometimes oxygen. They may also be named "chlorinated hydrocarbons" or "chlorinated insecticides". They comprise a notorious group of insecticides, among which are DDT and BHC; both of these were synthesized more than a hundred years ago, but forgotten. It was only around 1940 that their insecticidal properties were recognized. This event gave birth to the era of synthetic organic pesticide manufacture.

DDT became famous for its efficacy against flies, mosquitoes, body lice and fleas, which as vectors transmit human diseases such as malaria, yellow fever, typhus and bubonic plague. DDT was also used on a large scale in agriculture and horticulture. Because of its low cost, it probably was the most economical insecticide ever sold. Four chemical classes of organochlorine compounds may be distinguished :

**(a) Diphenyl aliphatics**

| | |
|---|---|
| chlorbenside | DDT |
| chlorfenethol | dicofol |
| chlorobenzilate | metoxychlor |

DDT has a long residual life or persistence in the soil and in aquatic environments. Also, because it accumulates in the tissues of animals and plants, it is banned for agricultural use. However, its use continues in health programmes for mosquito control. The other five compounds are very effective miticides, and do not have the long persistency of DDT.

DDT

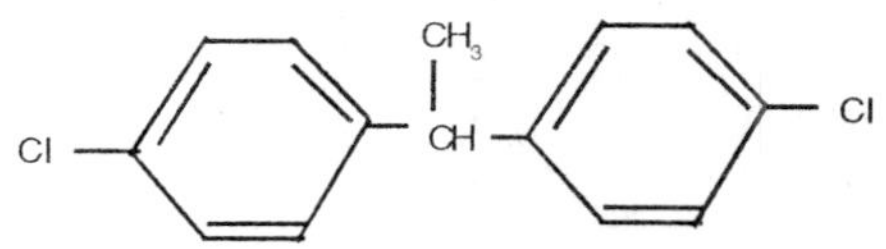


1,1,1, -trichloro-2,2 -bis(*p* -chlorophenyhethane

**(b) Benzene derivatives**

benzene hexachloride (BHC, HCH)
lindane (Gamma BHC)
pentachlorophenol

BHC is a chlorinated benzene consisting of a mixture of five isomeres, of which only the Gamma-isomer was found to have insecticidal properties; the other four being insecticidally inactive ingredients. A product containing 99 per cent gamma-isomer, namely lindane, is highly effective, but too expensive for large-scale crop use. The four inert isomers have a musty flavour that persists in animal and plant tissues as well as in the soil. Hence, normal mixture BHC, containing only 12 per cent Gamma-isomer, affects the taste of root crops and vegetables. Because the Gammaisomer is odorless, lindane was previously widely used in the control of storage pests.

HCH (BHC)

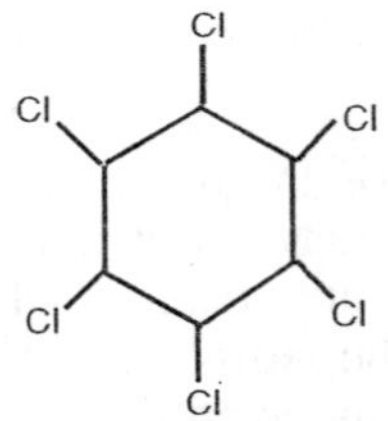


1, 2, 3, 4, 5, 6-hexachlorocyclohexane

**(c) Cyclodienes**

chlordane
chlordecone
endosulfan
endrin
heptachlor
mirex

Generally, cyclodienes are persistent soil insecticides, mainly used against coleopterous insects and termites; they also are generally photostable. Use of cyclodienes is progressively being cancelled or banned (aldrin and dieldrin) for reasons of resistance in insects, fish toxicity and serious environmental hazard. In Western countries, only endosulfan is still registered for use on field crops.

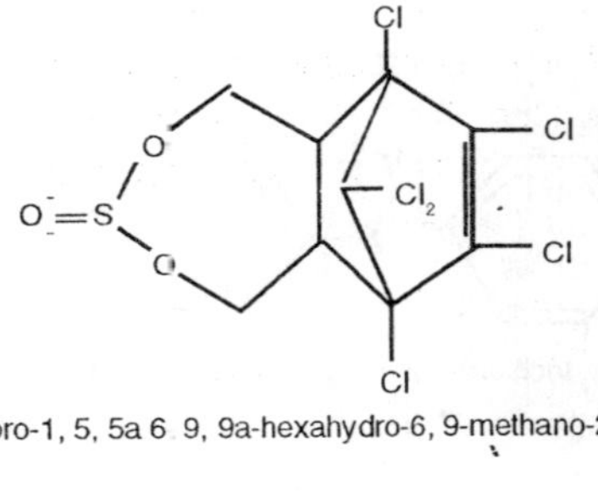


6, 7, 8, 9, 10, 10-hexachloro-1, 5, 5a 6, 9, 9a-hexahydro-6, 9-methano-2.4, 3-benzodioxathiepin 3-oxide

### (d) Polychloroterpenes

*camphechlor (Toxaphene)*

For 25 years until 1980, Toxaphene had the greatest use of any single insecticide in agriculture. In cotton cultivation, it was widely used in mixtures initially with DDT and later with parathion-methyl. Although Toxaphene is persistent in the soil, it evaporates from plant surfaces within weeks. It has low mammalian toxicity, but is toxic to fish.

**Organophosphorus insecticides** are all esters of phosphoric acid ($H_3PO_4$) and are also called organo-phosphates ($OP_s$) or phosphours esters. They comprise a large group of compounds that have two characteristics : organophosphates are generally acutely toxic to man and vertebrate animals, and they are non-persistent. Most of them have a short residual activity, which is desirable in keeping down on food crops, but is often a problem when longer protection is desired. Repeated applications may then be necessary. Organophosphates are nerve-poisons, acting through inhibition of the cholinesterase enzyme.

**Phosphate :**

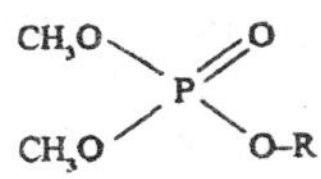

**Phosphorothioate :**

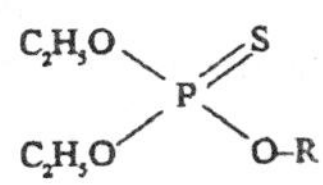

**Phosphorothiolate :**

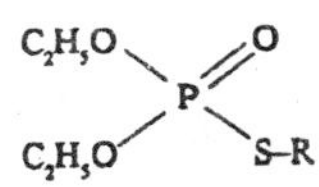

**Phosphorodithioate :**

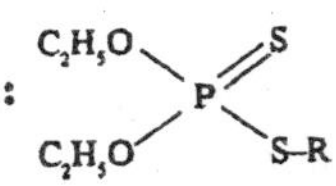

**Phosphonate :**

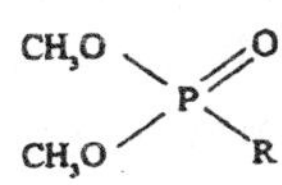

**Phosphoroamidate :**

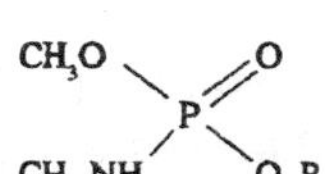

Phosphorus esters have distinctive combinations of oxygen, carbon sulphur and nitrogen attached to the phosphorus atom. The names of the phosphor molecules above are part of much more complicated chemical names for the compounds that contain these building blocks (moieties).

There are three chemical classes of organophosphorus insecticides namely :

* Aliphatic derivatives having a carbon chain structure.
* Phenyl derivatives containing a benzene ring with one hydrogen atom in the ring being replaced by the phosphorus moiety.
* Heterocyclic derivatives also containing a ring structure and the phosphorus group. In a heterocyclic carbon ring, however, one or more carbon atoms are displaced by oxygen, nitrogen or sulphur and the ring may consist of three, five or six atoms.

(a) **Aliphatic Organophosphates**

The oldest and best known insecticide of this class is malathion. Because of its high efficacy against many insect pests and its low mammalian toxicity, it has been used for almost 40 years on a large scale for agriculture, public health and the control of storage and household pests. Little resistance against malathion has developed among insect species and thus, it is still very useful.

MALATHION

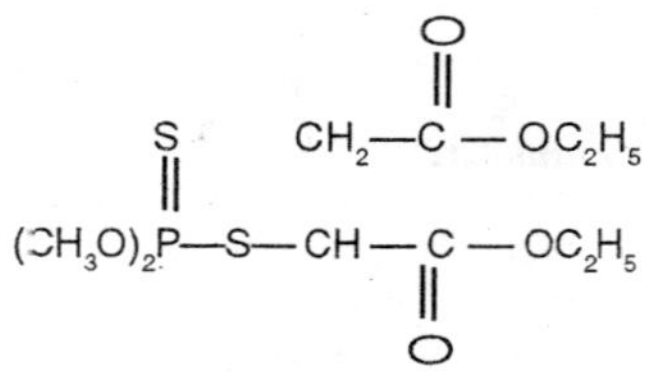

O, O-dimethyl-S-1, 2-di (carboethoxy) ethyl phosphorodithioate

Naled is another safe OP-compound having a very short residual action and a fumigant quality. As is the case with malathion, it is widely used for the control of mosquitoes, flies and ecto-parasites of domestic animals.

Several aliphatic OPs, such as monocrotophos, demeton and dimethoate, have a systemic action and are particularly effective against sucking insects.

Some aliphatic OP-insecticides – although being highly toxic – have such a very short residual activity that they are preferred for use on vegetables. Examples are listed hereunder (generally superseded compounds are not included in the list of examples shown) :

| | |
|---|---|
| acephate | methamidophos |
| demeton | mevinphos |
| demeton-methyl | monocrotophos |
| dichlorvos | naled |
| dicrotophos | omethoate |
| dimethoate | oxydemeton-methyl |
| disulfoton | phorate |
| ethion | phospharmidon |
| formothion | thiometon |
| malathion | trichlorfon |

(b) **Phenyl organophosphates**

These compounds are generally more stable than aliphatic ones and more persistent. Parathion-ethyl was introduced in 1974; with widespread use, it came to be known as parathion. Because of its dangerously high toxicity, it has largely been replaced by the slightly less toxic and broader acting parathion-methyl.

METHYL PARATHION

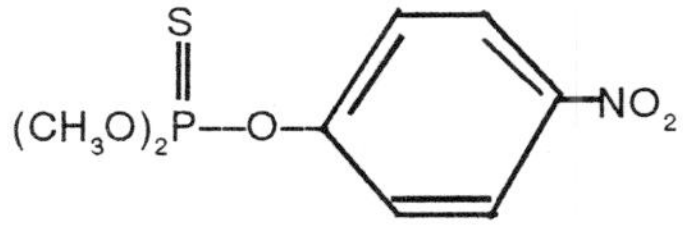


O,O dimethyl o-p-nitrophenyl phosphorothioate

Several older members of this class, such as fenitrothion and tetrachlorvinphos, are widely used in agriculture, horticulture and public health programmes. Included in this group are :

| | |
|---|---|
| bromophos | parathion |
| carbophenothion | parathion-methyl |
| chlorefenvinphos | phenthoate |
| edifenphos | phosalone |
| fenamiphos | phoxim |
| fenitrothion | profenofos |
| fensulfothion | prothiofos |
| fenthion | tempephos |

fonofos
isofenphos
tetrachlorvinphos
triazophos

**(c) Heterocyclic organophosphates**

Heterocyclic compounds have complicated molecular structures and are generally longer lasting than most of the aliphatic and phenyl derivatives. Upon degradation they may break down into many metabolites which may be difficult to analyse; some are very effective against mites and soil insects. Examples of this group are :

azinphos-ethyl
chlorpyrifos
chlorpyrifos-methyl
diazinon
dioxathion
etrimfos
isoxation
mephosfolan
methidation
phosmet
pirimiphos-methyl
pyrazophos
quinalphos

PIRIMIPHOS-METHYL

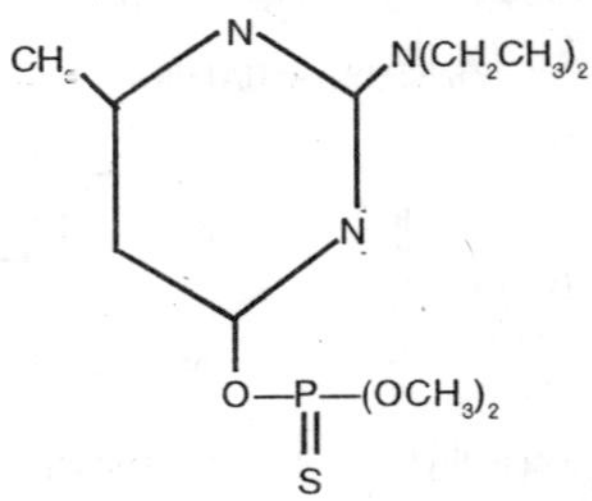


O-[2-(diethylamino) -6-methyl-4-pyrimidinyl]

C,O-dimethylphosporothioate

TETRADIFOR

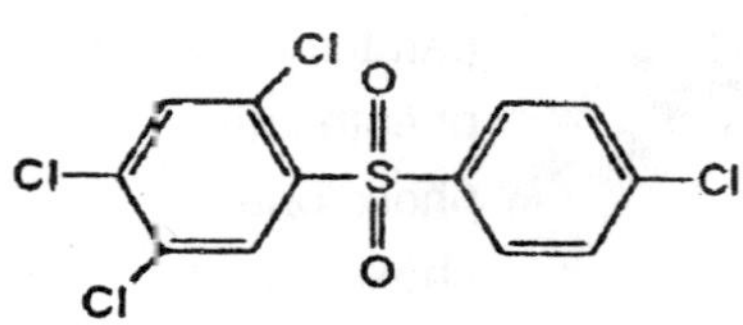


p-chlorophenyl 2, 4, 5-trichlorophenyl sulfone

**Organosulphur compounds** contain a dominant sulphur atom and commonly two phenyl rings. Sulphur alone has a good efficacy against mites but, in combination with the two phenyl rings, its acaricidal or miticidal effect is enormously enhanced. Organouslphurs combine this high toxicity to mites with a remarkably blow toxicity to insects; thus, they are very selective miticides and useful in integrated pest management. Examples of this group are :

| | | |
|---|---|---|
| ovex | propargite | tetradifon |

## Carbamates

These compounds resemble closely the organo-phosphates inbiological activity and, like them, they inhibit the cholinesterase enzyme required for nerve function in animals.

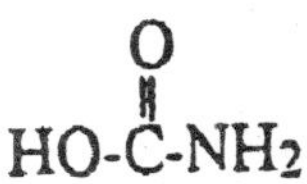

CARBARYL

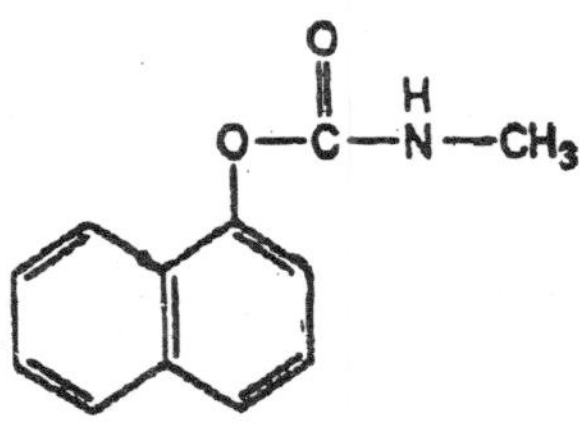

1-naphthyl N-methyl carbamate

Carbamates are esters of carbamic acid. They generally have a short residual activity and a very broad-spectrum effectivity as insecticides, miticides, nematicides and molluscicides. The carbamate group also includes herbicides such as diallate and propham. (The group of thiocarbamates and dithiocarbamates are considered under herbicides and fungicides, respectively). Among the carbamates, three classes of compounds may be distinguished :

(a) Methyl carbamates with phenyl-ring structure

| | |
|---|---|
| aminocarb | methiocarb |
| BPMC | metocarb (MTMC) |
| carbaryl | mexacarb |
| isocarb | promecarb |
| isoprocarb (MICP) | propoxur |

Carbaryl has become very popular in horticulture because of its low toxicity and broad spectrum efficacy. The carbamates propoxur, bendiocarb and dioxacarb are used to control mosquitoes, household and storage pests because of their rapid knock-down effect and long residual efficacy on wall surfaces.

CARBOFURAN

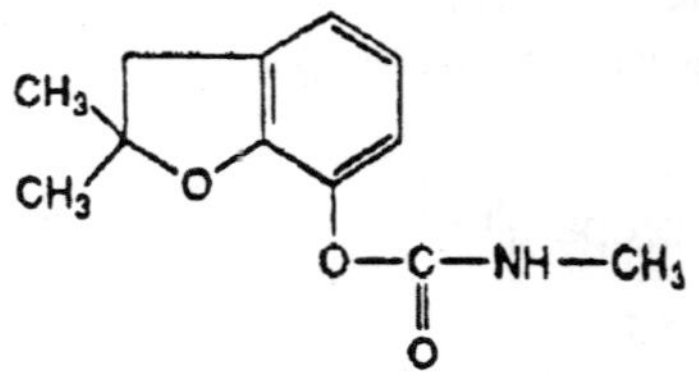

2, 3-dihydro 2, 2-dimethyl-7-benzofuranyl methyicarbamate

**(b) Methyl carbamates and dimethyl carbamates with heterocyclic structure**

| | |
|---|---|
| Bendiocarb | dioxacarb |
| carbofuran | pirimicarb |
| dimetilan | |

**(c) Methyl carbamates of oximes having a chain structure**

| | |
|---|---|
| aldicard | oxamyl |
| methomyl | thiodicard |

ALDICARB

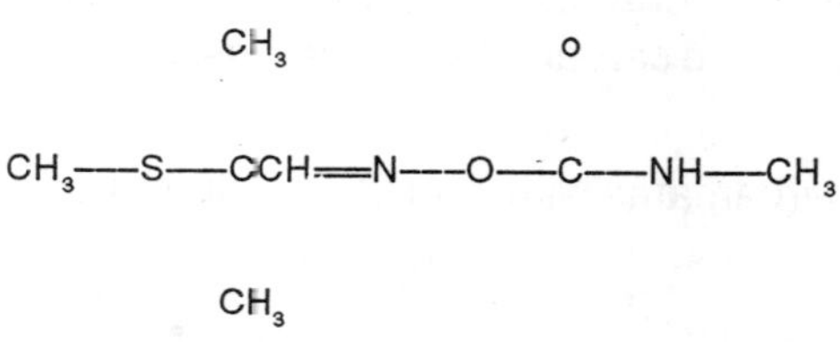

**2 methyl-2 (methylthio) propionaldehyde O (methylcarbamoyl) oxime**

Thiodicard is a relatively new compound with a double carbamate molecule linked with a sulphur atom; it has a long residual activity of up to 14 days.

**Formamidines** form a class of insecticideacaricide having the characteristic nitrogen structure-N=CH-N. They are very effective against eggs and very young caterpillars as well as against most stages of mites and ticks. Formamidines are valuable for the control of insects resistant to OPs and carbamates. Examples are :

amitraz
chlordimeform (restricted use)
formetanate

**Dinitrophenols** are derivatives of phenol with two nitro ($NO_{2)}$-radicals attached. The group has broad spectrum toxicity as insecticides, ovicides, herbicides and fungicides. Below are outstanding miticides :

binapacryl　　dinocap
dinobuton　　dinoterbon

**Organotions** are tin-based organic compounds which generally exhibit miticidal as well as fungicidal activity. Cyhexatin ;and fenbutatin-oxide are very selective miticides with long residual effectively.

cyhexatin　　fenbutatin-oxide

**Pyrethroids** are synthetic compounds, the chemical structure of which is patterned after pyrethrins (extracted from the chrysanthemum flower). a mixture of six esters named cincrim I and II, jasmolin I and II and pyrethrin I and II. The synthetic pyrethroids mimick the broad efficacy of the botanical, but, as they contain only one of these esters, insect species tend to develop resistance to them. Compared with the botanical pyrethrum, which contains all six ester properties, no resistance has yet been observed as it becomes very difficult for insects to develop the requisite combination of alternative pathways to these six properties.

Generally, pyrethroids show low mammalian toxicity, but like pyrethrum, they are highly toxic to fish and bees. They are anoxic nerve poisons. Their residues in crops do not cause problems.

Pyrethrum and the older synthetic pyrethroids are very sensitive to sunlight, because their molecules split under ultra-violet light. Therefore, they are not suited to agricultural use, but some of them have good volatility and are very effective against indoor insect pests. For household use they are formulated as aerosols together with piperonyl butoxide for synergistic action. Example are :

allethrin　　phenothrin
bioallethrin　　resmethrin
bioresmethrin　　tetramethrin

From the early 1970s, pyrethroids have been produced which have better photostability with low volatility; therefore, they may be used for agricultural purposes. Example are :

| | |
|---|---|
| deltamethrin | permethrin |
| fevalerate | |

The latest group of synthetic pyrethroids are photo-stable as well as extremely toxic to insects. Their efficacy is so good that a dose of only 10-40 g active ingredient per hectare is required. These new pyrethroids are not mixed with synergists. Example are :

| | |
|---|---|
| befenthrin | fenpropathrin |
| cyfluthrin | flucythrinate |
| cyhalothrin | fluvalinate |
| cypermethrin | tralomethrin |

FENPROPATHRIN

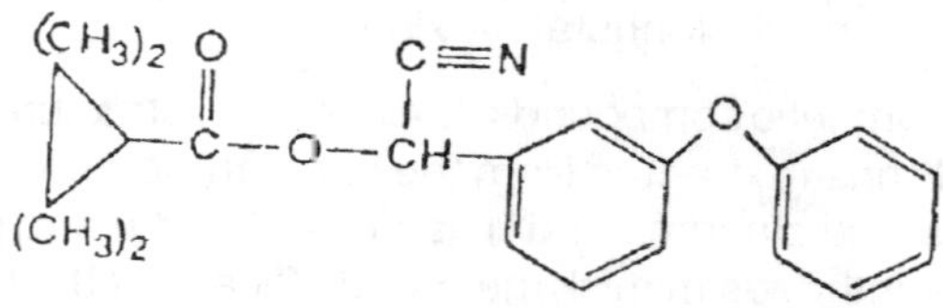

A-Cyano-3-phenoxybenzyl 2,2,3,3-tetramethyl cyclopropanecarboxylate

**Fumigants** are substances or a mixture of them which produce gas, vapour, fumes or smoke intended to kill insects, nematodes, bacteria or rodents. Usually, fumigants are volatile liquids or solids, or gaseous substances already consisting of small molecules, which often contain halogen radicals (C1-, Br- or F-). They are used to disinfect buildings, stored produce or the soil. Toxicity varies; however, the substances rapidly absorbed by the lungs and act through inducing narcosis (unconsciousness which may lead to death). Example are :

| | |
|---|---|
| chloropicrin | methyl bromide |
| ethylene dibromide | naphtalene |
| formaldehyde | phosphine |

Chlorophicrin has a strong irritating "tear gas" effect and may be added to methyl bromide as a warning agent.

**Petroleum oils,** also referred to as mineral oils, have been used for many years as insecticides and miticides. Only light applications of refined paraffinic oils, formulated with an emulsifier, can be safely made to trees in leaf and plants. These so called "white oil" or "summer oil" treatments are made against aphids, mites and scale crawlers. "Winter washes" of semi-refined and more aggressive oils of lower viscosity have greater efficacy against the eggs of spider mites and aphids as well as against scale insects, but such treatment can be tolerated only by dormant or deciduous trees in winter. Furthermore, certain petroleum oils are herbicides by themselves or may be used as solvents or adjuvants to other pesticides. Examples are "Actipan" and "Fyzol".

**Antibiotics** are chemical substances, such as penicillin, produced by micro-organisms and having bactericidal and fungicidal activity. Abamectin, produced by a *Streptomyces* spp. fungus, is the only antibiotic with good insecticidal, miticidal and nematicidal efficacy. Because it possesses some systemic activity, it provides good control of leafminers and of various mites attacking citrus, even on the underside of the leaves.

ABAMECTIN

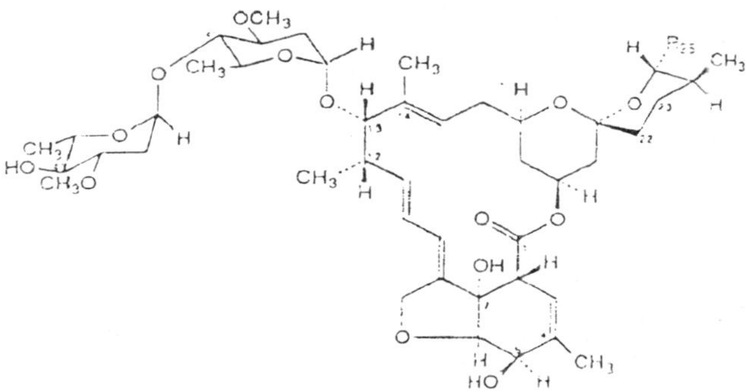

## Classification of insecticides by mode of action

Insecticides may also be classified according to the various ways they enter or affect pests. Once on or inside a pest organism, an insecticide may act upon one or more of the life processes. The result may be death, illness or a change in the behaviour, growth, metabolism or reproductive capabilities of the pest. The following are some examples of this method of classification :

* Stomach toxicants generally enter a pest's body through the mouth during feeding (ingestion) and are absorbed through the digestive tract.

* Contact toxicants generally penetrate a pest's body as a result of contact with the legs or other external portions and treated surfaces such as sprayed leaves.
* Fumigants are volatile and enter a pest's body through the respiratory system and kill at lethal concentration.
* Systemic toxicants are characterized by high water solubility, by which property they can readily be taken into the plant through its roots, stems or leaves. Once inside the plant, systemics move through the plant's vascular system to other untreated parts from where insects acquire the translocated insecticide during feeding. Systemic insectices are particularly effective against sucking, boring and mining insects and nematodes and are also used to control pests of livestock.
* Suffocating materials, usually oils, clog the respiratory mechanism of pests.

## CLASSIFICATION OF FUNGICIDES

The term "fungicides" strictly taken, refers to chemicals capable of preventing or eradicating diseases caused by fungi. Bacteria, the pathogens of bacterial plant diseases, may sometimes by controlled with bactericides or antibiotics. However, in the classification below, this distinction is not rigidly applied. Fungicides are generally not effective against virus diseases. However, because many virees diseases are transmitted by insects, mites or nematodes, their control is sometimes possible by using insecticides, miticides and nematicides to destroy these vectors.

### Classification of Fungicides by Chemical Nature

Fungicides can also be classified into main chemical groups consisting of inorganic or organic synthesized compounds.

### Inorganic Fungicides

Inorganic fungicides are derived from elemental sulphur or rather simple metal salts and do not contain carbon. Generally, they are stable, almost insoluble in water and persistent.

**Sulphur,** in its elemental form, is probably the oldest known cure against plant diseases. Originally, finely ground flowers of sulphur (the form of sulphur resulting from sublimation following the heating of crude sulphur and rapid cooling of the fumes) was applied as a fungicidal dust. It proved to be effective against powdery mildews and spider mites. Currently, elemental sulphur is mostly formulated as a wet paste or a "flowable" prepared from colloidal sulphur particles of 0.2 – 10 micrometers in diameter. The third form is a wettable sulphur powder which is mixed with a wetting agent during the milling process.

Previously, a liquid lime-sulphur mixture was widely used for orchard spraying against powdery mildews, anthracnose leafspot and brown rot diseases. This mixture is prepared by boiling sulphur and slacked lime in the ratio of 2 : 1 in five parts of water. Lime sulphur, however, cannot be sprayed in combination with organo-phosphates, copper compounds or other metal-containing pesticides.

The efficacy of sulphur against powdery mildews and mites is by direct contact and also by fumigant action; it has no systemic effect. For good fumigant action, the temperature should be above 20°C however, above 32°C sulphur vapour becomes phytotoxic. Because spores of powdery mildew germinate in the absence of a water film on the leaves, this fumigation effect is important for killing the fungus.

Sulphur is a cheap and safe fungicide, but outside temperatures need to be monitored during the time of application. Formulations of sulphur are Elosal, Kumulus S and Thiovit.

**Copper Fungicides**

Another early discovery was the fungicidal effect of Bordeaux mixture (a watery solution or slurry of copper sulphate and hydrated lime). Bordeaux mixture, with 12 per cent copper, is a safe fungicide with low mammalian toxicity; it controls a wide range of diseases such as downy mildews and late blight of potatoes. The product has been largely replaced by "fixed coppers" in which a copper compound of low-solubility is packed in a form that is stable in storage and readily dispersable in water. The copper compound is usually a basic cupric salt with a bright red, blue, green or yellow colour. The solubility and the rate of release of the toxic copper ion (Cu-radical) are decisive for providing efficacy against the fungi and for preventing phytotoxicity to the host plant.

In general, protective fungicides have a low rate of ionization. However, if a film of water is present at the spot of infection where the fungal spore germinates, a portion of the fungicide residue may go into solution. The small quantity of Cu-ions absorbed by the germinating spore is then replaced in the solution from the residue. The spore accumulates the toxic Cu-ions and is killed in the process. Such compounds are less phytotoxic than Bordeaux mixture, but their fungicidal efficacy tends to be less. Copper oxychloride is the most widely used compound against *Phytophthora* diseases. Examples of fixed coppers are ;

| | |
|---|---|
| Cupric carbonate | copper sulphate |
| copper hydroxide | cuprous oxide |
| copper oxychloride | |

Inorganic fungicides containing heavy metals, such as mercury, nickel, zinc and chromium ions, have strong fungicidal properties and have been in wide use over the past 35 years. These metal salts are generally very toxic to all forms of life and they are rather persistent in the soil and on treated surfaces. For these reasons, inorganic mercurial and other heavy metal fungicides have been banned in many countries. Manufacturing of such fungicides has been discontinued, except for some special purpose formulations, e.g. mercuric oxide is used as a paint against bark cankers and for sealing bark injuries, and insoluble mercurous chloride is still used for seed treatment.

**Organic Fungicides**

Since the development in 1931 of the first organic sulphur compound, thiram, a wide range of synthetic organic fungicides have gradually replaced the less selective inorganic compounds. Currently, about 150 synthetic fungicides are available or under development. A common feature is their high efficacy at rather low dosages, their long residual activity and a greater safety to crops, animals and the environment. Generally, the organic fungicides are broken down by soil micro-organisms and leave no persistent toxic metabolites.

**Dithiocarbamates** are derivatives of the sulphur-containing dithiocarbamic acid. For half a century, these fungicides have been among the most effective and popular ones in use. In combination with metallic salts such as zinc salt (ziram), ferric salt (ferbam) and manganous salt (maneb), these organic sulphur compounds offer a particular effectivity, better stability and less phytotoxicity than elemental sulphur. They have no systemic activity. Since they provide a good cover, several dithiocarbamates are used as seed protectants against soil-borne diseases. Their toxic effect to fungi probably stems from the isothiocyanate-radical (-N=C=S-) which is formed as a break-down component.

THIRAM

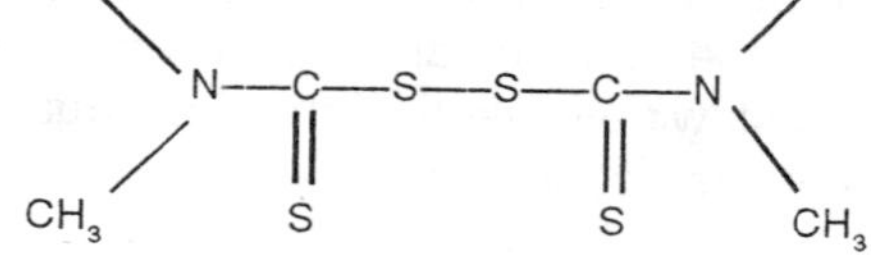


bis(dimethylthio-carbamoyl)disulfide

Additionally, chelates are formed within the fungal cells when dithiocarbamates or heavy metal fungicides are applied. When an excess quantity of such chelates is present, they may interfere with enzymatic and metabolic processes within the fungal cells. Heavy metal dithiocarmates thus have great killing power. Example are :

| | |
|---|---|
| ferbgam | propineb |
| maneb | thiram |
| metham-sodium | zineb |
| nabam | ziram |

mancozeb : a complex of zinc (2-5% Zn) and maneb (20% Mn). This ready-to-use fungicide combines the benefits of both maneb and zineb.

### Organometallic Compounds

**Mercury fungicides** were popular because of their efficacy against fungi, their good disinfective and protective action, and often considerable volatility which properties made them very well suited for seed treatment. However, because of their high mammalian toxicity, all organic and inorganic mercurial fungicides have lost their registration and are no longer available for any purpose.

**Organocopper compounds** include organic salts of acetate, naphthenate, oleate and quinolinate. Copper acetate was first developed in 1889 and became the first factory made basic copper fungicide. Copper compounds are not easily washed from leaves by rain, since they are relatively insoluble in water, and thus give longer protection against disease than do most of the organics. They are relatively safe to use and require no special precautions during spraying. The currently accepted theory for the mode of action fungistatic action is its nonspecific denaturation of protein. The $Cu^{++}$ion reacts with enzymes having reactive sulfhydryl groups–which would explain its toxicity to all forms of plant life.

| | |
|---|---|
| Copper 8-quinolinate | cuprobam |

**Organotin compounds** are truphenyl tin (fentin) salts, which are both toxic and phytotoxic. They demonstrate good control of blast diseases in rice, late blight in potatoes, coffee berry disease and brown spot disease in tobacco. The most widely used organotin fungicides are :

| | |
|---|---|
| fentin acetate | fentin hydroxide |
| fentin chloride | |

**Substituted aromatics** are derivatives of the benzene or phenol ring with hydrogen atoms replaced by chlorine, nitrogen or oxygen atoms. Possessing fungicidal properties, most of them are suited for seed treatment and soil treatment to control soil-borne fungi such as smut and damping-off diseases of seedings. Example are :

| | |
|---|---|
| chloroneb | hexachlorobenzene |
| | HCB pentachloroni-trobenszene, PCNB |
| dicloran, DCNA | pentachlorophenol, PCP |
| etridiazole | tochlophosmethyl |

Chlorothalonil and dicloran are used as protectants on foliage and fruits; PCNB and HCB for seed treatment; etridiazole and tochlophosmethyl for soil-treatment.

**Dicarboximides** constitute a group of fungicides which have the basic chemical structure shown in the diagram below; they contain a sulphur and nitrogen atom at the central position.

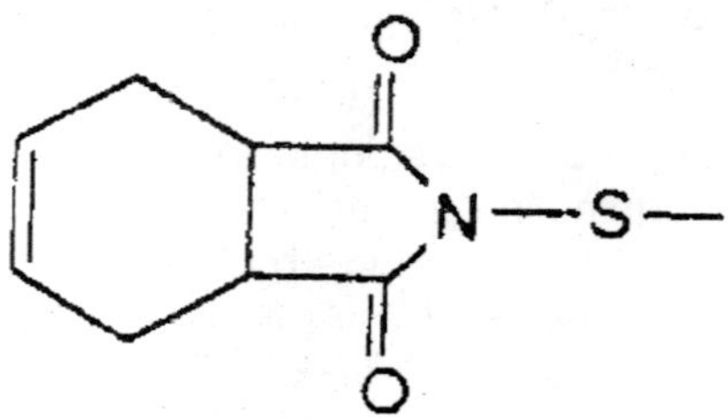

The group is also referred to as "sulfenimides". In general, they are considered to be among the safest pesticides and are used for seed treatment and for protectant sprays against *sclerotinia* diseases :

| | |
|---|---|
| chlozolinate | procymidone |
| iprodione | vinchlozolin |
| metomeclan | |

**Phtalamides** and related compounds are non-systemic fungicides with broad spectrum activity against many foliar diseases in fruit crops, vegetables and ornamentals. Captan is used on a large scale in tropical cultures; its use for food crops, however, is progressively being restricted :

| | |
|---|---|
| captafol | folpet |
| captan | tolyfluanid |
| dichlofluanid | |

**Dinitrophenol fungicides** with a non-systemic but specific action against powdery mildews are :

| binapacryl | dinocap |
|---|---|

**Triazines** comprise a group of compounds with herbicidal activity; they are reviewed below. Only anilazine is a fungicide; it is used for protectant application on vegetables.

## Systemic Fungicides

These compounds are absorbed by the plant by translocation of the active ingredient through the cuticle of leaves; hence they are taken into the vasculr system. These toxicants are transported via the sapstream towards the foliage and the apical (growth) point. The direction of transport is generally towards the leaf tips, but not downwards to the stem base and the roots. Some systemics can be applied to the soil and are slowly absorbed through the roots to give prolonged disease control. Systemic fungicides give a much better protective effect than the non-systemic protectant fungicides which need to be sprayed evenly onto the plant surface where they remain, essentially where they are deposited. Most systemics also exert a curative (therapeutic) effect against pathogens that have already invaded the plant.

There are many systemic fungicides on the market, which may be classified in one of the groups below :

*** Oxathiins**

| Carboxin | methfuroxam |
|---|---|
| furmecyclox | oxycarboxin |

Carboxin and related oxathiin fungicides control mainly pathogens of the Basidiomycetes, a class of fungi which includes such important pathogens as smuts and rusts of cereals, and the soil fungus *Rhizoctania solani.* Methfuroxam and furmecyclox control *R. Solani* in cotton and potatoes.

*** Benzimidazoles and thiophanates**

| benomyl | thiabendazole |
|---|---|
| carbendazim | thiophanate-methyl |
| fuberidazol | |

This group contains highly effective, systemic, broad-spectrum fungicides which are widely used in many tropical crops. However, intensive and exclusive use has caused resistance in major crops. Fuberidazol is an important replacement for organomercury compounds as a seed dresser. Thiabendazol controls post-harvest diseases in fruits. These fungicides are not effective against Phycomycetes (*Phytophthora, Pythium* and *Perenospora* spp.)

*** Pyrimidines**

| | |
|---|---|
| bupirimate | ethirimol |
| dimethirimol | fenarimol |

*** Acylalanines**

| | |
|---|---|
| furalaxyl | metalaxyl |

*** Ergosterol biosynthesis inhibitors (EBIs)**

| | | |
|---|---|---|
| (a) Imidazoles : | fenapanil | prochloraz |
| | imazalil | triflumizole |
| (b) Piperazine, compounds : | pyridine-and | pyrimidine |
| | buthiobate | pyrifenox |
| | fenarimol | triforine |
| | nuarimol | |
| (c) Morpholins : | aldimorph | tridemorph |
| | dodemorph | trimorphamide |
| | fenpropimorph | |

The morpholine fungicides demonstrate a systemic, specific activity against powdery mildews of cereals, bananas, rubber and ornamental plants.

| | | |
|---|---|---|
| (d) Triazoles : | bitertanol | myclobutranil |
| diclobutrazol | penconazol | |
| etaconazole | propiconazol | |
| fluotrimazol | triadimefon | |
| flusilazol | triadimenol | |
| flutriafol | triflumazol | |

The EBIs are a chemically heterogeneous group of systemic fungicides, grouped together because of a similar mode of action. They are also called sterol biosynthesis-inhibiting fungicides (SBIs) or demethylation inhibitors (DMIs). Most of these compounds have systemic, protective and curative properties, and are effective against powdery mildews and rust fungi which are important diseases of cereals and many other crops. They are also effective against many other leaf spot pathogens such as *Pyrenophora* spp., Venturia spp. and Septoria spp.

* Organophosphates

| | |
|---|---|
| ESBP | pyrozophos |

iprobenfos
edifenphos
ditalimfos
tolclofos-methyl
trimiphos

These compounds display protective as well as curative activity because of their systemic property. ESBP (Inezin), iprobenfos (Kitazin P) and edifenphos (Hinosan) are applied against rice blast; the others, against powdery mildews. Tolclofos'-methyl controls soil-borne diseases, especially *Rhizoctonia solani.*

*** Phenylamides and other fungicides against**

*Oomycetes*

**Phenylamides**

benalaxyl
cyprofuram
furalaxyl
metalaxil
ofurace
oxadixyl

**Others (including carbamates)**

cymoxanil
fosetyl
hymexazol
propamocarb
prothiocarb

This is a heterogeneous group of fungicides sharing the property of resistance against *Oomycetes,* the causal fungi of important root and foliar diseases such as *Perenospora, Plasmopara* and *Phytophtora.* Owing to their highly specific and systemic activity, resistance of this class of fungi to phenylamides may occur.

*** 2-Aminopyrimidines**

bupirimate
dimethirimol
ethimirimol

A small group of systemic fungicides with high efficacy against powdery mildews *(Erysiphaceae).*

*** Quinones**

benodanil
chloranil
dichlone
futonil
mepronil

**Other organic compounds**

There are important fungicides which do not belong to one of the chemical groups above; they comprise a random collection of fungicides with non-related chemical structures. Example are :

| | |
|---|---|
| anilazine | etridiazol, (echlomezol) |
| chlorfentezin | fenaminosulf |
| chlorothalonil | guazatine |
| dichlofluanid | pencycuron |
| dasomet | quinomethionate |
| dodine | see butylamine |
| | thiocyclam |

Most of these compounds are non-systemic protective fungicides. Pencycuron is specifically active against *Rhizoctonia solani,* sheath blight of rice, in particular. Dazomet is a soil fumigant with a broad spectrum activity, whereas etridazole and fenaminosulf are soil fungicides with restricted use, mainly against Phycomycetes spp.

Guazatin and oxine-copper are applied in seed dressings, whereas the main use of secbutylamine is for the control of post-harvest fruit-rotting fungi, for which purpose guazatin is also used.

**Antibiotics**

There are certain chemical substances produced by micro-organisms, such as bacteria and fungi (molds), that have the capacity, in very dilute concentrations, to inhibit the growth of or to kill bacteria and certain fungi that cause diseases in animals and plants.

To date, several hundred antibiotics have been discovered, but relatively few have been developed into commercial products. The Actinomycetals (an order of lower plants) constitute the largest source of fungicidal antibiotics. In particular, the family of Streptomycetaceae has become widely known for its members :

* *S. griseus* from which streptomycin and cycloheximide are produced that are used as bactericides for fruits, tobacco, maize and ornamentals. Their use is limited for toxicological reasons.

* *S. avermitilus,* from which abamectin is produced.

* *S. griseochromogenes,* which after fermentation yields the active substance of blasticidin–S.

* *S. Kasugaenis,* from which kasugamycin is produced.

* *S. cacaoi,* which after extraction yields polyoxins.

Of the latter three Japanese antibiotics, the first two are effective against blast diseases of rice and the third against rice sheath blight.

Abamectin has insecticidal, miticidal and nematicidal, but very little fungicidal, effectivity. Other antibiotics, such as penicillin, bacitracin and tetracycline, are used against bacterial diseases in man and livestock. Tetracyclines appear also to help control some mycoplasma-like plant diseases.

Cycloheximide, the least complicated antibiotic compound, affects the growth of yeast and fungi by inhibitin of protein-and DNA-synthesis. Its growth regulating properties are used for promoting the abscission of fruits such as oranges and olives. Streptomycin specifically disturbs the build-up of the vital nucleic acids DNA and RNA. Cycloheximide (Acti-dione) is the most toxic fungicide ($LD_{50}$, oral, rats, is 2 mg/kg) and an extremely strong repellent to rats (it is a restricted use product).

Antibiotics having fungicidal and bactericidal activity which are used for agricultural purposes are :

cycloheximide streptomycin

Antibiotics that have fungicidal action only are :

blasticidin-s polyoxins

kasugamycin validamycin

**Classification of fungicides by mode of action**

Fungicide sprays are of two types, protectants and eradicants.

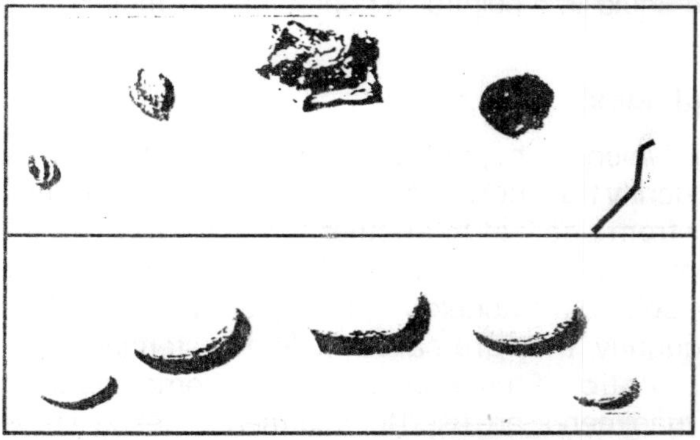

*In the process of seed coating, a water-based solution of an insecticide and/or fungicide is applied around each seed and is fixed with a polymeric sticker. The film coat that is formed on the seed is not soluble in water, thus providing continued close protection when the seed germinates in the humid soil. Film coating reduces up to 90 per cent of the dosage needed for the control of soil pests. (Bare seed above and pelleted seed below).*

## Protectant Fungicides

Several "classic" or conventional fungicides do not penetrate into plants. Instead, when applied as spray, dust or siurry, they provide a film of fungicide over the surface of plants and seeds that kills fungal spores upon germination. Plants are thus protected during stages when they are vulnerable to inoculation by pathogens before there is any evidence of disease. As most fungicides have no systemic activity, it is necessary that a uniform coating be deposited on upper-and under-sides of the leaves and on other external surfaces. This is best achieved with high volume sprays with wetting agents and stickers admixed, or by dusting. For protection over longer periods, the application may have to be repeated. Protectant fungicides are effective in preventing leaf sports, mildews and rusts on foliage, blemishes on flowers and post-harvest rot of fruits and vegetables. Examples are copper fungicides, captan and maneb.

## Curative or Eradicant Fungicides

To kill a fungus which has already invaded a plant, fungicides need to exert a curative or chemotherapeutic effectivity. Generally, a fungal disease can be cured only in its early stage of infection. Once they are well established and syptoms have appeared, fungal diseases are difficult to control. Only a few fungicides have curative action, among them are benomyl, dichlone, dodine, liquid lime-sulphur, fenepropimorph, metalaxyl, propicinazol and triadimefon.

## Systemic Fungicides

Fungicides which after application are absorbed by the foliage or roots and are subsequently transported over long distances within the plant (from root to shoot or from one leaf to another) are called systemic. The highly effective systemic fungicides discovered so far are mostly taken along through the vessels and tracheids of the xylem by the transpiration sap stream, consequently, they are called xylem-systemics. An example is benomyl for the control of fusarium diseases. Some systemics, such as fuberidazol and triadimenol, are used for treatment of seeds. Those fungicides which after having been absorbed show only a limited spread from the site of application into the tissues are termed locosystemics.

In practice, systemic fungicides are generally applied as foliar sprays and exert their disease-controlling activity mostly by direct contact between germinating fungal spores and the toxic deposit. Within the leaves, if pemetration is sufficient, the translaminar transport of the systemic will stop the infection process in the unsprayed parts of the leaf in a curative action. Thus, systemic fungicides provide superior protection as compared with non-systemic protectants and they have a vital role to play in controlling fungi. This is particularly so if a crop is valued for its appearance, as is the case with vegetables, fruits and flowers. With such crops, fungicides must be applied preventively in advance of infection by damaging pathogens.

## CLASSIFICATION OF HERBICIDES

A herbicide is a chemical intended for killing plants or interrupting their normal growth. They may either have a certain selectivity by chemical property by was of application in the control of weeds, grass or brush in cropland, rangeland or forests, or they may be "total herbicides" for use on industrial sites and rights-of-way locations.

### CLASSIFICATION BY CHEMICAL NATURE

#### Inorganic herbicides

Most inorganic herbicides are salts, they have been used for decades. In particular, sodium arsenite solutions were very popular as herbicides and arsenic trioxyde as a soil sterilant until the 1960s, when they were banned for ecotoxicological reasons. Also iron- and copper sulphates as well as ammonium sulphamate were favoured herbicides for foliar application. Sulphuric acid was, atone time, used for selective weeding in cereal crops, and pre-emergence in horticultural crops however, it is very corrosive to spray machinery. These compounds are usually highly water-soluble and easily leach from the soil. They cause scorching of leaves by inducing plasmolysis and desiccation in the plant cells. Borates, i.e. various sodium salts of boric acid, are absorbed through th roots and are non-selective herbicides. Sodium chlorate can used as a total herbicide at higher doses or for foliar application at lower ones.

| | |
|---|---|
| ammonium sulphamate | sodium borate |
| sulphuric acid | sodium chlorate |

#### Organic herbicides

Organic arsenicals are still being used, because they are much less toxic to mammals than inorganic arsenic salts. They act by inhibiting metabolic processes in the plant as they compete with phosphate in essential chemical reaction. Examples are:

| | |
|---|---|
| disodium | methanearsonate(DSMA) |
| monosodium | methanearsonate |

**Phenoxy aliphatic acid**

This group comprises a series of compounds in which the phenoxy-nucleus is linked with acetic-, propionic-and butyric acids. Their solubility in water is generally high in comparison with other groups of herbicides. These herbicides have a selective, hormone-type effect on broadleaf weeds, which disturb their normal growth, but grasses are very tolerant. Absorption takes place through the roots or shoots and the chemicals are readily translocated throughout the plants. 2,4-D and 2,4,5-T and MCPA have been immensely popular and were once regarded as being very safe.

**2,4-D**

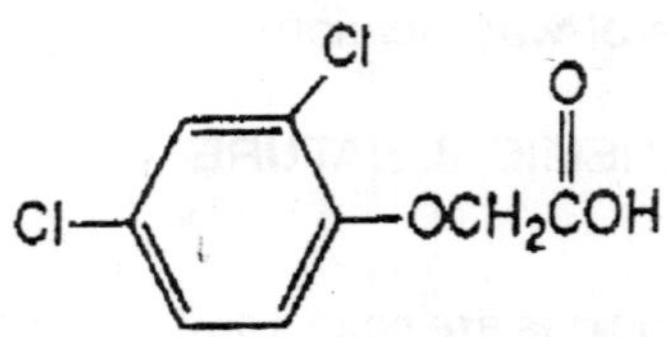


(2.4-dichlorophenoxy) acetic acid

Around 1970, however, the 2, 4, 5-T compound was suspected of being contaminated with dioxin, an extremely toxic impurity. Therefore, its registration was cancelled. However, 2, 4-D and MCPA have remained in wide use because of their low mammalian toxicity and their rapid degradation.

| | |
|---|---|
| 2, 4-D | dichlorprop ( 2, 4-DP) |
| 2, 4, 5-T | fenoprop (2, 4, 5-TP |
| MCPA | mecoprop (MCPP) |
| MCPA | |

**Substituted amides** constitute a large group of organic nitrogenous herbicides which include two sub-groups :

**(a) Amides**

The compounds in this sub-group act primarily in the soil against annual grass weeds, causing severe stunting of shoots. Amides are of low mammalian toxicity. Diphenamid is relatively persistent in the soil. Propyzamide has a selective and systemic effectivity against annual weeds. Quinonamid kills algae in lowland rice. Examples of amides are :

| | |
|---|---|
| chlorthiamid | propyzamide |
| diphenamid | quinonamid |

### (b) Anilides

compounds of this numerous sub-group vary greatly in type of action and in the range of weeds they control. Propanil is a post-emergence herbicide, which controls annual grasses and broadleaf weeds through inhibition of photosynthesis, after absorption through the leaves. Other closely related compounds include propachlor, alachlor, butachlor, metazachlor and metolachlor. They are applied pre-emergence for control of germinating annual weeds, including grasses. Perfluidone has a similar pre-emergence effect, but in addition it may also induce strong retardation in the development of underground buds of Cypereus rotundus and C. esculentus. All the products in this group have a low mammalian toxicity. Persistence in the soil usually lasts not longer than a few weeks. Example are :

alachlor
butachlor
metolachlor
metazachlor
propachlor
propanil
perfluidone

### Diphenylethers

These compounds possess two benzene rings joined through oxygen or a more complex chain of molecules. Nitrofen and fluorodifen are sprayed pre-emergence on the soil against germinating annual grasses and broadleaf weeds.

**NITROFEN**

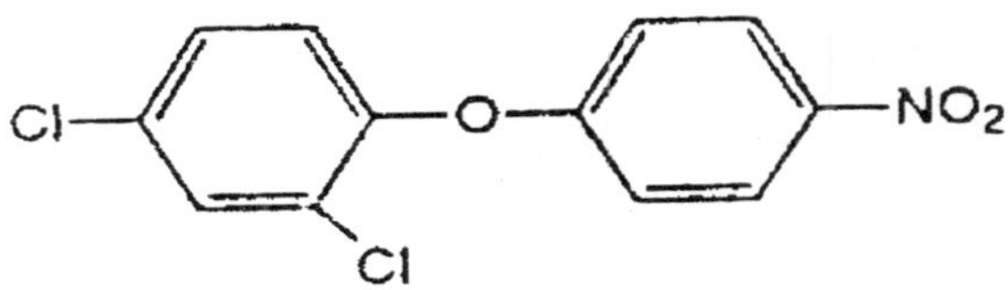


2, 4-dichlorophenyl p-nitrophenylether

Uptake is through foliage and by the roots. Bromofenoxim and lactofen are selective post-emergence herbicides for broadleaf weeds. Diphenylethers inhibit respiration and photosynthesis in plants, resulting in chlorosis, deformation and death of seedings and the scorching of foliage. The mammalian toxicity of this group is fairly low. The compounds are relatively insoluble in water and do not easily leach from the top soil. Persistency in the soil may last up to several months. Example are :

acifluorfen-sodium
bromofenoxim
diclofop-methyl
fluorodifen
lactofen
oxyfluorfen

**Dinitroanalines** are probably the most heavily used group of herbicides in agriculture. These herbicides, which have a similar dinitro-aniline-nucleus in common, are very effective against annual grasses and broadleaf weeds, when they are applied pre-emergence and incorporated into the soil. They even affect the underground buds and stolons of perennial weeds. These compounds and trifluralin and benfluralin, in particular, must be incorporated into the soil owing to the loss which occurs because of photo-decomposition and volatilization. Trifluralin is only slightly soluble in water, a property which minimizes leaching.

## TRIFLURALIN

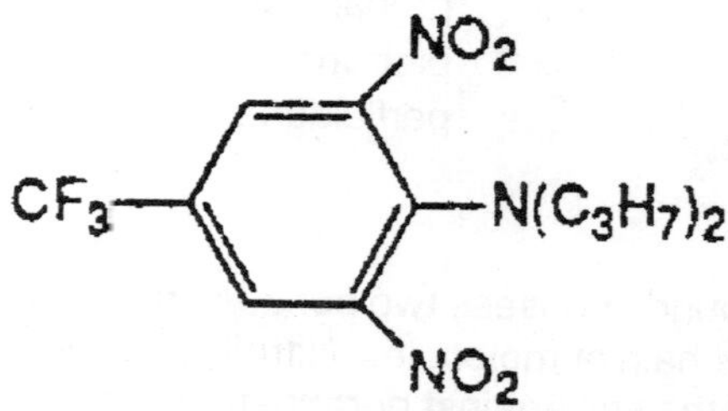


α,α,α-trifluoro-,6-dinitro- *N,N*-dipropylp- toluidine

Its efficacy stems from an inhibition of cell division in plants, which causes stunting of shoots and roots. Mammalian toxicity is low. The persistence in the soil ranges from a rew weeks for low doses upto one year for high doses. Examples are :

| | |
|---|---|
| benfluralin | oryzalin |
| fluchloralin | pendimethalin |
| nitralin | trifluralin |

**Substituted ureas**

compounds of this group are based upon the simple nitrogen-containing molecule of urea, but have the hydrogen atoms at both sides replaced with various carbon-chain and ring structures.

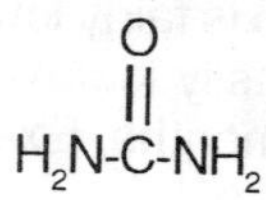


After the discovery around 1950 of monuron as a total herbicide, a large number of urea derivatives were developed as herbicides. The much used substituted ureas are primarily active as selective pre-emergence herbicides and are strongly absorbed to the soil. After absorption by the roots, they show a good efficacy against the majority of annual weeds. Some compounds can also be sprayed post-emergence if surfactants are added to the spray mixture. Control of susceptible weeds results from inhibition of photosynthesis, which causes chlorosis of the leaves, stoppage of growth and finally death. The mammalian toxicity of urea derivatives is low. The persistence generally lasts a few weeks in the soil, but efficacy is influenced by ecological factors (soil, rain, temperature). Example are :

| | |
|---|---|
| chlorbromuron | linuron |
| chloroxuron | methabenzthiazuron |
| chlortoluron | metobromuron |
| diuron | metoxuron |
| fenuron | monolinuron |
| isoproturon | thiazafluron |

**Carbamates**

The ester structure of this group has been explained previously under carbamate insecticides. Since the discovery of the herbicidal activity of propham, many more products have been developed in the carbamate group. Phenmedipham and barban are post-emergence herbicides; asulam pre- and post-emergence. The other compounds in this group are soil-active and are to be applied pre-emergence. Uptake occurs through roots or foliage and translocation within the plant is good. Carbamates are effective in controlling annual grasses and some annual broadleaf weeds. They act through the inhibition of germination and cell division; phenmedipham inhibits photosynthesis. Carbamates are of low mammalian toxicity; persistence in the soild is short. Some examples are :

| | |
|---|---|
| asulam | phenmedipham |
| barban | propham |
| chlorpropham | |

**Thiocarbamates**

The thio-and dithiocarbamates belong to the group of carbamates which contain sulphur. They are selective herbicides for pre-emergence or pre-planting application. Because of their volatility, the compounds must be incorporated into the soil. Uptake through the roots is followed by retarded growth and failure of the plant to emerge properly. Control of annual grasses and broadleafs is good. Di-allate and tri-allate act specifically against wild oats (Avena fatua); molinate, against water-grass (Echinochloa crusgalli) in rice. The -allate compounds are persistent for many months in the soil; the other thiocarbamates persist for a much shorter period. Metham-sodium acts as a soil fumigant by being converted in the soil to methyl isothiocyanate. Examples in this group are :

| | |
|---|---|
| EPTC | pebulate |
| di-allate | thiobencarb |
| metham-sodium | tri-allate |
| molinate | vernolate |

**Heterocyclic nitrogens** are compounds with a ring structure in which carbon atoms have been replaced by nitrogen and occasionally by sulphur. The main groups are as follows :

**a. Triazines** have a ring structure consisting of six atoms of which three are nitrogen atoms (hence its name tri-azine) to which two amino groups are commonly attached. The compounds demonstrate strong efficacy against annual grasses and broadleaf weeds coupled with a remarkable selectivity.

TRIAZINE NUCLEUS

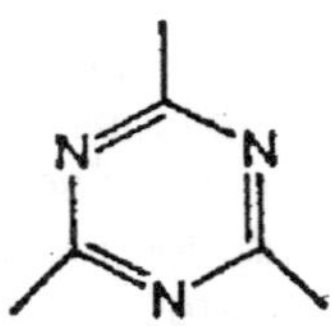


SIMAZINE

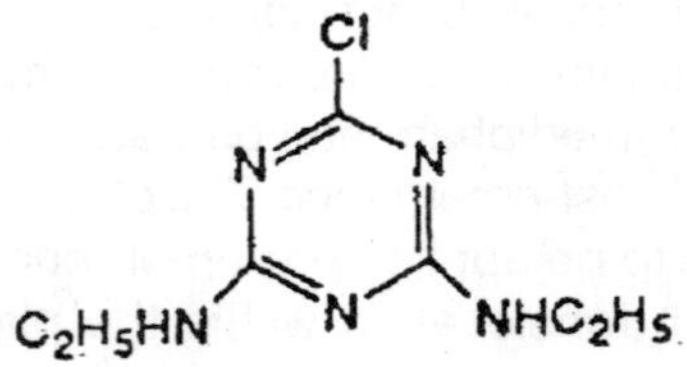


1-(4-chlorophenyl) 3-(2,6-difluorobenzoy)urea

This selectivity depends on the ability of tolerant plant species to metabolize the triazine compound, whereas susceptible plants do not metabolize the compound. Triazines are applied to the soil, primarily being absorbed through the roots and translocated inside the plants. Germination and emergence of the crop and the weeds are not affected but as soon as green leaves are formed, the activity causes severe inhibition of photosynthesis and chlorosis. Solubility in water is low, thus leaching from the soil is limited. The mammalian toxicity of triazine is generally low. Chlorotriazines and, in general, the "-azine compounds" such as atrazine, are very persistent in the soil and can be used for weed control in perennial crops and total weeds control with higher doses. The methylthiotriazines, generally the "-tryn compounds" such as ametryn, exhibit a soil-persistence of only a few weeks and therefore can be used in the crops having a short vegetation period and rapid rotation.

As of this writing however, it is expected that the use of atrazine in maize will be restricted in Western Europe, because serious contamination of groundwater (the source of drinking water) has resulted from intensive applications over the years. Example of this group are :

| | |
|---|---|
| atrazine | ametryn |
| cyanazine | dimethametryn |
| propazine | prometryn |
| simazine | simetryn |
| terbutylazin | terbutryn |

**b. Triazinones** also have a six-member ring and are closely related. Hexazinon is used for weed control on non-cropland and industrial sites. Mtribuzin is used for weed control in potatoes, tomatoes, tobacco and soybeans. Example are :

| | |
|---|---|
| hexazinon | metribuzin |

**c. Triazoles** are compounds containing a five-member ring in which three nitrogen atoms have replaced the carbon atoms. They are effective against broadleaf weeds in many crops and have a contact and slight systemic activity. Examples are :

| | | |
|---|---|---|
| amitrole | bentazon | oxadiazon |

**d. Pyridines** are chemicals derived from the pyridine molecule, a six-member ring with one carbon atom replaced by nitrogen. The best known is picloram, which is very effective against deep-rooted herbaceous weeds and woody shrubs.

PYRIDINE

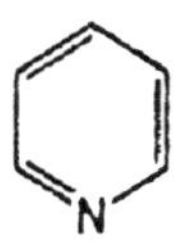


PICLORAM

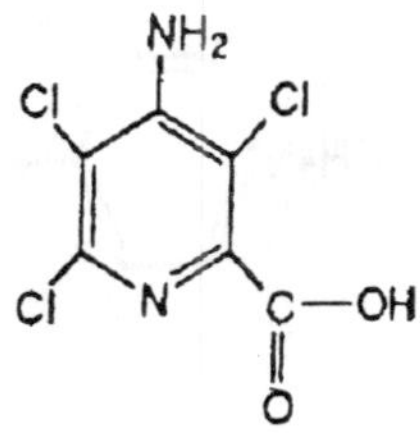


4-amino- 3,5,6-trichloropicolinic acid

Most grasses are resistant. Triclopyr is another related selective brush killer. Applied post-emergence, they may be taken up by either the roots or foliage. They act through stimulation of growth, resulting in elongation of cells, proliferation of tissues and formation of numerous rootlets. They are marketed for brush control in rangeland and utility rights-of-way. Example are :

fluroxypyr picloram triclopyr

**e. Uracils** are derived from the uracil nucleus, another substituted six-member ring with two nitrogen atoms and a double bond. Primarily for pre-emergence application and uptake mainly via the roots, they are very effective in controlling annual grasses and broadleaf weeds over an extended period by inhibition of photosynthesis. Mammalian toxicity is low; at higher doses, they may remain in the soil for up to 12 months. Example are :

bromacil lenacil terbacil

**Bipyridiliums** are composed of two pyridyl-rings and thus they are also termed pyridines. The two best known members of this group are diquat and paraquat. These herbicides have a strong contact action on above-ground plant parts. Within the plant, the chemicals are reduced to free radicals, which destroy tissue under light. Wilting and drying out of the folliage follow within hours, making these herbicides useful pre-harvest desccants for seed crops. Paraquat is particularly effective against grasses. Both are quickly deactivated in the soil due to strong adsorption to soil particles. However, because paraquat very slowly degrades in the soil, its use will soon be restricted in Western Europe.

**PARAQUAT**

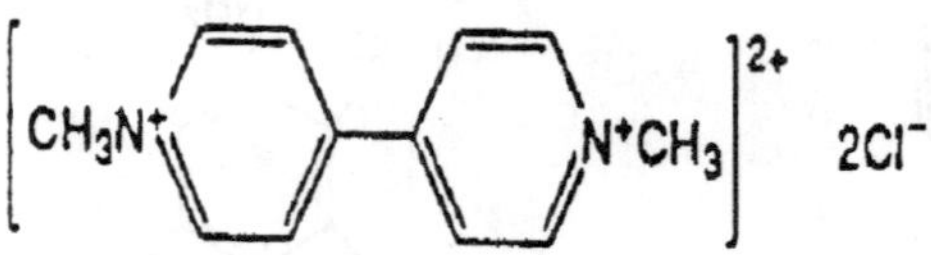


1,1'-demethyl-4,4'-bipyridylium ion (dichloride)

Both compounds are hazardous and need to be applied with great care, as no antidote is available for diquat and paraquat when swallowed. In many developing countries, paraquat is a major cause of fatal pesticide poisoning. It is much safer to use glyphosate (see sector under miscellaneous herbicides), a herbicides that is still more expensive, but which kills deep-rooted grasses as well as paraquat.

## Aliphatic Acids

Two heavily used herbicides of this group are chlorinated derivatives of acetic acid (TCA) and propionic acid (dalapon). They exhibit system action after having been absorbed by roots and leaves. They are effective against annual and perennial grasses. Used for non-cropland and forestry applications, they kill by causing precipitation of protein within the cells.

trichloroacetic acid (TCA) dalapon

## Phenol Derivatives

Compounds of this group are highly toxic, selective foliar herbicides. These are two sub-groups :

### (a) Dinitrophenols

These are primarily contact herbicides, but have also some effect via the soil against annual broadleaf weeds. The dinitrophenols are not translocated within the plant and are used as selective pre-and post-emergence herbicides. They inhibit respiration and photosynthesis within the cells. Some other dinitrophenol compounds are discussed above in the paragraphs about insecticides and fungicides. Example are :

| | |
|---|---|
| dinoseb (DNBP) | dinoterb |
| dinoseb-acetate | DNOC |

### (b) Chlorinated Phenols

The only herbicide in this sub-group is pentachlorophenol (PCP or Penta), which is also a termiticide and a wood protectant. PCP is a restricted use product. The use of dinoseb and dinosebacetate is banned in the United States, and Western Europe.

Benzonitrilles or substituted nitrilles consist of a benzene ring containing a cyanide (C-N) - radical. They show a broad spectrum activity, and act by various processes of inhibition of growth and tissue disruption. Effective against annuals grasses and broadleaf weeds. Examples are :

bromoxynil dichlobenil ioxynil

## Miscellaneous Herbicides

These are solitary compounds derived from rather unrelated chemical structures. Examples in wide use are :

| | |
|---|---|
| allozytdim-sodium | glufosinate-ammonium |
| bensulide | glyphosate |
| bentazone | methyl bromide |

| | |
|---|---|
| dimethazone | quizalofop-ethyl |
| endothal sodium | pyridate |
| difenzoquat | sethoxydim |
| fluazifop-butyl | |

Endothal sodium (Aquathol) is a preferred aquatic weed killer because of its low toxicity to fish, although it is toxic to mammals. Also, it is used as a systemic pre-and post-emergence herbicide against annual grasses and broadleaf weeds in field crops. Glyphosate is an important non-selective, non-residual, post-emergence herbicide for the control of deep-rooted grass and broadleaf weeds and woody shrubs. It is a foliar-applied systemic that is effective against all stages of weed growth. Action is through inhibition of protein and aromatic acid synthesis. Alloxydim sodium, sethoxydim, fluazifop-butyl and quizalofop-ethyl are new selective and systemic herbicides against annual and perennial grasses for post-emergence application.

## Classification of Herbicides by Mode of Action

Herbicides may also be classified according to the various ways they are being used or in which they act.

* Selective action. Compounds which kill weeds without harming crops.
* Non-selective action when all vegetation is killed.
* Contact action. Those plant parts are killed to which the herbicide is applied.
* Systemic action. The herbicide is taken up either by the roots or above-ground parts of plants and translocated throughout the tissues. They are particularly important for the control of perennial weeds, which continue growing from year to year.
* Pre-planting : Applied after the soil has been prepared but before seeding.
* Pre-emergence (contact) : Non-residual dosages are used after seeding but before emergence of the crop seedings.
* Pre-emergence (residual) : Applied at the time of seeding or just prior to crop emergence; the compound kills weed seeds and germinating seedings.
* Post-emergence : Application after emergence of the crop.

## Classification of Biological Pest Control Agents

Biological pest control agents are naturally occurring or genetically modified agents that are distinguished from conventional pesticides by their unique modes of action, low use volume and target species-specificity. Two major catagories may be distinguished :

* Biochemical pest control agents, such as hormones and growth regulators.
* Microbial pest control agents, such as bacteria viruses and fungi.

### Biochemical Pest Control Agents

A chemical must meet the following two criteria in order to be classified as a biotechnical pest control agent and meet the data requirements for this class of compounds :

* The chemical must exhibit a mode of action other than direct toxicity in the target pest (e.g. growth regulation, mating disruption). Botanical insecticides such as nicotine and pyrethrum kill and thus are not considered biochemical pest control agents.
* A biochemical must be naturally occuring, or if the chemical is synthesized by man, then it must be structurally identical to a naturally occuring chemical. Identical in this sense means the molecular structure of the major component of the synthetic chemical must be the same as the molecular structure of the naturally occurring analog.

Minor differences among stereochemical isomers are acceptable unless an isomer is found to have significantly different toxicological properties than another isomer.

In cases of doubt, such as if the exact molecular structure of the naturally occurring compound is unknown, or if the mode of action is different in the target compared with non-target organisms, a country's regulatory authority should rule on a case-by-case basis whether such chemicals should be classified as a bio-chemical pest control agent or as a conventional pesticide.

Biochemical pest control agents fall into four general biologically functional classes :

**(a) Semiochemicals**

These are chemicals emitted by plants or animals which modify the behaviour of receptor organisms of like or different kind. They include pheromones, allomones and kairomones.

* **Pheromones** are substances emitted by members of one species which modify the behaviour of others within the same species. Even at extremely low concentrations, these chemical messages induce insects to aggregate, help them to find a partner, provide an alarm signal or lead them to sources of food. The most common pheromones are sex attractants excreted by abdominal glands of the female to attract males for the purpose of mating; and the aggregation pheromones which are produced by one or both sexes of an insect species which bring both sexes together for feeding and reproduction. Sex hormones are common among moths and butterflies; the aggregation hormones, among beetles.

* **Allomones** are chemicals emitted by one species which modify the behaviour of different species to the benefit of the emitting species. Many plants produce secondary substances that repulse insects and prevent them from feeding; these are classified as allomones. The oil of *Citronella* grass has long been used by man as an insect-repellent applied to the skin.

* **Kairomones** are chemicals emitted by an animal organism which, at very low concentration, modify the behaviour of individuals of a different species to the disadvantage of the emitting and the benefit of the receptor species. For instance, an animal parasitoid may be guided by it in finding a host. Kairomones, like pheromones, can be used to attract insects to traps for the purpose of monitoring or catching them.

### b. Hormones

Hormones are biochemical agents that are synthesized in one part of an organism and traslocated to another part, where they have controlling, regulating or behavioural effects. The major groups of hormones have been identified; they are :

** Molting hormones or ecdysteroids*

These comprise a group of closely related water-soluble steroids in insects, of which several active analogs are found in plants. As yet, no effective control of insects through feeding or topical application of either natural or plant-derived ecdysteroid analogs could be obtained. Morever, as their synthesis appears to be obtained. Moreover, as their synthesis appears to be prohibitively expensive, the commercial production of ecdysteroids still remains in the research phase.

*** Juvenile hormones**

Four very similar juvenile hormones are produced by insects in the process of their immature development, which maintain the insects in their nymphal or larval form. These juvenile hormones, as well as many hundreds of synthesized active analogs-the so-called Juvenoids-are able to affect insect development almost equally well by anymode of application. Conforming to their mode of action, these juvenile hormones and juvenoids are also designated as insect growth regulators (IGRS).

Table 2.1:

**Five juvenoid compounds that are currently registered for use against insect pests**

| *Compound* | *Registered for use against* |
|---|---|
| diflubenzuron | *Lepidoptera, Diptera,* |
| fenoxycarb | mosquitoes fruit tree leafroller, fire ants |
| PRO-DRONE | fire ants |
| methoprene | flies, fleas, mosquitoes, pharao ants, stored food pests and tobacco pests |
| hydroprene | cockroaches |
| kinoprene | homopterous pests in greenhouses |

The natural hormones do not have enough environmental stability and are too costly to be synthesized; thus, they were not developed into commerical products. But the synthesis of their analogs, the juvenoids, turned out to be very productive and yielded many active compounds of often enhanced selectivity. To date, only five juvenoids have been registered for use against insect pests; they are listed in table 2.1. It appears that the listed juvenoids are used in protected environments; only fenoxycarb can be used in a field crop situation. This is one of several drawbacks of juvenoids; others can e summarized as follows :

- The instability of these compounds, when exposed to sunlight and wind as a foliar residue. Fenoxycrab is the most stable of the five compounds in the field application.

- Except for kinoprene, the juvenoids do not cause direct mortality in the target insects.
- The juvenoids are able to affect the target insects only during two distinct but short periods of their life. These brief periods, the so-called windows of sensitivity, co-incide with the last larvel instar and with early embryonic development in the egg-phase. Application of juvenoids in the last larval instar inhibits the process of metamorphsis. An excess of juvenile hormone or juvenoid results in the development of intermediate forms between nymphs and adults which, if they survive the molt, are incapable of reproduction. Application to the egg stadium causes an ovicidal effect that may result in abnormal embryo development, failure in hatching or death after emergence.

The advantages of juvenoids as chemical insect control agents are found in the following characteristics :

- Juvenoids demonstrate a rather extreme selectivity for insects, in which they affect receptor systems that do not exist in other forms of life and an often very high but selective activity on sensitive target species.
- These compounds have an extremely low toxicity to non-target organisms and mammals.
- Little cross-resistance is as yet expected to exist against these juvenoids.

Juvenoids which show neither a repelling nor direct killing action, as most conventional insecticides do, have proven to be very effective against social insects such as fire ants and pharao ants. Baiting with fenoxycard and methoprene generally gives good control since juvenoids brought into the nest by returning workers affect the brood and the social interactions.

* **Diflubenzuron** is a synthetic compound with contact and stomach activity that interferes with chitin deposition at the time of molting and prevents the shedding of the old skin. This leads to the death of the larvae and pupae, or to the development of non-viable adults. It also prevents hatching of insect eggs. Diflubenzuron is effective against lepidopterous caterpillars, grasshoppers, fly and mosquito larvae and weevils. It has no systemic activity and thus sucking insects are in general not affected. This forms the basis of its selectivity in favour of many insect predators. The trade name is Dimilin. Another promising IGR showing similar activity is teflubenzuron (Nomolt).

DIFLUBENZURON (Dimilin®)

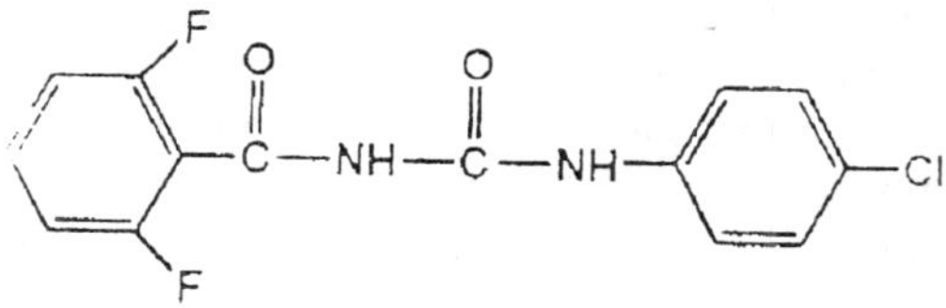

1-(4-chlorophenyl) 3-(2,6-difluorobenzoyl)urea

* **Kinoprene** is a juvenile hormone mimic that, when applied to larvel stages, prevents their metamorphosis into viable adults. Uses include the control of stored product pests and indoor insect pests, but it is particularly effective against insects of the order Homoptera such as white fly, aphids, mealybugs and scale insects in greenhouses. Although this compound had provide highly effective for pest control on ornamentals in greenhouses, it appears to have been withdrawn from the market as its market share was too small to justify the cost of keeping it available.

* **Methoprene** is also a juvenile hormone mimic with similar activity; it was registered in 1975 as a commerical IGR for use against mosquito larvae. Other uses include control of storage pests, homopterous fleas, leafminers and pharao ants. Juvenoids such as hydroprene and methoprene are very useful in confined environments such as greenhouses, houses and storage buildings.

(c) **Natural plant regulators**

Natural plant regulators are chemicals produced by plants that have inhibitory, stimulatory, or other modifying effect on the same or other species of plants. Some of these are termed "plant hormones" or "phytohormones".

Some examples of plant growth regulators (PGRs) are as follows :

* **Auxines-compounds** induce elongation in the cells of shoots. In 1934, it was discovered that auxins enhance the rooting of cuttings. Further uses of this PGR are for the thinning of fruits and the increasing of flowering. Auxins are formed within the plants from auxin precursors. Manufactured products with similar activity are indoleacetic acid, B-naphthaleneacetic acid and 2, 4-D.

* **Gibberellins** or gibberellic acid derivatives are substances which stimulate cell division and cell elongation through the induction of increased enzyme production in the cell. They occur naturally in all plants. Gibberellins

are used to increase stalk length, delay yellowing, break dormancy in seed potatoes, increase fruit set and yields etc.

* **Cytokinins** are naturally occurring or manufactured substances that induce cell division and the regulation of differentiation in plant parts. These compounds were discovered in 1955 and their usefulness lies in prolonging the storage life of green vegetables, cut flowers and mushrooms. Zeatin is a natural substance whereas kinetin and adenine are synthetic cytokenins.

* **Inhibitors** are substances that interfere with a physiological process in plants regulating growth, germination of seeds, or the action of hormones, gibberellins and auxines. Inhibitors that occur naturally in plants are usually hormones. Substances with inhibiting or retarding action are used to prevent sprouting of bulbs and tubers, prevent sucker growth on tobacco plants and induce shorter stem growth in grains. Naturally occurring inhibitors are benzoic acid, gallic acid, cinnamic acid and abscisic acid. There are also synthetic inhibitors such as maleic hydrazide.

**(d) Enzymes**

In this context, enzymes are defined as protein molecules that (1) are the instruments for the expression of gene action and that (2) catalyze chemical reactions.

## Microbial Pest Control Agents

The pesticides referred to as microbial pest control afents include formulations either of naturally occurring, infective micro-organisms, such as bacteria, fungi, protozoa and mycoplasmas, and viruses, or genetically modified micro-organisams that are used to achieve natural control of pests.

These pathogens and parasites are isolated and mass produced for use as a commercial pesticide. The basic general principie required for their registration is that the product should demonstrate effectiveness and not present unacceptable hazard to user, consumers of treated foods and the environments.

Microbial insecticides are preparations based on disease-including organisam (entempopathogens) or parasites which normally infect or poison an insect or mite and ultimately cause its death. Microbial insecticides are usually rather specific to certain orders of insects or mites and non-toxic to man, other mammals and plants.

Microbial insecticides have already been used for many years among a wide range of crops, forests and mosquito habitats where they are applied using conventional spraying techniques. They are often applied in combination with chemical insecticides and other means of control, within an integrated pest management approach.

Their main advantages are their environmental safety and highly specific action, but a major drawback is their lack of biological persistency under field conditions. Therefore, these microbial insecticides could not compete on the commerical market with more persistent and effective chemical pesticides, such as the successful synthetic pyrethroids. However, recent developments in the field of biotechnology, in particular in the areas of protein and genetic modification, have sparked a renewed interest in all groups of biological control agents.

Biotechnology appears to create new opportunities to overcome some of the long-standing disadvantages of microbial insecticides, such as their rapid breakdown, inconsistency of activity and costly production. In 1988, the world market for microbial insecticides was estimated at $US 70 million, or 1 per cent of the total insecticide market. The new developments seem to offer a possibility for show expansion of the market share of microbially based products to an estimated $US 300 million by 1992. In addition to the microbial insecticides, other microbial pesticides have already been developed that demonstrate a fungicidal, nematicidal or herbicidal activity.

**Bacteria** are the most researched and most widely exploited pathogens for pest control, mainly because of the high efficacy of certain strains of the infectious bacterium *Bacillus thurigiensis* (Bt), against susceptibel species of insects of the orders Lepidoptera, Diptera, Homoptera and (very recently) also Colcoptera.

The bacterium Bt forms within its cell an oval endospore and at the same time a proteinaccous inclusion commonly called a "crystal". This crystal, which represents up to 40 per cent of the dry weight of the bacterium cell at the time of sporulation, contains an endoroxin. Upon ingestion by an insect, this endotoxin may break down in an alkaline, midgut environment under the action of enzymes to release a smaller, active protoxin. This lethal protoxin damages the lining of the mid-gut wall leading to membrane rupture and lysis. The bacterial spores are thus released in the abdominal cavity of the insect where they multiply, eventually killing the insect. Furthermore, a cessation of feeding occurs usually within hours of ingestion owing to paralysis of the mouthparts.

The selectivity of Bt strains appears to depend on the acidity (pH-value) of the mid-gut content. Insects having an alkaline mid-gut content of pH 8-10 are susceptible (e.g. lepidopteran larvae). But the desert locust, *Schistocerca gregaria,* having a more acidic mid-gut content of pH 6.2-7.1

is non-susceptible as the known Bt endotoxins remain insoluble and hence inactive under such acidic conditions.

The microbial insecticides that have found widespread use against caterpillars and beetle grubs are produced from *B. thurigiensis* var. *kurstaki* under trade names such as Bactospeine, Thuricide and Dipel. Those microbials produced from *Bt* var. *israelensis* are most effective against larvae of mosquitoes and black fly; brand names are Bactimos and Teknar.

Vigorous research over recent years has yielded many new varieties of Bt which are effective against a number of different insect species. Some of the new discoveries are more than 10 times as effective as those used in traditional Bt formulations. A serious drawback of traditional Bt formulations has been their instability under field conditions; they break down quickly when exposed to ultra-violet light. By means of genetic manipulation, an ingenious solution to this problem of short persistency has been recently developed and patented under the tradename "Cellcap" (refer to box on the next page).

*Bacillus sphaericus* also produces a crystalline toxin, and several strains have proven to be effective against larvae of mosquitoes. No appearance of resistance in larvae against these toxins has as yet been observed either in the field or during laboratory tests at sub-lethal doses.

**Fungal microbial insecticides** contain parasitic fungi which are capable of penetrating the insect cuticle directly. After piercing the cuticle – often by means of enzymes that break down chitin and protein – the fungus multiplies inside the insect, producing lethal metabolites. Peak mortality normally occurs 5-10 days after application, depending on dose and insect size.

**Microbial insecticides** are formulated, for instance, with the use of the following fungi : *Beauveria bassiana, Verticillium lecanii, Entemophaga asiatica, E. grylli, Metharizium anisopliae, Zoophthora radicans.* Parastic fungi, generally, have host-specific strains and are not hazardous to non-target organisms. They are cheap to produce and may be formulated and applied in a way similar to chemical insecticides. Since these fungi broach directly through the insect cuticle, they have a contact action without having to awaitingestion by the target insects. By this property, a fungal microbial avoids a prolonged exposure to ultra-violet light, low relative humidity and other adverse climatic conditions which may inactivate it. Thus, waiting for the pest to ingest the pathogen is a critical limitation for the use of microbials based on viruses, bacteria and protozoa.

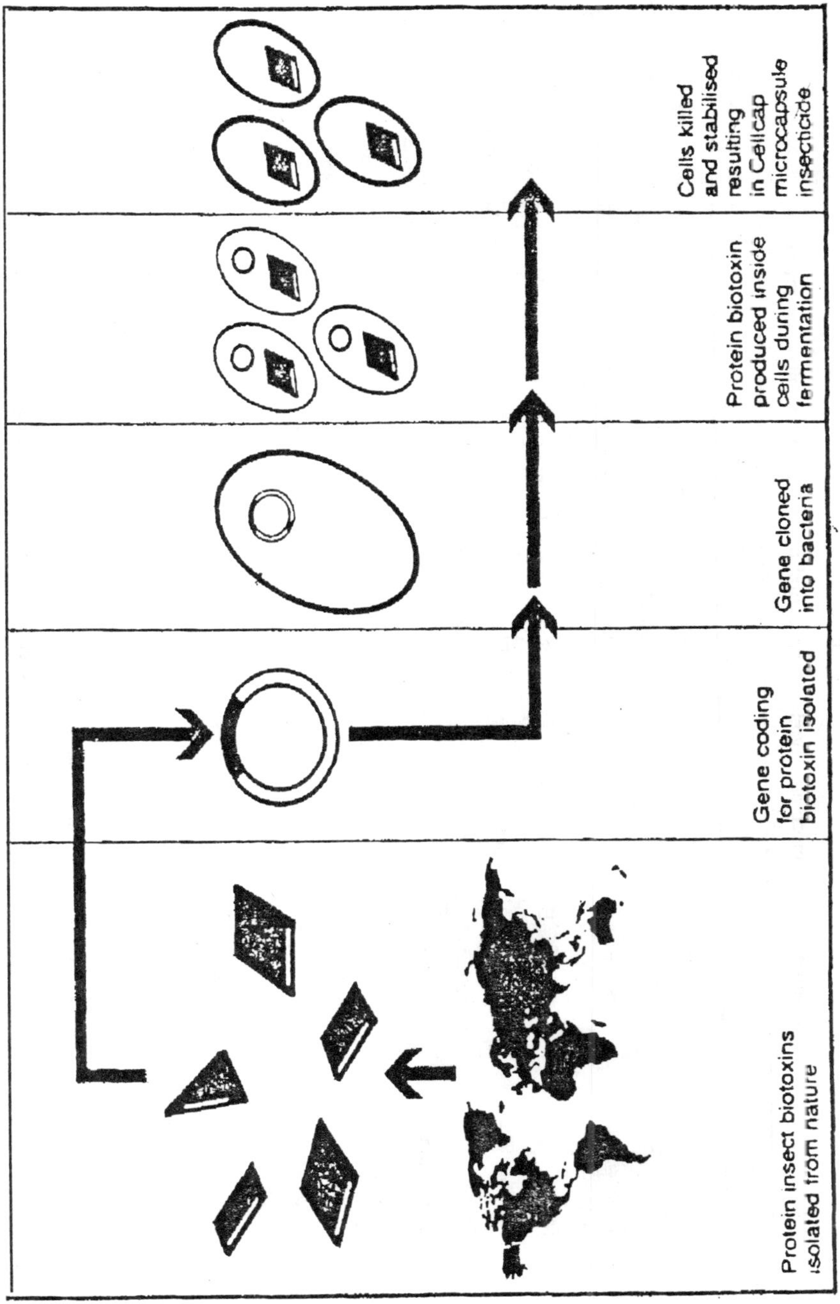
Protein insect biotoxins isolated from nature
Gene coding for protein biotoxin isolated
Gene cloned into bacteria
Protein biotoxin produced inside cells during fermentation
Cells killed and stabilised resulting in Cellcap microcapsule insecticide

**Table 2.2**

**Examples of commercially available microbial insecticides and their target pests**

| *Product* | *P1athogen* | *Target* | *Company (country)* |
|---|---|---|---|
| Dipel | Bacteria Bt *var. kurstaki* | Lepidopterous larvae | Abbot Labs. (USA) |
| MVP | Bacteria Bt *var. kurstaki* | Lepidopterous larvae | Mycogen Corp. (USA) |
| Skeetal (Denmark) | Bacteria Bt *var. israelensis* | Mosquito and blackfly larvae | Novo Bio Control |
| M-one | Bacteria Bt *var. san diego* | Colorado patato beetle | Mycogen Corp. (USA) |
| Nemasys | Nematode/bacterium | Black vine weevil | Agricultural Genetics (UK) |
| Biosafe | nematode *Steinernema* spp. | Soil insects | Biosys (USA) |
| Mamestrin | MbNPV[1] | *Heliothis* spp. | Calliope (France) |
| Spodopterin | SINPV[2] | *Spodoptera* spp. | Calliope (France) |
| Virox | NsNPV[3] | *Neodiprion sertifer* | Oxford Virology (UK) |
| Nolo bait | Protozoan : *Nosema locustae* | Rangeland grasshoppers | Evans Bio Control (USA) |
| Vertalec* | Fungus : *Erynia neoaphidis* | Aphids | Microbial Resources (UK) |
| Mycotal* | Fungus : *Verticillium lecanii* | Glasshouse whitefly | Microbial Resources (UK) |
| Development Product | Fungus : *Neozygites* | Spider mites | Ecogen (USA) |

*Notes :* [1]*Mamestra brassicae* nuclear polyhedrosis virus; [2]*S. littoralis* nuclear polyhedrosis virus; and [3]*Neodiprion sertifer* nuclear polyhedrosis virus. Product withdrawn from the market.

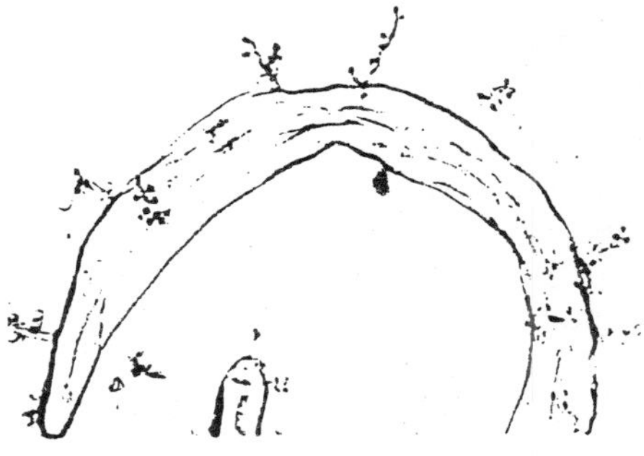

*A nematode infected with and killed by a Verticillium lccanii fungs (Photo courtesy of PD, the Netherlands)*

Close observation, however, has revealed that under adverse conditions a pathogen such as *Beauveria* will kill a target insect only if it either hits the insect directly or contacts it quickly after application, but before it is inactivated. Past attempts to induce epidemics from single applications were not successful, as the disease did not automatically increase to epidemic levels. A high relative humidity is required for the production of spores. When low humidity prevails, the disease cannot spread and a high kill would only be obtained through a highly effective initial application. Constraints which apply to pathogen use are similar to those limiting effective chemical pesticide use; formulation and application technology are critical.

Recently, it has been found that the use of oil-based fungal pathogen formulations hold much greater promise than water-based formulations that evaporate very rapidly under dry conditions. In dose-response studies on a weevil pest, *Beauveria bassiana* was over 30 times more effective by topical application when formulated in a vegetable oil. The suggested reason is that insect cuticles are lipophilic (fat-loving), so that the oil spreads out over the cuticle and penetrates into the thin membranes at the articulating surfaces of the joints, carrying the spores to the most vulnerable part of the cuticle. By contrast, water-based fungal formulations run off and the spores are lost. Thus, much interest exists in the development of oil-based fungal formulations for low and ultra-low volume application. Further examples of fungal insecticides are :

Hirsutella thompsonii, a parasitic fungus from which a spore-formulation is produced that kills the citrus rust-mite and also infects spider mites. Formulations of *Verticillium lecanii* control aphids, scales, thrips and red spider mites in greenhouse crops (see also table 2.2). Furthermore, a number of other fungi are currently being investigated to determine their potential microbial value : *e.g. nomureae* spp. and *Paecilomyces* spp.

**Viral microbial insecticides** are formulated on the basis of nuclear polyhedrosis viruses.

A virus is a sub-microscopic infectious agent existing as a nucleo-protein entity that is composed of protein and a nucleic acid, RNA or DNA. The protein surrounds, as a crystalline shell (capsid), the nucleic acid component which transfers the genetic information. Owing to their lack of organ structures, viruses are able to replicate only within the living cells of a host. Since viruses contain only DNA or RNA and lack their own metabolism, they are not recognized as being organisms.

Nuclear polyhedrosis viruses infect the destructive *Heliothis* spp. caterpillars, such as the cotton bollworm and tobacco budworm, which damage many types of crops. Nuclear polyhedrosis viruses are very specific and highly virulent and can survive for years because of their protective capsid. Following ingestion by an insect, the protein capsid dissolves in the insect's alkaline mid-gut juices. The infectious, individual, mature virus particles, the virions, permeate the gut lining and eventually enter into the bloodstream they multiply rapidly and take over control of susceptible cells. This results in the death of the insect within two to nine days, depending on the stage of development of the insect.

The baculovriuses include the group known as polyhedrosis viruses. Production of these viruses involves rearing them on living insects, which is a costly process.

**Nematodes,** which occur naturally in the soil and parasitize soil-insects, are excellent material for the formulation of microbial insecticides. Once released into the soil, they are able to disperse over short distances and they are attracted to their insect hosts. The infective juvenile stages of genera such as *Steinernema* and *Heterorhabditis* are usually ingested by the insects, but they may also enter via the anus or spiracles. From the gut of the insect they pass through the gut wall into the circulatory system, where they release bacteria. These released bacteria reproduce rapidly and cause the insect's death within one to two days.

Active nematodes need to be surrounded all the time by a water film; only some genera are able to survive drought conditions in a particular cyst-form. Thus, the use of nematodes as microbials has been mainly restricted to the soil environment, or protected habitats where they are able to survive. Above the soil surface they are easily exposed to ultra-violet light and desiccation, which prohibits their use against foliar-feeding insect pests.

*Neoplectana carpocapsae* is a nematode that acts as a vector in transmitting a pathogenic bacterium lethal to termites. Commercial microbial formulations are already on the market.

# 39

# Bio-Protection in Fields : Extracts from Novel Pesticides

Applications of biotechnology in agriculture range from genetic improvement in cash-crops to production of environmentally friendly biopesticides. Novel biopesticides are being created and tested in the laboratories around the world. Apart from trying out viruses and bacteria or even toxins and enzymes as biocontrol agents, scientists are also trying to genetically transform the plants so that they become inherently resistant to pests. On paper, the idea is simple enough. All it takes is to identify the genes endowing resistance to a particular pest in a resistant species of plant and to transfer them into the genome of the vulnerable variety. Of course, this is not as easy as it sounds.

Plants which have had a foreign gene 'stitched' into their genome are called transgenic plants. One can have 'tailored' plants to suit one's requirements. Flavour, colour, ripening and other genetically determined characteristics may be altered at will. But how do scientists ferry genes in and out of plants?

Micronjection is a method of introducing foreign DNA into plants. But as this often damages the protoplasm in the cells, this method is not very popular. Sometimes DNA is encapsulated in closed vesicles, called 'liposomes' which are then introduced into the cell. The liposomes fuse with the plasma membrane and empty their contents into the protoplasm. Electroporation has also been used to introduce foreign DNA into the cell. The process involves passing of short pulses of electric current which makes the cell membrane temporarily permeable to molecules such as DNA. Sometimes DNA is 'shot' into plant cells using what is called a 'gene gum'. Using virus as a molecular ferry to transfer genes is also an option that scientists have. The tumour inducing **plasmid** of *Agrobacterium tumefaciens* which is a circular piece of DNA has also been used by scientists to suit their purpose. However, in all fairness, it must be admitted that the integration of foreign genes into plant chromosomes during genetic manipulations occurs at very low frequencies.

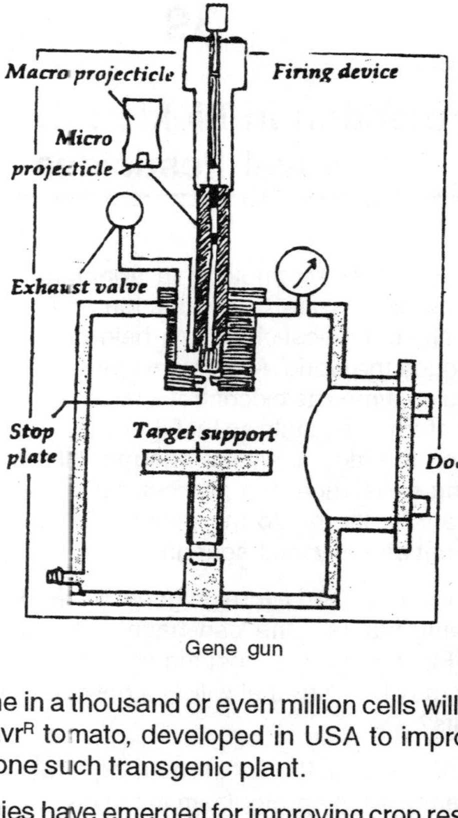


Gene gun

May be only one in a thousand or even million cells will carry the gene stably. The Flavr Savr[R] tomato, developed in USA to improve the flavour quality of tomato is one such transgenic plant.

Several strategies have emerged for improving crop resistance. These include the manipulation of resistance specially if this characteristic is governed by a single gene. Resistance that is governed by more than one gene. Resistance that is governed by more than one gene or regulatory mechanisms are of course, a bit more difficult to manipulate.

For many years it was known that BT could be useful for biological control of insects because it produced toxins against insects. Therefore, it represented a potential transgenic solution for insect control. The "pesticidal" plants are the closest transgenic application to commercialization. In China, a lot of effort is being expended to develop virus-resistant rice. Hopefully, by the turn of the century, insect resistant maize, wheat and rice will be available in the market. However, success of transgenic plants in the fields may pose the two potential problems of biosafety and destabilization of natural ecosystems. Currently the insect control market is dominated by BT toxin. BT is considered to be environmentally benign, though some insects, for example, Cotton Bollowrm are becoming resistant to its action. But there are vulnerable insects and the market remains vast.

Before introducing new chemical pesticide in agro-industry, serious thought has to be given to the projected market. This covers the costs of discovery, production, registration and of course, the product should be reasonably profitable. Normal time required from identification of a new chemical to its marketing as a pesticide is around eight years. Registration alone can cost more than $20 million. On the other hand, for biopesticides the lead time can be less than five years and the registration cost is also very little. The advantages of biopesticides therefore speak for themselves.

## Essential Characteristics of Effective Biocontrol Agents

**Speed** to enable pathogen to develop resistant structures.

**Longevity,** enough to protect plant during its vulnerable period, whatever that may be.

**Environmental tolerance,** to sustain activity under different soil and climatic conditions.

**Mode of action,** varies from pathogen to pathogen, physical contact, chemical nature of killing component.

While using natural enemies, it is important to have fast growing biocontrol organism in the fields which can eventually make the conditions unfavourable for the pathogens proliferation.

## Requirements for Commercialization

**Viable market size,** broad spectrum activity is preferable.

**Safety,** non-toxicity to plants and mammals, and no-effect on non-target species.

**Stability, minimum tow years shelf life at - 5C to + 30C.**

**High performance and consistency,** effect has to be comparable to that of chemical pesticides.

**Cost and practically,** use of cheap substrates such as agricultural waste for production, stable when dry and be easily formulated, insensitive to light and dry climate.

**Application,** should not change the present day agricultural practices.

Longer lasting stability of the biopesticide under field conditions is essential to protect crops during its vulnerable period. Spraying or irrigation time depends on the site and mode of biopesticide attack on the pathogen. Preventive approach is no good for heavily infested fields.

One of the significant factors in the success of newly developed biopesticides is the education and knowledge of the farming community about the pest and its developmental cycle.

For biochemicals such as antibiotics and hydrolytic enzymes, the storage stability is the main concern. To get licence for genetically engineered biopesticides, strict regulations are followed.

Quality control of agro-industry needs due consideration. To avoid marketing of substandard biocontrol agents, coordinated efforts are necessary by the industry and food growers. To improve the quality of the biocontrol agents many different aspects require careful attention. Quality control of the biopesticides includes stringent regulation of production standard, production facility and field performance.

Although lot of experimental evidence is available on biocontrol agents, very few of these, have actually seen the light of commercialization. Bacteria, viruses and fungi have been used as biocontrol agents in agriculture. However, the greatest impact has been made only by BT.

At present more than 13 microbial pesticide agents, have been approved and registered with the Environmental Protection Agency. These registered organisms are marketed in around 75 different products for use in agriculture, forestry and insects control.

Since 1975, co-ordinated efforts for the biocontrol of pest and weed have been made by the Indian Council of Agricultural Research and other Indian Laboratories and Universities with some success. The future therefore, does seem replete with the possibility of safe biocides at last.

# 40

# Suppliers of Plant and Equipments

## STORAGE TANKS

**Air Flow Pvt. Ltd.**
13/1090
Naiwalan, Karol Bagh
New Delhi - 110005
Tel : + 91 (0) 11 5721236
Fax : + 91 (0) 11 5752267
E-mail: airflow@del3.vsnl.net.in

**Alpha Process Vessels Pvt. Ltd.**
A-90,1st Flr., Amar city.
New Delhi-110024
Tel :+ 91 (0) 11 6427087
Fax : + 91 (0) 11 6467084

**Ark Industrial products pvt. Ltd.**
S-255, Greater kailash-II
New Delhi-110048
Tel :+ 91(0)11 6236892
Fax :+91(0)11 6236898
E-mail :
akashyap@ndb. vsnl.net.in

**Asm-Technoxi Air System Inc.**
P. O. Box 4317
New Delhi-110018
Tel :+ 91(0) 116489275

**Bays India**
1767, Nai Basti
S P Mukherjee Marg.
Delhi-110006
Tel :+91(0)11 5588796
Fax:+91(0)11 5588807
E-mail : bays @de13.Vsnl.net. in

**Bhiwadi Chemical Pvt Ltd.**
184, New Okhla Indl. Cmplx.,
Phase-I, Okhla Indl. Area
New Delhi - 110020
Tel : + 91(0) 11 6813624
Fax : + 91(0)11 6474340

**Dynamic Engineers**
C-12, yadav Ngr.
New Delhi-110042
Tel : + 91(0) 11 7214104

**Engineers Syndicate**
A-2, F.F., Ring Rd.
Rajouri Garden
New Delhi - 110027
Tel :+ 91(0) 11 5122357
Fax : + 91(0) 11 5124396
E-mail :
engrsynd@ndb.vsnl.net.in

**Garg Rototechnik**
14A/B, WEA, Karol Bagh,
New Delhi - 110005
Tel : + 91 (0) 11 5746509
Fax : + 91 (0) 11 5195721

**Indcon Boilers Ltd.**
D-170, Phase-I
Okhla Indl. Area
New Delhi - 110020
Tel : + 91 (0) 11 6811440
Fax : + 91 (0) 11 6812425
E-mail : indcon@vsnl.com

**Alfa Fluid piping Systems**
Pvt. Ltd.
E-27, Phase-VII
SIDCO Indl. Est.
Hosur, Karnataka-635109
Tel : + 91 (0) 4344 76417
Fax : + 91 (0) 4344 76417
E-mail : alfafluid@eth.net

**Arul Rubbers Pvt. Ltd.**
B-5, SIDCO Indl. Est.
Hosur, Karnataka - 635126
Tel : + 91 (0) 4344 76650
Fax :+ 91(0) 4344 77504
E-mail : aspl@bgl.vsnl.net.in

**Steelite Engg. Ltd.**
103/5, Blackle House
Opp. GPO, VT
Walchand Hirachand Marg
Mumbai, Maharashtra-400001
Tel : + 91(0) 22 2324093
Fax: + 91(0) 22 2610803
E-mail :
samir@steelitegroup.com

**Abros Enterprises**
12/8, D-1
MIDC, Chinchwad
Pune, Maharashtra - 411019
Tel : + 91(0) 20 7475687
Fax : + 91(0) 20 7470673

**Albaj Engg. Corp.**
340, Clover Centre
Moledina Rd.
Pune, Maharashtra - 411001
Tel : + 91(0) 20 631511
Fax : + 91(0) 20 6137255
E- mail : albaj@vsnl.com

**Alpha Beta Engg. Construction Pvt. Ltd.**
222, Swastik Chmbrs.
CST Rd., Chembur
Mumbai, Maharashtra-400071
Tel : + 91 (0) 22 5224527
Fax : + 91 (0) 22 5224237
E-mail: alpha.beta@lwbbs.net

**Amalgamated Industrial Composites Pvt. Ltd.**
Unit No. 111/112
Ashok Service Indl. Est.
L B S Marg
Bhandup (W)
Mumbai, Maharashtra-400078
Tel : + 91 (0) 22 5904565
Fax : + 91 (0) 22 5913611
E-mail : maheshwary@amalgamated.wiprobt.ems.vsnl.net.in

**A K Tech Engg. Works**
B-24, Sect. 10
Noida, Uttar Pradesh-201301
Tel : + 91 (0) 120 543863

**Abdul Karim & Co.**
D-21, Indl. Area, Sect. 17
Kavi Ngr.
Ghaziabad, U.P. - 201003
Tel : + 91 (0) 120 4702282

**Anand Dis-Brew Engg. Works**
5, Rajinder Ngr. Indl. Area
Mohan Ngr.
Ghaziabad, U. P. - 201007
Tel : + 91 (0) 120 4627318
Fax : + 91 (0) 120 4721508

**Ananda Fabrications (CBE) Pvt. Ltd.**
"Anand Nilayam", 70,
Bharathi Park, Rd. No. 2
S B Mission P. O.,Coimbatore,
Tamil Nadu - 641011
Tel : + 91 (0) 422 866034
Fax : + 91 (0) 422 455990

**Anandha Fabrications (Cbe) Pvt. Ltd.**
Nr. Sankara Polytechnic
Chinnavadampatti (Post)
Coimbatore,
Tamil Nadu - 641006
Tel : + 91 (0) 422 446213
Fax : + 91 (0) 422 866634
E-mail :
anandhafabrications@usa.net

**Baalu Fabrication Works**
K-15, Indl. Est., Ambattur
Chennai, Tamil Nadu-600058
Tel : + 91 (0) 44 6252685

**Campion Plastic Industries Pvt. Ltd.**
37, Postal Cly., 3rd St.
West Mambalam
Chennai, Tamil Nadu-600033
Tel : + 91 (0) 44 4853173

## COOLING TOWERS

**Delta Cooling Towers Pvt. Ltd.**
1st Flr., Bhagwati Sadan
Plot No. 8, Comm. Centre,
BH Block, Shalimar Bagh
Delhi - 110088
Tel : + 91 (0) 11 7495801
Fax : + 91 (0) 11 7495804
E-mail :
delta@deltactowers.com

**Ocean FRP Cooling Towers**
14, Flyover Complx. Mkt.
Defence Cly.
New Delhi - 110024
Tel : + 91 (0) 11 4602359
Fax : + 91 (0) 11 6228804

**Airtech Engineers**
B-93
Phase-II, Okhla Indl. Area
New Delhi - 110020
Tel : + 91 (0) 11 6912711
Fax : + 91 (0) 11 6920649
E-mail : airtek@vsnl.com

**Armec Group of Organizations**
Armec Corner, T-5, 12
Ajanara Savita Vihar Mkt.
Delhi - 110092
Tel : + 91 (0) 11 2162488
Fax : + 91 (0) 11 2158736

**Armec Cooling System Pvt. Ltd.**
208, Anilkunj
Paldi, Char Rasta
Ahmedabad, Gujarat-380006
Tel : + 91 (0) 79 6577598
Fax : + 91 (0) 79 6576716

**Artech Cooling Towers**
5021, GIDC Indl. Area
Ankleshwar, Gujarat-393002
Tel : + 91 (0) 2646 50302
Fax : + 91 (0) 2646 50302
E-mail :
udayshah99@yahoo.com

**Bhagwati Engg. Works**
102, Por, Ramangamdi
Vadodara, Gujarat-391243
Tel : + 91 (0) 265 830943
Fax : + 91 (0) 265 830665

**Cool-Tech Cooling Towers**
105 & 106, Calico Ngr.
Narol-Sarkhej Highway, Narol
Ahmedabad, Gujarat-380405
Tel : + 91 (0) 79 5716060
Fax : + 91 (0) 79 5715085
E-mail :
cooltech@wilnetonline.net.

**Cooling Tower Corp.**
40 B, GIDC,
Makarpura
Vadodara, Gujarat-390010
Tel : + 91 (0) 265 642337
Fax : + 91 (0) 265 642337
E-mail : acs_brd@yahoo.co.in

**Parag Fans & Cooling Systems Ltd.**
Plot No. 1/2B & 1B/3A
Indl. Area No. 1
A B Rd., Dewas,
Madhya Pradesh - 455001
Tel : + 91 (0) 7272 58131
Fax : + 91 (0) 7272 30273
E-mail :
paragb@bom2.vsnl.net.in

**Suony Fibre Glass (I) Pvt. Ltd.**
315-316
Manas Bhavan Extn.
RNT Marg, Indore,
Madhya Pradesh - 452001
Tel : + 91 (0) 731 519298
Fax : + 91 (0) 731 529804

**DBR Cooling Towers Pvt. Ltd.**
56, Jatin Das Rd.
Kolkata, West Bengal-700029
Tel : + 91 (0) 33 4647062
Fax : + 91 (0) 33 4662976

**Paharpur Cooling Towers Ltd.**
8/1/B
Diamond Harbour Rd.
Kolkata, West Bengal-700027
Tel : + 91 (0) 33 4792050
Fax : + 91 (0) 33 4792188
E-mail: pctccu@paharpur.com

**Blue Stars Cooling Tower**
No. 4, 1st Flr., D 1 Blk.
Mahalakshmi Apts.
Secretariet Cly. Main Rd.
Adambakkam
Chennai, Tamil Nadu - 600088
Tel : +91 (0) 44 2456865

**Cope Industries**
TS-73, SIDCO Tiny Sect.
Thiru-Vi-Ka Indl. Sect.
Ekkattuthangal
Chennai, Tamil Nadu - 600097
Tel : +91 (0) 44 2323787
E-mail : copeex@usa.net

**GEA Cooling Tower Technologies (I) Pvt. Ltd.**
443, Anna Salai
Teynampet
Chennai, Tamil Nadu - 600018
Tel : + 91 (0) 44 4326171
Fax : + 91 (0) 44 4360576
E-mail : gct@md4.vsnl.net.in

**Gem Cooling Towers Pvt. Ltd.**
SF. No. 100/A
Arasur, Coimbatore,
Tamil Nadu - 641407
Tel : + 91 (0) 422 887059
Fax : + 91 (0) 422 888247
E-mail :
gemcool@md2.vsnl.net.in

**Aqua Cooling Towers**
Rao Compound, Nr. Pneucon
B B Patil Marg, Kolshet
Thane, Maharashtra - 400607
Tel : + 91 (0) 22 5384727
Fax : + 91 (0) 22 5384727
E-mail: actamol@hotmail.com

**Blue Chip Cooling Towers Pvt. Ltd.**
123, New Sonal Indl.
Est. No. 2
Kanchpada, New Link Rd.
Malad (W), Mumbai,
Maharashtra - 400064
Tel : + 91 (0) 22 8805089
Fax : + 91 (0) 22 8805164

**Bright Engineers**
4, K A Kamal Est.,
Opp. Ruby Coach Factory
M V Rd., Marol Naka
Andheri (E), Mumbai,
Maharashtra - 400059
Tel : + 91 (0) 22 8524572
Fax : + 91 (0) 22 8501466
E-mail: bintl@bom9.vsnl.net.in

**Canara Engineers Pvt. Ltd.**
203, Hill Green, 149
Marol Maroshi Rd.
Andheri (E), Mumbai,
Maharashtra - 400059
Tel : + 91 (0) 22 8500020
Fax : + 91 (0) 22 8501704
E-mail :
canara@bom5.vsnl.net.in

**Choksi Group**
F-Bajsons Indl. Est.
Cardinal Gracious Marg
Andheri (E), Mumbai,
Maharashtra - 400099
Tel : + 91 (0) 22 8326964
Fax : + 91 (0) 22 8366598
E-mail :
choksi@choksi-india.com

## BOILERS

**L G Thermoflo Systems Pvt. Ltd.**
Ground Flr., Paigah Plaza
Basheerbagh
Hyderabad,
Andhra Pradesh - 500029
Tel : + 91 (0) 40 3240024

**LG Thermoflo Systems Pvt. Ltd.**
Ground Flr., Paigah Plaza
Basheer Bagh
Hyderabad,
Andhra Pradesh - 500029
Tel : + 91 (0) 40 3242468

**Babcock Power (Overseas Projects) Ltd.**
906-906A,
International Trade Tower
Nehru Place
New Delhi -110019
Tel : + 91 (0) 11 6446118
Fax : + 91 (0) 11 6446538
E-mail :
aniray.del@mitsuibabcock.co.in

**Bharat Heavy Electricals Ltd. Jeevan Tara Bldg.**
5, Sansad Marg
New Delhi -110001
Tel : + 91 (0) 11 3347331
Fax : + 91 (0) 11 3342769

**Crupp Metals**
Kh. No. 56/1
Mundka, Rohtak Rd.
New Delhi - 110041
Tel : + 91 (0) 11 5183085
Fax : + 91 (0) 11 5183085

**Flare Combustion Systems**
A-18, Hauz Khas
New Delhi -110016
Tel : + 91 (0) 11 6868382
Fax : + 91 (0) 11 6868382
E-mail :
flarecombustion@ic.eth.net

**NSW India Ltd.**
Plot No. 43-44, Sect. 34
EHTP
Gurgaon, Haryana - 122001
Tel : + 91 (0) 124 6371106
Fax : + 91 (0) 124 6372859
E-mail :
pnarang@del2.vsnl.net.in

**Sterling Strips Ltd.**
2/10, Meghal Service Indl. Est.
Devidayal Rd., Mulund (W)
Mumbai, Maharashtra-400080
Tel : + 91 (0) 22 5605588
Fax : + 91 (0) 22 5916496
E-mail: ssl@bom3.vsnl.net.in

**BMT Industrial Machines Ltd.**
15-16-17
Neelkanth Shopping Arcade,
1st Flr.
Nr. Vijaya Bank, R C Marg
Chembur
Mumbai, Maharashtra-400071
Tel : + 91 (0) 22 5288035
Fax : + 91 (0) 22 5281136
E-mail: bmt@bom2.vsnl.net.in

**Chhatrapati Engg. Ltd.**
Chatrapati House, 128/1B
Paud Rd.
Pune, Maharashtra - 411029
Tel : + 91 (0) 20 339388
Fax : + 91 (0) 20 331939

**Forbes Marshall Ltd.**
Bombay-Pune Rd.
P.O. Box 29
Kasarwadi
Pune, Maharashtra - 411034
Tel : + 91 (0) 20 7145595
Fax : + 91 (0) 20 7147413

**Bharat Heavy Electricals Ltd.**
Fossil Boilers, Tiruchirapalli,
Tamil Nadu - 620014
Tel : + 91 (0) 431 520713
Fax : + 91 (0) 431 520642
E-mail: aksrajan@bheltry.co.in
www.utilityboiler.com

**Bharat Heavy Electricals Ltd.**
Industrial Power Products
Tiruchirapalli,
Tamil Nadu - 620114
Tel : + 91 (0) 431 520215
Fax : + 91 (0) 431 520233
E-mail: siva@bheltry.co.in

**ISGEC John Thompson**
A-4, Sec. 24
Noida, Uttar Pradesh - 201301
Tel : + 91 (0) 120 4524072
Fax : + 91 (0) 120 4551686
E-mail : ijtsales@isgec.com

**Saraswati Industrial Syndicate Ltd.**
A-4, Sect. 24
Noida, Uttar Pradesh - 201301
Tel : + 91 (0) 120 4524071
Fax : + 91 (0) 120 4542072
E-mail: exports@isgec.com

**Heiza Boilers (I) Pvt. Ltd.**
P-7, Grahams Land
Kolkata, West Bengal-700040
Tel : + 91 (0) 33 4711526
Fax : + 91 (0) 33 4711526

## MIXERS

**Base Industries**
Plot No. 138-B, IDA
Mallapur, Hyderabad,
Andhra Pradesh - 501507
Tel : + 91 (0) 40 7823073
Fax : + 91 (0) 40 7823073
E-mail :
enfabs@hd1.vsnl.net.in

**Coppral Agencies**
7-1-246/2, Balkampet
Hyderabad,
Andhra Pradesh - 500016
Tel : + 91 (0) 40 3730549

**Jogindra Engg. Works**
70, Rama Rd.
New Delhi -110015
Tel : + 91 (0) 11 5442112
Fax : + 91 (0) 11 5453836
E-mail :
jogindra@ndf.vsnl.net.in

**Karamson Engg. Corp.**
3/24, Kirti Ngr. Indl. Area
New Delhi -110015
Tel : + 91 (0) 11 5417621
Fax : + 91 (0) 11 5433577
E-mail: kencor@usa.net

**Rank & Co.**
A-95/3, Wazirpur Indl. Est.
Delhi -110052
Tel : + 91 (0) 11 7456101
Fax : + 91 (0) 11 7234126
E-mail :
vkmrank@del3.vsnl.net.in

**Sukriti Engineers Pvt. Ltd.**
55, Phase-I, DSIDC
Okhla Indl. Area
New Delhi -110020
Tel : + 91 (0) 11 6817546
Fax : + 91 (0) 11 6821812

**Gems Engg. Works**
7/B, Gujarat Laghu Udyog
Vikas Mandal,
Dudheshwar Rd., Dhobighat
Ahmedabad, Gujarat-380004
Tel : + 91 (0) 79 5622594
Fax : + 91 (0) 79 6423061

**Hind Pulverizer Works**
B-3/2, Ambica Indl. Est.
Nagarvel Hanuman Rd.
Sukhramnagar
Ahmedabad, Gujarat-380023
Tel : + 91 (0) 79 2747451
Fax : + 91 (0) 79 2747451

**Kevin Engg. Pvt. Ltd.**
A/1/3706, GIDC, Phase-IV
Vatva Indl. Area
Ahmedabad, Gujarat-382445
Tel : + 91 (0) 79 5891503
Fax : + 91 (0) 79 5894243
E-mail : info@kevinindia.com

**Adam Fabriwerk Pvt. Ltd.**
203, Rajguru Apts.
New Nagardas Rd.
Andheri (E), Mumbai,
Maharashtra - 400069
Tel : + 91 (0) 22 8380548
Fax : + 91 (0) 22 8390195
E-mail: adamfab@vsnl.com

**Dipesh Engg. Works**
3, Sheroo Villa, 87, J P Rd.
Andheri (W), Mumbai,
Maharashtra-400053
Tel : + 91 (0) 22 6336729
Fax : + 91 (0) 22 6315507
E-mail :
kjpatel_71@hotmail.com

**Argus Industrial Equipment Pvt. Ltd.**
K-19, Ambattur Indl. Est.
Chennai,
Tamil Nadu - 600058
Tel : + 91 (0) 44 6251668
Fax : + 91 (0) 44 6250226

**Iyappan Engg. Industries Pvt. Ltd.**
107-A, SIDCO Indl. Est.
Ambattur, Chennai,
Tamil Nadu - 600098
Tel : + 91 (0) 44 6252073
Fax : + 91 (0) 44 6250192
E-mail : iyappan@vsnl.com

**Pugazh Industries**
39, 2nd Main Rd.
Indl. Est., Chennai,
Tamil Nadu - 600058
Tel : + 91 (0) 44 6251909
Fax : + 91 (0) 44 6248372
E-mail :
pugazh@md4.vsnl.net.in

**Advance Equipment**
B-18, Sect.7
Noida,
Uttar Pradesh - 201301
Tel : + 91 (0) 120 4545560
Fax : + 91 (0) 120 4535160
E-mail: meera@del3.vsnl.net.in

**Sathe Engg. Company Pvt. Ltd.**
E-198/199
Kavinagar Indl. Area
Ghaziabad,
Uttar Pradesh - 201002
Tel : + 91 (0) 120 4700252
Fax : + 91 (0) 120 4700316
E-mail : sathe@del3.vsnl.net.in

## STEEL TANKS STAINLESS

**Anil Chemical Equipments**
Plot A-18, IDA, Rd. No. 18
Nacharam, Hyderabad, Andhra Pradesh - 500076
Tel : + 91 (0) 40 7175230
Fax : + 91 (0) 40 7175230

**GEI Godavari Engg. Ltd.**
Mumbai National Highway 9
Patancheru, Medak,
Andhra Pradesh - 502319
Tel : + 91 (0) 8455 42715
Fax : + 91 (0) 8455 42692
E-mail :
godavari@hd2.vsnl.net.in

**Industrial Construction Co.**
A 115, Vikas Marg
Shakarpur
Delhi - 110092
Tel : + 91 (0) 11 2231497
Fax : + 91 (0) 11 2231497

**Maharaja Casting**
Plot No. 86A/2, Gali No. 8
Anand Parbat Indl. Area
New Delhi - 110005
Tel : + 91 (0) 11 5731276
Fax : + 91 (0) 11 5437988
E-mail : maharajanap@delhi-industry.com

**Satwant Tanks & Vessels**
C-186, Phase-I
Naraina Indl. Area
New Delhi - 110028
Tel : + 91 (0) 11 5794729
Fax : + 91 (0) 11 5466565

**Vishkarma Machine Tools**
A-6, Phase-II
Mayapuri Indl. Area
New Delhi - 110064
Tel : + 91 (0) 11 5402815
Fax : + 91 (0) 11 5132815

**Aero Engineers**
Plot No. 3419
Phase-IV, GIDC
Vatva, Gujarat-382445
Tel : + 91 (0) 79 5831556
Fax : + 91 (0) 79 5891041
E-mail : aero@icenet.net

**Annapurna Trollies Pvt. Ltd.**
312, Anandmangal-II
C G Rd., Navrangpura
Ahmedabad, Gujarat - 380014
Tel : + 91 (0) 79 6462389
Fax : + 91 (0) 79 6462389
E-mail: jet_2000in@yahoo.com

**HDO Process Equipment & Systems Ltd.**
5/1/2, GIDC
Vatva, Gujarat-382445
Tel : + 91 (0) 79 5830591
Fax : + 91 (0) 79 5833286
E-mail: patfilt@ad1.vsnl.net.in

**Round-Tech Engg. Co.**
24, Madhuram Park,
Nr. Gauri Cinema,
National Highway Rd.
Odhav, Gujarat - 382415
Tel : + 91 (0) 79 2875989
Fax : + 91 (0) 79 2875989
E-mail: roundtech@yahoo.com

**The Indian Sugar & General**
Engg. Corp. Pressure Vessel
Divn.Yamuna Nagar,
Haryana -135001
Tel : + 91 (0) 1734 51700
Fax : + 91 (0) 1734 51495
E-mail: pvd_sales@isgec.com

**Vee Aar Fabricators**
464-465
Phase-III, Udyog Vihar
Gurgaon, Haryana-122016
Tel : + 91 (0) 124 6342846

**Bora Bros. Industries**
76-79-A
Indl. Area, Govindpura
Bhopal,
Madhya Pradesh - 462023
Tel : + 91 (0) 755 586112
Fax : + 91 (0) 755 586378
E-mail :
vijay_bora@hotmail.com

**Engg. Craft Industries**
33-B, Sect. H, Indl. Area
Govindpura, Bhopal
Madhya Pradesh - 462023
Tel : + 91 (0) 755 784130

**Machine Well**
16-C, `Dalal Sadan'
Madhuiban
Udaipur, Rajasthan - 313001
Tel : + 91 (0) 294 529970

**AKS Engg. Co.**
468, SIDCO Indl. Est.
Ambattur, Chennai,
Tamil Nadu - 600098
Tel : + 91 (0) 44 6250052
Fax : + 91 (0) 44 6258618

**Ananda Fabrications (CBE) Pvt. Ltd.**
"Anand Nilayam", 70,
Bharathi Park, Rd. No. 2
S B Mission P. O.
Coimbatore,
Tamil Nadu - 641011
Tel : + 91 (0) 422 866034
Fax : + 91 (0) 422 455990

**Indian Commerce & Industries Company Ltd.**
Beehive Bldg., 57 (Old 29)
Prakasam Rd.
Chennai, Tamil Nadu - 600108
Tel : + 91 (0) 44 5231477
Fax: + 91 (0) 44 5228833
E-mail: beehive@earthling.net

**Sri Ram Fab**
11/2, Thadagam Rd.
Edayarpalayam Post
Coimbatore,
Tamil Nadu - 641025
Tel : + 91 (0) 422 400078

## LABORATORY EQUIPMENTS & SUPPLIERS

**Intel Systems**
5-234/2
H P Rd., Moosapet
Hyderabad,
Andhra Pradesh - 500018
Tel : + 91 (0) 40 3711379
Fax : + 91 (0) 40 3713567
E-mail :
intelarch@mantraonline.com

**Thermal Instruments & Equipments**
2-1-478, St. No. 7
Nallakunta, Hyderabad,
Andhra Pradesh - 500044
Tel : + 91 (0) 40 7667645

**Accumax India**
C-5A/184, Janak Puri
New Delhi - 110058
Tel : + 91 (0) 11 5501092

**Avante Global Services**
225, Prakash Mohalla
East of Kailash
New Delhi - 110065
Tel : + 91 (0) 11 6233259
Fax : + 91 (0) 11 6443097
E-mail : avante@vsnl.com

**J Mitra & Company Ltd.**
A-180, Phase-I
Okhla Indl. Area
New Delh - 110020
Tel : + 91 (0) 11 6818971
Fax : + 91 (0) 11 6818970
E-mail : jml@del2.vsnl.net.in

**Mittal Enterprises**
2151, T-7C
New Patel Ngr.
New Delhi - 110008
Tel : + 91 (0) 11 5702784
Fax : + 91 (0) 11 5408375
E-mail :
mittalenterprises@vsnl.com

**Globe Scientific Glass Industries**
B/h Amar Ice Factory
Nr. Chhani Jakat Naka
BEI Compound
Vadodara, Gujarat - 390002
Tel : + 91 (0) 265 773131
Fax : + 91 (0) 265 773625

**Inox India Ltd.**
4th Flr., ABS Towers
Old Padra Rd.
Vadodara, Gujarat - 390007
Tel : + 91 (0) 265 343125
Fax : + 91 (0) 265 333398
E-mail : inox@inoxindia.com

**Hemraj Enterprises**
227, Sonal Link Est.
Bldg. No. 2, Link Rd.
Malad (W), Mumbai,
Maharashtra - 400064
Tel : + 91 (0) 22 8628727
Fax : + 91 (0) 22 8628727
E-mail:
sales@hemrajindia.com

**Pathak Electrical Works**
208 & 214
Bhola Bhagwan Indl. Est.
I B Patel Rd.
Goregaon (E), Mumbai,
Maharashtra - 400063
Tel : + 91 (0) 22 8733209
Fax : + 91 (0) 22 8749162
E-mail: pthk@vsnl.com

**Eastern Instruments**
Mercantile Bldg., 3rd Flr.
C-Block, 9/12
Lal Bazar St.
Kolkata, West Bengal-700001
Tel : + 91 (0) 33 2435219
Fax : + 91 (0) 33 2481653
E-mail :
easterninstruments@yahoo.com

**Hardson S D & Co.**
106B, Raja Dinendra St.
Kolkata, West Bengal-700004
Tel : + 91 (0) 33 5545366
Fax : + 91 (0) 33 5545366
E-mail:
sdhardson@hotmail.com

## DISTILLATION COLUMMS & TOWERS

**Base Industries**
Plot No. 138-B,
IDA, Mallapur
Hyderabad,
Andhra Pradesh - 501507
Tel : + 91 (0) 40 7823073
Fax : + 91 (0) 40 7823073
E-mail : enfabs@hd1.vsnl.net.in

**Dhopeshwar Chem-Tech Group**
A-16, Co-op. Indl. Est.
Balanagar, Hyderabad,
Andhra Pradesh - 500037
Tel : + 91 (0) 40 3771579
Fax : + 91 (0) 40 3772450
E-mail :
dhopesh@hd2.dot.net.in

**Dhopeshwar Engg. Pvt. Ltd.**
A-16, CIE, Balanagar
Hyderabad,
Andhra Pradesh - 500037
Tel : + 91 (0) 40 3771579
Fax : + 91 (0) 40 3772450
E-mail :
dhopesh@hd2.dot.net.in

**Ablaze Glass Works Pvt. Ltd.**
E/52-2
Sardar Indl. Est., Ajwa Rd.
Vadodara, Gujarat - 390019
Tel : + 91 (0) 265 561241
Fax : + 91 (0) 265 564341
E-mail: ablaze@satyam.net.in

**Atin Industries**
C 1/4412, Phase-IV
GIDC, Vatva
Ahmedabad,
Gujarat - 382445
Tel : + 91 (0) 79 5830714

**Cadam Enterprise A Zydus Group Co.**
3708/B, Phase-IV,
GIDC, Vatva
Ahmedabad,
Gujarat-382445
Tel : + 91 (0) 79 5891824
Fax : + 91 (0) 79 5834923

**Amir Tanks & Vessels Pvt. Ltd.**
84-85-B, Sect. F
Sanwer Rd.
Indore,
Madhya Pradesh - 452015
Tel : + 91 (0) 731 422849
Fax : + 91 (0) 731 422936
E-mail :
nadkarni@sancharnet.in

**Febchem Engg. Works**
A/2, Sect. A, Indl. Area
Sanwer Rd.
Indore,
Madhya Pradesh - 452015
Tel : + 91 (0) 731 720467
Fax : + 91 (0) 731 723087

**Indian Sugar & General Company Ltd.**
Yamuna Nagar,
Haryana - 135001
Tel : + 91 (0) 1732 51700
Fax : + 91 (0) 1732 50250
E-mail : isgec@ch1.dot.net.in

**Jain Scientific Glass Works**
2580/29
B/h S D Public School
Gian Marg, Ambala Cantt.,
Haryana - 133001
Tel : + 91 (0) 171 643090
Fax : + 91 (0) 171 643246
E-mail : jsgw@sancharnet.in

**The Indian Sugar & General Engg. Corp. Foundry Divn.**
Yamuna Nagar,
Haryana - 135001
Tel : + 91 (0) 1732 51700
Fax : + 91 (0) 1732 51495
E-mail: pvd_sales@isgec.com

## BLENDER : CHEMICAL

**Base Industries**
Plot No. 138-B
IDA, Mallapur
Hyderabad,
Andhra Pradesh - 501507
Tel : + 91 (0) 40 7823073
Fax : + 91 (0) 40 7823073
E-mail :
enfabs@hd1.vsnl.net.in

**Coppral Agencies**
7-1-246/2, Balkampet
Hyderabad,
Andhra Pradesh - 500016
Tel : + 91 (0) 40 3730549

**Jogindra Engg. Works**
70, Rama Rd.
New Delhi -110015

Tel : + 91 (0) 11 5442112
Fax : + 91 (0) 11 5453836
E-mail :
jogindra@ndf.vsnl.net.in

**Karamson Engg. Corp.**
3/24, Kirti Ngr. Indl. Area
New Delhi - 110015
Tel : + 91 (0) 11 5417621
Fax : + 91 (0) 11 5433577
E-mail : kencor@usa.net

**Kevin Engg. Pvt. Ltd.**
A/1/3706
GIDC, Phase-IV
Vatva Indl. Area
Ahmedabad, Gujarat - 382445
Tel : + 91 (0) 79 5891503
Fax : + 91 (0) 79 5894243
E-mail : info@kevinindia.com

**Navyug Industries**
C-1/363, GIDC Est.
Odhav, Gujarat - 382415
Tel : + 91 (0) 79 2871945
Fax : + 91 (0) 79 2871959
E-mail:
navyug@wilnetonline.net

**Molly Enterprises**
Major Indl. Est., Ollur
Trichur, Kerala-680306
Tel : + 91 (0) 487 352446

**Standard Engineers**
3rd Flr., Sharda Sadan
Opp. Gunbow St.,
Fire Brigade, 11,
S A Brelvi Rd., Mumbai,
Maharashtra - 400001
Tel : + 91 (0) 22 2614419
Fax : + 91 (0) 22 2626152

**Sterling Equipments Pvt. Ltd.**
A-141, H Block, MIDC
Pimpri
Pune, Maharashtra - 411018
Tel : + 91 (0) 20 770308
Fax : + 91 (0) 20 774241
E-mail :
ramnad@satyam.net.in

**Argus Industrial Equipment Pvt. Ltd.**
K-19, Ambattur Indl. Est.
Chennai, Tamil Nadu - 600058
Tel : + 91 (0) 44 6251668
Fax : + 91 (0) 44 6250226

**Iyappan Engg. Industries Pvt. Ltd.**
107-A, SIDCO Indl. Est.
Ambattur
Chennai, Tamil Nadu - 600098
Tel : + 91 (0) 44 6252073
Fax : + 91 (0) 44 6250192
E-mail : iyappan@vsnl.com

**Advance Equipment**
B-18, Sect.7
Noida, Uttar Pradesh - 201301
Tel : + 91 (0) 120 4545560
Fax : + 91 (0) 120 4535160
E-mail :
meera@del3.vsnl.net.in

**Sathe Engg. Company Pvt. Ltd.**
E-198/199
Kavinagar Indl. Area
Ghaziabad,
Uttar Pradesh - 201002
Tel : + 91 (0) 120 4700252
Fax : + 91 (0) 120 4700316
E-mail : sathe@del3.vsnl.net.in

**Neomachine Mfg. Company Pvt. Ltd.**
39/2A, Purna Das Rd.
Kolkata, West Bengal - 700029
Tel : + 91 (0) 33 4644568
Fax : + 91 (0) 33 4647254
E-mail :
neocota@satyam.net.in

**Precision Balance (I)**
6, Wood St.
Kolkata, West Bengal-700016
Tel : + 91 (0) 33 2403476
Fax : + 91 (0) 33 2400168

## GRINDERS

**Dharam Engg. Works**
A-142
Wazirpur Indl. Area
New Delhi -110052
Tel : + 91 (0) 11 7418645

**Indian Machine Tools**
B-163, DDA Shed, Phase-I
Okhla Indl. Area

New Delhi -110020
Tel : + 91 (0) 11 6817999
Fax : + 91 (0) 11 6818378
E-mail :
imtindia@del3.vsnl.net.in

**Consortech Tools (I) Ltd.**
308, Patil Plaza
Mitra Mandal Corner
Pune, Maharashtra-411009
Tel : + 91 (0) 20 4002414
Fax : + 91 (0) 20 4443838
E-mail :
constech@pn2.vsnl.net.in

**Alex Machine Tools**
8, Gaiwadi Indl. Est., S V Rd.
Goregaon (W), Mumbai,
Maharashtra - 400062
Tel : + 91 (0) 22 8743744
Fax : + 91 (0) 22 8757319
E-mail: amt@vsnl.com

**Elgi Equipments Ltd.**
Trichy Rd., Singanallur
Coimbatore,
Tamil Nadu - 641005
Tel : + 91 (0) 422 574691
Fax: + 91 (0) 422 573697
E-mail : export@elgi.jet.co.in

**Vimal Trading Co.**
181, Bharathiar Rd.
P N Palayam
Coimbatore,
Tamil Nadu - 641037
Tel : + 91 (0) 422 214364

**Parishudh Machines Pvt. Ltd.**
C-26, Indl. Area
Meerut Rd., Ghaziabad,
Uttar Pradesh - 201003
Tel : + 91 (0) 120 4712268
Fax : + 91 (0) 120 4714111
E-mail : goindi@vsnl.com

**SRB Machines Pvt. Ltd.**
59/2/1, Site-IV
Indl. Area, Sahibabad,
Uttar Pradesh - 201010
Tel : + 91 (0) 120 4771540
Fax : + 91 (0) 120 4774748
E-mail :
srbmachines@satyam.net.in

## DRYER CHEMICAL

**Enfab Industries Pvt. Ltd.**
C-2, Shanthi Niwas
Mettuguda
Secunderabad,
Andhra Pradesh - 500017
Tel : + 91 (0) 40 7824343
Fax : + 91 (0) 40 7830010
E-mail :
enfabs@hd1.vsnl.net.in

**Bry-Air (Asia) Pvt. Ltd.**
20, Rajpur Rd.
Delhi -110054
Tel : + 91 (0) 11 3912800
Fax : + 91 (0) 11 3915127
E-mail :
enquire@pahwa.com www.
bryair.com

**Malik Chemi Process Pvt. Ltd.**
D-37, Kirti Ngr.
New Delhi -110015
Tel : + 91 (0) 11 5195892
Fax : + 91 (0) 11 5195892
E-mail :
mcppldd@nde.vsnl.net.in

**Smid Engg. Co.**
25-A, Rama Park Bus Stop,
Nr. Medicine Factory
Uttam Ngr.
New Delhi -110059
Tel : + 91 (0) 11 5649063
Fax : + 91 (0) 11 5635908

**Acmefil Engg. Systems Pvt. Ltd.**
93/D, Aspha Mill Compound
Opp. Mardia Steel, Phase-I
GIDC, Vatva,
Gujarat - 382445
Tel : + 91 (0) 79 5893294
Fax : + 91 (0) 79 5893294
E-mail : acmefil@icenet.net

**Febchem Engg. Works**
A/2, Sect. A, Indl. Area
Sanwer Rd.
Indore,
Madhya Pradesh - 452015
Tel : + 91 (0) 731 720467
Fax : + 91 (0) 731 723087

**Pharmaceutical Machinery Manufacturing Works**
47/B, Laxmibai Ngr.
Indore,
Madhya Pradesh - 452006
Tel : + 91 (0) 731 410963
Fax : + 91 (0) 731 410071
E-mail :
pharmamach@satyam.net.in

**Dipesh Engg. Works**
3, Sheroo Villa
87, J P Rd., Andheri (W)
Mumbai, Maharashtra - 400053
Tel : + 91 (0) 22 6336729
Fax : + 91 (0) 22 6315507
E-mail :
kjpatel_71@hotmail.com

**Arrowhead Seperation Engg. Pvt. Ltd.**
159(0), Amar Brass Compound
S G Barve Marg, Vidya Nagari
Kalina, Mumbai,
Maharashtra - 400098
Tel : + 91 (0) 22 6526495
Fax : + 91 (0) 22 6528385

**Bectochem Engineers**
5C/204
Sanjay Bldg. Mittal Indl. Est.
Andheri (E), Mumbai,
Maharashtra-400059
Tel : + 91 (0) 22 8500008
Fax : + 91 (0) 22 8506785
E-mail: bectochem@vsnl.com

**Pratish Driers & Chemicals**
C/o Jay Deep Enterprises,
Room No. 36, 2nd Flr., 5/1
Clive Row
Kolkata, West Bengal - 700001
Tel : + 91 (0) 33 2204726
Fax : + 91 (0) 33 2205935

# 41

# Suppliers of Raw Materials

**NAPHTHALENE**

**Porwal Tar Products Pvt. Ltd.**
200/C, Indl. Area Sect.-C
Urla, Raipur,
Madhya Pradesh - 493221
Tel : + 91 (0) 771 324031
Fax : + 91 (0) 771 526687

**Central Chemicals Industries**
12, Kopal Wadi, M.G. Rd.
Ghatkopar (W), Mumbai,
Maharashtra-400086
Tel : + 91 (0) 22 5118585
Fax : + 91 (0) 22 5162843

**Himadri Chemicals & Industries**
23-A, 8th Flr., Room No. 15
N S Rd.
Kolkata, West Bengal - 700001
Tel : + 91 (0) 33 2209953
Fax : + 91 (0) 33 2209051
E-mail : hil@vsnl.com

**Kanoi Chemicals Ltd.**
8th Flr., Suryarath
Nr. White House
Panchvati
Ahmedabad, Gujarat-380006
Tel : + 91 (0) 79 6421833
Fax : + 91 (0) 79 6569627
E-mail :
ahmkanoindia@wilnetinline.net

**Natraj Chemicals**
Plot No. C1/24
Phase 4, GIDC Est.
Vapi, Gujarat - 396195
Tel : +91 (0) 260 22174

**Swastik Laboratory & Indl. Chemicals Pvt. Ltd.**
217, Phule Baug
Sadashiv Peth
Pune, Maharashtra-411030
Tel : + 91 (0) 20 4331140

**Sabari Aromatics Pvt. Ltd.**
Plot No. 2303
Sub Post Office, GIDC Est.
Ankleshwar, Gujarat - 393002
Tel : + 91 (0) 2646 50253
Fax : + 91 (0) 2646 50353

**Sodium Metal Pvt. Ltd.**
Plot No. 21, GIDC Est.
Nandesari, Gujarat-391340
Tel : + 91 (0) 265 840241
Fax : + 91 (0) 265 840893
E-mail: smfinechem@vsnl.com

**Synthetic Drugs & Intermediates**
Plot No. 6503, GIDC Est.
Ankleshwar, Gujarat-393002
Tel : + 91 (0) 2646 51406
Fax : + 91 (0) 2646 336567

**PARAFFIN WAX**

**D K Traders**
C-198, Phase-II
Mayapuri Indl. Area
New Delhi -110064
Tel : + 91 (0) 11 5400331
Fax : + 91 (0) 11 5786602

**Bahubali Chemical Industries**
No. 4, "The Emperor", 1st Flr.
Fatehgunj Main Rd.
Vadodara, Gujarat - 390002
Tel : + 91 (0) 265 791449
Fax : + 91 (0) 265 793607
E-mail :
nikunjchem@satyam.net.in

**Gujarat Microwax Ltd.**
6th Flr., Motilal Centre
Ashram Rd.
Ahmedabad, Gujarat - 380009
Tel : + 91 (0) 79 6582944
Fax : + 91 (0) 79 6581316
E-mail : gppl@ad1.vsnl.net.in

**Gujarat Parachlor Pvt. Ltd.**
6th Flr., Motilal Centre
Ashram Rd.
Ahmedabad, Gujarat - 380009
Tel : + 91 (0) 79 6585033
Fax : + 91 (0) 79 6581316
E-mail : gppl@ad1.vsnl.net.in

**Associated Petrochem Pvt. Ltd.**
49-6 Km
Delhi - Rohtak Rd.
Sampla, Haryana-124501
Tel : + 91 (0) 12626 7019003
Fax : + 91 (0) 12626 7022591
E-mail :
thymolindia@hotmail.com

**Alka Chemical Industries**
B/6, Sidhpura Indl. Est.
LBS Marg, Ghatkopar (W)
Mumbai, Maharashtra-400086
Tel : + 91 (0) 22 5008875
Fax : + 91 (0) 22 5008646
E-mail : aci@bom5.vsnl.net.in

**Devi Organics Pvt. Ltd.**
65, Atlanta, Nariman Point
Mumbai, Maharashtra-400021
Tel : + 91 (0) 22 2825200
Fax : + 91 (0) 22 2872796
E-mail: rishi@bom2.vsnl.net.in

**Indian Wax Industries**
14-16, Bhandari St.,3
Mahavir Dharshan
Mumbai, Maharashtra-400003
Tel : + 91 (0) 22 3422673
Fax : + 91 (0) 22 3448412
E-mail : indianwax@vsnl.com

**Pals Petrochem**
109, Nainiappa Naicken St.
Chennai, Tamil Nadu-600003
Tel : + 91 (0) 44 5355623

## BENZOIC ACID

**Canton Laboratories**
110-B, GIDC Est.
Makarpura
Vadodara, Gujarat - 390010
Tel : + 91 (0) 265 643119
Fax : + 91 (0) 265 643515
E-mail :
canton@wilnetonline.net

**Citron Organics Ltd.**
17, Dwarakadish Chmbrs.
Kevada Baug
Vadodara, Gujarat-390001
Tel : + 91 (0) 265 433286
Fax : + 91 (0) 265 438665

**Gayatri Minerals & Chemicals**
34-A, Shastrinagar,
Nizampura
Vadodara, Gujarat-390002
Tel : + 91 (0) 265 781284
Fax : + 91 (0) 265 780228
E-mail :
info@gayatrionline.com

**Gujarat Organic Chemicals**
Plot No. 32, GIDC
Vithal Udyognagar,
Gujarat - 388121
Tel : + 91 (0) 2692 36205
Fax : + 91 (0) 2692 36446

**Indiana Chem-Port**
349, GIDC Est.
Makarpura
Vadodara, Gujarat-390010
Tel : + 91 (0) 265 642067
Fax : + 91 (0) 265 644717
E-mail:
indiana@wilnetonline.net

**Medilux Laboratories Pvt. Ltd.**
201, B C Chmbrs., 47
Jaora Compound
Indore,
Madhya Pradesh - 452001
Tel : + 91 (0) 731 702891
Fax : + 91 (0) 731 463188
E-mail :
medilux@bom4.vsnl.net.in

**Benzo Organics (I) Pvt. Ltd.**
1421, Marker Chmbr.
Nariman Point
Mumbai, Maharashtra-400021
Tel : + 91 (0) 22 2821664
Fax : + 91 (0) 22 2871476

**Ganesh Benzoplast Ltd.**
Ganesh House, Marol
Andheri (E)
Mumbai, Maharashtra-400059
Tel : + 91 (0) 22 8382096
Fax : + 91 (0) 22 8391529

**Daurala Sugar Works A Divn. of DCM Shriram Industries**
Kanchenjunga Bldg.,18
Barakhamba Rd.
New Delhi - 110001
Tel : + 91 (0) 11 3324580
Fax : + 91 (0) 11 3315424
E-mail :
chemicalsud@dcmsr.com

**Sabari Aromatics Pvt. Ltd.**
Plot No. 2303
Sub Post Office, GIDC Est.
Ankleshwar, Gujarat-393002
Tel : + 91 (0) 2646 50253
Fax : + 91 (0) 2646 50353

**Sabari Chemicals Pvt. Ltd.**
A/2, 236, GIDC, Tagore Ngr.
Nandesari, Gujarat - 391340
Tel : + 91 (0) 265 840429
Fax : + 91 (0) 265 840143
E-mail :
sabari_chemicals@hotmail.com

**Natasha International**
4-Bunglow, 162
Park St., Andheri (W)
Mumbai, Maharashtra-400053
Tel : + 91 (0) 22 6313195
Fax : + 91 (0) 22 6311395
E-mail : ninte@roltanet.com

**Pankaj Aero Chemicals Pvt. Ltd.**
203, Himalaya House, 79
Palton Rd., Fort
Mumbai, Maharashtra-400001
Tel : + 91 (0) 22 2619182
Fax : + 91 (0) 22 2611580
E-mail : hemani@vsnl.com

**Plasti Pigments Pvt. Ltd.**
401, Sai Chmbrs., 367
Narsi Natha St.
Mumbai, Maharashtra-400009
Tel : + 91 (0) 22 3437890
Fax : + 91 (0) 22 3424780
E-mail :
plastic.pig@hotmail.com

**Roma Chemicals**
Mehjabeen Arcade, No. 305
Chakla St. Cross Lane
Opp. Patel Roadways
Masjid (W), Mumbai,
Maharashtra - 400003
Tel : + 91 (0) 22 3441013
Fax : + 91 (0) 22 3448273
E-mail : romachem@vsnl.com

**Subhash Chemical Industries**
Shed W-2, S-Block, MIDC
Bhosari
Pune, Maharashtra - 411026
Tel : + 91 (0) 20 7120632
Fax: + 91 (0) 20 7122554

**Tapan Chemicals**
402, Ramnivas-A
G B Indulkar Rd.
Vile Parle (E), Mumbai,
Maharashtra - 400057
Tel : + 91 (0) 22 8252616
Fax : + 91 (0) 22 8345159
E-mail :
sales@tapanchemicals.com

**Ujwal Pharma Pvt. Ltd.**
1421, Maker Chmbrs. V, 221
Nariman Point
Mumbai, Maharashtra-400021
Tel : + 91 (0) 22 2040232
Fax : + 91 (0) 22 2871476

**Daurala Sugar Works A Divn. of DCM Shriram Industries**
Kanchenjunga Bldg., 18
Barakhamba Rd.
New Delhi -110001
Tel : + 91 (0) 11 3324580
Fax : + 91 (0) 11 3315424
E-mail:
chemicalsud@dcmsr.com

## FUNGICIDES

**Makam Agrochem Pvt, Ltd.**
A-280, 2nd stage
6th Main Rd., Peenya Indl.Est.
Bangalore, karnataka-560058
Tel : + 91 (0) 80 8360178
Fax : + 91(0) 80 8360824
E-mail : makam@vsnl.com

**S S Crop Care Ltd.**
10,Indl. Area Govindpura
Bhopal,
Madhya Pradesh-462023
Tel : + 91 (0)755 586826
Fax : + 91(0)755 588571
E-mail :
sscc@sscropcare.com

**Cee sulfons Ltd.**
B/7, Rajratan Apts.
Service Rd., Jogeswari ( E)
Mumbai, Maharashtra- 400060
Tel : + 91 (0) 22 8377186
Fax : + 91(0) 22 8202283

**Cheminava**
Bandra (E), Mumbai,
Maharashtra - 400051
Tel : + 91 (0) 22 6542209
Fax : + 91(0) 22 6542655

**Excel Industries Ltd.**
184-87
Swami Vivekanand Rd.
Jogeshwari (W) Mumbai,
Maharashrta - 400102
Tel : + 91 (0) 22 6788258
Fax : + 91(0) 22 6783657
Email :
excelmumbai@excelind.com

**Heranba Industries Ltd.**
101, Kanchanganga Bldg.
Factory Lane, Borivali (w)
Mumbai, Maharashtra-400092
Tel : + 91 (0) 22 8987912
Fax : + 91(0) 22 8993948
Email :
heranba@bom4.vsnl.net.in

**Indofill Chemicals Company A Divn. Of Modipon Ltd.**
Nirlon House
Dr. Annie Besant Rd.,worli
Mumbai, Maharashtra-400025
Tel :+ 91 (0) 22 4937391
Fax :+91(0)22 4937073
Email :
indofill@ giasbmo.1 vsnl.net.in

**Rallis India Ltd.**
Ralli House, P.O. Box 166, 21
D S Marg, Mumbai,
Maharashtra - 400001
Tel : + 91 (0) 2078221
Fax : + 91 (0) 2077755
Email : rallis@tata.com

**RPG Life Sciences Ltd. Formerly Searie (1) Ltd.**
21, D S Marg
Mumbai, Maharashtra-400001
Tel : + 91 (0) 22 2077731
Fax : + 91(0) 22 2077202

**Western Agro & Hygiene Chemicals Pvt Ltd.**
75, Moty st., Fort
Mumbai, Maharashtra-400001
Tel : + 91 (0) 22 2611174

**Coromandel Indag Products India Ltd.**
62, Spur Tank Rd.
Chetput
Chennai, Tamil Nadu-600031
Tel : + 91 (0) 44 8227908
Fax : + 91(0) 44 8227908

**Fungicides (I) Ltd.**
H-88, Vidya palace, Ist Flr.
New Delhi - 110049
Tel : + 91 (0) 11 4626551
Fax : + 91 (0) 11 4633874
E-mail :
fungicid@del2.vsnl.net.in.

## ETHYL ALCOHOL

**Sir Shadi Lal Enterprises Ltd.**
4-A, Hansalaya, 15
Barakhamba Rd.
New Delhi -110001
Tel : + 91 (0) 11 3316409
Fax : + 91(0) 11 3722193

**Yeast Alco Enzymes Ltd.**
1st Flr., Divya Apts.
Nr. Mithakhali Underbridge
Navrangpura
Ahmedabad, Gujrat - 380009
Tel : + 91 (0) 79 6563265
Fax : + 91(0) 79 6569203

**Mojj Engg.Systems Ltd.**
81-B/15,MIDC
Bhosari
Pune, Maharashtra - 411026
Tel : + 91 (0) 20 7120330
Fax : + 91 (0) 20 7122836
E-mail : mojjpune@ip.eth.net

**Dharamsi Morarji Chemical Company Ltd.**
317/21, 3rd flr., prospect
Chmbrs., Dr. D N Rd.
Mumbai, Maharashtra-400001
Tel : + 91 (0) 22 2048881
Fax : + 91 (0) 22 2843230
E-mail :
dharamsi@bom2.vsnl.net.in.

**Highland International**
61, Panvel Indl, Est.
Panvel, Maharashtra-410206
Tel : + 91 (0) 21546 7503682
Fax : + 91 (0) 21546 6481356
E-mail : pigment@vsnl.com

**Mangalam Drugs & Organics Ltd.**
2nd Flr., 292,Nr. Flyover
Pricess St.
Mumbai, Maharashtra-400002
Tel : + 91 (0) 22 2087968
Fax : + 91(0) 22 2087074
E-mail :
mangalam_drugs@vsnl.com

**Moraya Global Pvt Ltd.**
Plot A-42
Marol Indl. Area (MIDC)
St.No.2, Andheri (E)
Mumbai, Maharashtra- 400093
Tel : + 91 (0) 22 8375234
Fax : + 91(0) 22 8364491
E-mail : ffc@vsnl.com

Sarigon Organics Ltd.
60, Balaji Villa, Green Garden
Acharyangar, W T Patil Rd.
Govandi
Mumbai, Maharashtra-400088
Tel : + 91 (0) 22 5511814
Fax : + 91 (0) 22 8364491
E-mail :
sarigon@bom3.vsnl.net.in

**Somaiya Group**
Warden House, 3rd Flr.
Sir P M Rd., Fort
Mumbai, Maharashtra-400001
Tel : + 91 (0) 22 2884635
Fax : + 91(0) 22 2884636
E-mail :
mokashi@somaiya.com

**Somaiya Organics (I) Ltd. A Somaiya Group Co.**
Agra Bldg., 2nd Flr., 121
Mahatma Gandhi Rd.
Mumbai, Maharashtra-400023
Tel : + 91 (0) 22 2673780
Fax : + 91 (0) 22 2673264

**Somaiya Organo-Chemicals Ltd.**
Fazalbhoy Bldg., 45-47
M G Rd., Fort
Mumbai, Maharashtra-400023
Tel : + 91 (0) 22 2048272
Fax : + 91 (0) 22 2047297

**Srinivas Chemicals Industries Pvt. Ltd.**
201-203, Arjun Centre
B S D Marg, Deonar
Mumbai, Maharashtra-400088
Tel : + 91 (0) 22 5512545
Fax : + 91 (0) 22 5561723
E-mail :
scipl@bom5.vsnl.net.in

**The Somaiya Group of Industries**
Fazalbhoy Bldg., 45-47
M G Rd., Fort
Mumbai, Maharashtra-400001
Tel : + 91 (0) 22 2048272
Fax : + 91 (0) 22 2047297

**Va-Sudha Chemicals Pvt. Ltd.**
5th Flr., Sai Ashish 'A'
B R Rd., Mulund (W)
Mumbai, Maharashtra-400080
Tel : + 91 (0) 22 5684382
Fax : + 91 (0) 22 5643680
E-mail :
vasudha@bom3.vsnl.net.in

**Govardhan Spinners Pvt. Ltd.**
No. 12, Bharani Cly.
Saligramam
Chennai, Tamil Nadu-600093
Tel : + 91 (0) 44 4834494
Fax : + 91 (0) 44 4836998

**IFB Agro Industries Ltd.**
Plot No. 5, Sect. I
East Calcutta Township
Kolkata, West Bengal-700078
Tel : + 91 (0) 33 4781503
Fax : + 91 (0) 33 4787339

## DISTILLED - WATER

**Sukla Enterprises**
214, E Rd., Sonary (W) Layout, Sonary
Jamshedpur, Bihar-831011
Tel : + 91 (0) 657 228518

**Ashoka Pure Chemicals**
A-93/15-18
Wazirpur Indl. Area
Delhi - 110052
Tel : + 91 (0) 11 7222444

**Tanha Laboratories**
A-31, Dahima Ngr
Dandi Rd., Rander
Surat, Gujarat - 395005
Tel : + 91 (0) 261 685764

**Kalpus Distillery Works**
13/-, BGT Rd.
Nr. Mico Adugodi Post
Bangalore, Karnataka-560030
Tel + 91 (0) 80 2239676

**Accurate Minerals**
9/10, Adi House
Opp. Portuguese Church
Gokhale Rd. (N), Dadar (W)
Mumbai, Maharashtra-400028
Tel : + 91 (0) 22 4371408
Fax : + 91 (0) 22 4312475

**United Industries**
325 Nana Peth
Pune, Maharashtra-411002
Tel : + 91 (0) 20 653782

**The Modern Distilled Water & Acid Supply Co.**
5-36/221/B
Prashanthi Ngr., Kukatpally
Hyderabad,
Andhra Pradesh - 500037
Tel : + 91 (0) 40 3077531

## FRAGRANCES

**Aerol Formulations Pvt. Ltd.**
201, Shivam House
Karampura Comml. Cmplx.
New Delhi - 110015
Tel : + 91 (0) 11 5433375
Fax : + 91 (0) 11 5459768
E-mail :
headoffice@aerotech.wipro.net.in

**Bhaion Ki Dukan**
899, Chowk Qutab Rd.
Sadar Bazar
Delhi - 110006
Tel : + 91 (0) 11 3624700
Fax : + 91 (0) 11 3624706
E-mail : sandy74@id.eth.net

**Delta Exports India**
293, Dhanmill Rd.
Chattarpur Pahadi
New Delhi - 110030
Tel : + 91 (0) 11 6800561
Fax : + 91 (0) 11 6800384
E-mail : info@deltaexports.com

**Denour Speciality Chemicals**
703, Vishal Tower
District Centre, Janakpuri
New Delhi - 110058
Tel : + 91 (0) 11 5531619
Fax : + 91 (0) 11 5599125

**Star Aromatics**
1/2360, Shanti Bldg.
Ram Ngr., Mandoli Rd.
Shahdara, Delhi - 110032
Tel : + 91 (0) 11 211170

**Atul Ltd. Member of the Lalbhai Group**
P.O. Atul
Atul, Gujarat-396020
Tel : + 91 (0) 2632 330261
Fax : + 91 (0) 2632 330241

**Chemical Centre**
1631, 2nd Flr., Sewka's Wadi
Nr. Sadhna School, Khadia
Ahmedabad, Gujarat-380001
Tel : + 91 (0) 79 6741913

**Mittal Perfumery Industries**
2, Aerodrome Rd.
Chatrapati Ngr.
Indore,
Madhya Pradesh - 452002
Tel : + 91 (0) 731 411377

**Omkar Fine Organics Pvt. Ltd.**
23/2, Mangalam Rd., Villianur
Commune, Uruvaiyar
Pondicherry - 605110
Tel : + 91 (0) 413 666429
Fax : + 91 (0) 413 666305
E-mail :
omkar@md2.vsnl.net.in

**Khandari Beverages Pvt. Ltd.**
177 F, Indl. Area I
Chandigarh, Punjab-160002
Tel : + 91 (0) 172 650152

**Aar Aar Enterprises**
9, Sapphire, Chheda Ngr.
Chembur,
Mumbai, Maharashtra-400089
Tel : + 91 (0) 22 5286697
Fax : + 91 (0) 22 5283897
E-mail :
aaraar@bom4.vsnl.net.in

**Acme Synthetic Chemicals**
308, Veer Savarkar Marg
Dadar,
Mumbai, Maharashtra-400028
Tel : + 91 (0) 22 4465127
Fax : + 91 (0) 22 4440282
E-mail: acmechem@vsnl.com

**Akshay Oils**
Kanchannagar, Nakshtrawadi
Paithan Rd., Aurangabad,
Maharashtra - 431002
Tel : + 91 (0) 240 337803
Fax : + 91 (0) 240 354842
E-mail: novitdn@vsnl.com

**Asian Chemical Works**
"Asian House", 29
Off Andheri-Kurla Rd.
Ramkrishna Mandir Rd.
Andheri (E), Mumbai,
Maharashtra - 400059
Tel : + 91 (0) 22 8343491
Fax : + 91 (0) 22 8380164

**Attar Mohd. Afaque & Sons**
2nd Flr., 267, Nagdevi St.
Mumbai, Maharashtra-400003
Tel : + 91 (0) 22 3400458
Fax : + 91 (0) 22 3415596
E-mail : afague@vsnl.in

**Astrra Chemicals**
11, Moores Rd.
Moores Garden
Chennai, Tamil Nadu - 600006
Tel : +91 (0) 44 8273947
Fax : +91 (0) 44 8235838
E-mail: astrra@md3.vsnl.net.in

**Attar Mohd. Dawood & Bros.(Madras)**
A-13 & 14
Madras Export Processing Zone
Chennai, Tamil Nadu-600045
Tel : + 91 (0) 44 2368102
Fax : + 91 (0) 44 2368125
E-mail :
attarmoh@md4.vsnl.net.in

**Dev Chemicals**
Siddhi Sadan
Tiraha Tubewell Cly.
Moradabad, U. P. -244001
Tel : + 91 (0) 591 417531
Fax : + 91 (0) 591 417530

**Fragona International**
11/9, Selimpur Rd.
Dhakuria
Kolkata, West Bengal-700031
Tel : + 91 (0) 33 4127992
Fax : + 91 (0) 33 4733282
E-mail : fragona@vsnl.com

## CASTOR OILS

**TGV Group**
6-2-1012, TGV Towers
Khairthabad, Hyderabad,
Andhra Pradesh - 500004
Tel : + 91 (0) 40 3313841

**India Vitamins Ltd.**
107/108, Chenoy Trade Centre
Parklane, Secunderabad,
Andhra Pradesh - 500003
Tel : + 91 (0) 40 7844986
Fax : + 91 (0) 40 7844999

**Aditi Global Enterprise**
27, New Jagnath Plot
Rajkot, Gujarat - 360001
Tel : + 91 (0) 281 443057
Fax : + 91 (0) 281 450558
E-mail :
aditibhatt@netscape.net

**Bahubali Chemical Industries**
No. 4, "The Emperor", 1st Flr.
Fatehgunj Main Rd.
Vadodara, Gujarat-390002
Tel : + 91 (0) 265 791449
Fax : + 91 (0) 265 793607
E-mail :
nikunjchem@satyam.net.in

**Acme Synthetic Chemicals**
308, Veer Savarkar Marg
Dadar, Mumbai,
Maharashtra - 400028
Tel : + 91 (0) 22 4465127
Fax : + 91 (0) 22 4440282
E-mail: acmechem@vsnl.com

**Bhavnagar Oil & Chemical Industries Pvt. Ltd.**
414, Rewa Chmbrs.
Sir Vithaldas
Thackersey Marg
New Marine Lines
Mumbai, Maharashtra-400020
Tel : + 91 (0) 22 2054045
Fax : + 91 (0) 22 2065605
E-mail :
mitco@bom5.vsnl.net.in

**Raj Agro Mills Ltd.**
Nr. Civil Airport
V.P.O. Pawa, G T Rd.
Ludhiana, Punjab - 141020
Tel : + 91 (0) 161 844423
Fax : + 91 (0) 161 844811
E-mail : raml@del3.vsnl.net.in

**Rahul Industries**
E-96, MIA, Phase-II
Basni
Jodhpur, Rajasthan-342005
Tel : + 91 (0) 291 742564
Fax : + 91 (0) 291 742491

**Shri Ram Oils & Chemical Industries**
Plot No. C-62, Rd. No. 1C
Vishwakarma Indl. Area
Jaipur, Rajasthan - 302013
Tel : + 91 (0) 141 332504

**Progressive Producers Corp.**
Merchantile Bldg., 2nd Flr.
B Block, 9, Lal Bazar St.
Kolkata, West Bengal-700001
Tel : + 91 (0) 33 2202976

## CREOSOTE

**STP Ltd.**
STP House, Plot No. 570
Phase-V, Udyog Vihar
Gurgaon, Haryana - 122016
Tel : + 91 (0) 124 343204
Fax : + 91 (0) 124 343206
E-mail : udyog@del.stp.co.in

**Porwal Tar Products Pvt. Ltd.**
200/C, Indl. Area Sect -C
Urla, Raipur,
Madhya Pradesh - 493221
Tel : + 91 (0) 771 324031
Fax : + 91 (0) 771 526687

**Himadri Chemicals & Industries**
23-A, 8th Flr., Room No. 15
N S Rd.
Kolkata, West Bengal-700001
Tel : + 91 (0) 33 2209953
Fax : + 91 (0) 33 2209051
E-mail : hil@vsnl.com

**S K Tarchem Development Company Pvt. Ltd.**
113, 6th Flr., Park St.
Kolkata, West Bengal-700016
Tel : + 91 (0) 33 2293084
Fax : + 91 (0) 33 2295292

## LINSEED OIL

**Eastern Tar Pvt. Ltd.**
41, Circuit House Area (N-W)
Jamshedpur, Bihar-831011
Tel : + 91 (0) 657 426669
Fax : + 91 (0) 657 310666

**Haritha Chem India**
15, Sellaperumal St.
Kossapalayam, Pondicherry,
Pondicherry - 605013
Tel : + 91 (0) 413 225380

**Punjab Alkalies & Chemicals Ltd.**
SCO-125-127
P.O. Box 152, Sect. 17-B
Chandigarh, Punjab-160017
Tel : + 91 (0) 172 703645
Fax : + 91 (0) 172 704797

**Chemfab Alkalies Ltd.**
Temple Tower, 4th Flr., 476
Anna Salai
Chennai, Tamil Nadu-600035
Tel : + 91 (0) 44 4330449
Fax : + 91 (0) 44 4344104
E-mail : colmktg@vsnl.com

**Chemicals India**
SIDCO Indl. Est., 93D/E
Menam Bedu Rd.
Nr. Devon Machine Plant-II
Ambattur
Chennai, Tamil Nadu-600098
Tel : + 91 (0) 44 5351434
Fax : + 91 (0) 44 5354914

**Balrampur Chini Mills Ltd.**
"FMC Fortuna",
234/13A, 2nd Flr.
A J C Bose Rd.
Kolkata, West Bengal-700020
Tel : + 91 (0) 33 2474749
Fax : + 91 (0) 33 2403083

**Durgapur Chemicals Ltd.**
6, Little Russel St.
Kolkata, West Bengal-700001
Tel : + 91 (0) 33 2471556
Fax : + 91 (0) 33 2400340

**Bilt Chemicals Ltd.**
31/A, Sarojini Devi Rd.
Secunderabad,
Andhra Pradesh - 500003
Tel : + 91 (0) 40 7805231
Fax : + 91 (0) 40 7707717
E-mail :
info@biltchemicals.com

**Padma Agencies**
2-4-41, M G Rd.
Secunderabad,
Andhra Pradesh - 500003
Tel : + 91 (0) 40 7848018
Fax : + 91 (0) 40 7844943

## CASEIN

**Classik Casein**
178/10, Chandreshwar
Bhavan, Sion Main Rd.
Sion (W), Mumbai,
Maharashtra - 400022
Tel : + 91 (0) 22 4071318
Fax : + 91 (0) 22 4092718

**Indus Chemie**
174, Samarat Bhavan
R. No. 3, Gujarat Society
Sion (W), Mumbai,
Maharashtra - 400022
Tel : + 91 (0) 22 4071318
Fax : + 91 (0) 22 4092718
E-mail :
classikcasein@hotmail.com

## BORAX

**Sisco Research Labs Pvt. Ltd.**
2F, `C' Wing
FC Satam Indl. Est.
Dr. Cardinal Gracious Rd.,
Chakala, Andheri (E)
Mumbai, Maharashtra-400099
Tel : + 91 (0) 22 8203882
Fax : + 91 (0) 22 8380998
E-mail: srl@bom3.vsnl.net.in

**Indo Borax & Chemicals Ltd.**
5-A/113, Mittal Indl. Est.
M V Rd.,
Andheri (E), Mumbai,
Maharashtra - 400059
Tel : + 91 (0) 22 8504012
Fax : + 91 (0) 22 8504493
E-mail :
indoborax@hotmail.com

**Haritha Chem India**
15, Sellaperumal St.
Kossapalayam, Pondicherry,
Pondicherry - 605013
Tel : + 91 (0) 413 225380

**Ram Agro Chemical Industries Ltd.**
196/6, Govindappa Naick
St. Parrys
Chennai, Tamil Nadu-600001
Tel : + 91 (0) 44 5248913
Fax : + 91 (0) 44 5323095

**Allipo Chemicals**
49, GIDC
Makarpura
Vadodara, Gujarat-390010
Tel : + 91 (0) 265 642908
Fax : + 91 (0) 265 642708
E-mail : allipo@satyam.net.in

**Indiana Chem-Port**
349, GIDC Est.
Makarpura
Vadodara, Gujarat-390010
Tel : + 91 (0) 265 642067
Fax : + 91 (0) 265 644717
E-mail :
indiana@wilnetonline.net

## ROSIN

**India Rosin Industries**
F-18, Sipcot Indl. Cmplx.
Gummidipoondi,
Tamil Nadu - 601201
Tel : + 91 (0) 4119 22156
Fax : + 91 (0) 4119 5240339

**Dujodwala Products Ltd.**
812/813, Tulsiani Chmbrs., 212
Nariman Point
Mumbai, Maharashtra-400021
Tel : + 91 (0) 22 2824089
Fax : + 91 (0) 22 2841284
E-mail :
power@bom3.vsnl.net.in

# 42

# Packing Materials

## GLASS BOTTLES

**Ahlcon Parenterals (I) Ltd.**
3rd Flr., 4,
Comm. Centre
Saket, New Delhi - 110017
Tel : + 91 (0) 11 6514262
Fax : + 91 (0) 11 6852036
E-mail : ahlcon@gndel.global net.ems.vsnl.net.in

**Haryan Sheet**
HSG House
D-3, Prashant Vihar
New Delhi - 110085
Tel : + 91 (0) 11 7860621
Fax : + 91 (0) 11 7876993

**Haryana Sheet Glass Ltd.**
F-24, D B Gupta Mkt.
Karol Bagh
New Delhi - 110005
Tel : + 91 (0) 11 7778437
Fax : + 91 (0) 11 3550913

**Owens Brockway (I) Ltd.**
Thapar House, 1st Flr.
Western Wing
Janpath Lane, 124, Janpath
New Delhi - 110001
Tel : + 91 (0) 11 3342611
Fax : + 91 (0) 11 3367981
E-mail:
hariom_sharma@aci.com

**Bhagwati Glass Containers Ltd.**
338, Spectrum 1
Nr. Relief Cinema
Ahmedabad, Gujarat-380001
Tel : + 91 (0) 79 5501386

**K-Jhil Scientific Glass**
Plot No. 198/2
Opp. Vapi Paper Mill, GIDC
Vapi, Gujarat-396195
Tel : + 91 (0) 260 421442
Fax : + 91 (0) 260 421442
E-mail: info@k-jhil.com

**United Glass Bottle Manufacturing Co. Ltd.**
Avalahalli's Anajanapura Post
Bangalore, Karnataka-560062
Tel : + 91 (0) 80 642335
Fax : + 91 (0) 80 6654979

**Victory Glass & Industries Ltd.**
205, 2nd Flr., Midford Hse.
(off M G Rd.)
Midford Gardens
Bangalore, Karnataka-560001
Tel : + 91 (0) 80 5589475
Fax : + 91 (0) 80 5584064
E-mail:
vgil.glass@gems.vsnl.net.in

**Magnum Glass Works**
G-289, Main Avenue
Panampilly Ngr.
Kochi, Kerala-682036
Tel : + 91 (0) 484 321116
Fax : + 91 (0) 484 319273
E-mail:
magnum@magnumglass.com

**East India Glass**
Bottle House, Shanker Ngr.
Raipur,
Madhya Pradesh - 492007
Tel : + 91 (0) 771 424289

**Oberoi Glass Industries**
Vill Chherikhedi
P.O. Mandir Hasod
Raipur,
Madhya Pradesh - 492002
Tel : + 91 (0) 771 426289
Fax : + 91 (0) 771 425524

**Bharat Glass Works**
Tilak Ngr., Chembur
Mumbai, Maharashtra-400089
Tel : + 91 (0) 22 5521870
Fax : + 91 (0) 22 5527171

**Excel Glasses Ltd.**
Parijat House, 2nd Flr.
1076, Dr. E Moses Rd., Worli
Mumbai, Maharashtra-400018
Tel : + 91 (0) 22 4933050
Fax : + 91 (0) 22 4937743

**Glass Ventures Pvt. Ltd.**
Shed No. 3/A
Parekh Ngr., S V Rd.
Kandivli (W)
Mumbai, Maharashtra-400067
Tel : + 91 (0) 22 8053582
Fax : + 91 (0) 22 8019719

**Haldyn Glass Ltd.**
Off Western Express Highway
Goregaon(E)
Mumbai, Maharashtra-400063
Tel : + 91 (0) 22 8730311
Fax : + 91 (0) 22 8735231
E-mail:
vintar@giasbm01.vsnl.net.in

**Krishna Glass Ltd.**
P.O. Box 16, S V Rd.
Majiwada
Thane, Maharashtra-400607
Tel : + 91 (0) 22 5342418

**Paisa Fund Glass Works**
Talegaon Dabhade
Pune, Maharashtra-410507
Tel : + 91 (0) 2114 23685
Fax : + 91 (0) 2114 23685
E-mail:
paisafund@hotmail.com

**Pragati Glass Works Ltd.**
C/309, Raj Deep
Opp. Sheetal Cinema
L B S Marg, Kurla (W)
Mumbai, Maharashtra-400070
Tel : + 91 (0) 22 5164922
Fax : + 91 (0) 22 5153677

**R G Glass Industries**
244, Maulana Azad Rd. (N)
Nagpada
Mumbai, Maharashtra-400008
Tel : + 91 (0) 22 3086984
Fax : + 91 (0) 22 3010223
E-mail:
rgglass@bom5.vsnl.net.in

**Star Glass Works**
299, Kurla Andheri Rd.
Jari Mari

Mumbai, Maharashtra-400072
Tel : + 91 (0) 22 8511211
Fax : + 91 (0) 22 8511686

**Shree Durga Glass Ltd.**
PO Barang
Cuttack, Orissa-754005
Tel : + 91 (0) 671 440049
Fax : + 91 (0) 671 401199

**Mohan Crystal Glass Works**
Mohan Ngr., Ghaziabad,
Uttar Pradesh - 201007
Tel : + 91 (0) 120 732502
Fax : + 91 (0) 120 734704

**Universal Glass**
Plot No. 17, Site IV
Indl. Area,Sahibabad,
Uttar Pradesh - 201010
Tel : + 91 (0) 120 770911
Fax : + 91 (0) 120 770124

**Andhra Glass Factory**
51-12-12-C3, Bellary Rd.
Karnool,
Andhra Pradesh - 518003
Tel : + 91 (0) 8518 21086
Fax : + 91 (0) 8518 21700

**Ashok Enamel & Glass Works Pvt. Ltd.**
1st Flr., 34 A, Metcalfe St.
Kolkata, West Bengal-700013
Tel : + 91 (0) 33 2362513
Fax : + 91 (0) 33 2155063
E-mail:
manju@giascl01.vsnl.net.in

**B D J Glass Industries Pvt. Ltd.**
1, Palace Court, Lift No.2,
1st Flr., KYD St.
Kolkata, West Bengal-700016
Tel : + 91 (0) 33 2296566
Fax : + 91 (0) 33 2172838

**BDJ Glass Industries Pvt. Ltd.**
34 A, 1st Flr., Metcalfe St.
Kolkata, West Bengal-700013
Tel : + 91 (0) 33 2362513
Fax : + 91 (0) 33 2155063
E-mail: sales@ashoke.com

**Hindustan Sanitaryware & Industries Ltd.**
2, Red Cross Place
Kolkata, West Bengal-700001
Tel : + 91 (0) 33 2487406
Fax : + 91 (0) 33 2487045

**Hindusthan National Glass & Indutries Ltd.**
2, Red Cross Place
Kolkata, West Bengal-700001
Tel : + 91 (0) 33 2482341
Fax : + 91 (0) 33 2482367
E-mail: hngi@cal.vsnl.net.in

**Labott Pvt. Ltd.**
Lakar Bldg.
Arithang Rd.
Gangtok, West Bengal-737101
Tel : + 91 (0) 3592 22963

**Saraf Glass Pvt. Ltd.**
P-23/24, Radha Bazar St.
Kolkata, West Bengal-700001
Tel : + 91 (0) 33 2429515

## ALUMINUM CONTAINERS

**Almin Extrusion**
876/1, GIDC Est.
Makarpura
Vadodara, Gujarat-390010
Tel : + 91 (0) 265 643441
Fax : + 91 (0) 265 642043

**Karti Extrusion & Colours Pvt. Ltd.**
Plot No. 244/25
GIDC Est.
Umbergaon, Gujarat - 396171
Tel : + 91 (0) 26354 63818

**Minimax Metals Pvt. Ltd.**
Hanuman Gate, Jagadhri
Yamuna Nagar,
Haryana - 135001
Tel : + 91 (0) 1732 43404
Fax : + 91 (0) 1732 43403
E-mail :
minimaxmetals@vsnl.com

**Drawcans Pvt. Ltd.**
16, 8.5 KM
Bannerghatta Rd.
Bangalore, Karnataka-560076
Tel : + 91 (0) 80 6581203
Fax : + 91 (0) 80 3461204
E-mail :
drawcans@satyam.net.in

**Gloria Extrusions Pvt. Ltd.**
C-71 & 72
KSSIDC Indl. Est.
Hosur Rd., Veerasandra
Bangalore, Karnataka-562158
Tel : + 91 (0) 80 8422397
Fax : + 91 (0) 80 3303191
E-mail : ahok@blr.vsnl.net.in

**Klas Engg. Pvt. Ltd.**
No. 22, BSK Stage-II
Indl. Layout
Bangalore, Karnataka-560070
Tel : + 91 (0) 80 6630692
Fax : + 91 (0) 80 6642420
E-mail : info@klaseng.com

**Prithvi Fabrications Pvt. Ltd.**
189, 11th Main, 2nd Cross
Phase-III, Peenya Indl. Area
Bangalore, Karnataka-560058
Tel : + 91 (0) 80 3355431
Fax : + 91 (0) 80 3355431
E-mail : pfpl@vsnl.com

**Shiba Containers Pvt. Ltd.**
8-30, KSSIDC Indl. Est.
Yelahanka
Bangalore, Karnataka-560084
Tel : + 91 (0) 80 8460330
E-mail : shiba@quillnet.net

**Super Tech Industries**
No. 3/2/2, 1st Cross
M C Rd. Extn., Vijayanagar
Bangalore, Karnataka-560079
Fax : + 91 (0) 80 3386485

**Vijaya Seamless Containers Pvt. Ltd.**
189, Indl. Area, Peenya
Bangalore, Karnataka-560058
Tel : + 91 (0) 80 8395203
Fax : + 91 (0) 80 3305138
E-mail :
drawcans@satyam.net.in

**Al-Can Exports Pvt. Ltd.**
Sheetal Indl. Est.
Kashmira Rd., Bhayander (E)
Thane, Maharashtra-401105
Tel : + 91 (0) 22 8193122

**Cosmos Containers**
41, Panchratna Bldg.
Opp. Rly. Stn., Bhayandar (E)
Thane, Maharashtra - 401105
Tel : + 91 (0) 22 8195410
Fax : + 91 (0) 22 8191630
E-mail :
cosmoscontainers@rediffmail.com

**K K Cans & Allied Products Pvt. Ltd.**
B-5, MIDC Area, Ajanta Rd.
Jalgaon, Maharashtra-425003
Tel : + 91 (0) 257 210750
Fax : + 91 (0) 257 210950
E-mail : kkcans@vsnl.com

**Premier Spares Pvt. Ltd.**
C-48, MIDC Indl. Est.
Hingna
Nagpur, Maharashtra-440028
Tel : + 91 (0) 712 523797
Fax : + 91 (0) 712 526069
E-mail :
engg@premierindia.com

**Sales Win Containers Pvt. Ltd.**
S-25, MIDC, Bhosari
Pune, Maharashtra-411026
Tel : + 91 (0) 20 7122137

**Deccan Container & Metal Pvt. Ltd.**
1-A/1, Sidco Indl. Est.
Ambattur
Chennai, Tamil Nadu-600098
Tel : + 91 (0) 44 6253682
Fax : +91 (0) 44 6257138

**Nikata Containers Pvt. Ltd.**
3, 4th Flr., Gokul Arcade, No. 2, Sardar Patel Rd., Adyar
Chennai, Tamil Nadu-600020
Tel : + 91 (0) 44 4917977
Fax : + 91 (0) 44 7917948

**Vijaya Seamless Containers Pvt. Ltd.**
189, Indl. Area, Peenya
Bangalore, Karnataka-560058
Tel : + 91 (0) 80 8395203
Fax : + 91 (0) 80 3305138
E-mail :
drawcans@satyam.net.in

**P Gopal Chettiar Rolling Works**
1033, T H Rd., Kaladipet
Chennai, Tamil Nadu-600019
Tel : + 91 (0) 44 5950209
Fax : + 91 (0) 44 5953718

**Sterling Containers Pvt. Ltd.**
C-87/4, Sect. 4
Noida, Uttar Pradesh-201301
Tel : + 91 (0) 120 4520381

**Bottle Closures**
L-26, Katedan
Hyderabad,
Andhra Pradesh - 500077
Tel : + 91 (0) 40 4015514

**High Finish Technologies**
Opp. IDPL Project, 6/25
Balanagar, Hyderabad, Andhra Pradesh - 500037
Tel : + 91 (0) 40 3770260
Fax : + 91 (0) 40 3773613

**Impact Metals Ltd.**
Plot No. 7, Sunrise Apts.
Naveen Ngr.
Hyderabad,
Andhra Pradesh - 500004
Tel : + 91 (0) 40 3399501
Fax : + 91 (0) 40 3399054
E-mail : rama@hd1.vsnl.net.in

**SEC Industries Pvt. Ltd.**
Opp. IDPL Project
Balanagar, Hyderabad, Andhra Pradesh - 500037
Tel : + 91 (0) 40 3770260
Fax : + 91 (0) 40 3773613
E-mail :
secind@secglobemail1.com

**Sri Venkataratna Metals Pvt. Ltd.**
Flat No.401, Satya Sai Apts.
Srinivasa Ngr. Cly. (E)
Ameerpet,
Hyderabad,
Andhra Pradesh - 500016
Tel : + 91 (0) 40 3736924
Fax : + 91 (0) 40 3736926

**Vishnu Metals & Alloys Pvt. Ltd.**
Plot No. 54 & 55
IDA, Phase-III, Jeedimetla
Hyderabad,
Andhra Pradesh - 500055
Tel : + 91 (0) 40 3098089
Fax : + 91 (0) 40 3097299

## SHRINK - FILM

**A-Garg Exim Pvt. Ltd.**
42, DLF Indl. Area
Kirti Ngr.
New Delhi - 110015
Tel : + 91 (0) 11 5417831
Fax : + 91 (0) 11 5195721
E-mail : pawan@garg.org

**Allied Polybags Pvt. Ltd.**
A-4/3, Phase-II
Mayapuri Indl. Area
New Delhi - 110064
Tel : + 91 (0) 11 5404595
Fax : + 91 (0) 11 5404595

**Apex Polyfilm**
1B. Rudravan Apts.
Nr. ExperimentalSchool, Parle Point, Athwalines
Surat, Gujarat-395007
Tel : + 91 (0) 261 610569
Fax : + 91 (0) 261 872709

**Arihant Gujarat Plastic Industries**
L-60/9, GIDC Est.
Nr. Blue Star
Narmadanagar,
Gujarat - 392015
Tel : + 91 (0) 2642 46941

**Pee Kay Polymer**
354, Friends Cly.
Rly. Rd., Pravesh Marg
Faridabad, Haryana-121002
Tel : + 91 (0) 129 5268644
Fax : + 91 (0) 129 5279778

**Synthetik Wraps**
Dr. Kalki's Compound, 57/3
Kamakshipalya, Magadi Rd.
Bangalore, Karnataka-560079
Tel : + 91 (0) 80 3484237
Fax : + 91 (0) 80 8361616

**Kalpak Products**
E - 9, Indl. Area, Govindpura
Bhopal,
Madhya Pradesh - 462023
Tel : + 91 (0) 755 568807

**Dear Packaging Pvt. Ltd.**
B1 & 2
Laghu Udyog Kendra
I B Patel Rd.
Goregaon (E), Mumbai,
Maharashtra - 400063
Tel : + 91 (0) 22 8764434
Fax : + 91 (0) 22 8760237
E-mail : info@dearpack.com

**Apex Polyfilm**
1B. Rudravan Apts.
Nr. ExperimentalSchool, Parle Point, Athwalines
Surat, Gujarat - 395007
Tel : + 91 (0) 261 610569
Fax : + 91 (0) 261 872709

**Arihant Gujarat Plastic Industries**
L-60/9, GIDC Est.
Nr. Blue Star
Narmadanagar,
Gujarat - 392015
Tel : + 91 (0) 2642 46941

**Sri Kaleeswarar Industries**
103, Salai St., Olugaret
Pondicherry,
Pondicherry - 605010
Tel : + 91 (0) 413 273140

**Shree Ram Polymers**
392, Indl. Area-A
Ludhiana, Punjab - 141003
Tel : + 91 (0) 161 667669
Fax : + 91 (0) 161 662055

**Chellsons Fine Arts**
2nd Flr., 43, Sembudoss St.
Chennai, Tamil Nadu-600001
Tel : + 91 (0) 44 5223415
Fax : + 91 (0) 44 5260505

**Shreepack**
A-15, Phase-III, Indl. Est.
Guindy
Chennai, Tamil Nadu - 600032
Tel : + 91 (0) 44 2342567

**Sri Krishna Packaging**
B-36, Sect. 2
Noida, Uttar Pradesh - 201301
Tel : + 91 (0) 120 4548345
Fax : + 91 (0) 120 4548178

**PBS Packaging**
405, Narayani Bldg.,
4th Flr., 47, Brabourne Rd.
Kolkata, West Bengal-700001
Tel : + 91 (0) 33 2427087
Fax : + 91 (0) 33 2427642

**Penguin Plastics**
76, Christopher Rd.
Kolkata, West Bengal-700046
Tel : + 91 (0) 33 3292091
Fax : + 91 (0) 33 3282668

## CONTAINERS : AEROSOL

**Drawcans Pvt. Ltd.**
16, 8.5 KM
Bannerghatta Rd.
Bangalore, Karnataka-560076
Tel : + 91 (0) 80 6581203
Fax : + 91 (0) 80 3461204
E-mail :
drawcans@satyam.net.in

**Super Tech Industries**
No. 3/2/2, 1st Cross
M C Rd. Extn., Vijayanagar
Bangalore, Karnataka-560079
Tel : + 91 (0) 80 3304165
Fax : + 91 (0) 80 3386485

**Bharat Containers Pvt. Ltd.**
Cecil Court, Apollo Bunder
Mahakavi Bhushan Marg
Mumbai, Maharashtra-400039
Tel : + 91 (0) 22 2020021
Fax : + 91 (0) 22 2028124

**Deepak Industries**
1280, Ashok Chowk
Sangamnet, Sangamner,
Maharashtra - 422605
Tel : + 91 (0) 2425 25007
Fax : + 91 (0) 2425 25007
E-mail:
dmaniyar@bom6.vsnl.net.in

**Ishan Exporters**
9/10-A-Wing
Satyam Shopping Centre
Ghatkopar (E)
Mumbai, Maharashtra-400077
Tel : + 91 (0) 22 5125172
Fax : + 91 (0) 22 5163791
E-mail:
jayraj@bom4.vsnl.net.in

**Ishan Industries**
9/10A,
Wing Satyam Shopping Cmplx.
Ghatkopar (E), Mumbai,
Maharashtra - 400077
Tel : + 91 (0) 22 5102484
Fax : + 91 (0) 22 5163791
E-mail: jairaj@bom4.vsnl.net.in

**Jayraj Industries Ltd.**
9/10,
Satyam Complx., A-Wing
M G Rd., Ghatkopar (E)
Mumbai, Maharashtra-400077
Tel : + 91 (0) 22 5102484
Fax : + 91 (0) 22 5163791

**Maa Container Industries**
W-186, Phase-II, MIDC
Dombivili (E),
Maharashtra - 421203
Tel : + 91 (0) 251 470281
Fax : + 91 (0) 251 456156

**Metal Impact Ltd.**
2, Shivaji Mandir
N C Kelkar Rd., Dadar
Mumbai, Maharashtra-400028
Tel : + 91 (0) 22 4306197
Fax : + 91 (0) 22 4301020

**Rajdeep Cans Pvt. Ltd.**
202, Rinku Apts.
B Bhagve Rd., Navagaon
Dahisar (W)
Mumbai, Maharashtra-400068
Tel : + 91 (0) 22 8942520
Fax : + 91 (0) 22 8068538
E-mail: info@can_makers.com

**Sara-Chem (I) Pvt. Ltd.**
D-42, Sara House
Arenja Cmplx., Sect. 8
C B D, Navi Mumbai,
Maharashtra - 400614
Tel : + 91 (0) 22 7671256
Fax : + 91 (0) 22 7571689
E-mail :
rkjain@bom5.vsnl.net.in

**Shatrunjay Extrusions Ltd.**
135, Shivkrupa
LBS Marg, Vikhroli (W)
Mumbai, Maharashtra-400083
Tel : + 91 (0) 22 5790802
Fax : + 91 (0) 22 5773055

**Bharat Containers**
1/11101, Subhash Park
Shahdara
Delhi - 110032
Tel : + 91 (0) 11 2271718

**Containers Point**
1/11101, Subhash Park
Shahdara
Delhi - 110032
Tel : + 91 (0) 11 2271718
Fax : + 91 (0) 11 2271920

## PET BOTTLES

**Crystal Polymers**
Plot No. 6
Electronic Cmplx. Extn.
ECIL X Rds.
Hyderabad,
Andhra Pradesh - 500062
Tel : + 91 (0) 40 7131491
E-mail : psraocrystal@usa.net

**Mold-Tek Plastics Ltd.**
303, C-Block, 7-1-27,
Srinivasa Cmplx., Ameerpet
Hyderabad,
Andhra Pradesh - 500016
Tel : + 91 (0) 40 3734409
Fax : + 91 (0) 40 3731834
E-mail :
moldtek@hd2.dot.net.in

**Pavani Polymers**
Plot No. 35, IDA, Phase-IV
Jeedimetla
Hyderabad,
Andhra Pradesh - 500055
Tel : + 91 (0) 40 3096478
Fax : + 91 (0) 40 3193369

**Hans Mouldings Pvt. Ltd.**
W-15, Phase-II
Okhla Indl. Area
New Delhi - 110020
Tel : + 91 (0) 11 6911518

**Himanshu Plastics**
D-30, DSIDC Indl. Cmplx.
Rohtak Rd., Nangloi
New Delhi - 110041
Tel : + 91 (0) 11 5476203

**Innovative Tech Pack Ltd.**
1109-10-11, Chiranjiv Tower,
43, Nehru Place
New Delhi - 110000
Tel : + 91 (0) 11 6427394
Fax : + 91 (0) 11 6477929
E-mail :
inpack@del2.vsnl.net.in

**Jauss Polymers Ltd.**
602-603, Pragati Towers
26, Rajendra Place
New Delhi - 110008
Tel : + 91 (0) 11 5783012
Fax : + 91 (0) 11 5823628

**Alpha Containers**
Plot No. 374
Sect. C, Alpha Industrial Park
Athiawad, Dabhel
Daman, Gujarat - 396210
Tel : + 91 (0) 236 52978

**Alpha Packaging Pvt. Ltd.**
1, Jash Mkt., Ring Rd.
Surat, Gujarat - 395002
Tel : + 91 (0) 261 623714
Fax : + 91 (0) 261 623545
E-mail:
alpha@alphabags.com

**Classic Blowtechnik Pvt. Ltd.**
K1/802/20
GIDC, Sect. 28
Gandhinagar,
Gujarat - 382028
Tel : + 91 (0) 2712 21403
Fax : + 91 (0) 2712 20287
E-mail :
angelpkg@icenet.net

**Kee Pet Container**
29, Haribhai Mkt., Crosslane
Revdibazar, Kalupur,
Ahmedabad, Gujarat - 380002
Tel : + 91 (0) 79 2131768
Fax : + 91 (0) 79 2111590
E-mail :
keepet900@yahoo.com

**Blow Moulders India**
6, MSR Indl. Est., Gokula Extn.,
Mathikere
Bangalore,
Karnataka - 560054
Tel : + 91 (0) 80 3446748
Fax : + 91 (0) 80 3442956

**Manjushree Extrusions Ltd.**
143, C-5
Bommasandra Indl. Area
Hosur Rd., Hebbagodi
Bangalore,
Karnataka - 562158
Tel : + 91 (0) 80 33478
Fax : + 91 (0) 80 33819
E-mail : melbng@bgl.vsnl.net.in

**Radix Impex Pvt. Ltd.**
314, BG, Scheme No. 74C
Vijay Ngr. Indore,
Madhya Pradesh - 452010
Tel : + 91 (0) 731 223066
E-mail : radix@bom4.vsnl.net.in

**Yash Petequip (I) Pvt. Ltd.**
12, Sect. G
J K Rd., Govindpura
Bhopal,
Madhya Pradesh - 462023
Tel : + 91 (0) 755 584702
Fax : + 91 (0) 755 781966

**Amishree Industries**
Lachwad Basement # 1
South Pond Rd.,
Vile Parle (W), Mumbai,
Maharashtra - 400056
Tel : + 91 (0) 22 6178235
E-mail :
amishreeb@relip.com

**Aristo Pet**
2, Sonawala Chawl
Sonawala X Rd.
Goregaon (E), Mumbai,
Maharashtra - 400063
Tel : + 91 (0) 22 8731484

**Beekay Containers**
55, Grants Bldg. Annexxe
1st Flr., Nr. Strand Cinema
Colaba, Mumbai,
Maharashtra - 400005
Tel : + 91 (0) 22 2820337
Fax : + 91 (0) 22 2845345

**Clair Packaging Pvt. Ltd.**
23, Veena Beena Shopping
Centre, Guru Nanak Rd.
Bandra (W), Mumbai,
Maharashtra - 400050
Tel : + 91 (0) 22 6409855
Fax : + 91 (0) 22 6425214

**Dhaval Cans Pvt. Ltd.**
201, Prashanti Devidas
Borivali (W), Thane,
Maharashtra - 400103
Tel : + 91 (0) 22 8090519
E-mail :
canmakers@yahoo.com

**Master Plastic Bottle Manufacturers Pvt. Ltd.**
163, Sneh Sadan, G-2, Ground
Flr., Colaba P.O.
Mumbai, Maharashtra-400005
Tel : + 91 (0) 22 2186173
Fax : + 91 (0) 22 2152875
E-mail :
mastpet@bom5.vsnl.net.in

**Shree Nath Techno Products Pvt. Ltd.**
94, Dashmesh Cly. Township
Rajpura, Punjab-140401
Tel : + 91 (0) 1762 25625

**Jai Polypan Pvt. Ltd.**
C-64, Bais Godam Indl. Est.
Jaipur, Rajasthan - 302006
Tel : + 91 (0) 141 211687
Fax : + 91 (0) 141 213981
E-mail :
vishal@jp1.dot.net.in

**Noble Packaging**
71-A, Sect. II
Pithampur, Rajasthan-454773
Tel : + 91 (0) 7292 63055
Fax : +91 (0) 7292 40425
E-mail: noblepet@yahoo.com

**Livia Polymer Bottles Pvt. Ltd.**
Mandaiyur Salai, Mandaiyur
Pudukkottai,
Tamil Nadu - 622515
Tel : + 91 (0) 4339 50418
Fax : + 91 (0) 4339 50580
E-mail:
livia@md3.vsnl.net.in

**St. Antony's Plastics**
Shed No. B-6
SIDCO Indl. Est.
Kodungaiyur, Chennai,
Tamil Nadu - 600118
Tel : +91 (0) 44 5542667

**Tass Polymer**
7A, Warren Rd.
Mylapore, Chennai,
Tamil Nadu - 600004
Tel : + 91 (0) 44 4951614
Fax : + 91 (0) 44 4970283
E-mail : tass3@vsnl.com.

**Goldmine Polymers Ltd.**
B-22 & 23
Sect. 6, Noida,
Uttar Pradesh - 201301
Tel : + 91 (0) 120 533054
Fax : + 91 (0) 120 526355

**Injex Poly Products**
D-136, Indl. Area
Bulandshahr Rd.
Ghaziabad,
Uttar Pradesh - 201001
Tel : + 91 (0) 120 4700886
Fax : + 91 (0) 120 4702668

**Sunshine Polypet Pvt. Ltd.**
Plot No. 9
Punjab Expeller Compound
Meerut Rd.
Ghaziabad, Uttar Pradesh-
201001
Tel : + 91 (0) 120 4713722

**Pearl Poly Industries Pvt. Ltd.**
7-A, Middleton St.
Kolkata,
West Bengal - 700071
Tel : + 91 (0) 33 2400157
Fax : +91 (0) 33 2407758

**Rock Pet Chem Pvt. Ltd.**
1, 4th Flr., Rawdon St.
Kolkata,
West Bengal - 700017
Tel : + 91 (0) 33 240289
Fax : + 91 (0) 33 2402891

**Sunrise Plastic Industries**
11, 1st Flr., Pollock St.
Kolkata,
West Bengal - 700001
Tel : + 91 (0) 33 2350419
Fax : + 91 (0) 33 2350419

117. MANUFACTURE OF TIN CONTAINERS
118. MANUFACTURE OF STORAGE TANKS, PRESSURE VESSELS, HEAT EXCHANGERS
119. MARK II HAND PUMPS
120. MARUTI WORKSHOP CUM - SERVICE STATION
121. MECHANICAL JACKS
122. METAL CUTTING DIE DESIGN
123. METAL CUTTING OF AND GRINDING WHEELS (ABBRASIVE CUTTING WHEELS)
124. METAL HOOKS & CLIPS
125. METAL SEPARATION (COPPER, TIN, LEAD) FROM SPENT WASH ACID
126. METALLIC RING JOINTS
127. METALLIC GASKET (SPIRAL WOUND)
128. MICROVEE & ABSOLUTE FILTER
129. MICROWAVE OVEN
130. MILD STEEL INGOTS
131. MINI STEEL PLANT
132. MODERN VEHICLE WORKSHOP
133. MOPED
134. M.S.HINGES
135. M.S.INGOT AND HR. STEEL STRUCTURALS
136. M.S.INGOT BY INDUCTION FURNACES
137. M.S.PIPES
138. M.S. WELDING ELECTRODE
139. MUFFLERS & SILENCERS FOR THREE WHEELERS
140. NAIL CUTTER WITH FILER & MANICURE
141. NICHROME WIRE
142. NICKEL LINED SCREENS
143. NON-FERROUS ALLOY ROLLING
144. NON-FERROUS FORGING
145. NON-FERROUS FOUNDRY
146. NON PRESSURE
147. INCANDESCENT LAMP
148. NUMBER COMBINATION LOCKS FOR LUGGAGES
149. NUTS & BOLTS
150. PAPER COATED ALUMINIUM AND COPPER WIRE
151. PETROMAX CONTAINER
152. PHOTO ETCHING OF STAINLESS STEEL PLATES
153. PIPE GALVANIZING PLANT
154. PISTON RING-AUTOMOBILE
155. PLANT PROTECTION EQUIPMENTS
156. PLATINUM LABORATORY APPARATUS
157. PRESSURE COOKER & ALUMINIUM UTENSILS
158. PRESSURE COOKER (ALUMINIUM)
159. PRESSURE DIE CASTING
160. PRINTED ALUMINIUM COLLAPSIBLE TUBES
161. PRINTED TIN CONTAINERS
162. PRINTING PRESS (CYLINDER MACHINE)
163. PUMPS FOR CHEMICAL INDUSTRY (SPECIAL)
164. RAILWAY SLEEPERS (M.S.)
165. RAZOR TWIN BLADE
166. R.C.C SPUN PIPES
167. RECONDITIONING OF M.S. DRUMS/BARRELS
168. RE-ROLLING COPPER AND BRASS SHEET AND RODS
169. RE-ROLLING MILLS
170. RESIN COATED SAND
171. RESIN CORED SOFT SOLDER WIRES
172. ROLLING MILL (BY INDUCTION FURNACE) & MANUFACTURE OF BARS, ANGLES, SQUARES, TUBES AND OTHERS
173. ROLLER BEARING & FORGING
174. ROLLING OF STAINLESS STEEL PATTA
175. RUBBER INSULATED PLIERS (HAND TOOLS)
176. RUBBING COMPOUND FOR AUTOMOBILES
177. SCIENTIFIC LABORATORY EQUIPMENTS
178. SCOOTER ASSEMBLING
179. SECONDARY LEAD EXTRACTION BY SCRAP BATTERY PLATES,PIPES & SHEET
180. SEAMLESS M.S. TUBES & PIPES
181. SELF TAPPING STEEL SCREW
182. SEWING NEEDLES
183. S.G. IRON & ALLOY STEEL
184. SHEET METAL PRODUCTS, (FERROUS/NON-FERROUS)
185. SHIP/MARINE CONTAINER
186. SHOCK ABSORBERS
187. SHOE EYELETS
188. SHOT AND GRITS BY AUTOMIZATION PROCESS
189. SHOVELS
190. SILICO MANGANESE ALLOYS
191. SILENCERS (MUFFLERS) EXHAUST & TAIL PIPE FOR ALL TYPES OF VEHICLES
192. SINTERED BEARING
193. SINTERED BUSHES
194. SINTERED METAL PRODUCTS
195. SOFT AND HARD FERRITES
196. SPANNERS
197. SPARK PLUGS
198. STEEL PLANT (ELECTRIC ARC FURNACE BASED- EAF)
199. SPHERIODAL GRAPHITE CAST IRON
200. SPRAY DRYER
201. STAINLESS STEEL HINGES
202. STAINLESS STEEL SHEET ROLLING TO PRODUCE STAINLESS STEEL UTENSILS
203. STAINLESS STEEL UTENSILS
204. STAPLE PINS,PAPER PIN , GEM CLIPS ETC.
205. STEEL CASTINGS
206. STEEL CHAIN
207. STEEL FOUNDRY
208. STEEL FURNITURES AND ELECTRICAL APPLIANCES
209. STEEL PLANT (MINI)
210. STEEL RODS AND COILS FROM SCRAPS
211. STEEL ROLLING MILL
212. STEEL STRIPS (COLD ROLLED) SILICON WITH GRAIN RIENTED FOR ELECTRIC USE
213. STEEL TRANSMISSION LINE TOWERS & ROLLING MILL TO PRODUCE STEEL SECTION
214. STEEL FURNITURES AND ELECTRICAL APPLIANCES
215. STEEL WIRE DRAWING AND GALVANIZING
216. STEEL WOOL
217. SUBMERGED ARC WELDED PIPES
218. SUBMERSIBLE PUMP MANUFACTURING
219. SUPER ENAMELLED COPPER WIRE
220. THREE WHEELERS
221. TIE-ROD ENDS
222. TIN CONTAINERS
223. TOOLROOM AND SHEET METAL PRODUCTS
224. TRACTOR TRAILERS
225. TRANSMISSION POWER FITTING
226. TUBULAR POLES
227. SUPER ENAMELLED COPPER WIRES
228. TUBULAR POLES FOR ELECTRICAL TRANSMISSION (BY FABRICATION PROCESS)
229. TUBULAR POLES OF M.S. & HIGH TENSILE STEEL
230. VACUUM CLEANERS
231. VACUUM FLASK (STAINLESS STEEL)
232. VALVES FOR REFRIGERATION AND AIR-CONDITION
233. VEHICLE WELDING & PAINTING
234. VENETION BLIND
235. WASHING MACHINES (AUTOMATIC & COMPUTERISED)
236. WATER CONTROLLER (AUTOMATIC)
237. WATCH STRAPS/CHAINS/ BRACELETS/BELT BRASS & STAINLESS STEEL
238. WATER COOLERS
239. WELDED WIRE MESH
240. WELDING ELECTRODES
241. WICK STOVES
242. WIND MILL WINDOW FRAME (FERROUS & NON-FERROUS)
243. WRIST WATCH

# LIST OF FEW READILY AVAILABLE 'DETAILED PROJECT REPORTS' OUT OF 30,000 REPORTS

## CHEMICALS (ORGANIC & INORGANIC)

244. ACETIC ANHYDRIDE
245. ACETIC ACID FROM ETHANOL
246. ACETYLENE BLACK
247. ACETYLENE GAS
248. ACETYLENE GAS & OXYGEN (INTEGERATED UNIT)
249. ACID SLURRY BY MANUAL PROCESS
250. ACTIVATED ALUMINA
251. ACTIVATED BLEACHING EARTH (ACTIVATED FULLERS EARTH)
252. ACTIVATED CARBON FROM CASHEWNUT SHELL
253. ACTIVATED CARBON FROM RICE HUSK
254. ACTIVATED CARBON FROM RICE HUSK, COCONUT SHELL & COCONUT POWDER
255. ACTIVATED CARBON FROM WOOD
256. ACTIVATED CARBON POWDER & GRANULES FROM COCONUT SHELL
257. ACTIVATED CARBON & SODIUM SILICATE FROM PADDY & RICE HUSK
258. ALUM FOR WATER TREATMENT
259. AEROSOL INSECTICIDES SPRAY (BAYGON, HIT, MORTEIN TYPE)
260. AGARBATTI SYNTHETIC PERFUMERY COMPOUNDS
261. ALCOHOL FROM POTATO
262. ALCOHOL FROM RICE GRAINS
263. ALCOHOL FROM RICE HUSK
264. ALCOHOL FROM MOLASSES
265. ALCOHOL, BEER, STARCH, LIQUID GLUCOSE, DEXTROSE, SORBITOL, VITAMIN-C, GERM OIL, CATTLE FEED ETC. FROM MAIZE
266. ALKYD RESIN
267. ALKYLATED PHENOL LIKE NONYL PHENOL, DODECYL PHENOL
268. ALUM (NON FERRIC)
269. ALUM (FERRIC)
260. ALUMINIUM INGOT BY BAUXITE
261. ALUMINIUM PHOSPHIDE
262. ALUMINIUM PHOSPHATE
263. AMINES & ALLIED PRODUCTS
264. AMMONIA GAS
265. AMMONIA GAS BOTTLING
266. AMMONIA LIQUOR
267. AMMONIUM CHLORIDE (PURE & TECHNICAL)
268. ANILINE
269. ARGON GAS
270. ARIEL TYPE DETERGENT POWDER
271. ANTHRAQUINONE
272. ANTIMONY TRIOXIDE
273. AZODICARBONAMIDE
274. BAKING SODA FROM ASH
275. BARIUM CARBONATE
276. BARIUM COMPOUNDS
277. BARIUM PEROXIDE
278. BARIUM-THIO-SULPHATE BANZENE
279. BARYTE POWDER
280. BEER PLANT
281. BELT PASTE (WITH BFS OIL)
282. BENZYL ACETATE, BENZYL BENZOATE, BENZYL ALCOHOL
283. BETA NAPHTHOL
284. BENTONITE POWDER
285. BENZIDINE
286. BIO GAS PLANT
287. BIO GAS FILLING IN CYLINDER
288. BI-CHROMATE OF SODIUM, POTASSIUM & AMMONIUM
289. BI-FUNCTIONAL BLACK MFGR. REACTIVE DYE (DYE FROM COTTON YARN DYEING)
290. BITUMINOUS ROAD EMULSION
291. BLACK PHENYL
292. BLACK SULPHUR
293. BLEACHING POWDER (STABLE)
294. BONE CRUSHING PLANT
295. BONE MEAL (CALCINED) ENRICHMENT WITH CALCIUM & PHOSPHORUS
296. BORIC ACID
297. B.O.N. ACID
298. BRANDY
299. BUTANOL
300. 1,4, BUTANEDIOL
301. BUTYL ACETATE
302. CAFFEIN FROM TEA WASTE
303. CALCINED LIME (DEAD BURNT DOLOMITE)
304. CALCINING OF MAGNESITE & DEAD BURNT MAGNESITE
305. CALCIUM ALUMINATE
306. CALCIUM CARBIDE
307. CALCIUM CARBONATE
308. CALCIUM CARBONATE (PRECIPITATED) FROM BY PRODUCT (LIME SLURRY & CARBON DIOXIDE)
309. CALCIUM CARBONATE (ACTIVATED & PRECIPITATED)
310. CALCIUM CHLORIDE
311. CALCIUM GLUCONATE
312. CALCIUM NITRATE
313. CALCIUM SILICATE BRICKS
314. CAMPHOR POWDER (SYNTHETIC)
315. CARBON DIOXIDE
316. CARBON BLACK FROM FERTILIZER WASTE
317. CARBOXY METHYL CELLULOSE (CMC)
318. CASEIN AND BY PRODUCTS
319. CASEIN FROM MILK
320. CATIONIC SOFTNER (STEARIC ACID BASED)
321. CAUSTIC SODA
322. CAUSTIC SODA FROM TRONA
323. CAUSTIC SODA, CHLORINE AND HYDROGEN GAS BY ELECTRO-LYSIS OF BRINE SOLUTION
324. CELLULOSE ACETATE MOULDING POWDER
325. CELLULOSE POWDER & MICRO CRYSTALLINE CELLULOSE POWDER
326. CEMENT COLOUR
327. CEMENT FROM FLY ASH & LIME
328. CEMENT TILES (GLAZED)
329. DOUBLE FIRING (HEATING)
330. CHELATED ZINC (ZN EDTA)
331. CHEMICALS FROM PRAWN HEAD
332. CHITIN & CHITOSAN FROM PRAWN SHELL WASTE
333. CHLORAL HYDRATE
334. CHLORAMPHENICOL
335. CHROMIC ACID (WITH POLLUTION CONTROL)
336. CHROMIC ACID (OXIDE) & BLUE OXIDE
337. CHLORINATED PARAFFIN WAX (CPW)
338. CHROMIC ACID
339. CEMENT PAINT & DISTEMPER
340. CITRIC ACID FROM LEMON
341. CITRIC ACID FROM MOLASSES
342. CLEANING OF COOLING SYSTEM AND BOILER
343. COAL TAR DISTILLATION
344. COBALT OCTOATE
345. COMPOST FOR MUSHROOM
346. COPPER OXYCHLORIDE
347. COPPER PHTHALOCYANINE BLUE & GREEN
348. CORRECTION FLUID
349. CYANURIC CHLORIDE
350. DEFOAMING AGENT FOR PAPER INDUSTRY
351. DE-NICKELING (ELECTROLYTIC PROCESS)
352. DETERGENT CAKE & POWDER
353. DETERGENT POWDER
354. DETERGENT CONCENTRATE (IDET 10)
355. DEXTROSE MONOHYDRATE & DEXTROSE ANHYDROUS POWDER FROM TAPIOCA STARCH
356. DI-BASIC LEAD STEARATE
357. DI CALCIUM PHOSPHATE
358. DICLOFENAL SODIUM SLOW RELEASE (SR) TABLES 100MG.

CRUDE NAPHTHA
570. TRIMETHYL AMMONIUM CHLORIDE
571. TRIPHENYL PHOSPHITE (T.P.P)
572. ULTRAMARINE BLUE (LIQUID)
573. UREA FORMALDEHYDE & MELAMINE FORMALDEHYDE POWDER
574. UNDECYLINIC ACID
575. VINYL ACETATE MONOMER
576. VITAMIN C
577. VITAMIN E
578. WASTE WATER TREATMENT PLANT FOR INDUSTRIAL SECTOR IN INDIA (ONLY MARKER SURVEY)
579. WIRE DRAWING LUBRICANT
580. WIRE ENAMEL
581. XANTHATES
582. YELLOW DEXTRIN
583. ZINC CHLORIDE
584. ZINC OXIDE
585. ZINC PHOSPHATING BY COLD PROCESS
586. ZINC SILICATE
587. ZINC STEARATE
588. ZINC SULPHATE
589. ZINC SULPHATE MONOHYDRATE
590. ACID BLACK
591. AURAMINE'O'
592. AZO DYES STUFF
593. DYE & DYE INTERMEDIATE
594. DYE INTERMEDIATES
595. MALACHITE GREEN
596. METHYLENE BLUE
597. PHTHALOCYANINE BLUE
598. PHTHALOCYANINE BLUE & GREEN
599. REACTIVE DYES
600. SULPHUR BLACK DYE
601. VAT DYES
602. WATER CHILLING PLANT
603. WADDING OIL (100%) FOR WADDING OF COTTON HOSIERY CLOTH IN THE DYEING PROCESS
604. WHITE OIL
605. WAX FLOOR POLISH

## ELECTRICAL, ELECTONICS, COMPUTERS AND INFOTECH/IT PROJECTS

606. AIR CONDITIONING
607. ALUMINIUM ALLOY CONDUCTOR
608. ALUMINIUM CABLE
609. ALUMINIUM ELECTROYTIC CAPACITORS
610. AUDIO CASSETTE ASSEMBLING & RECORDING
611. AUDIO CASSETTES DUPLICATING RECORDING
612. AUDIO CASSETTES & AUDIO STUDIO
613. AUDIO CASSETTES PLANE & RECORDED
614. AUDIO MAGNETIC HEADS
615. AUDIO MAGNETIC TAPE
616. AUDIO/VIDEO CASSETTES
617. AUTO BULB/LAMPS
618. AUTOMATIC VOLTAGE STABILIZER
619. BATTERY PLATES
620. BACK OFFICE (Rs. 5000/-)
621. B/W TV & COMPUTER MONITOR PICTURE TUBE
622. BREAD BOARDS
623. CALL CENTRE
624. CAMERA (35 MM)
625. CAPACITORS
626. CARBON ELECTRODE USED FOR BATTERY CELL
627. CARBON POTETIOMETERS
628. CEILING FAN
629. CERAMIC INSULATOR
630. CHILDREN INFOTECH TRAINING INSTITUTE (Rs. 5000/-)
631. CHOKE AND PATTI
632. CHOKE AND STARTER
633. CHOKE USED FOR FLUORESCENT LAMPS
634. COLOUR TELEVISION
635. COLOUR AND BLACK & WHITE TELEVISION
636. COMPACT DISC
637. COMPACT DISC PLAYER (AUDIO/VIDEO)
638. COMPUTER EDUCATION INSTITUTE
639. COMPUTER ASSEMBLY
640. COMPUTER HARDWARE
641. COMPUTER KEYBOARD
642. COMPUTER PERIPHERALS
643. COMPUTER PRINTERS
644. COMPUTER RIBBON
645. COMPUTER RIBBON REINKING OR REFILLING
646. COMPUTER STATIONERY
647. COMPUTER STATIONERY &

IMPORTED HARDWARE PARTS
648. COMPUTER TERMINALS
649. COMPUTERISED WASHING MACHINE (AUTOMATIC)
650. COMPUTER SOFTWARE
651. CONDENSER FOR MOTOR USING MPP FILM
652. CONTENT DEVELOPMENT CENTRE (EOU) (Rs. 5000/-)
653. CONTROL PANEL BOARD
654. COOLING COIL FOR AIR CONDITIONERS
655. COPPER STRIP COIL FROM SCRAP
656. CORDLESS TELEPHONES
657. CYBER CAFE
658. CYBERKIOSK (Rs. 5000/-)
659. DATA PROCESSING CENTRE (Rs. 5000/-)
660. D.C. MICRO MOTORS
661. D.G.SETS
662. DISH ANTENNA AND CABLE T.V. NETWORK EQUIPMENT
663. DISTRIBUTION TRANSFORMERS & REPAIRS
664. DOMESTIC ELECTRICAL APPLIANCES- ROOM COOLER, WASHING MACHINE, WATER HEATER, ELECTRIC ROOM HEATER
665. E-SCHOOL
666. E-COMMERCE/BUSINESS
667. ELECTRIC ENERGY METER
668. ELECTRIC FANS
669. ELECTRIC HORN FOR AUTOMOBILE
670. ELECTRIC LAMP/GLS (INCANDESCENT LAMP)
671. ELECTRIC MIXER
672. ELECTRIC MOTORS UP TO 10 HP. REWINDING OF ALL TYPES OF MOTORS WATER PUMPS
673. ELECTRIC MOTOR WINDING (FOR FAN, MIXIES, ETC.)
674. ELECTRIC STEAM IRON
675. ELECTRICAL APPLIANCES
676. ELECTRICAL FIXTURES
677. ELECTRICAL STAMPING
678. ELECTROLYTIC CAPACITORS
679. ELECTROMAGNETIC RELAY
680. ELECTRONIC BALAST/CHOK
681. ELECTRICAL CHOKE
682. ELECTRONIC DIGITAL WATCHES
683. ELECTRONIC DIGITAL WEIGHING MACHINE
684. ELECTRONIC FIRE ALARM
685. ELECTRONIC GAS STOVE LIGHTERS
686. ELECTRONIC PRESSURE INDICATORS, ELECTRICALS, ELECTRONIC LIQUID LEVEL INDICATORS, ELECTRONIC TEMPERATURE INDICATOR, DIGITAL TACHOMETER
687. ELECTRONIC TELEPHONE INSTRUMENTS
688. ELECTRONIC TOYS
689. ELECTRONIC WATCHES & CLOCKS
690. FAX MACHINES
691. F.H.P MOTORS
692. FLOPPY DISKETTES
693. FLUORESCENT LAMP STARTER
694. FLUORESCENT TUBULAR

**Price Rs. 4200/- for each "Detailed Project Report" Payable in advance through Draft/Cash/ M.O. in favour of *"ENGINEERS INDIA RESEARCH INSTITUTE"*. 4449, Nai Sarak (D), Main Road Delhi - 110 006 *OR Ask by V.P.P.* ● Ph : 3918117, 391 6431, 392 0361, 396 0797 ●Fax : 91-11- 391 6431 ●E-Mail : eirisidi@bol.net.in ● WebSite : www.startindustry.com**

LAMPS WITH INTRODUCTION TO MERCURY VAPOUR LAMP
695. FRANCHISEE COMPUTER EDUCATION CENTRE (Rs. 5000)
696. GAS DETECTOR (L.P.G)
697. GENERATOR SET & PUMP SETS
698. GENERATOR (BATTERY OPERATED)
699. GIS SERVICE CENTRE (GEOGRAPHICAL INFORMATION SYSTEMS)
700. HARDWARE FITTING FOR TRANSMISSION LINE (OVERHEAD LINE MATERIAL
701. HEADERS FOR TRANSISTOR ICS SEMI CONDUCTOR
702. H.T & L.T INSULATORS
703. H.T & M.V INDUSTRIAL CUBICAL SWITCH BOARD
704. INFORMATION MOVING DISPLAY (L.E.D TYPE)
705. INSURANCE CLAIM PROCESSING CENTRE (EOU) (Rs. 5000/-)
706. INTEGRATED CIRCUITS
707. INTERNET BASED STOCK TRADING (Rs. 5000/-)
708. INTERNET SERVICE PROVIDER (I.S.P.)
709. JELLY FILLED TELEPHONE CABLES
710. LAP TOP COMPUTERS
711. LEAD ACID BATTERIES
712. LEAD ACID BATTERY PLATES AND ASSEMBLING OF BATTERY
713. LEGAL TRANSCRIPTION & SECRETARIAL SERVICES CENTER (EOU)(Rs. 5000/-)
714. LIGHT EMITTING DIODES (L.E.D)
715. LINEAR ICS TRAINER KIT
716. LOUD SPEAKER
717. L.T TRANSFORMER REPAIRING
718. MEDICAL TRANSCRIPTION CENTRE
719. METAL FILM RESISTORS
720. METALLISED POLYPROPYLENE, POLYESTER FILM CAPACITOR
721. MICA BASE ELECTRONIC COMPONENTS
722. MICA PAPER WASTE PAPER FROM MICA WASTE
723. MICRO PROCESSORS TRAINER KITS BASED ON MICRO PROCESSORS
724. MINI COMPUTER (PERSONAL COMPUTER)
725. MINIATURE CIRCUIT BREAKER (M.C.B)
726. MINIATURE WATCH BATTERIES (BUTTON CELL)
727. MIXER/GRINDER (MIXI)
728. MONO CHROME COMPUTER MONITOR
729. MOTOR START ELECTROLYTIC CAPACITOR
730. MULTI LAYER P.C.B
731. MULTIPLE RELAY FOR LOW VOLTAGE
732. NEON INDICATOR
733. NEON SIGN MANUFACTURE
734. OPTICAL FIBRE CABLES
735. ON LINE SHOPPING MALL (Rs. 5000/-)
736. OPTO MECHANICAL & ELECTRICAL EQUIPMENTS
737. PHOTO COLOUR LAB
738. PICTURE TUBE (B/W)
739. PLAIN PAPER COPIER
740. PLASTIC FILM CAPACITORS
741. POLYESTER CAPACITORS
742. PORTABLE GENERATOR SET
743. PORTAL
744. PORTABLE TELEVISION(TV)
745. POWER CAPACITORS
746. POWER INVERTERS
747. POWER PLANT
748. POWER TRANSFORMERS UP TO 600 KVA
749. PRINTED CIRCUIT BOARD
750. PVC WIRES & CABLES
751. RE-CONDITIONING OF PICTURE TUBE
752. RESIN CAST CT & PT (1 KV)
753. SEMI CONDUCTOR DEVICE
754. SEMI CONDUCTORS FOR TRANSISTORS & DIODES
755. SETTING UP OF A VIDEO STUDIO
756. SMOKE DETECTORS
757. SOLAR CELLS
758. SOLAR MODULES
759. SOLAR PHOTO VOLTAIC SYSTEM
760. SOLDER FLUXES
761. SOLAR WATER HEATING PANELS
762. STEEL FURNITURE & ELECTRICAL APPLIANCES
763. STEREO AMPLIFIERS
764. STEREO CASSETTE RECORDERS/PLAYERS
765. STREET LIGHT FITTINGS SURGE SUPPRESSOR
766. TANTALUM CAPACITORS
767. TEFLON COATED ELECTRIC CABLE
768. TELEMEDICINE (DISTANCE HEALTH CARE) (Rs. 5000/-)
769. TELEPHONE CORD/CABLE
770. TELEPHONE (PUSH BUTTON TYPE)
771. TELEPHONE (PUSH BUTTON & CORDLESS)
772. TELEVISION (CTV & B/W)
773. TELEVISION (3-D)
774. TELEVISION DEFLECTION COMPONENTS
775. TELEVISION SIGNAL BOOSTERS
776. TELEVISION TUNERS
777. TRACTION BATTERIES
778. TRAINING INSTITUTE OF MEDICAL TRANSCRIPTION
779. TRANSFORMER FOR B/W TV
780. TRANSFORMER FOR VOLTAGE STABILIZER & E.H.T
781. TRANSMISSION POWER LINE FITTING
782. TRANSMISSION TOWER FITTING
783. TV AUDIO EQUIPMENT CABINETS & THEIR ASSEMBLING UNIT
784. UN-INTERRUPTED POWER SUPPLY (U.P.S)
785. VARIABLE FREQUENCY
786. VARIABLE VOLTAGE A.C. DRIVE
787. VIDEO CASSETTES (COMPLETE MANUFACTURING & ASSEMBLING)
788. VIDEO CASSETTES RECORDER (V.C.R)
789. VIDEO FILM STUDIO
790. VOLTAGE REGULATOR FOR AUTOMOBILES
791. VOLTAGE STABILIZERS
792. VOLTAGE STABLIZER & T.V. GAIN BOOSTER
793. WAX AND CHEMICAL COATED, BRAIDED TINSEL WIRE
794. WEBSITE DESIGN & E-MAIL REGISTERING
795. WELDING ELECTRODES
796. WIND ENERGY POWER PROJECT (10 MW) WIRE WOUND POTENTIOMETERS

## FOOD, AGRO FOOD, PROCESSED FOOD, AGRO PLANTATION, CULTIVATION, FARMING, DAIRY/MILK, TOBACCO/PAN MASALA, BREWERY & DISTILLERY, EDIBLE OILS, EOU FOOD PRODUCTS AND ALLIED PRODUCTS

797. ALCOHOLIC BEVERAGES & VENEGAR FROM COCONUT WATER
798. ALCOHOL DRINKS FROM ETHYL ALCOHOL BY MIXING OF VARIOUS FLAVOURS
799. ANTI SCALE COMPOUND FOR ADDING INTO SUGAR JUICE BOILING
800. APPLE JUICE CONCENTRATED & DEHYDRATED FRUIT & VEGETABLES
801. ARTIFICIAL FISH MEAL FOR POULTRY FEED
802. AUTOMATIC BISCUIT PLANT
803. BABY CEREAL FOOD AND MILK POWDER
804. BACTERIA FOR CANE JUICE
805. BAKER'S YEAST
806. BAKERY INDUSTRY
807. BANANA PUREE
808. BEER & WINE
809. BEER PLANT (BREWERY)
810. BIDI
811. BIDI & CIGARETTE
812. BISCUIT PLANT

813. BREAD (AUTOMATIC PLANT)
814. BLACK PEPPER (SPICES)
815. BREAD AND BISCUITS
816. BREEDING FARM
817. BROILER CHICKEN
819. BUTTON MUSHROOM CULTIVATION & PROCESSING
820. CANNING OF RASAGULLAS IN METAL CANS
821. CAFFEIN FROM TEA WASTE
822. CANNING OF FRUITS & VEGETABLES
823. CASEIN AND BY-PRODUCTS
824. CASHEW FRUIT JUICE FROM CASHEW FRUIT APPLE
825. CASHEWNUT KERNEL EXTRACTION FROM CASHEWNUT FRUIT
826. CASHEWNUT SHELL LIQUID & KERNEL PROCESSING
827. CASHEW FENI
828. CATECHEU (BY CHEMICAL PROCESS)
829. CATTLE FEED FROM TAPIOCA
830. CHEWING & BUBBLE GUM
831. CHICKEN/SHEEP MEAT PROCESSING
832. CHOCOLATE (MILK)
833. CIGARETTE AND BEEDIES
834. COCOA BUTTER FROM COCOA MASS
835. COCONUT PRODUCTS & BY PRODUCTS PROCESS COMPLEX
836. COLD/SOFT DRINKS
837. COLLECTION OF MILK AND MILK MAKING POWDER
838. COLLECTION OF MILK AND PACKING IN POLYTHENE POUCH (1/2 KG.1 KG. & 2 KG.)
839. CONDENSED MILK (SWEETNED)
840. CONFECTIONERY INDUSTRY (TOFFEE & CANDY, SEMI-AUTOMATIC PLANT)
841. COUNTRY LIQUOR FROM MOLASSES
842. CIGARETTE
843. DAIRY FARM AND DAIRY (MILK) PRODUCTS (PASTEURISED MILK, BUTTER, GHEE, PANEER)
844. DAIRY FARM TO PRODUCE MILK & PACKING IN POUCHES (50%) & CAN(50%)
845. DAIRY FOR MILK PROCESSING
846. DAIRY FARM (BUFALO)
847. DAL (PULSE) MILL UNIT
848. DEHYDRATION OF CARROT & GARLIC
849. DEHYDRATION & CANNING OF FRUITS & VEGETABLES
850. DEHYDRATION OF FIGS
851. DEHYDRATION OF FRUITS AND VEGETABLES
852. DEHYDRATED ONIONS AND ONION POWDER
853. DRY ICE BY BREAKING OF AIR
854. DRYING OF RED CHILLIES, HALDI, DHANIA, AND GREEN PEAS
855. EGG POWDER (40,000 EGGS PROCESSING PER DAY)
856. EXPORT OF PROCESSED FOODS AND MARINE PRODUCTS
857. FISH CANNING & POUCHING
859. FISH FARMING (PRAWN & OTHER MARINE PRODUCTS)
860. FISH MEAL
861. FLOUR MILL AND MUSTARD OIL
862. FOOD COLOUR & ORASTED GROUNDNUT GRAM PEAS, ETC IN POUCHES
863. FROG LEGS PROCESSING
864. FROZEN MEATS PROCESSING
865. FOOD FLAVOURS (WHISKY) VODKA, GRAPE, BUTTER SCOTCH)
866. FOOD PRODUCTS COMPLEX (DEHYDRATED ONIONS, GARLIC POWDER & FLAKES, CATTLE FEED, TOMATO POWDER, TOMATO PRODUCTS, CANNED FRUITS & VEGETABLES, TOMATO PURE, GROUN NUT OIL, REFIND OIL, DEHYDRATED GRAPES, BANANA POWDER & WAFFERS)
867. FRUIT JUICE, JAM, JELLIES & ALLIED PRODUCTS
868. FRUIT JUICE, PICKLES PROCESSING AND CANNING
869. FRUIT JUICE MAKING & PACKING IN PLASTIC CONTAINER/POUCHES
870. FRUIT PROCESSING (JAM & JELLIES)
871. FRUIT PULP & JUICE CONCENTRATES
872. FRUIT & VEGETABLE DRYING (FREEZE DRYING METHOD)
873. GOAT & SHEEP FARMING
874. GRAM DALL/PULSE MILL
875. GRAPE DEHYDRATION
876. HARD BOILED CANDY (TOFFEE & CANDY)
877. HERBAL CIGARETTES
878. HONEY PROCESSING & PACKAGING
879. ICE CREAM OF DIFFERENT FLAVOURS
880. ICE CREAM STABILIZER
881. ICE MAKING PLANT
882. INDIAN MADE FOREIGN LIQUOR (I.M.F.L)
883. INSTANT FOOD (IDLI MIX, DOSA MIX, GULAB JAMUN MIX)
884. INSTANT FOOD (INSTANT FOOD & FAST FOOD PARLOUR)
885. INSTANT NOODLES
886. INSTANT TEA
887. INSTANT TEA FROM BLACK TEA
888. INTEGERATED STARCH BAKING POWDER/YEAST INDUSTRY
889. IODIZED SALT
890. IODIZED SALT (ORDINARY MOISTURE-LESS/FREE FLOWING IN PLASTIC BAGS AND CONTAINERS)
891. JAM, JELLIES, FRUIT JUICE & ALLIED PRODUCTS
892. KATHA AND CUTCH
893. KHANDSARI SUGAR
894. KHANDSARI SUGAR & IMFL
895. LACTIC ACID FROM WHITE SUGAR BY FERMENTATION PROCESS
896. LACTOSE & BY PRODUCTS PROCESSING FROM MILK
897. LIQUID GLUCOSE AND ITS BYE PRODUCTS
898. MACRONI AND VERMICILLI
899. MALT EXTRACTION FROM BARLEY
900. MANGO PROCESSING (MANGO PULP, JUICE & SLICES)
901. MAYUR BRAND TYPE CHEWING TOBACCO
902. MINERAL WATER
903. MILK PRESERVATION & MARKETING TO WHOLE SELLERS (INPOUCH PACKING BY UHT TECHNOLOGY)
904. MILK PROCESSING AND PACKAGING OF MILK PRODUCTS
905. MILK PRODUCTS (CASEIN, LACTOSE, GHEE & WHEY POWDER)
906. MILK TOFFEE
907. MINI FLOUR MILL
908. MINI SUGAR PLANT
909. MISRI (PEARL SUGAR CANDIES)
910. MODERN RICE MILL
911. MURABBA
912. MUSTARD OIL EXTRACTION & REFINING
913. MUTTON TALLOW
914. NAMKEEN INDUSTRY (BHUJIA, CHANA CHUR ETC.)
915. NAMKEEN & SWEETS
916. NON-BASMATI RICE FROM PADDY
917. OLEORESIN, ESSENTIAL OIL, DYES & POWDER OF SPICES
918. OLEORESIN EXTRACTION FROM DIPTERO-CARPUT TURMINATUS AND PINUS KHASYANA
919. OLEORESIN EXTRACTION FROM CHILLI
920. PAN MASALA AND POUCH

1059. BUFFALO HORN TIP, HOOF
1060. BANQUET HALL
1061. BUTTON
1062. CALCINED PETROLEUM (C.P) COKE
1063. CANVAS SHOES
1064. CANVAS SHOES, JUNGLE BOOTS
1065. CARBON BRUSH, BRUSH HOLDER & SLIP RING
1066. CEMENT SHEETS WITH COIR FIBRE & OTHER SEGMENTS
1067. CERAMIC TILES (GLAZED) BY DOUBLE FIRING/HEATING
1068. CHILDREN RECREATION CENTRE
1069. COAL BRIQUETTES
1070. COLD STORAGE & ICE
1071. COLD STORAGE FOR FRUITS AND VEGETABLES
1072. COMPRESSOR (HERMETIC) FOR AIR CONDITIONER
1073. COSTUME JEWELLERY/ IMITATION JEWELLERY
1074. DECORATIVE LAMINATED SHEET (SUNMICA)
1075. DIAMOND CUTTING & EXPORTS
1076. DRINKING STRAW FROM PROPYLENE
1077. ENGINEERING COLLEGE
1078. ENTERTAINMENT CLUB
1079. FASHION TECHNOLOGY INSTITUTE
1080. FAST FOOD PARLOUR
1081. FAST FOOD (INSTANT FOOD & FAST FOOD PARLOUR)
1082. FIRE EXTINGUISHERS (SODA ACID TYPE)
1083. FISH NET
1084. FLORICULTURE (CUT FLOWER ROSE) WITH GREEN HOUSE
1085. FLOOR COVERING SHEET
1086. FILM STUDIO (VIDEO)
1087. FLUSH DOOR, CHIP BOARD, WOOD WOOL & OTHER INSULATING BOARDS
1088. GAS DETECTORS OF L.P.G
1089. GEMS MANUFACTURING
1090. GLASS BOTTLE BY SCRAP
1092. GOAT & SHEEP FARMING
1093. GOLD ELECTROPLATING
1094. GOLD JEWELLERY (E.O.U)
1095. GOLD PLATED SILVER JEWELLERY & CUTLERY
1096. GRANITE SLAB AND TILES
1097. GREEN HOUSE
1098. HARD CHROMIUM PLATING
1099. HEALTH CLUB AND BEAUTY PARLOUR CUM HAIR SALOON WITH SONA BATH
1100. HEALTH CLUB CUM BEAUTY PARLOUR TRAININGINSTITUTE
1101. HORN TIP,HOOVE BUTTON
1102. HOSPITAL
1103. HOSPITAL (100 BEDS)
1104. HOSPITAL (200 BEDS)
1105. ICE MAKING PLANT
1106. IMITATION AND COSTUME
1107. JEWELLERY (NECKLACE, EARRINGS EAR TOP ETC.)
1108. INITMATE SCENT CHEMICALS FROM ALL TYPES OF FLAVOUR
1109. INVESTMENT CASTING
1110. JUTE, COIR, GLASS ROPE/ SUTLI
1111. JUTE TWINE
1112. L.P.G BOTTLING PLANT
1113. L.P.G REGULATOR (DOMESTIC PURPOSE)
1114. LAMINATED PARTICLE BOARD & HARD BOARD
1115. LAMINATED SAFETY AND TOUGHENED GLASS
1116. LEASING & HIRE PURCHASE
1117. LICHEN (CHARILA)
1118. MANILA ROPES
1119. MEDICAL COLLEGE
1120. MATCH UNIT FROM WAXED PAPER
1121. MEDIUM DENSITY FIBRE BOARD
1122. MELAMINE CROCKERY
1123. MINERAL WATER
1124. MINI CEMENT PLANT
1125. MIRROR SILVER, GOLDEN, PINK, BLACK & SMOKES
1126. MODERN ADVERTISING AGENCY WITH DTP & FILM STUDIO
1127. MOTEL/SMALL HOTEL
1128. MULTI COLOUR PRINTING
1129. MULTI STOREY COMMERCIAL COMPLEX ALONGWITH RESIDENTIAL AND DELUX FLATS FOR FOREIGN TOURISTS & REVOLVING RESTAURENT AT THE TOP
1130. MULTIPLE LAMINATION INDUSTRY
1131. MUSHROOM GROWING AND PROCESSING (BY DEEP FREEZING METHOD)
1132. NEWS PAPER PRINTING
1133. NICKEL LINED INDUSTRIAL SCREEN
1134. OFFSET COLOUR PRINTING PRESS (SIX COLOUR)
1135. OFFSET PRINTING PRESS
1136. P.C.C ELECTRIC POLES
1137. PHOTOGRAPHIC DEVELOPER & FIXER
1138. PVC EXTRUSION PROFILE (DOOR & WINDOWS)
1139. POP-CORN
1140. PHOTO ETCHING OF S.S.
1141. PRE STRESSED CEMENT CONCRETE PIPES
1142. PILFER PROOF CAPS
1143. PILFER PROOF CAPS AND CROWN CAP
1144. POUCH MAKING & GRAVURE PRINTING (ROTO PRINTING)
1145. POULTRY & FISH FARMING (INTEGERATED UNIT)
1146. PRINTING OF TIN SHEETS
1147. READYMADE GARMENTS
1148. RESTAURANT
1149. ROSE PLANTATION AND ROSE OIL EXTRACTION
1150. ROTOGRAVURE PRINTING
1151. SAFETY BELTS
1152. SAFETY MATCHES
1153. SHOE LACES
1154. SILKCOCOON CULTIVATION (GROWING OF SILK COCOON WARM)
1155. SILK SCREEN PRINTING FORMULATIONS FOR PLASTIC, PAPER & CLOTH
1156. SPIKENARD (JATAMANSI)
1157. STENCIL COATING SOLUTION
1158. SUGAR CANDY (MISRI)
1159. SUGAR CANE PLANTATION
1160. SUGAR CANE JUICE PRESERVATION
1161. SURAT ZARI
1162. SYNTHETIC SHOES & SOLES
1163. TEA PACKAGING INDUSTRY
1164. TENNIS BALLS
1165. THREE STAR HOTEL
1166. TRAVELLING AGENCY
1167. TRAYS, TROLLEYS FOR HOSPITAL WITH SCRATCHLESS COATING
1168. WAX EXTRACTS (TANNING POWDER)
1169. WIRE ROPE SLINGS
1170. WOOD WOOL SLAB
1171. WOODEN CANE FURNITURE WITH EXPORT POTENTIAL
1172. WOODEN FURNITURE
1173. WOODEN PANEL INCLUDING KILN SEASONING
1174. WOODEN FURNITURE
1175. WATCH CASE BUFFING
1176. WATCH DIAL
1177. WRIST WATCHES
1178. WATCHES (ELECTRONIC)
1179. ZEDOARY (KACHUR)

## EDIBLE OILS, ESSENTIAL OILS LURICATIING OILS, GREASES, VEGETABLE OILS, WAXES, CAMPHOR, PERFUMES & PERFUMERY COMPOUNDS AND REFINED OILS ETC.

1180. AROMATIC PERFUMERY COMPOUND
1181. AEROSOL
1182. AGARBATTI PERFUMERY COMPOUND
1183. BEES WAX MANUFACTURE
1184. CAMPHOR
1185. CARDANOL FROM CASHEW NUT SHELL LIQUID
1186. CASTOR OIL
1187. CASTOR OIL DERIVATIVE OLEORESINS
1188. CHILLI OIL
1189. CITRONELLA OILS
1190. CLOVE OIL
1191. CONCENTRATE OF ROSE JASMINE & LILY ETC.
1192. COLOURED FLAME CANDLE

1193. CANDLES (SEMI-AUTOMATIC)
1194. CORN OIL (MAIZE OIL)
1195. DEHYDRATED CASTOR OIL
1196. EUGENOL FROM CINNAMON LEAF OIL
1197. EXTRACTION OF ESSENTIAL OIL (CARDAMON, JEERA, AJOWAN, GINGER OILS ETC. & PACKAGING OF GROUND SPICES)
1198. EXTRACTION OF JASMINE ESSENCE
1199. EXTRACTION OF ESSENTIAL OILS BY SUPER CRITICAL FLUID METHOD FROM FLOWERS, HERBS & SPICES
1200. EUCALYPTUS OIL
1201. EXTRACTION OF OIL FROM OIL SEED EXPANDEREXTRUSION TECHNOLOGY)
1202. FAT LIQUOR SULPHATED OIL
1203. FLAVOURS FOR FOOD
1204. GARLIC OIL & POWDER
1205. GINGER OIL, SANDALWOOD OIL AND NAGARMOTHA OIL
1206. GINGER OIL
1207. GINGER OIL & GINGER DUST
1208. INTEGERATED WAX COMPLEX
1209. IONONE FROM LEMON GRASS OIL
1210. JASMINE & LILLY FLOWER OIL
1211. LEMON GRASS OIL
1212. LIQUID PARAFFIN
1213. LUBE OIL & GREASE
1214. LUBRICATING OIL
1215. MENTHOL CRYSTALS
1216. MENTHOL OIL & CRYSTAL
1217. MICRO CRYSTALLINE WAX
1218. MUSTARD OIL (EDIBLE OIL)
1219. OIL FROM ARTEMISIA HERBS
1220. PALM OIL CRUSHING UNIT
1221. PAN MASALA
1222. PARAFFIN WAX
1223. PARAFFIN WAX FROM SLACK WAX
1224. REFINED OIL-SUN FLOWER OIL, GROUNDNUT OIL, STAFF FLOWER OIL & COTTON SEED OIL
1225. REFINED VEGETABLE OIL
1226. RECLAMATION OF USED ENGINE OIL
1227. RICE BRAN OIL (R.B.O)
1228. ROSE OIL EXTRACTION
1229. SMOKE LESS CANDLE
1230. SPICE OIL & OLEORESINS
1231. SOLVENT EXTRACTION PLANT (OIL CAKE BASED)
1232. SYNTHETIC ALMOND OIL
1233. SYNTHETIC TALLOW
1234. SYNTHETIC GHEE
1235. VEGETABLE OIL EXTRACTION & REFINING
1236. WADDING OIL (100%) FOR WADDING OF COTTON HOSIERY CLOTH IN DYEING PROCESS
1237. WAX EMULSION FOR TEXTILE
1238. WAX FLOOR POLISH

## PAINT, ENAMEL, SOLVENTS, THINNERS, INKS & VARNISH

1239. ACRYLIC EMULSION PAINTS
1240. ALUMINIUM PAINT
1241. AUTOMOBILE PAINTS
1242. BALL POINT PEN REFILL INK
1243. BITUMINIOUS ROAD EMULSION
1244. BITUMEN
1245. BITUMINIOUS FELTS FOR WATER & DAMP PROOFING
1246. BITUMINIOUS ROAD EMULSION RAPID MEDIUM & SLOW SETTING
1247. BUFFING & POLISHING
1248. CEMENT PAINT FOR WHITE & GREY CEMENT

1249. DISPERSANT
1250. DRY DISTEMPER
1251. DRY DISTEMPER & CEMENT PAINT
1252. DUPLICATING INK BLACK FOR GESTNER DUPLICATOR
1255. EMULSION PAINTS (WATER BASED)
1256. HAMMERTONE PAINT
1257. INSULATING VARNISH & WIRE ENAMEL
1258. IRON OXIDE PIGMENTS
1259. INSULATING VARNISH (POLY VINYL BUTYRAL BASED, FFC GRADE)
1260. LIME COLOUR (CEMENT COLOUR)
1261. SYNTHETIC RED OXIDE FOR FLOORINGS
1262. SOLVENT & THINNERS
1263. MARKING INKS (WATER PROOF)
1264. METAL NAPHTHANATE (AS DRIER FOR PAINTS)
1265. N.C.PUTTY
1266. OFFSET PRINTING INK
1267. OIL BOUND DISTEMPER PAINT
1268. PAINT BRUSHES
1269. PAINT REMOVERS
1270. PAINT INDUSTRY
1271. PAINT & VARNISH
1272. PICTURE VARNISH
1273. POWDER COATING PAINT
1274. PRINTING INKS (OFFSET, FLEXO & ROTO GRAVURE)
1275. PRIMER PAINT & ENAMEL PAINT
1276. PUTTY & WATER PROOFING PAINT
1277. PRINTING INKS (FLEXO-GRAPHIC INK)
1278. PUTTY (METAL CASEMENT)
1279. RED OXIDE PRIMER (ANTI CORROSIVE)
1280. REFRECTORY PAINT (GRAPHITE BASED)
1281. SCREEN PRINTING INKS
1282. SILK SCREEN PRINTING INK FORMULATION FOR PLASTIC, PAPER, CLOTH
1283. STAMP & PAD INK
1284. STOVING PAINT
1285. SPIRIT SOLUBLE MALEIC RESIN
1286. TEXTURE PAINT
1287. THINNERS AND ITS ALLIED PRODUCTS
1288. TONER INK
1289. VARNISH THINNER (SOLVENT)
1290. VACUUM METALLIZING LACQUERS
1291. WOOD PRIMER

## PHARMACEUTICAL, DRUGS, AYURVEDIC/HERBAL COSMETICS & MEDICINES, HOMOEOPATHIC MEDICINES, DISPOSABLE SYRINGE, DENTAL COLLEGE & FINE CHEMICALS ETC.

1292. AROMATIC FILLS
1293. ASPIRIN
1294. AYURVEDIC PAIN BALM OINTMENTS
1295. AYURVEDIC CHURAN AND TABLETS
1296. AYURVEDIC TABLETS (HAJMOLA TYPE)
1297. AYURVEDIC HERBAL PHARMACY
1298. AYURVEDIC SHERBATS
1299. AYURVEDIC PRODUCTS
1300. BULK DRUGS (E.O.U)
1301. BLOOD BAGS
1302. CALCIUM GLUCONATE
1303. CAPSULE, TABLET & INJECTION WITH MODERN INSTRUMENTS
1304. CASHEW FENI
1305. CHLOROQUINONE PHOSPHATE (BULK DRUGS)
1306. CLINICAL THERMOMETER
1307. DENTAL CLINIC

1308. DENTAL COLLEGE
1309. DENTAL GRADE EUGENOL
1310. DEXTROSE MONOHYDRATE, LIQUID GLUCOSE
1311. DEHYDRATED ONION & ONION POWDER
1312. DEXTROSE POWDER (ANHYDROUS FROM STARCH)
1314. DEXTROSE SALINE SOLUTION
1315. DISTILLERY (I.M.F.L)
1316. DISPOSABLE NEEDLES FOR SYRINGES
1317. DISPRIN
1318. DISTILLED WATER
1319. EMPTY HARD GELATINE CAPSULES
1320. FILLING & PACKING OF CAPSULES
1321. GLUCOSE - D - POWDER
1322. GLYCERINE
1323. HERBAL COSMETICS
1324. HERBAL SHAMPOO
1325. HERBAL HAIR OILS (AYURVEDIC)
1326. HOMOE & BIO-MEDICINES WITH MOTHER TINCTURE
1327. HOMOEPATHIC MEDICINES
1328. HYPODERMIC NEEDLES
1329. I.V. FLUIDS
1330. IBUPROFEN
1331. INFUSION & TRANSFUSION SETS (I.V. SET)
1332. INJECTABLE FOR PHARMACEUTICALS
1333. INJECTION AMPOULES PACKAGING BOX
1334. INTEGERATED SURGICAL COTTON
1335. ICE MAKING PLANT
1336. ICE & COLD STORAGE
1337. LACTOSE & BY PRODUCTS PROCESSING FROM MILK
1338. LICHEN (JATAMANSI CHARILA)
1339. LIQUID GLUCOSE AND ITS BY-PRODUCTS
1340. L-LYSINE MONOHYDRO CHLORIDE
1341. LIQUID GLUCOSE FROM POTATOES
1342. MEDICAL COLLEGE
1343. NICOTINE FROM TOBACCO WASTE
1344. OINTMENT-AYURVEDIC (YELLOW & WHITE)
1345. PHARMACEUTICAL AND FOOD GRADE GELATINE
1346. PHARMACEUTICAL INDUSTRY (TABLETS, CAPSULES, LIQUID, GEL, OINTMENT POWDER INJECTABLE)
1347. PHARMACEUTICAL UNIT (EOU) WITH FORMULA TIONS, INJECTABLES, ETC. PYRIDINE & DERIVATIVES
1348. SALT (IODIZED SALT)
1349. SALINE & INJECTION WATER
1350. SALINE WATER & DEXTROSE SOLUTION (I.V.FLUID IN PLASTIC BOTTLES)
1351. SORBITOL
1352. STARCH (MAIZE)
1353. SURGICAL ADHESIVE PLASTER
1354. SURGICAL BANDAGES
1355. SURGICAL GLOVES
1357. SURGICAL COTTON
1358 SURGICAL COTTON AND BANDAGE
1359 SYNTHETIC CAMPHOR POWDER
1360 TABLETS & CAPSULES
1361 TISSUE CULTURE
1362 TINCTURE FROM RECTIFIED SPIRIT
1363 TRIMETHOPIME
1364 VETERENARY MEDICINES (ONLY FORMULATIONS)
1365 VITAMIN 'C', SORBITOL' ANHYDROUS DEXTROSE, STARCH

## PULP, PAPER, STRAW/GREY BOARD, KRAFT PAPER, PACKAGING, PAPER CARRY BAGE, PAPER FROM AGRO WASTE & STATIONERY ETC.

1366. AMMONIA PAPER
1367. AUTOMATIC BOOK BINDING
1368. ADHESIVE (FEVICOL TYPE)
1369. ALL PIN & GEM CLIPS
1370. CARBON PAPER
1371. CARD BOARD
1372. CARBON LESS PAPER
1373. CELLPHANE PAPER
1374. COMPUTER FORMS & SECURITY PRINTING PRESS
1375. CORRUGATED BOARD & BOX (PRINTED & LAMINATED)
1376. CORRUGATED BOARD AND BOXES FROM FROM CARD BOARDS
1377. CORRUGATED CARTONS FROM PLAIN PAPERS
1378. CORRUGATRED PACKING & MATERIAL (BULB & TUBES PACKING)
1379. DESK TOP PUBLISHING
1380. DEFOAMING AGENT FOR PAPER PLANT
1381. DRINKING STRAW PAPER
1382. D.T.P CUM OFFSET PRESS
1383. EGG TRAYS
1384. EXERCISE NOTE BOOK, REGISTER AND PAD
1385. FLEXOGRAPHIC INK
1386. GREETING CARD BY OFFSET PRESS
1387. HAND MADE PAPER FILTER PAPER
1388. HARD BOARD
1389. INJECTION AMPOULES PACKAGING BOXES
1390. INSULATIING PAPER
1391. KRAFT PAPER
1392. KRAFT PAPER FROM BAGASSE
1393. LAMINATED PACKAGING PAPER WITH PRINTING
1394. LAMINATION & COATING ON PAPER
1395. M.G. PAPER FROM WASTE PAPER
1396. MILL PAPER FROM WASTE PAPER
1397. MILL BOARD FROM RICE & WHEAT STRAWS
1398. MILL BOARD FROM WASTE PAPER
1399. MINI PAPER PLANT FROM SISAL
1400. MINI PAPER PLANT
1401. MULTI WALL PAPER SACKS
1402. NEWS PAPER FOR CHILDREN
1403. NEWS PRINT PAPER FROM RICE STRAW BAGASSE
1404. NEWS PAPER CHILDRENS
1405. NEWS PRINT PAPER
1406. OFFSET AND TREADLE TYPE PRINTING PRESS
1407. MILL BOARD BASED ON RICE STRAW
1408. PAPER AND BOARD FROM STRAW
1409. PAPER & PAPER PRODUCTS
1410. PAPER ENVELOPES
1411. PAPER CARRY BAGS
1412. PAPER BOARD CARTON
1413. PAPER CONES FOR LOUD SPEAKERS
1414. PAPER FROM AKRA
1415. PAPER FROM BAGASSE WITH CORRUGATED BOARD & BOXES
1416. PAPER FROM BAMBOO
1417. PAPER GLASSES FOR BEVERAGES
1418. PAPER FROM RICE HUSK & WHEAT HUSK
1419. PAPER FROM TREE BARK, EUCALYPRUS WOOD
1420. PAPER PRODUCTS
1421. PAPER PLANT (WHITE WRITING & NEWS PAPER FOR PULP & WASTE PAPER)
1422. PAPER PLATES, PAPER GLASS
1423. PAPER CONES & TUBES
1425. PAPER PLANT WITH DTP & PRINTING & PUBLISHING UNIT
1426. PAPER BASED PHENOLIC SHEET
1427. PAPER CUP FOR ICE CREAM
1428. PAPER TUBES SPIRAL WINDING COMPOSIT CONTAINER
1429. PAPER LABLE FOR BEER BOTTLES
1430. PARTICLE BOARD & BLACK BOARD WITH SANDING & LAMINATION OF PARTICLE BOARD
1431. PARTICLE BOARD FROM RICE HUSK
1432. POUCH FILLING & MAKING FOR TOMATO SAUCE
1433. POUCH MAKING &

INSULATION & SHEETS GRADES)
1550. P.V.C GRANULES FROM PVC SCRAPS (WITH POLLUTION CONTROL)
1551. P.V.C HOSES
1552. P.V.C LEATHER CLOTH
1553. P.V.C FLEXIBLE PIPES
1554. P.V.C PIPES AND FITTINGS
1555. POLYTHENE BAGS (PRINTED)
1556. PVC PLASTICS FILM SHEET SOFT/RIGID
1557. PVC RESIN AND COMPOUND
1558. PVC RULAR
1559. PVC STABLIZERS (SINGLE PACK SYSTEM)
1560. PVC WIRE AND CABLES
1561. PAPER BASED PHENOLIC SHEET FOR ELECTRICAL
1562. PHENOL FORMALDEHYDE RESIN
1563. PHENOLIC RESIN
1564. PLASTIC BEADS FROM PLASTIC SCRAPS
1565. PLASTIC BUTTONS
1566. PLASTIC CANS
1567. PLASTIC COLLAPSIBLE TUBE
1568. PLASTIC CORRUGATED SHEET & BOXES
1569. PLASTIC FILM AND SHEETS WITH PRINTING FLEXO & ROTO/LDPE/HDPE/PP/HM/PVC
1570. PLASTIC FILTER MASTER BATCH & OTHER MASTER BATCHES FOR VARIOUS PLASTICS
1571. PLASTIC JERRY CANS
1572. PLASTIC GRANULES OR POWDER FROM PLASTIC SCRAP
1573. PLASTIC INJECTION MOULDED T.V. CABINETS
1574. PLASTIC ITEMS MANUFAC TURE FROM POWDER MELAMINE
1575. PLASTIC GOODS
1576. PLASTIC PIPES & TARPAULINES
1577. PLASTIC SHEET FROM SCRAP
1578. PLASTIC PLANT (BLOW MOULDING & INJECTION MOULDING)
1579. PLASTIC PRODUCTS (GOLD, SILVER, NICKEL)
1580. PLASTIC TOYS
1581. POLYESTER BEADING
1582. POLYESTER FILM
1583. POLYTHENE BAGS & AUTOMATIC PRINTING
1584. POLYTHENE PRINTED BAGS
1585. POLYURETHANE FOAM AND ITS PRODUCTS
1586. PROPYLENE FILM (PRINTED) & BAG MANUFACTURING
1587. PLASTIC MATS
1588. RAINBOW COLOUR ON PVC FILM & SHEET
1589. RED MUD PVC PIPES AND FITTINGS
1590. RE-RUBBERISED OF SOLID TYPE
1591. RESIN COATED SAND REXINE
1592. REXINE CLOTH & ALLIED PRODUCTS
1593. RUBBER ADHESIVE
1594. RUBBER AUTO PARTS
1595. RUBBER BELTING
1596. RUBBER MOULDING UNIT INCLUDING LINING RUBBER SHEETING
1597. RUBBER RECLAIMING
1598. RUBBER ROLLERS FOR TEXTILE MILLS & PAPER INDUSTRIES
1599. RUBBER & PLASTIC SHEETS, MATS & FLAPS
1600. RUBBER SHEET AND ALLIED HOSPITAL RUBBER GOODS
1601. RUBBERIZED PVC GASKET
1602. RUBBERISED COIR
1603. RUBBER COMPOUND FOR AUTOMOBILES
1604. SAFETY BELTS
1605. SILVER AND GOLD PLATING ON PVC AND NYLON-6
1606. SILICONE RUBBER NIPPLES/ TEATS
1607. SPECTACLE FRAMES (PLASTIC)
1608. SPUNGE RUBBER
1609. SURGICAL EXAMINATION GLOVES
1610. SYNTHETIC PEARL COATING ON POLYSTYRENE BEADS
1611. SYNTHETIC RUBBER ADHESIVE
1612. TEFLON MANUFACTURING
1613. TEFLON TAPE
1614. TEFLON TAPES & CABLES
1615. THERMOCOLE SHEET AND MOULDED PRODUCTS EXPANDED POLYESTERENE EXTRUSION PROFILES
1616. THERMOFORMED PACKAGING (BLISTER PACKAGING & POUCH PACKAGING)
1617. THERMOPLASTIC POLYURETHANE
1618. THERMOFORMED CUPS, PLATES & GLASS WITH HIPS SHEET
1619. THERMOCOLE
1620. THERMOCOLE BASED DISPOSABLE GLASS, CUPS & PLATES
1621. TOOTH BRUSHES
1622. TOY BALLOON, DECORA TIVE & INDUSTRIAL BALLOONS
1623. TREAD RUBBER
1624. TYRE RETREADING (HOT)
1625. TYRE RETREADING BY COLD PROCESS
1626. TYRE TUBES & FLAPS
1627. TYRE & TUBES
1628. UNSATURATED POLYESTER FOR REXINE
1629. V-BELT AND FAN BELT
1630. VINYL ASBESTOS AND PVC WALL PAPER
1631. VITON (FLUORO ELASTOMER)

## SOAP, COSMETICS & PERFUMS

1632. ACID SLURRY, SYNTHETIC DETERGENT POWDER
1632. ACID SLURRY
1633. AGARBATTI SYNTHETIC, PERFUMERY COMPOUND
1634. AFTER SHAVE LOTION
1635. ANTISEPTIC CREAM
1636. BETA IONONE
1637. BLEACHING POWDER
1638. BLUE DETERGENT POWDER
1639. CLEANING POWDER (VIMTYPE)
1640. COLD CREAM
1641. COLOURED FLAME & PERFUMED CANDLES (RED, BLUE, GREEN FLAME)
1642. COSMETIC INDUSTRY (MODERN)
1643. COSMETIC INDUSTRY (SHAMPOO, SPRAY PERFUME, TALCUM POWDER
1644. DETERGENT POWDER (ARIEL TYPE)
1645. DETERGENT POWDER (NIRMA TYPE) FULLY AUTOMATIC PLANT
1646. DETERGENT WASHING POWDER
1647. FISH OIL SOAP
1648. GLYCERINE TRANSPARENT SOAP
1649. HAIR REMOVING CREAM
1650. HERBAL COSMETICS
1651. HERBAL SHAMPO & CREAM
1652. HERBAL/AYURVEDIC COSMETICS
1653. INCENSE POWDER, INCENSE STICKS & INCENSE CAKE
1654. OPTICAL WHITENERS
1655. ROSE OIL EXTRACTION
1656. SHAMPOOS (COCONUT OIL BASED COLD PROCESS)
1657. SHAVING CREAM
1658. SINDUR (KUMKUM)
1659. SOAP COATED PAPER
1660. SPRAY DRIED DETERGENT POWDER
1661. STAIN REMOVER
1662. TALCUM POWDER (FACE & TOILET POWDER)
1663. TOILET AND HERBAL SOAP
1664. TOOTH PASTE & POWDER
1665. WASHING DETERGENT POWDER AND WASHING SOAP
1666. WASHING POWDER LIQUID DETERGENTS, LOTION & SHAMPOO

ENTERTAINMENT CLUB WITH 4 STAR HOTEL
1779. HOSPITALS
1780. ICE CREAM PARLOUR
1781. INTERNET SERVICE PROVIDER (I.S.P.)
1782. MEDICAL COLLEGE
1783. MEDICAL COLLEGE, HOSPITAL & RESEARCH INSTITUTE
1784. MEDICAL TRANSCRIPTION CENTRE
1785. MENTAL RETARDATION HOSPITAL & CEREBRAL PALSY
1786. MOTEL/SMALL HOTEL
1787. MULTISTOREY COMMERCIAL COMPLEX
1788. MULTISTOREY RESIDENTIAL COMPLEX
1789. NURSERY SCHOOL
1790. NATURE CARE CENTRE
1791. NURSING HOME
1792. ONLINE SHOPPING MALL (RS. 5000/- REPORT)
1793. PORTAL
1794. REHABILITATION CENTRE FOR AGED & NEEDY PERSONS
1795. RESIDENTIAL CUM COMMERCIAL COMPLEX
1796. RESTAURANT
1797. RESTAURANT WITH PUB
1798. SCHOOL (PRIMARY)
1799. SCHOOL (HIGHER SECONDARY)
1800. THREE STAR HOTEL
1801. TOURIST CLUB
1802. TRAINING INSTITUTE FOR MEDICAL TRANSCRIPTION
1803. VIDEO FILM STUDIO
1804. WARE HOUSE
1805. WEBSITE DESIGN & E-MAIL REGISTERING

## AGRO BASED INDUSTRIES

1806. COAL BRIQUETTES FROM AGROWASTE
1807. FURFURALFROM RICEHULL
1808. MUSHROOM CULTIVATION & PROCESSING (BUTTON)
1809. MUSHROOM GROWING & PROCESSING WITH AIR CONDITIONING
1810. MUSHROOM CULTIVATION & PROCESSING UNIT DEHYDRATION & PACKAGING OF OYSTER & PADDY STRAW MUSHROOMS
1811. ORGANIC MANURE
1812. PAPAYA CULTIVATION
1813. PAPAYA & TOMATO CULTIVATION
1814. PROCESSING & UTILISATION OF COCONUT
1815. PROCESSING OF SHEEP HAIR TO PRODUCE WOOL

## BAKERY, CONFECTIONERY & FOOD PRODUCTS

1816. AGROLACTOR SOYA MILK
1817. APPLE FRUIT JUICE WITH CANNING BOTTLING
1818. AYURVEDIC SHARBAT
1819. BAKERY UNIT (PASTRIES, BREAD, BUNS, CAKE, TOFFEE ETC.)
1820. BAKING POWDER
1821. BANANA & ITS BY PRODUCTS
1822. BANANA POWDER
1823. BANANA WAFERS
1824. BANANA CULTIVATION
1825. BEER INDUSTRY
1826. DEHULLING OF JAUN FOR BEER
1827. BEER & WINE
1828. BEER, ALCOHOL, IMFL
1829. BESEN PLANT
1830. BISCUIT PLANT
1831. BREAD & BISCUIT PLANT
1832. BOTTLING PLANT COUNTRY LIQUOR FROM RECTIFIED SPIRIT
1833. BRANDY
1834. BREAD RUSKS
1835. CANNED FRUITS & VEGETABLES
1836. CANNING & PRESERVATION OF MEAT
1837. CANNING & PRESERVATION OF VEGETABLES
1838. CANNING OF MANGO PULP & MANGO SLICES
1839. CARBONATED BEVERAGS
1840. CASHEW FENI
1841. CASHEW NUT (DRIED & FRIED)
1842. CATTLE BREEDING
1843. CATTLE BREEDING & DAIRY FARM TO PRODUCE MILK
1844. CATTLE FEED FROM TAPIOCA
1845. CHEWING GINGER & AMLOKI
1846. CHEWING GUM
1847. CHILLI SAUCE
1848. CHILLI POWDER
1849. CHOCOLATE
1850. CIDER PLANT
1851. COCOA POWDER
1852. COCOA BUTTER & COCOA POWDER
1853. COCONUT SHELL POWDER
1854. COCONUT WATER
1855. COCONUT SWEET (WATERY)
1856. COCONUT MILK POWDER (DEHYDRATED)
1857. COCONUT PRODUCTS & BY PRODUCTS (INTEGRATED PLANT)
1858. COLD DRINK
1859. CURRY POWDER
1860. DAIRY FOR MILK PROCESSING (GHEE, BUTTER & PANEER)
1861. DAIRY PRODUCTS
1862. DAIRY PRODUCTS MILK PACKAGING IN POUCH (GHEE, BUTTER, ETC.
1863. DAIRY FARM TO PRDUCE MILK WITH PACKAGING (COW)
1864. DAIRY FARM TO PRDUCE MILK WITH PACKAGING (BUFALLOE)
1865. DAIRY FARM & MILK PRODUCTS
1866. DAL MOTH, CHANACHUR & BHUJIYA
1867. DEHYDRATION OF FRUITS & VEGETABLE
1868. DESICCATED COCONUT POWDER FROM COCONUTS
1869. DEHYDRATION & CANNINGOF FRUITS & VEGETABLES
1870. DRY FRUIT ROASTING & PACKAGING
1871. DRYING OF RED CHILLIES, HALDI, DHANIYA, PEAS & GROUND NUT
1872. EGG POWDER
1873. FISH CANNING IN TIN & POUCHES
1874. FISH DEHYRATION (DRYING OF FISH)
1875. FISH MEAL
1876. FISH PROCESSING (BEAST FREEZING PROCESSES)
1877. FLAVOURS FOR FOOD INDUSTRIES
1878. FLOUR MILL (ROLLER)
1879. FROZEN MEAT
1880. FOOD DEHYDRATION (FRUITS & VEGETABLES)
1881. FRIED & ROASTED GROUND NUT, GRAMS, PEAR ETC.
1882. FRUIT JUICE MAKING & PACKAGING IN PLASTIC CONTAINER
1883. FRUIT JUICE IN TETRA PACK (DRINKS)
1884. FRUIT JUICE, SQUASHES, SAUCE & KETCHUP, JAM, JELLY, VINEGAR ETC.
1885. GARLIC FLAKES
1886. GARLIC POWDER
1887. GHEE & BUTTER
1888. GINGER (PULVERISED)
1889. GINGER GLAZING & PRESERVATION
1890. GINGER STORAGE
1891. GINGER PROCESSING
1892. GINGER OIL & GINGER DUST
1893. GINGER POWDER (DRY) & OLEORESIN
1894. GRAPE DEHYDRATION
1895. GRAPE CULTIVATION
1896. GRAPE JUICE
1897. HONEY PROCESSING & PACKAGING
1898. ICE CREAM & ICE CANDY
1899. ICE CUBE
1900. INVERT SUGAR
1901. IDLI MIX, DOSA MIX SAMBHAR MIX, VADA MIX, GULAB JAMUN MIX
1902. INSTANT COFFEE & INSTANT TEA

1903. INSTANT NOODLES
1904. INSTANT SOUPS
1905. IODIZED SALT FROM CRUDE SALT
1906. JAM CHUTNEY PICKLES & SQUASHES
1907. KATHA MANUFACTURING
1908. LECITHIN (SOYA BASED)
1909. LEMON & ITS PRODUCTS
1910. MACARONI MANUFACTURING
1911. MACARONI, SPAGHETTI, VERMICELLI & NOODLES
1912. MAIZE & ITS BY PRODUCTS MALTING PLANT
1913. MANGO PAPPAD (AAM PAPPAD)
1914. MANGO POWDER RIPE
1915. MANGO POWDER
1916. MANGO PROCESSING & CANNING (MANGO PULP)
1917. MEAT PROCESSING (CHICKEN MUTTON)
1918. MEAT PROCESSING (BUFFALO)
1919. MENTHOL BOLD FROM MENTHOL FLAKES
1020. MILK POWDER
1921. MILK POWDER & GHEE
1922. MILK POWDER, GHEE & SPICES
1923. MILK PRESERVATION & MARKETING TO WHOLE SELLERS
1924. MILK PRESERVATION & MARKETING TO WHOLE SELLERS (IN POUCHES)
1925. MILK TOFFEE MANUFACTURES
1926. MINERAL WATER
1927. MINERAL WATER IN POUCHES
1928. MINI FLOUR MILL ATTA MAIDA, SUJI & WHEAT BRAN
1929. MITHAI/HALWAI (SWEET & NAMKEEN)
1930. MUTTON PROCESSING
1931. PAN MASALA (MEETHA, SADA, ZARDA) MAKING & PACKING
1932. PAN MASALA AND POUCH MAKING
1933. PANEER (CHEESE)
1934. PAPAD & BARIYAN
1935. PAPAD PLANT
1936. PEPSICOLA IN POLYTUBES
1937. PETHA PACKAGING
1938. PICKLES
1939. PIGGERY/MEAT/CHICKEN PROCESSING
1940. PINE APPLE JUICE CANNING
1941. POTATO & ONION POWDER
1942. POTATO & ONION FLAKES
1943. POTATO CHIPS
1944. POTATO GRANULES
1945. POUCH FILLING FOR SAUNF SUPARI ILAICHI ETC.
1946. PRESERVATION OF RAWS MANGO JUICE
1947. PROCESSED CHEESE & MARINE PDTS.
1948. PULP FROM TARMARIND
1949. READYMATE PROCESSED FOOD
1950. RICE & CORN FLAKES
1951. RICE BASMATI (TRADING)
1952. RICE POLISHING & PACKAGING IN POUCH
1953. ROASTED/SALTED/MASALA/ CASHEW NUTS ALMONDS & PEA NUT
1954. ROLLER FLOUR MILL

## INFOTECH/IT PROJECTS

1955. MEDICAL TRANSCRIPTION
1956. E-COMMERCE
1957. CYBERCAFE
1958. INTERNET SERVICE PROVIDER (ISP)
1959. COMPUTER EDUCATION CENTRE
1960. PORTAL (WEBSITE DESIGN)
1961. CALL CENTRE

# TERMS AND CONDITIONS

## FOR INDIA

1. Price Rs. 4200/- (Rs. Four Thousand Two Hundred Only) for Each *Market Survey Cum Detailed Techno Economic Feasibility Report.* Payable in advance through Draft/M.O./Cash in favour of 'ENGINEERS INDIA RESEARCH INSTITUTE', Delhi. Delivery by Regd.post within 2 Days. (Postage Free)

2. Reputed Firms/Companies may place their orders by V.P.P. for full amount in India Only.

## FOR OVERSEAS

1. Price US $ 250/- (US Dollars Two Hundred Fifty Only) for Each *Market Survey Cum Detailed Techno Economic Feasibility Report.*

2. Payable fully in advance through Draft in favour of 'ENGINEERS INDIA RESEARCH INSTITUTE', Delhi (Payable in India) Delivery by Regd. Air Mail Post within 2 Days.


# ENGINEERS INDIA RESEARCH INSTITUTE

4449, Nai Sarak (D), Main Road, Delhi - 110 006 (India)
Ph:. 91-11-3918117, 3916431, 3920361, 3960797
Fax: 91-11-3916431 E-Mail : eirisidi@bol.net.in
Website:www.startindustry.com
Also at : 4/27, Roop Nagar, Near Roop Nagar No. 1 School, Delhi - 110 007 (India) Ph:. 396 0797, 392 0361